ANTIQUES
Handbook
& Price Guide

Miller's Antiques Handbook & Price Guide
By Judith Miller

First published in Great Britain in 2011 by Miller's, a division of Mitchell Beazley,
imprints of Octopus Publishing Group Ltd, Endeavour House,
189 Shaftesbury Avenue, London, WC2H 8JY.
www.hachette.co.uk

Miller's is a registered trademark of Octopus Publishing Group Ltd.
www.millersguides.com

ISBN 9781845336363

A CIP record for this book is available from the British Library

Set in Frutiger

Printed and bound in China

Editorial Director Tracey Smith
Project Manager Katy Armstrong
Copy Editor Julie Brooke
Editorial Assistant Rhea Finnie
Indexer Hilary Bird
Advertising Sales Christine Havers

Art Director Jonathan Christie
Design and Prepress Ali Scrivens, TJ Graphics

Production Manager Peter Hunt

Photograph of Judith Miller by Chris Terry

Page 1: An Inuit stone and ivory "Dancing Polar Bear" figure, by Pauta Saila. £25,000-35,000 WAD
Page 3: A 1920s Muller Frères stork table lamp. £1,000-1,500 QU
Page 4 from left to right: A Meissen chocolate pot and cover. c1745 £5,000-7,000 TEN; A 19thC Japanese ivory and wood figure of an elderly man
gathering wood. £2,500-3,500 LHA; An early 19thC Russian Empire Neo-classical mahogany veneer armchair. £6,000-8,000 DOR; A Goldscheider figure
of a dancing girl, by Josef Lorenzl. £1,800-2,200 WW
Page 5 from left to right: An Attic black-figured amphora, in the manner of the Antimenes Painter. c530-520BC £60,000-70,000 SOTH; A Beeson O
gauge electric 3-rail 0-4-4 No.440 tank locomotive. £8,000-10,000 TEN; A late 1940s Joseff of Hollywood "Sungod" brooch. £400-500 PC; A WMF
pewter mounted wine jug. £1,000-1,500 L&T

ANTIQUES
Handbook
& Price Guide

Judith Miller

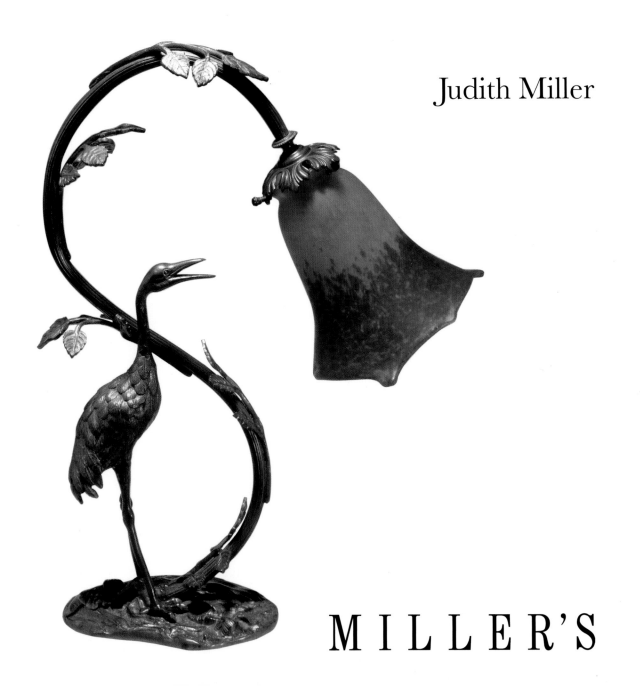

MILLER'S

Contents

PORCELAIN — 8-55

Berlin | Bow | Caughley | Chelsea and Girl in a Swing | Coalport | Copeland | Derby | Dresden | Liverpool | Longton Hall | Lowestoft | Meissen | Minton | Nantgarw | New Hall | Paris | Samson | Sèvres | Vienna | Worcester | Other Factories

POTTERY — 56-89

Delft | Faience | Maiolica | Slipware | Creamware | Pearlware | Lustreware | Transfer-printed | Staffordshire Figures | Toby Jugs | Mason's Ironstone | Wedgwood | Stoneware | Redware | Mocha Ware | Other Factories

ORIENTAL — 90-157

CERAMICS

Marks | Ancient Ceramics | Blanc-de-Chine | Celadon | Sang de Beouf | Monochrome | Blue-and-White | Famille Verte | Famille Rose | Rose Medallion | Famille Noir | Famille Jaune | Armorial | Doucai | Wucai | Chinese Polychrome | Japanese Imari | Satsuma | Other Japanese Ceramics | Korean | Other Ceramics

WORKS OF ART

Chinese Cloisonné | Chinese Metalware | Japanese Metalware | Other Metalware | Ivory | Netsuke | Horn | Jade | Coral | Lapis Lazuli | Other Hardstones | Wood | Bamboo | Lacquer | Glass | Snuff Bottles | Paintings | Embroidery & Textiles

FURNITURE

Chairs | Tables | Cupboards | Screens

FURNITURE — 158-263

Country Chairs | Dining Chairs| Side Chairs | Hall Chairs | Corner Chairs | Stools | Open Armchairs | Upholstered Armchairs | Sofas | Other Chairs | Refectory Tables | Gateleg Tables | Pedestal Tables | Extending Tables | Drop-leaf Tables | Breakfast Tables | Centre Tables | Console Tables | Side Tables | Occasional Tables | Library Tables | Writing Tables | Sofa Tables | Pembroke Tables | Games Tables | Tea Tables | Dressing Tables | Lowboys | Tripod Tables | Work Tables | Other Tables | Dressers | Cupboards | Corner Cupboards | Linen Presses | Coffers | Chests | Chests-of-Drawers | Commodes | Chests-on-Stands | Chests-on-Chests | Tall Chests | Secrétaires | Secrétaire Bookcases | Bureau Bookcases | Breakfront Bookcases | Library Bookcases | Low Bookcases | Cabinets-on-Stands | Display Cabinets | Side Cabinets | Credenzas | Chiffoniers | Sideboards| Beside Cabinets | Desks | Bureaux | Davenports | Canterburies | Mirrors | Étagères | Dumb Waiters | Teapoys | Wine Coolers | Jardinières | Torchères | Trays | Screens | Beds | Other Furniture

BOXES — 264-275

Tea Caddies | Work Boxes | Table Cabinets | Writing Boxes | Dressing Boxes | Knife Boxes | Other Boxes

CARVINGS

CLOCKS, BAROMETERS & SCIENTIFIC INSTRUMENTS — 276–310

CLOCKS

Bracket Clocks | Longcase Clocks | Mantel Clocks | Lantern Clocks | Other Clocks | Garnitures | Wall Clocks

WATCHES

Pocket Watches | Wristwatches

BARMOMETERS

Stick Barometers | Wheel & Banjo Barometers | Aneroid Barometers

SCIENTIFIC INSTRUMENTS

Chronometers | Microscopes | Telescopes | Barographs | Engines | Globes

MUSIC BOXES

NAUTICAL ANTIQUES

METALWARE — 311-340

Silver Candlesticks | Silver Cups | Silver Teapots | Silver Coffee Pots | Silver Tea & Coffee Sets | Silver Jugs | Silver Sauceboats | Silver Tea Caddies | Silver Caddy Spoons | Silver Spoons & Tongs | Silver Tureens | Silver Flatware | Silver Baskets | Silver Bowls | Silver Cruets | Silver Novelties | Silver Wine Antiques | Other Silver | Silverplate | Other Metalware

GLASS — 341-348

Wine Glasses | Other Glass | Paperweights | Bohemian Glass

LIGHTING — 349-355

Candlesticks | Chandeliers | Lanterns | Wall Lighting | Lamps

JEWELLERY — 356-368

Early Jewellery | Georgian | Victorian | Art Nouveau | Edwardian | Arts and Crafts | Art Deco | Costume Jewellery

OBJETS DE VERTU   369-393

Silver Vinaigrettes | Silver Card Cases | Other Card Cases |
Snuff Boxes | Treen | Vesta cases | Inkstands | Enamels | Ivory |
Miniatures | Other Objets De Vertu

RUSSIAN ANTIQUES

Cloisonné | Fabergé | Silver | Other Russian Antiques

ARCHITECTURAL   394-401

Fire Surrounds | Fire Grates | Fire Accessories |
Other Architectural Antiques | Weathervanes | Trade Signs

TEXTILES   402–429

Persian Rugs & Carpets | Caucasian Rugs & Carpets | Turkish
Rugs & Carpets | Other Rugs & Carpets | Quilts | Tapestries |
Silk Embroideries | Wool Embroideries | Samplers | Fans | Other
Textiles | Costume | Couture | Handbags & Trunks | Shoes

BOOKS AND PRINTS   430–438

Classics | Modern First Editions | Maps | Other Ephemera

DOLLS, TOYS & MODELS   439–453

Dolls | Dolls' Houses | Automata | Money Boxes | Tinplate |
Teddy Bears | Other Toys | Trains | Models

SPORTING ANTIQUES   454–458

Football | Cricket | Golf | Other Sports

TRIBAL ART   459–469

Africa | Inuit | The Americas | Oceania

ARMS & ARMOUR   470–481

Guns | Edged Weapons | Powder Horns | Medals | Badges |
Armour & Uniform

ANTIQUITIES   482–483

MUSICAL INSTRUMENTS   484–485

DECORATIVE ARTS   486-587
CERAMICS

Amphora | Arequipa | Clewell | Chelsea | Clarice Cliff |
William de Morgan | Doulton | Goldscheider | Lenci |
Majolica | Marblehead | Martin Brothers | Minton |
Moorcroft | Bernard Moore | William Morris | Newcomb |
North Dakota | George Ohr | Pewabic | Quimper | Rookwood |
Roseville | Royal Dux | Ruskin | Teco | Van Briggle | Louis Wain |
Walrath | Wedgwood | Weller | Wemyss | Zsolnay | Other
Ceramics | Studio Ceramics

FURNITURE

Aesthetic | Gothic Revival | Arts and Crafts | Art Nouveau | Art Deco

GLASS

Daum | Gallé | Lalique | Loetz | Murano | Tiffany | Other Glass |
Stained Glass | Perfume Bottles

CLOCKS

LIGHTING

Tiffany | Roycroft | Other Lighting

METALWARE

Liberty & Co | Tiffany | Georg Jensen | Roycroft | WMF | Other
Silver | Other Copper | Other Metalware

SCULPTURE

TEXTILES

MODERN DESIGN   588-624

Furniture | Ceramics | Glass | Lighting | Sculpture | Textiles

PERIOD CHART   625

CLASSIFIED ADVERTISING   626-631

KEY TO ILLUSTRATIONS   632-633

DIRECTORY OF AUCTIONEERS   634-636

DIRECTORY OF SPECIALISTS   637-640

INDEX TO ADVERTISERS   640

INDEX   641-648

LIST OF CONSULTANTS

At Miller's we are extremely lucky to be able to call on a large number of specialists for advice. My colleagues and friends on the BBC Antiques Roadshow have a wealth of knowledge and their advice on the state of the market is invaluable. It is also important to keep in touch with dealers as they are really at the coalface dealing directly with collectors. Certain parts of the market have been extremely volatile over the past year, so up to date information is critical.

CERAMICS

John Axford
Woolley & Wallis
51-61 Castle Street
Salisbury SP1 3SU

Fergus Gambon
Bonhams
101 New Bond Street
London W1S 1SR

Steven Moore
Anderson & Garland
Anderson House, Crispin Court,
Newbiggin Lane
Westerhope,
Newcastle upon Tyne NE5 1BF

John Howard
Heritage
6 Market Place, Woodstock
OX20 1TA

DECORATIVE ARTS

Michael Jeffrey
Woolley & Wallis
51-61 Castle Street
Salisbury, SP1 3SU

John Mackie
Lyon & Turnbull
33 Broughton Place
Edinburgh EH1 3RR

Will Farmer
Fieldings
Mill Race Lane
Stourbridge DY8 1JN

Mike Moir
www.manddmoir.co.uk

FURNITURE

Lennox Cato
1 The Square, Edenbridge
Kent TN8 5BD

Lee Young
Lyon & Turnbull
33 Broughton Place
Edinburgh EH1 3RR

ORIENTAL

John Axford
Woolley & Wallis
51-61 Castle Street
Salisbury SP1 3SU

Robert McPherson
40 Kensington Church Street
London W8 4BX

GLASS

Jeanette Hayhurst
www.antiqueglasslondon.com

SILVER

Alistair Dickenson
90 Jermyn Street
London SW1 6JD

JEWELLERY

Trevor Kyle
Lyon & Turnbull
33 Broughton Place
Edinburgh EH1 3RR

Steven Miners
Cristobal
26 Church Street
London NW8 8EP

CLOCKS & BAROMETERS

Paul Archard
Derek Roberts
25 Shipbourne Road
Tonbridge TN10 3DN

MODERN DESIGN

Mark Hill
Miller's
189 Shaftesbury Avenue,
London WC2H 8JY

John Mackie
Lyon & Turnbull
33 Broughton Place
Edinburgh EH1 3RR

HOW TO USE THIS BOOK

Running head Indicates the sub-category of the main heading.

Caption The description of the item illustrated, including when relevant, the period, the maker or factory, medium, the year it was made, dimensions and condition. Many captions have **footnotes** which give explain terminology or give identification or valuation information.

Essential Reference Gives key facts about the factory, maker or style, along with stylistic identification points, value tips and advice on fakes.

Page tab This appears on every page and identifies the main category heading as identified in the Contents List on pages 4-5.

Closer Look Does exactly that. This is where we show identifying aspects of a factory or maker, point out rare colours or shapes, and explain why a particular piece is so desirable.

The object The antiques are shown in fulll colour. This is a vital aid to identification and valuation. With many objects, a slight colour variation can signify a large price differential.

The price guide These price ranges give a ball park figure of what you should pay for a similar item. The great joy of antiques is that there is not a recommended retail price. The price ranges in this book are based on actual prices, either what a dealer will take or the full auction price.

Source code Every item has been specially photographed at an auction house, a dealer, an antiques market or a private collection. These are credited by code at the end of the caption, and can be checked against the Key to Illustrations on pages 632-633.

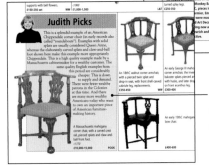

Judith Picks Items chosen specially by Judith, either because they are important or interesting, or because they're good investments.

INTRODUCTION

I am delighted to introduce the new edition of Millers Antiques Handbook and Price Guide - I hope you like the changes we've made to the format and the information. Of course, the book is still packed with over 8,000 beautiful full-colour photographs, detailed descriptions and price ranges, but this year's guide also features more information to help with identification and valuation.

We have, I hope, put the GUIDE back into Price Guide! It's often confusing to see two quite superficially similar chests of drawers with quite different price ranges - so we explain why. We also look at the problem of fakes and how to tell if something is genuine.

I've also chosen some areas which I think are good buys and tried to explain the problem with objects that are out of fashion. I find on the BBC Antiques Roadshow that people are often astounded that, for example, many floral Victorian tea sets are worth comparatively little. I try to explain that, although they are over a hundred years old and beautifully decorated, they are out of fashion. However this is a good area to buy into if you believe that the trend will reverse and you like the piece.

We are experiencing one of the worst global recessions and there is no denying that the antiques market has had a very difficult time. Many antiques shops have closed and dealers have retired or gone out of business. However other dealers and auctioneers are reporting strong sales, particularly at the top end of the market. Any rare piece in good original condition, with good provenance will find a ready market. The Chinese booming economy has meant that the pace and phenomenal rise in value of 18thC Imperial porcelain and jade is unprecedented and does not look set to abate.

At the other end of the scale, mid-range and low-end pieces have seen falling or stagnant sales. "Brown furniture" is nearly impossible to shift. So it's a very good time to buy. A colleague on the Antiques Roadshow furnished his son's college flat from local auctions and antiques shops for surprisingly little money.

A Ron Arad "Big Easy" sofa, upholstered in red wool. Designed 1988 72in (183cm) wide £1,500-2,000 DRA

These items may also prove to be a good investment in the longer term, as fashions will change and prices will undoubtedly rise.

Other areas that have seen strong sales are Arts and Crafts and Art Deco where interesting examples, of furniture, ceramics or glass have seen strong competition between collectors. This competition ensures a healthy, buoyant market, as demand outstrips supply. The 20thC Design market has seen strong sales, with Mid Century Modern still attaining record prices. I find it amusing that when I was interviewed two years ago by a journalist from a national US newspaper and mentioned that the interest in mid-century modern was still strong, she said her editor had banned them writing about it, as it was "so last season". Well, last season it is not – as prices for good original pieces continue to rise.

This year I've attended antiques shows in both the US and the UK and have found prices to be realistic enough to be very tempting. As always, when I leave home my husband attempts to curb my enthusiasm – "repeat after me, we do not need one more single chair" – but he tends not to notice the mid-20thC glass candlestick, the Stanley Hagler brooch, or the small 18thC creamware table salt!

It is, as I said, a great time to buy.

A pair of Chinese Qianlong period Imperial jade elephants 7.5in (19cm) long 26.5lb (12kg) £1,000,000+ WW

THE PORCELAIN MARKET

There has been some nervousness in the porcelain market, fuelled by porcelain collectors' very real concerns about the economy. However, there are many indicators that collectors are prepared to buy when rare and high-quality items are on offer.

The last few years have seen very little change to the market. The leaders – Sèvres and Meissen – have remained very much in demand, particularly early 18thC examples. The "golden age" of Meissen, from the early years of the factory to the end of the Seven Years War (1710-1759), was represented in Bonhams' sales of part of the Hoffmeister and Gustav von Klemperer collections. The von Klemperer pieces had been badly damaged in the Dresden bombing during World War II, but such is the provenance and rarity of the pieces they all sold very well. Stand out pieces included a jester with part of his face missing, which sold for £10,200 (more than ten times the low estimate) and a Harlequin figure, which sold for £108,000 (five times the low estimate). When quality is offered, buyers respond even in an uncertain economic climate.

Later 18thC pieces have tended to struggle, unless the piece has some rare features. Dresden and Limoges pieces have to be particularly impressive to sell well at the moment. The Paris factories have also struggled, and buyers are suspicious of many so-called "Samson" pieces that do not have the quality of the true Samson copies of original pieces.

Another area that is still in the doldrums is British blue-and-white porcelain from both the 18thC and 19thC. What buyers really want are pieces in exceptional condition and with a rare, early pattern. Large platters are also in demand, but not if they have a common transfer-printed pattern. Worcester has been in demand, but only the First Period Dr. Wall pieces with rare hand-painted patterns. Later transfer-printed pieces have struggled to find pre-recession prices, with many auctioneers combining pieces in job lots. If you are considering beginning a collection of 18thC English porcelain, this is a good time to start. However, Lowestoft has really bucked the trend, particularly rare shapes and pieces, such as the cygnet shown on page 28. Unrecorded early Derby figures always excite the market. Royal Worcester ewers and vases painted by artists such as Charles Baldwin and Harry Davis still have their collectors and prices have remained steady.

It is always good to buy from a reputable dealer or auction house, as there are many fakes on the market. Marks alone will not guarantee authenticity. The Meissen crossed-swords mark, for example, has been applied to many Dresden pieces, and can appear on 18thC soft-paste English porcelain and other European hard-paste examples. Study as many good Meissen examples as possible to appreciate the superb quality of the modelling and decoration.

Top Left:
A Caughley dish.
See page 13.

Left: A Derby
campana vase.
See page 22.

PORCELAIN

An 18thC Berlin candlestick, modelled as a putto holding a scrolling support, standing on a triform base, with sceptre mark and impressed "G", some restoration.

9.75in (25cm) high

£200-300   **WW**

ESSENTIAL REFERENCE - BERLIN

The Berlin porcelain factory was founded in 1761, in Berlin, Germany, by Johan Ernst Gotzkowky. He hired many employees of an earlier Berlin factory, as well as several Meissen craftsmen, notably modeller Friedrich Elias Meyer and painters Karl Wilhelm Böhme, Johann Balthasar Borrmann and Karl Jakob Christian Klipfel.

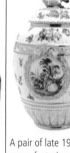

● When the factory went bankrupt in 1763, it was acquired by Frederick the Great. He renamed it the Royal Porcelain Manufactory.

● Early pieces were strongly influenced by Meissen's Rococo style. Such pieces featured pierced rims, trelliswork and floral painting.

● The Empire style of Sèvres (with gilding and solid-coloured bands) was used from the early 19thC. Dinner wares and vases were particularly popular, but biscuit porcelain statuettes and busts were also made.

● Vases with fine landscape painting and richly decorated "cabinet" wares are noteworthy.

● In the late 19thC fc large porcelain plaques were produced, often painted with copies of famous paintings and mounted in gilt frames.

● Pieces are marked "KPM" for Königliche Porzellan-Manufaktur. The sceptre mark was used from 1763.

● The factory was renamed Staatiliche Porzellan Manufaktur Berlin in 1918. It is still active.

A late 18th/early 19thC Berlin ornithological plate, painted with three woodland birds perched on a hawthorn bush amidst butterflies and insects, the rim gilded and reticulated, with blue sceptre mark.

9.75in (25cm) diam

£250-350   **WW**

A Berlin gilt and polychrome enamel plate, featuring the Podewil coat-of-arms and Indian flowering branches, the edge with six gilt shells, with underglaze blue sceptre mark to reverse.

c1800   *9in (23cm) diam*

£3,000-4,000   **DOR**

A pair of late 19thC Berlin covered vases, featuring painted scenes of courting couples within gilt wreaths, set in a floral decorated ground, with eagle finials, with blue sceptre mark.

11.5in (29cm) high

£600-800   **LHA**

One of a pair of late 19thC Berlin urns, decorated with alternating panels, one side decorated with philosophers, the other mythological scenes, separated with four panels of allegorical scenes of putti representing the four seasons, with underglaze sceptre mark and over painted Royal Vienna shield mark.

26.25in (66.5cm) high

£20,000-30,000 pair   **LHA**

A Berlin coffee service, consisting of a coffee pot with lid, a milk jug with lid, a jug, six cups with saucers, the body with gilt edging, basketweave relief, polychrome and gilt painted monogram with crown, with underglaze blue sceptre mark, red orb mark and "KPM", dated 1900, 1903, 1905, 1907, 1912, 1914.

According to court records this service was formerly owned by Emperor Wilhelm II. Provenance (identifying a piece's origins or history) adds interest and can add value.

Coffee pot 7in (18cm) high

£8,000-12,000   **DOR**

A mid-19thC Berlin oval painted plaque, depicting a vestal virgin holding an oil lamp, impressed "KPM" and sceptre marks, in a decorative giltwood frame.

17in (43cm) high

£4,000-6,000   **TEN**

A late 19thC Berlin painted plaque, depicting a maiden in exotic attire standing near a well, with gilt decoration, impressed "KPM" and sceptre mark, incised "916", in a giltwood frame.

9in (23cm) high

£3,000-4,000   **LHA**

A late 19thC Berlin painted plaque, depicting a woman with cockatoo, impressed "KPM" and sceptre marks, incised "9.6", in giltwood frame.

9.5in (24cm) high

£3,000-4,000   **LHA**

A Berlin painted plaque, depicting a brunette woman in peasant blouse, signed "Giel", with impressed "KPM" and sceptre marks.

7in (18cm) high

£1,500-2,500   **LHA**

A late 19thC Berlin oval painted plaque, depicting a young child in bedclothes kneeling at prayer, in a modern giltwood frame.

5.75in (14.5cm) high

£1,200-1,800   **FRE**

A late 19thC Berlin painted plaque, depicting a barefoot peasant woman at a shrine, signed "Emil Echarkdt, Dresden", impressed "KPM" and sceptre marks, in a giltwood frame.

12.5in (32cm) high

£1,500-2,500   **FRE**

A Berlin painted plaque, depicting "Psyche at the Sea" after W. Kray, signed lower right "F. Wagner, Vienna", with gilt wooden frame, impressed sceptre mark.

Wilhelm Kray (1828-1889) studied portrait and landscape painting at the Berlin Academy under Julius Schrader and Wilhelm Schirmer, before settling in Vienna in 1878. His art has a lyrical, elegiac quality, and he specialised in romantic wood nymphs and mermaids in fantastical natural surroundings. He also painted portraits, such as King Wilhelm I and the poet, Ernst Moritz Arndt.

1908   *9in (23cm) high*

£8,000-12,000   **DOR**

A late 19thC Berlin oval painted plaque, depicting a dark haired girl wrapped in a blanket, impressed mark.

7in (18cm) high

£500-700   **GORL**

An 18thC Bow figure of a shepherd playing a pipe, restored.

6in (15cm) high

£1,000-1,500   **GORL**

A small Bow figure of a recumbent hound, the flat base highlighted with manganese dashes, some chips.

Early Bow figures are always desirable. This example is in excellent condition, with good colouration. The subject matter, being a dog, also adds to the value.

c1750   *2.25in (5.5cm) wide*

£2,500-3,500   **WW**

A Bow two-handled cup, painted with exotic birds, insects and a caterpillar, applied forget-me-nots issuing from the handles.

c1755-58   *5in (12.5cm) high*

£700-1,000   **WW**

A large Bow figure of Flora, after Farnese, the goddess draped in a yellow robe painted with floral motifs, raised on a marbled and flower encrusted base, repairs.

c1760   *18in (45.5cm) high*

£3,000-4,000   **WW**

A Bow white-glazed salt, modelled as a large shell resting on a mass of smaller shells from which a small crab protrudes.

c1755   *6in (15cm) wide*

£1,500-2,500   **WW**

One of a pair of large Bow plates, painted in the Oriental style with pink and blue flowers issuing from rockwork.

c1758-60   *13in (33.5cm) diam*

£1,000-1,500 pair   **WW**

A Bow figure of a grape seller, repairs.

c1760   *5in (12.5cm) high*

£300-400   **WW**

A Bow vase, modelled between two putti, painted with flower sprays and butterflies, applied flower garlands trailing from the neck to the foot, some restoration.

Although restored, the two putti make this vase rare.

c1765   *7in (18cm) high*

£800-1,200   **WW**

A pair of Bow models of a musician and his companion, modelled on scroll bases, he playing the bagpipes, she the cymbal.

c1765   *8.75in (22cm) high*

£1,500-2,500   **DN**

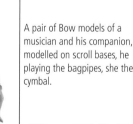

A pair of Bow candlesticks, modelled *en rocaille* as groups of pheasants within bocage, with anchor and dagger marks, some restoration.

c1765   *9.75in (25cm) high*

£1,500-2,500   **DN**

ESSENTIAL REFERENCE - CAUGHLEY

The Caughley factory was established near Broseley in Shropshire, England, c1750. Although initially a pottery factory, it began producing porcelain (known as Salopian ware) after it was taken over by Thomas Turner in 1772.

- Painted wares are generally earlier than printed ones.
- In 1775, transfer printing was introduced by Robert Hancock, formerly of Worcester.
- Caughley deliberately imitated Worcester pieces, both in pattern and shape, so it can be difficult to distinguish the work of the two factories.
- Caughley's soapstone type-body shows orange to transmitted light (Worcester's shows pale green). Its blue pigment is also slightly brighter than Worcester's.
- From the 1780s many pieces were highlighted with gilding.
- It was bought in 1799 by John Rose of the nearby Coalport factory.
- The Caughley Works closed in c1812.
- The blue printed patterns are generally marked with a crescent (in imitation of Worcester's earliest mark – see p47) or with "S" for Salopian.

Used c1775-90. Shaded crescent used on printed pieces.

"S" mark for Salopian. Used c1775-90 (printed).

A Caughley lobed-shaped dish, painted in underglaze blue with the "Man in Sanpan" pattern, with pseudo-Chinese character mark and "C".
c1775-80   *10in (25.5cm) wide*
£500-700   SWO

A Caughley blue-and-white spoon, painted with flowers.
c1775   *4.25in (11cm) long*
£350-450   DN

A Caughley blue-and-white coffee pot and cover, printed to both sides with the "Fisherman" pattern beneath an inverted trefoil border.
c1775-80   *9.75in (25cm) high*
£400-600   WW

A Caughley heart-shaped dish, painted in underglaze blue with the "Man in Sanpan" pattern, with pseudo Chinese character mark and "C".
c1775-80   *12in (30.5cm) wide*
£400-600   SWO

A late 18thC possibly Caughley leaf-moulded jug, with wrythen neck, painted with floral sprigs in gilt and with oak leaf banding, restored.
7.5in (19cm) high
£200-300   DA&H

A rare late 18thC Caughley cup, of ogee form, polychrome painted with the "Dragon in Compartments" pattern.
2.25in (5.5cm) high
£180-220   AH

An early 19thC Caughley jug, with spiral fluted body and painted with a view of Tongcastle and Church Salop, within gilded borders.
7.25in (18.5cm) high
£400-600   GORL

PORCELAIN

Judith Picks: Goat-and-Bee Jugs

In comfortably-off households in the mid 18thC, afternoon and after-dinner tea and coffee were typically served by the lady of the house in the drawing room. By the date that the Chelsea porcelain factory made its "goat-and-bee" cream jugs, black teas were more popular in Britain than green teas. Like coffee, fermented black tea was usually drunk with milk or cream, and often sweetened with sugar.

What makes these jugs particularly special is that they are among the earliest dated English porcelain. It is likely they were designed and modelled by Nicholas Sprimont (1716-1771), the manager of Chelsea. A visitor to England said of Chelsea's earliest years that "an able French artist" (Sprimont was from a French-speaking part of Flanders) supplies "or directs the models of everything manufactured there". Sprimont had been a silversmith, and the motif of two goats, placed parallel but facing in opposite directions, occurs on silver bearing his sponsor's (or "maker's") mark.

BEWARE!

Although £5,000-7,000 is still an impressive sum, there is no denying that it is substantially less than the value of the polychrome jug on this page. Why? Well, quite simply this is due to the later decoration, which is on top of the glaze, rather than beneath it. Collectors of these early jugs are interested in originality, and any later modifications, such as over-painting, makes a piece significantly less desirable.

A Chelsea "Goat-and-Bee" jug, with incised triangle mark, some restoration with some overpainting to the neck, the decoration may be later.

c1745-47   *4in (10cm) high*
£5,000-7,000   **WW**

A Chelsea white-glazed "Goat-and-Bee" jug, the pear-shaped body moulded beneath the spout with a flowering plant, the lower part modelled with two recumbent goats, incised triangle mark.

3in (7.5cm) high
£7,000-10,000   **TEN**

A Chelsea "Goat-and-Bee" jug, the pear shaped body moulded beneath the spout with a brightly enamelled flowering plant, the ground painted with a moth and ladybird, the lower part modelled with two recumbent goats, incised triangle mark.

c1745-49   *4.25in (11cm) high*
£12,000-15,000   **SOTH**

A Chelsea white-glazed beaker and matched trembleuse saucer, the beaker moulded with tea-plant sprays, the saucer with prunus, applied raised anchor to the saucer, damages.

Even damaged, the rarity of this extremely early raised anchor beaker and saucer make them very desirable to collectors.

c1747   Saucer 5in (12.5cm) diam
£2,000-3,000   **WW**

A Chelsea octagonal beaker and saucer, painted in the Kakiemon palette with alternating panels of scrolls and peony on white ground and foliate S-scrolls on red ground, with raised anchor pad to beaker.

c1748-52   Saucer 6in (15cm) diam
£1,200-1,800   **WW**

A Chelsea fruit-painted dessert plate, with feather-moulded rim picked out in iron red and gilt, painted with a sprig of fruiting raspberry, bordered by insects, with red painted anchor mark and inscribed "Chelsea C. 1758", with old label of A.J. Filkins.

c1752-56   9in (23cm) diam
£1,000-1,500   **TEN**

A Chelsea bird and flower dessert plate, with scroll-moulded rim, the rim panels alternately incised with waves and Oriental birds, the central field scattered with sprays and sprigs of flowers, with red painted anchor mark and old label.

c1752-56
£300-400   **TEN**

A rare Chelsea peach-shaped jug, with a stalk handle, painted with polychrome flower sprays and scattered leaves, with brown line rim.

c1750-52   3.5in (9cm) high
£2,500-3,500   **WW**

CLOSER LOOK - CHELSEA FINGER BOWLS

The red anchor period at Chelsea ran from 1752-56.

The scalloped (lobed) rims are typical of the period.

The cool white paste of the body was often left undecorated, or featured a restrained use of colour.

These exotic birds may have been painted in the workshop of James Giles, an independent ceramic decorator who worked in London.

The fact that these are a pair more than doubles the value.

A pair of 18thC Chelsea finger bowls and stands, the bowls with scalloped rims and cylindrical, slightly waisted bodies, all decorated with exotic birds at a river with a tree.

Stand 6in (15cm) diam
£22,000-28,000 pair   **L&T**

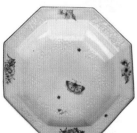

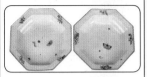

A pair of Chelsea octagonal plates, in the Meissen style, painted with scattered flowers and insects and moulded in relief with flowers, the butterflies with shadows, with a brown-line rim.

c1750-55   9in (23cm) diam
£1,000-1,500   **DN**

A pair of Chelsea peony dishes, each modelled as a large bloom picked out in pink and purple, beneath a heavily veined leaf, the stalk of which forms the handle, with red anchor marks.

c1755   9in (23cm) wide
£8,000-12,000   **WW**

A Chelsea botanical plate, painted with a large spray of *Artemisia Annua* (Sweet Wormwood) amidst scattered insects and butterflies, with red anchor mark.

The botanical painting on this plate is probably taken from Philip Miller's "Figures of the Most Beautiful, Useful and Uncommon Plants Described in the Gardener's Dictionary" (1755). Philip Miller was the chief gardener at the Chelsea Physic Garden, which inspired many Chelsea botanical pieces.

c1755   8in (20cm) diam
£2,500-3,500   **WW**

A Chelsea ècuelle, cover and stand, painted with flower stems and sprays, the cover finial modelled as a large blossoming bud, the handles formed as green-tinged leaves, with red anchor marks.

c1755   Stand 8in (20cm) diam
£2,000-3,000   **WW**

A pair of Chelsea vine leaf dishes, painted with flowers, the edges tinged with green and yellow, with pink veins, with red anchor marks, damages.

c1755   8in (20cm) long
£500-700   **WW**

A Chelsea écuelle and cover, enamelled after a Meissen original with butterflies, moths and beetles, with rose knop, with red anchor mark under base.

c1755   7in (18cm) wide
£4,000-6,000   **H&L**

A miniature Chelsea figure of a hunter, with red anchor mark, restored.

c1755-58   2.25in (5.5cm) high
£500-700   WW

An unusual Chelsea figure of Winter, modelled by Joseph Willems as a bearded man in a white greatcoat and fur-lined hat, with red anchor mark, restored.

c1755   5.25in (13cm) high
£1,500-2,500   WW

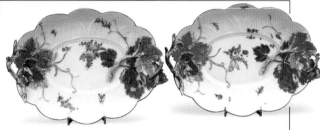

A pair of Chelsea oval two-handled dessert dishes, painted with flowers and insects and modelled with twig handles and vine-leaf terminals, one with red anchor mark, one with chipped handle.

c1756   11in (28cm) long
£2,500-3,500   DN

A Chelsea plate, painted with three colourful exotic birds perched in fruiting branches and on rockwork, within a feather-moulded border, brown anchor mark.

c1757   9in (23zm) diam
£500-700   WW

A Chelsea plate, of scalloped circular form, the border panels painted with birds in the Meissen style, the central field with flowers, red line rim, red anchor mark.

c1758   8in (20cm) diam
£800-1,200   TEN

A Chelsea oval dish, painted with three colourful birds perched on a rocky stump and within leafy branches, feather moulded rim, brown anchor mark.

c1757   11in (28cm) wide
£300-500   WW

A pair of Chelsea vine dishes, modelled as overlapping leaves with twig-form handles and applied flowerheads and painted with floral sprigs within a pale green border.

c1760   8in (20cm) long
£1,000-1,500   FRE

A Chelsea dessert plate, a gilt band to the slightly raised rim, centrally painted in colourful enamels with a pheasant and a blue bird amongst shrubs, within three main floral trails, with gilt anchor mark.

c1765   9in (23cm) diam
£400-600   TEN

A pair of Chelsea "The Imperial Shepherds" figures, the figures against encrusted flowering shrubs from Rococo scroll bases, enriched in gilt throughout, both with impressed "R" and gold anchor marks.

c1765   Tallest 13in (33.5cm) high
£3,500-4,500   TEN

A Chelsea Meissen-style basket, with pierced outscrolled leaf handles and trellis borders, painted with scattered flowers and sprigs, openwork feet, with gold anchor mark.

c1770   10in (25.5cm) wide
£300-400   TEN

PORCELAIN

Judith Picks: Triple Scent Bottle

There is an adage about antiques that you should "always buy the best you can afford", and that is what you are looking at here. The Girl-in-a-Swing factory produced expensive "toys": scent bottles, étuis, patch boxes, seals etc. These early examples of high-quality English porcelain are rare and desirable – the quality of modelling, design, detailing and colouring is exceptional. Always check the condition – especially extremities such as heads, fingers, toes, ears and finials– because, due to the fineness of the potting, they are often damaged. Because of the rarity, damaged pieces still sell, but pristine pieces command a premium. The stamped gilt-metal foliate mounts on this bottle are of typically high quality. The

complexity of the design adds to it desirability – a triple-headed scent bottle is extremely rare. Difficult to find, these treasures do turn up, but beware: there are late 19thC Samson fakes. These are identifiable by the hard paste porcelain body and inferior modelling, so study as many originals as possible.

A Girl-in-a-Swing triple-headed scent bottle, modelled as chickens standing on a log, raised on a domed base delicately painted with flowers, with gilt metal mounts.

c1750-59

3in (7.5cm) high

£3,500-4,500   WW

ESSENTIAL REFERENCE - GIRL-IN-A-SWING

Many pieces originally attributed to the Chelsea factory have since been reattributed to a rival London firm, referred to as the "Girl-in-a-Swing" factory after two soft-paste porcelain figures that were probably made between 1749 to 1754.

- **Charles Gouyn (who had been a partner at Chelsea until 1749) may have been this factory's director.**
- **Girl-in-a-Swing pieces have a similar glassy paste body to the triangular wares of Chelsea, but have a greater percentage of lead. They also have some modelling differences.**
- **Typical wares include perfume bottles, étuis and patch boxes, but some figures (such as the girl in the swing) were also made.**

A Girl-in-a-Swing double scent bottle, modelled as a putti and a small dog, raised on a domed base, finely painted with flowers to both sides, restoration.

c1750-59   3in (7.5cm) high

£1,500-2,500   WW

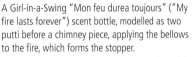

A Girl-in-a-Swing "Mon feu durea toujours" ("My fire lasts forever") scent bottle, modelled as two putti before a chimney piece, applying the bellows to the fire, which forms the stopper.

c1750-59   3.25in (8.5cm) high

£2,500-3,500   WW

A Girl-in-a-Swing "L'Heure du berger fidèle" ("The hour of the faithful shepherd") scent bottle, modelled with a clock face amidst pink roses, supported by Venus and Cupid, some restoration, the stopper sealed shut.

c1750-59   3in (7.5cm) high

£2,000-3,000   WW

A pair of 19thC Coalport vases and covers, encrusted with finely modelled enamelled flowers, arranged around panels of painted bouquets, the handles, feet and pierced covers highlighted with blue and gilt.

11.5in (29cm) high

c1800

£1,000-1,500   WW

A rare Coalport coffee can, painted with an artist's palette and brushes between a wide band of fuchsia, titled "Romney".

The name on this can probably relates to the portrait painter, George Romney (1734-1802).

c1800   *3.5in (9cm) high*

£600-800   WW

A pair of Coalport vases, painted with bouquets of flowers on a white ground, raised on gilt-decorated bases, with swan handles.

c1820   *11in (28cm) high*

£1,500-2,500   WW

A Coalport Rococo-style vase and cover, of ogee outlined pedestal baluster form, the domed cover moulded with radiating panels of husks, depicting three exotic birds in a landscape, on an ogee swept foot, richly gilded throughout, restoration.

c1830   *15in (38cm) high*

£350-450   TEN

A pair of early 19thC Coalport-style vases, painted with flowers on a dark brown ground, between elaborate gilded borders.

7in (18cm) high

£300-500   WW

One of a pair of Coalport Rococo Revival twin-handled pedestal ice-pails, covers and liners, painted with panels of flowers on a blue ground, damages.

c1825   *13in (33.5cm) high*

£1,200-1,800 pair   DN

A pair of mid-19thC Coalport Imari pattern vases, on gilt claw and ball feet.

8.5in (21.5cm) high

£250-350   WW

An early 20thC large Coalport plate, decorated by Frederick H. Chivers, with fruit on a mossy bank, within a broad blue border with an undulating border pattern and dentil rim, with blue printed mark and "5351/R" in gilt, impressed "8C20", signed.

12in (30.5cm) diam

£500-700   TEN

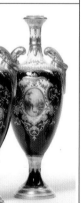

A pair of Coalport urn-shaped vases, painted with Warwick Castle and Windermere in oval panels, gilt cartouches on a blue ground with gilt borders, wreath and scroll handles, initialled "PHS", with printed marks and retailer's mark for Townsend & Co, Sunderland.

c1900   *11.75in (30cm) high*

£600-800   TEN

A Coalport ten-piece British topographical-view dessert service, decorated by Edward Oakes (Ted) Ball, painted with vignettes within scroll framed reserves against midnight blue grounds enriched with gilt, comprising six dessert plates, and four serving dishes, all named in script and with gilders mark "X2289", all signed "E Ball", with blue printed crown mark.

Edward Oakes (Ted) Ball was a landscape painter born in Jackfield, Shropshire. He trained at the Coalport Pottery and became one of its principal landscape painters.

c1900-10

£1,000-1,500   TEN

Judith Picks: Parian

We see quite a few parian figures on the Antiques Roadshow and in autumn 2010 an example of "The Bride" was brought in for evaluation. The interesting thing about the bust was that it had been relegated to the garden shed – another example of the unpopularity of Victorian sentimentality. However this is a fine-quality piece and, treated sensitively, can look good in a more modern environment. The value of this example, in particular, has seen an increase of late. The overtly Classical pieces are still, in my opinion, undervalued.

A Copeland parian bust of "The Bride", after Raffaelle Monti, made for the Ceramic and Crystal Palace Art Union of London, mounted on a concave-sided circular base, impressed "Crystal Palace Art Union", the bust with incised signature "R. Monti", "1861", and "Copeland".

c1861   *15in (38cm) high*

£1,500-2,500   **TEN**

A Copeland parian group of "Emily and the White Doe" after F.M. Miller, impressed marks.

c1860   *19in (48cm) high*

£1,200-1,800   **SWO**

ESSENTIAL REFERENCE - SPODE

The Spode factory was established in 1776 by Josiah Spode and initially produced pottery. Early pieces are marked with an impressed or painted "Spode", or with a Pattern number.

- Spode is generally credited with the invention of bone china in around 1796–97.
- During the Regency period, Spode used brilliantly coloured Japanese patterns highlighted with gilding.
- In 1833 it was taken over by William Copeland and Thomas Garrett, who had previously managed Spode's London shop. They renamed the company Copeland & Garrett, and began to produce new, modern designs.
- Copeland were arguably the first to make parianware (Minton & Co. claimed to have discovered the secret simultaneously and were certainly also making parian porcelain in the 1840s), and these white figures dominated output during the mid-19thC. Elaborately decorated table-services were also made, as well as household crockery.
- The factory is still operating today under the name Spode Ltd (which it adopted again in 1970). It continues to produce many of its 19thC patterns.
- The famous "Caramanian" and "Indian Hunting" series of printed wares remain extremely collectable.

c1784-1805

c1790-1820

EARLY 20THC

A Copeland parian figure of "Venus", after John Gibson, the standing figure holding an apple and her tunic mantle (with gilt and tinted borders), on a stepped base, impressed "Copeland".

17in (43cm) high

£200-300   **TEN**

A Copeland parian figural comport, depicting the Three Graces supporting a pierced circular dish on a tripartite stand with acanthus leaf and shell moulding picked out in gold, some repairs.

c1870   *18in (45.5cm) high*

£800-1,200   **H&L**

A Copeland parian bust of "The Mother", after Raffaele Monti, impressed "Crystal Palace Art Union", the bust with incised "R. Monti" signature and "1871", stamped "Ceramic and Crystal Palace Art Union, Copeland 074".

This bust is the companion piece to "The Bride".

1871   *15in (38cm) high*

£2,000-3,000   **TEN**

A Copeland parian figure of "Musidora", after William Theed, made for the Ceramic and Crystal Palace Art Union, impressed "Ceramic and Crystal Palace Art Union W Theed pubd 1867", and "Copeland 076".

This is the companion figure to Malempré's "Shepherd Boy", and is based on the marble statue executed for the Prince of Wales in 1866.

17in (43cm) high

£600-800   **TEN**

PORCELAIN

A rare pair of Derby models of parrots, their plumage picked out in green, yellow and orange enamels, perched on rocky stumps.

c1755　　　5.5in (14cm) high

£10,000-20,000　　　WW

An unrecorded Derby "dry-edge" figure of Columbine, concealing a slapstick behind her left arm, her right foot outstretched.

These "dry-edge" figures are the most notable of Derby's early wares, produced c1750-55. In order to stop the glaze running under the base during the firing process, these early figures were held upside down in a liquid glaze and then either wiped clean after dipping, or only partially dipped, during the process. This left the white biscuit edge visible. Peter Bradshaw's *Derby Porcelain Figures* records a pair of dry-edge figures of Harlequin and Columbine but there are several differences in the pose of this figure to the one in the book.

c1753　　　5in (12.5cm) high

£2,000-3,000　　　WW

A Derby figure of Minerva, with plumed helmet and shield resting on a pile of books, with an attendant owl, on gilt scrolling base, missing spear.

c1760-69　　　14in (36cm) high

£450-550　　　H&L

A Derby figure of Juno and the peacock, some restoration.

The goddess is explaining to the bird that he cannot have both beauty and song.

c1765　　　8in (20cm) high

£300-400　　　WW

A large Derby figure of Diana, carrying a quiver of arrows on her back, her hound at her side, raised on a flower encrusted base, damages.

c1765　　　10in (25.5cm) high

£500-700　　　WW

A pair of Derby models of shepherds, she with an apron full of flowers and a lamb at her feet, he with a long red cloak over one shoulder, raised on scrolling bases, some restoration.

c1765　　　9in (23cm) high

£500-700　　　WW

A pair of Derby candlesticks, each with two lovebirds in a flower-encrusted bower, looking down on a small dog, damages.

c1765-70　　　8in (20cm) high

£450-550　　　WW

A matched set of Derby models of the Infant Seasons, after Meissen, the cherubs seated with their seasonal attributes of flowers, corn, grapes and fire, some restoration.

c1765　　　Tallest 6in (15cm) high

£1,200-1,800　　　WW

A mid-late 18thC Derby candlestick figure of a seated dandy, a dove perched on his right hand, a dog seated by his left knee, before flowering bocage, restoration.

11in (28cm) high

£500-700 WW

A pair of Derby figures of a shepherd and shepherdess, he with a dog at his side against flower encrusted shrub, she with a garlanded lamb, in typical soft coloured enamels, enriched in gilt, on Rococo scroll bases, restored.

c1770-1780 *Tallest 6in (15cm) high*

£200-300 TEN

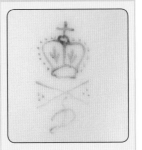

A Derby Mansion House dwarf, raised on a flower-encrusted base, incised "No 227", restored.

c1770-80 *7in (18cm) high*

£350-450 WW

Derby
Used: c1782-1825 (painted)

Bloor Derby
Used: c1820-40 (printed)
The earliest Bloor Derby mark

A pair of Derby leaf-shaped sauce boats, enamelled with bouquets and sprays beneath a green tinged rim, restoration.

c1760-70 *5in (12.5cm) long*

£400-500 H&L

A Derby figure of Autumn, from the "French Seasons", personified as a young girl carrying a basket of grapes, raised on a circular base.

c1775 *9in (23cm) high*

£350-450 WW

A Derby group of two Bacchantes adorning a bust of Pan, after engraving by Francesco Bartolozzi, incised "N196", restoration.

c1775

£400-600 WES

Bloor Derby
Used: c1825-40 (printed)

A pair of Derby two-handled urns and covers, decorated with a striped enamel blue and gilt ground, with painted panels depicting a study of a fashionable woman and landscape panels, incised "59".

c1780 *9in (23cm) high*

£700-1,000 DN

A Derby dessert plate, the central vignette painted with a putto astride a shepherd's crook holding a flaming torch, within a broad gilded and blue enamel border, with puce painted crown, crossed batons, dots, "D", and pattern number "177".

c1800 *9in (23cm) diam*

£700-1,000 TEN

Royal Crown Derby
Used: c1890 onwards (printed)
"Made in England" replaced "England" c1921

A garniture of three Derby campana vases, painted with a spray of flowers against a midnight blue ground enriched with motifs in gilt, with looped serpent handles, upon vine decorated circular pedestals, gold painted crown and "D" mark.
c1810   *Tallest 8in (20cm) high*
£1,000-1,500 set   **TEN**

A pair of Derby two-handled vases, each painted with a landscape scene of Classical ruins, on a gilded cobalt blue ground, each titled in red "Near Naples" and "Near Glasgow", crowned crossed baton marks.
c1810-20   *9in (23cm) high*
£1,500-2,500   **WW**

A large Derby campana vase, painted with panels of flowers on a blue simulated shagreen ground, the gilt loop handles issuing from masks of Pan.
c1815   *18in (45.5cm) high*
£5,000-7,000   **WW**

A Bloor Derby topographical vase, of Neo-classical pedestal baluster form, with a frontal octagonal solid gilt framed reserve painted with a view of "Earl Spencer's, St James's Park", against a dark blue ground enriched in gilt, with red printed crown and circle mark and "Bloor Derby".
c1820   *11in (28cm) high*
£1,000-1,500   **TEN**

A Bloor Derby plate, enamelled after the original Nantgarw plate by Claude Lorrain with a Mediterranean scene of merchants on a quayside, within narrow gilt and continuous landscape borders, with red circular backstamp, paper label "Mitchell-Hedges Collection No. 241".
c1820-40   *9in (23cm) diam*
£550-750   **H&L**

A Bloor Derby plate, painted by William Corden after the original Nantgarw plate decorated by James Plant, with children throwing snowballs in a winter landscape, within narrow gilt and continuous landscape borders, with red circular backstamp.
c1820-40   *9in (23cm) diam*
£1,500-2,500   **H&L**

A Bloor Derby Imari-pattern 120-piece dinner service, comprising plates, dishes, tureens, stands, bowls and a wine cooler, with red painted crown, crossed batons, dots and D mark.
c1820   *Cooler 6in (15cm) high*
£1,200-1,800 set   **TEN**

A Derby vase, of flared cylindrical form, decorated in gilt and enamel, with beaded accents, raised on a circular foot.
6.5in (16cm) high
£120-180   **LHA**

An unusual Crown Derby reticulated scent bottle and stopper, the neck and shoulder, decorated with turquoise and white "jewelling" and reserved on a pink ground, the pierced lower section tinted turquoise, with printed mark.
c1880   *9in (23cm) high*
£1,000-1,500   **DN**

A Royal Crown Derby Sèvres-style two-handled vase and cover, decorated by Desire Leroy, painted with a panel of flowers signed "Leroy" on a dark-blue, turquoise and gilt ground, with iron-red printed mark.

1892   *6in (15cm) high*
£2,500-3,500   **DN**

A Royal Crown Derby 17-piece dessert service, comprising a tazza, two oval shaped dishes, two lobed dishes and 12 plates, gilded and decorated with bands of cobalt blue, turquoise and green, with printed marks.

This dessert service is extremely good value, when you consider the work that went into making it, and the 17 individual pieces it comprises. However, much like "brown furniture", it is not currently in fashion, and is, therefore, relatively affordable.

c1900
£800-1,200   **GORL**

A Royal Crown Derby "Old Imari" matched 75-piece dinner and tea service, comprising two comports, 55 plates, seven tea cups and saucers and four other pieces, decorated with pattern 1128.

c1900
£2,000-3,000 set   **GORL**

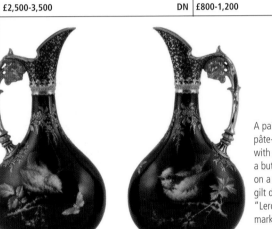

A pair of Royal Crown Derby pâte-sur-pâte ewers, enamelled with a bird on a branch, watching a butterfly, flowers and fungi on a cobalt blue ground with gilt decoration, each inscribed "Leroy" in the glaze, with printed marks and date codes.

1901   *10in (25.5cm) high*
£5,000-7,000   **WW**

A Royal Crown Derby Sèvres-style pedestal vase and cover, decorated by Desire Leroy with panels of flowers and trophies, on a dark-blue and gilt ground with turquoise "jewels", with shape number "F468/1414" and iron-red printed marks and date code.

1906   *8in (20cm) high*
£4,500-5,500   **DN**

A pair of Royal Crown Derby ewers, painted by Cuthbert Gresley with floral garlands between raised gilded columns of stylised foliage and trefoils, with printed marks and date codes.

1914   *9in (23cm) high*
£1,500-2,500   **WW**

A Royal Crown Derby two-handled vase and cover, painted by Albert Gregory with a band of flowers on burgundy and pale pink ground, with pine cone finial, signed, printed marks and date codes.

1918   *8in (20cm) high*
£1,000-1,500   **WW**

A Royal Crown Derby "Gold Aves" eight place dinner, tea and coffee service, comprising 25 plates, eight hors d'oeuvres dishes, two covered tureens, gravy boat, eight consommé cups and stands, eight tea cups and saucers, tea pot, coffee pot, cream jug, sucrier, octagonal fruit bowl, and a pair of candlesticks, with printed marks and date codes.

1937/8
£2,500-3,500 set   **SWO**

A 19thC Dresden group of dancers, the five dancers modelled on and around a rocky mound, on gilt-highlighted scrolling base, with blue crossed swords mark in underglaze blue.

13in (33.5cm) high

£800-1,200   ROS

A large 19thC Dresden vase and cover, with flower-encrusted garlands to the body and cover and painted with floral bouquets and butterflies, the finial in the form of a woman, with crossed swords mark in underglaze blue.

26in (66cm) high

£500-700   ROS

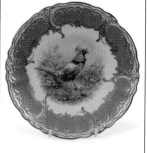

A 19thC Dresden part dessert service, the four plates decorated with a game bird, within a green and gilt border.

9in (23cm) diam

£200-250 set   CHT

A late 19thC Dresden "Nodder" figure, after the Meissen model, the seated figure with moving head and hands, with Dresden mark in underglaze blue.

10.5in (27cm) high

£800-1,200   LHA

A late 19thC Dresden reticulated part dessert service, after an original by Meissen, comprising a pair of tazzas, 16 plates, and three large dishes, each painted with harbour scenes, against floral decorated white ground enriched with gilt, crowned blue "D" mark.

£1,500-2,500 set   L&T

A late 19thC Dresden group, depicting five characters in Louis XVI style costume celebrating, with crowned "S" mark.

20in (51cm) wide

£1,500-2,500   LHA

A late 19thC Dresden figural group, depicting a parlour scene with a woman with two children and a courting couple beside a piano.

24in (61cm) wide

£1,800-2,200   LHA

A late 19thC Potschappel-Dresden Carl Thieme centrepiece, the pierced basket above a columnar standard, decorated with applied putti, with all-over foliate and gilt decoration.

In the late 19thC and early 20thC, there were at least 40 workshops or *hausmalers* (home decorators, who decorated white porcelain from elsewhere) in and around the city of Dresden. Many of them worked in the Meissen style. In 1872 Carl Thieme, a former *hausmaler*, founded the Saxon Porcelain Manufactory in Potschappel to manufacture his own porcelain pieces.

16.5in (42cm) high

£800-1,200   LHA

A late 19thC Potschappel-Dresden Carl Thieme jardinière, with pierced lattice work decoration, and applied flowers and figures of the four seasons, raised on four scrolled legs, with mark in underglaze blue.

42in (107cm) high

£400-600   LHA

A late 19thC cabinet with Potschappel-Dresden Carl Thieme porcelain decoration, the black lacquered wooden cabinet decorated with lattice rocailles, flowers, raised turquoise and pink leaves, and various models of women and children.

81in (214cm) high

£18,000-22,000   DOR

A late 19thC Dresden mirror frame, with raised light turquoise, pink and gilt leaf rocailles, garlands of flowers, with depiction of "The Five Senses", Cupid, cherubs and five children.

35in (90cm) high

£1,500-2,500   DOR

An early 20thC Dresden floral encrusted mirror frame, with applied musical putti and flowers, the mirror flanked by side panels with foliate scroll candle arms.

33in (85cm) high

£1,000-1,500   FRE

A large late 19thC/early 20thC Dresden mirror frame, with stepped pediment centred by a plaque painted with a lover's tryst, the other sides applied with musical cherubs, birds, and figures.

65.5in (166cm) high

£2,000-3,000   FRE

A pair of 20thC Dresden ice pails, covers and liners, painted with polychrome flower sprays amidst single scattered blooms, printed and impressed marks.

12in (30.5cm) high

£1,200-1,800   WW

An early 20thC Dresden centrepiece, the central oval basket supported by a flower-encrusted column with putti attendants on a moulded base, with crossed swords mark.

14in (36cm) high

£150-250   GORL

A Dresden "In The Garden" painted plaque, painted with a young Classical woman within a gilded frame, flanked by decorative panels of stags and vases in turquoise and deep salmon pink, with blue printed "Dresden Germany" and lamb symbol, titled "IM Garten" in black script.

c1900   *10in (25.5cm) wide*

£500-700   TEN

A pair of late 19thC Dresden flower-encrusted bottle vases, painted with panels of Watteauesque scenes and flowers.

12in (30.5cm) high

£250-350   DN

Two early 20thC Dresden cabinet plates, painted by E.Volk with portraits of maidens within duck egg blue borders.

Largest 10in (25.5cm) diam

£1,000-1,500   GORL

A mid-late 20thC Dresden figural group, depicting three seated maidens over a naturalistic flower encrusted base, set on a base fitted as a lamp.

15in (38cm) wide

£600-800   LHA

PORCELAIN

ESSENTIAL REFERENCE - LIVERPOOL

Several porcelain factories were established in 1750s Liverpool. Many used copies of Worcester's porcelain formula, leading to confusion over attribution of their wares.

- Richard Chaffers & Partners c1754-65: The most successful Liverpool porcelain maker. Chaffers bought Worcester's porcelain recipe in 1755, and produced thin teawares decorated with blue-and-white Chinese-style patterns.
- Philip Christian c1765-76: Took over from Chaffers.
- James, John and Seth Pennington c1769-99: Brothers with separate works around the city. Majority of Pennington wares in blue-and-white. The glaze is sometimes tinted.
- Samuel Gilbody c1764-61: Rarest of all Liverpool wares.
- William Reid c1755-61: Mainly blue-and-white wares with crude, semi-opaque body. Declared bankrupt in 1761.
- William Ball c1755-69: Took over from Reid. Decoration often resembled delftware.

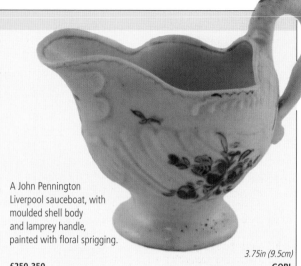

A John Pennington Liverpool sauceboat, with moulded shell body and lamprey handle, painted with floral sprigging.

3.75in (9.5cm)

£250-350   GORL

A Chaffers Liverpool blue-and-white vase and cover, of hexagonal panelled baluster shape, the neck painted with lozenge trellis, the shoulder panels and base centred by lotus blossoms alternately against cellular backgrounds, with ovoid finial.

This vase is part of an unrecorded garniture of Chaffers Liverpool.

c1755-60   12in (30.5cm) high
£6,000-8,000   TEN

A pair of small Chaffers Liverpool baluster shape mugs, the chinoiserie landscapes incorporating pylon and bubble trees, with lattice borders.

c1770   2.5in (6.5cm) high
£2,500-3,500   TEN

A John and Jane Pennington Liverpool cannonball-form teapot, decorated in underglaze blue, red, pink and gold, with a scroll bordered panel containing an exotic bird, verso a chrysanthemum bloom and a fence.

c1770-94   7in (18cm) high
£200-250   H&L

A Liverpool saucer dish, painted with bold flowers.

c1770   6.75in (17cm) diam
£100-150   SWO

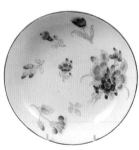

A Liverpool teabowl and saucer, painted with flowering prunus and chrysanthemum issuing from rockwork, within a hatched border.

c1775   Saucer 5in (12.5cm) diam
£350-450   WW

LEFT: A mid-18thC Longton Hall dish, modelled as overlapping cabbage leaves with puce veining and wide green edges, with a stalk handle.

9.75in (25cm) long

£1,500-2,500 **FRE**

RIGHT: A mid-18thC Longton Hall dish, modelled as overlapping leaves edged in yellow and green with pink veining, with a stalk handle.

9.75in (25cm) long

£1,000-1,500 **FRE**

A Longton Hall melon tureen and cover, the ridged body moulded with raised veins, glazed in green and yellow, with a vine stem finial, with workman's "W" mark.

c1755 *5in (125cm)*

£2,000-3,000 **WW**

A Longton Hall cabbage leaf sauceboat, with double branch moulded handles, the interior painted with flower spray and insect, the exterior in puce and bright green.

c1755 *8in (20cm) wide*

£1,500-2,500 **TEN**

A Longton Hall vase and cover, the Rococo-moulded body and cover applied with large flower heads above panels of painted butterflies and insects.

c1755 *10in (25.5cm) high*

£400-600 **WW**

A Longton Hall blue-and-white sparrowbeak jug, with a chinoiserie landscape, with angular handle, with painter's number "3".

c1775 *3in (7.5cm) high*

£700-1,200 **TEN**

A Longton Hall blue-and-white coffee cup, painted with birds and a house in a mountainous landscape.

c1755-60 *3in (7.5cm)*

£350-450 **WW**

A Longton Hall strawberry dish, the rim moulded with three sprigs of fruiting strawberry plant between three leaves, the well painted with flower sprays and scattered blooms.

c1756-57 *9in (23cm) diam*

£1,500-2,500 **WW**

A Longton Hall ovoid mug, printed by Sadler of Liverpool with the arms of the Society of Bucks, the print inscribed "Sadler Liverpool".

It is thought possible that Sadler bought many Longton Hall mugs in the white as a vehicle for its prints.

c1760 *6in (15cm) high*

£2,000-3,000 **DN**

An early Lowestoft blue-and-white bell-shaped mug, painted with a pagoda amongst trees and pierced rocks, beneath a berry border.

c1765-68
6in (15cm) high
£1,200-1,800   A&G

A rare Lowestoft model of a cygnet, from the same mould as a Lowestoft swan, the feathers painted in sepia enamel, the beak and eyes naturally painted.

The Lowestoft porcelain factory was founded in Suffolk in 1757 and closed c1800. It specialised in simple-form tablewares, painted or printed in underglaze blue, largely with chinoiserie designs. The Worcester porcelain factory was a major influence on shape and design, but Lowestoft porcelain is coarser and more prone to staining. Many pieces pre-1775 are numbered inside the footrim or on the base. Birth tablets and pieces inscribed for the local market are sought after. This cygnet is particularly rare and desirable.

c1785   *2.25in (5.5cm) long*
£12,000-18,000   **LOW**

A late 18thC Lowestoft coffee pot, of baluster shape, painted with peonies issuing from rockwork on one side, a spray of peonies on the other, with cushion knop.

9in (23cm) high
£1,200-1,800   **TEN**

A Lowestoft inkwell, painted with flowers and "A Trifle from Lowestoft".
c1800
2.75in (7cm) diam
£6,000-8,000   **POOK**

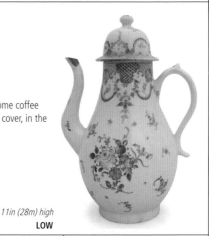

A Lowestoft polychrome coffee pot and high-domed cover, in the "Curtis" pattern.

11in (28m) high
£5,000-7,000   **LOW**

A rare Lowestoft custard cup and cover of bulbous form, painted with blue and gilt sprigs, with flower knop to cover.
£4,500-5,500   **LOW**

A Lowestoft powder blue coffee pot and cover.
£2,500-3,500   **LOW**

A Lowestoft moulded jug, the body painted with Oriental island and man on bridge, with mask beneath the lip of a bearded man, deep fine border, with unusual pierced hole in footring, with decorator's mark "5".
10in (25.5cm) high
£2,500-3,500   **LOW**

A Lowestoft blue-and-white plate, painted with standing woman with parasol in a fenced garden with a large urn.
9in (23cm) diam
£1,000-1,500   **LOW**

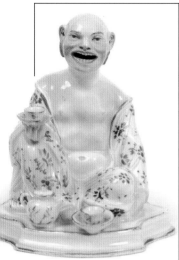

A Meissen pagoda figure, holding a tea bowl and saucer in his right hand, a further tea bowl and teapot in front of him, enamel decoration and later painted overglaze blue crossed swords mark, and "KJ" and three dots.

Early 18thC Meissen pagoda figures were copied from original Chinese blanc-de-chine examples. The figures gradually evolved, with the popular nodding head variant (first created by J. J. Kandler) being introduced c1730.

c1730   *4in (10cm) high*
£8,000-12,000   **TEN**

CLOSER LOOK - MEISSEN PART TEA AND COFFEE SERVICE

Meissen was the only European factory producing quality hard-paste or true porcelain at this date.

This is a rare and desirable set from the company's golden age.

The *laub-und-bandelwerk* borders exhibit the skill of gilder "T".

The typical harbour, rustic and sea-battle scenes are painting in miniature – the quality is exceptional.

An early 18thC Meissen part tea and coffee service, comprising 12 pieces painted with rustic and harbour scenes, including two nocturnal views, within *laub-und-bandelwerk* borders incorporating Böttger-lustre, with underglaze-blue crossed swords mark and gilder's mark "T".

Coffee pot 8.25in (21cm) high
£50,000-70,000   **SOTH**

A Meissen white teapot, the gently fluted body with semi-sculptural foliate branches on the lid, body and branch handles, with underglaze blue crossed swords mark.

This is after a Chinese model.

c1730   *3.5in (9cm) high*
£9,000-11,000   **DOR**

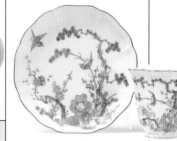

A Meissen Kakiemon-style fluted beaker and saucer, of bracketed circular form, painted with the "Three Friends" pattern, within brown line rims, with blue crossed swords mark and pressnummer 24.

c1735
£3,000-4,000   **TEN**

ESSENTIAL REFERENCE - MEISSEN

Meissen (est. 1710) became Europe's first porcelain factory, with the discovery of hard-paste porcelain by Johann Böttger.

- **Its great period began in 1720 with the appointment of J. G. Höroldt as chief painter. Meissen became Europe's foremost porcelain factory in the 1730s, with its shapes, decoration and crossed swords mark (introduced 1723) widely copied.**
- **J. J. Kändler became chief modeller in 1733; he helped produce some of its finest figures, such as the Monkey Band (see p31).**
- **Early decoration showed Oriental influence. Naturalistic flowers known as *Deutsche Blumen* ("German flowers") were popular from c1740.**
- **From the early 19thC, pieces in popular styles, such as Empire, Gothic Revival and Rococo, were produced in quantity.**
- **The Art Nouveau and Art Deco periods saw Meissen producing new and original designs by Paul Scheurich and Max Esser.**
- **The factory is still active.**

A rare Meissen Böttger porcelain fluted bowl and cover, Dutch-decorated in the famille rose palette with three Chinese figures beneath willow and flowering prunus, the cover moulded with fourteen impressions containing flower motifs, the underside painted with a peony.

c1720   *6in (15cm) high*
£5,000-7,000   **WW**

A Meissen cup and saucer, with segmented underglaze blue rims, borders, double rings, rosettes, saucer with tendrils in relief, the underside with two underglaze blue leaf tendrils, with underglaze blue crossed swords mark.

c1735   *cup 2in (5cm) high*
£2,000-3,000   **DOR**

A Meissen teabowl and saucer, the bowl exterior painted with a continuous band of Höroldt-style chinoiserie figures, the interior and saucer with figures holding fly swats, within gilded borders, with crossed swords marks.

c1735   Saucer 5in (12.5cm) diam
£2,500-3,500   **WW**

A Meissen armorial hot milk jug, from the Mauro D'Averso service, decorated in the manner of Bonaventura Gottlieb Haüer, the main body decorated in colours with estuary scenes and merchants discussing business, the gilded wishbone handle with shell thumb-piece, the armorial painted beneath the spout, with blue crossed swords mark.

The arms are Mauro D'Averso of Naples quartering Branciforte and Collonna of Naples, the Pucci of Florence and the Crespi of Venice. D'Averso is the only Neapolitan known to have ordered an armorial service from the Meissen factory.

c1740   5in (12.5cm) high
£7,000-10,000   **TEN**

A Meissen figure of a Turkish woman with lute, the model by J. J. Kändler and Peter Reinicke, with underglaze blue crossed swords.

c1744   6in (15cm) high
£5,000-7,000   **DOR**

A Meissen chocolate pot and cover, the body decorated with a continuous harbour scene with figures discussing business, the cover with base-metal hinged handle and sliding escutcheon, the crabstock handle with turned wood socket grip, enriched with leafy florets, with blue crossed swords mark, impressed dreher's mark of a quatrefoil flower, gilder's numeral "28".

c1745
£5,000-7,000   **TEN**

A pair of Meissen figures of a dancing country couple, with underglaze blue crossed swords mark on reverse of plinth.

c1745   7.5in (19cm) high
£15,000-20,000   **DOR**

A Meissen figure of a town crier with map of the Duchy of Silesia, from the "Cris de Paris" series by Peter Reinicke, with blue crossed swords on unglazed base.

c1745   6.5in (16cm) high
£25,000-35,000   **DOR**

A miniature Meissen vase, from the Saxon Court, painted with two dragons in iron-red and gilt above stylised motifs, with blue crossed swords mark and "KHC" in purple.

KHC stands for Königliche Hof-Conditorei (Royal Court Pantry). Pieces marked with these initials were designated for use on the Saxon palace dessert table.

c1745   2.5in (6.5cm) high
£1,500-2,500   **WW**

A Meissen warrior group, in the centre the standing God of War, to the side two putti and Cupid with lion's pelt, shield and the club of Hercules, with blue crossed swords on unglazed base.

c1750   8in (20cm) high
£8,000-12,000   **DOR**

A Meissen porcelain potpourri vase and cover, modelled by J.J. Kändler, the baluster form mounted with flowering vines, below a lady and cupid gather flowers, on a Rococo scroll base, with underglaze blue crossed swords mark.

c1750   13.75in (35cm) high
£2,000-3,000   **FRE**

A Meissen porcelain plate, decorated with an image of a military camp from the Seven Years' War, with painted flowers, with underglaze blue crossed swords, impressed "56".

c1756-1763   9in (23cm) diam
£1,500-2,500   **DOR**

ESSENTIAL REFERENCE - MEISSEN MONKEY BAND

Meissen's monkey band was created for Count Brühl, Chief Minister of Frederick Augustus II of Saxony and director of the Meissen factory 1733-1763.
Brühl is also well known to Meissen lovers for commissioning a figure of his tailor riding a goat (see below).

- All 21 monkey figures were modelled by J. J. Kändler. Together they form an orchestra (including a singer and a conductor with a music stand), dressed in 18thC court costume.
- Copies are still being made, both at Meissen and at other European factories.

A Meissen monkey band double bass player figure, model by J. J. Kändler and Peter Reinicke, on raised gilt base with rocailles, with blue crossed swords mark.

c1765-1766   *4.75in (12cm) high*

£2,000-3,000   DOR

A mid-18thC Meissen figure of a dancing peasant, perhaps modelled by J. J. Kändler, raised on a square base applied with flowers, with crossed swords mark to the reverse, black "F" to the base, restoration.

7.25in (19cm) high

£4,000-6,000   WW

Three Marcolini Meissen pictorial plates, decorated with scenes from the fables of La Fontaine, *L'Agne et le Sanglier*, *Le Loup et la Brebis*, *Le Singe et le Renard*, within gilt and light green and white painted bands, with underglaze blue crossed swords and star.

c1780   *9in (23cm) diam*

£2,500-3,500   DOR

A pair of late 18thC Meissen bison hunting groups, modelled by J. J. Kändler, raised on flower encrusted bases, with crossed swords marks, restoration.

9in (23cm) wide

£5,000-7,000   WW

A Marcolini Meissen ornithological coffee can and saucer, the can painted with two oval reserves in vivid enamels with tropical birds, the saucer centred by an eagle owl being mobbed by four birds, within tooled gilt lines with brown beaded borders, linked by swags of husks, with solid gilt banded rims, with blue crossed swords and star mark.

c1790   *Saucer 5in (12.5cm) diam*

£1,200-1,800   TEN

A pair of 19thC Meissen parrots, enamelled in turquoise, yellow, orange and purple, with underglazed blue crossed swords mark.

13in (33.5cm) high

£2,500-3,500   AH

A pair of 19thC Meissen crested cockatoos, after models by J. J. Kändler, enamelled in pinks and yellows, perched on mossy tree stumps, incised "57a", impressed "34" and "32", with crossed swords marks.

10in (25.5cm) high

£1,200-1,800   WW

A large 19thC Meissen figure of Count Bruhl's tailor, riding a goat, after a model by J. J. Kändler.

17.5in (44cm) wide

£12,000-18,000   GORL

A pair of large Meissen figures of "The Gardener" and "The Gardener's Wife", modelled after Johann Carl Schönheit, on square scrolling bases, the bases with blue crossed swords mark and incised "2868" and "B.65", damages.

Tallest 20in (51cm) high

£4,000-5,000   H&L

BEWARE!

Just because a piece has a crossed swords mark, does not mean it's Meissen. So great was the quality and success of Meissen that there were few 18th and 19th century factories that did not attempt to pass off their wares as Meissen. This mark is from a mid-late 18thC Worcester saucer (yes, even Worcester: one of England's best 18thC factories stooped this low).

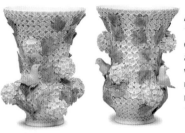

A pair of early 19thC Meissen "snowball" vases, the body encrusted with white flowers and flowering branches, each with two seated yellow birds, underglaze blue crossed swords mark, model "2760", modeller "80", painter "10", restoration.

7.75in (19.5cm) high

£3,500-4,500 DOR

A mid-late 19thC Meissen model of "Apollo and Daphne", modelled by J. J. Kändler c1745, the raised purple base with rocailles covered with green leaves, with underglaze blue crossed swords mark, model "2900", and painter "33".

Unable to escape from Apollo's love, the nymph Daphne begged her father Peneus (the river god) to save her. She was transformed into a laurel tree, and since Apollo could no longer marry her, he vowed to tend her tree, promising that her leaves would decorate the heads of leaders as crowns and would be depicted on weapons.

18in (45.5cm) high

£10,000-15,000 DOR

A large 19thC Meissen figure group of Apollo and Minerva, after a model by J.J. Kändler, the gods attended by Cupid, a nude male figure and dragon below, raised on a stepped shaped base, with blue crossed swords and incised marks.

15in (38cm) high

£6,000-8,000 FRE

A pair of Meissen pedestal pot pourri vases and covers, encrusted with figures, painted with Watteauesque figures in a woodland glade and flower sprays, framed by encrusted flowers and flanked by a pair of infants, the other, with tall encrusted flower finials, with crossed swords mark in underglaze blue, one with incised "2707".

c1870 *17in (43cm) high*

£3,500-4,500 TEN

A pair of Meissen flower-encrusted figural chambersticks, depicting a dancing couple in 18thC costume, on scroll-edged Rococo plinths, with underglaze blue painted crossed swords mark, impressed "91" and incised "166".

c1875 *9in (23cm) high*

£1,200-1,800 TEN

A late 19thC Meissen figural group, depicting two women with cherubs.

9.75in (25cm) high

£1,500-2,500 LHA

A Meissen tiger baiting group, modelled as three dogs attacking a tiger, cancelled crossed swords mark and incised "2678", damages.

c1870 *9in (23cm) wide*

£400-600 SWO

A late 19thC Meissen figure of a putto, holding a scroll of "Eirath's Contract" in one hand and a shoe behind his back, with underglaze blue crossed sword mark, impressed "136".

10.75in (27.5cm) high

£1,800-2,200 LHA

A late 19thC Meissen model of Venus and Cupid, with crossed swords mark, incised "1346", impressed "93", marked "5".

12.75in (33cm) high

£1,200-1,800 LHA

A late 19thC Meissen figural group, depicting two ladies and two putti fishing, with underglaze blue crossed swords mark, incised "635".

12.25in (31cm) high

£1,500-2,500 LHA

A late 19thC Meissen figural centrepiece, in two parts, the main section in the form of a gallant and his lady, the pedestal base raised on four scroll feet, with underglaze blue crossed swords mark, and incised "2772".

22.5in (57cm) high

£4,000-6,000   LHA

A late 19thC Meissen figure of the apostle James, after a model by J.J. Kändler, on an incurved square pedestal base, the side panels decorated with the Hasburg-Lorraine coat of arms, with gilt details, with underglaze blue crossed swords mark.

19.25in (49cm) high

£5,000-7,000   FRE

A large late 19thC Meissen figural group of the "Conqueror of Olympia", she holding a wreath (lacking) while a putto reaches for the straps held in the man's hand, on an oval base with underglaze blue crossed swords and impressed mark, incised "O.179".

17in (43cm) high

£7,000-10,000   FRE

A late 19thC Meissen figural group of Columbine and Scaramouche, with underglaze blue crossed swords mark, incised "250", impressed "150".

A late 19thC Meissen figure of Cupid, standing beside a mask topped pedestal, writing on a tablet with his arrow, with underglaze blue crossed swords mark.

8.75in (22cm) high

£1,000-1,500   LHA

A late 19thC Meissen figural group, depicting a figure on an eagle, with underglaze blue crossed swords mark, with impressed "125", incised "530".

10.5in (27cm) high

£600-800   LHA

7.25in (18.5cm) high

£1,000-1,500   LHA

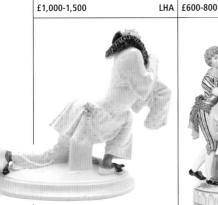

A late 19thC Meissen figure of a kneeling harlequin, on an oval base, with underglaze blue crossed swords mark, impressed "143", incised "D283".

7in (18cm) high

£1,200-1,800   LHA

A Meissen figure group of an amorous couple, with crossed swords mark, pressnummer "100", and incised "J60".

c1900   *12in (30.5cm) high*

£2,000-3,000   TEN

A late 19thC/early 20thC Meissen figural group of vintners, with underglaze blue crossed swords and impressed marks, incised "F2".

12in (30cm) high

£4,000-6,000   FRE

A large early 20thC Meissen flower stand, the shaped top painted with floral sprigs and applied flowers and foliage, on scrolled feet, with crossed swords mark to underside.

26.25in (66.5cm) long

£1,200-1,800   FRE

A Minton parian figure of Sir Robert Peel, standing beside a cloth-draped pillar, with incised ermine mark and year cypher.

1858   *19in (48cm) high*

£1,200-1,800   **TEN**

CLOSER LOOK - A MINTON PARIAN FIGURE

This group was conceived as a companion to "Ariadne on a Panther".

The full-scale statue, also known as "Purity", was included in the sculpture section of the Great Exhibition in 1851.

The subject is from Spencer's poem "The Faerie Queene". Una, who personifies True Religion, following her separation from the Red Cross Knight, is given protection by a lion who represents England. "The Lyon would not leave her desolate, but with her went along, as a strong gard of her chast person" ("The Faerie Queene", Book I, canto iii).

The diamond mark appears to have been registered at the Patent Office on 4th October 1847.

A Minton parian figure of "Una and the Lion", after John Bell, shape number 184, made for Summerley's Art Manufacturers, on a glazed shaped rectangular plinth, applied "Felix Summerley and John Bell" cartouche, also applied registered diamond and "Minton" impressed mark "N", "CM2" and "SJ" incised.

c1850-60   *14in (36cm) high*

£700-1,000   **TEN**

A pair of mid-19thC Minton figural candlesticks, he holding a tray of apples, she with an apron full of flowers, raised on circular Rococo bases, incised ermine marks, some restoration.

8in (20cm) high

£400-600   **WW**

A late 19thC Minton part-dessert service, comprising two tazzae and 12 plates, painted with a central arrangement of pink roses, within blue diaper borders, interspersed with rose wreaths, with impressed marks.

Largest plate 10in (25.5cm) diam

£350-450 set   **WW**

A Minton parian figure of a water nymph, after John Thomas 1861, impressed "Minton", year cypher and "T".

The original stone statue was exhibited at the Royal Academy in 1861 as "Nymph: Property of HM The Queen". It is now in the Royal Dairy at Frogmore.

31in (79cm) high

£1,200-1,800   **TEN**

A Minton parian figure of "Lalage", after John Bell, part-glazed and green-tinted figure, the maiden holding a floral garland, with incised title and "John Bell", impressed "Minton" and year cypher.

1868   *16in (40cm) high*

£500-700   **TEN**

A Minton lettuce leaf dish, a small rabbit with black ears nibbling at one fold, various marks, damages.

1869   *9in (23cm) long*

£200-300   **WW**

A pair of late 19thC Minton pâte-sur-pâte ewers, decorated and gilded with wild roses and ivy, with gilded marks.

11.25in (28.5cm) high

£1,200-1,800   **GORL**

A pair of Minton cabinet plates, by Henry Mitchell, painted with differing river scenes within blue and gilt surrounds the pierced rim with gilt Greek key pattern banding, each monogrammed "H M".

9.25in (23.5cm) diam

£300-400   **DA&H**

A pair of Nantgarw small tureens, covers and stands, London decorated with flowers, moulded with scrolling foliate panels and impressed marks to the stands.

c1814-23   *Tureens 7in (18cm) high*
£10,000-15,000   WW

A Nantgarw Sèvres-style plate, London-decorated, possibly in the Sims workshop, with flowers within a floral border reserved on a seeded blue ground, impressed "Nant-Garw C.W.".

c1818-20   *9in (23cm) diam*
£800-1,200   DN

A Nantgarw Sèvres-style square dish, with scattered floral bouquets and moulded in relief with borders of scrolling foliage, impressed "Nant Garw C.W.".

c1818-20   *9in (23cm) wide*
£1,500-2,000   DN

ESSENTIAL REFERENCE - NANTGARW

The Nantgarw porcelain factory was founded in South Wales by William Billingsley in 1813. The factory moved to Swansea in 1814. Billingsley and his partner William Weston Young returned to Nantgarw as decorators in 1817.

- **Pieces are marked "NANTGARW" with impressed "C.W." (china works). Many forgeries have a red painted mark.**
- **Billingsley was known for his high-quality rose painting. Much rich decoration was done by decorators in London.**
- **Nantgarw closed in 1822, reopening as a pottery factory 1833-1920.**

A Nantgarw plate, of the Macintosh Service type, painted in London by Robbins and Randall, with a bird within an elaborate gilt border, with four C-scroll panels of flowers, impressed "Nant Garw CW".

According to W.D. John, other services with this sort of decoration are known. The so-called Macintosh Service was owned by the Priest Richards Family of Plas Newydd, and passed through marriage to the Macintosh of Macintosh.

c1818   *9in (23cm) diam*
£4,500-5,500   DN

A Nantgarw Sèvres-style plate, with apple-green border with gilt scroll-edged floral reserves around a central spray of fruits and flowers, impressed mark "Nantgarw C.W.".

c1817   *8in (20cm) diam*
£1,500-2,500   TEN

A Nantgarw plate, of the Duke of Cambridge Service type, London decorated with flowers, birds, fruit and landscapes, impressed "Nant-Garw C.W.".

The service was thought to have been purchased from Mortlocks by the Prince Regent for the Duke of Cambridge in 1818 on the occasion of his marriage.

1818-20   *9in (23cm) diam*
£3,500-4,500   DN

A Nantgarw square dish, from the MacIntosh service, painted with a wading bird between aquatic plants, within borders of floral sprays and gilt shell and foliate motifs.

The painting on plates and dishes from this service is now believed to have been executed by Thomas Martin Randall at the establishment of Messrs. Robins & Randall, after engravings from Le Vaillant of Paris (c.1801-06).

c1818-20   *10in (25.5cm diam*
£3,000-4,000   WW

One of a pair of Nantgarw dessert plates, from the Cardiff Castle service, probably decorated by Thomas Pardoe, in a Canton enamel style with birds beneath a blue and floral ground band, with lobed panels of birds, impressed marks "NANT-GARW CW".

c1820   *8in (20cm) diam*
£4,000-6,000 pair   DN

A pair of Nantgarw plates, painted with floral sprays, impressed mark to reverse.

c1813-22   *8.5in (21.5cm) diam*
£1,500-2,500   GORL

A Nantgarw square dessert dish, painted in the manner of Morris, with flowers and and insects within a flower and gilt leaf meander border on a turquoise ground, with impressed marks.

c1820   *8.75in (22cm) wide*
£1,000-1,500   TEN

ESSENTIAL REFERENCE - NEW HALL

Established in Staffordshire, England, in 1781, New Hall originally produced porcelain wares elaborately decorated in imitation of Chinese export wares. Simpler patterns, such as sprigs of flowers in famille rose colours, were used from 1791 under the direction of key decorator Fidelle Duvivier.

- The factory was founded to exploit an improved version of Richard Champion's hard-paste porcelain patent. The resulting "hybrid hard paste" could be thinly potted. However, it did not produce a satisfactorily white body, so New Hall turned to "bone china" in c1815.
- The glaze tends to be thick, dull and greenish-grey.
- New Hall was the first porcelain manufacturer to assign pattern numbers to its designs. The printed mark was introduced c1812.
- Wares were aimed at the mass-market, with tea and coffee services providing the bulk of the range. More expensive pieces, such as figures and vases, were avoided.
- The factory closed in 1835.
- Later pieces are not as collectable as earlier examples.

An early 19thC New Hall dessert service, comprising nine plates, four trefoil dishes, two quatrefoil dishes, each with a vignette of working peasants within flower-moulded borders highlighted in grey and gilt, marked with pattern number "2229".

£400-600 set　　　　　　　　　　　　　　　　　　　AH

A large early 19thC New Hall floral bowl, pattern number 1373, the internal ground with blossoms in enamels and gilt, within gilded rim band, exterior with lobed and arched repeat panels, restored.

13in (33.5cm) diam

£300-500　　　　　　　　　　　　　　　　　　　　TEN

A pair of New Hall leaf-shaped serving dishes, painted with flowers, with ribbon-bow handles, one with painted pattern number "3371".

c1830　　　　　　　　　　　　　*8in (20cm) wide*

£150-250　　　　　　　　　　　　　　　　　　　　DN

A mid-19thC Paris part coffee service, painted with scenes of Paris within square gilt panels on a green ground, with printed marks "P.L. Dagoty & E. Honoré".

£3,500-4,500　　　　　　　　　　　　　　　　　　WW

A pair of Paris figural vases, with applied figures of huntsmen and hounds, each flared vase with leaf-moulded rim, some restoration.

c1860　　　　　　　　　　　　*16in (40cm) high*

£450-550　　　　　　　　　　　　　　　　　　　BELL

A pair of late 19thC Paris Empire-style twin-handled pedestal vases, with central figural landscape panels (reverse with flowerheads) surrounded by green ground with gilt flowerheads, with twin swan neck handles, and paw supports.

10in (25.5cm) high

£250-350　　　　　　　　　　　　　　　　　　　ROS

A 19thC Samson armorial wine cooler, the coat of arms surmounted by a coronet and surrounded by painted floral and gilt decoration, with a diaper band at the rim and shell-form handles.

9in (23cm) diam

£1,000-1,500   **FRE**

One of a pair of 19thC Samson famille jaune-style ewers and covers, the ribbed bodies painted with panels containing vases and auspicious objects, with "S" marks.

7in (18cm) high

£600-800 pair   **WW**

A pair of mid- to late 19thC Samson models of cockatoos, after Meissen, in plumage picked out in grey, yellow and orange, perched on tree stumps, with crossed swords marks.

19in (48cm) high

£1,200-1,800   **WW**

ESSENTIAL REFERENCE - SAMSON ET CIE

Edmé Samson's factory was established in Paris in 1845 with the aim of making exact copies of European and Oriental porcelain for collectors and museums.

- **Prior to this he had great success making replacements for broken pieces of dinner services.**
- **The factory is particularly well known for its excellent copies of Meissen and Chinese porcelain. English soft-paste porcelain copies are easier to detect due to the Continental hard-paste body.**
- **Samson wares can also be distinguished by a lack of sharp modelling and inaccurate palettes.**
- **French faience, Dutch Delft and some Strasbourg wares, as well as enamel and ormolu pieces, were also copied.**
- **Samson et Cie did not intend their replicas to be passed off as the real thing. Reportedly each piece was made with a letter "S" contained within the copied factory's mark. However, this can be easily removed.**
- **The factory closed in 1969. Its moulds were sold in 1979.**
- **Today Samson pieces are sought after in their own right, due to their decorative qualities.**

A large Samson famille verte-style vase and cover, painted with panels of figures, birds, flowers and rockwork, on a gilded powder blue ground, with lozenge mark.

c1880   *17in (43cm) high*

£350-450   **WW**

A probably Samson Sèvres-style fruit bowl, decorated with flowers between a mesh of green strapwork within solid banded borders with gilt *oeil de perdrix* motifs, with overglaze blue interlaced "LL" mark.

c1890   *12in (30.5cm) diam*

£400-600   **TEN**

A pair of mid-late 19thC Samson Bolognese terriers, after Meissen, decorated with patches of grey.

For an example of the Meissen originals see *Miller's Antiques Handbook & Price Guide 2010-2011*, p30.

13in (33.5cm) high

£700-900   **WW**

A pair of Samson Kakiemon-style vases and covers, of shouldered hexagonal form, decorated with flowers and foliage, between turquoise and blue foliate line borders, with hunting horn and cross marks in iron-red.

c1900   *13in (33.5cm) high*

£2,000-3,000   **TEN**

ESSENTIAL REFERENCE - VINCENNES

The Vincennes factory – which moved to Sèvres in 1756 – was established in c1740. It soon gained a 20-year exclusive privilege to produce porcelain from Louis XV. In 1753 the king restricted the use of subjects, colours and gilding by other French factories.

- Early wares were inspired by Meissen, with typical pieces featuring small flower sprays in soft colour palettes.
- Rococo shapes and patterns were introduced around 1750.

A mid-18thC Vincennes sucrière and cover, gilded with panels of birds in flight within shaped panels of foliage, on deep blue ground, with chrysanthemum finial, blue interlaced Ls mark.

5in (12.5cm) high
£3,500-4,500   **WW**

A Sèvres porcelain écuelle, cover and stand, the dark blue ground richly gilded, later painted with six reserves of harbour scenes, with blue interlaced "L's" mark enclosing "AA" over "M".
c1770   Écuelle 8in (20cm) wide
£2,500-3,500   **TEN**

A Sèvres cup and saucer, painted by Jean-Louis Morin with panels of marine subjects, on a dark blue ground with gilt borders of medallions, floral swags and foliate scrolls, interlaced "L's" mark, date letters "AA" and script painter's mark "M".
1778
£3,500-4,500   **DN**

A Sèvres cup and saucer, painted by Louis-Gabriel Chulot, the cup with an oval panel of grapes, the saucer with a trophy, both with S-scroll borders, the saucer with blue semi-quavers decorator's mark, the cup incised "TB".
c1780
£1,800-2,200   **DN**

A Sèvres cup and saucer, decorated by Charles-Nicolas Dodin, the cup painted with three musicians, the saucer a music room scene, both against dark blue grounds with gilt scroll, paterae and floral swag decoration, blue interlaced "L's" enclosing "AA", painter's mark "K", gilder's mark for Michel-Barnabe Chauvaux.
1778   Cup 3in (7.5cm) high
£10,000-15,000   **TEN**

All In The Mark

You can tell a lot from a mark if you know how to read it.

1. The interlaced "L's" shape signifies the factory: Sèvres.
2. The "KK" is a date mark, signifying the year 1787.
3. What looks like a "119" is actually an "NQ" signalling the painter, Nicquet (1764-1792).
4. The gilt "L" is the gilder's mark, for Louis-Francois Lecot.

A Sèvres cup and saucer, painted by Jean-Louis Morin, with marine scenes reserved on a turquoise ground, gilt with scrolling foliage, interlaced "L's" marks and script painter's mark "M".
c1780
£1,500-2,500   **DN**

A Sèvres potpourri canopic jar, the body with pierce-cut stars, gilt decoration and banding, with a central floral medallion flanked by a floral band, marked "M. Imp le Sèvres" in red ink.
1804-1809   11in (28cm) high
£2,000-3,000   **LHA**

A Sèvres cup and saucer, painted with panels of flowers reserved on a pale-yellow ground with swagged ornament and foliage.
£1,500-2,500   **DN**

A pair of 19thC Sèvres low bowls, with gilt and polychrome floral decoration, each with interlaced "L's" mark.

9.5in (24cm) diam

£1,500-2,500   LHA

A pair of late 19thC Sèvres-style gilt bronze mounted vases, depicting courting scenes, the magenta body with gilt foliate decoration.

19in (48cm) high

£1,500-2,500   LHA

A Sèvres-style pedestal baluster vase, painted to the front with a panel depicting two lovers in the manner of Émile Lessore, the reverse depicting a castle, on a dark blue ground with gilt, with overglaze blue interlaced "L's" marks centred by "L".

c1870   *29in (74cm) high*

£1,500-2,500   TEN

A pair of Sèvres-style portrait plaques, of Marie Antoinette and, probably, Madame de Pompadour, signed "Lebre", within ormolu frames, signed "Lebre".

c1875   *Plaques 9in (23cm) high*

£1,500-2,500   TEN

A pair of late 19thC Sèvres-style gilt metal-mounted covered urns, depicting pastoral scenes, on dark ground, mounted on four-legged bracket foot, with pineapple finial, marked inside the lids and under the feet.

26in (66cm) high

£5,000-7,000   LHA

A late 19thC Sèvres-style urn, depicting two winged putti, with raised and gilt swags to sides and lion mask handles, raised on gadrooned foot upon metal mount, signed.

21in (53.5cm) high

£1,200-1,800   LHA

A late 19thC Sèvres-style iridescent, gilt and ormulu mounted vase, the neck with reserves depicting profile portraits, the body painted with sea nymphs and cherubs, mounted on a square gilt metal base with paw feet, signed.

23in (58cm) high

£2,500-3,500   FRE

A set of six 19thC Sèvres allegorical plates, each painted with a scene of Classical maidens attended by putti, within a silver, foliate scroll and gilt border, inscribed with Sèvres marks.

10in (25.5cm) diam

£1,200-1,800   FRE

A large late 19thC Sèvres-style ormulu-mounted urn, painted with a scene of women attended by putti, the reverse with Cupid caught in a web, on a cobalt ground with gilt accents, with berry finial, signed "C(harles) Fuches".

34.25in (87cm) high

£6,000-8,000   FRE

A late 19thC Sèvres-style ormulu mounted urn and cover, of baluster form, decorated with a Classical maiden, signed "Poitevin".

37.5in (95cm) high

£6,000-8,000   LHA

PORCELAIN

A pair of large late 19thC Sèvres-style pot pourri vases and covers, painted with floral sprays, with twin winged female bust handles, floral painted fluted and gilded.

15.5in (39cm) high

£1,500-2,500　　　　　**GORL**

CLOSER LOOK - A SÈVRES ORMOLU-MOUNTED URN

This piece is of such high quality – it may have been produced for an exhibition.

A. Collot was a famous French porcelain painter and artist, known for his high-quality work at Sèvres in the late 19thC.

The size – 41.5ins (105cm) – is particularly large and impressive.

The piece is beautifully painted with cherubs, a gracious lady, flowers, a sea god and a fantastical fish.

The ormolu mounts are of the highest quality.

A late 19thC Sèvres ormolu-mounted urn, the body painted with a Classical scene, signed "Collot".

41.5in (105cm) high

£12,000-18,000　　　　　**LHA**

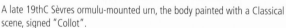

A late 19thC Sèvres-style ormolu-mounted urn, painted with a garden scene of a young couple in 18thC dress, raised on a square foot with scrolled feet.

39in (99cm) high

£3,500-4,500　　　　　**FRE**

A late 19thC Sèvres-style ormolu-mounted urn, decorated with a courting couple on a bench, verso with a landscape, signed "Carle", mounted as a lamp.

21.5in (55cm) high

£1,200-1,800　　　　　**LHA**

A pair of late 19thC Sèvres ormolu-mounted vases, decorated with mythological scenes, signed "Lebrum".

26in (66cm) high

£4,500-5,500　　　　　**LHA**

A pair of late 19thC Sèvres-style ormolu-mounted urns, depicting a pastoral scene and courting couples, one signed "E. Dalex", the other "Cor Biere", with raised scrolling gilt decoration.

20.5in (52cm) high

£1,200-1,800　　　　　**LHA**

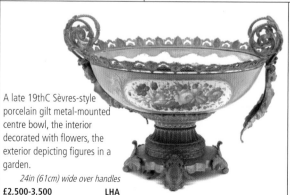

A late 19thC Sèvres-style porcelain gilt metal-mounted centre bowl, the interior decorated with flowers, the exterior depicting figures in a garden.

24in (61cm) wide over handles

£2,500-3,500　　　　　**LHA**

A large late 19thC/early 20thC Sèvres ormolu-mounted urn, painted with oval reserves of courting couples and landscapes, with raised gilt decoration, pinecone finial, and blue crossed interlaced "L's" mark.

33in (84cm) high

£4,000-6,000　　　　　**FRE**

ESSENTIAL REFERENCE - VIENNA

Claudius Du Paquier founded the first porcelain factory in Vienna, Austria, in 1718 with the assistance of defectors from Meissen. Early pieces were strongly influenced by Meissen.

- In 1744 Du Paquier sold the factory to the State. Chief modeller Johann Josef Niedermayer introduced a wide variety of figures, and other Rococo shapes.

- Sörgel von Sorgenthal was made director in 1784. The Rococo style was phased out in favour of the Neo-classical. Typical pieces include urn-shaped vases, richly painted and gilded.

- By 1820 the factory was in decline, and in 1864 it was closed by the Emperor.

A rare Vienna white figure of a farmer with vegetables, with underglaze blue Austrian shield, some firing cracks.

c1760   8in (20cm) high

£1,200-1,800   **DOR**

A Vienna white figural group of Summer, modelled by O. Dioniusius Pollion, depicting three reapers discovering a bird's nest in a cornfield, with underglaze blue Austrian shield.

c1760   8in (20cm) high

£2,500-3,500   **DOR**

A Vienna white figural group of a dancing harlequin family, modelled by F. Joseph Dangel, the plinth covered with flowers, with faint blue Austrian shield, some firing cracks and restoration.

c1765   9in (23cm) high

£2,000-3,000   **DOR**

CLOSER LOOK - VIENNA FIGURAL GROUP

This Classical figural group was modelled by F. Joseph Dangel, one of the most highly regarded porcelain modellers at the Vienna factory, who worked there from 1762 to 1804.

The group exhibits the great fluidity and fine detailing that is typical of this period.

Condition is crucial with these figure groups – check all extremities: bocage, fingers, toes for damage.

The rocaille base is typical of the Rococo styling of this period.

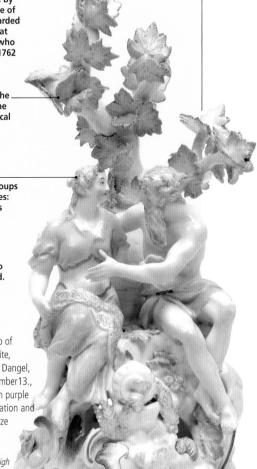

A Vienna figural group of Neptune and Amphitrite, modelled by F. Joseph Dangel, painted by painter number13., the pierced plinth with purple and gilt rocaille decoration and foliage, with underglaze blue Austrian shield.

c1765   11in (28cm) high

£4,000-5,000   **DOR**

A Vienna figural group of the "Santiago" pilgrim family, painted by painter number 24 Konrad Haab, the base covered with flowers, with underglaze blue Austrian shield, some firing cracks and restoration.

c1765   7in (18cm) high

£2,000-3,000   **DOR**

A Vienna cup and saucer, painted by Anton Schaller, the cup depicting "Aglaia enamoured of Cupid" after Angelica Kauffmann, the saucer with three lozenges with polychrome attributes of Summer, on dark blue ground, gilded, with underglaze blue Austrian shield.

1802 *5.25in (13cm) diam*

£3,500-4,500 **DOR**

CLOSER LOOK - VIENNA CUP AND SAUCER

The raised gilt handle has rolled flower and leaf terminals.

Due to the importance of this cup and saucer, all the artists are identified, including gilt painter number154 Ignatz Obenbiegler.

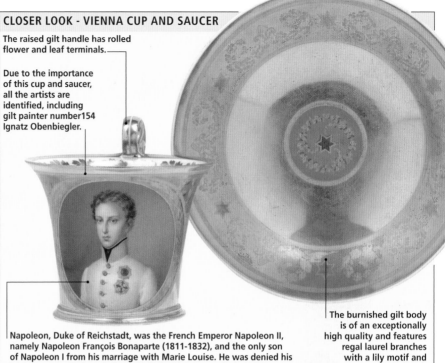

Napoleon, Duke of Reichstadt, was the French Emperor Napoleon II, namely Napoleon François Bonaparte (1811-1832), and the only son of Napoleon I from his marriage with Marie Louise. He was denied his inheritance in 1817, and given the Bohemian monarchy in 1818.

The burnished gilt body is of an exceptionally high quality and features regal laurel branches with a lily motif and stars on a matt gilt band.

A Vienna portrait cup and saucer, depicting the Duc de Reichstadt, the burnished gilt body with gilding to the interior, with underglaze blue and impressed Austrian shield.

1830 *Saucer 7in (18cm) diam*

£5,500-6,500 **DOR**

A Vienna Veduti cup and saucer, the cup with polychrome view "Vue du chateau I. R. Belvedere, vers le Bassin à Vienne", with raised gilt ear handle, the saucer in emerald green enamel, gilded by Johann Teufel, with underglaze blue Austrian shield.

This is a very rare view of Vienna.

1817 *3.75in (9.5cm) high*

£6,000-8,000 **DOR**

A Vienna pictorial plate, depicting "Diana and Endymion" with burnished and matt gilt borders, by Franz Schulz, with underglaze blue Austrian shield.

1823 *9in (23cm) diam*

£4,000-5,000 **DOR**

A pair of Austrian Vienna-style pedestal vases and covers, depicting scenes from mythology (one titled "Samson und Delilah"), against a gilt dark blue ground, each with printed underglaze blue beehive mark and blue shield stamp "FD Vienna Austria".

c1870 *12in (30.5cm) high*

£1,200-1,800 **TEN**

A pair of German Vienna-style pedestal vases, depicting figures in medieval costume, gilded with iridescent blue metallic finish to the neck, shoulder and base, each with beehive mark in underglaze blue and faint red original titles.

c1870 *15in (38cm) high*

£3,500-4,500 **TEN**

A German Vienna-style octagonal "Pandora and Prometheus" cabinet plate, within a panelled border, gilt throughout, with blue painted beehive mark and titled in red script.

c1890   *14in (36cm) wide*

£1,500-2,500   **TEN**

A pair of Continental Vienna-style vases and covers, decorated with frontal oval reserves printed with classical scenes after Angelica Kauffmann, against a turquoise jewelled, solid-gilded and powdered-ruby ground.

c1900   *14in (36cm) high*

£800-1,200   **TEN**

A late 19thC Vienna covered urn on stand, decorated with mythological scenes and mounted as a lamp.

19.5in (50cm) high

£1,000-1,500   **LHA**

A pair of late 19thC Vienna-style lidded vases, with central band of Classical scenes, signed "Wagner" on central panel, the undersides of both with cobalt blue beehive mark.

12.5in (32cm) high

£2,200-2,800   **LHA**

A late 19thC Vienna "jewelled" vase, with portrait of Erbluth, after Asti, the reverse with cupids, signed Otto Zwierzina, on a blue green iridescent and gilded ground, with floral decorator's overmark and blue beehive mark with red serial numbers, on carved giltwood base.

Vase 17.25in (44cm) high

£10,000-15,000   **FRE**

A German Vienna-style painted cabinet plate, "Der Gerbruchene Krug", painted with a young girl within a midnight blue border with gilt swans and foliage, signed "Volk", with blue printed beehive mark, titled in gilt and numbered "D202".

c1900   *14in (36cm) diam*

£2,000-3,000   **TEN**

A late 19thC Vienna-style three piece garniture, each decorated with Classical scenes.

23.5in (59cm) high

£1,200-1,800   **LHA**

An early 20thC Vienna covered urn, the frieze painted with a Classical scene, surrounded by gilt foliage, on concave fluted legs with paw feet on stepped circular base, with blue beehive mark.

17.5in (44cm) high

£3,000-4,000   **FRE**

PORCELAIN

Judith Picks: Worcester

People always want to know about antiques as an investment, and over the last 30 years many antiques have performed well compared with traditional investments. But it all depends when you have to sell. The value of antiques is affected by many things – and one of the most fickle is fashion.

I have been collecting early English porcelain since the early 1970s, and First Period Worcester is one of my favourite collecting subjects. I have an example of this blue-and-white chestnut basket and the equivalent polychrome example.

It seems that First Period Worcester pieces have slipped in value over the last few years, and while rare painted patterns from the 1750s have continued to increase in value, common patterns have struggled. Condition is also paramount.

Many auctioneers are grouping small pieces of the more common First Period Worcester printed patterns together in job lots. In short, it's a great time to buy.

These early English porcelains are over 200 years old and document the early years of English soft-paste porcelain manufacture.

A First Period Worcester blue-and-white basket and cover, the pierced lid above flower head trellis body, the well printed with gourds and flowers.
c1770   *8in (20cm) wide*
£700-1,000   **L&T**

A First Period Worcester blue-and-white shell-shaped pickle dish, painted with the "Two Peony Rock Bird" pattern, with workman's mark.
c1754-65   *5in (12.5cm) long*
£200-300   **H&L**

A large First Period Worcester blue-and-white tankard, painted in the "Prunus Fence" pattern, with grooved strap handle.
c1755-60   *6in (15cm) high*
£800-1,200   **H&L**

A large pair of First Period Worcester blue-and-white cornucopia wall vases, painted with branches of prunus beneath curlicue borders, one with crossed swords mark.
c1757-60   *12in (30.5cm) long*
£800-1,200   **WW**

A small First Period Worcester blue-and-white globular teapot, printed with the "Mother and Child" pattern, with hatched crescent mark.
c1775   *5in (12.5cm) high*
£400-600   **DN**

A First Period Worcester transfer-printed bowl, with three vignettes comprising milkmaid and gallant at a five-bar gate, "The Milkmaids", and an amorous couple, inside centre with two swans and a cygnet.

Bearing a Bayley Collection orange paper label, and vestiges of older label with ink inscription From Col Foster, Hornby Castle.
c1760   *6in (15cm) diam*
£250-350   **TEN**

A First Period Worcester transfer-printed sparrow beak jug, with a lady watering a garden and L'Amour in a garden with a Neptune fountain.

Bearing a Bayley Collection orange paper label.
c1760   *4in (10cm) high*
£400-600   **TEN**

A First Period Worcester transfer-printed baluster jug, by Robert Hancock, printed *en grisaille* with three chinoiserie subjects, "Le Feu", "La Terre" and "L'Oiseau Chinois".

c1765   *7in (18cm) high*
£1,500-2,500   **DN**

A rare early Worcester coffee cup, painted in Japanese Kakiemon-style with a branch of flowering prunus blossom, the double scroll handle with curled thumbrest.

c1752   *2.5in (6.5cm) high*
£2,000-3,000   **TOV**

A Worcester sauce boat, enamelled in the Meissen style with brightly coloured sprays of flowers and sprigs, with brown line rim, and spurred scroll handle.

c1760   *6.75in (17cm) long*
£500-700   **TEN**

A Worcester teabowl and saucer, printed and painted with the "Red Cow" pattern.

c1760
£200-300   **DN**

A small Worcester vase, of hexagonal pear-form, printed and painted with Chinese figures, damages.

c1765   *5in (12.5cm) high*
£1,200-1,800   **SWO**

A fine Worcester trio, painted with Budai and attendants in bright enamels and gilding.

c1765
£1,000-1,500   **SWO**

A Worcester blue scale soup plate, painted with gilt cartouches containing flowers, with blue seal mark.

c1765   *9in (23cm) diam*
£300-400   **WW**

A Worcester leaf-moulded cream jug, the outside decorated with the "Stag Hunt" pattern, the inner rim with underglaze blue leaves.

This may be an example of early Chamberlain decoration.

c1765   *3.5in (9cm) high*
£1,000-1,500   **SWO**

A Worcester trio, painted with exotic birds and insects in shaped panels on a yellow scale ground, with crossed swords marks.

c1770
£1,000-1,500   **SWO**

A Worcester double leaf-moulded dish, painted with chrysanthemum and prunus in the Imari palette, restoration.

c1770   *10.25in (26cm) wide*
£200-300   **WW**

A Worcester blue scale mug, painted on each side with a spray of flowers within gilt scroll edged shaped reserve, with gilded rim, with hatched square mark.

6in (15cm) high
£600-800   **TEN**

PORCELAIN

A Worcester teapot and cover, each side painted with a Chinese lady and her two children beneath a tree, bordered by panels of foliate tendrils.

c1770   *7in (18cm) high*
£350-450   **WW**

A Worcester teacup and saucer, painted with gilt-edged panels of colourful birds and insects on a blue scale ground, seal marks.

c1770-75   *5in (12.5cm) diam*
£300-400   **WW**

A Worcester dessert plate, with a scalloped rim, painted by Jefferyes Hammett O'Neale with a lion and lioness within a band of flowers, fruit, garlands and exotic birds, with blue open crescent mark.

c1775   *9in (23cm) diam*
£1,200-1,800   **SWO**

A Worcester teapot and cover, painted with two Chinese figures before a table, a third looking out of a window beside flowering prunus, a minute chip to the underside of the cover.

c1770-80   *7.5in (19.5cm) high*
£300-400   **WW**

A Worcester plate, painted with a dry-blue floral spray and swags in shades of turquoise and purple within gilt foliate scroll borders.

c1770-80
£500-700   **WW**

A Worcester lozenge-shaped dish, painted with flowers within a scroll and trellis gilded frame and deep blue border, with underglaze blue painted hatched square mark, restoration.

c1775   *10.25in (26cm) wide*
£200-300   **TEN**

A Worcester coffee pot and cover, painted with sprays of pink and yellow flowers, the spout and handle with gilt foliage.

c1780   *9.25in (23.5cm) high*
£300-400   **WW**

A fluted Worcester trio, decorated in the Kakiemon palette with a "Scarlet Japan" pattern.

c1775-80   *5in (12.5cm) diam*
£200-300   **WW**

A Worcester teapot and cover, painted in a version of the "Scarlet Japan" pattern with alternating panels of Chinese figures with birds, and Oriental flowers between orange stripes with chrysanthemum.

c1775-80   *7in (18cm) high*
£200-300   **WW**

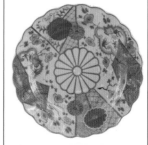

One of a pair of 18thC Worcester petal rim dishes, in the green dragon brocade pattern, with gold crescent mark.

8.5in (21.5cm) diam
£500-700 pair   **GORL**

A Worcester Barr, Flight & Barr urn, painted with views of Nantmellon, Wales and The Esk River, Scotland.

c1807-1813   *4.25in (11cm) high*
£1,000-1,500   **GORL**

One of a pair of Worcester Barr, Flight & Barr bulb jars, of demi-lune form, painted with panels of grazing sheep, each with three pierced covers.

c1810   *5in (13cm) high*
£1,500-2,500 pair   **POOK**

A pair of Worcester Flight, Barr and Barr mantle urns, with landscape roundels of Windsor Castle, Salisbury Cathedral, North Castle, Glamorganshire and Kirkham Priory Gateway.

c1815   *8in (20cm) diam*
£3,000-4,000   **POOK**

A rare Worcester Flight, Barr & Barr two-handled cabinet cup and saucer, enamelled with a profile portrait of the Duke of Wellington within a raised gilt border reserved on a blue ground, with puce Worcester and London House script marks.

The portrait of Wellington is not shown in this photograph but is, combined with the quality and maker, the primary reason this piece is worth as much as it is.

c1830   *3.25in (8.5cm) high*
£2,000-3,000   **H&L**

A pair of Grainger's Worcester reticulated vases, decorated with scrolling jasmine within "jewelled" borders, one pink and one blue, with printed marks.

c1870   *8.75in (22cm) high*
£600-800   **GORL**

A pair of Kerr and Binns Worcester vases, painted with dead game birds within gilt strapwork and leaf scroll border, with ring handles, painted marks.

9.75in (25cm) high
£600-700   **TEN**

WORCESTER MARKS

First Period Worcester
Used: c1755-92 (painted/or printed).

First Period Worcester
Used: c1755-75 (painted)

Flight period
Used: c1788-92 (painted)

Barr, Flight & Barr
Used: c1807-13 (impressed)

Flight, Barr & Barr
Used: c1813-40 (printed)

Royal Worcester
Used: 1891-1943 (printed)

PORCELAIN

PORCELAIN

A Chamberlain's Worcester crested part dessert service, the 14 pieces decorated with the "Dragons in compartments" pattern, the centre with an antelope crest, with iron-red script marks and painted pattern No 75.

c1800 Plates 8.5in (21.5cm) diam
£2,000-2,500 set   DN

A set of six Chamberlains Worcester plates, decorated with the "Bengal Tiger" pattern within double-lined gilt borders, with painted marks in grey and iron-red.

c1810   10in (25.5m) diam
£1,200-1,800   TEN

A Chamberlain's Worcester match pot or spill vase, enamelled after Thomas Baxter, with a gilt-framed rectangular panel of feathers reserved on a cream ground, painted mark in puce "Chamberlains Worcester".

c1820   4in (10cm) high
£600-800   H&L

A Chamberlain's Worcester part dessert service, the 25 pieces printed and painted with a variation of the "Two Quails" pattern, marked.
c1820
£1,000-1,500   DN

An early 19thC Chamberlain's Worcester composite part dinner service, in "Dragons in Compartments" pattern, comprising soup tureen, cover and stand, three oval dishes and six dinner plates, with printed and impressed marks.
£1,500-2,500   DN

ESSENTIAL REFERENCE - CHAMBERLAIN'S

A former head of decorating at Worcester, Robert Chamberlain (c1736-1798) left to start his own porcelain decorating business in 1783. It was soon successful, with Nelson placing an order in 1802, and the Prince Regent issuing a Royal Warrant in 1807.

● Chamberlain's & Co. took over former rivals Flight, Barr & Barr in 1840. The pieces from the period 1840-51 feature outstanding decoration.

● William Kerr took over in 1851.

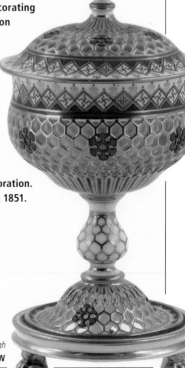

A Chamberlain's Worcester double-walled reticulated vase and cover, raised on a honeycomb knopped stand and three claw feet, puce factory marks.

A pair of Chamberlain's Worcester tureens and covers, with green and cream ground and painted with flowers.
c1835   8in (20cm) high
£800-1,200   DN

c1840-50   7in (18cm) high
£1,000-1,500   WW

An unusual Royal Worcester vase, possibly painted by James Callowhill, modelled with three samurai, verso trophies of war, impressed and printed mark with date code.

1878   *13.25in (34cm) high*

£800-1,200   **WW**

A 19thC Royal Worcester flower trough, moulded with shells and decorated with a lustre glaze, with central figure of a young boy and small dog, with impressed mark and raised registration mark.

                                    18in (45.5cm) high

£400-600   **WW**

A Royal Worcester pedestal vase and cover, decorated in applied white enamels with a heron amongst lilies and reeds, with handles terminating in grotesque animal masks, with puce marks, pattern number "1764" and date code.

1896   *16in (40cm) high*

£2,000-3,000   **H&L**

A Royal Worcester blush ivory figure of a dancing lady wearing a star-covered robe on a gilt rockwork base, with puce printed mark to the base and "no. 1441" with impressed marks.

                        23.5in (59.5cm) high

£800-1,200   **DUK**

A Royal Worcester pot pourri vase, inner lid and cover, painted by Charles Baldwyn with six swans in flight, signed, the base moulded with basket weave, with printed mark and date code.

1902   *8in (20cm) high*

£5,000-7,000   **WW**

A pair of Royal Worcester pedestal vases, shape number 2256, painted by Harry Davis with a ram, sheep and lamb by the edge of a loch, against an gilt and apricot ground, signed, with puce printed crown and wheel mark and year mark.

1907   *10in (25.5cm) high*

£2,000-3,000   **TEN**

A Royal Worcester vase, painted by Harry Stinton, shape number "G.405", with pierced rim, painted with two highland cattle in a misty mountain landscape, signed, with green painted crown and wheel mark and year mark.

1907   *4.5in (11.5cm) high*

£1,000-1,500   **TEN**

A Royal Worcester ewer, painted by Charles Baldwyn, shape number 1309, with four swans above raised gilt foliage on a bright sky blue ground, the reverse with two swallows, raised on a foot moulded with acanthus leaf lappets, signed, with printed marks and date code.

1907   *16in (40cm) high*

£10,000-15,000   **WW**

A Royal Worcester ewer, shape number 789, painted by Harry Davis with sheep beside a mountain tarn, the foliate handle issuing from a mask and terminating in a dolphin head, signed, with printed mark and date code.

1908   *13in (33.5cm) high*

£4,000-5,000   **WW**

An early 20thC Royal Worcester fruit painted vase, by William Ricketts, shape number "G42", with pierced-strapwork, gilded neck and leaf and knurl feet, with green printed crown and wheel mark.

8.75in (22cm) high

£800-1,200   **TEN**

A large Royal Worcester vase and cover, painted by John Stinton Jr with three Highland cattle in mountain landscape, shape number 1481, the reverse with a stream, signed, printed mark and date code.

The Stinton family are Royal Worcester's best-known artists. Henry Stinton was employed by Grainger's. His son, John Snr joined the factory in 1840, and quickly became one of the most important and respected artists. Two of his sons became major artists, John Jr (for Highland cattle) and James (for gamebirds). John Jr's son, Harry joined Worcester in 1896, and is highly regarded for his purple-hued Highland cattle scenes.

1910   *19in (48cm) high*

£4,000-5,000   **WW**

A large Royal Worcester two-handled vase, shape number 1969, painted by Harry Davis with three sheep by a stream, raised on a gilded and ribbed foot, signed, printed mark and date code.

1912   *16in (40cm) high*

£6,000-8,000   **WW**

A Royal Worcester "Ivory and Gold" Eastern water carrier, shape number 2/125, on a blush-ivory circular base, with green printed crown and wheel mark and year cipher.

1912   *20.5in (52cm) high*

£800-1,200   **TEN**

A small Royal Worcester two-handled pedestal vase, shape number 1969, painted by Harry Stinton with Highland cattle in a mountainous landscape, with matt green highlighted scroll lug handles and canted square base, signed, with printed mark in puce.

1913   *6.75in (17cm) high*

£1,000-1,500   **TEN**

A large Royal Worcester pot-pourri vase, cover and inner lid, painted by Edward Townsend with Highland cattle amongst heather, signed with black printed mark and painted shape number.

Edward Townsend, or Ted, started at the Royal Worcester factory in 1918 and stayed there until he retired in 1971. A member of the Terrible Seven (a group of apprentices who, in the most playful and harmless of manners, would terrorise the other Royal Worcester workers and leave work to play football whenever the opportunity arose). He loved painting fruit, but was also skilled in many other areas. He became assistant foreman to Harry Davis, and became foreman in 1954 when Davis retired.

13.25in (34cm) high

A Royal Worcester square scalloped dish, by Richard Sebright, the border decorated with gilt shells, flowers and foliage reserved on a pale ground, the well decorated with fruit and flowers, signed, with puce painted mark.

1917   *9.5in (24cm) wide*

£300-500   **L&T**

A Royal Worcester circular tapered pot pourri vase, shape number 2048, with richly painted roses and foliage and raised gilt ornamentation, with vegetable pattern finial, signed Sedgley and with date code.

1919   *17.5in (44cm) high*

£1,000-1,500   **A&G**

A pair of Royal Worcester pedestal vases, shape number 2120, painted by James Stinton with pheasants in a wooded landscape, raised on short fluted gilt pedestals and square plinth bases, signed and dated.

1919   *5.5in (14cm) high*

£1,000-1,500   **FLD**

£1,500-2,500   **WW**

A large pair of Royal Worcester vases, shape number 1410, painted by John Stinton Jr with Highland cattle by a mountain stream, with mask head handles, signed, with printed marks and a date code.

1920   *15in (38cm) high*
£6,000-8,000   **WW**

A Royal Worcester two-handled pot pourri vase and cover, shape number 1428, painted by John Stinton Jr with Highland cattle, mounted on a rocaille-moulded, low-pedestal, solid-gilded foot, with puce printed crown and wheel mark, year cypher.

1921   *13in (33.5cm) high*
£6,000-8,000   **TEN**

A fine Royal Worcester twin handled vase, painted by W. A. Hawkins with fruit and flowers, on a gilded dark blue ground, twin gilded handles and base, with date code.

1921   *12.5in (32cm) high*
£4,000-5,000   **GORL**

A Royal Worcester vase, painted by Harry Davies, pattern number 2491, sheep amongst bluebells in a woodland landscape, with puce backstamp and date code.

1926   *6in (15cm) high*
£2,000-3,000   **H&L**

A Royal Worcester lidded vase, painted by John Freeman with fruit, of bellied form with pointed finial and gilded mask, raised on gilded foot, with black mark.

John Freeman was born in 1911 and joined the Royal Worcester factory in 1925. He became an extremely talented fruit and still-life painter, and was probably the most prolific of all the fruit painters of his time. He stayed at the Royal Worcester factory throughout his long working life and became the senior fruit painter in the mens' painting room. John Freeman was known among his colleagues as "The Fruit Machine", due to the speed of his output.

14in (36cm) high
£4,000-6,000   **HT**

A small Royal Worcester circular plaque, painted with five sheep in a Highland landscape, the sun setting, with printed mark and date code.

1929   *2.75in (7cm) diam*
£400-600   **WW**

A Royal Worcester fruit painted bowl, shape number 2577, painted by Richard Sebright, with a gilded narrow rim band, externally with solid black glaze, signed, with blue printed crown and wheel mark, and year mark.

The choice and quantity of fruits shown, the arrangement, and the painter, are all factors that affect the value of this type of porcelain.

1931   *12in (30.5cm) diam*
£2,000-3,000   **TEN**

A Royal Worcester vase, shape number F126, painted by Harry Stinton with Highland cattle, signed "H Stinton", below moulded and gilded foliate border and cup-shaped neck, dated.

1933   *4.75in (12cm) high*
£800-1,200   **FLD**

A Royal Worcester fruit-painted jar and cover, shape number 2826, painted by Horace Price, with milled-gilt rim bands, signed, with puce printed crown and wheel mark, year mark.

1938   *6in (15cm) high*
£1,500-2,500   **TEN**

A Bristol two-handled cup and saucer, with osier-moulded rims, painted with a garland of flowers including rose and nigellus, painted "B4" mark.

c1775 *6in (15cm) high*

£350-450 **WW**

A Plymouth porcelain mug of baluster form, with ribbed strap handle, enamelled with flowers beneath a gilt and brown rim, with pale blue cross mark.

c1770 *5in (12.5cm) high*

£500-700 **H&L**

A Plymouth mug, painted with three large colourful birds amidst rich green foliage, the other side with two kingfishers in flight, with gilt rim.

England's first hard-paste porcelain was produced at the Plymouth porcelain works in 1768 by chemist William Cookworthy. Unfortunately, due to technical difficulties, many pieces made during Plymouth's short period of production (1768-70) show distortions (e.g. cups have handles askew) and a smoky, spotted glaze. In 1770 Cookworthy moved the factory to Bristol and, in 1774, he assigned his patent to Richard Champion, who sold it to New Hall (see p36).

c1768-70 *6in (15cm) high*

£2,500-3,500 **WW**

A pair of possibly Ridgway vases, one painted with a maiden milking a goat or ewe, the other with a satyr and a goat, on a matt blue and gilt ground, the handles formed as twin serpents.

Brothers Job and George Ridgway established their factory in 1794, moving it to Cauldon Place, Shelton, England in 1802. The factory, which was run by Job's sons John and William after his death in 1813, produced porcelain and blue-and-white decorated stone china, which became known as "Cauldon ware". The latter became extremely popular, with much exported to the USA with new patterns developed specially for the market. William set up his own factory in 1830, which produced similar wares. The Cauldon factory exhibited gilt and polychrome porcelain at the Great Exhibition in 1851.

c1815-20 *11in (28cm) high*

£1,500-2,500 **WW**

A Rockingham pedestal bowl, painted with four floral posies within blue borders gilded with ears of barley, with red printed griffin mark, "Rockingham Works Brameld", and red script "CL.7".

c1826-30 *11in (28cm) diam*

£600-800 **TEN**

A Rockingham raised comport, from the service supplied to William IV, decorated with flowers, with puce gryphon mark.

By descent to the present owner from his ancestor William Newman, land agent to Earl Fitzwilliam, patron of the Rockingham Works. Due to manufacturing faults it is possible that the naive painting could have been executed by a local, amateur hand.

c1830-40 *11.5in (29cm) high*

£1,000-1,500 **DN**

Judith Picks: Wedgwood tête-à-tête

This is the type of item that can disappoint visitors to the Antiques Roadshow. It seems to tick lots of boxes: excellent maker (Wedgwood), over 100 years old (c1880), hand-painted, on a good "cracked-ice" ground. So why is it worth so little? Unfortunately I blame my daughters and their generation. Who makes formal tea these days? We use mugs and put them in the dishwasher. The floral painting is out of fashion in today's minimalist interiors. Victorian teasets (unless a very rare and desirable pattern) are very poor sellers.

Will this trend reverse? On a recent visit to New York I heard that certain trendy hotels have had a revamp – out with the minimalist and back with some tasteful Victorian style. They have even started serving traditional afternoon tea using 19thC crockery. It's only a beginning, but these prices could be at an all-time low. And, as they say, they're not making them anymore!

This set comprises a tray, a teapot and cover, a sugar box and cover, two cups and saucers and a milk jug. The teapot and jug are cracked.

A Wedgwood tête-à-tête part tea service, painted with panels of flowers reserved on a black and gilt "cracked-ice" ground, printed "Portland vase" mark.
c1880
£50-100   DN

A Staffordshire figure of T.D. Rice in the role of "Jim Crow", partially coloured and gilded, on a square base inscribed "Jim Crow".

Thomas Dartmouth Rice (1806-60), American vaudeville performer. Jim Crow was his most famous character. In 1836 he visited England and performed a song and dance routine as Jim Crow at the Royal Surrey Theatre in London, which was a great success and lead to the vogue for so-called "nigger minstrels" in England at that time.

c1836
£400-600   DN

A pair of mid-19thC Staffordshire models of greyhounds, one with a hare at its feet, the other with a recumbent spaniel, restoration.
5.5in (14cm) high
£250-350   DN

A Swansea dessert plate, painted with a central bouquet of flowers possibly by William Pollard, with gilt lappet-band border.
c1814-22   8in (2cm) diam
£1,000-1,500   DN

A Swansea two-handled sucrier, London-decorated with pink roses and scattered insects.
c1822   7.5in (19cm) diam
£1,500-2,500   DN

A pair of Chantilly cylindrical boxes and covers, painted in the Kakiemon palette with beetles and flowers, metal mounts to the lids, hunting horn mark to one.

c1740-50   *3in (7.5cm) high*

£3,500-4,500   **WW**

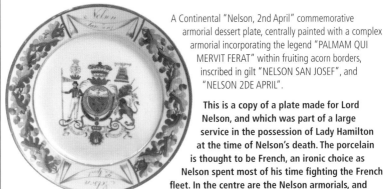

A Continental "Nelson, 2nd April" commemorative armorial dessert plate, centrally painted with a complex armorial incorporating the legend "PALMAM QUI MERVIT FERAT" within fruiting acorn borders, inscribed in gilt "NELSON SAN JOSEF", and "NELSON 2DE APRIL".

This is a copy of a plate made for Lord Nelson, and which was part of a large service in the possession of Lady Hamilton at the time of Nelson's death. The porcelain is thought to be French, an ironic choice as Nelson spent most of his time fighting the French fleet. In the centre are the Nelson armorials, and various dates, including 14th February (the date of his 1797 victory at Cape St Vincent). The original service remained in Lady Hamilton's possession until 1813, when she was forced to sell all her effects.

8.75in (22cm) diam

£1,500-2,500   **TEN**

A pair of mid-to-late 18thC Höchst figures of a hunter and his companion, with blue wheel marks, one incised "HM", restorations.

6.75in (17cm) high

£1,500-2,500   **WW**

A Frankenthal figure of Diana, raised on a mossy base, with painted factory mark and that of Adam Bergdoll, some restoration.

c1765-70.   *7in (18cm) high*

£1,000-1,500   **WW**

A mid-18thC Furstenburg figure of Harlequin, seated on a marble plinth, with blue "F" mark to the plinth, damages, the plinth and figure possibly associated.

6in (15cm) high

£1,200-1,800   **WW**

A matched pair of 18thC Höchst figures of a Turk and his companion, raised on grassy bases, with blue wheel marks, one crowned.

He 7.25in (18.5cm) high

£3,000-4,000   **WW**

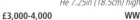

A Ludwigsburg group of Pierrot and Violetta from the "Venetian Mass", with impressed marks.

3in (7cm) high

£2,000-3,000   **DOR**

A pair of Sitzendorf figures of Napoleonic soldiers.

Taller 13.75in (35cm) high

£400-600   **GORL**

A pair of early 20thC Sitzendorf flower-encrusted vases, with painted and printed panels, within green flowers with rustic twin handles.

8.5in (21.5cm) high

£500-700   **GORL**

A set of 14 Royal Copenhagen "Flora Danica" teacups and saucers, finely painted with botanical specimens, identified in Latin on the reverse, with gilt enhanced borders, with printed and painted factory marks.

Cups 3in (7.5cm) high

£5,000-7,000   **FRE**

A mid-18thC Capodimonte cup and saucer, painted in the manner of Giovanni Caselli, with distant buildings behind sparse trees issuing from rockwork in a purple monochrome palette, with fleur de lys marks in underglaze blue.

5in (13cm) diam

£1,200-1,800   **WW**

A mid-18thC Cozzi figure of a couple beneath a tree, she seated with a book and tambourine, he wearing a yellow hat, damages.

6in (15cm) high

£1,200-1,800   **WW**

A pair of Doccia white-glazed bas-relief portrait plaques, modelled with the bust of a man and a lady in Biblical dress, within moulded Rococo frames.

c1745   *8in (20cm) high*

£8,000-12,000   **WW**

A rare Doccia figure of Il Capitano, from the *Commedia dell'arte*, raised on a small square base,

Il Capitano (The Captain) is typically a cowardly figure, masking his many negative traits under feigned bravado. He is usually portrayed as Spanish: a reference to the Spanish domination of Italy during the Renaissance and into the 18thC.

c1760-65   *5.25in (13cm) high*

£2,000-3,000   **WW**

ESSENTIAL REFERENCE - DOCCIA

The Doccia porcelain factory was founded in 1735 near Florence, Italy, by Carlo Ginori. He brought with him former employees of Du Paquier's Vienna factory.

- The factory produced a greyish, rough-textured hybrid hard-paste porcelain. Its glaze often lacks brilliance.
- Its most successful pieces were on a large scale. The grand and imposing figures were derived from models intended for bronze statuettes. Some of its best-known tableware designs of this period feature coats of arms or a pattern called *a tulipano*.
- A whiter body and glaze were introduced in 1765. Sèvres-style pieces were produced. Wares *a doppia parete* (double-walled) became a speciality.
- From 1850, Doccia moved towards a more industrial mode. From 1860, it also became increasingly influenced by the French Limoges factory.
- Large and impressive Art Nouveau pieces were produced from the 1890s until the early 20thC.
- Gio Ponti served as artistic director 1923-1930, and produced many Art Deco designs. He was suceeded by Giovanni Garibaldi.
- The factory is still active today.

An early Doccia teapot and cover, each side painted with a central orange flower within green foliage and smaller flower sprays, the spout modelled as a serpent, cracked.

From the collection of Anthony Ray (1926-2009), ceramic historian and, by repute, formerly in the collection of Arthur Lane (1909-1963).

c1740-45   *7.75in (19.5cm) high*

£600-800   **WW**

THE POTTERY MARKET

As with most areas of the antiques market, pottery collectors have been affected by the economic climate. Having said that, when good, rare, early pieces come fresh to the market, top prices are paid. In contrast to this, mid-priced and low-end pieces have struggled.

John Howard, chairman of the Cotswold Antiques Dealers Association, says that the American market for British pottery is stronger than the British market at the moment. Business is mainly conducted on the internet, because there are fewer American buyers travelling to Britain than in the past. He also mentions that there is a strong interest in pre-1830 pottery. Victorian pottery and Staffordshire figures either have to be exceptionally rare, or very cheap, to attract any interest.

There is also the problem of fake "Staffordshire" figures which are being manufactured in China. These are made from porcelain rather than pottery, and are really quite easy to spot (see page 76). If in any doubt you should buy from a reputable dealer or auction house. I recently spotted about a hundred of these "Staffordshire" figures lying on the grass at a large antiques and collectables fair. They were very cheap and I think the old adage applies: if something looks too good to be true, it normally is!

Delftware, again, has to be early and a rare shape to achieve strong prices. For the more modest collector interested in delft and slipware, this is an excellent time to buy. At many sales there is strong competition for the top-end pieces, but the market is generally sluggish for the more common pieces.

There have been some dramatic prices paid for some early pottery, particularly the Italian maiolica istoriato ware plates and dishes created in the 16thC. A few pieces sold at Sotheby's, London had the added attraction of the must-have provenance in this field: the Isabella D'este Service – billed as quite simply "the most celebrated istoriato service in existence".

One such charger, boldly emblazoned with the arms of the ruling Gonzaga family of Mantua, and painted by Nicola da Urbino, sold for £165,000. The value was further helped by its rarity: this is one of just four pieces in private hands from the 23 known to have survived, the others being in museums.

Interest in good and early (16thC) Hispano Moresque pottery remains strong – but little comes to the market. In general buyers are looking for pieces that are in excellent condition, feature strong colours and are of rare design.

American stoneware continues to have a strong collectors' market, particularly for rare shapes and makers. Redware has seen a sluggish period, where only the most unusual pieces fetch high prices. Early spatterware, such as the platter featured on page 89, continues to fetch substantial prices.

Above: A redware Bennington lion. See page 86.

Top Left: A Spode pearlware plate. See page 73.

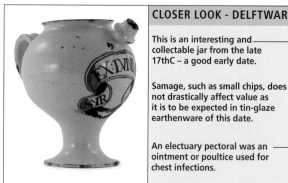

A delftware wet drug jar, simply decorated with a ribbon banner below the onion spout, titled "SYR. EX:LVIVLAE".

c1660-70   *9in (23cm) high*

£2,000-3,000   **WW**

CLOSER LOOK - DELFTWARE DRY DRUG JAR

This is an interesting and collectable jar from the late 17thC – a good early date.

Samage, such as small chips, does not drastically affect value as it is to be expected in tin-glaze earthenware of this date.

An electuary pectoral was an ointment or poultice used for chest infections.

The initials "I.G" are believed to relate to James Glover, a wealthy apothecary who made gifts to the Apothecaries' Society from the mid-17th century. He last appears in their records in 1702.

A late 17thC delftware dry drug jar, painted with an angel with outspread wings holding a banner titled "E: PECTORAL", above the initials "I.G".

8in (20cm) high

£3,500-4,500   **WW**

A late 17thC delftware dry drug jar, painted in blue with the haloed head of Apollo between two peacocks above a cartouche bearing the inscription "E:MITHRIDAT".

Mithridatum was a pharmaceutical preparation used as an antidote to poisons.

7in (18cm) high

£3,000-4,000   **WW**

An unusual 18thC delftware wet drug jar, painted in manganese with "a disturbance at the heron house" pattern around the inscription "Syr. De Cydonys".

Syrup of Quince has many uses including soothing digestive complaints and throat infections. Plutarch, among others, recommended it to newly weds as an early form of aphrodisiac.

8in (20cm) high

£500-600   **WW**

An early 18thC delftware dry drug jar, titled "U:TUTIAE" within a cartouche of songbirds and a basket of fruit.

Unguentum de Tutia or "tutty" was an ointment of zinc oxide commonly used for eye complaints.

7in (18cm)high

£1,000-1,500   **WW**

An unusual late 17thC/early 18thC delftware dry drug jar, painted with a flying wyvern beneath a shell and fruit topped cartouche, titled "C:ABSINTH:R".

The Museum of London holds a collection of 24 drug jars which feature a flying wyvern, and possibly relate to the arms of the Apothecaries Society which feature Apollo (the god of healing) killing Python as the dragon of disease.

7in (18cm) high

£3,500-4,500   **WW**

An early 18thC delftware wet drug jar, with flanged spout, the title "S.LIMONUM" surrounded by song birds and a pipe-smoking man.

9in (23cm) high

£1,500-2,500   **WW**

A 17thC delftware fuddling cup, probably Southwark, London, the three interlocked vessels of baluster form, painted with blue stylised flowers, connected by twisted handles.

5in (12.5cm) high

£3,500-4,500 WW

An 18thC delftware puzzle jug, with typical pierced neck and floral painted panels, inscribed with a verse.

This jug demonstrates the classic form of puzzle jug, which reached its heyday in the Georgian era. The pierced decoration around the neck of the jug makes it impossible to pour liquid through the spout without spilling most of the contents. A number of further spouts and holes around the rim, along the handle and sometimes concealed elsewhere, would need to be discovered and blocked before a drinker could sip from the one remaining uncovered aperture. A short rhyme (in the form of a challenge to the drinker) is also typical.

7in (18cm) high

£1,000-1,500 GORL

An early 18thC delftware oak leaf charger, painted with a central leaf with blue veins, surrounded by leaves and fruit, with blue-dash border.

14in (36cm) diam

£3,500-4,500 L&T

ESSENTIAL REFERENCE - DELFT

Tin-glazed earthenware was produced across the Netherlands from the late 15thC. By the late 17thC, Delft was the most important centre of manufacture.

- Dutch Delft has a gritty texture and thick glaze with "peppering" (due to exploding air bubbles). Early decoration was based on Chinese blue-and-white porcelain, but a wide range of colours and designs had been introduced by the late 17thC.
- Britain's "delftware" was produced from the mid-16thC, with important centres of production springing up in Lambeth, London, Liverpool, and Bristol. Delftware is typically less finely potted than Dutch Delft ware, and the glaze is often tinged with blue or pink. By the early 18thC British delftware had become more refined, with a smoother glaze than Dutch wares. Patterns included floral designs and landscapes, predominantly in blue-and-white.

An early 18thC Bristol delftware silver-shaped loving cup, painted in blue with a faux gadrooned lower section and a band of meandering flowers, the scroll handles with blue dashes, cracked and rivetted.

c1725 *5in (12.75cm) high*

£4,000-5,000 DN

A 17thC/18thC delftware campana vase, each side moulded with an open-mouthed mask between swags, decorated in white, some restoration.

9.5in (24cm) high

£1,500-2,500 WW

An 18thC Lambeth delftware charger, painted in blue and white with a central "acrobatic bird" roundel surrounded by a manganese ground border with fish, restored.

13.5in (34cm) diam

£1,500-2,500 GORL

A Lambeth delftware charger, enamelled in blue, green and manganese with the London balloon ascent of Vincenzo Lunardi, within a feathered border with foliate swags and husks, damages.

c1785 *14in (36cm) diam*

£1,500-2,500 H&L

POTTERY

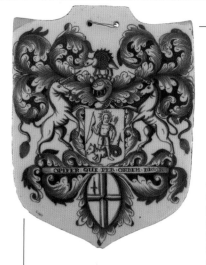

An unusual late 17thC delftware shield-shaped pill slab, painted with the arms of the Worshipful Society of Apothecaries, the top with two holes, some restoration.

While slabs of this type had a functional purpose, many believe that they were often used purely to display an apothecary's credentials.

12in (30.5cm) high

£7,000-10,000   WW

A mid-18thC Liverpool delftware plate, painted with sprays of mimosa in blue, sage and yellow.

9in (23cm) diam

£250-350   SWO

A set of four 18thC delftware sweetmeat dishes, probably Liverpool, comprising two matching pairs, fitting together to form a scalloped circle with central hole, painted in the Chinese style with peonies and foliage.

Each 5in (12.5cm) long

£800-1,200   WW

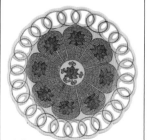

A delftware basket, probably Liverpool, decorated in blue with a stylised flowerhead, and lotus blossoms, on a dense scroll ground, with the openwork rim.

c1760-70   *8.75in (22cm) diam*

£1,500-2,500   WW

A late 18thC delftware octagonal pill slab, painted in blue with the arms of the Worshipful Society of Apothecaries and their motto "Opiferque Per Orbem Dicor", the edges with traces of manganese glaze.

12in (30.5cm) long

£2,500-3,500   WW

A delftware mug, painted with a polychrome spray of flowers, scattered flowerheads and stylised leaves.

c1760-70   *3in (7.5cm) high*

£550-650   WW

A late 18thC/early 19thC delftware baluster vase, titled "Tonka" within a cartouche, the base inscribed "W-VB (?) /4", with brass cover.

10in (25.5cm) high

£400-600   CHT

A delftware spoon tray, probably Liverpool, painted in blue with a scroll and Oriental flora and foliage.

c1770   *6.5in (16cm) high*

£1,500-2,500   WW

A set of four small late 18thC delftware drug jars with metal covers, titled within cartouches of peacocks, fruit baskets and angel masks, with metal lids.

These jars would have been used to store ginger, rosemary, arnica and bitterwood. The metal lids date them to the end of the 18thC when such covers were used to replace the more traditional tied-on parchment.

5in (12.5cm) high

£1,500-2,500   WW

A pair of Dutch Delft vases, decorated in blue with chinoiserie designs, marked "GK".

The mark "GK" is a workshop monogram, indicating the workshop Drie Posteleyne Astonne, which was active from 1655-c1803.

c1690　　　　　　　　　　　　12.25in (32cm) high
£3,500-5,500　　　　　　　　　　　　　　WKA

A Dutch Delft Royal Portrait dish, painted with a half length portrait of William of Orange, with the initials "W R", damages.

c1680　　13.75in (35cm) diam
£1,000-1,500　　　　DA&H

A Dutch Delft inverted baluster jar, decorated in the Transitional style with Chinese figures in a landscape, lacks cover, damages.

c1700　　　　11in (28cm) high
£800-1,200　　　　　　DN

An early 18thC Dutch Delft plate, painted in blue with a couple in a park, verso painted "6".

9in (23cm) diam
£400-600　　　　　　DN

An 18thC/19thC Dutch Delft five-piece garniture, painted in blue with tiers of compartments containing flowers and rockwork, possibly matched.

Tallest 15in (38cm) high
£2,000-3,000 set　　　　　　WW

A mid-late 18thC Dutch Delft vase, painted in blue with flying ducks amidst large floral sprays, damages.

10in (25.5cm) high
£400-600　　　　　WW

A pair of 18thC/19thC Dutch Delft double gourd-shape vases, painted in blue with a continuous floral design between scrolling stylised foliate borders.

17in (43cm) high
£1,500-2,500　　　　　WW

A Dutch Delft model of a boar, with a a stylised floral spray on its back, with retrospective De Grieksche A factory "AK" monogram in blue over "35".

c1900　　　7in (18cm) high
£500-700　　　　TEN

POTTERY

An early 18thC probably French faience book-shaped hand-warmer, decorated in blue with foliage and strapwork, the pages and spine similarly decorated.

6in (15cm) high

£700-1,000   H&L

A large early 18thC possibly French faience tray, decorated in blue with garlands, swags, cornucopia and shell motifs around a central eight-pointed star surmounted by a mask head crest, damages.

22in (56cm) wide

£3,000-4,000   WW

A Rouen faience tureen, decorated with polychrome birds and butterflies.

1760   *11in (28cm) long*

£400-600   DCB

A French Revolution faience plate, painted with the execution of Louis XVI, and an inscription reading "I'an second de la République Française. Execution de Louis Capet 21 janvier 1793", marked "RF" to base.

It's very unusual that something with such historical significance did not sell for more. This may be a later copy.

9in (23cm) diam

£250-350   ROS

A pair of 19thC French faience flagons, modelled as portrait busts of Royals.

12in (30.5cm) high

£1,200-1,800   GORL

A late 19thC Nove faience baluster urn, cover and stand, with two mythical beast handles and decorated with birds and flowers, "G.B. Viero" mark, repairs.

31in (79cm) high

£600-800   DN

A late 19thC French faience dolls' house partial dinner service, Paris, decorated in colours with fish, butterflies, ducks, turkeys, cockerels, insects and flowers, edged in blue, some pieces marked.

£25,000-30,000   PIA

A German Arnstadt faience barber's bowl, painted in blue with a rabbit and floral decoration, with old label for the Eckert Collection.

c1650   11.5in (29cm) diam
£1,500-2,500   WKA

ESSENTIAL REFERENCE - GERMAN FAIENCE

There is evidence that Germany's first tin-glazed earthenware was produced by stove-makers in the south of Bavaria and the Tyrol in the early 16thC. However, most German faience dates from the later 17thC, after the arrival of Dutch potters in Frankfurt and Berlin.

- Early German faience was produced in Hanau (from 1661), Frankfurt (from 1666), and Berlin (1678).
- Much was decorated in blue-and-white with Chinese-style designs, although some local themes are found. Some pieces are also decorated with manganese and yellow.
- Typical pieces include contoured dishes and hollow-wares, as well as *enghalskrugen* (narrow-necked jugs).
- More potteries were established in the 18thC, particularly in south Germany. Notable regions include Ansbach, Nuremberg, Bayreuth, Brunswick, Fulda, Höchst and Crailsheim.
- Chinese designs were increasingly replaced by more native subjects, such as buildings, figures, landscapes and coats of arms, in a high-fired palette of blue, yellow and red.
- The *walzenkrug* (cylindrical tankard) is the characteristic form of 18thC German faience.
- Some figures were made, mostly in Brunswick and Münden.
- The popularity of British creamware forced many factories to close in the late 18thC, but at least one factory remained open until c1860.

A German Hanau pewter-mounted faience jug, painted by Leonard John Priess, the cream-coloured body decorated in blue with an image of a castle in a landscape, marked "P", the lid with engraved monogram "AL" and year.

1779   13.5in (34cm) high
£2,500-3,500   WKA

A German faience pewter-mounted tankard, the ochre-coloured body decorated in blue with an image of St Simon.

c1700   11.25in (28.5cm) high
£1,200-1,800   WKA

An 18thC German faience pewter-mounted tankard, with polychrome decoration of a horse in a floral landscape.

10.5in (27cm) high
£2,000-3,000   WKA

A pair of Italian faience apothecary jars, decorated in dark blue with flowers and titled "CARBON D'AMM" (ammonium carbonate) and "OLIO DI CAMOMIL" (chamomile oil), restored.

6.75in (17cm) high
£1,200-1,800   WKA

A large 18thC Italian Savone faience round dish, decorated in blue with a knight on horseback surrounded by buildings and foliage.

18in (45.5cm) diam
£2,000-3,000   CSB

A late 18thC Continental faience model of a seated dog, decorated.

The separately moulded legs are a sign of quality on this charming piece. Add to this its appealing expression, and an enthusiasm amongst collectors (myself included) for dogs, and you have a piece worth £3,000+.

8in (20cm) high
£3,000-4,000   WW

POTTERY

A rare late 14thC/early 15thC Hispano-Moresque maiolica albarello, Malaga or Manises, painted with bands of Arabic script and various panels in gold lustre and blue, damages.

13in (33.5cm) high

£20,000-30,000   **L&T**

A late 15thC/early 16thC Italian maiolica albarello, probably Faenza, polychrome painted with stylised leaves and scrolls and titlted "Trifera Perhicha", with symbols on base.

Tryphera Persica is a medicinal paste made from senna leaves, larch agaric, rhubarb, thyme dooder, hops and other ingredients. Used as a mild purgative, as an antidepressant, and to treat jaundice.

c1490-1520   5in (12.5cm) high

£1,500-2,500   **L&T**

A small early 16thC Italian Montelupo maiolica pill jar, polychrome painted with Persian palmettes, titled "Pll.Cotie" below the coat of arms of the Aldobrandini di Lipo family, marked "Bo".

1500-20   5in (12.5cm) high

£3,000-4,000   **L&T**

An Italian Faenza *berettino* ground dish, painted with musical and military trophies against a deep blue *berettino* ground, the reverse painted with various blue geometrical signs.

c1520   10in (25.5cm) diam Est

£14,000-18,000   **SOTH**

An Italian Faenza *berettino* ground dish, probably by the workshop of Piero Berganti, the centre painted with a female figure pouring water, the broad border with winged cherub heads and dolphin heads, the reverse with stylised flower heads.

c1525-30   9.5in (23.5cm) diam

£20,000-25,000   **SOTH**

A 16thC Italian Montelupo maiolica albarello, titled "DiANBRA" (made from Ambergris) above an urn and with resist daisy heads and incised scrolling.

c1530-40   7in (18cm) high

£3,000-4,000   **L&T**

A 16thC Italian Castelli maiolica albarello, possibly Pompei workshop, painted in colours with a profile bust of a bearded balding man, titled "Conte Pru", with simple spirals and a central plant to reverse.

1545-60   8in (20cm) high

£15,000-25,000   **L&T**

A mid 16thC Italian Castel Durante maiolica albarello, painted in colours with a drug label in gothic script between a crest of a cockerel and a pharmacy badge.

The crest may be for the El Gallo pharmacy in Milan.

6in (15cm) high

£2,500-3,500   **L&T**

An early 16thC Italian maiolica albarello, probably from Faenza, titled "Dia Maluahi" between a star and a pharmacy label "CA/G", decorated with trophies and scrolling foliage, with symbols on the base.

1500-1525   6in (15cm) high

£3,500-4,500   **L&T**

A mid-late 16thC Hispano Moresque Valencia maiolica albarello, Narbonne, painted with an allover leaf design in ruby lustre and blue, damages.

11in (28cm) high

£18,000-22,000   **L&T**

A 16thC Italian Venice maiolica albarello, probably from the workshop of Domenego Da Venezia, painted with a band of stylised flowers and foliage with incised sgraffito scrolls, with borders of foliate scrolls on the shoulder.

c1560-1580   6in (15cm) high

£3,500-4,500   **L&T**

A 16thC Italian Castel Durante maiolica albarello, titled "AD.PRVIS" (odeps prunus – prune grease), with a frame containing panels of trophies and with bold scrolling foliage to the reverse, dated.

1566   8in (20cm) high

£4,000-5,000   **L&T**

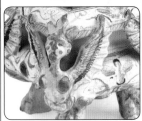

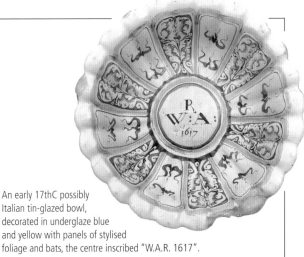

An early 17thC possibly Italian tin-glazed bowl, decorated in underglaze blue and yellow with panels of stylised foliage and bats, the centre inscribed "W.A.R. 1617".

This large bowl was previously thought to have been made in London, particularly in view of the way the initials and date are inscribed. However, it is now believed that an attribution to the Faenza workshops of Leonardo & Antonio Bettisi can be made, as although the inscription is unusual for an Italian piece, the decoration is very similar to that found on known Bettisi pieces.

An Italian Tuscan maiolica salt from Montelupo or Pisa, decorated *a compendiario*, with applied moulded female caryatid to each corner, the centre with a winged grotesque below a black cameo, with swags of fabric, pearls and cameos to the exterior.

c1590-1610   5in (12.5cm) wide

£2,000-3,000   L&T

A 17thC Italian Sicilian maiolica albarello, probably Caltagirone, painted in shades of blue, green, ochre and yellow with a stylised floral motif amidst incised scrolls.

10in (25.5cm) high

£1,000-1,500   WW

1617   15in (38cm) diam

£3,500-4,500   H&L

A mid-17thC Spanish dish, Talavera or Puente del Arzobispo, painted in shades of ochre and blue with a gentleman in a plumed hat.

11.25in (28.5cm) diam

£5,000-7,000   WW

A 17thC/18thC Spanish plate, painted in blue, ochre and umber with a central roundel of a bird, within concentric bands of flowers and foliage.

12.5in (31cm) diam

£1,500-2,500   WW

A large 18thC Italian maiolica urn, polychrome decorated with a scene of a soldier on horseback and a beggar, with leaf and strap moulded handles mounted with masks, the reverse with cipher and dated.

1702   17.25in (43cm) high

£2,000-3,000   FRE

An 18thC possibly Spanish maiolica ovoid vase, decorated in green, manganese, yellow and blue with repeat flowerheads and leaves, on a solid blue background.

8in (20cm) high

£500-700   TEN

A mid-18thC Spanish maiolica dish, Talavera or Puente del Arzobispo, painted with a prancing horse in shades of green, ochre and umber.

15in (38cm) diam

£1,200-1,800   WW

One of a pair of late 19thC Italian maiolica *istoriata* chargers, one depicting the Rape of the Sabines, the other depicting a Biblical scene.

24in (61cm) diam

£1,200-1,800 pair   FRE

A North Devon slipware fuddling cup, with sgraffito decoration of stylised flowers, damages.

The challenge of the fuddling cup is to drink from the vessel in such a way that the beverage does not spill. To do this successfully, the cups must be drunk from in a specific order.

1705   *6in (15cm) wide*

£4,000-5,000   **WW**

An unusual 18thC/19thC slipware costrel, decorated with a mottled brown glaze with incised lines of decoration.

Costrels, or pilgrims' flasks, as they have often been called, are flattened vessels made from silver, pewter, wood, leather or earthenware, with ears by which they could be suspended from the shoulder or belt. Chaucer mentions one in his "Good Woman".

8in (20cm) high

£500-700   **WW**

A rare early 18thC small thistle-shaped slipware cup, decorated with seven brown circular dots on a creamish ground.

3.25in (8.5cm) high

£2,500-3,500   **WW**

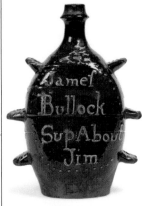

A West Country slip-decorated pottery harvest flask, with three pierced tab handles to each side, inscribed on one side with "this life is but a span and Henry will be the best man", on the other "James Bullock Sup about JIM", impressed "EX" at the base.

c1800   *9in (23cm) high*

£800-1,200   **TEN**

An early 19thC Sussex Slipware flask, inscribed "For Henrey Funnell of Piddinghoe, Sussex" and dated "April 23rd 1832, made by John Figgery of Herstmonceux", with various other verses.

1832   *6.25in (15.5cm) high*

£800-1,200   **GORL**

A North Devon slipware sugar jar, inscribed "If aney shuger you have got pray put it in this Little pot 1813", between scrolling and zigzag borders.

1813   *6in (15cm) high*

£1,200-1,800   **WW**

A probably Victorian 17thC-Staffordshire-style slipware commemorative charger, depicting William of Orange in trailed decoration, signed "MA Maker" and bearing the motto "God Save The King".

19in (48cm) diam

£700-1,000   **LSK**

A mid-18thC Staffordshire creamware pineapple-moulded teapot, decorated with coloured glazes.
£2,500-3,500   DN

A mid-18thC Staffordshire creamware cabbage-leaf-moulded teapot, of hexagonal section and decorated with green, brown and ochre glazes.
£1,500-2,500   DN

CLOSER LOOK - LEEDS COFFEE POT

David Rhodes was an independent enameller and a partner in the firm of Robinson & Rhodes of Leeds, a company which often decorated Wedgwood's creamware pieces.

The entwined strap handle has flower and leaf terminals in red and green enamels.

The spout is moulded with acanthus leaves and a female head in high relief.

The body and cover are decorated in a pattern derived from textiles, incorporating bold stripes and scaled lozenge, cellular and arrowhead motifs.

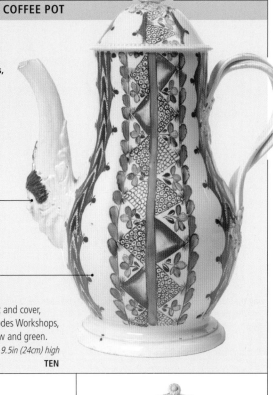

A Leeds creamware coffee pot and cover, probably decorated in the Rhodes Workshops, decorated in purple, red, yellow and green.
c1775   9.5in (24cm) high
£2,500-3,500   TEN

A pair of mid-late 18thC Wedgwood creamware vases, painted in sepia tones with baskets of fruit and flowers below an oak leaf garland border, the neck moulded with grapevine and lappets, one impressed "WEDGWOOD" mark.
6in (15cm) high
£500-700   WW

A probably Yorkshire creamware teapot, decorated in vivid enamel colours with stylised chinoiserie figures amongst furniture on a veranda, moulded bead strings to the rims, with trumpet flower finial.
c1770   6in (15cm) high
£800-1,200   TEN

A probably Leeds creamware punch pot, engine turned with vertical fluting, entwined and grooved strapwork handles with moulded terminals, with sunflower finial.
c1775   15in (38cm) long
£350-450   TEN

A small Leeds creamware coffee pot, the body painted with flowers in puce *en camaïeu*, with entwined reeded strap handle with floret and leaf terminals, inside cover impressed "HM".
c1775   5.5in (14cm) high
£300-400   TEN

A Leeds creamware milk jug, probably decorated in the Rhodes Workshops with a lansdcape within a scroll and flower border, with entwined strapwork handle, restored.
c1775   5.5in (14cm) high
£300-400   TEN

A Wedgwood creamware mug, printed with a man herding sheep and cattle, inscribed "John Peter and Ann Du Port, Guernsey, 1786", impressed "Wedgwood" mark.
1786   5in (12.5cm) high
£600-800   WW

A "Duke of York" creamware jug, printed in brown with "His Royal Highness Frederick Duke of York", verso with a drunk man entitled "Dear Tom this brown jug".
1793   8.25in (21cm) high
£600-700   HANDC

A 19thC creamware cauliflower-moulded teapot, with crack to the base.

7in (18cm) high

£450-550 WW

A creamware "Poor Jack" jug, printed in black with a scene of drinkers around a table, the reverse with a couple in front of a frigate and inscribed with a verse.

c1800 7in (18cm) high

£250-350 GHOU

An English creamware cow creamer, painted with dark brown and mustard spots and dark brown horns, on a concave-sided, green-glazed, flat, integral plinth.

c1800 4in (10cm) high

£300-400 TEN

ESSENTIAL REFERENCE - CREAMWARE

Creamware (cream-coloured earthenware) was developed in the mid-18thC by potteries in Staffordshire. By adding flint to the clay, it could be modelled as thinly as porcelain, while still being durable and relatively cheap.

- The close-grained body was very receptive to underglaze blue, overglaze enamelling and transfer printing.
- The clay was mixed with flint to produce a fine surface, and then covered with a thin layer of ivory-tinted lead glaze.
- Thomas Astbury, Enoch Booth and Josiah Wedgwood are all associated with its invention. In 1765 Wedgwood developed an improved type of creamware, which he named "Queensware" in honour of Queen Charlotte (wife of George III) who had ordered a Wedgwood creamware tea service, and who later granted him a Royal Warrant.
- Some ornamental wares and figures were produced for the aristocracy. Catherine the Great of Russia had a 926-piece service, known as the "Frog" service (due to a bright green frog set in its borders). However, most creamware took the form of everyday table- and teawares.
- By the late 18thC, creamware had become the standard household pottery throughout Britain, Continental Europe and North America. Consequently, many tin-glazed earthenware factories went out of business.
- Pearlware is a porcellaneous version of creamware.

A John Warburton creamware cruet set, the pierced body supporting six pedestal gourd-shaped condiments (four with original stoppers, and two later matched covers), the stem with four moulded female masks, impressed (twice) "Warburton".

c1810 14in (36cm) high

£400-600 TEN

A Herculaneum Creamware Liverpool Amnesty Jug, printed in black with "GR III 50" and figures of History and Britannia holding an inscribed scroll over an equestrian statue and prison with inscription, the reverse with the Royal coat of arms.

This rare print celebrates the Grand Nation Jubilee and the Jubilee Amnesty at which deserters and all those who had committed offences in the armed forces were pardoned, a subscription was raised to discharge insolvent debtors, and amnesty was given to all prisoners of war – except the French.

c1809 9.25in (24cm) high

£1,000-1,500 TEN

A Regency Yorkshire creamware figure of a lion, with sponged polychrome decoration, on rectangular base with scrolling foliate decoration.

9.5in (24cm) long

£4,000-6,000 GORB

A Yorkshire pearlware puzzle jug, with three trumpet spouts, pierced with one floral and two lozenge trellis body panels, painted in underglaze blue with two gentlemen, marked "666".

c1790   *7in (18cm) high*

£1,200-1,800   **TEN**

A Regency pearlware group of lovers, depicting a boy and girl on a garden seat with a King Charles spaniel between them, damages.

c1800   *7in (18cm) high*

£450-550   **SWO**

A pearlware bust of Minerva, wearing her plumed helmet and raised on a marbled socle, impressed "MINERVA" to the reverse.

c1800   *12in (30.5cm) high*

£1,000-1,500   **WW**

A pearlware figure of Hercules and the Cretan Bull, Hercules wearing his lion-skin robe, raised on a flower encrusted base, some good restoration.

c1800   *6in (15cm) high*

£500-600   **WW**

An English pearlware tea or punch puzzle pot, with two handles and two spouts, the inside of novel construction with a smaller pot and spout, printed in blue with a version of the "Willow" pattern, old repairs.

The "Willow" pattern is a consistently popular chinoiserie design, comprising a willow tree, a Chinese temple, a bridge with figures on it, a boat, birds in flight and a distant island. It was designed for printing on ceramics in c1780 by Thomas Minton, probably for Caughley, but it was soon used by a large number of Staffordshire factories.

c1800   *9in (24cm) high*

£600-800   **DN**

A pearlware loving cup, painted with the instruments of a tailor beneath the inscription "Robert Kirby 1805", within floral sprays, some restoration.

1805   *7in (18cm) high*

£500-700   **WW**

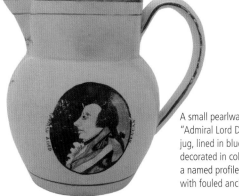

A small pearlware "Admiral Lord Duncan" jug, lined in blue, decorated in colours with a named profile oval, verso with fouled anchor.

c1797   *4.25in (11cm) high*

£350-450   **HANDC**

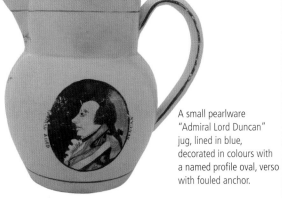

A rare "1821 Coronation" pearlware mug, printed in brown with a named, inscribed and dated portrait, sunbleached.

1821   *3.25in (8cm) high*

£1,200-1,400   **HANDC**

An early 20thC pearlware pepperpot of a woman in the Suffragette (WSPU) colours, her mob cap forming the pepper caster.

The Suffragettes adopted the colours purple (violet), white and green in 1908. These symbolised dignity (purple), purity (white), and hope (green), and not (as is commonly believed) the acronym GWV: "Give Women Votes".

5.25in (13cm) high

£1,000-1,500   **WW**

POTTERY

Judith Picks: Cow Creamers

I bought my first cow creamer in the early 1970s and have since bought many more. They are great examples of the naive qualities of early 19thC British pottery.

Staffordshire creamers were made in salt-glazed stoneware, creamware, glossy black "Jackfield ware", pearlware and bone china. Lustre glazes were used, but the most common finish was tan dappled in green, black, yellow, blue or orange.

Early Welsh pieces were in splashed lustreware, and later ones had transfer-printed rural scenes. Yorkshire cows had oblong, waisted bases with chamfered corners, and colourful lustreware creamers were usually made in Sunderland.

Creamers have been widely copied, so be careful when buying, especially "Jackfield" cows with golden horns or hooves – prime candidates for Edwardian reproduction. Run your finger round the outside: those made before 1830 tend to be rough to the touch. They also look mottled pink in soft light, but show gold in the sunshine.

Beware heavy gilding on horns or hooves; it may well conceal a repair. A missing or replacement stopper will cut the value dramatically, so make sure the stopper fits well and is a perfect match in glaze and body. Crude modelling is a feature of early cows, and only adds to their charm, but damaged or missing horns will devalue them.

A Yorkshire pearlware cow creamer, with calf, both sponge decorated in ochre and manganese, some good restoration.

c1800   7in (18cm) wide
£600-800   **WW**

An English pearlware cow creamer, Staffordshire or Yorkshire, the cow being milked by a milkmaid, sponged in brown, blue and green, repairs.

c1820   6in (15cm) long
£400-600   **DN**

A Swansea pearlware cow creamer, Cambrian Pottery, painted with pink-lustre and iron-red patches, impressed "D", restoration.
c1840
£350-450   **DN**

A late 18thC Enoch Wood pearlware figure of a lion, glazed in browns on green, cream and brown moulded base.

7.5in (19cm) long
£2,000-3,000   **GORB**

An English pearlware model of a cockerel, with orange, yellow and black plumage, on an integral square stand with spheres at the corners.
c1800   9in (23cm) high
£1,500-2,500   **TEN**

A pearlware figure of a horse, probably North East Potteries, with dappled coat, on a green-washed, canted, rectangular, flat plinth, restored.
c1810   6in (15cm) high
£1,000-1,500   **TEN**

A probably Scottish pearlware figure of a lion, standing on a high base inscribed "Nero" between moulded florets.
c1820   9in (23cm) long
£1,500-2,500   **SWO**

A rare Sunderland yellow-ground lustre jug, printed with an eagle, an American ship and figures including George Washington and Benjamin Franklin around a map of the United States, dated.

1804   *11in (28cm) high*

£4,500-5,500   **WW**

An unusual "William IV in Memoriam" pink lustre mug, printed in black and enamelled in yellow, green and red with a named, inscribed and dated portrait.

1837   *4in (10cm) high*

£1,200-1,800   **HANDC**

A Sunderland lustre mug, decorated with the high level bridge Newcastle upon Tyne on one side, the reverse with a three-masted man o'war, both within splodged pink borders.

c1850   *4.25in (11cm) high*

£500-700   **TEN**

A rare Dawson & Co. Sunderland pink and copper lustre and transfer-printed jug, printed in sepia with a Masonic print of the Temple of Solomon and verse "the world is in pain...", the reverse with coloured South East Bridge View, with initials "H.M.T.".

6in (15cm) high

£600-800   **A&G**

A Sunderland pink lustre frog chamber pot, painted with a figure within and "Keep me Clean and use me well and What I see I will not tell", with additional text to the exterior.

8.5in (21.5cm) diam

£350-450   **DA&H**

POTTERY

A large 19thC blue-printed meat dish, with draining channels, printed with Classical peasants and animals in a river landscape, some small chips.

20in (51cm) wide

£150-250   **WW**

A 19thC blue-printed soup bowl, decorated with an image of the Catskill Mountains.

10.25in (26cm) diam

£350-450   **POOK**

A 19thC Staffordshire blue-printed platter, depicting the Pennsylvania Hospital, Philadelphia.

Although on the opposite page I mention that the market for blue-and-white transfer-printed platters is in the doldrums, this is not the case for platters that were specifically designed with scenes for the American market: Niagara, the Catskills, the cities series of Detroit and Sandusky, Columbus, Indianapolis, Chillicothe, and Louisville, and the Eastern "greats" including New York, Philadelphia, Boston and Baltimore, carried many a "back home" picture along with the West-bound pioneer.

  The Churches of America series includes New York's "old St. Patrick's" and the "Church on Murray Street". College views included Harvard, Yale, and the University of Maryland. Among the homes sketched are the Lawrence Mansion, the Hancock House, the White House, Mount Vernon and Harrison's log cabin.

18.5in (47cm) wide

£1,500-2,500   **POOK**

A 19thC Staffordshire blue-printed platter, depicting Winter View, Pittsfield, Massachusetts.

16.5in (42cm) wide

£1,800-2,200   **POOK**

A 19thC Staffordshire blue-printed jug, decorated with the Seal of the United States.

5.75in (15cm) high

£1,200-1,800   **POOK**

A 19thC Staffordshire purple-printed platter, depicting the Residence of the late Richard Jordan, New Jersey.

17.75in (45cm) wide

£350-450   **POOK**

A T. Lakin & Sons pearlware blue printed eggcup stand with six eggcups, lion's head finial carrying handle, printed with scrolling foliage, the cups and borders with diaper bands.

c1810

£200-300   **DN**

A rare Woods & Brettle pearlware blue printed supper set, in a version of the "Bird's Nest" pattern, comprising a tureen and four hors d'oeuvres dishes, each with lion finials, in a mahogany oval tray with brass handles, impressed "W & B" to bases.

1818-23   *Tureen 9in (23cm) long*

£1,000-1,500   **TOV**

A rare blue printed Christening (or betrothal) egg, depicting a three masted ship, scene of Scottish courtship and initials "G.B B.R".

2.5in (6.5cm) long

£400-500   **A&G**

A blue printed "The Bridge of Lucano" dog's bowl, of canted rectangular form, with a floral and foliate border, impressed "00".

9in (23cm) long

£500-700   **H&L**

Judith Picks: Transfer-printed platter

I bought my first blue-and-white transfer printed platter in Edinburgh in the late 1960s for a few pence. It was a very typical country house scene, with a lake in front with a few cows, potted somewhere in Staffordshire in the mid-19th century. A few years ago I would have been able to sell it for £300-350. Today I'd be lucky to get £50-80. The market has held up rather better in America.

This is merely fashion. These blue-and-white platters are considered more "granny's taste" and not suited to today's modern interiors.

However, even in Britain, rare shapes are still highly desirable, and the rarer patterns are selling for more. Spode's "Indian Sporting" series (produced 1815-33), seen here, is one of the more sought after. For more information and examples see *Millers Collectables Handbook & Price Guide 2012-2013*.

Standard patterns, like my country house and cows, have never been cheaper, though. So, what a great time to buy—before some fancy interior designer decides that four or six platters grouped on a white wall are the latest must-have eye-candy.

A Spode pearlware blue printed "Dooreahs leading out dogs" meat plate, from the "Indian Sporting" series, with printed and impressed marks.

c1815   *19in (48cm) long*
£400-600   **DN**

A Staffordshire blue-printed "Durham Ox" meat plate, with restored crack.
c1820   *21in (53cm) wide*
£700-1,000   **SWO**

An Adams blue-printed "Lions" platter, with impressed factory marks to base.
c1820   *13in (33.5cm) long*
£650-750   **TOV**

A Ridgway pearlware blue-printed "Eastern Port" boughpot and pierced cover.
c1820   *6in (15cm) wide*
£400-600   **DN**

A Wedgwood pearlware brown-printed dinner and dessert service, each piece with extensive chinoiserie lakeland landscape within floral borders.
c1830   *Dinner plates 10in (25.5cm) diam*
£4,000-6,000   **TEN**

An unusual pair of mid-late 18thC Staffordshire cats, painted with red wheels of fire, one with repairs.

7in (18cm) long

£300-500   WW

A Ralph Wood-style Bacchus jug, the god's hair entwined with vine leaves and grapes, the spout formed as a mythical beast above him.

c1775   *5in (12.5cm) high*

£400-600   WW

A pair of Ralph Wood Staffordshire figures of seated hounds, each seated on a tasselled cushion with brown decoration on a cream ground and green-glazed bases.

c1790   *7.25in (18.5cm) high*

£3,500-4,500   POOK

A Staffordshire figure of a swan, with yellow, green and brown decoration on a cream ground.

c1790   *4.5in (11.5cm) high*

£800-1,200   POOK

An early 19thC Isaac Walton Staffordshire figural group "Return from Egypt", modelled as Mary, Joseph and the infant Christ, with donkey, with a floral bocage back, moulded signature to reverse.

8in (20cm) high

£500-700   GORB

Judith Picks

I love early Staffordshire figures, particularly small animals, such as this squirrel. And I'm not alone! Add to the detailed, crisp modelling, the naive charm and the good colouration and THE name in 18thC modelling – Ralph Wood – and you have a hit. There were actually two Ralph Woods and both were important in the development of the Staffordshire potteries into an organised industry. Ralph Wood I (1715-1772), one of the first English potters to impress his name onto his work, was making very well-modelled figures decorated with coloured glazes by c1760. Ralph Wood II (1748-1795) produced similar figures decorated with enamels.

A Ralph Wood Staffordshire figure of a squirrel, with green, yellow and brown decoration on a cream ground.

c1770   *7.25in (18cm) high*

£5,000-7,000   POOK

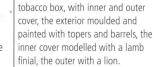

A Staffordshire pearlware figure of John Liston, in the role of the mischievous gossip, Paul Pry carrying his umbrella, some good restoration.

Paul Pry was the eponymous character of a busybody turned hero from John Poole's comedy of 1826. He carried an umbrella which he deliberately left behind him in order to have an excuse to return and eavesdrop.

c1826-30   *6in (15cm) high*

£250-350   WW

An early 19thC Staffordshire model of a frog.

2in (5cm) high

£800-1,200   GORL

An early 19thC Staffordshire lustre model of a baby in cradle.

5in (12.5cm) long

£550-650   SK

A rare early 19thC Staffordshire tobacco box, with inner and outer cover, the exterior moulded and painted with topers and barrels, the inner cover modelled with a lamb finial, the outer with a lion.

6.25in (15.5cm) high

£1,500-2,500   WW

A Prattware "Peace" jug, moulded with oval panels entitled "Peace" and "Plenty", decorated in blue, green and yellow.

Two late 18thC Prattware models of Spring and Autumn, personified as Classical figures holding a cornucopia of flowers and wheat sheaf respectively, raised on tall square bases.

10.25in (26cm) high

£800-1,200   **WW**

Although undated, the crispness of the moulding would suggest this jug was made at the time of the Peace of Amiens (1802).

c1802   *6.25in (16cm) high*

£450-550   **HANDC**

ESSENTIAL REFERENCE - PRATTWARE

Prattware is a cream-coloured earthenware (similar to Pearlware), characterised by a strong high-temperature palette of blue, green and yellow, over relief decoration.

- **It takes its name from the Staffordshire factory F. & R. Pratt, founded by William Pratt c1775.**
- **Other factories, including Leeds and Bristol, are known to have produced similar pieces.**
- **In the 1840s Pratt's factory became the leading manufacturers of pot lids. These are also collectable.**

An early 19thC Yorkshire Prattware model of a ram, on a grassy base encircled with a border of black and ochre splashes, restoration.

With paper labels for the Jonathan Horne collection.

5.75in (14.5cm) wide

£800-1,200   **WW**

A Staffordshire Prattware "Shephardess" (sic) group.

c1810   *6in (15cm) high*

£1,500-2,500   **SWO**

A pair of Prattware cow groups, the cows with blue, ochre and manganese sponged markings, one with a farmer and dog, the other with a milkmaid and calf, on sponged mound bases.

A late 18thC Staffordshire Prattware milking group, with sheep and milkmaid with blue, yellow and brown decoration on a cream ground.

6.25in (16cm) high

£800-1,200   **POOK**

c1810   *5.75in (14.5cm) high*

£1,500-2,500   **TEN**

A pair of 19thC Staffordshire models of recumbent lions, raised on rectangular bases.

5in (12.5cm) long

£600-800 pair   WW

A pair of mid-19thC Staffordshire spill vases modelled as bull mastiffs.

6in (15cm) high

£700-1,000   DN

A 19thC Staffordshire model of a greyhound, with dead hare, on a light blue base, restored.

11in (28cm) long

£500-700   WW

A pair of 19thC Staffordshire cat and kitten groups, with tiger coats and blue collars, on oval bases.

These cats are so appealing. They have lovely, expressive faces, which clearly encouraged someone to buy them – and maybe several people to bid for them. There are many cat collectors out there, and to have achieved such a high price there must have been more than one interested party. Groups of cats and kittens are significantly rarer than single cats.

7in (18cm) high

£800-1,200   TEN

A pair of 19thC Staffordshire models of a cockerel and hen, with yellow, brown and orange plumage, on grassy bases raised on hatched plinths.

7.5in (19cm) high

£1,200-1,800   WW

A pair of mid-19thC Staffordshire models of sporting hounds, painted with black patches, one repaired.

£1,000-1,500   DN

A pair of 19thC Staffordshire zebras, painted in white and black, with bridles, standing on a green, brown and yellow moulded ground, with gilt line to base.

These zebras were made using exactly the same moulds that were used for horses. The designers had never seen a zebra in real life, and so didn't know zebras were shaped differently.

8in (20cm) high

£400-600   MOR

BEWARE!

Staffordshire figures are still being made today and the unscrupulous can sell new pieces as antique. Modern examples are lighter and more thinly potted than originals, with brash colours and bright gold gilding. They also look too refined and are made from porcelain.

A late 20thC "Staffordshire" flatback figure of a circus horse.

8in (20cm) high

£20-30   PC

A 19thC Staffordshire model of Benjamin Franklin, standing and holding his tricorn hat in his left hand, a document in his right, titled to the base.

15in (38cm) high

£300-400 WW

A pair of Staffordshire figures of Queen Victoria and Prince Albert, on shaped square bases with bows at each corner.

c1840 *He 7in (18cm) high*

£350-450 DN

A rare mid-19thC Staffordshire figure of Captain Cook, modelled after a portrait by Nathaniel Dance, in full dress uniform, with a manuscript, on gilded base.

7in (18cm) high

£700-1,000 GORL

A rare mid-19thC Staffordshire group of two boys, with spill vase, the smaller boy riding on the other's shoulders, beside a tree.

14in (36cm) high

£300-400 SWO

A mid-19thC Enoch Wood Staffordshire figure of Billy Waters, modelled with wooden leg, playing a fiddle, leaning against a bollard.

Billy Waters was one of the more famous of London's numerous street entertainers. A former African-American slave, and identifiable from his military-style clothing and wooden leg, he played outside the Adelphi Theatre in The Strand during the 1780s and was immortalised by George Cruickshank the caricaturist. He spent his last months at the St Giles' Workhouse, where he was elected "King of Beggars".

8.25in (21cm) high

£600-800 GORL

A pair of mid-19thC Staffordshire models of wire-coated dogs and pups.

9in (23cm) high

£1,200-1,800 DN

A pair of Staffordshire models of hares, on a naturalistic bases.

c1860 *3in (7.5cm) long*

£400-500 SWO

One of a pair of Staffordshire elephant spill vases, with orange sashes, on shaped base.

c1860 *6.5in (16cm) high*

£700-1,000 pair SWO

A Staffordshire figure of Garibaldi and his horse, the grassy base inscribed "Garibaldi", damages.

15in (38cm) high

£250-350 SWO

One of a pair of Victorian Staffordshire flatback models of ptarmigan, the birds perched on grassy mounds.

12.5in (32cm) high

£400-600 pair GORL

A matched pair of Victorian Staffordshire figures of Queen Victoria and Albert Prince of Wales (later Edward VII), decorated with enamel and gilding.

17.5in (44cm) high

£200-300 CAPE

POTTERY

A late 18thC Toby mug, depicting a seated gentleman.

9.25in (23.5cm) high

£200-300   **LHA**

A Neale & Co. creamware Toby jug, painted with coloured enamels, impressed "NEALE & CO", restored.

c1790   *10in (25.5cm) high*

£700-1,000   **DN**

A 19thC Staffordshire-style Toby jug, covered in yellow, brown and green glaze.

11in (28cm) high

£700-1,000   **AH**

A pearlware sailor Toby jug, the sailor seated in a chair over travelling trunk, holding a jug and a beer glass, on an acanthus-trimmed, shaped base, restored.

c1800   *11in (28cm) high*

£1,500-2,500   **TEN**

An early 19thC pearlware Toby jug, with a pimpled and toothless visage.

9in (23cm) high

£350-450   **WW**

An early 19thC Staffordshire sailor Toby jug, seated on a sea chest with raised moulded ship, restored.

11in (28cm) high

£450-550   **SWO**

CLOSER LOOK - THIN MAN TOBY JUG

Toby jugs were made from the mid-18thC, mainly by Staffordshire potteries. Many of the best were made by the Wood family (see p74).

Extremities, such as Toby's pipe, can be easily damaged, so make sure you check before you buy. Damage will reduce value considerably.

The "Toper" (ale drinker) is the most common form. The "Thin Man" is one of the rarer variations, and consequently is more sought-after.

Impressed marks or labels usually increase desirability.

An early Thin Man Toby jug, highlighted in blue, black and brown enamels, some restoration.

c1780   *9.75in (24.75cm) high*

£2,000-3,000   **WW**

A Winston Churchill creamware Toby jug, modelled by Leonard Jarvis, the figure holding a palette and giving a "V" sign, with incised inscription, including number "156".

This jug has a certificate, which is dated 1953, signed by the artist, and states that it is one of 350 copies. A truly limited edition, such as this, is likely to increase in value if there are more potential buyers than there are objects.

1953   *7in (18cm) high*

£1,000-1,500   **SWO**

A large Mason's Ironstone ewer, the body with elaborate moulded gilt mask and shell decoration and two gilt putti to the base of the neck, with two panels enamelled and painted with peacocks, with impressed mark to base.

1800-1825   *26in (66cm) high*

£1,800-2,200   ROS

A pair of early 19thC Mason's Patent Ironstone pot pourri vases, painted with Chinese figures in a landscape, with pierced covers and gilded ram's head mask handles, with printed Royal coat of arms mark and "Patent Iron Stone China Warranted", one with damages.

£2,500-3,500   A&G

A Mason's Ironstone part dinner service, comprising a tureen and cover, a sauce tureen, cover and stand, four rectangular dishes, six soup plates and twenty six plates in three sizes, painted in the Imari palette with the "Old Schoolhouse" pattern.

c1820

£2,500-3,500   WW

A Mason's Ironstone part dessert service, comprising two comports, two vases, eight serving dishes and ten plates, painted in the Imari palette, with impressed marks.

c1825

£1,500-2,500   DN

A large early-to-mid-19thC Mason's Ironstone octagonal jug and bowl, painted in the Imari palette with flowers and cartwheel motifs, the handle modelled as a lion/dragon hybrid, with impressed mark to the bowl.

Jug 12in (30.5cm) high

£250-350   WW

A mid-19thC Mason's Ironstone three-vase garniture, printed with chinoiserie landscapes with enamel highlights, with swan's neck handles, printed mark and inscribed "197".

9in (23cm) high

£400-500   SWO

One of a pair of mid-19thC William Ridgway Ironstone soup tureens, covers and stands, in the Imari pattern with vases issuing flowering shrubs, with royal coat of arms mark, one tureen cracked.

Stands 13in (33.5cm) diam

£1,500-2,500 pair   DN

A mid-19thC Mason's Ironstone vase, of shouldered square section form with a pair of gilt "sea-dragon" handles, decorated in the Cantonese enamel style, with pseudo Chinese seal mark, base cracked.

22in (56cm) high

£700-1,000   DN

POTTERY

ESSENTIAL REFERENCE - JASPERWARE

The most famous form of Wedgwood stoneware, Jasperware was introduced in 1774/5.

- It was made by adding sulphate of barium to the usual clay. This produced a fine-grained, hard and slightly translucent material that was pure white.
- It could easily be stained a variety of colours, including the famous Wedgwood blue, as well as sage green, olive green, lilac, lavender and black.
- Early Jasperware saw the colour mixed with the body. This resulted in what is now known as "solid jasper". From 1777, the colour was applied to the surface in washes ("jasper dip"), which left the applied relief ornament in white.
- Pieces were usually Classical in style, both in form and decoration. Artists including John Flaxman and George Stubbs produced designs based on excavated Greek and Roman pieces.
- Pieces made before 1860 are marked with "Wedgwood" and a single letter. From 1860 a three-letter mark was used to denote the month, the potter and the year. 1891-1908 pieces were marked "Wedgwood" and "England"; 1908-1969 "Wedgwood" and "Made in England". Modern japserware is stamped "Wedgwood Made in England".

A 19thC Wedgwood black jasper dip "Apotheosis of Homer" vase and cover, with applied white relief of Classical figures within borders of anthemion and stylised foliage, the cover with Pegasus finial, with impressed mark.

24.5in (62cm) high

£7,000-10,000 SK

An early 19thC Wedgwood blue jasper dip Borghese vase and cover, with applied white Classical figures in relief between foliate, gadroon and fruiting grapevine borders, with impressed mark.

18.5in (47cm) high

£6,000-8,000 SK

A pair of Victorian Wedgwood ormulu-mounted three-colour jasper dip vases and covers, decorated with central lavender classical roundels within white swags on a green ground, damages and heavy restoration.

11in (28cm) high

£500-700 GORL

A pair of early 19thC Wedgwood white jasper models of a chess king and queen, each mounted atop a raised, circular, dark blue-dipped base, impressed marks.

4.5in (11.5cm) high

£2,500-3,500 SK

An early 19thC Wedgwood dark blue jasper dip tripod vase and cover, and applied white acanthus and bell flowers, gadroons and florets, the legs with lion masks, with impressed mark.

8in (20cm) high

£1,800-2,200 SK

A late 19thC Wedgwood black jasper dip vase, with applied personifications of the Arts.

15in (38cm) high

£500-700 GORL

A late 19thC Wedgwood blue jasper dip copy of the Portland or Barberini vase, impressed mark.

10in (25.5cm) high

£1,500-2,500 DN

A pair of late 19thC Wedgwood three-colour jasper dip vases and covers, with applied white relief on ochre-green ground and with lilac medallions decorated with Classical figures, impressed mark.

12.75in (32.5cm) high

£4,000-6,000 pair SK

A late 19thC Wedgwood black jasper dip Portland Vase, with applied white Classical figures in relief, a man wearing a Phrygian cap under the base, impressed mark.

10in (25.5cm) high

£1,200-1,800 SK

A 19thC Wedgwood gilded black basalt ewer, with Triton holding the horns of a marine monster, with aquatic festoons, with impressed mark to base.

15in (38cm) high

£3,500-4,500 LHA

An early 19thC Wedgwood encaustic-decorated black basalt vase, bottle-shape with iron red and black, with musician below a band of palmettes, with impressed mark.

7in (18cm) high

£1,800-2,200 SK

An early 19thC Wedgwood encaustic-decorated black basalt calyx-krater vase, decorated in iron red and black enamel with figures, with impressed mark.

11in (28cm) high

£3,500-4,500 SK

ESSENTIAL REFERENCE - BLACK BASALT

Josiah Wedgwood introduced his "Black Basaltes" (pottery with a black stoneware body) in 1768. It was made from a reddish-brown clay that burned black in firing.

● **Other "Egyptian Black" wares had been produced in the area before this date, but the colour of Wedgwood's black basalt was superior due to the addition of manganese.**

● **It was used to produce vases, portrait medallions, plaques, library busts and candlesticks in Classical shapes inspired by antique originals.**

● **Two new forms of decoration were patented for black basalt: bronzing, and encaustic painting in the style of ancient Greek and Roman vases, although Wedgwood used a greater variety of colours than the red and black of the originals.**

● **Black basalt pieces are still made by Wedgwood today.**

A mid-19thC Wedgwood black basalt bust of George Stephenson, with impressed marks.

14in (36cm) high

£500-600 SWO

A Wedgwood encaustic-decorated black basalt vase, by George Eyre, decorated in iron red, black and red enamel with figures to either side, with signed artist monogram and date, impressed mark.

1858 *6in (15cm) high*

£3,000-4,000 SK

A pair of 19thC Wedgwood black basalt wine and water ewers, water with Triton and a marine monster, with aquatic festoons; wine with Bacchus and a ram, with fruiting grapevine, impressed marks.

15in (38cm) high

£1,800-2,200 SK

Two Wedgwood figures of John Jorrocks, modelled by Montague A. Weaver-Bridgeman, one in black basalt, the other in enamelled bone china, with impressed and printed marks.

c1825 *7.5in (19cm) high*

£2,000-3,000 SK

A late 19thC Wedgwood creamware part service, decorated with long-billed birds, large butterflies and flower stems, within a shaped reticulated border, impressed marks.

Plates 9in (23cm) diam

£500-700 WW

A pair of Wedgwood Queensware ewers, the design attributed to Hugues Protat, decorated by Emile Lessore, each with an enamelled depiction of a battle, artist signed and impressed marks.

1861 *14.5in (37cm) high*

£6,000-8,000 SK

A Wedgwood Queensware peace plaque, decorated in polychrome enamel with a Latin verse surrounding a portrait of Bellona: goddess of war, with impressed mark.

c1919 *22in (56cm) diam*

£1,500-2,500 SK

A Wedgwood Egyptian-style red stoneware teapot, with applied winged scarabs, sphinxes and other motifs, with a crocodile finial, impressed mark.

c1790 *9.25in (23.5cm) wide*

£1,000-1,500 WW

A 19thC Wedgwood Imari palette part luncheon service, with 25 pieces, impressed "Wedgwood".

Tureen 9in (23cm) high

£1,200-1,800 set FRE

An early 19thC Wedgwood *rosso antico oenochoe* ewer, with foliate moulded spout, with handle terminating in a satyr mask, decorated in enamel with flowers, impressed mark.

17.25in (43.5cm) high

£1,800-2,200 SK

A Wedgwood parian bust of Byron, after a marble by E. W. Wyon, on a socle and base, impressed "Wedgwood, Byron, E W Wyon".

c1845 *18in (44.5cm) high*

£600-800 SWO

A pair of Wedgwood marine-decorated pearlware vases, attributed to John Holloway, with coiled snakes to scrolled handles, gilt trim and polychrome enamelled central panels with sailing ships, impressed marks.

c1875 *14.5in (37cm) high*

£10,000-15,000 SK

A Rhenish stoneware Bellarmine jug, with applied bearded mask, chips.

c1680   *5in (12.5cm) high*

£450-560   **SWO**

A late 17thC German stoneware Bellarmine, decorated in blue with three dated crests and rampant lions, restored.

16in (41cm) high

£600-800   **GORL**

CLOSER LOOK - STONEWARE TANKARD

In his search to discover the secret of hard-paste porcelain at Meissen, Johann Friedrich Böttger produced a fine brownish-red stoneware c1706-07. It was extremely hard and finely textured, and is described as "jaspisporzellan" or jasper porcelain.

One of the first artists to be involved in the modelling of the material was the court goldsmith Johann Jakob Irminger (1635-1724) and many pieces, such as this one, were based on gold and silver designs.

The cover is engraved with the arms of Schütz von Mossbach of Saxony. Almost all pieces produced were commissions for the aristocracy, or the Elector of Saxony himself.

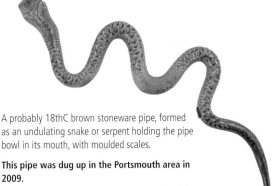

A rare Böttger silver-gilt-mounted red stoneware tankard and hinged cover, covered with a brushed brown slip, the cover engraved with the arms of Schütz von Mossbach of Saxony, the mounts with stiff leaf borders around the foot and half-gadrooned ball thumbpiece.

c1715-20   *8.75in (22cm) high*

£60,000-80,000   **SOTH**

A probably 18thC brown stoneware pipe, formed as an undulating snake or serpent holding the pipe bowl in its mouth, with moulded scales.

This pipe was dug up in the Portsmouth area in 2009.

10.5in (27cm) long

£1,000-1,500   **WW**

An English saltglazed stoneware silver-mounted mug, probably London, the top half brown-glazed, incised "2 Û 12".

c1700   *9in (23cm) high*

£500-700   **DN**

A German Westerwald pewter-mounted stoneware tankard, bearing the coat of arms for the Kingdom of Great Britain.

c1707-14   *7in (18cm) high*

£700-1,000   **WW**

A large stoneware jug, inscribed "1783 Sml Leonard, With good old Cyder or October, Pray treat your Friends but keep them Sober", damages.

1783   *10in (25.5cm) high*

£700-1,000   **WW**

A George III silver-mounted stoneware jug, the applied reliefs include a hunting scene, a woman riding a donkey, Charlotte mourning at the tomb of Werther, Isaac Walton, a cockerel and hen, hallmarked London.

1793   *9in (23cm) high*

£700-1,000   **SWO**

POTTERY

Judith Picks

As a generalisation, most of the utilitarian stoneware produced in North America in the late 18thC, but particularly the 19thC, is much sought-after by collectors.

Much was made in the North-eastern state of Vermont – mainly by the Norton family of Bennington. The most common forms are the standard "crock" with ear handles, and the standard jug. The piece illustrated here is more desirable as it's a water cooler. It would originally have been fitted with a spigot. Other forms to look out for are covered pots, chamber pots and spittoons.

Decoration was rare before c1830, and varied only subtly for the rest of the 19thC. It is typically in underglaze cobalt blue painted in a naïve fashion, sometimes over a scratched design. Images include flowers (most common), insects, birds, animals, landscapes and, most desirable, commemorative designs. Collectors also look out for more unusual makers or retailers, and so these typically add value.

Condition is of prime importance, as stoneware can chip and crack. These valuable objects can still sometimes be found in yard and estate sales.

A rare 19thC stoneware water cooler, impressed "Wells & Richards Reading Berks Co. PA".

19in (48cm) high

£8,000-12,000   **POOK**

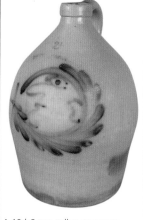

A mid-19thC stoneware water cooler, cobalt-decorated with a hand with pointing finger, inscribed "Ohio", also marked "7" "Quigley & Sons", with Albany slip-glazed interior, cracked,

15.75in (39.5cm) high

£8,000-12,000   **SK**

A 19thC two-gallon stoneware jug, impressed "Cowden & Wilcox Harrisburg PA", with cobalt decoration of the man in the moon.

13.5in (34cm) high

£4,000-6,000   **POOK**

A late 18thC/early 19thC stoneware churn, with incised flower and bird decoration, with applied beehive-form handles, and brown-manganese-highlighted incised decoration, the reverse with the initials "MP" or "MS".

20in (51cm) high

£5,000-7,000   **SK**

A 19thC stoneware jug, with cobalt floral decoration.

9in (23cm) high

£800-1,200   **POOK**

A small 19thC stoneware jug, probably by Richard Remmey, with cobalt floral decoration.

6.75in (17cm) high

£1,500-2,500   **POOK**

A 19thC stoneware mug, inscribed "J.A. Perkins".

4.5in (11.5cm) high

£700-1,000   **POOK**

A 19thC stoneware jug, with cobalt floral decoration.

8.5in (21.5cm) high

£300-400   **POOK**

A 19thC stoneware mug, attributed to Shenfelder of Reading, Pennsylvania, with hand-painted cobalt flower.

3.25in (8.5cm) high

£1,200-1,800   POOK

A 19thC stoneware presentation mug, made by Daniel Shenfelder of Reading Pennsylvania, handpainted "Charles Krick" with cobalt flower.

4.25in (11cm) high

£3,000-4,000   POOK

A 19thC stoneware jug, with cobalt floral band.

10.25in (26cm) high

£1,800-2,200   POOK

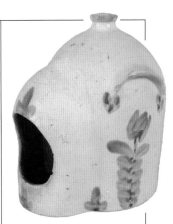

A 19thC stoneware chicken feeder, Philadelphia, impressed "Thos. Haig 975 N. 2nd St. Phila.", with cobalt tulip decoration.

9in (23cm) high

£700-1,000   POOK

A 19thC stoneware jug, Pennsylvania, with cobalt floral decoration.

10.75in (27.5cm) high

£800-1,200   POOK

A 19thC stoneware batter jug, impressed Cowden & Wilcox, Harrisburg, with cobalt decoration.

8.5in (21.5cm) high

£700-1,000   POOK

A 19thC stoneware jug, Harrisburg, Pennsylvania, stamped "Cowden & Wilcox Harrisburg PA" and "4", with cobalt decoration of a bird.

17in (43cm) high

£4,500-5,500   POOK

A large 18thC three-gallon stoneware pitcher, Pennsylvania, attributed to Richard Remmy, with cobalt decoration of large flowers around the date "1726".

1726   16.5in (42cm) high

£5,000-7,000   POOK

A 19thC 16-gallon stoneware crock, Pennsylvania, inscribed "J. Hamilton & Co. Greensboro", with stencilled eagle decoration.

23.5in (60cm) high

£400-600   POOK

A late 19thC stoneware jar, decorated with a cobalt duck, "COWDEN & WILCOX HARRISBURG PA," cracks.

9.75in (25cm) high

£1,000-1,500   SK

POTTERY

A 19thC redware pig flask, Pennsylvania, with manganese splash decoration.

5.25in (13cm) wide

£1,800-2,200   **POOK**

A 19thC redware jug, with profuse manganese splash decoration.

8.75in (22cm) high

£1,000-1,500   **POOK**

A redware flint enamel lion, Bennington, Vermont, impressed "Lyman Fenton & Co.", with coleslaw mane.

c1850   *11in (28cm) wide*

£6,000-8,000   **POOK**

A rare redware urn, by James C. Mackley, Maryland, with S-scroll handles and applied florettes, above a coggled stepped base, signed and dated.

While the works of Mackley's mentor Anthony Bacher can be found in numerous public and private collections, only a few signed examples by Mackley are known.

1874   *8.5in (21.5cm) wide*

£12,000-18,000   **POOK**

A late 19thC redware wall pocket, attributed to S. Bell & Sons, Shenandoah Valley, with relief bird perched on a floral branch with green glaze.

7in (18cm) high

£4,000-6,000   **POOK**

A 19thC redware pitcher, by Jacob Medinger, with incised stag decoration.

7.75in (19.5cm) high

£1,800-2,200   **POOK**

ESSENTIAL REFERENCE - CHALKWARE

A 19thC chalkware rooster, with a polychrome surface.

6.25in (15.5cm) high

£2,000-3,000   **POOK**

Hand-decorated chalkware animals were common ornaments in 18thC and 19thC American homes.

- The name derives from the chalky appearance of the figures, rather than the actual material used. In fact, chalkware figures were made from moulded and air-dried plaster of Paris.
- It was typically painted with watercolours or oil paints.
- Chalkware figures were sold cheaply, given away at funfairs, or peddled door-to-door.
- Many 19thC pieces imitated early Staffordshire animal figures, particularly dogs or farmyard groups, as these were popular with wealthier Americans.
- Chalkware was also made during the Great Depression, and these figures are typically more jocular than their 18thC/19thC counterparts.

A 19thC chalkware figure of a cat.

9in (23cm) high

£1,800-2,200   **POOK**

An early 19thC sgraffito redware charger, Bucks County, Pennsylvania, attributed to Conrad Mumbouer, with tulip decoration.

13.25in (34cm) diam

£5,000-7,000   POOK

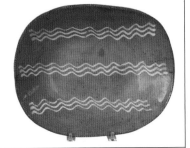

A 19thC redware pie plate, with yellow slip decoration.

9in (23cm) diam

£500-700   POOK

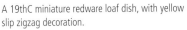

A 19thC redware loaf dish, Pennsylvania, with yellow slip wavy line decoration.

15.75in (40cm) wide

£700-1,000   POOK

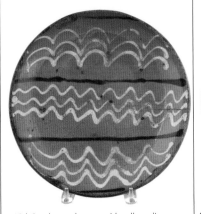

A 19thC redware charger, with yellow slip swag decoration, signed indistinctly on underside.

12.25in (31cm) diam

£800-1,200   POOK

A 19thC redware charger, with unusual yellow slip decoration.

12.25in (31cm) diam

£600-800   POOK

A 19thC miniature redware loaf dish, with yellow slip zigzag decoration.

4in (10cm) wide

£2,000-3,000   POOK

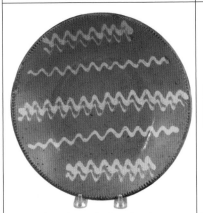

A rare 19thC redware pie plate, New Jersey, stamped "J. McCully Trenton", with yellow slip squiggle line decoration.

10in (25.5cm) diam

£1,000-1,500   POOK

A 19thC redware charger, Southeastern Pennsylvania, with yellow slip decoration in a swag motif.

13in (33.5cm) diam

£2,500-3,500   POOK

A redware shallow bowl, by Isaac S. Stahl, the turquoise glaze with central pinwheel within a swag border, signed on reverse within German inscription, dated.

1945   *8.25in (21cm) diam*

£800-1,200   POOK

POTTERY

ESSENTIAL REFERENCE - MOCHA WARE

Mocha ware, or mocha pottery, is a type of earthenware made to resemble moss agate (also known as Mocha stone), a milky coloured stone with green and red/brown mossy markings. This effect was produced by dripping "mocha tea" (a mix of tobacco juice, stale urine and turpentine) onto the wet pottery before firing. The tea immediately diverged into feather-like mossy shapes.

- Other decoration was provided with coloured bands of specially prepared slip.
- Mocha ware was originally made in Staffordshire in the 1780s for the American market, and was made throughout the 19thC in the UK, America and France.
- It was mainly used in taverns and humble homes.

A mocha ware pepper pot, with earthworm decoration on a tan ground with brown and cream stripes.

4.25in (11cm) high

£700-1,000   POOK

A mocha ware barrel-form jug, with green and brown stripe decoration.

6.5in (16cm) high

£3,000-4,000   POOK

A mocha ware jug, with green, brown and orange stripe and line decoration on a cream ground.

c1820   *6.75in (17cm) high*

£3,000-4,000   POOK

A 19thC mocha ware pepper pot, with blue and brown bands.

4.75in (12cm) high

£1,000-1,500   POOK

A large 19thC mocha ware bowl, with earthworm decoration on an orange ground with blue wavy lines.

9.75in (25cm) diam

£2,000-3,000   POOK

A large 13thC/14thC jug, the ribbed baluster body decorated in a mottled greenish glaze, with a wide strap handle, some restoration.

11.25in (28.5cm) high

£2,000-3,000   WW

A Donyatt puzzle jug, decorated with a yellow and green glaze, incised with a drinking poem above tulips, with the inscription "W F Bartlett May 29 1834".

1834   *7in (18cm) high*

£800-1,200   WW

A Donyatt moneybox, decorated in a mottled yellow and green glaze, inscribed "Alice G Summers 1871; keep within compass and you shall be sure to avoid many troubles which others endure. Donyatt Pottery", the finial modelled as a tricorn hat.

1871   *7in (18cm) high*

£600-800   WW

CLOSER LOOK - SPATTERWARE PLATTER

Spatterware (or sponged ware) was a form of 19thC pottery. Its bright colours were applied with a sponge to give a splotchy effect. It was predominantly made in Staffordshire and exported to America.

Large flat pieces of spatterware, particularly chargers, are hard to find and display the pattern well.

The "rainbow" colourway is hard to find.

The star burst pattern has immense visual appeal.

A rare 19thC five colour rainbow Spatterware platter.

15.25in (39cm) wide

£25,000-35,000   **POOK**

A Davenport terracotta wine cooler, moulded with vines and a pair of Bacchus-mask handles, partially decorated in a green enamel, impressed anchor mark.

c1810

£800-1,200   **DN**

A Mexborough Pottery house moneybox, raised on four bun feet, inscribed "Sophia Hayes July 21th 1844", restoration.

The Mexborough Old Pottery was established in Yorkshire in the late 18thC by Robert Sowter and William Bromley, who produced transfer-printed pottery under the name "Sowter & Co". It was purchased in 1804 by Peter Barker, originally from Staffordshire, whose family ran it until 1844.

1844   *7 in (18cm)*

£800-1,200   **WW**

A twin-handled chemist's drug jar and cover, possibly by Samuel Alcock, titled "Tamarinds" in gold on a green ground, cover repaired.

c1850   *12in (30.5cm) high*

£1,000-1,500   **SWO**

A pair of Gladstone and Disraeli earthenware figures, hand-painted and on marble effect bases, with impressed marks "W & R", "L", and 19thC registration mark.

The "W&R" mark was thought for some time to be for Wayte & Ridge of Staffordshire, who produced pottery figures. It is now thought to be Messrs Wittman & Roth Importers of London 1870-1896.

£1,500-2,500   **LC**

A Measham-style two-handled mug, with kidney shape appliqué with impressed blue enamelled inscription "William Frogatt 1883", frog applied internally.

1883   *4in (10cm) high*

£500-700   **TEN**

THE ORIENTAL MARKET

In a depressed economic climate, Oriental works of art shine as a beacon of hope. It seems that not a week passes without some record being broken, whether for jade or ceramic.

The most exciting news over the last year was the winning bid of £43 million (£51.6 million including buyer's premium) for the Qianlong vase found in a bungalow in Pinner, Middlesex, England. The 16in (40.5cm) high reticulated double-walled vase, or yang cai, with famille rose decoration would have been a commission for one of the palaces of the Qianlong Emperor (1736-95), probably the summer palace or the Forbidden City. The vase combines various different decorative elements reminiscent of pieces made in Tang Ying's directorship of the Imperial manufactory at Jingdezhen – a period of remarkable technical achievement.

Meanwhile, Woolley & Wallis in Salisbury, Wiltshire, England, posted total sales of Oriental works of art to the staggering sum of £22.6 million last year. A good percentage of that came from just four jade carvings, which each sold for excess of £1 million.

Anderson & Garland in Newcastle upon Tyne, England, sold a 3in- (7.5cm-) high carved celadon glazed "flying clouds" water pot, from the Kangxi period and with a six-character mark, for £270,000 to a Chinese dealer who flew in from Beijing to view the piece in person.

A Qianlong-dynasty scroll painting sold in Toulouse, south-west France, for a record 22.1 million euros (£18.5 million), the latest in a series of big-ticket auction prices pledged by Asian bidders keen to buy back China's heritage. Toulouse also saw the sale of an Imperial Qianlong dynasty 4in (10cm) white jade seal, surmounted by carvings of intertwined dragons, which was one of those used by the Qianlong Emperor to sign his calligraphic paintings. Like the scroll, it was thought to have been looted from the Forbidden City in 1900. Competed for by seven Chinese bidders, it sold for 12.4 million euros (£15 million), exceeding an estimate of 1 million to 1.5 million euros.

At Clars Auction Gallery, Oakland, California, a well-carved Chinese celadon jade oval plaque measuring just 6in (15cm) high was expected to sell for £1,000. Even Clars' expert Asian specialists could not believe it when the price escalated in heated bidding to an "astonishing" final selling price of £60,000 (sixty times its high estimate!) going to a Taiwanese collector.

A large and important Chinese blue-and-white Ming-style vase bearing a Qianlong seal mark and dating from the period was sold by Freeman's in Philadelphia, Pennsylvania. This Ming-style vase is a tremendous example of the distinctive artfulness and skill employed at Qianlong's imperial kiln. It sold for £865,000 in March 2011.

Left A Chinese Qianlong period famille rose reticulated double-walled vase, made for the Emperor. 16in (40.5cm) high £52,000,000+ BAIN

Far Left: A 19thC Japanese ivory netsuke. See page 135.

ORIENTAL

CHINESE REIGN PERIODS AND MARKS

Imperial reign marks were adopted during the Ming dynasty, and some of the most common are illustrated here. Certain emperors forbade the use of their own reign mark, lest they should suffer the disrespect of a broken vessel bearing their name being thrown away. This is where the convention of using earlier reign marks comes from – a custom that was enthusiastically adopted by potters as a way of showing their respect for their predecessors.

It is worth remembering that a great deal of Imperial porcelain is marked misleadingly, and pieces bearing the reign mark for the period in which they were made are, therefore, especially sought after.

EARLY PERIODS AND DATES

Xia Dynasty	c2000 - 1500BC	Three Kingdoms	221 - 280	The Five Dynasties	907 - 960
Shang Dynasty	1500 - 1028BC	Jin Dynasty	265 - 420	Song Dynasty	960 - 1279
Zhou Dynasty	1028 - 221BC	Northern & Southern Dynasties	420 - 581	Jin Dynasty	1115 - 1234
Qin Dynasty	221 - 206BC	Sui Dynasty	581 - 618	Yuan Dynasty	1260 - 1368
Han Dynasty	206BC - AD220	Tang Dynasty	618 - 906		

MING DYNASTY REIGNS

Hongwu	1368 - 1398	Jingtai	1450 - 1457
Jianwen	1399 - 1402	Tianshun	1457 - 1464
Yongle	1403 - 1424	Chenghua	1465 - 1487
Hongxi	1425 - 1425	Hongzhi	1488 - 1505
Xuande	1426 - 1435	Zhengde	1506 - 1521
Zhengtong	1436 - 1449		

MING DYNASTY MARKS

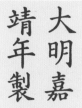

Jiajing	Longquing	Wanli	Tianqi	Chongzhen
1522 – 1566	1567 – 1572	1573 – 1619	1621 – 1627	1628 – 1644

QING DYNASTY MARKS

Shunzhi	Kangxi	Yongzheng	Qianlong	Jiaqing	Daoguang
1644 – 1661	1662 – 1722	1723 – 1735	1736 – 1795	1796 – 1820	1821 – 1850

Xianfeng	Tongzhi	Guangxu	Xuantong	**REPUBLIC PERIOD**
1851 – 1861	1862 – 1874	1875 – 1908	1909 – 1911	Hongxian (Yuan Shikai) 1915 – 1916

ESSENTIAL REFERENCE - EARLY CHINESE CERAMICS

Low-fired earthenwares were made in China during the Neolithic period. Early pieces were painted with zoomorphic, geometric or curved designs in red and black.

- Kiln firing was mastered in the Shang period (1500-1028BC) and the first stoneware and feldspathic glazes were made.
- Lower-temperature lead glazes were produced towards the end of the Zhou dynasty (1028-221BC).
- During the Han dynasty (206BC-220AD) many funerary models were made. Subjects included houses, farms and people.
- The Tang dynasty (618-906AD) is known for its fine, white-bodied wares, which led to the discovery of true porcelain c9thC.
- The most characteristic Tang pottery wares are the "sancai" (three colour) funeral goods, on which the glaze has been allowed to drip and run. The best of these are well-modelled horse and camel figures.

A Chinese Han dynasty model of a Shitzu dog, with studded neckstrap around his chest, with TL test.

26in (66cm) high

£1,500-2,500   **L&T**

A Chinese Tang dynasty unglazed and painted pottery model of a court lady, with elaborate hairstyle and flowing robes, with TL test.

618-906 AD   *14in (36cm) high*

£3,500-4,500   **WW**

A large Chinese Tang dynasty pottery model of a matron, with flowing robes, rouged cheeks and upturned toes, with TL test.

618-906AD   *19in (48cm) high*

£2,000-3,000   **WW**

A large Chinese Tang dynasty pottery model of a white horse, with TL test.

A Chinese Tang dynasty sancai-glazed pottery model of a female equestrian, raised on a rectangular base, with TL test.

618-906AD   *17in (43cm) high*

£6,000-8,000   **WW**

A Chinese Tang dynasty treacle-glazed pottery model of a Bactrian camel, with TL test.

618-906 AD   *20in (51cm) high*

£3,500-4,500   **WW**

TL (thermoluminescence) testing measures the amount of natural radiation absorbed over the lifetime of an object, and from this an approximate date is obtained. This horse's age report was issued from Oxford Authentication in 2004. Authentication reports are increasingly important, due to a large number of fake Chinese pieces entering the market, causing a lack of public confidence in buying. However, false positives can occur, as a result of the deliberate insertion of genuine fragments into modern pieces (typically porcelain into the base) or artificial exposure to the same amount of radiation as a geniune piece would have absorbed over its lifetime.

618-906AD   *19in (48cm) high*

£5,000-7,000   **WW**

ORIENTAL

Judith Picks: Chinese North Song Dynasty

Together with "guan", "ge", "Ru", and "Ding" wares, "Jun" ware is one of the "five famous wares of the Song dynasty".

"Jun" lotus bud waterpots of this elegant form and distinctive opalescent glaze are held in major public and private collections worldwide.

The heavy potting and thick glaze of "Jun" ware are best suited to simple, fluid forms, such as this waterpot.

Qingbai pottery was made in the Song Dynasty. It has a bluish tint. Unlike most pottery of the era, which was made specifically for Imperial use, Qingbai was used by ordinary people.

The large lion embodies male and female attributes through its brocade ball (thrown into a group of male admirers to help a woman choose a husband – the catcher was victorious) and cub respectively.

The fierce expressions, pre-eminent eyebrows, triangular teeth, and well-modelled fur are characteristic of the lions made in the Hutian kilns of Jingdezhen.

A Chinese North Song Dynasty "Jun" "Lotus Bud" waterpot, covered with a thick lustrous glaze of milky lavender colour, which thins at the rim to a pale mushroom colour.

3.5in (9cm) high

£120,000-180,000 **SOTH**

A rare Chinese Northern Song Dynasty Qingbai Buddhist, lion-shaped pillow, the lion with a brocade ball and a small cub, on an oval base carved with lotus petals, supporting a kidney-shaped upper surface.

Ceramic pillows first appeared in the Sui Dynasty (581-618), reaching their apotheosis of production and use in the Song, Jin and Yuan dynasties (10thC-14thC).

8.25in (21cm) wide

£300,000-500,000 **SOTH**

A Chinese Tang dynasty sancai-glazed ovoid jar.
618-906AD *6in (15cm) high*
£4,000-5,000 **WW**

A Chinese Tang dynasty sancai-glazed ovoid jar and cover, decorated with green and amber splashed glazes.
618-906AD *9in (23cm) high*
£3,000-4,000 **WW**

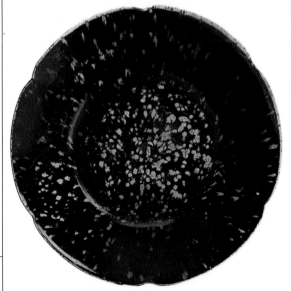

A large Chinese Five Dynasties black wine ewer, the body rising to a thin neck with wide cylindrical rim, with a thin handle, two square-shaped lug handles, and a rooster-head spout.
907-960AD *12in (30.5cm) high*
£1,000-2,000 **RTC**

A 10thC Chinese Yu cylindrical box and cover, covered inside and out with crackled celadon glaze, the cover incised with a lotus flower.
6.75in (17cm) diam
£4,500-5,500 **WW**

A Chinese Northern Song Dynasty Ding-type russet-splashed black-glazed foliate dish, with flared petal-lobed rim and raised foot.

The dish is decorated with an irregular pattern of small splashes of iron oxide, which creates the effect of small "partridge-feather" mottles: something often seen on black-glazed conical-form bowls of the Northern Song period. This dish is unusual for its flower shape, and no similar example appears to be recorded. However, the type is known from vessels covered in a deep russett glaze.

7.75in (19.5cm) diam

£350,000-450,000 **SOTH**

A Chinese late Ming dynasty blanc-de-Chine figure of Guanyin, seated with her hands folded into her robe.

6in (15cm) high

£4,000-6,000   **L&T**

A 17thC Chinese blanc-de-Chine incense burner, with a flared rim and three feet.

8in (20cm) diam

£1,000-1,500   **WW**

An 18thC Chinese Qing dynasty blanc-de-Chine censer, the sides with horizontal fluting, on three lingzhi fungus feet.

4in (10cm) diam

£1,000-2,000   **RTC**

An unusual Chinese blanc-de-Chine model of two Europeans, wearing tricorn hats and holding fans, with a jardinière and a dog, some restoration.

c1700   *6.5in (16cm) high*

£2,500-3,500   **WW**

A pair of 18thC blanc-de-Chine models of elephants and riders.

7.25in (18.5cm) high

£4,000-6,000   **GORL**

A Chinese blanc-de-Chine figure of Lohan, flanked by deer and rock work, with gourd and square seal mark to base.

15in (38cm) high

£3,500-4,500   **FRE**

A Chinese blanc-de-Chine figure of Guanyin, holding a lingzhi fungus sprig in her hand, with a deer carrying a basket of flowers.

24in (61cm) high

£1,500-2,500   **SK**

A Chinese Yuan dynasty celadon vase, Longquan, reduced from a yen yen vase, moulded with scrolling peony leaves and flowers above a band of stiff leaves.

11in (28cm) high

£1,500-2,500   WW

A Chinese Yuan dynasty carved celadon charger, of rounded U-shape form, with central medallion of carved and applied dragon, with orange foot and glazed base, impressed foliate mark.

13.5in (34cm) diam

£6,000-8,000   FRE

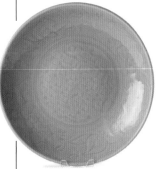

A Chinese Ming dynasty carved celadon bowl, Zhejiang, the interior with a diamond pattern surrounded by a band of alternating peonies and peaches.

14.25in (37cm) diam

£1,800-2,200   RTC

A Chinese Ming dynasty carved celadon barbed charger, central medallion carved to show lotus blossoms issuing from thin reeds, with ribbed wall, unglazed orange foot.

16in (40cm) diam

£2,500-3,500   FRE

A Chinese Ming dynasty carved celadon censer, with white/orange buff interior and crisscross-carved outer-wall, raised on three mask and claw feet, with unglazed base.

11.5in (29cm) diam

£1,200-1,800   FRE

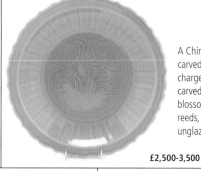

A large 19thC Chinese carved celadon vase, carved to show Indian lotus flowers and leaf scrolls within dentil bands to shoulder, raised on circular white-glazed foot.

24in (61cm) high

£4,000-5,000   FRE

A Chinese Kangxi period oxblood bowl, in 19thC French ormolu mounts with loose ring handles.

5.25in (13cm) diam

£1,500-2,500   LHA

A Chinese Yongzheng period Imperial aubergine-glazed saucer dish, the centre incised with two cranes beneath a pine tree and flanking a fungus, the reverse with bats and lingzhi clouds, the base with a six-character Yongzheng mark.

5in (13cm) diam

£4,000-5,000   WW

A small Chinese Yongzheng period pink-enamelled bowl, with white interior, with underglaze blue four-character mark, with wood stand.

3.5in (9cm) diam

£1,800-2,200   SK

A pair of Chinese Qianlong period sang de boeuf saucer dishes, both with underglaze blue six-character Qianlong seal mark, each with fitted box and hardwood stand.

7in (18cm) diam

£2,000-3,000   WW

A Chinese Qianlong period sang de boeuf stem bowl, the glaze draining from the rim, the base with six-character Qianlong seal mark.

8in (21cm) diam

£2,000-3,000   WW

A pair of Chinese Qianlong period sang de boeuf bottle vases, the crimson glaze thinning to white around the rim, the interior and the base of clear glaze, with underglaze blue Qianlong six-character mark.

6in (15cm) high

£1,500-2,500   SK

A rare Chinese Qianlong period flambé-glazed bottle vase, with moulded horizontal ribs, covered in a reddish-purple flambé glaze mottled with milky pale blue, with unglazed foot and brown-glazed base, with impressed six-character Qianlong seal mark.

The present piece is notable for its impressive size and the brilliance and depth of the glaze. Vases of this type derived from guan ware of the Song dynasty (960-1279), but the Qing craftsmen also made innovations and developments on some of the traditional Song glazes. These flambé glazes are derived from "Jun" wares. The form of this vase was first revived by the Yongzheng emperor and covered in Song-inspired glazes.

16in (40cm) high

£500,000-700,000   SOTH

A Chinese Qianlong period coral-ground brushwasher, modelled to simulate coral and decorated with calligraphy in gilt, the interior turquoise, the base with a six-character gold Qianlong mark.

3.25in (8.5cm) high

£15,000-25,000   WW

A pair of Chinese Republican period pink-enamelled vases, with gilt rim, old label to the base.

12in (30.5cm) high

£1,500-2,500   SK

ORIENTAL

Judith Picks: "Ge" Brushwasher

Delicate potting and a glaze that thins at the rim to reveal the black body, and that has a prominent crackled effect, are characteristic of "ge" wares produced from the Song dynasty into the Yuan period. "Ge" is a connoisseur's term known only from post-Song texts, and does not refer to a production area. It is used for ceramics similar to "guan" wares but with a more opaque, buff glaze. The crackle effect is distinctively stained black, interspersed with some rust-red or light-brown crackles. Nigel Wood in "Chinese Glazes" (London, 1999, p.87) notes that it is likely that both "ge" and "guan" wares were issued simultaneously from the same kilns, showing natural variations of atmosphere, temperature and cooling.

The form of this brushwasher continues a Song dynasty type produced at the official (guan) kilns located within the palace walls in the Song capital of Hangzhou, Zhejiang province. It is closely related to a "guan" washer from the Kempe collection that has been attributed to the Song period.

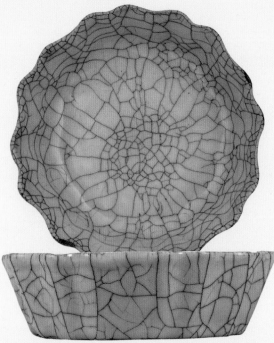

A rare Chinese Yuan dynasty "Ge" brushwasher, the lobed, flaring sides rising from a slightly concave base to an everted rim, covered overall with a thick, grey crackle glaze, the base with six spur marks.

5in (12.5cm) diam

£1,000,000+   **SOTH**

FAKE ALERT!

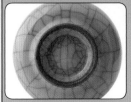

This example is a modern fake. At first glance it looks quite convincing however there are numerous clues that all is not as it should be.

- The shape is wrong for the period.
- Period wares had black bodies- this has a reddish brown body.
- The base has no spur marks, which are a result of the pieces being stacked in the kiln.
- It is too thickly potted.
- The piece is too heavy.
- Glaze covers the whole piece evenly (apart from footrim).

A rare Chinese Song dynasty ding yao pillow, modelled as two boys sleeping back to back, restoration.

7in (18cm) long

£8,000-12,000   **WW**

A Chinese probably Song dynasty Ding yao shallow bowl, incised with ducks swimming amidst reeds and flowers, their heads tilted, with a flaring border and unglazed rim.

This Song design, emblematic of fidelity and a happy marriage, is particularly associated with the Ding wares from the Hebei province during the Northern Song period. It appears on various shapes including Ding bowls and dishes.

8in (20cm) diam

£18,000-22,000   **WW**

An 18thC Chinese Guan-type cong-shaped vase, moulded with 15 horizontal flanges around each corner, covered with pale olive-green crackle glaze.

9in (23cm) high

£2,500-3,500   **SK**

One of a pair of 19thC Chinese white-glazed vases, of ladded yen yen form.

26in (66cm) high

£2,000-3,000 pair   **FRE**

A Chinese Yuan dynasty blue-and-white footed bowl, the interior with lotus pads and blossoms tied with ribbon, the exterior with a band of stylised ruyi and lappets near the foot.

6.75in (17cm) high

£10,000-15,000   **IMC**

A rare Chinese Yuan dynasty blue-and-white octagonal-section vase, Yuhuchunping, moulded with facets and painted with panels of peony, lotus and diaper designs, the neck with panels of "Three Friends of Winter", the base with Buddhist emblems.

11.75in (30cm) high

£18,000-22,000   **WW**

A rare Chinese Jiajing period blue-and-white square dish, with central design of five-clawed dragons flanking a tower of auspicious symbols, within floral and foliate border, with Jiajing mark.

10.5in (27cm) wide

£3,000-4,000   **IMC**

A Chinese Jiajing period blue-and-white charger, of U-shape, the interior decorated with the "Three Friends of Winter", lotus scroll and wave band, the exterior with lotus scroll band above key band.

14in (36cm) diam

£5,000-7,000   **FRE**

A large Chinese Jiajing period blue-and-white bowl, the exterior painted with the "Eight Treasures", foliage and lotus flower heads beneath a key-fret border, the interior with a similarly decorated panel, base with six-character Jiajing mark, cracks.

13in (33.5cm) diam

£4,000-6,000   **WW**

A large Chinese late Ming dynasty Swatow blue-and-white bowl, the interior painted with a bird and large blossoms flanked by floral panels, with mark.

Swatow ware is a common name for a group of mainly late Ming Dynasty export porcelains intended for the South East Asian market. Swatow ware is typically coarse, crudely potted and often under-fired. Blue-and-white decoration is by far the most common.

15.25in (38.5cm) diam

£800-1,200   **IMC**

A Chinese Ming dynasty blue-and-white meiping vase, painted with a band of lotus scroll, a border of rocks and cresting waves around the foot, and a band of peonies within gadroon panels at the shoulder.

With glaze degradation probably due to sea immersion.

9.75in (25cm) high

£2,000-3,000   **WW**

ORIENTAL

ESSENTIAL REFERENCE - CHINESE EXPORT PORCELAIN

From the 16thC, much blue-and-white porcelain was made in China for export to the West. Such pieces are similar to those produced for the home market, but can be of inferior quality and often lack symbolically significant decoration.

● Concessions to European habits were made: plates had wide rims, teacups had saucers, and garnitures were made.

● Our knowledge of this sort of porcelain has been greatly improved by the recovery of cargo from several shipwrecked trading vessels, such as the Nanking Cargo, which was rediscovered 1986.

● The quality of porcelain exported to Europe declined in the 19thC.

A large Chinese Kraak bowl, the exterior painted with alternating panels of chrysanthemum and auspicious objects, the interior with a tied scroll, cracks, with wooden stand.

Kraak ware (named after the carracks – Portuguese ships – in which it was transported) is an early type of Chinese export porcelain produced from the Wanli period until around 1640.

c1620   *15.25in (38.5cm) high*
£2,500-3,500   WW

A small Chinese Wanli period blue-and-white octagonal jar, painted in blue outline with a pictorial frieze of mounted figures, with a pair of moulded lion handles.

5in (12.5cm) high
£1,200-1,800   FRE

A Chinese Wanli period blue-and-white openwork porcelain model of a scholar's rock garden scene, with two moulded figures to the front.

9.5in (24cm) high
£1,000-1,500   IMC

A large 18thC Chinese Wanli-style blue-and-white covered jar, decorated with cartouches of boys at play, buff unglazed base.

19in (48cm) high
£1,500-2,500   FRE

A Chinese Wanli period blue-and-white compressed circular vase, painted with birds in flight in a pine and bamboo grove, the rim reduced and with a metal fitting, cracks, with wooden cover.

10.25in (26cm) high without cover
£3,500-4,500   WW

A Chinese Wanli period blue-and-white compressed circular vase, with a wide band of phoenix in flight, peony blooms and serpentine scroll, the shoulder with peony and chrysanthemum on a complex geometric ground.

10in (25.5cm) wide
£3,500-4,500   WW

A Chinese Wanli period blue-and-white bowl, the interior painted with a standing dignitary in front of a kneeling warrior, with lingzhi mark.

5.75in (14.5cm) diam
£1,200-1,800   WW

A Chinese Wanli period blue-and-white Guan jar, the heavily potted body cobalt-painted with four-clawed dragons between a band of lotus flowers above, and a rock and water design below, base unglazed.

11.75in (30cm) high
£12,000-18,000   SK

A large Chinese late Ming dynasty blue-and-white cylindrical brushpot, with straight sides slightly flared towards the mouth, painted in underglaze blue with a scene from a romance, extensive damage and restoration.

c1630-40　　　　*8.75in (22cm) high*

£10,000-15,000　　　　**WW**

A Chinese transitional period blue-and-white ewer, painted with a band containing houses on stilts in a rocky, watery landscape, the spout formed as an animal's head.

c1640　　　　*8in (20cm) high*

£1,000-1,500　　　　**WW**

A large Chinese Kangxi period blue-and-white "soldier" vase, painted with a central band of dragons in reserve with stylised scrolling ruyi on a blue ground, between bands of lotus scrollwork, leaves at the neck and lotus at the foot.

36in (91.5cm) high

£150,000-250,000　　　　**SOTH**

A 17thC Chinese blue-and-white bowl, the interior with scene of a lone fisherman, the exterior with a covered boat, carrying a nobleman and attendants, with panel of calligraphy inscription and Ming Cheughua mark, with wood stand.

7.25in (18.5cm) high

£1,500-2,500　　　　**IMC**

A Chinese Shunzhi period blue-and-white sleeve vase, painted with a scene depicting a warrior and two attendants consulting a sage in front of mountains, with four cranes, all between An hua bands of flowers and chevrons, some restoration.

17in (43cm) high

£8,000-12,000　　　　**WW**

A 17thC Chinese blue-and-white bowl, painted with flowerheads divided by five shou characters, and with another character and peaches to the interior, with lozenge mark.

7in (18cm) diam

£500-700　　　　**WW**

A Chinese Kangxi period blue-and-white meiping vase, underglaze blue painted with the "Three Friends of Winter", the base with a four-character Chenghua mark.

9in (23cm) high

£7,000-10,000　　　　**WW**

A Chinese Kangxi period copper, blue-and-white "dragon and phoenix" beaker vase, painted with four-clawed dragons, and medallions of phoenix, with alternating carved foliate medallions, cross-hatched band to foot and rim, glazed, recessed base.

17.5in (44cm) high

£15,000-25,000　　　　**FRE**

A pair of Chinese Kangxi period blue-and-white hexagonal-form vases, painted with panels of figures and precious objects, with very rare "CD" European monogram.

12in (30.5cm) high

£15,000-25,000　　　　**SWO**

A Chinese Kangxi period blue-and-white vase, with panels of flowers.

An early price label on the base states that this vase with a damaged companion was sold for £13 10d.

11in (28cm) high

£2,500-3,500　　　　**SWO**

A Chinese Kangxi period blue-and-white bottle vase, painted with six precious objects, including pairs of scrolls, a lucky knot and vases on stands, some restoration.

11.75in (30cm) high

£2,000-3,000   WW

A Chinese Kangxi period blue-and-white yen yen vase, painted in underglaze blue with a dignitary and his servant being approached by a peasant with a gift, and other figures, some damages.

18in (45.5cm) high

£6,000-8,000   WW

A Chinese Kangxi period blue-and-white export Gu vase, divided into three registers, the upper with two dignitaries and their attendants in a garden, the middle with figures dining, the lower with Confucian scholars and attendants, with blue painted fungus mark within parallel line circle.

18in (45.5cm) high

£15,000-25,000   TEN

A pair of Chinese Kangxi period blue-and-white baluster-form vases, with moulded lotus petal and landscape decoration.

8in (20cm) high

£3,000-4,000   LHA

One of a pair of Chinese Kangxi period blue-and-white vases and covers, painted with precious objects, covers matching.

Larger 8in (20cm) high

£4,000-6,000 pair   SWO

A Chinese Kangxi period blue-and-white ovoid vase, painted with two phoenix amidst peony blossoms, with later wood stand and cover, the cover damaged.

8in (20cm) high

£1,200-1,800   WW

A Chinese Kangxi period blue-and-white bowl, the exterior decorated with phoenix and fauna amongst rockery, the cavetto with large peony blooms, with mark to base.

7.75in (19.5cm) diam

£1,800-2,200   RTC

A Chinese Kangxi period blue-and-white bowl, the rim with citron cartouches to geometric band, the interior with central medallion, the exterior with figural court scene, raised on circular foot, Kangxi six-character mark to base.

8in (20cm) diam

£4,000-6,000   FRE

A large Chinese Kangxi period blue-and-white bowl, with a cavetto depicting a stylised lotus bloom with ruyi leaves, the exterior with a band of interlocking ruyi outlines, base with six-character Xuande mark.

8in (20cm) diam

£3,000-4,000   RTC

A large Chinese Kangxi period blue-and-white bowl, of shallow U-shape form with barbed foliate rim, central medallion of deer among pine trees enclosed by butterflies, ruyi and foliate blossoms, sprigs to the underside.

14.5in (37cm) diam

£1,800-2,200   FRE

A Chinese Kangxi blue-and-white bowl, the interior painted with three boys at play, the exterior with ladies and dignitaries on a terrace and in interiors, with a six-character Jiajing mark.

6in (1cm) diam

£2,500-3,500   WW

ORIENTAL

A large Chinese Kangxi period blue-and-white cistern, decorated with cranes and deer within wave and stylised foliate borders, the rim with panels of pine trees, the sides with unglazed Shi Shi-mask handles.

25.5in (65cm) diam

£30,000-40,000   DUK

A Chinese Kangxi blue-and-white jar, painted with boys at play, with wood cover.

8.5in (21.5cm) high

£4,000-6,000   FRE

A Chinese Kangxi period blue-and-white stem cup, the exterior with coral red five-clawed dragons amid waves, foot with waves and "earth" motif, with Xuande mark.

c1700   *5.5in (14cm) high*

£2,000-3,000   IMC

A Chinese Kangxi period blue-and-white porcelain ewer, painted with archaic vessels, prunus, peonies and Buddhistic precious objects, handle and spout painted with cloud wisps, with six-character Jiajing mark within double concentric circle, lacking cover.

6.25in (15.5cm) high

£2,000-3,000   TEN

A Chinese Kangxi period blue-and-white cup and cover, painted with two panels enclosing a landscape scene, on a high, curved foot, damages.

6.25in (15.5cm) high

£2,000-3,000   WW

A Chinese Kangxi period blue-and-white brush pot, decorated in underglaze blue with a famous prose "Ode to the Sound of Autumn" written by Ou Yangxiu (1007-1072) in the year 1059, and an iron-red seal, the base with a wide unglazed ring encircling a small recessed centre.

8in (20cm) diam

£5,000-7,000   SK

A Chinese Kangxi period blue-and-white plate, painted with three figures in an interior, with six-character Jiajing mark.

8in (20cm) diam

£1,000-1,500   WW

A Chinese Kangxi period blue-and-white spiral-moulded dish, painted with panels of fish and crustacea, with a flower head mark within a double ring.

11in (28cm) diam

£800-1,200   WW

One of a pair of Chinese Qianlong period blue-and-white dragon dishes, decorated with dragons amidst wave patterns, each with a six-character Qianlong seal mark, both damaged.

7in (18cm) diam

£6,000-8,000 pair **WW**

CLOSER LOOK - QIANLONG LANTERN VASE

This vase was memorably used as an umbrella stand by the vendors, who had no idea of its true value. It was almost certainly acquired from Embly Court, Hampshire (home of Florence Nightingale, who might conceivably have owned this vase).

The use of copper-red, and the masterful execution of the continuous landscape, suggests that this vase was manufactured in the Imperial kilns under the direction of Tang Ying during the early years of Qianlong's reign. Tang Ying was multi-talented, skilled at script-writing, painting, engraving seal script, and poetry, as well as working with ceramics. He made a significant contribution to Chinese porcelain during the Yongzheng and Qianlong periods.

The painting style of the landscape is reminiscent of the work of Wang Hui (1632-1717), who played a key role in reinvigorating past traditions of landscape painting. It is possible this vase's decoration is derived from his masterwork: a series of 12 monumental scrolls depicting the Kangxi Emperor's Southern Inspection Tour of 1689.

A small Chinese Yongzheng period blue-and-white lobed vase, painted with leafy trailing gourd vines.

2.25in (5.5cm) high

£2,500-3,500 **WW**

A Chinese Qianlong period "Lantern" vase, with decoration in underglaze blue, copper-red and passages of An hua, the neck with bands of prunus, flowers and bamboo shoots over a continuous mountainous landscape, the tallest peak with two impressed characters, the base with seal mark of Qianlong, damage.

18.5in (47cm) high

£800,000-1,200,000 **DUK**

One of a pair of Chinese Qianlong period blue-and-white bowls, each decorated with five leaf-and-fruit roundels punctuated by pomegranate motifs, a repeat band of ruyi heads to the basal rim, each with Qianlong seal mark.

Each bowl is internally pasted with an old pen-and-ink label, and with an additional label reading "Tell Sir John the reading of that mark on his two bowls is 'Made in the Chienlung period of the great Xing Dynasty. This fixes their date as being between 1736 and 1795'."

6in (15cm) diam

£6,000-8,000 pair **TEN**

A Chinese Qianlong period blue-and-white square-section teapot and cover, decorated with reticulated panels and complex diaper designs.

6.75in (17cm) high

£1,800-2,200 **WW**

A Chinese Jiaqing blue-and-white jar and cover, with steep sided bowl and shallow domed cover topped with a Fu-dog knop, with six-character Jiaqing mark.

5.25in (13cm) high

£250-350   RTC

A Chinese blue-and-white export square-section vase, decorated with a continuous lakeland scene, cover lacking.

c1800   *13in (33.5cm) high*

£1,200-1,800   TEN

A large 19thC Chinese blue-and-white Hu-shaped vase, the handles modelled as sections of bamboo, the body decorated with a continuous lotus scroll beneath bands of waves, leaves, shou characters, cell diaper and other border designs.

21in (53.5cm) high

£10,000-15,000   WW

A pair of large Chinese late Qing dynasty blue-and-white dragon vases, with foliate rim, narrow neck, applied qilong to shoulders.

24in (61cm) high

£3,000-4,000   FRE

A pair of 19thC Chinese Qing Dynasty blue-and-white covered vases, decorated with figural and landscape images framed by lingzhi borders.

13.5in (34cm) high

£1,800-2,200   FRE

A Chinese Guangxu period blue-and-white yuhuchunping, painted with stylised bamboo, plantain and rockwork, the base with a six-character Guangxu mark.

11.5in (29cm) high

£8,000-12,000   WW

A Chinese blue-and-white cylindrical jar and cover, the body painted with a scene outside a walled city within lappet and ruyi head borders, the shoulders with Buddhistic precious objects, the cover with hilly lakeland landscape scene.

c1850-80   *14in (36cm) high*

£1,200-1,800   TEN

A Chinese, probably Daoguang period, blue-and-white vase, the body with band of the "Eight Buddhist Emblems", lotus below and scrolling lotus above, with moulded archaistic mask mock-ring handles, with Qianlong seal mark.

22in (56cm) high

£1,000-1,500   IMC

A mid 19thC Chinese blue-and-white jardinière, painted with dragons on a ground of scattered flowers between lappet and rui borders.

13.5in (33.5cm) high

£1,200-1,800   GORB

A 19thC Chinese blue-and-white vase and cover, painted with panels containing fans, and precious objects, divided by lotus and peony sprays, and flower head borders.

12in (30.5cm) high

£1,000-1,500   WW

A large Chinese late Qing dynasty blue-and-white jardinière, with moulded mask handles, ruyi band to collar, bird and foliate sprigs.

14in (36cm) diam

£1,500-2,500   **FRE**

A pair of 19thC Chinese blue-and-white garden seats, painted with lotus scrolls and moulded with studs, restored.

18in (45.5cm) high

£2,500-3,500   **WW**

An early 20thC Chinese blue-and-white jardinière, decorated with lotus blossoms and meandering foliage, ruyi-shaped band to rim and foliate lappets to base.

15.5in (39cm) high

£300-400   **IMC**

A large early 20thC Chinese blue-and-white brush pot, painted with two panels containing auspicious objects divided by shou characters.

8in (19.5cm) high

£150-250   **WW**

A Chinese blue-and-white moonflask vase, decorated with figures in gardens.

12in (30.5cm) high

£300-500   **GORL**

An early 20thC Chinese blue-and-white hand warmer, the oval-section cylinder painted with a continuous lotus scroll, with four-character Daoguang mark.

6in (15cm) long

£300-400   **WW**

An early 20thC Chinese blue-and-white dragon jar, decorated with two writhing dragons amid pearls and clouds.

7.5in (19cm) high

£150-250   **IMC**

One of a pair of Chinese blue-and-white vases, decorated with stylised scrolling floral motifs, each with inventory mark inscribed to base, with later silver-plated lids.

6in (15cm) high

£600-800 pair   **GORB**

One of a pair of early 20thC Chinese ginger jars, decorated with prunus and cracked ice, with wood covers.

8in (20cm) high

£300-400 pair   **SWO**

A Chinese baluster vase and cover, decorated in underglaze blue with dragons and lotus amongst clouds.

c1900   *17in (43cm) high*

£400-600   **DN**

A Chinese Kangxi period famille verte brush pot, decorated with figures in a garden, the base with wide foot rim with concave glazed medallion at centre.

5.5in (14cm) high

£3,500-4,500   **LHA**

ESSENTIAL REFERENCE - FAMILLE VERTE

Chinese porcelain is often categorised by its colour palette. Famille verte (literally "green family") was introduced during the Kangxi period (1662-1722). It was still used into the 20thC.

- **Its main colours are bright green and iron-red, with blue, yellow and aubergine. These were mainly overglaze colours.**
- **Typical designs include landscapes and gardens, figures, the "Eight Precious Things", and the "Eight Buddhistic Emblems".**
- **Many famille verte pieces were commissioned by wealthy European families. Such pieces may include coats of arms.**

An 18thC Chinese famille verte bowl, decorated in underglaze blue and overglaze colours with a dragon and a pair of phoenix amongst foliage, with Buddhistic emblems to the rim, internally with central sky dragon roundel, with six-character Kangxi mark.

6in (15cm) diam

£7,000-9,000   **TEN**

A pair of 18thC Chinese famille verte figures of Dogs of Fo, one with a puppy, the other with a brocade ball, enamelled on the biscuit, on rectangular bases.

14in (36cm) overall

£2,000-3,000   **DN**

A large Chinese Kangxi period famille verte dish, decorated with a scene from a romance, depicting nine beautiful young ladies, with artemesia leaf mark, extensively restored.

14.5in (37cm) diam

£3,000-4,000   **WW**

A pair of Chinese famille verte lidded temple jars, depicting scenes of a figural procession.

17in (43cm) high

£2,500-3,500   **LHA**

A Chinese Kangxi period famille verte vase, with enamelled Shou characters to neck over peony and birds amongst rock work and foliate sprigs, butterflies and song birds verso, with double rings to base.

16.75in (43cm) high

£4,000-6,000   **FRE**

A pair of Chinese Kangxi period famille verte plates, each decorated with the "Eight Horses of Mu Wang" in a landscape, the borders with rockwork and prunus, each with a Ding mark.

9.75in (22cm) diam

£3,500-4,500   **WW**

A large Chinese Kangxi period famille verte dish, painted with two birds amidst peony and lotus, above a pond with an egret, carp and large crustacean, some restoration.

14in (36cm) diam

£2,000-3,000   **WW**

ORIENTAL

A pair of Chinese Kangxi period famille verte figures of boys, each standing and holding a lotus in a vase.

11in (28cm) high

£1,800-2,200   DN

A Chinese Kangxi period famille verte cylindrical brushpot, painted with two long-tailed birds perched on a flowering hydrangea, the reverse with two small flying insects.

5in (12.5cm) high

£3,000-4,000   WW

A large Chinese Kangxi period famille verte brushpot, with pale celadon glaze decorated with calligraphy and swimming fish, signed "QIAO-YIN", dated.

1712   *7in (18cm) diam*

£4,000-6,000   RTC

A large 18thC Chinese famille verte vase, decorated with a continuous frieze of an equestrian bowman and his groom in a hilly landscape, between horizontal bandings of lozenge and tasselled jewelled motifs.

24in (61cm) high

£3,500-4,500   TEN

A Chinese Qing dynasty famille verte octagonal bottle vase, with iron red and green archaic scrolls and geometric band to neck, above panels of immortals, mark flanked by green enamelled dragons.

15.75in (40cm) high

£5,000-7,000   FRE

A pair of Chinese famille verte baluster vases, each with four applied dragons on shoulders and applied double Fu dog handles to neck.

25in (63.5cm) high

£2,500-3,500   LHA

A Chinese Qing dynasty famille verte fish bowl, internally painted with goldfish amongst aquatic weeds, externally with a continuous palace complex interior scene between diapered border bands.

c1870   *18in (45.5cm) diam*

£5,000-7,000   TEN

A large 19thC Chinese Qing Dynasty famille verte fishbowl, heavily potted and of deep U-form with hidden foot ring, decorated with "One Hundred Antique Vases" and with four medallions depicting different songbirds amongst florals and rockery.

24in (61cm) diam

£10,000-15,000   RTC

An early 20thC Chinese famille verte brushpot, in the "Hundred Boys" pattern.

The "Hundred Boys" represent the Chinese desire for many sons to carry on the family name and bring honour to the family. There are many traditions associated with achieving this wish, such as offering young brides candied lotus seeds at the New Year celebrations, and adding an arrowroot bulb (which resembles a baby boy's penis) into the New Year's cooking.

7.25in (18.5cm) diam

£2,500-3,500   WW

A large Chinese famille rose Hu-form vase, enamelled with a landscape and figure verso, with script, with black glazed elephant handles.

c1700   *15.25in (39cm) high*

£15,000-25,000   **FRE**

A Chinese Qianlong period export famille rose hexagonal panelled vase, the panels alternating between families on verandas and birds amongst trees and rockwork, with arches of scrolls to the shoulder and reserve panels of mythological animals, further shaped oval panels to the base.

19.25in (49cm) high

£1,500-2,500   **TEN**

CLOSER LOOK - "SOLDIER" VASES

A high level of craftsmanship was vital to produce such large vases, not only in the potting, but also in managing the firing of the wood-fuelled kiln.

These vases are notable for their finely composed and detailed designs that successfully occupy and enhance the elegant form.

These "soldier" or "dragoon" vases are so-named because Augustus the Strong of Saxony once traded 151 porcelain pieces against a regiment of fully equipped soldiers (Dragoneers). A set of (probably) 16 large vases formed the most important part of the barter.

A pair of Chinese Qianlong period famille rose "soldier" vases and covers, enamelled with birds on rockwork between lotus-lappets and a lambrequin collar, the neck with quatrefoil landscape panels on a prunus and cracked-ice ground.

48in (122cm) high

£150,000-250,000   **SOTH**

A Chinese Qianlong period famille rose Tibetan-style benbaping (altar vase), painted with eight Buddhist emblems and eight stylised lotus blooms on a ruby ground, the base with six-character iron red Qianlong mark, lacking top section.

8.25in (21cm) high

£70,000-100,000   **WW**

A 19thC Chinese famille rose "Three Boys" vase, with moulded figures of boys, and lotus and scrolls over yellow and ruby ground, with red Qianlong mark.

12.5in (32cm) high

£25,000-35,000   **FRE**

A large pair of 19thC Chinese export famille rose vases, with moulded neck, the body enamelled with figural landscapes over a ground of foliate sprigs.

24in (61cm) high

£3,500-4,500   **FRE**

A 20thC Chinese famille rose vase, with ruyi band to rim, Indian lotus and gilt shou symbols to shoulder, the body worked to show detailed enamelled butterflies, iron-red Guangxu mark to base.

15.5in (39cm) high

£4,000-6,000   **FRE**

One of a pair of Chinese Republic period gilded famille rose vases, enamelled with landscape cartouches within blue and gilt lotus ground Qianlong mark.

8.5in (21.5cm) high

£6,000-8,000 pair   **FRE**

A Chinese famille rose ovoid vase, by Zhai Xiaoxiang, painted with bamboo, roses, magnolia and butterflies, the reverse with calligraphy, the base with a four-character seal mark for Jing de zhen zhi, 1995, cased and with artist's and Olympia exhibition certificates.

1995   *10in (25.5cm) high*

£3,500-4,500   **WW**

ORIENTAL

A Chinese Yongzheng famille rose peony bowl, the exterior with a large and small flowering branch, and a yellow flower sprig, the interior with single pink bloom, the base with a six-character Yongzheng mark.

8in (20cm) diam

£1,500-2,500   **WW**

A rare Chinese Qianlong period famille rose "Hunting and Farming" export punch bowl, the interior with a continuous landscape of European huntsman and hounds, the exterior with Chinese figures in paddy fields.

13in (33.5cm) diam

£3,500-4,500   **TOV**

A Chinese Jiaqing famille rose bowl, cover and liner, decorated with figures in rocky gardens, with gilt-metal handles, with iron red six-character Jiaqing mark.

Provenance: Acquired by John Reeves after his arrival in Canton in 1812.

7in (18cm) wide

£7,000-10,000   **WW**

A Chinese gold-ground famille rose bowl, cover and stand, enamelled with court ladies in a pagoda, each piece with an iron-red six-character mark for Jiang Zheng long zhi (Made by Jiang Zhenglong).

Provenance: Acquired by John Reeves after his arrival in Canton in 1812.

c1820   *4in (10cm) diam*

£5,000-7,000   **WW**

One of a pair of Chinese Daoguang period famille rose deep bowls, with central cavetto of a lotus medallion, the exterior with medallions containing Buddhist symbols, Immortals and sacred animals below a band of shou (longevity) characters and Buddhist emblems, base with two-character Baragon Tumed mark, with hardwood stands.

Part of the wedding service of the daughter of the Daoguang Emperor to the Mongol prince, Baragon Tumed.

5in (12.5cm) diam

£6,000-8,000 pair   **RTC**

A pair of rare Chinese late Daoguang period famille rose pomegranate bowls, the exterior with a pomegranate tree, the bases surrounded by lingzhi fungus, the interior with a single bloom, bases with enamel red Shen de Tang mark.

Provenance: Purchased from the former Ho residents of Na Za Zai in Beijing in the early 1970s.

5in (12.5cm) diam

£30,000-40,000   **RTC**

A Chinese Guangxu period famille rose bowl, enamelled with flowering prunus branches and red berries, the reverse with calligraphy and three pink seals, the base with underglaze blue six-character Guangxu mark.

4.75in (12cm) diam

£2,500-3,500   **WW**

One of a pair of Chinese famille rose bowls, with floral decoration on a glazed pink reserve with interspersed circular cartouches, with gilt seal mark on underside.

6in (15cm) diam

£1,200-1,800 pair   **LHA**

One of a pair of Chinese famille rose bowls, with yellow reserves.

5.5in (14cm) diam

£5,000-7,000 pair   **LHA**

An 18thC Chinese famille rose figure of a maiden, wearing a brightly coloured robe and holding a vase, minor repairs.

10in (25.5cm) high

£1,000-1,500   **WW**

One of a pair of 18thC Chinese export famille rose tureens and covers, with canted corners and flared feet, scroll handle to the cover and boars' head handles to the body, decorated with spear-head borders, flowers and rockwork.

15in (38cm) wide

£3,000-4,000 pair   **L&T**

CLOSER LOOK - FAMILLE ROSE BASIN

This piece is a large and well-painted basin in the highly collectable famille rose palette.

The carp holds specific significance in Chinese art and literature. This symbolic image, has been one of the most popular themes in Chinese paintings.

The carp can jump 8-10ft (2.5-3m) in the air and symbolise a sudden uplifting in one's social status, as when one ascended into the upper society or had found favour with the royal or a noble family.

The fish are usually coloured in gold or pink, shimmering with an unmistakably auspicious tone.

A pair of Chinese Yongzheng period famille rose saucer dishes, painted with large peony and other flower sprays and flying insects, bases with six-character Yongzheng marks, some restoration.

6in (15cm) diam

£1,500-2,500   **WW**

A large 18thC Chinese famille rose basin, enamelled with iron-red and famille rose carp among green aquatic sprigs, with copper insert and later hardwood stand.

Basin 30in (76cm) high

£20,000-30,000   **FRE**

A pair of rare Chinese Qianlong period famille rose moulded teapots, painted with panels of figures in boats in watery landscapes on wide green and black enamel floral bands.

c1740   *6in (15cm) high*

£1,500-2,500   **WW**

A 20thC Chinese famille rose U-shaped cup, painted with a boy and chicken in a garden between blue rockwork and flowers, the reverse with calligraphy, the base with six-character Qianlong mark.

3.25in (8.5cm) diam

£700-1,000   **WW**

A rare Chinese Qianlong/Jiaqing period faux bois, woodgrain and famille rose brush pot, the interior rim and base with painted faux grain, the centre enamelled with a fishing hamlet landscape, on wood stand.

5.5in (14cm) high

£6,000-8,000   **FRE**

A 19thC Chinese famille rose cockerel teapot and cover, with brightly enamelled plumage, and standing on large yellow feet, restoration.

7.25in (18.5cm) high

£5,000-7,000   **WW**

One of a pair of 19thC Chinese famille rose models of recumbent lion dogs, vases rising from their backs, enamelled with flowers and leaves.

7in (18cm) long

£2,000-3,000 pair   **WW**

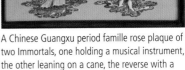

A Chinese Guangxu period famille rose plaque of two Immortals, one holding a musical instrument, the other leaning on a cane, the reverse with a yellow ground with two incised dragons chasing the flaming pearl, all in a hardwood frame.

Framed 26in (66cm) wide

£4,000-6,000   **L&T**

A 19thC Chinese rose medallion bowl, Canton, of deep U-shape form, the interior with gilt figural Canton palette, on circular foot.

21in (53cm) diam

£6,000-8,000   FRE

A large pair of 19thC Chinese export rose medallion vases, with enamelled figural cartouches to typical rose medallion ground, with foliate barbed rim, and moulded and gilded Fu lion handles and qilong to shoulder, on wood stands.

Vase 35in (89cm) high

£10,000-15,000   FRE

A Chinese rose medallion centre bowl, decorated with alternating panels of figures in interiors and birds on flowering branches, raised on a hardwood stand.

14in (36cm) diam

£800-1,200   LHA

A pair of late 19thC Chinese export rose medallion vases, enamelled with panels of ladies at leisure and foliate sprigs, with gilt Fu lions and qilong to the neck.

23.5in (60cm) high

£1,500-2,500   FRE

A late 19thC Chinese export rose medallion ormulu-mounted bowl, enamelled with Chinese figures in an interior scene, the interior depicting wrestlers, on pierced and beaded base with patera.

15in (38cm) diam

£2,500-3,500   FRE

A pair of famille noir rouleau vases, decorated with birds and flowers above rocks, with black enamel six-character reign mark on underside in a double circle.

17.5in (44cm) high

£1,200-1,800   LHA

A pair of 19thC Chinese famille noir club-form vases, with underglaze blue six-character Kangxi mark within the inset base, with hardwood stand.

£1,000-1,500   WES

One of a pair of 19thC Chinese famille jaune moonflasks, decorated with dragons and chrysanthemums on a turquoise reserve.

12in (30.5cm) high

£1,200-1,800 pair   GORL

A 19thC Chinese famille jaune vase and cover, painted with pheasants on rockwork amongst a floral ground, with four-character mark.

22in (56cm) high

£1,000-1,500   GORL

A Chinese Qianlong period armorial plate, painted with the arms of Field of Stanstedbury, in Hertfordshire.

c1755   *9in (23cm) diam*

£1,200-1,800   **WW**

ESSENTIAL REFERENCE: DOUCAI

Doucai (literally "contrasting colours") is a type of delicate porcelain, introduced during the Chenghua period (1465-1487).

● The design is outlined in soft underglaze blue then filled in with overglaze enamels in a wide range of translucent enamel colours.

● The technique saw a resurgence during the early 18thC.

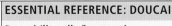

A rare Chinese Yongzheng period doucai butterfly and flowers conical bowl, the exterior enamelled with floral medallions of the flowers of the "Four Seasons", the interior painted with two butterflies and a flower sprig encircled by a double-line border repeated at the rim, base with six-character Yongzheng mark.

9in (23cm) diam

£25,000-35,000   **WW**

A pair of Chinese Imari armorial plates, each with a central coat of arms containing a castle, the borders with flowers and foliage.

9in (23cm) diam

£1,000-1,500   **WW**

An 18thC Chinese famille rose armorial punch bowl, with foliate border and floral spray at centre.

14in (36cm) diam

£3,000-4,000   **LHA**

A rare Chinese probably Kangxi period eggshell doucai month cup, thinly potted, decorated with a peach tree with scattered blossoms (taohua) with a poem on the reverse, with Kangxi mark.

2in (5cm) high

£5,000-7,000   **RTC**

A rare Chinese Kangxi period doucai dragon and phoenix bowl, enamelled with two dragons, a phoenix and flaming pearls on a yellow ground, the base with a six-character Kangxi mark within a double circle.

6in (15cm) diam

£10,000-15,000   **WW**

A 17thC Chinese doucai vase, decorated with a pheasant on pierced rockwork amongst peony and chrysanthemum.

8in (20cm) high

£1,200-1,800   **DN**

A Chinese 19thC doucai jar, painted with boys playing in a garden, below a band of ruyi collar lappet, base with underglaze blue Jiajing six-character mark.

5.75in (14.5cm) high

£1,200-1,800   **SK**

A Chinese Transitional period wucai jar, with 18thC French ormulu mounts, enamelled to show horses, blue rocks and green leaves, over an S- and C-leaf scroll ormulu base.

Total 19.5in (50cm) high

£7,000-10,000   FRE

CLOSER LOOK - WUCAI VASE

The deer is a traditional Chinese symbol of longevity, due to its being the only animal capable of finding the lingzhi fungus of immortality.

As a result, it is often depicted with Shoulao, the God of Longevity.

The Chinese word for "deer" sounds the same as their word for "emolument" or "civil service salary". This pattern consequently represents a sucessful career in government service in Imperial China.

A Chinese Wanli period wucai "Hundred Deer" vase, enamelled in green, yellow, iron-red and brown with the "Hundred Deer" design above stylised lappets and below hanging motifs, scrollwork and floral sprays, with Wanli mark.

£50,000-70,000

13.5in (34cm) high

SOTH

A Chinese late Ming dynasty wucai vase and cover, decorated in underglaze blue and enamels with horses leaping among Buddhist emblems between tall rocks against which crash waves, restoration.

15in (38cm) high

£2,000-3,000   WW

A small Chinese Shunzi period wucai vase, decorated in underglaze blue and enamels with a scene from a romance.

7.25in (18.5cm) high

£2,500-3,500   WW

A rare Chinese Kangxi period wucai charger, with six cartouches and central medallion of iron-red, yellow, green and purple enamelled fruit, lotus, and foliate sprigs, with six-character mark to base.

13in (33.5cm) diam

£2,500-3,500   FRE

A 17thC Chinese wucai jar, the shoulder with six moulded lugs, the body painted with dignitaries with young female attendants in an interior, repairs.

11.5in (29cm) high

£5,000-7,000   WW

A Chinese Kangxi period wucai dish, the centre with four lanca characters in a quatrefoil amidst flowers and foliage, the exterior with stylised flowers and leaves, with six-character Chenghua mark.

Reign marks can help date a piece, but can easily mislead as many Chinese potters and decorators used the marks of earlier reigns. This was not done to defraud (even when the piece in question mimicked the style of the mark period), but as a form of venerating ancestors. A six-character mark such as this (read right column down, left column down) reads: "da" (great), dynasty, the emperor's reign title (two characters), "nian" (period), and "zhi" (made/manufactured), which translates as "made in the reign of [emperor's reign title] in the Great [dynasty name] dynasty".

6in (15cm) diam

£2,000-3,000   WW

A Chinese Qianlong period wucai dragon and phoenix bowl, decorated with three dragons and two stylised phoenix, the base with a six-character Qianlong mark, restoration.

5in (12.5cm) diam

£5,000-7,000   WW

CLOSER LOOK - YONGXHENG TEA BOWL AND SAUCER

To the Chinese the significance behind the decoration was obvious. The two lovers are wishing that they were the chickens and the boy is holding a rui sceptre, which can mean "may your wishes come true".

Eggshell porcelain was introduced during the Yongle period (1403–24), reappearing during the reigns of Chenghua (1465–87), Wanli (1573–1619) and Yongzheng (1723-35).

Detailed interior scenes are particularly desirable.

A Chinese Yongzheng period eggshell teabowl and saucer, painted with a pair of young lovers watching copulating chickens, a boy approaching from one side, the rim with gold and brown lotus.

£2,500-3,500   SWO

A Chinese Jiajing square dragon bowl, overall glazed yellow, each side painted in underglaze blue and burnt-black with a dragon rising above crashing waves, the interior with floral scroll, with Jiajing six-character mark.

7.5in (19cm) wide

£3,500-4,500   SK

A Chinese Yongzheng period bowl, the exterior with a green-glazed scene of young boys playing in a garden courtyard over yellow, with iridescence, with Yongzheng mark.

6in (15cm) diam

£5,000-7,000   IMC

A Chinese late Qianlong period celadon bowl, painted with two quail amidst rockwork and chrysanthemum, and with two bats to the reverse, the interior with three further bats, base with six-character Qianlong seal mark.

7in (18cm) diam

£1,500-2,500   WW

A rare Chinese Daoguang period green and aubergine dragon bowl, for a concubine of the fifth rank, the exterior incised with two dragons above waves in pursuit of flaming pearls, base with underglaze blue six-character Daoguang seal mark.

4in (10cm) diam

£2,000-3,000   WW

A pair of Chinese Jiaqing period iron-red glazed bowls, with scalloped rim, decorated with swallows amongst branches of prunus blossom, with red painted Jiaqing seal mark.

4.75in (12cm) diam

£1,500-2,500   L&T

A large mid-19thC Chinese Canton punch bowl, the interior with a band of fruit and flowers on a gilt ground, with female figures in a garden below, the exterior with a band of small figures above a scene of warriors, attendants and dignitaries.

16in (40cm) diam

£4,500-5,500   L&T

One of a pair of Chinese Guangxu period bowls, with enamelled butterflies among gilt-painted shou symbols on yellow ground, raised on shallow foot ring, with Guangxu mark.

4.25in (11cm) diam

£1,200-1,800 pair   FRE

A Chinese Guangxu mark medallion bowl, with four panels containing dragon and phoenix on a yellow ground with a flowering gourd vine, the base with a six-character Guangxu mark.

8.25in (21cm) diam

£4,000-6,000   WW

A Chinese fishbowl, depicting figures seated at a table.

15in (38cm) diam

£2,000-3,000   LHA

ORIENTAL

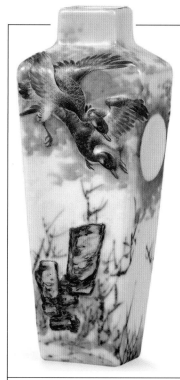

An 18thC Chinese vase, moulded with geese flying above rockwork chasing a full moon, painted in overglaze enamel, reserved on a blue-and-white ground of afterglow and reeds, base with Yongzheng four-character mark.

6.75in (17cm) high

£18,000-22,000　　SK

A Chinese gourd-form vase, with underglaze copper-red decoration of scrolling foliate design.

10.5in (27cm) high

£2,500-3,500　　LHA

A large 19thC Chinese hexagonal-section vase, the sides painted with young ladies between bands of complex diaper grounds, with four-character Kangxi mark.

22.5in (57cm) high

£5,000-7,000　　WW

A large 19thC Chinese moulded bottle vase, relief-moulded with five bifid dragons climbing amidst lingzhi fungus on a celadon ground, below a band of ruyi heads and above moulded lappets painted in underglaze blue and red with black detailing.

24in (61cm) high

£12,000-18,000　　WW

A large 19thC Chinese Canton vase, painted with four panels of figures in shallow relief on a blue ground, with gilt lion-dog handles and applied chilong dragons, some restoration.

35in (90cm) high

£4,000-6,000　　WW

A large 19thC Chinese Canton vase, the body painted with four panels containing figures and smaller panels of birds and fish on a diaper ground, with applied lion-dog handles and chilong dragons, some restoration.

35in (90cm) high

£2,000-3,000　　WW

A pair of late 19thC Chinese cong vases, painted in the Dowager Empress style *en grissaille* with flowers on a turquoise ground, with elephant-head handles and with underglaze blue six-character Qianlong seal marks.

12in (30.5cm) high

£2,500-3,500　　WW

A late 19thC Chinese moulded vase, relief-moulded with a variety of antique objects, with flowers and foliage issuing from each object, on a turquoise ground, with galleried mouth rim.

14in (36cm) high

£1,500-2,500　　SK

A pair of Chinese Republic period vases, painted to one side with Zhong Kui putting a flower in a lady's hair, with an attendant carrying a basin, the reverse with poetic inscriptions.

The Chinese Republic period refers to the period 1912-1916, between the Xinhai Revolution (which saw the end of the Qing Dynasty) and the War Lord Era. Good quality wares from this recent period in Chinese porcelain-making have seen a leap in value recently, particularly when compared to some lesser-quality late 19thC wares.

8in (20cm) high

£2,000-3,000　　SK

A Chinese Ming dynasty pottery roof tile in the form of a temple guardian, standing on a cloud with one fist raised, glazed in yellow, green and aubergine.

16in (41.5cm) high

£800-1,200   **L&T**

A Chinese Ming dynasty pottery roof tile in the form of a warrior on horseback, decorated in green and ochre glaze.

15in (38cm) high

£1,000-1,500   **L&T**

An 18thC Chinese hen and chicks ewer, decorated with green, yellow and aubergine enamels, the cover lacking.

6in (15cm) wide

£3,000-5,000   **WW**

A Chinese Daoguang pottery figure of Zhongli Quan, seated on a cloud, holding a palm leaf fan in one hand and a ball in the other, his head and hands gilt, his robes turquoise with gilt, pink and blue details, on carved wood stand.

17in (43cm) high

£3,500-4,500   **L&T**

A Chinese Liao dynasty-style pottery figure of a Lohan, seated with hands clasped, glazed in green and yellow, on a pierced green stand.

Figure 15in (38cm) high

£600-800   **L&T**

One of a pair of late 19thC Chinese Ho-Ho boys, with polychrome enamelled robes, each with vase and water dropper, on carved wood bases.

7.75in (19.5cm) high

£800-1,200 pair   **LHA**

A large Chinese Qianlong period "Double Dragon" dish, with two yellow-glazed dragons on dark blue ground to edge, and central medallion of a single five-clawed dragon among clouds and flaming pearls, decoratively similar to reverse, with white-glazed base, blue Qianlong mark.

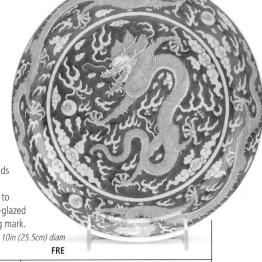

10in (25.5cm) diam

£10,000-15,000   **FRE**

A large 19thC Chinese brush washer, the interior underglazed in blue and copper-red, with lotus sprigs and blossoms, strong red glaze to outer-wall, white-glazed base with Qianlong mark, with wood stand.

9in (23cm) diam

£2,000-3,000   **FRE**

A pair of Chinese Qing dynasty reticulated wedding lanterns, decorated with solid roundels containing enamelled floral scenes, bases glazed turquoise.

16in (41cm) high

£5,000-7,000   **LHA**

A pair of Chinese Republican period cups, exteriors enamelled with Immortals riding on waves with a crane, interiors with three bats in iron-red, bases with Yongzheng mark.

3in (7.5cm) diam

£1,500-2,500   **SK**

ORIENTAL

ESSENTIAL REFERENCE - IMARI

A type of Japanese porcelain made at Arita on Kyushu, and shipped from the port of Imari (from which it takes its European name) from the late 17thC.

- It has a characteristic palette of underglaze blue and iron-red with gold or silver gilding. However, green, yellow, brown and (rarely) turquoise can also be used.
  - Decoration may have been based on brocade (silk with gold silk thread). The finest examples feature panels decorated with conflicting themes.
    - Most Imari pieces are decorative, with many intended exclusively for display.
    - It was thickly potted, and is not easily cracked.
    - In the late 17thC and 18thC, the most common objects were high-shouldered covered jars, beaker vases and saucer dishes.
      - From the 18thC, Chinese copies (Chinese Imari) were produced for export.
      - From the 19thC, the style was also copied by European factories – in porcelain by Meissen and Derby, pottery by Mason's Ironstone, and in tin-glazed earthenware in the Dutch city of Delft.

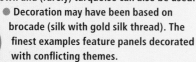

A large Japanese Imari baluster vase and cover, Arita, decorated with panels of hydrangea, peony and a flowering tree, the shoulder with panels of dragons, repairs.

c1700   *27.5in (70cm) high*

£2,000-3,000   **WW**

A pair of early 18thC Japanese Imari trumpet vases, each painted with panels of birds, pavilions, bamboo and flowers, within floral borders.

16in (41cm) high

£1,000-1,500 pair   **TOV**

An early 18thC Japanese Imari barber's bowl, Arita, decorated with a vase of peonies and other flowers.

11in (28cm) diam

£700-1,000   **WW**

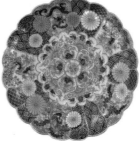

A pair of Japanese Imari chrysanthemum-shaped dishes, decorated with phoenix, prunus, birds and brocade patterns, gilding.

c1880   *12in (30.5cm) diam*

£800-1,200   **WW**

A pair of 19thC Japanese Imari faceted vases and covers, decorated with panels of phoenix, flowers and vases.

19in (48cm) high

£1,000-1,500   **WW**

A late 19thC set of one large and four small Japanese Imari fish dishes, painted in blue, iron red and gold, each with a six-character mark.

Largest 14.5in (37cm) long

£800-1,200   **WW**

A 19thC Japanese Imari lotus-flower bowl, with segmented scenic borders and central vase decoration.

13.25in (34cm) diam

£300-500   **GORL**

ESSENTIAL REFERENCE - SATSUMA

Satsuma wares take their name from a feudal province in southern Kyushu, which benefited from an influx of Korean master potters after Japan's invasion of Korea in 1597. They began to make Satsuma's first notable ceramics: simple Karatsu-style tea ceremony wares, typically glazed in yellow over a cream ground. In the late 18thC the potters learned decorative techniques, such as enamelling and gilding, from potters in Arita and Kyoto.

- Most of what we call "Satsuma" today was made at Kyoto for export to the West from c1850.
- The cream-coloured pottery has a clear, yellowish, crackled glaze, decorated with polychrome enamels and gilding.
- Most Satsuma artists bought glazed blanks and decorated them freehand with traditional Japanese motifs and patterns, including foliage and flowers (typically chrysanthemums, hydrangeas, lotus, prunus blossom and bamboo), landscapes, real and mythical birds and beasts, and figures performing ceremonial, military or everyday domestic activities. These scenes are typically surrounded by well-decorated borders of flowers, diaper or fretwork.
- Quality varies from early pieces, which might take a master painter months to decorate using a single rat's hair, to more recent gaudy items created for the mass-market.

A Japanese Meiji period Satsuma shallow dish, by Shoko Takebe, decorated to the interior with a scene of a royal procession below key-band at rim, with crimped rim, with gilt seal mark "Thomas B Blore commission".

8.75in (22cm) diam

£2,500-3,500   FRE

A Japanese Satsuma bowl, by the Kinkozan family, decorated in gilt and polychrome enamel, the interior with image of "Seven Lucky Gods".

5in (12.5cm) diam

£4,000-6,000   FRE

A Japanese Meiji period Satsuma bowl, by Gyokuzan, decorated to exterior with butterflies and to the interior with alternating swirling bands of butterflies and a diaper pattern.

5in (12.5cm) diam

£1,000-1,500   FRE

A Satsuma foliate bowl, centrally decorated with a procession of figures in a landscape on a scattered floral ground, signed.

6.5in (16cm) diam

£2,000-3,000   DN

A Japanese Meiji period Satsuma plate, by Matsumoto Hozan, interior decorated with a rectangular image of a temple and its grounds in springtime, surrounded on all sides to rim with chrysanthemum ground.

10in (25.5cm) diam

£1,800-2,200   FRE

A Japanese Satsuma square tray, probably by Ryozan, depicting a figure with the Goddess of Mercy pouring out mercy to a crouching demon holding an alms bowl, the border with raised gilt decoration with a key fret border, signed in overglaze red.

15.75in (40cm) wide

£2,500-3,500   LHA

ORIENTAL

A pair of Japanese Satsuma vases, with alternating sides of landscape decoration and ladies, with signature on bases in cartouches with black reserves.

4.75in (12cm) high

£2,000-3,000 LHA

A Japanese Satsuma triangular-form tea caddy, with landscape and figural decoration, signed in gilt script on underside.

5.5in (14cm) high

£2,000-3,000 LHA

A late 19thC Japanese Satsuma flask-form tea caddy, with landscape decoration, flanked by scrolled handles, signed on base.

5in (12.5cm) high

£3,000-4,000 LHA

Judith Picks: Satsuma

Miyagawa (Makuzu) Kozan (1842-1916) was artist to the Japanese Imperial household and one of the greatest potters of the Meiji era. He came from a long line of potters based in Kyoto, and took over the family business aged just 18. In 1870 he opened a workshop in Yokohama, and arrived at his artistic height in the 1880s. Pieces signed "Makuzu Kozan" were made into the early 20thC. This piece has fine and varied decoration with auspicious cranes and finely detailed deities.

A Japanese Satsuma vase, by Kozan Sei, decorated with alternating bands of cranes, creatures, deities, figures and rakan, with gilt seal mark.

6.25in (15.5cm) high

£5,000-7,000 FRE

A Japanese Satsuma reticulated vase, Yasuda, with two raised panels to sides enamelled to depict beauties in different settings, and two other panels reticulated in hexagonal knot pattern, with red and gold mark.

7in (18cm) high

£1,800-2,000 FRE

A Japanese Satsuma covered double-gourd vase, by Ryozan, Kyoto, signed, the flared mouth and cover supported by two cylindrical, vertical posts that rise from shoulder of body, decorated with figures and geometric and floral grounds, signed.

8.25in (21cm) high

£1,800-2,200 FRE

A small Japanese Satsuma censer, attributed to Yabu Meizan, with a single cartouche of figures in an interior and an image of an open book with butterflies, with multicoloured band to rim, petal-like tripod feet and a reticulated cover.

4in (10cm) high

£3,000-5,000 FRE

A Japanese Satsuma jar, by Yabu Meizan, with raised petal-form band below neck and mouth ring, decorated in gilt and polychrome enamel with figures between bands of flowers, with gilt seal mark.

2.25in (5.5cm) high

£2,500-3,500 FRE

A Japanese Satsuma covered vase, by the Kinkozan family, decorated with alternating bands of seated figures and chrysanthemum blossoms, with impressed mark.

6in (15cm) high

£2,500-3,500 FRE

A Meiji Period Japanese Satsuma baluster vase, with two cartouches containing pheasants and chickens, surrounded by a cobalt ground, gilt decoration at base and rim, base signed in gilt on a red cartouche.

12.5in (32cm) high

£1,800-2,200 LHA

An unusual late 17thC Japanese Ko-Kutani shallow dish, enamelled with a pheasant perched on a leafy maple branch, the iron-red diaper border with three panels of "Three Friends of Winter", the base with a Fuku mark.

The history of Kutani ceramics dates back to the early Edo period, around the year 1655. Maeda Toshiharu, the first Lord of Daishoji, encouraged the development of pottery by investigating the pottery techniques of Hizen Arita. The establishment of Kutani kilns began with the adoption of this new skill. The kilns in Kutani suddenly disappeared around 1730. The ceramics fired during this period are now known as "Ko-Kutani". Representing Japanese Iro'e (multicoloured over-glazed) porcelain, it is highly rated for its unique, vigorous, formal beauty.

7in (18cm) diam

£3,000-5,000   WW

A rare mid-17thC Japanese Ko-Kutani heart-shaped dish, enamelled in iron-red, green and yellow with tied ribbons, brown line rim.

6.5in (16cm) wide

£2,000-3,000   WW

A 19thC Japanese famille jaune jardinière, decorated with reserves of ducks and lotus on a floral ground.

14in (36cm) high

£1,000-1,500   GORL

A pair of 19thC Japanese famille jaune figures of infant boys, holding rui sceptres, on hardwood stands.

6.5in (16cm) high

£3,500-4,500   GORL

A pair of 19thC Japanese ormolu-mounted table lamps, Arita, stamped "BRIGHT LATE ARGAND & Co 37 BRUTON ST", one cracked.

19in (48cm) high

£2,000-3,000   WW

A 19thC Japanese figure of a kneeling bejin, Arita, with ball at feet, her kimono decorated with a floral motif.

14.5in (37cm) high

£600-800   FRE

An early 20thC Japanese Seifu meiping-form vase, the cream-glazed body worked to show white-carved and low-relief blossoms, with white foot and unglazed rim, signed Seifu.

15in (38cm) high

£20,000-30,000   FRE

A pair of large early 20thC Japanese vases, decorated with opposed underglaze blue bird and flower panels and smaller landscape and floral panels, the rest clobbered in brown and gilt, base with blue painted character mark.

25in (64cm) high

£1,500-2,500   L&T

A Japanese Fukagawa vase, painted with cranes over the water on a light blue ground, signed in red.

c1875   *18in (45.5cm) high*

£1,000-1,500   SWO

An 18thC Japanese Edo period E-Garatsu ware sake ewer, decorated with cream crackle glaze with willow tree panel on one side, plovers and susuki grass on the other, the lid with five stylised hollyhock crests of Toyotomi family.

The pail-form handle imitates that of a metal water kettle.

7.5in (19cm) high

£700-1,000   RTC

ORIENTAL

KOREAN DYNASTIES

United Silla Dynasty (668-935AD)
The result of the unification of the three kingdoms of the Korean peninsula: Silla, Paekche, and Koguryo. The art of this period used flowing lines and soft contours. Richly decorated tiles featured lotus flowers and complex floral patterns.

Koryo Dynasty (935-1392)
During this period Korea began to form distinct cultural traditions that separated it from the rest of East Asia. The aristocracy led an extravagant lifestyle, and demanded elegant, beautiful objects. Ceramics improved dramatically in this period, with the development of luminescent celadon glazes and the use of delicate inlays.

A 12thC Korean Koryo dynasty celadon wine cup and associated stand, the sides inlaid in slip with flower heads, restoration.

5.75in (14.5cm) high
£2,000-3,000　　　**WW**

Choson Dynasty (1392-1910)
also known as the Yi dynasty. Choson potters rejected the opulence of the Koryo dynasty. The early years of this dynasty were characterised by an informally decorated ware known as Punch'ong, and simple white porcelains, inspired by the Chinese. By the mid-15thC, white pieces painted in blue, brown, and red with whimiscal designs were also produced.

An 18thC Korean Choson dynasty blue-and-white jar, decorated in underglaze blue with a dragon among clouds, below a band of lappet around the neck.

16.25in (41cm) high
£1,000-1,500　　　**SK**

A 13thC Korean Koryo dynasty celadon stoneware vase, of maebyeong shape, with sangam inlay of white and black in a design of floral sprigs and reserves of children.

13in (33.5cm) high
£20,000-30,000　　　**SK**

A Korean Koryo dynasty celadon conical bowl, the interior incised with three phoenix above a floral medallion.

7in (18cm) diam
£800-1,200　　　**FRE**

An 18thC Korean Choson dynasty wine bottle, decorated in underglaze blue with birds and a rose bush.

8.5in (21.5cm) high
£3,000-5,000　　　**SK**

A Korean late Choson dynasty blue-and-white maebyong vase, decorated with a pair of birds among prunus, bamboo and floral features.

7in (18cm) high
£1,000-1,500　　　**FRE**

A large 18thC Korean Choson dynasty white jar, of wide shoulder form supporting tall straight rim, with drilled base.

14.5in (37cm) high
£5,000-7,000　　　**FRE**

An 18thC Korean Choson dynasty water dropper, the double-walled vessel carved and pierced with lotus flowers and leaves, decorated with underglaze blue decoration, with perforations for brushes.

3.5in (9cm) diam
£1,500-2,500　　　**SK**

A 10th-12thC Persian pottery bowl, decorated in iron-red and brown with broad, stylised leaf motifs, the centre with script, restored.

8in (20cm) diam

£800-1,200   **DN**

A Persian lead-glazed pottery bowl, decorated in brown and green slip with a symmetrical design on a cream ground, restored.

9.25in (23.5cm) diam

£800-1,200   **DN**

An unusual 17thC Safavid ewer, painted in blue with black outlines, depicting a deer and a bird above a band of floral lappets, flower heads and leaves, with painted mark to the base, the spout reglued.

7in (18cm) high

£800-1,200   **WW**

An 18thC Safavid shallow dish, painted with a figure and flowering bushes, within a border of vine leaves, the reverse with kraak design and a hatched mark.

9.5in (24cm) diam

£1,500-2,500   **WW**

A 16thC Vietnamese charger, Le Dynasty, probablu My Xa Kilns, the exterior enamelled with lotus lappets, the cavetto with a carp surrounded by waterplants and quatrefoil lozenges.

13.75in (35cm) diam

£2,500-3,500   **RTC**

A 16thC Turkish Iznik jug, painted in red, turquoise and blue with stylised tulips, carnations and fruit medallions, damages.

c1580   *8.75in (22cm) high*

£7,000-10,000   **L&T**

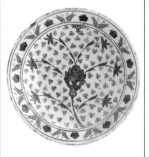

A rare 17thC Turkish Iznik dish, painted in blue, red, green and black with flowering stems issuing from a central flowerhead, amidst spiral trefoils.

12in (30.5cm) diam

£8,000-12,000   **L&T**

An early to mid-17thC Turkish Iznik jug, painted to the body and neck in red, green, turquoise and blue with stylised tulips and carnations, with black spiral border.

9.25in (23.5cm) high

£3,500-4,500   **L&T**

A 17thC Turkish Iznik dish, painted with a central saz leaf, carnations, roses and a blue tulip surrounded by a black ammonite scroll border.

12in (30.5cm) diam

£3,500-4,500   **L&T**

An early 19thC Middle Eastern vessel in the form of a camel.

7in (18cm) wide

£3,500-4,500   **GORL**

An early 19thC Middle Eastern vessel in the form of a lion.

9in (23cm) wide

£4,000-6,000   **GORL**

ORIENTAL

ESSENTIAL REFERENCE - CHINESE CLOISONNÉ

Cloisonné is a decorative enamel technique. Thin strips of metal are soldered onto an object's surface to form individual cells (or cloisons), which are filled with powdered enamel, fired in a kiln and polished.

- It was first practised in China in the 14thC.
- Early pieces used dark green, cobalt blue, red, yellow and white enamels on a turquoise ground. Pink was added in the 18thC.
- Qing emperors commissioned imposing pieces with much gilding. Animal and bird figures were popular in this period.
- Chinese cloisonné was exported to Europe from the 16thC.

A pair of Chinese Ming dynasty gilt-bronze and cloisonné near hu-form vases, the shoulders with two lion masks and free-moving ring handles, enamelled with Indian lotus on dark blue ground.

13.5in (34cm) high

£5,000-7,000   FRE

A large Chinese Wanli period cloisonné cushion-shaped box and cover, with key-pattern borders, the lid with goats in a landscape within a border of cellular panels and flowers, the interior with blossom on cracked-ice ground.

15.25in (39cm) diam

£30,000-40,000   DUK

One of a rare pair of Chinese Qianlong period Imperial ormolu and cloisonné "Tree and Bird" groups and stands, cast in mirror image, the trunks and branches patinated in green, brown and parcel gilt, with cloisonné magpies, raised on matching patinated ormolu stands.

24in (61cm) high

£700,000-1,000,000 pair   SOTH

A Chinese Qianlong period cloisonné and gilt-copper tripod censer, enamelled with Indian lotus flowers issuing from scrolling leaves, with insert gilt plate with Qianlong mark.

4.75in (12cm) diam

£5,000-7,000   FRE

A Chinese Qianlong period cloisonné shallow bowl, decorated with four panels of peonies separated by stylised lotus on a pale blue ground, base with six-character Qianlong mark.

6.5in (16cm) diam

£50,000-70,000   WW

An 18thC Chinese ormolu and cloisonné moon flask vase, the mouth flanked by two ormolu Qilong, above two gilt wire-worked panels of butterflies and plants.

12in (30.5cm) high

£10,000-15,000   FRE

A Chinese Qianlong period cloisonné circular box and cover, decorated with stylised lotus flowers with scrolling leaves and tendrils reserved on a turquoise ground, with gilding to interior, borders and base, base with a Qianlong mark.

2.75in (7cm) diam

£30,000-50,000   WW

A Chinese Qianlong perod cloisonné jue-shape wine vessel, enamelled with stylised lotus flowers, inset with semi-precious beads, on a circular stand, base with Qianlong four-character mark.

8.5in (21.5cm) high

£15,000-25,000   SK

A pair of Chinese Qianlong period cloisonné stupas, the body decorated with an enclosed lanca character and stylised lotus below a band of masks and hanging pendant, the base with lotus petals, reserved on a turquoise ground.

7.5in (19cm) high

£50,000-70,000   SOTH

Judith Picks: An Enamel Stem Bowl

Some objects scream quality and desirability. I have always laboured against the "it speaks Qianlong enamel to me" school of appraisal (preferring a more academic approach!), but this small stem bowl and cover is an exquisite example of the quality of the mid-to-late 18thC Chinese enamellers. The provenance is also quite impressive, coming from the collection of Sackville George Pelham, 5th Earl of Yarborough (1888-1948).

One panel depicts Ceres, Pomona and Flora beneath a tree, another shows Vertumnus and Pomona with Cupid at their feet. The third detail is possibly also Vertumnus and Pomona.

The European subject matter of this piece means it was specially commissioned by a European merchant.

A rare Chinese Qianlong period enamel stem bowl and cover, painted with three panels depicting Europeans in Classical dress on a ground of flowers, leaves and scrolls, foot and cover with bands of fruit and foliage and with four pink bat motifs encircling the top.

5in (12.5cm) high

£200,000-300,000   WW

A pair of 18thC Chinese cloisonné pricket candle stands, decorated with flowers and foliage on a turquoise ground.

15in (38cm) high without pricket

£3,500-4,500   L&T

A Chinese cloisonné bowl, with foliate decoration throughout, the centre roundel with landscape scene on a blue reserve, with gilt copper rims.

c1800   *8.75in (22cm) diam*

£3,000-4,000   LHA

A 19thC Chinese ormolu Daoist group of two Immortals on a cloisonné stand, the stand with lotus petal and geometric ground.

9in (23cm) high

£4,000-6,000   FRE

A pair of Chinese Qing dynasty cloisonné and bronze-mounted vases, with four detailed masks supporting ring handles, enamelled with Indian lotus flowers and leaves over shield-form cartouches, on wood metal-lined stands.

Vase 28in (72cm) high

£15,000-25,000   FRE

One of a pair of early 20thC Chinese gilt-metal and cloisonné tripod elephant censers, based on Qianlong examples, the base raised on three red enamel elephant heads, supporting a blue-ground basin.

17.5in (44cm) high

£1,500-2,500 pair   FRE

ORIENTAL

A rare Chinese Tang dynasty chased and engraved silver jar and cover, the cover with flying mythical beasts among scrolling foliage, the body with scrolling lotus flowers above panels of phoenix and flowers, base with stylised flowerhead.

6in (15cm) high

£2,500-3,500 L&T

A Chinese Ming dynasty or later bronze two-handled censer, with tao tieh masks, animal heads and various geometric bands and keyfret patterns, base with four-character Xuande mark, with carved wood cover and stand.

12in (30.5cm) high

£1,800-2,200 L&T

A Chinese Ming dynasty gilt and bronze tripod censer, the domed cover with mouse finial, base with gilded seasonal panels and mask handles, over gilded straight legs.

5.5in (14cm) high

£2,500-3,500 FRE

An 18thC Chinese gilt-bronze figure of Guandi, sitting on a bench and raised on a plinth, losses.

Guandi, the God of War, was based on the famous historical 3rdC military commander Guan Yu. He personifies honour, loyalty, integrity, justice, courage and strength.

7in (18cm) high

£12,000-18,000 WW

An 18thC Chinese gold-splashed bronze vase, with a wide flared neck, body with cast lion heads, foot with lappets, the base with a 26-character inscription, including the date geng zi.

12in (30.5cm) high

£2,500-3,500 WW

A 18thC Chinese ormolu figure of Amitayus Buddha, on a rectangular base with a detachable flaming aureole, base with incised six-character mark.

8in (20cm) high

£5,000-7,000 WW

A large 18thC Chinese Qianlong period bronze vase, with continuous row of leaf tips below archaic characters and Fo dog mask cast shoulder handles, thunder pattern banding to rim and foot, 12-character Qianlong mark, lacking handle rings.

c1760 *24in (61cm) high*

£7,000-10,000 TEN

A large 18thC Chinese silver-inlaid bronze figure of Quanyin, with inlaid script verso, on wood stand.

bronze 23.5in (60cm) high

£22,000-28,000 FRE

A large Chinese Chien-form bronze jardinière, with five free moving rings above tao tie masks and scroll ground, raised on tall, barbed, circular foot.

16in (40cm) diam

£2,500-3,500 FRE

A pair of large Chinese gilt-metal Guardian figures, both with ribbon halo issuing from their shoulders, with detailed robes above rock-work base.

47in (119cm) high

£2,500-3,500 FRE

A Japanese Meiji period hexagonal-form cloisonné vase, attributed to the Hayashi Kodenji studio, decorated with a peacock and peahen, and songbirds with prunus blossom.

10in (25.5cm) high

£3,000-4,000   L&T

One of a pair of Japanese Meiji period cloisonné vases, Hayashi Kodenji studio, decorated with prunus blossom and birds in flight, on a dark blue ground, base with lozenge mark.

7.5in (19cm) high

£3,000-4,000 pair   L&T

A Japanese Meiji period bronze figure of a warrior, with gold overlays.

6.75in (17cm) high

£2,500-3,500   LHA

A Japanese Meiji period cloisonné tray, by Namikawa Sosuke, depicting a cockerel and hen, in mostly wireless technique on a grey reserve, reverse with plum-blossom decoration and seal of Namikawa Sosuke.

1890-1900   12.25in (31cm) high

£8,000-12,000   LHA

A Japanese Meiji period bronze figure of a mother walking with a small child on her back, on a circular base, signed.

24.5in (62cm) high

£2,500-3,500   LHA

A late 19thC Japanese patinated bronze bear, with incised fur.

22in (56cm) long

£6,000-8,000   FRE

A 19thC Japanese Meiji period bronze articulated model of a crab, fully articulated, realistically textured and with a rich brown patina.

8.5in (21.5cm) wide

£1,500-2,500   FRE

A 19thC Japanese Meiji period bronze model of a snake, textured with a dark patina and applied gilt eyes.

3.5in (9cm) high

£1,800-2,200   FRE

A Japanese cloisonné covered koro, by Namikawa Yasuyuki, decorated with five song birds among sprigs of chrysanthemums, with silver rim, base and signed silver tablet to base.

3in (7.5cm) high

£6,000-8,000   FRE

ORIENTAL

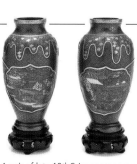

One of a pair of Japanese Meiji period bronze vases, inlaid with silver, gold and enamel with roundels of flowers and foliage beneath stylised butterflies.

8in (20cm) high

£2,500-3,500 pair   **WW**

A pair of late 19thC Japanese vases, Kyoto, with gilded Greek-key band over a collar of applied silver and gilt work "grape and vine" design, with cartouche of a fishing hamlet framed by a single fan enclosing birds, signed, on stands.

Vase 6in (15cm) high

£3,000-4,000   **FRE**

A pair of Japanese bronze urns, with floral decoration and elephant-form handles, set in silvered metal mounts as lamps.

11.5in (29cm) high

£1,200-1,800   **LHA**

A Japanese Meiji period bronze vase, with raised sinuous dragons holding rock crystal spheres in their claws, flying through the clouds above Mount Fuji.

28in (71cm) high

£2,500-3,500   **LHA**

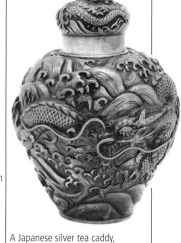

A Japanese white metal and Shibayama two-handled bowl, with enamel and mother-of-pearl and set with panels, one with Hotei and the other with a lady and attendant, with pierced dragon handles, signed, on wood stand.

Shibayama is the art of inlaying carved, semi-precious material (such as mother-of-pearl, semi-precious stones and tortoiseshell) in lacquer and ivory pieces. The result stood out in relief from the flat ground. This technique was named after Shibayama Dosho, who introduced it to Japan in the 18thC, and was used exclusively on export pieces.

A 19thC Japanese silver, enamel and applied covered vase, the reverse with applied panels to lattice walls, the cover with bird finial.

6.25in (15.5cm) high

£1,800-2,200   **FRE**

c1900

£2,500-3,500   **DN**

7in (18cm) high

A Japanese silver tea caddy, decorated with a sinuous dragon in high relief.

5.75in (14.5cm) high 9oz (255g) approx

£1,500-2,500   **LHA**

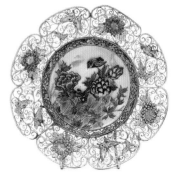

A Japanese enamelled silver filigree dish, with eight panels of flowers and butterflies, the interior with two birds among flowering peonies, reverse with applied cartouche with three-character mark.

c1900   *8in (20cm) diam*

£5,000-7,000   **LHA**

A Japanese silver and Shibayama dish, with silver wirework and scalloped ivory and lacquer panels, inlaid mother-of-pearl, coral, ivory, and tortoiseshell decoration, interior with a cockerel on gilt lacquered reserve, reverse with mother-of-pearl cartouche with three-character mark.

12.25in (31cm) diam

£4,000-6,000   **LHA**

A 19thC Japanese Kyoto gold and iron plate, with emerging demonic figure in low relief, signed.

10in (25.5cm) diam

£2,000-3,000   **FRE**

An 11th-13thC Western Tibetan/Ladakh figure of Manjusri, holding a sword in his right hand,

Manjusri, is the oldest of the Bodhisattvas (beings dedicated to achieving complete Buddhahood) with many manifestations. He is the Bodhisattva of wisdom, and is represented as a beautiful youth of golden yellow colour. In his right hand he has a sword which cuts through ignorance, a book, and in his left hand he has a stem of lotus blossom which bears the inscription, "perfection of wisdom". He is a popular deity and looked upon as the bringer of civilization to the Himalayas. Just as the Dalai Lama is regarded as an incarnation of Avalokitesvara, outstandingly wise rulers in East Asia have been regarded as incarnations of Manjusri.

6in (15cm) high

£3,500-4,500   WW

A 14thC Tibetan gilt bronze seated figure of Buddha Akshobya, in virasana (lotus position) on a high double-lotus base.

5.5in (14cm)

£2,500-3,500   RTC

An 18thC Tibeto-Chinese ormolu model of Avalokitesvara, standing on an oval lotus-moulded plinth.

12in (30.5cm) high

£15,000-25,000   WW

A fine Sino-Tibetan Qing dynasty ormolu model of Vajrasattva, polychrome-decorated, with crown, flowing mantle and partially-enamelled jewels, on double-lotus base.

10.25in (26cm) high

£7,000-10,000   FRE

A large 19thC Sino-Tibetan silver bottle vase, decorated with a floral pattern and with four raised floral-decorated cartouches, four silver-wire applied flowers to shoulder.

19.5in (50cm) high

£1,500-2,500   FRE

A 19thC gilt bronze Tibetan figure of Kubera, the God of Wealth in Indian-form as Jambhala the King of the Gandharvas, with his jewel-spitting mongoose companion, the sealed base with double vajra mark, on wood stand.

4in (10cm) high

£2,000-3,000   RTC

A 19thC Sino-Tibetan gilt bronze seated figure of a Karmapa Lama, possibly by Thekchok Dorje (1798-1868), seated before a dorje embedded in the double-lotus base in reference to a manifestation of Aksobhya Buddha in elaborate robes, with seal.

7.5in (19cm) high

£2,000-3,000   RTC

A 19thC Sino-Tibetan parcel-gilt bronze figure of Yamantaka, in yab-yum with his consort, wearing his skull crown and standing atop four supplicants, on separate lotus base, with wood stand.

8in (20cm) high

£1,000-1,500   IMC

A Tibetan tantric lama's skull, decorated with silver skull and dragon ornaments, lined with silver.

Lama is a high priest.

6.75in (17cm) high

£2,500-3,500   LHA

A pair of Sino-Mongolian turquoise- and coral-inset silver scent flasks, with orange agate ball finials, each side with a pierced jade panel and jade loop handles.

10in (25.5cm) high

£1,500-2,500   GORL

ORIENTAL

A Chinese Ming Dynasty ivory figure of a scholar, in long robes, playing the flute, on wood stand.
Ivory 11in (28cm) high
£1,800-2,200   **IMC**

An 18thC Chinese ivory figure of a luohan, with a staff and begging bowl, with small loss.
13.25in (34cm) high
£2,500-3,500   **SK**

A pair of 18thC Chinese polychromed ivory figures of luohans with a foo dog.
5.5in (14cm) high
£10,000-15,000   **SK**

A 19thC Chinese ivory group of two Buddhist saints and a lion.
5.5in (14cm) high
£5,000-7,000   **SK**

The figure's headdress is carved with a miniature Buddha – a very auspicious sign.

The base has a seal mark.

She is holding a branch in one hand and a basket of fish and lotus in the other.

The phoenix by her side has a tied scroll hanging from its beak.

This figure is magnificently carved, with extraordinary attention to detail.

At 33.5in (86cm) high this is a dramatic piece of carving – meant for an important location.

A tall Chinese ivory figure of Guanyin, in flowing robes draped in beaded garlands, with seal mark, on wood stand.
33.5in (86cm) high
£10,000-15,000   **IMC**

A Chinese late Qing dynasty ivory figure, possibly of the philosopher Zhuangzi, holding a pair of lotus flowers and a dragon-head staff, from which hangs a double gourd.
15in (38cm) high
£2,000-3,000   **FRE**

An early 20thC Chinese ivory figure of Quanyin, in flowing beaded robes and crown with image of the Buddha, with small deity on double lotus throne, scroll in right hand, jar in left.
26.25in (66.5cm) high
£7,000-10,000   **FRE**

A Chinese ivory figure of a graceful beauty, draped in layered robes with a butterfly tassel, holding a fan, on wood pedestal stand.
18in (45.5cm) high
£4,000-6,000   **IMC**

A Chinese ivory figure of Avalokitesvara, seated on a triple lotus throne, well carved verso.
10in (25.5cm) high
£3,000-5,000   **FRE**

A pair of Chinese ivory figures of an emperor and empress, with carved decoration to their robes, on wood stands.
Figure 36in (91.5cm) high
£6,000-8,000   **LHA**

A Japanese Meiji period ivory okimono of a screen maker, seated on bamboo matting, his robe with geometric and floral patterns, signed in inlaid red lacquer tablet.

2.25in (5.5cm) high

£1,500-2,500   L&T

A 19thC Japanese ivory and wood figure of an elderly man gathering wood, with inset ivory signature.

13.75in (35cm) high

£2,500-3,500   LHA

A 19thC Chinese ivory model of a dragon boat, with various figures and a pavilion.

22in (56cm) long

£8,000-12,000   SK

ESSENTIAL REFERENCE - JAPANESE IVORY

Although Japanese ivory carvings were made from around c1700, the best figures were produced in the late 19thC. With the decline of traditional costume, Buddhist images, and ornamental weaponry, Japanese craftspeople began to produce more ornamental objects for the foreign market.

- All Japanese ivory carvings were made from imported supplies.
- As well as figures, fruit was a popular subject for Japanese carvers. Such pieces were often stained in realistic colours.
- Decoration included gilding and inlay.
- Some pieces combined ivory and carved wood.
- Ivory absorbs oils and stains as it ages – polishing and handling produces a golden to dark-brown patina. Be aware, that this effect can be replicated with tea-stains.
- Many ivorene fakes have appeared. Ivorene feels slightly warmer to touch and does not contain the irregular growth lines of ivory. A very unpopular test (with anyone selling ivory!) is that a hot needle will pierce ivorene but not ivory.

A Japanese Meiji Period ivory figure of a fisherman, Tokyo School, with amber and horn eyes.

10.75in (27.5cm) high

£5,000-7,000   LHA

A Japanese Meiji period ivory okimono group of an elderly man mobbed by three young boys, each with individualized portraits, signed to base, repairs.

15in (38cm) high

£4,000-6,000   TOV

A Chinese Shibayama elephant, the ivory body covered with strings of "jewels" and saddle cloth in horn, mother-of-pearl and stained ivory, repairs, on carved softwood stand.

c1880   *6in (15cm) wide*

£1,500-2,500   SWO

A pair of Chinese ivory archers and chariots, the bases of naturalistic form comprised of carved ivory tiles.

Each 14in (36cm) long

£3,500-4,500   LHA

A Chinese ivory model of a dragon boat, on a carved wood base.

Ship 47in (119cm) long

£6,000-8,000   LHA

A large 19thC Chinese ivory brushpot, with reticulated figural design of court scenes, with lacquered interior, on openwork wood stand.

9.5in (24cm) high

£5,000-7,000   IMC

A large Japanese Meiji period Shibayama tusk vase, decorated with a cockerel with prunus blossom, verso with foliage and flowers, signed Masayuki on oval green inset hardstone, on hardwood stand.

12in (30.5cm) high

£1,500-2,500   L&T

A pair of 19thC Chinese ivory vases, carved in relief with figures and palace gardens.

9.5in (24cm) high

£5,000-7,000   SK

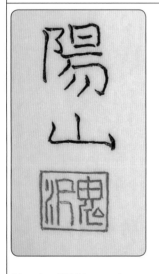

A large late 19thC Japanese ivory tusk vase, carved with a troop of monkeys in relief, with polychrome peach branches, on wood stand.

14.75in (37.5cm) high

£2,000-3,000   IMC

A pair of Chinese ivory urns and covers, carved in relief with equestrian noblemen and warriors on a dense ground of dragons, phoenix and clouds, with seal marks, on wood stands.

22.75in (58cm) high

£4,000-6,000   IMC

A Japanese ivory, gilt and patinated metal vase, decorated with butterflies and birds.

15in (38cm) high

£1,500-2,500   LHA

A pair of Chinese polychrome-decorated ivory-covered vases, with reticulated cylindrical bases and elephant finials.

17in (43cm) high

£1,500-2,500   FRE

A large Chinese Qing dynasty ivory seal, carved in medium relief with coiled dragons and scrolling clouds, incised chop.

6in (15cm) high

£1,500-2,500   **FRE**

A Chinese Qing dynasty ivory wrist rest, of bamboo form, interior carved with birds in a tree above bamboo, exterior carved with bamboo.

6.25in (15.5cm) long

£5,000-7,000   **FRE**

A Chinese Qing dynasty ivory and inkwork table screen, carved with a figural landscape and detailed script verso, on fitted bracket ink work and scroll-carved stand.

11in (28cm) high

£3,000-4,000   **FRE**

A 19thC Chinese elephant tusk, carved with warriors and naturalistic scenes, on carved wood base.

Tusk 22.5in (57cm) long

£3,000-4,000   **LHA**

An early 19thC Chinese ivory letter holder, Canton, with double dragon carved crest over seven "day" sleeves all carved with figural landscape above arrow-form crest.

16in (41cm) high

£5,000-7,000   **FRE**

A late 19thC Chinese carved and reticulated ivory plaque, decorated with birds amongst bamboo, blossoms and persimmon, signs of black pigment, on wire inlaid wood stand.

Ivory 10.5in (27cm) long

£3,000-4,000   **FRE**

A Chinese ivory tusk, with a carved panel depicting two dragons, on hardwood stand.

30in (76.5cm) long

£1,200-1,800   **LHA**

A pair of Chinese mounted elephant tusks, the uncarved tusks mounted on square malachite pillars, with filigree silver collars.

27in (69cm) high

£2,000-3,000   **FRE**

A large Chinese ivory tusk, carved with ten immortals among foliage, with Guanyin at centre seated atop a Buddhistic lion.

49in (124cm) long

£5,000-7,000   **LHA**

A Chinese ivory table screen, carved with figures in a boat under trees in relief, with bamboo on the reverse.

6.5in (16cm) high

£1,500-2,500   **LHA**

ORIENTAL

A Chinese late Ming/early Qing ivory "bamboo trunk" brushpot, carved in medium relief with cicada and grasshopper, and detailed script verso, with two seal marks, together with bone, horn and horsehair brush.

Pot 4.75in (12cm) high

£1,800-2,200 FRE

A pair of early 19thC Chinese quail-shaped ivory boxes and covers, carved with detailed plumage, on carved wood stands.

6in (15cm) long

£4,000-6,000 WW

A pair of late 19thC Japanese Shibayama whist markers, decorated in gilt and hardstones with partridges amongst flowers and foliage, the pegs decorated with birds or insects in mother-of-pearl and hardstones, in a leather case inscribed with gilt Prince of Wales feathers and "Christmas 1894".

The box containing these whist markers is inscribed with the Prince of Wales' feathers which suggests that it was either a gift to or from keen gambler Albert Edward the Prince of Wales (later Edward VII). On 8th September 1890, he and Sir William Gordon-Cumming were among the guests at a house party at which baccarat (then illegal in England) was played. Sir William was observed apparently cheating, and, although he agreed to sign a pledge that he would never play cards again in exchange for an agreement that the matter would be kept secret, the news was made public and Sir William was consequently shunned by society. He decided to take his accusers to court, where the Prince of Wales was forced to admit his participation in the events. Sir William lost and the Prince of Wales gave up baccarat and took up whist instead.

Each 3.75in (9.5cm) long

£1,200-1,800 L&T

A pair of mid-late 19thC Chinese ivory wrist rests representing Day and Night, carved with scholars on on a rocky mountain track and a scholar at work (Day) or slumped asleep on his desk (Night), the reverse in low relief with figures under the sun and moon respectively, on wood stands.

14in (36cm) long

£10,000-15,000 TEN

A pair of late 19thC/early 20thC Chinese ivory phoenix, with stained and carved feathers, seated on a profusely carved cascade of flowers and on a white-metal inlaid-wood stands.

Ivory 10in (25.5cm) high

£1,200-1,800 L&T

A pair of fully articulated ivory crab okimono, with inlaid eyes, inscribed on oval mother-of-pearl reserves, in hardwood case.

9.5in (24cm) wide

£2,000-3,000 IMC

A pair of tortoiseshell and ivory cricket cages, with pierced lattice carving throughout with applied carved ivory fish, plants and flowers, on carved wood stands.

8.25in (21cm) high

£1,500-2,500 LHA

A large Chinese ivory "jewelled" and jadeite-mounted pagoda censer, base on three claw-feet with green jadeite ring handles, supporting three-tier pagoda enclosing seated Buddhas, on wood stand.

Ivory 34in (86.5cm) high

£1,500-2,500 FRE

ESSENTIAL REFERENCE - NETSUKE

Netsuke are small, decorative carvings which were used as a toggle as part of traditional Japanese dress from the 16thC. Inro boxes could be hung from them.

● Designs range from a simple disc (manju toggle) to figural pieces, in the shape of animals, people, ghosts and masks. All were smoothly carved, so as not to damage the clothes.

● Although wood and bone were also used, most netsuke were carved from ivory and these are the most collectable. The most sought-after ivory examples have finely carved details; good, stained highlights; and an artist's signature.

● Moulded resin fakes began to appear on the market in the late 20thC. These typically have poorly defined details, and feel warm and light in comparison to genuine ivory.

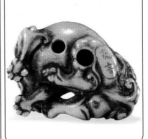

A 19thC Japanese ivory netsuke of a Shi Shi, signed Tomo____(?) in an oval reserve, on wood stand.
£2,500-3,500   IMC

A late 18thC ivory netsuke of a snarling mother Shi Shi, with loose ball in her mouth, a young cub on her back, with fine patina, on inlaid wood stand.
£1,200-1,800   IMC

A late 19thC Japanese parcel-stained ivory netsuke of a tiger and young, with inlaid eyes to one, attractive patination, on wood stand.
£1,000-1,500   IMC

A Japanese ivory netsuke of three intertwined tigers fighting, a small cub hiding beneath, each with inlaid eyes, signed "Tomo" in an oval reserve.
£2,000-3,000   IMC

A 19th Japanese ivory netsuke of a Shi Shi, with loose ball in mouth.
£1,800-2,200   IMC

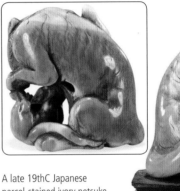

A Japanese ivory netsuke of a Shi Shi, sitting up with a ball, with inlaid eyes and loose ball in its mouth, signed Mitsuharu in an oval reserve.
£2,500-3,500   IMC

A Japanese ivory netsuke of a Shi Shi, in a playful stance crouched low in the front with its back reared up, with inlaid eyes.
£1,800-2,200   IMC

A 19thC ivory netsuke of a Shi Shi hugging a ball, with a loose ball in its mouth, with double inlaid eyes.
£2,000-3,000   IMC

ORIENTAL

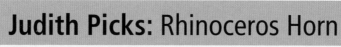

Judith Picks: Rhinoceros Horn

While everyone should be totally opposed to the killing of endangered rhinoceroses for their horns to be used in Chinese medicine, we must not forget that rhinoceros horn has been prized as a precious material in China since ancient times, and carvings are still considered national treasures today. The 2011 ban on trading rhinoceros horn applies only to unworked horns - these beautiful pieces meanwhile have clearly been worked by Ming and Qing master craftsmen at the time when rhinoceros horn was more expensive than gold.

Rhinoceros horn carvings not only display brilliant technical artistry, they are also very rare. Most of the pieces are elaborately carved with a variety of naturalistic, decorative and auspicious motifs, including flowers, fruits, birds, landscapes, mythical creatures, and the eight Daoist Immortals. The most common organic form is the lotus, one of the "Eight Treasures of Buddhism", and you can see several examples of this decoration below.

Before the Wanli period (1573-1619), rhinoceros horn carvings were only allowed to be owned by the Emperor because they were so rare and precious.

A large 17thC Chinese rhinoceros horn libation cup, exterior deeply carved with four chilong dragons amidst bamboo and lingzhi fungus, the handles as bamboo stems.

Provenance: Acquired by John Reeves after his arrival in Canton in 1812.

7in (18cm) wide

£30,000-50,000　　　　　　　　　WW

A Chinese late Ming dynasty rhinocerous horn libation cup, one side with gibbons staring at the moon, the other with two deer, both with multi-layered rockery and foliage from the "Three Friends of Winter".

6.75in (17cm) long

£40,000-60,000　　　　　　　　　RTC

An 18thC Chinese Qing dynasty rhinocerous horn libation cup, with Greek keyfret borders inside and out, the sides with two large taotie masks, the handle carved with a large kuei dragon and three smaller ones, of dark toffee tones, on wood stand.

6.25in (15.5cm) long

£50,000-70,000　　　　　　　　　RTC

An 18thC Chinese Qing dynasty rhinocerous horn libation cup, with mythical beasts bordered by a keyfret pattern inside and out, with three flanges dividing two archaistic taotie masks and two small beasts, of rich walnut tones.

6.25in (15.5cm) long

£50,000-70,000　　　　　　　　　RTC

A 17thC/18thC Chinese rhinoceros horn libation cup, carved as a large lotus leaf resting on breaking waves, from which rise leaves and flowers.

The lotus is one of the more popular decorative themes of rhinoceros-horn carving. It is a symbol of purity and summer, growing from the mud and yet remaining unsullied, and one of the "Eight Treasures of Buddhism".

4in (10cm) wide

£5,000-7,000　　　　　　　　　WW

An 18thC Chinese rhinoceros horn libation cup, carved as a lotus leaf, with incised veins and naturalistic "leaf" edge, the outer wall carved with lotus buds, leaves and veins.

5in (12.5cm) long

£10,000-15,000　　　　　　　　　FRE

CLOSER LOOK - JADE BRUSH POT

The ten small figures are arranged in four groups, the one shown here is of a sage with two attendants carrying fruiting branches and a lingzhi sceptre, beneath rocks besides steps leading up the mountain.

The second is of two figures beneath steps leading to a pagoda, the third of a sage holding a staff and a small boy carrying a peach spray, and the fourth two figures on a mountain bridge, looking out over the landscape.

The depth and quality of the carving indicate that the pot was made by a highly skilled artist.

The provenance adds to its value.

A Chinese Qianlong period Imperial spinach-green jade brush pot, the "Buchanan-Jardine Bitong", the thick sides deeply carved with scenes of Daoist immortals in a tree-lined mountain landscape, on hardwood stand reticulated and carved with peaches, bamboo and chrysanthemum amidst rocks.

Sir John William Buchanan-Jardine (1900-1969), a Baronet, had a distinguished military career and later became the head of Jardine-Matheson. During his time as head of what was one of the most powerful organisations of the British Empire in the early 20thC, he had access to exceptional Chinese art works at a time when many pieces from the Imperial Collection were dispersed. Buchanan-Jardine bought this brushpot from Spink & Son in 1952.

6in (15cm) high

£500,000-700,000   WW

An 18thC Chinese white jade Pi ritual shaped disk, with russet marking, one side with five kylin, the other with the "Eight Buddhist Emblems". in a foliate scroll, rope border, and a comma-carved edge, on a cloud-carved hardwood stand, boxed with extensive inscription.

Disk 8in (20cm) diam

£70,000-100,000   SK

A Chinese Yuan or early Ming dynasty pale green jade toggle of a boy, with light russet markings, depicting the boy flying above clouds and holding a scarf above his head.

2in (5cm) wide

£4,000-6,000   LHA

An 18thC Chinese pale green jade vase, carved with dragons, pearls, flowers, bats, and small children in swirling clouds, on a hardwood stand with silver inlay.

3.75in (9.5cm) high

£70,000-100,000   SK

A pair of Chinese Qianlong period Imperial jade elephants, from a throne-room group of the Emperor Qianlong, the ears incised, with four-character Qianlong mark.

In China, the elephant is a symbol of strength, astuteness and happiness. They existed in China during the Bronze Age, but were soon hunted to extinction. In the Ming dynasty, there were stables in the Forbidden City for the elephants that were given as gifts to the Ming emperors from the rulers of Burma. During the Qing Dynasty elephants carrying vases on their backs appeared in processions to celebrate the Emperor Qianlong's birthday. The Qing rulers commissioned pairs of jade elephants, which along with a throne in the centre, a screen at the back, a standing fan, a luduan unicorn statue, and a vertical censer, formed what is now commonly referred to as a "throne-room group."

7.5in (19cm) long 26.5lb (12kg)

£1,000,000+   WW

ORIENTAL

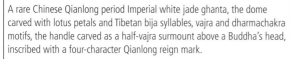

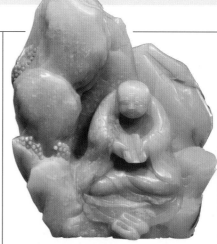

A rare Chinese Qianlong period Imperial white jade ghanta, the dome carved with lotus petals and Tibetan bija syllables, vajra and dharmachakra motifs, the handle carved as a half-vajra surmount above a Buddha's head, inscribed with a four-character Qianlong reign mark.

The bell (or ghanta) represents the female aspect of wisdom and supreme knowledge. The bell and the thunderbolt (or vajra) are the most important symbols in Tibetan Buddhism. Together they represent the perfect union of wisdom and compassion, the two principles necessary for attaining enlightenment. Other ritual objects include the dagger or phurba, skull-cup, and thigh-bone trumpet.

7in (18cm) high

£2,000,000+   WW

A rare Chinese Qianlong period celadon jade boulder carving, carved with a solitary luohan, incised (with traces of gilding) with a poem, and with five seal marks including Qianlong Chenhan.

The poem reads: **"Liao Yi Qie Fa Can Ru Shi Jing/ Shui Liu Shi Leng Feng Guo Hua Xin/ Shi Hu Lun Di Shi Guang Ming Zang/ Li Yi Sao Chu Shi Wei Li Zhang"** which roughly translates as: **"To understand the universe One can study from Buddhist classics,/ When water runs through stones The stone becomes cold/When wind blows through flowers It draws out their perfume/ If you understand all It will bring you brightness and wisdom".**

7.25in (18.5cm) high

£500,000-700,000   WW

A large Chinese Qianlong period spinach-green jade brush pot, carved in deep relief with a continuous scene depicting three Immortals with a single acolyte in a landscape.

6.25in (15.5cm) high

£150,000-250,000   WW

A rare Chinese Qianlong period Imperial spinach-green jade Bi disc, the "Bruce Imperial Bi Disc", carved with nine dragons and chilongs around the central aperture, the reverse with small raised circular bosses.

Bi discs, or stone rings, were made by the people of eastern China as early as the fifth millennium BC. Jade discs have been found carefully laid on the bodies of the dead in tombs of the Hongshan culture (about 3800-2700 BC), a practice which was continued by later Neolithic cultures, presumably to assist the spirit in the afterlife. After the Shang period they are usually more ornate, carved with dragons, snakes or fish, and used in ritual ceremonies. This rare bi disc was reputedly made to celebrate the Qianlong Emperor's 60th birthday.

8in (20cm) diam

£300,000-500,000   WW

An 18thC Chinese white jade bowl.

5.5in (14cm) diam

£15,000-25,000   **LHA**

An 18thC near-white jade openwork finial, with a partial russet skin in some areas, deeply carved with foliage and birds throughout, with hollow centre.

2.75in (7cm) high

£10,000-15,000   **LHA**

A Chinese Qianlong period spinach jade archaistic tripod incense burner and cover, carved with confronting phoenix, with lion mask and paw legs and pierced phoenix handles suspending loose rings, with coiled dragon finial.

8.25in (22.5cm) high

£40,000-60,000   **SOTH**

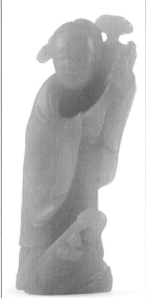

A Chinese Qianlong period celadon jade carving of a robed figure, carrying large ruyi sceptre, with a crane.

4in (10cm) high

£5,000-7,000   **WW**

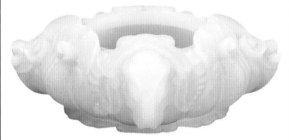

A Chinese Qianlong period white jade brush-washer, the hollow circular recess framed by ram's head handles, carved with scrolls, raised on a foliate base.

6.5in (16cm) wide

£50,000-70,000   **FRE**

An 18thC yellow jade inkstone, with impressed well area and carving of bats at the corners, on a fitted hardwood stand.

3.5in (9cm) long

£6,000-8,000   **LHA**

An 18thC Chinese spinach jade covered jar and stand, decorated with with stylised lotus patterns, with elephant-form jump rings, topped with open lotus flower.

10in (25.5cm) high

£20,000-30,000   **SK**

An 18thC Chinese jade carving of Shoulao, seated holding a peach amidst a rocky outcrop, watching a bat, with hardwood stand.

3.25in (8.5cm) wide

£3,500-4,500   **WW**

An 18thC Chinese Qing dynasty white jade brush washer, in the shape of a ribbon-tied sack, with a small monkey clinging to the rim.

3.75in (9.5cm) wide

£2,500-3,500   **TEN**

A Chinese Qianlong/Jiaqing period white and spinach jade, gold- and gem-mounted deity, with later opal, red stone, diamond and gold mounts.

9in (23cm) high

£25,000-35,000   **FRE**

ORIENTAL

ESSENTIAL REFERENCE - CHINESE JADE

For many thousands of years, the Chinese have prized jade, originally as a symbol of human virtue, later for its aesthetic qualities. The earliest worked jade dates from c4500BC, with the first collectors of ancient jade emerging in the Han period (206BC-220AD).

- "Jade" properly refers to only two minerals: nephrite and jadeite. Nephrite, from which most Chinese jades are made, is typically yellow, white, black or green. Stronger colours (sometimes in mixtures) often indicate jadeite.
- Jade is extremely hard and can only be carved using saws, discs and drills and abrasive powders.
- It is either worked in formal style (including archaic shapes, geometric patterns and motifs) or in a natural style (featuring animals, humans and later plants).
- The more elaborate and heavy a piece is, the more likely it is to be of recent manufacture.

An 18thC Chinese celadon jade figure the Buddha, on wood stand.

11in (28cm) high

£250,000-350,000 SK

An unusual 19thC Chinese celadon jade vessel of squat archaic form, with dragon carved "C" handle, the pierced hardwood cover with a carved carnelian figural finial.

4.75in (12cm) long

£3,500-4,500 FRE

A Chinese Qianlong period jade covered jar and stand, carved with scholars, the finial carved with dragons and clouds, with lion-mask handles, jump rings, and chains, base with Qianlong mark, stand marked Ping Yu Shu Shuang Chih Yu.

15in (38cm) high

£30,000-40,000 SK

An 18thC Chinese white jade group of three quail, nestled together each biting onto the same large spray of millet, with incised feather detailing.

5.5in (14cm) long

£4,000-6,000 IMC

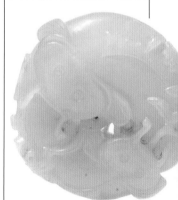

A 19thC Chinese lavender jadeite censer and cover, with Fu dog and pup finial over archaic scrolls and Greek key band, base with two wide masks and free moving rings, beaded scrolls work to body, on wood stand.

Jade 8.5in (21.5cm) wide

£8,000-12,000 FRE

An 18thC Chinese celadon jade censer, with mask-and-ring handles, and lion form finial, raised on three squat legs.

8in (20cm) wide

£6,000-8,000 LHA

An 18thC/19thC Chinese yellow jade vase, carved with qilong.

6in (15cm) high

£6,000-8,000 FRE

A 19thC Chinese Qing Dynasty celadon jade catfish pendant, naturalistically carved.

2.5in (6.5cm) diam

£2,000-3,000 TEN

An 18thC Chinese white jade carving of a horse, the jade of slightly-green hue with few russet inclusions, on well-carved wood stand.

6in (15cm) long

£10,000-15,000   FRE

A large 18thC Chinese spinach jade plate, with graduating sloping wall, raised on short wide circular foot.

11.5in (29cm) diam

£2,000-3,000   FRE

An 18thC/19thC Chinese celadon jade peach-form water coupe, with relief and open-carved peach boughs, and free-hanging rings attached to bat-form handles, on carved wood frame.

7in (18cm) wide

£5,000-7,000   FRE

A 19thC Chinese celadon jade vase, with some areas of spinach green tone, with floral finial and raised scrolling decoration, carved with a central scene of birds and plants, on fitted jade stand.

8.25in (21cm) high

£12,000-18,000   LHA

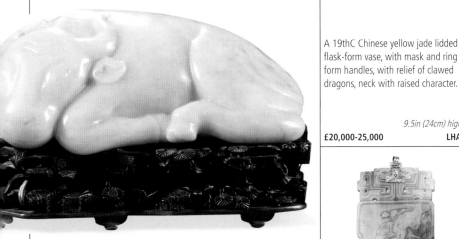

A 19thC Chinese jade boulder in the shape of a reclining water buffalo, on carved hardwood stand.

7in (18cm) wide

£40,000-60,000   SK

A 19thC Chinese yellow jade lidded flask-form vase, with mask and ring form handles, with relief of clawed dragons, neck with raised character.

9.5in (24cm) high

£20,000-25,000   LHA

A 19thC Chinese apple green and white jadeite pendant, the scroll-carved panel top over two panels carved with a frog and bird in low relief, on gilt metal bracket.

2.25in (5.5cm) high

£2,500-3,500   FRE

A 19thC Chinese white jade toggle, depicting lingzhi fungus amongst a lotus seed pod, with pierced carving throughout.

2.25in (5.5cm) long

£1,200-1,800   LHA

A 19thC Chinese Mughal-style yellow-green jade censer, thinly carved with various floral scrolls, highly translucent.

7.75in (19.5cm) high

£15,000-25,000   SK

A 19thC Chinese white jade mountain, of boulder form, the carved grotto enclosing an Immortal and framing pine trees.

5in (12.5cm) high

£3,500-4,500   FRE

A late 19thC Chinese jadeite covered vase, the cover with scrolling qilong and scroll finials, the body with lappet band to neck, above archaic masks.

10in (25.5cm) high

£6,000-8,000   FRE

ORIENTAL

A 19thC Chinese coral group of a warrior and another figure, with waving banners in the background, on wood stand.

5.5in (14cm) high

£1,500-2,500   **LHA**

A large 19thC Chinese coral group of a young woman and a Fu dog, with free-moving ring to collar, on wood stand.

9in (23cm) high

£2,500-3,500   **FRE**

A 20thC coral figure of a meiren, on wood stand.

A Chinese coral figure of a woman holding a vase of flowers, on wood base.

c1800   *9.25in (23.5cm) high*

£4,000-6,000   **LHA**

A 20thC coral figure of a dancing meiren, with regal robes and a large sunflower by her side, on wood base.

6in (15cm) high

£1,000-1,500   **RTC**

5in (12.5cm) high

£500-700   **RTC**

A Chinese coral figure of a young woman in long flowing robes, waving a sash and holding a flower in the wind, on wood stand.

6.25in (15.5cm) high

£2,500-3,500   **IMC**

A Chinese coral figure of a woman holding a flowering branch, on carved wood stand.

Overall 6.25in (15.5cm) high

£1,500-2,500   **LHA**

A rare 18thC Chinese Qing dynasty lapis lazuli bowl or brush washer, carved with a continuous band of ten lingzhi fungi issuing from a single tuft above which a bat flies.

The lingzhi fungus has great medicinal qualities and was believed to be able to revive the dead, thus it is called the fungus of immortality. It is found in every medium in Chinese art. Ling is also a pun for "age". Together with the bat, Fu, it can be interpreted as "may your mind be clear when blessings arrive".

5.25in (13.5cm) wide

£120,000-180,000 WW

A large 18thC Chinese Qing dynasty Imperial lapis lazuli boulder carving, one side with a luohan with a squirrel and incised and gilded poem, on later ormolu stand.

The poem can be translated as: "Imperial inscription in praise of the Luohan,/ The ten thousand things are complete in me; all comers are like the family,/ In my hand I hold a squirrel; I rejoice that it is good-natured./ Being good-natured, it is not disturbed; being joyful it has no regrets,/ And together with all sentient beings, we wander in the land of Buddha."

Overall 10.25in (26cm) high

£200,000-300,000 WW

A Chinese Qianlong lapis lazuli table screen, deeply carved with two cranes, the reverse with incised and gilded calligraphy titled "Yuzhi he shi" (An Imperial poem in praise of cranes), on carved hardwood stand.

Plaque 9in (23cm) high

£7,000-10,000 WW

A small Chinese Qianlong period Imperial lapis lazuli mountain carving, inscribed with a poem by the Qianlong emperor, on carved wood stand.

Poem reads: "Yu Zhi Xu Ting Na Cui / Xu Ting Ruo Yi Ju Chui Yi Ceng Bu Chuang Ling/ Mian Mian Shi Zuo Zhe Ying Zhi You Bie Jie Tu Ta Feng Cui Na Wu Yi". The term "Xu Ting" is a type of pavilion seen in Chinese gardens.

4in (10cm) high

£150,000-300,000 WW

A Chinese Qing dynasty lapis lazuli covered vase, featuring taotie masks and archaic decorations, mask handles with free rings at neck separated by raised and gilt-rubbed inscriptions, with Qianlong mark, on wood stand.

In China, lapis lazuli is known as qing jin shi (blue-gold stone). Although lapis beads which date to the Han dynasty have been excavated, there are no records of the use of lapis before the Qing dynasty.

14.25in (36.5cm) high

£10,000-15,000 FRE

One of a pair of large 19thC Chinese huanghuali-framed dreamstone panels, a grey and white marble panel with script above white marble panel with detailed poetic script from Wen Jien-MIng by Zhang Yu Guangxu, titled "Landscape from West Lake", with metal hanging hooks.

c1825 *26in (66cm) high*

£18,000-22,000 pair FRE

A pair of Chinese Western-style lapis dogs, carved with collars with bells at front, on carved hardwood stands.

Overall 7.5in (19cm) high

£3,500-4,500 LHA

A Chinese turquoise scholar's rock (lusongshi), of slim, bent form with large projection at the top, on wood stand.

13in (33.5cm) high

£1,500-2,500 IMC

A carved agate toggle, depicting of a lotus pod, a shell and a dragonfly, with areas of transparency and opaque white and black coloured stone.

2in (5cm) wide

£3,000-4,000 LHA

ORIENTAL

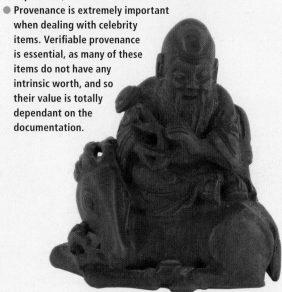

A small 18thC/19thC Chinese bamboo carving of Shoulao, holding a ruyi sceptre, seated on a deer.

Provenance: Acquired by John Reeves after his arrival in Canton in 1812.

2.5in (6.5cm) high

£5,000-7,000   WW

A large 18thC Chinese bamboo brushpot, deeply carved with a mountainous landscape containing pagodas, leafy trees and small figures, cracks.

7in (18cm) high

£6,000-8,000   WW

A Chinese Qing dynasty wooden jar cover, carved to show a group of rams over rockwork.

8.5in (21.5cm) diam

£2,000-3,000   FRE

A 19thC Chinese Qing dynasty octagonal hardwood box, carved with central lotus bloom surrounded by dragons, the sides with stylised lotus lappets.

13in (33.5cm) diam

£1,200-1,800   RTC

A 19thC Huanghuali brush pot, with straight walls, central plug in base.

7.5in (19cm) diam

£3,000-4,000   LHA

A 19thC Japanese carved wood group of farmers harvesting grain, on inscribed and dated base, under associated glass dome.

1863   *7in (18cm) high*

£2,000-2,500   GORL

A Chinese carved wood figure of Guanyin, seated on a lion.

6.5in (16cm) long

£3,000-4,000   LHA

A Chinese bamboo brush pot, with figural carving throughout.

7.25in (18.5cm) high

£1,800-2,200   LHA

ESSENTIAL REFERENCE - LACQUER

Oriental lacquer is prepared from the sap of the lacquer tree (rhus vernicifera), which is native to China, Korea and Japan.

- Thin layers of lacquer are applied to a base (typically of wood or cloth). The resulting hard surface can be carved, and is resistant to water and heat.
- The 13thC and 14thC saw inventions such as red lacquer (by adding cinnabar), gold lacquer and new styles of carving, including the guri scroll pattern.
- Carved polychrome lacquer with mother-of-pearl inlay was popular in the Ming dynasty.
- The Qing dynasty (particularly Emperor Qianlong) favoured carved red lacquer.
- Chinese lacquer was exported to Europe from the 16thC.

A rare Chinese Yuan/Ming dynasty two-tone lacquer foliate dish, the interior carved with peony sprigs and four birds in flight over a red ground, underside also carved.

11.5in (29cm) diam

£8,000-12,000　　FRE

A pair of 18thC Chinese cinnabar lacquer paste boxes, carved to show phoenix over scrolling clouds, with black interior.

1.5in (4cm) diam

£2,000-3,000　　FRE

One of a pair of Chinese red cinnabar lacquer vases, with panels of figures on a ground of flowers and foliage, bases with six-character Qianlong marks, but later.

8.75in (22cm) high

£6,000-7,000 pair　　WW

A large Chinese Qing dynasty Lac Burgaute lacquered tray, the rim inlaid with foliate cartouches on geometric ground, the central panel with Immortals over scrolling seat.

14.5in (37cm) long

£2,000-3,000　　FRE

A rare Chinese Ming/Qing dynasty red and black tixi lacquer and dry-lacquered square dish, carved tixi panels frame a gilt- and black-lacquered panel depicting deer and a pine grove.

12.5in (32cm) wide

£1,500-2,500　　FRE

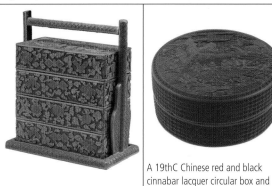

A rare Chinese Ming dynasty red cinnabar lacquer picnic box, of four tiers, the cover carved in medium relief to show scholars with attendants nearby, the sides with Buddhistic symbols, peach, shells and foliate sprigs.

11.5in (29cm) high

£8,000-12,000　　FRE

A 19thC Chinese red and black cinnabar lacquer circular box and cover, the cover with five figures led by Lao Tzu the founder of Daoism in a mountainous landscape, two carrying an enormous peach, and with a sixth figure and deer below, sides with swastika diaper designs, damages.

7in (18cm) diam

£3,000-4,000　　WW

ESSENTIAL REFERENCE - BUDDHIST EMBLEMS

The "Eight Buddhist Emblems" are:

- The Wheel of Law (falun), the inexorable expansion of the Buddha's teaching.
- The Conch Shell (luo), majesty, felicitous journey, the voice of the Buddha.
- The Umbrella (san), spiritual authority, reverence, purity.
- The Canopy (gai), royal grace.
- The Lotus (hua), purity, truthfulness in adversity.
- The Vase (ping), eternal harmony, the receptacle of lustral water, the nectar of immortality.
- The Paired Fish (shuangyu), conjugal happiness, fertility, protection, spiritual liberation.
- The Endless Knot (panchang), eternity.

A large 18thC Chinese red cinnabar lacquer quatrefoil box and cover, the cover with figures in a mountainous landscape, the sides with panels of flowers and the "Eight Buddhist Emblems", damages.

13in (33.5cm) diam

£10,000-20,000　　WW

A pair of 18thC Chinese (Peking) glass vases, with red overlay over yellow bases, carved with pagodas, a resting scholar and workmen crossing a bridge.

7.75in (19.5cm) high

£1,500-2,500 **LHA**

An 18thC Chinese (Peking) glass lidded ginger jar, with blue overlay over white ground, carved with a lotus plant with foliage and flower above waves as well as two cranes, with four-character Qianlong mark.

5.75in (14.5cm) high

£800-1,200 **LHA**

An 18thC Chinese (Peking) purple glass cup, carved with a dragon facing a flaming pearl, with four-character reign mark.

3.5in (9cm) high

£2,000-3,000 **LHA**

A pair of 19thC Chinese (Peking) Imperial yellow glass square bowls, carved on two sides with facing dragons, the others with dragon faces.

2.5in (6.5cm) high

£1,200-1,800 **LHA**

ESSENTIAL REFERENCE - CHINESE GLASS

Glass was made in China before the Qing dynasty, but is rare. The Peking Imperial Palace glassworks were founded in 1680 by the Kangxi emperor (1662-1722). Three main types of glass, all influenced by European glassmaking, were produced.

- **Plain glass, enamelled by porcelain painters.**
- **Monochrome carved glass, of which the best known is "Imperial yellow" glass, the colour of the ceramic glaze used for the Emperor.**
- **Cased/overlay glass. 18thC examples are almost exclusively red over white. Popular 19thC combinations include blue-on-white (reminiscent of porcelain) and red-on-yellow (carved hornbill). Multiple overlay (multiple layers) and multi-coloured overlay (different colours applied to different areas) were also used.**

A 19thC/20thC Chinese (Peking) yellow glass vase, carved with a wide band of debased taotie masks.

8in (20cm) high

£1,200-1,800 **WW**

An early 20thC Republican period European-subject enamelled-glass vase, the neck with flanking lug handles, both sides decorated with a European lady and attendant.

4.5in (11.5cm) high

£1,500-2,500 **RTC**

A Chinese (Peking) Imperial yellow glass vase, carved with three Immortals one with a rooster, the recessed foot containing a four-character reign mark in a square.

8.5in (21.5cm) high

£800-1,200 **LHA**

A Gu Yuexuan-style (Peking) glass snuff bottle, painted with a pheasant and peony, iris and aster, with Qianlong mark to base.

3in (7.5cm) high

£2,500-3,500 RTC

An 18thC Chinese rock crystal snuff bottle, carved as a Spanish coin, probably the work of the Imperial atelier, with matching stopper.

2in (5cm) high

£6,000-8,000 SK

A late 18thC Chinese celadon jade snuff bottle, one side with a russet skin.

3in (7.5cm) high

£8,000-12,000 WW

An 18thC Chinese yellow jade snuff bottle and tray, bottle relief-carved with Liu Hai and his frog, reverse with scholar viewing a cliff from a boat.

2.5in (6.5cm) high

£12,000-18,000 SK

An 18thC Chinese coral snuff bottle, carved in relief with two chilong dragons.

2.5in (6.5cm) high

£1,000-1,500 WW

A late 18thC Chinese pale celadon jade octagonal snuff bottle.

2.25in (5.5cm) high

£7,000-10,000 WW

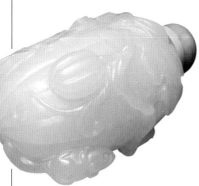

A white jade melon-form snuff bottle, deeply carved with vines and hanging fruit around the exterior of the bottle, with coral and turquoise stopper.

1.75in (4.5cm) long

£4,000-6,000 LHA

A Canton enamel European-style snuff bottle, with panels of quail amid puce and beige ground trellis diaper patterns, with four-character Jiaqing mark.

3in (7.5cm) high

£800-1,200 RTC

An 18thC/19thC Chinese glass snuff bottle, painted to show a chicken and birds amongst foliate sprigs, with three marks to base.

2.5in (6.5cm) high

£2,500-3,500 FRE

A celadon jade melon-form snuff bottle, carved with ribs, butterflies, leaves and bats, with faceted purple quartz stopper.

2.5in (6.5cm) high

£2,500-3,500   LHA

CLOSER LOOK - GLASS SNUFF BOTTLES

The quality of these snuff bottles suggest that they can be attributed to the Imperial Palace Workshops, Jingdezhen.

The opaque white and yellow in the famille rose palette made it possible to create the delicately shaded clothing on the figures. This was not possible using the transparent colours of the famille verte palette.

The bottles have a smooth, bluish-white glaze and neatly drawn enamelling.

The execution of the decoration – in particular the depiction of the Immortals – has retained the quality of the earlier Kangxi (1622-1722) examples.

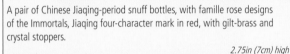

A pair of Chinese Jiaqing-period snuff bottles, with famille rose designs of the Immortals, Jiaqing four-character mark in red, with gilt-brass and crystal stoppers.

2.75in (7cm) high

£60,000-80,000   SK

An enamelled-glass snuff bottle, with four-character enameled mark on underside, on hardwood stand.

c1800   *3in (7.5cm) high*

£2,500-3,500   LHA

An 18thC/19thC Chinese celadon jade vasiform snuff bottle, with Fu dog handles.

2.25in (5.5cm) high

£2,500-3,500   SK

An early 19thC ruby glass snuff bottle, with carved white jade stopper in the form of a parrot, on a green jade bi.

3in (7.5cm) high

£1,000-1,500   IMC

An early 19thC white jade lotus-form snuff bottle, with red glass stopper.

Overall 2.5in (6.5cm) high

£1,200-1,800   TEN

A 19thC Chinese russet-streaked celadon jade pebble snuff bottle, with jadeite stopper.

3.5in (9cm) high

£1,500-2,500   WW

A late 19thC Chinese amber and turquoise cameo glass snuff bottle, in relief with foil back fruiting gourds on a plain turquoise ground, with agate stopper.

3in (7.5cm) high

£1,200-1,800   TEN

A late 19thC Chinese coral snuff bottle, carved in high relief with two squirrels clambering amongst fruiting vines, with pale green jadite stopper.

2.25in (5.5cm) high

£1,500-2,500   TEN

ESSENTIAL REFERENCE - LIN FENGMIAN

Lin Fengmian (1900-1991) is considered a pioneer of modern Chinese painting, as he blended Chinese and Western styles. He spent his early career in Europe, studying painting in France, and holding solo exhibitions in Germany.

● In 1925 he returned to China and became the principal of the Beiping State Vocational Art School. In 1928, he helped found the precursor to the China Academy of Art, and became its first principal until the Japanese invasion in 1937. He steered the academy to be both modern and Chinese, exposing students to modern Western concepts and traditional Chinese painting.

● Many of Lin's more political works were destroyed during the Sino-Japanese War (1937-1945) and the Cultural Revolution (1966-1976), and he personally destroyed many more after criticism from both the Communist party and the Gang of Four in the early 1970s.

● Despite taking precautions he was still imprisoned for over four years.

● After his release in 1977 he moved to Hong Kong, where he began to recreate many of his destroyed works.

Lin Fengmian (1900-1991), "Lady Holding a Flower", ink and colour on paper, signed, with one seal of the artist, framed.

PROVENANCE: Purchased from the artist in Shanghai between 1963 and 1965.

26.75in (68cm) high

£300,000-400,000   SOTH

Jin Cheng (Chinese), landscape, colourwash and ink on paper, signed and dated, various seals.

1913   *47in (119cm) high*

£2,000-3,000   FRE

Fu Baoshi (Chinese, 1904-1965), long boat under the willow shade, wash and ink on paper, signed and with Alice Boney Collectors seal.

Fu Baoshi was born in China, but studied art in Japan, and he brought Japanese visual elements to the Chinese ink painting tradition. Although also praised for his figural work, he is best known for his landscape paintings, in which he recorded the splendors of the rivers and mountains of China. Such paintings employed a new technique of dots and inking derived from traditional rules. He was the leader of the so-called New Chinese Painting Movement, which reformed traditional Chinese painting after 1949.

21in (53cm) long

£70,000-100,000   FRE

Huang Bin-Hung (Chinese, 1864-1955), landscape, colourwash and ink on paper, with artist seal and Alice Boney Collectors seal.

69in (173.5cm) high

£7,000-10,000   FRE

Huang Hsiang Chien (Chinese, 17th century), landscape, colour and ink on paper, with Alice Boney Collectors seal.

20in (51cm) high

£3,500-4,500   FRE

Kao Feng-Han (Chinese, 1683-1743), stone, branch and plum blossom, colour and ink on paper, signed and with various seals, including Alice Boney collectors seal, bottom right corner, remounted.

58in (147cm)

£2,000-3,000   FRE

Ku-Yin (Chinese) two ladies in the room of treasures, colourwash on champagne silk.

1836   *65in (165cm) high*

£1,800-2,000   FRE

ORIENTAL

Shin-Lou-Shan-Jen (Chinese), landscape with gentleman leaning on pine tree, colourwash and ink on paper, script top left corner, several seals, including Alice Boney collector seal.

This was painted when the artist was 74.

54in (137cm) high

£4,000-6,000   **FRE**

Tso Tzu Yang (Chinese), spring outing in landscape, wash and ink, dated.

1850   *50in (127cm) high*

£2,500-3,500   **FRE**

Wang Chen (Chinese, 18th century), landscape, ink wash on paper, signed and with two artist seals and Alice Boney Collectors seal.

37in (94cm) high

£5,000-7,000   **FRE**

Wang Yi-Ting (Chinese), banana leaves and sparrows, colour and ink on paper, signed and dated either 1922 or 1982, various collectors seals.

47in (119cm) high

£2,000-3,000   **FRE**

Wang Yun (Chinese, 1888-1934), blue vase with plum blossom and teapot, colour wash and ink on paper, with seal of Alice Boney.

36in (91.5cm) high

£800-1,200   **FRE**

Wu Ku-Hsiang (Chinese, 1848-1903), landscape with detailed script, ink and colourwash on paper, with seal to top right corner.

55in (140cm) high

£2,500-3,500   **FRE**

A Chinese Ming dynasty framed scroll painting, depicting flowering lotus blossoms, signed.

33.75in (86cm) high

£3,500-4,500   **LHA**

A long 18thC/19thC Chinese scroll painting, depicting a procession including two yellow palanquins and figures on horseback crossing a bridge.

310in (788cm) wide

£3,000-4,000   **WW**

A Chinese Qianlong period Imperial embroidered panel, embroidered with nine gold dragons, the central frontally-faced dragon chasing a flaming pearl, on a pale yellow ground with clouds, scrolling flames and bats above waves and mountains, in later frame.

A 19thC Chinese embroidered silk panel, in the "Hundred Birds in a Garden" patttern, framed and glazed.

The dragons have been finely rendered in various tones and thickness of thread, which heightens the opulence of the piece.

40in (102cm) wide

£80,000-120,000   **SOTH**

29in (74cm) high

£1,800-2,200   **SK**

A Chinese embroidered silk kesi suit, in the style of Imperial parade armour, with metallic-thread five-claw writhing dragons amid clouds, above mountains, waves and lishui band, with allover gilt brass studs.

Sleeve to sleeve 60.5in (154cm) wide

£40,000-60,000   **IMC**

A Chinese embroidered silk dragon robe, depicting a five-clawed gilt dragon flanked below by two other dragons, bats and flowers, above a gilt pavilion, waves and "earth", on blue ground, mounted.

57.5in (146cm) long

£4,000-6,000   **IMC**

A Chinese embroidered silk robe, with design of five-clawed, gilt-thread dragons amid clouds, bats and emblems above the waves and the "earth", on dark blue ground.

52in (132cm) long

£5,000-7,000   **IMC**

An 18thC/19thC Chinese embroidered kesi silk robe, with design of five-clawed dragons amid clouds, bats and emblems above waves and "earth", all on red ground, with floral and butterfly cuffs, striped collar and bottom.

42in (107cm) long

£2,500-3,500   **IMC**

A 19thC Chinese brown embroidered silk robe, decorated with dragons and auspicious symbols above breaking waves, minor damages.

£2,000-3,000   **WW**

A Chinese embroidered blue silk surcoat, decorated with dragons, bats, shou characters and auspicious objects amidst cloud scrolls, above waves and vibrant stripes.

£3,500-4,500   **WW**

ORIENTAL

An 18thC Chinese huanghuali side chair, with veined grey marble-inset back splat and foliate-pierced lower panel, the seat with basketweave panel and open fretwork apron.

37in (94.5cm) high

£400-600   L&T

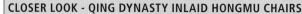

CLOSER LOOK - QING DYNASTY INLAID HONGMU CHAIRS

Dreamstones are pieces of polished marble which resemble Chinese landscape paintings. They are part of the Chinese literati tradition, along with scholars' rocks and furniture made of gnarled tree roots.

A dark brown wood, sometimes known as "black wood", hongmu is one of the most common Chinese hardwoods. It was used extensively for furniture from the mid-Qing dynasty, as supplies of huanghuali began to dwindle.

To the Chinese, the bat symbolised good fortune and great happiness.

A pair of Chinese late Qing dynasty inlaid hongmu chairs, back rest with a circular dreamstone under a bat- and lingzhi-carved shoulder strut, further dreamstones in armrests, all inlaid with mother-of-pearl foliate sprigs.

40in (102cm) high

£3,500-4,500   FRE

An unusual pair of probably 18thC Chinese hardwood "moon-gazing" chairs, each with a reclining back and pull out footrest, some damage.

£2,000-3,000   SWO

A pair of 19thC Anglo-Chinese foliate and floral-carved zitan chairs, with upholstered insert back panel and seat, on fluted front legs with casters and cabriole legs to rear.

41in (104cm) high

£10,000-15,000   FRE

A pair of mid-late 19thC Chinese foliate-carved hardwood armchairs, backs with circular inset marble splats, above panelled seats, on shaped tapered legs united by H-stretchers.

£1,000-2,000   L&T

One of a set of four 19thC Chinese huanghuali chairs.

£4,000-6,000 set   SK

One of a pair of Chinese Qing dynasty huanghuali and mixed-wood horseshoe chairs, with carved vertical splat, square insert seat and beaded apron, on straight, rounded, joined legs.

£5,000-7,000 pair   FRE

A 19thC Chinese carved huanghuali chair.

£1,800-2,200   SK

One of a pair of Ming dynasty-style huanghuali stools, probably from Hainan Island.

19in (48cm) high

£1,200-1,800 pair   LHA

ESSENTIAL REFERENCE - CHINESE FURNITURE

The earliest surviving Chinese wooden furniture dates from the Ming dynasty. Such pieces are made from huanghuali and other hardwoods. They are constructed with mortise and tenon joints, are solid and sparingly decorated. Qing furniture is similar, but is likely to have richer decoration.

- Chairs were originally used only by men (women sat on stools). They often have a box-framed base, a straight back and wide central splat. Round- and yoke-back chairs were generally used by the elite.
- From the Ming dynasty onwards, tables are typically waisted with recessed legs. Coloured stone was sometimes inset into the top.
- Very plain cupboards are typical, usually of slightly tapering form with two doors.
- Two types of screen are common: a single panel set on a stand, or several hinged panels.

An 18thC Chinese huanghuali recessed-leg table, the "ice-plate" top with scroll flanges above apron carved with dragons and foliate scrolls, pierced sides, on rounded and beaded straight legs.

76in (193cm) wide

£10,000-15,000   FRE

An 18thC Chinese lacquered table, painted with bird and flower reserves on a brocade-pattern ground.

56.5in (144cm) long

£15,000-25,000   SK

A late 18thC Chinese painted hongmu recessed-leg side table, the top set with shaped flanges, carved to show antiques, on straight, joined legs.

80in (203cm) long

£2,500-3,500   FRE

A late 18thC/early 19thC Chinese huanghuali altar table, the cleated rectangular top with open fret carved frieze above square-section legs with framed panels, spiral-carved capitals and similarly carved feet.

61in (155cm) wide

£2,000-3,000   L&T

A 19thC Chinese hongmu side table, with waisted, carved high apron worked to show archaic scrolls and bands, beaded edge to straight legs and hoof scroll-carved feet.

37in (95cm) long

£1,200-1,800   FRE

An early 19thC Chinese carved huanghuali altar table, with ornate pierced foliate-carved frieze, raised on stylised cabriole legs terminating in claw-and-ball feet.

41in (104cm) wide

£1,500-2,500   L&T

A 19thC Chinese huanghuali altar table, on four legs with stretchers, with carved openwork aprons centred by two dragons clutching pearls.

47.5in (120cm) long

£1,500-2,500   IMC

ORIENTAL

A 19thC Chinese marble-top hardwood table, with a carved and fret-pierced frieze, raised on moulded square legs ending in claw-and-ball feet.

44in (112cm) wide

£3,000-4,000   **L&T**

A pair of small Chinese Qing dynasty huanghuali wine tables, with rectangular top over slender rounded legs.

£4,000-6,000   **FRE**

A 19thC Chinese carved zitan and mixed-wood pedestal desk, the marble-insert rectangular top with three drawers with lotus leaf horn handles to frieze, over two pedestals with single drawer and cupboard door, carved with foliate blossoms and scrolls to three sides, on straight, joined legs with hoof feet.

37in (94.5cm) high

£20,000-30,000   **FRE**

A late 19thC Chinese carved hardwood bench or low table, on twin open-end supports with ornate pierced foliate-carved aprons.

80in (203cm) wide

£3,000-4,000   **L&T**

A 19thC Chinese carved hongmu and burlwood side table, the top with three burlwood inserts, over lingzhi-carved ends above dragon-carved apron, on straight, carved legs with lingzhi feet.

45.5in (115.5cm) long

£800-1,200   **FRE**

A Chinese nanmu and bamboo altar table, Shangxi province, the top with upright scroll ends, the legs, sides and frieze with bamboo openwork and fretwork panels.

c1890   *90in (229cm) long*

£1,500-2,500   **WW**

A late 19thC Chinese huanghuali circular low table, with shaped frieze carved with stylised dragons and insects, on shaped legs united by a peripheral stretcher, on lotus leaf-carved feet.

27in (69cm) diam

£1,200-1,800   **L&T**

A nest of late 19thC Chinese huanghuali quartetto tables, the tops with foliate-carved edge and ornate pierced and foliate-carved frieze, on conforming legs.

28in (71cm) high

£800-1,200   **L&T**

A 19thC Chinese huanghuali square table, with carved apron.

34in (86cm) square

£1,200-1,800   **SK**

A Chinese hardwood two-tier marble-inset jardinere stand.

33in (85cm) high

£500-700   **DN**

A 19thC Chinese black lacquer miniature display stand, with eight compartments above three drawers, decorated in gilt and with painted chinoiserie landscapes, with ornately carved borders.

22in (56cm) high

£3,500-4,500 WW

CLOSER LOOK - HUANGHUALI CABINETS

Huanghuali wood was the principal hardwood employed by Chinese cabinetmakers during the classic period of Chinese furniture, between the mid-16thC and mid-18thC.

Huanghuali wood has a very attractive grain which exhibits patterns known as "friendly ghost faces"; its lustre also reflects the light. It is a fine-grained, fragrant and precious tropical hardwood only perhaps equalled in value by Zitan.

These cabinets are desirable to collectors who like traditional Chinese furniture, but are equally suitable in a minimalist interior.

The quality of these cabinets can be seen in the refined beading and scrolling edges.

A pair of Chinese late Qing/Republic period huanghuali cabinets, the carved gallery apron with beaded and scrolling edge over a gallery above two panelled cupboard doors, on square feet.

72in (183cm) high

£15,000-25,000 FRE

One of a pair of Chinese Qing dynasty huanghuali kang cabinets, Yuanjiao, the beaded doors with horizontal openwork panel carved to show lotus leaf scrolls, on rounded straight feet.

52in (132cm) high

£2,500-3,500 pair FRE

A near pair of early 20thC Chinese huanghuali pagoda-form side cabinets, with a single frieze drawer and two cupboard doors, with carved, stylised, geometric designs.

31.5in (80cm) high

£1,200-1,800 L&T

A pair of Chinese Qing dynasty carved huanghuali cabinets, with lattice-carved doors and side panels, above two cupboard doors carved with dragons within beaded edge, on square feet.

64in (162.5cm) high

£15,000-25,000 FRE

A part-19thC Chinese carved hongmu and giltwood panelled cabinet, carved with Greek keys and Fu bats enclosing gilded figural scenes, on scroll-carved feet.

85in (216cm) wide

£3,000-4,000 FRE

A Chinese Qing dynasty carved zitan display cabinet, the compartmentalised cabinet carved with export-style floral motifs, with double-hump top and open back, with single locking compartment.

£6,000-8,000 FRE

A Japanese Meiji period shakudo work kodanzu, with two doors decorated with a harvest scene, enclosing six lacquered drawers above a single drawers, on wave decorated stand.

Shakudo is a Japanese alloy metal comprised of 96% copper and 4% gold. It was traditionally used for sword guards and other sword fittings. A Kodanzu is a Japanese cabinet containing a chest of drawers. The best have decoration including lacquer, inset with mother-of-pearl or tortoiseshell.

11.5in (29cm) high

£15,000-25,000 GORL

ORIENTAL

CLOSER LOOK - QING DYNASTY PAINTED SCREEN

The birds in a landscape are beautiful, and also function as a metaphor for society. The phoenix (the sacred bird) usually featured in the centre and symbolised the emperor or empress. The other birds, the colourful (higher echelons) and smaller birds (commoners) are depicted paying homage to it.

Bird-and-flower painting was popular from as early as the Song dynasty, when under the patronage of the Northern Song emperor Huizong (r. 1101-1125) the Imperial Academy was established. Here, artists were encouraged to experiment with their painting style. Northern Song painter Cui Bo (active circa 1060-1085) is often credited with changing the direction of bird-and-flower paintings within the Academy, making them more animated and freer in style.

This type of screen was an important furnishing of halls and palaces. It would have been prominently placed either dividing the room or used as a background setting.

A rare 18thC Chinese Qing Dynasty 12-panel gouache on painted silk screen, depicting phoenix and cranes around a magnolia tree, amongst flowering peony, plantain and rockwork and swirling clouds beside a pond with mandarin ducks and birds, with bamboo, prunus and lingzhi fungus on the marshy banks.

Panels of this intense colouration and bold painting are extremely rare.

281in (714cm) wide

£120,000-180,000　　　　　　　　　　　　　　　SOTH

An 18thC Chinese four-panel floor screen, each rectangular panel decorated with silk dragon embroidery.

79.5in (202cm) high

£25,000-35,000　　　LHA

An 18thC Chinese celadon jade screen, carved with Shao Lao and attendants in a landscape, reverse with emblems of longevity, on boxwood stand carved with deer, the "Three Friends", pine, bamboo, prunus, and ling chih.

Screen 10in (25.5cm)

£80,000-120,000　　　SK

An 18thC Chinese celadon jade screen, carved with the Immortals, with quail and millet plants to reverse, on carved rosewood stand.

Screen 8in (20cm) diam

£50,000-70,000　　　SK

A Chinese Jiaqing period dry-lacquer six-panel screen, with six tall rectangular strutted panels, incised and gilded to show various figural landscapes.

72in (183cm) high

£2,000-3,000　　　FRE

A Chinese Qing dynasty hardwood and porcelain inset five-panel floor screen, on short, square legs.

62in (157.5cm) high

£25,000-35,000　　　FRE

A small Chinese ink-work on ivory table screen, decorated with a scholar in a mountainous landscape with script, reverse with detailed calligraphic script, on hardwood stand.

5in (12.5cm) high

£3,500-4,500　　　FRE

A 19thC Chinese carved "cameo"-layered inkstone tablescreen, decorated with a bamboo grove, scholar's rocks, flowers, small birds amid foliage, on wood stand with chilong flanges.

23in (58cm) high

£6,000-8,000　　　IMC

A Chinese five-panel "palace"-style tablescreen, set with carved spinach jade figural scenes, the main panel of Immortals quelling a dragon in front of a pavilion, in a wire-inlaid wood frame, on double-pedestal base.

22.25in (56.5cm) long

£2,500-3,500　　　IMC

A 19thC Chinese kingfisher feather and hongmu table screen and stand, depicting Immortals in a foliate garden, with applied rock work and peach grove, within lattice-carved fret-and-panel frame, the stand inlaid with polychrome ivory scenes.

Overall 27.5in (70cm) high

£6,000-8,000 FRE

A Chinese spinach jade table screen, carved in relief with scenes of a warrior and attendant outside a city gate, the reverse with inscribed character, in pierce-carved wood frame.

23.5in (59cm) high

£3,000-4,000 LHA

A 19thC Chinese Qing dynasty six-panel famille rose table screen, depicting the Daoist Immortals in leisurely pursuits, in hardwood reticulated peony frame and stand.

Plaques 6.25in (15.5cm) high

£1,500-2,500 RTC

A late 19thC Japanese six-panel screen, with ink and vibrant colours on paper, depicting a battle-by-the-water scene.

64.5in (164cm) high

£1,500-2,500 IMC

A 19thC Japanese four-panel screen, decorated in ink and colours on paper with three cranes by a pond, on gilt ground, with repoussé dragon corner mounts.

67in (170cm) high

£1,800-2,200 IMC

A 19thC Chinese carved and pierced pine six-fold barrier screen, with fretted medallions and trelliswork above a planked apron.

This screen has been converted from the sliding doors in the courtyard of a merchant's house in Southern China.

965in (2450cm) high

£3,500-4,500 L&T

A Japanese hardwood, ivory and bone two-fold screen, each fold with six shaped panels of birds and flowers above rectangular panels, the reverse with two large panels of sparrows in flight.

c1900 *74in (188cm) high*

£15,000-25,000 DN

THE FURNITURE MARKET

The furniture market is really a play in two acts. The first would feature the "UK Antique Furniture Index", published by the Antiques Collectors' Club in January 2011. It showed that prices fell by eight per cent in 2010, the largest ever twelve-month fall in the index in four decades. Some sources are actually claiming a 20 to 30 per cent fall. "Georgian brown", or just brown, furniture has nose-dived in value, whereas 20thC furniture, especially Mid-Century Modern, has continued its renaissance.

On the other hand, the second act would be opened by the Harrington marquetry commode, attributed to Thomas Chippendale, which sold for £3.35 million at Sotheby's, London, in December 2010, a new record for English furniture.

The reasons for the decline in value of "average", mid-range furniture is complex, but may be at least partially attributed to fashion and a lack of really good-quality examples on the market. Additionally, many vendors are naturally reluctant to enter good antique furniture to auction while prices are depressed.

Pieces that are too bulky for modern interiors need to be of exceptional quality to attract buyers. There is no doubt that Georgian and Regency pieces sell better than their heavy Victorian counterparts. Additionally, pieces such as the davenport, Canterbury and bureau, have no real function in today's interiors.

Many dealers also record that American buyers are still not coming to Britain in their previous numbers, and this has had a dramatic effect on export sales.

So has the low- to mid-range furniture market reached its nadir? Some of the prices achieved at auction are ridiculously low for pieces made from solid wood, by craftsmen, and not merely fashioned out of MDF (medium-density fibreboard – which is quite simply wood fibres, combined with wax and a resin binder). Well, there are some indicators that prices may be beginning to climb slightly.

People are being persuaded that "antiques are green" and that recycling old furniture is more responsible than cutting down more of the Amazon jungle or Scandinavian pine trees.

Also, with some prices so low, younger buyers are looking at auctions when furnishing their first flat or house.

Sturdy, good-quality, highly functional pieces are excellent value for money: a solid mahogany, Victorian, chest-of-drawers can be found at around £100. These pieces could well provide good investment potential, as prices must surely increase with a strengthening economy – whenever that happens. Also, if you get tired of the piece, you can re-sell it and should get your money back – or even make a profit. Try that with a piece of flat-pack!

Above: A lady's cylinder bureau, by François Linke. See page 196.

Left: A late 18thC Italian commode, by Giovanni Maffezzoli. See page 224.

A mid-18thC Georgian oak Windsor armchair, the underside retaining a brass plaque detailing the chair's history, including its trip to the Colonies aboard the packet ship of Joshua Fisher and its descent in the Fisher family.

£2,500-3,500   **POOK**

A Lancaster County, Pennsylvania sack-back Windsor armchair, retaining an old finish.

c1770

£2,500-3,500   **POOK**

An early 19thC American ash Windsor armchair, with a curved comb-back and continuous arms, on later turned legs and stretchers, traces of green paint.

£450-550   **WW**

A possibly Lisbon, Connecticut, black-painted sack-back Windsor chair, with carved knuckle handholds and boldly carved saddle seat, original surface.

c1790   *34in (86cm) high*

£5,000-7,000   **SK**

A set of three Lincolnshire 19thC yew Windsor elbow chairs, each stamped "G Wilson Grantham", the low double-bow backs with pierced splats and turned arm supports, elm seat, on turned legs with H-stretcher.

£2,500-3,500   **TEN**

A pair of 19thC fruitwood and elm Windsor wheel-back armchairs, damages.

£300-400   **WW**

An early 19thC yew and elm stick-back Windsor elbow chair, with pierced central splat, on turned and tapered splayed legs, united by a crinoline stretcher.

£400-600   **H&L**

An early 19thC green-painted elm stick-back chair, with comb-shaped top rail and outswept arms, with turned legs.

£1,200-1,800   **TEN**

An early 19thC ash and elm Windsor armchair, with a hoop back and a shaped seat edge, damages.

£150-250   **WW**

A mid-19thC Thames Valley ash and beech comb-back Windsor armchair, old repairs.
£220-280   DN

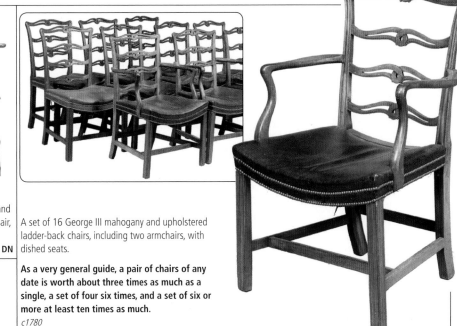

A set of 16 George III mahogany and upholstered ladder-back chairs, including two armchairs, with dished seats.

As a very general guide, a pair of chairs of any date is worth about three times as much as a single, a set of four six times, and a set of six or more at least ten times as much.
c1780
£30,000-40,000   DN

A mid-19thC Victorian yew and elm Windsor armchair, on turned tapered legs with crinoline stretcher.

£250-350   L&T

A pair of Victorian ash, fruitwood and elm hoop-back Windsor armchairs.
£200-300   WW

A Victorian elm and yew Windsor armchair, on turned tapered legs with H-stretcher.
c1860
£300-400   L&T

A 19thC Nottinghamshire yew Windsor armchair, the pierced splat between turned spindle arm supports, with moulded elm seat on turned spindle legs with crinoline stretcher.
c1860   *40in (102cm) high*
£200-300   TEN

A Georgian Chippendale-style fruitwood child's chair, with shaped toprail and pierced central vase-shaped splat, on square chamfered legs with stretchers.
£300-400   H&L

A 19thC Canadian red-painted rocking chair, with a woven seat.
£80-120   WW

One of a pair of early 19thC painted country side chairs, with rush seats.
£250-350 pair   WW

CLOSER LOOK - GILES GRENDEY CHAIRS

Giles Grendey was one of London's most successful 18thC furniture makers, yet compared with contemporaries such as Thomas Chippendale, relatively little is known of his work. Grendey set up shop in St. John's Square, Clerkenwell. It was far larger than most furniture shops, which suggests that Grendey was both ambitious and well funded. When his workshop was struck by fire in 1731 over £1,000 worth of stock destined for export was destroyed.

These chairs can be approximately dated by the style of the label which corresponds to the shorter of two versions employed by the Grendey workshop. Other furniture bearing this label can be dated on stylistic and technical grounds to the 1740s or later.

The ladder-back style derives from the so-called "Dutch chairs" of the early 18thC, which were imported from Holland in huge numbers and were widely copied by English chair-makers. These chairs are "polite" versions of the form, demonstrating its acceptance into mainstream English furniture-making.

This type of chair typically had rush or "matted" seats, a cheap and popular alternative to more expensive, upholstered, drop-in seats. The present boarded seats are replacements, installed some time before 1974. The rush seat fitted to one of the chairs was installed while it was on loan to the Victoria & Albert Museum in London.

Two chairs are stamped "T C" on the inside of the back rails: this stamp is hitherto unrecorded, but other chairs bearing Grendey's label are also stamped with various initials, assumed to be those of journeymen employed in Grendey's workshop.

A set of six George II walnut ladder-back dining chairs, by Giles Grendey.

£12,000-18,000 set

SWO

A set of seven mid-18thC-style carved mahogany dining chairs, including an open armchair, all with leather drop-in seats.

£700-1,000   WW

A set of six George III mahogany dining chairs, with drop-in seats.

c1780

£1,200-1,800 set   DN

A set of six George III mahogany dining chairs, the wavy shaped top rails with carved anthemion and shaped vertical splat, with drop-in seats, on square chamfered legs with stretchers.

£1,000-1,500 set   TEN

Two of a set of four George III mahogany dining chairs, the reeded X-form backs centred by palmette motifs, with overstuffed seats and reeded turned tapered legs.

c1790

£600-800 set   L&T

A Pennsylvania Chippendale walnut dining chair, the shell-carved crest with voluted ears above a pierced splat, on shell-carved cabriole legs with voluted returns and claw-and-ball feet.

c1790

£6,000-8,000   POOK

A set of six late 18thC Massachusetts Chippendale carved mahogany side chairs, with old refinish, restoration.

38in (96cm) high

£4,000-6,000   SK

Two of a set of four early 19thC mahogany dining chairs, with stringing and overstuffed seats, and ash seat rails.
£250-350 set   WW

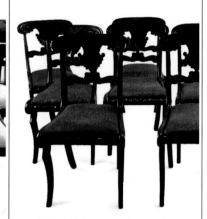

A set of eight Regency mahogany dining chairs, including two armchairs, all with acanthus leaf and panelled curved cresting rails above beige floral-upholstered seats, on turned and reeded legs.
£4,000-6,000 set   GORL

A set of eight Irish Regency mahogany dining chairs, with curved scroll and acanthus leaf backs and green-upholstered seats, on sabre legs.
£3,500-4,500 set   GORL

A set of four Regency mahogany dining chairs.
c1815
£150-250 set   DN

A set of ten Regency carved rosewood dining chairs, almost certainly by Gillows, including two armchairs with carved acorn and oak leaf brackets and klismos-shaped backs, all with green velvet upholstered drop-in seats, one stamped "K" to the seat rail.
c1815
£25,000-35,000 set   DN

A set of eight Scottish George IV mahogany dining chairs, attributed to Gillows, including two armchairs, the bar backs above drop-in seats covered in simulated shark skin, on reeded and turned legs with turned X-stretchers.
c1825
£6,000-8,000 set   L&T

A set of seven Regency mahogany dining chairs, including one armchair, faults.
c1820
£350-450 set   DN

Two of set of nine George IV mahogany dining chairs, with bar-backs and overstuffed seats, on turned, tapered legs, five chairs stamped on the seat rail "R.S.A/R".
c1825

£2,500-3,500 set L&T

Two of a set of six William IV mahogany dining chairs, including one armchair, all with later leatherette stuffed-over seats.

£500-700 set WW

ESSENTIAL REFERENCE - VICTORIAN STYLE

The Victorian age was dominated by revivals of historical styles. Initially Gothic and Classical styles were popular, fighting it out in what was known as the "battle of the styles". Later, Renaissance and especially Rococo revival became more common, as did exotic motifs. These revived styles were exaggerated and more luxurious than their original manifestations. Furniture was typically heavier, highly ornamented, curvaceous and richly upholstered, braided and tasselled.

● Due to the Industrial Revolution, mass-produced products designed for the middle classes were increasingly common.
● The Arts & Crafts movement of the mid-to-late 19thC was a reaction against the prevalence of historical styles and the poor quality of industrial manufacturers. Art Nouveau (from the late 19thC onwards) was an attempt to create a new style, rather than continually reviving old ones.

A set of eight Victorian mahogany dining chairs, including two armchairs, each with carved female figure stiles and leather upholstery with relief lion passants.

£10,000-15,000 POOK

Two of a set of six mid-19thC Scottish Victorian mahogany and upholstered dining chairs, in buttoned blue leather, with relief-carved thistle crestings, on moulded cabriole legs with hairy paw feet, restoration.

£3,000-4,000 set L&T

A set of six mid-to-late 19thC George III-style mahogany dining chairs, with leaf and palmette-carved and pierced splats, overstuffed seats, with leaf-capped cabriole legs, and claw-and-ball feet.

£1,000-1,500 WW

Two of a set of 12 Victorian mahogany and upholstered dining chairs, the shaped backs and overstuffed seats in buttoned green velvet, on reeded turned tapered legs, each stamped "1881".

c1880

£3,000-4,000 set L&T

FURNITURE

One of a set of eight George III-style mahogany dining chairs, including two armchairs, with foliate-carved shaped top rails, pierced splats and drop-in seats, on square chamfered legs with H-stretchers.

£1,000-1,500 set   **L&T**

A George III Chippendale-style mahogany dining chair.

£500-700   **GORL**

A set of six 20thC Queen Anne-style walnut dining chairs, with additional simulated figuring.

£350-450 set   **DN**

A set of ten late 19thC/early 20thC George III-style mahogany chairs, with tan leather upholstered seats.

£3,000-4,000 set   **DN**

Two of a set of 14 20thC George III-style mahogany dining chairs, including two armchairs, with pierced, interlaced, vase-shaped splats and drop-in seats, on square chamfered legs with H-stretchers.

£3,000-4,000 set   **L&T**

A set of 10 20thC George III-style mahogany dining chairs, including a pair of armchairs, all bearing maker's ivorine plaque "W.WALKER & SONS MANUFACTURERS, BUNHILL ROW, LONDON, E.o".

£1,200-1,800 set   **DN**

Two of a set of six early 20thC 18thC-Irish-style mahogany dining chairs, including two armchairs, all with carved and pierced splats and overstuffed seats, the cabriole front legs with tulips on a diaper ground terminating in paw feet.

£350-450 set   **WW**

Judith Picks:
Chippendale Revival

There is absolutely no doubt that Thomas Chippendale is one of the greatest chair designers. As Mies van der Rohe said in 1930, "The chair is a very difficult object. Everyone who has tried to make one knows that. There are endless possibilities and many problems – the chair has to be light, it has to be strong, it has to be comfortable. It is almost easier to build a skyscraper than a chair. That is why Chippendale is famous.".

Unfortunately, original sets of 18thC Chippendale style chairs are difficult to find and tend to be expensive (an average set of eight 18thC chairs would certainly be £100,000+). So a good alternative is to buy good late 19thC or early 20thC reproductions. They are elegant and tend to be of solid construction. This set of chairs is particularly good and therefore not inexpensive, but if you look at the other chairs on the page, bargains are to be had.

One of a set of eight Chippendale revival mahogany chairs, including a pair of armchairs, with pierced arched backs, and chamfered square legs with pierced spandrels.
c1880

£7,000-9,000 set   **DN**

An early 18thC upholstered walnut side chair, in floral foliate tapestry, on cabriole legs, with stretchers and pointed pad feet.
£1,500-2,500 H&L

A pair of George I oak and walnut side chairs.
c1720
£3,000-4,000 DN

One of a pair of English George II mahogany side chairs, with rolled crests over vertical pierced carved splats and upholstered seats, on carved cabriole legs with paw feet.

38.25in (97cm) high
£5,000-7,000 pair LHA

A pair of George II walnut side chairs, with arched shell-carved crest rail above pierced and shell-carved splat flanked by double C-scroll stiles, with velvet-upholstered seat and shaped gadrooned skirt, on acanthus leaf-capped cabriole legs with claw-and-ball feet.

This style of chair has been refered to as the "Kateshill Chair" as a set of four chairs and a similar settee were made for the Bury Family of Kateshill near Worcester, England, possibly by Thomas Chippendale.
c1750
£25,000-35,000 WES

A George III mahogany side chair, with a pierced vase-shaped splat and a later needlework-covered drop-in seat, repairs.
£400-600 WW

A matched pair of George III mahogany and petit point upholstered side chairs, in the manner of Giles Grendey, on carved cabriole legs, one stamped "W.F.".
c1770
£8,000-12,000 DN

Two of a set of four 19thC mahogany shield-back chairs, with drop-in seats.
£500-700 set WW

A Regency simulated rosewood and brass-mounted side chair, with a squab cushion above a cane seat and on sabre legs.
£200-300 WW

A pair of Regency mahogany side chairs, the reeded oval padded backs and overstuffed seats covered in red velvet, above foliate carved aprons, on cabriole legs with paw feet, surmounted by patera motifs.
c1820
£1,500-2,500 L&T

A set of six Biedermeier birch side chairs, with rounded crest rail over the upholstered seat, on square tapering legs.
35.5in (91cm) high
£2,000-3,000 set LHA

A pair of Victorian ebonised and mother-of-pearl-inlaid side chairs, the oval foliate-decorated backs flanked by twist columns above the caned seats.

37.5in (95cm) high

£600-800   LHA

A set of six Victorian mahogany side chairs, with carved scroll-husk top rails and drop-in seats.

£600-800   WW

Two of a set of four 19thC mahogany side chairs, with curved top rails inlaid with fans, the supports with bell flowers.

£150-250 set   WW

Two of a set of four Queen Anne-style inlaid walnut chairs, by Knight & Sons, Bath, the shaped splats inlaid with thistles and central motif depicting "John" and "Jesus" after the resurrection entitled "Noli Me Tangere", on foliate-inlaid square cabriole legs with stretchers.
c1900

£1,000-1,500 set   L&T

A 20thC Regency-style painted side chair, the central panel back with Grecian figures, with cane seat, on turned splay legs.

£250-350   WW

Judith Picks

This is a splendid example of an American Chippendale corner chair (in early records also called "roundabouts"). Examples with solid splats are usually considered Queen Anne, whereas the elaborately carved splats and claw-and-ball foot shown here make this example more appropriately Chippendale. This is a high quality example made by a Massachusetts cabinetmaker for a wealthy customer. The same quality English examples from this period are considerably cheaper. This is down to supply and demand. There were fewer wealthy patrons in the Colonies at this time. And there are many more wealthy Americans today who want to own an important piece of American furniture-making history.

A Massachusetts mahogany corner chair, with a carved crest rail, pierced splats and claw-and-ball front foot.
c1770

£10,000-15,000   POOK

An 18thC walnut corner armchair, with a pierced twin splat and drop-in seat, with front shell-carved cabriole leg, replacements.

£350-450   WW

An early George III mahogany corner armchair, the inverted baluster splats pierced and carved with husks, and later drop-in seat, on front acanthus leg.

£300-400   WW

An early 19thC mahogany smoker's bow chair.

£400-600   GORL

A mid-18thC mahogany hall chair.
c1750
£200-300   DN

A set of four George III mahogany hall chairs, each back centred by a painted armorial of a rampant leopard above a crown.
c1700
£1,000-1,500 set   DN

A pair of late George III mahogany hall chairs, attributed to John Reid of Leeds, the shaped carved backs with central heraldic oval above shaped solid seats, on tapered ring-turned legs, both stamped "I.K.", one stamped twice.

The workman's mark of I.K. is recorded on several pieces marked by John Reid of Leeds, and these chairs have the same legs and seats as marked examples by this maker.
£600-800   A&G

A pair of late George III mahogany hall chairs, the shield backs with inset vacant cartouches.
£400-600   GORL

A set of six Regency simulated rosewood and parcel gilt hall chairs, in the manner of Seddon, with trefoil finials, arcaded backs, caned seats and faux bamboo supports, re-decorated.
c1815
£2,000-3,000   DN

A pair of late Regency mahogany hall chairs, in the manner of Gillows, with carved shell backs on waisted scroll supports, on ring-turned and spiral-ribbed legs, one damaged.
£700-900   WW

A late Regency leather-upholstered hall porter's chair, decorated with round-headed nails, on short turned legs.
66in (167.5cm) high
£3,500-4,500   DUK

A Black Forest carved and stained wood musical hall bench, the hinged seat opening to a musical movement.
c1900   *39in (99.5cm) wide*
£4,000-6,000   DN

Miller's Compares George II stools

The carving on this stool is of poor quality. The seat rail in particular has carving that bears no relation to the very average quality of the legs and was probably associated in the early 20thC. The modern fabric is unsuitable. The wood has been refinished to an unfashionable "toffee" colour and has no evidence of original patination.

Meanwhile, the carving on this example is crisp and accomplished. The gadrooned rail is raised on deeply carved shell cabriole legs. The carving on the knees and lion-paw feet shows plenty of detail. The drop-in seat is upholstered in suitable, although not necessarily original, old needlework. The mahogany has a rich colour and the overall patina is excellent.

A George II mahogany stool, the upholstered top over a wave-carved frieze, on carved cabriole legs with claw-and-ball feet.

24.25in (62cm) wide

£600-800　　　　　　　　　　　　　　　　　**PC**

A George II mahogany dressing stool, the seat upholstered in old needlework fabric, carved with flowers, shells and leaves.

22in (56cm) wide

£4,500-5,500　　　　　　　　　　　　　　　　　**TEN**

A 19thC oak stool, on faceted legs, repairs.

16.5in (42cm) wide

£60-80　　　　　　**WW**

An unusual early 19thC possibly Russian mahogany piano stool, the adjustable seat covered in studded tan leather supported by stylised stiff leaves, on a triform platform base with squat bun feet.

20in (51cm) high

£600-800　　　　　　**L&T**

An early 19thC mahogany stool, the solid seat on ribbed tapering legs.

19.75in (50cm) high

£200-300　　　　　　**WW**

A Regency rosewood stool, faults.

c1815　　　　*24in (61cm) wide*

£250-350　　　　　　**DN**

A William IV rosewood X-framed stool, with lappet-carved finials and centred by carved rosettes.

c1835　　　　*17in (43cm) high*

£1,500-2,500　　　　　　**DN**

A 19thC possibly Barbadian soft wood stool carved in the shape of a tortoise, the overstuffed seat covered in simulated-shell velvet.

16in (40cm) wide

£700-1,000　　　　　　**L&T**

A Victorian rosewood high stool, on bun feet.

14.5in (37cm) high

£350-450　　　　　　**WW**

A late Victorian rectangular long stool, with buttoned, upholstered leather top, on turned mahogany legs.

56in (142cm) long

£800-1,200　　　　　　**WW**

A Victorian rosewood and uphostered stool, the serpentine seat covered in foliate-patterned needlework, on cabriole scroll legs with ceramic castors.
c1860   *44in (112cm) wide*
£600-800   **L&T**

A pair of Victorian walnut foot stools, designed by Thomas Jeckyll for Gillows & Co, the rectangular pierced back above studded green leather seats, on openwork moulded trestle end supports, stamped "Gillow 11439" and "11440", dated.

These stools formed part of a group of furniture designed by Thomas Jeckyll for the industrialist Edward Green and his wife Mary for their home The Old Hall, Heath, Yorkshire, England in the 1870s. The signature of F. Branscombe is thought to be that of the upholsterer. It is also thought that the original leather upholstery was brown.
1875   *14in (36cm) wide*
£1,500-2,500   **L&T**

An Austrian Revival-style walnut stool, by Constantin Drbal, carved with lion's heads and paws, the leather patterned with figures and ornament, and with ornamental brass nails.

Produced by the firm Constantin Drbal, Royal and Imperial purveyor, sculptor and specialist in patterned furniture leather.
c1880-90
£2,000-3,000   **DOR**

A late 19thC/early 20thC French Louis XVI-style carved and parcel gilt "Duchesse" day bed, formed from a pair of tub shaped armchairs and a stool.
£1,000-1,500   **DN**

A pair of Continental carved beechwood and parcel gilt stools, with serpentine front and a drop in seat.
25in (63.5cm) wide
£600-800   **WW**

A 20thC Regency-style carved mahogany and upholstered centre stool.
59in (150cm) wide
£600-800   **DN**

A matched pair of Irish George III mahogany window seats, upholstered in studded red leather.
c1780   *38in (96.5cm) wide*
£5,000-7,000   **DN**

A large 19thC gilt and gesso window seat, upholstered in buttoned green silk damask, on leaf-carved and fluted legs.
75in (190cm)
£2,000-3,000   **TEN**

A large mid-20thC Hepplewhite-style upholstered window seat, the buttoned floral chintz over square mahogany supports and stretchers.
66in (167.5cm) wide
£200-300   **WW**

FURNITURE

Judith Picks

For some time these heavy, carved, solid-oak armchairs were out of fashion – but no longer. A chair of this size and elaborate carving would have been made for an important nobleman. In its period, the early 17thC, chairs were still a status symbol. (In the medieval period the person of highest status had the chair – everyone else either sat on benches or stood. That is why we have the term chairman.)

The carving on this example is deep and accomplished. The colour (a very important element when assessing period oak) is rich and warm. From the style of the chair it would seem to hail from the West Country.

If you like the style but not the price there are a large number of 19thC copies, which are a fraction of the cost but unlikely to appreciate in value as much as a good period chair such as this.

A Charles I West Country carved oak armchair, the back with stylised fleur-de-lys frieze and arcaded guilloche panel, with guilloche-decorated seat rail on turned legs with stretchers, on block feet with gros point needlework loose cushion.

£4,000-6,000   **H&L**

An early 17thC Italian Renaissance walnut armchair, Rome, with turned armrests and supports, with leather upholstered seat and backrest with gold brocade border.

£5,000-7,000   **DOR**

A Charles II probably Derbyshire carved oak armchair, the back with central tulip flanked by leafy scrollwork above a geometric flower head and scrolling flower head frieze panel, on turned legs with strethers, on block feet.

£5,000-7,000   **H&L**

A Charles II and later oak panel-back chair.

£2,000-3,000   **DN**

A late 17thC and later possibly Gloucestershire carved oak panel-back armchair, the back carved with an arcade centred with stylised foliage, with down-scroll arms and an arcaded frieze, on conforming supports and stretchers.

£5,000-7,000   **WW**

A late 17thC oak chair, with carved panelled back and solid seat, on bun feet.

£2,500-3,500   **GORL**

A tall 18thC Baroque gilded armchair, carved with ornament and rocaille, the backrest with an armorial cresting in the form of a double eagle, with later upholstery.

£8,000-12,000   **DOR**

A pair of matched Italian 18thC Baroque gilded armchairs, Venice, carved with ornament and rocaille, with later and removable upholstery on the seats and backrests.

£10,000-15,000   **DOR**

An early 18thC and later walnut and needlework-upholstered armchair.

£800-1,200   DN

An early 18thC Continental open armchair, with carved walnut arms, turned supports and conforming front legs with H-stretcher, replacements.

£200-300   WW

A George I walnut and burr walnut shepherd's crook armchair, with shell-carved knees and claw-and-ball feet.
c1720

£5,000-7,000   DN

A Delaware Valley Queen Anne walnut armchair, the yoke crest above a vasiform splat and slip seat, on cabriole legs with slipper feet.
c1745

£3,000-4,000   POOK

A pair of Louis XVI giltwood armchairs, with lavender and gold upholstery in a Neo-classical French design.
38in (96cm) high

£3,000-4,000   LHA

A set of four 18thC Italian gilded armchairs, Genoa, the hardwood chairs with serpentine sides and laurel wreath decoration, with fluted bands, with later upholstery.

£35,000-45,000 set

DOR

A pair of Louis XVI giltwood fauteuils, with striped yellow Scalamandré upholstery with green foliate banding throughout.
38in (96cm) high

£3,000-4,000   LHA

An 18thC Continental parcel gilt and upholstered armchair, with pierced C-scroll cresting, on shell- and foliate-carved cabriole legs united by a conforming wavy apron.

£3,000-4,000   L&T

A George II mahogany and petit point-upholstered library chair, on leaf-carved cabriole legs.
c1750

£8,000-12,000   DN

A Georgian mahogany open arm chair, carved with honeysuckle motifs and scrolls, on carved scrolling legs.

£500-700   A&G

FURNITURE

CLOSER LOOK - "GAINSBOROUGH" ARMCHAIR

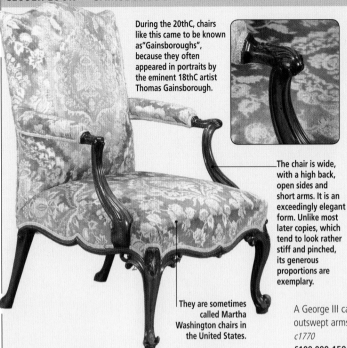

During the 20thC, chairs like this came to be known as"Gainsboroughs", because they often appeared in portraits by the eminent 18thC artist Thomas Gainsborough.

Contemporaries referred to it as a "French chair", as the most elaborate styles were based on French Rococo chairs from the Louis XV period.

The chair is wide, with a high back, open sides and short arms. It is an exceedingly elegant form. Unlike most later copies, which tend to look rather stiff and pinched, its generous proportions are exemplary.

The huge desirability is further enhanced by masterful foliate carving on the mahogany arms and cabriole legs.

They are sometimes called Martha Washington chairs in the United States.

A George III carved mahogany "Gainsborough" armchair, with carved outswept arms and slender carved cabriole legs.
c1770
£100,000-150,000   DN

An 18thC Chippendale-style painted armchair, with carved and pierced back support, arms and drop-in seat, on square fluted and tapering forelegs with block feet with understretcher.
£3,500-4,500   TEN

A Delaware Valley Queen Anne walnut armchair, with a shell-carved crest and solid splat above a slip seat, on shell-carved cabriole legs with trifid feet.
c1760
£5,000-7,000   POOK

A George III mahogany open armchair, upholstered in pale green damask, padded arms on spiral fluted supports, on moulded cabriole legs carved with foliage and berries.
£1,000-1,500   H&L

A pair of George III Chinese Chippendale-style mahogany cockpen open armchairs, with pierced fret-cut back and downswept arms, and drop-in seats, on square, chamfered legs with H-stretchers.
£5,000-7,000   TEN

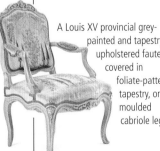

A Louis XV provincial grey-painted and tapestry-upholstered fauteuil, covered in foliate-pattern tapestry, on moulded cabriole legs.

Provenance: Baron Necker, part of a suite made for the Chateau Crans, Lake Geneva.
c1780
£1,000-1,500   L&T

A pair of George III Gillows mahogany and caned open armchairs, with upholstered cushions.
c1780
£10,000-15,000   DN

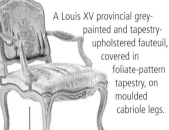

A late 18thC Italian Transition-style gilded armchair, Naples, carved ornament with portrait medallion in the frieze, with loose linen base covers, restoration.
£4,000-6,000   DOR

A set of four late 18thC French Louis XVI walnut-veneered armchairs, on conical fluted legs, with rich gilt grooved decoration, later loose upholstery.
£6,000-8,000   DOR

A pair of 19thC Swedish gilt-painted tub chairs, upholstered in striped fabric, the stiff leaf-shaped top rail between reeded downswept supports, with carved seat rail, on square, tapering front legs with hoof feet.
£2,500-3,500   TEN

Four of a set of ten Regency armchairs, painted in dark green, the scroll crest rail with parcel gilt Greek-key banding above a curule-form splat centred by a white-painted harlequin bust vignette, each caned seat with tufted champagne silk damask loose cushion, restoration.
c1815
£12,000-18,000 set   WES

CLOSER LOOK - RUSSIAN EMPIRE ARMCHAIR

Much of the style of Russian Empire was based on French Neo-classicism, particularly the work of Georges Jacob (1739-1814).

The style was popularised by the publication of La Mesangere's pattern book "Meubles et objets de gout" in 1802.

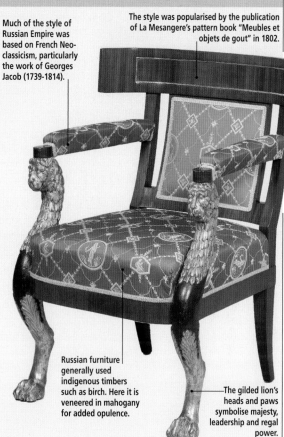

Russian furniture generally used indigenous timbers such as birch. Here it is veneered in mahogany for added opulence.

The gilded lion's heads and paws symbolise majesty, leadership and regal power.

An early 19thC Russian Empire Neo-classical mahogany veneered armchair, with carved and gilded front legs in the form of lion's heads and paws, with upholstered seat and backrest, with later covers.
£6,000-8,000   DOR

ESSENTIAL REFERENCE - THE ROYAL PAVILION

The Royal Pavilion, also known as the Brighton Pavilion after the English seaside town in which it was built, was designed for the then Prince of Wales, later Prince Regent, later George IV.

● Originally a farmhouse, it was redesigned in 1786 by Henry Holland as a Neo-classical marine pavilion. In the early 19thC the structure was extended, and a massive Indian-style stable block, designed by William Pordern, was built.

● In 1815, John Nash was hired to transform it into the Indo-Saracenic-style palace it is today.

● John C. Crace (1754-1819) was hired in 1788 to provide Chinese furniture, porcelain and other objects for the Pavilion. Between 1815 and 1822 his son Frederick (1779-1859) designed and executed the exotic chinoserie and Indian-style decorations of the main rooms, with the help of painter Robert Jones.

● George's sucessor, William IV continued to use the Pavillion, but Queen Victoria disliked it.

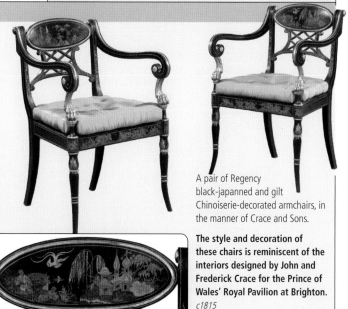

A pair of Regency black-japanned and gilt Chinoiserie-decorated armchairs, in the manner of Crace and Sons.

The style and decoration of these chairs is reminiscent of the interiors designed by John and Frederick Crace for the Prince of Wales' Royal Pavilion at Brighton.
c1815
£4,000-6,000   DN

FURNITURE

ESSENTIAL REFERENCE - HENRY PETERS

Henry Peters (d.1852) was an English cabinetmaker who arrived in Genoa in 1817. His pieces were predominantly inspired by the Regency style, but he also made Empire and Restauration pieces, working both for the court in Genoa and for middle-class patrons.

- He favoured mahogany, Indian walnut and boxwood in particular.
- He completed pieces of furniture for the Palazzo Reale and the Villa Durazzo dello Zerbino in Genoa, and the Palazzo Reale in Turin.
- In 1835, Peters was nominated "Maker of the Court" (of the house of Savoy) after completing a commission for the Palazzo Reale.

A pair of North Italian walnut and parcel gilt open armchairs, by Henry Thomas Peters, Genoa, with ornate shell and foliate scroll-carved bar-backs, the overstuffed seats in studded gold fabric, on reeded, turned, tapered legs, stamped "Peters Maker Genoa".
c1840
£4,500-5,500 L&T

A pair of Anglo-Indian rosewood open armchairs, with palmette-carved splats, the scrolling downswept arms above stuffed-over seats covered in buttoned suede, raised on reeded, turned, tapering legs.
c1830
£4,000-6,000 L&T

An Anglo-Indian carved hardwood library armchair, upholstered in floral patterned gold fabric, the top rail carved with fruit and foliage, on acanthus-carved scroll legs terminating in brass castors.

c1840
£600-800 L&T

A 19thC late 18thC-style carved walnut armchair.
£150-250 DN

A 19thC Italian specimen wood and bone-inlaid throne chair, on reeded and fluted legs united by an H-stretcher, on compressed bun feet.

52in (132cm) high
£350-450 TEN

A Victorian turned walnut open armchair, with a serpentine front seat.
£250-350 WW

A pair of 19thC French Regence-style open armchairs, with shaped tapestry-covered backs, padded arms and overstuffed seats, frames carved with shells and acanthus scrolls, on cabriole legs with scroll feet.
£3,500-4,500 DN

A pair of mid-19thC French armchairs, painted in white and gilded, with later upholstery, one piece indistinctly stamped "Jeanselme".

"Jeanselme" was an important 19thC French dynasty of cabinet makers. This stamp indicates a date from the period 1840-1853.

£6,000-8,000   DOR

A Victorian carved rosewood "Master of the Hunt" parlour armchair, the oval padded backrest within a frame carved with a stag hunt and oak leaves, acorns and C-scrolls, with boar's head hand-holds, hunt-themed still-life to apron, on cabriole legs with castors.

c1860   *44.5in (113cm) high*

£3,000-4,000   SK

A late 19thC 17thC-style French carved walnut and upholstered armchair, the arms carved with lion's masks.

£700-1,000   DN

A Henri II-style walnut open armchair, the tapestry-upholstered back and seat within carved scrolling arms, on turned legs with stretchers.

49.25in (126cm) high

£800-1,200   LHA

A pair of late 19thC walnut fauteuils, upholstered in cream and floral damask, with a scrolling leaf-carved top rail above outswept arms, on cabriole fore legs with scrolling toes.

37in (94.5cm) high

£1,000-1,500 pair   TEN

A set of four late 19thC French carved walnut fauteuils, with oval caned backs, padded scroll arms and cane seats, two damaged and with later applied covers.

£700-1,000   WW

A Henri II-style open armchair, with needlepoint-upholstered square back and seat within carved scrolling arms, on carved scrolling legs with X-form stretchers.

46.5in (118cm) high

£600-800   LHA

An American carved beechwood "Evolution" chair, the padded back flanked by carved Neanderthals above scroll arms and monkey supports, on foliate legs and a twin-beast front stretcher.

This chair is a reference to the 1925 trial of American high school teacher John T. Scope, who was accused of violating Tennessee's Butler Act, which made it unlawful to teach evolution. The trial drew intense national publicity, with reporters flocking to the small town of Dayton. William Jennings Bryan, (three-time Presidential candidate for the Democrats) argued for the prosecution, while the famed defence attorney Clarence Darrow spoke for Scopes. Scopes was found guilty, but the verdict was overturned on a technicality and he was never brought back to trial.

£700-1,000   WW

FURNITURE

ESSENTIAL REFERENCE - BERGÈRE ARMCHAIRS

The bergère armchair was first made in France in the 18thC. It features an upholstered back, or back and sides made from cane, and a deep seat, typically with a tailored squab cushion. It was light, which meant it could be moved around the room, rather than being kept against the walls as part of the décor.

● It was designed for lounging in comfort, and consequently has a deeper and wider seat than the typical French armchair (fauteuil).

● In the UK and US the term "bergère" generally refers to pieces with caned back and sides.

A pair of Regency mahogany bergère armchairs, with cane backs, sides and seats, with leaf-carved uprights and scrolling downswept arms, flower-carved spandrels, on sabre forelegs.

36in (91.5cm) high

£2,500-3,500   **TEN**

A late George III mahogany bergère armchair, with cane back, seat and sides, on turned tapering spindle supports and forelegs.

34in (86.5cm) high

£600-800   **TEN**

A Regency ebonised and parcel gilt bergère armchair, with cane back, sides and seat, on inverted sabre legs, with much of the original black and yellow gilt paint remaining.

35in (90cm) high

£2,000-3,000   **TEN**

A Regency mahogany and leather-upholstered library armchair, the caned back and padded arms above a loose, buttoned, cushion seat, on turned tapered legs.

c1830

£1,000-1,500   **L&T**

A George IV rosewood bergère library chair, with flared cresting rail above acanthus leaf-carved scrolling arm terminals, on turned tapering legs with castors.

£1,500-2,500   **A&G**

A mid-19thC mahogany bergère, with cane-filled arched overscrolled back and seat, padded arms on lotus- and acanthus-carved scroll supports, on decagonal baluster front legs with brass castors.

£600-800   **H&L**

An Edwardian mahogany bergère armchair, with caned back and seat, with carved husk decoration.

£80-120   **WW**

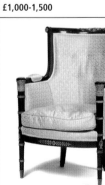

An Empire-style mahogany and gilt metal-mounted bergère, with cream upholstery and reeded columnar-form legs, with gilt metal mounts.

41in (104cm) high

£700-1,000   **LHA**

A George II mahogany easy chair, with serpentine crest and outward flaring wings, on cabriole legs with pad feet.

c1740

£3,000-5,000   POOK

A part-18thC George II-style carved walnut wing-frame armchair, upholstered in Dralon velvet, on shell- and scroll-decorated cabriole front legs with claw-and-ball feet.

£700-1,000   H&L

A red velvet-covered and upholstered throne chair, the back with applied 18thC raised needlework quartered coat of arms, with loose seat cushion, on X-form supports with stretchers.

46in (117cm) high

£1,500-2,500   L&T

ESSENTIAL REFERENCE - BIEDERMEIER

Biedermeier was a decorative style produced in Germany, Austria and Scandinavia mainly between c1805 and 1850.

- A simplified version of the French Empire style, it featured simple, clean lines and geometric shapes in light coloured woods. Elaborate ornamentation was eschewed in favour of large areas of flat veneer that showed off the grain of the wood. Upholstery was flat and square.
- Much Biedermeier furniture was made anonymously, although pieces are known by leading makers such as Josef Danhauser (1780-1829) of Vienna.
- It was primarily a middle-class style, but was also used in the private areas of some noble houses.
- By the mid-19thC, the style had begun to seem dowdy and was given the derogative name "Biedermeier", derived from a satirical term meaning "the decent, if slightly dull common man". However, it was revived in the early 20thC.

A George III and later mahogany and leather barrell-back arm chair.

c1770

£2,500-3,500   DN

A pair of Regency rosewood tub armchairs, with scrolling foliate inlay above green upholstered back and enclosed arms ending in scrolling handholds, on curved forelegs.

32.5in (83.5cm) high

£6,000-8,000   FRE

A William IV button-back upholstered library chair, on turned rosewood front legs, the front brass castors stamped "J.W. Lewty's patent", replaced back castors.

£300-400   WW

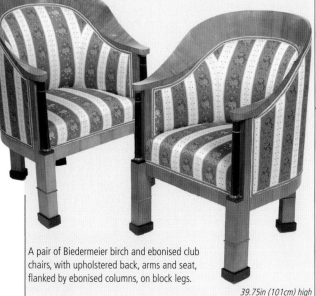

A pair of Biedermeier birch and ebonised club chairs, with upholstered back, arms and seat, flanked by ebonised columns, on block legs.

39.75in (101cm) high

£4,000-6,000   LHA

A William IV mahogany and leather buttoned upholstered adjustable armchair, bearing retailers ivorine plaque "LEVESON & SONS 19 OXFORD ST. W.C."

c1840

£2,500-3,500   DN

An early 19thC mahogany wing-frame armchair, upholstered, with splayed front legs with turned stretchers and castors.

£2,500-3,500   H&L

A 19thC Continental carved mahogany-frame armchair, with gadrooned top rail and shaped, upholstered, overstuffed sides and serpentine seat, on gadrooned and foliate-carved cabriole legs with scroll feet.

£350-450   H&L

A 19thC Empire-style green painted and parcel gilt tub-shaped armchair.

£3,000-4,000   DN

A pair of 19thC George I-style wing-back armchairs, upholstered in red velvet, with scrolling flared arm rests and squab cushions, on scrolling cabriole forelegs with hoof feet and wavy understretcher.

47in (119cm) high

£3,000-4,000   TEN

A Victorian button-back nursing chair, with rosewood scroll frame, on mahogany cabriole legs.

£100-150   WW

A Victorian carved walnut nursing chair.

£150-250   WW

A Victorian mahogany and upholstered tub armchair, with turned armfacing and ball finials, on baluster-turned legs terminating in brass caps and castors.

c1860

£500-700   L&T

A Victorian carved walnut and button-back upholstered armchair.

c1875

£250-350   DN

A Victorian leather upholstered armchair, covered in buttoned brown leather, on squat turned tapered legs ending in brass caps and castors.

c1880

£3,000-4,000   L&T

A pair of Victorian leather upholstered armchairs, in buttoned brown leather, on squat turned, tapered legs with brass caps and castors.
c1880
£5,000-7,000 L&T

A pair of late 19thC Continental beechwood tub armchairs, on ebonised square, tapering front supports, damages.
£250-350 WW

A late Victorian armchair, with worn and miss-matched upholstery, on turned supports with ceramic castors.
£40-60 WW

A late 19thC Queen Anne-style wing armchair, upholstered in cream silk damask, the squab cushion above a plain seat rail, on cabriole forelegs with scrolling feet and toes.
49in (124.5cm) high
£1,200-1,800 TEN

A late 19thC French Louis XVI-style walnut open armchair, the frame carved with trophies and acanthus leaf decoration, on turned fluted legs.
£500-700 GORL

One of a pair of early 20thC 17thC-style walnut and upholstered wing armchairs, covered in tapestry and striped fabric, on cabriole legs with wavy stretchers, with a pair of matching foot stools.
£2,500-3,500 pair L&T

An early 20thC George III-style mahogany wing armchair, on leaf-carved cabriole front legs and claw-and-ball feet.
£250-350 WW

An early 20thC Queen Anne-style wing armchair, on short walnut cabriole legs and a turned and block H-stretcher.
£600-800 WW

An early 20thC 18thC-style wing armchair, on cabriole legs and claw-and-ball feet.
£500-700 WW

FURNITURE

An 18thC Italian Rococo gilt carved softwood chair, Naples, the front with an angel's head, small losses.

This masterpiece is an outstanding example of Neapolitan furniture making, which stands more as a piece of sculpture than furniture.

55in (140cm) high

£20,000-30,000　　　　　　　　　　　　　**DOR**

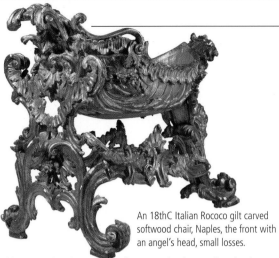

A Regency mahogany metamorphic library chair, attributed to Morgan & Stanley, with cane back and seat, on reeded sabre legs, the whole hinging open to reveal four leather inset treads.

c1810

£6,000-8,000　　　　　　　　　　　　　　**L&T**

A George IV mahogany metamorphic library armchair, attributed to Gillows, reeded and with shell carving, with original red leather squab seat, originally with caned seat.

The chair is stamped "H.H." on the front rail. Although H.H. has never been fully identified, it is generally accepted as the mark of the journeyman Henry Holmes. This example is part of a distinct group of furniture with strong connections to the Gillows workshops. The reeded sabre legs conform to the "Hackwood Variant" seen in the 1823 Gillows, Lancaster sketch book.

£6,000-8,000　　　　　　　　　　　　　　**A&G**

A rare Italian walnut metamorphic armchair, with pierced demi-lune fan-shaped splat, on turned, tapered legs, the whole opening to reveal an oval table.

c1820　　　　　*Chair 32in (81cm) high*

£2,500-3,500　　　　　　　　　　　　　　**L&T**

A Victorian mahogany revolving music seat, the rounded fret-cut back support with scrolling leaf-carved splat, upholstered in green floral velvet, on a turned mahogany support with brass collar and four scrolling legs.

32in (81cm) high

£700-1,000　　　　　　　　　　　　　　　**TEN**

A Victorian carved mahogany invalid's chair, by S. Heath, Bath.

£250-350　　　　　　　　　　　　　　　**GORL**

A 19thC Continental carved walnut throne armchair, incorporating earlier elements, the crest rail carved with a crown flanked by putti, the central panel with a heraldic crest and male and female profiles, with gryphon-carved arms.

80in (203cm) high

£500-700　　　　　　　　　　　　　　　**FRE**

A late 19thC stained pine Orkney chair, the curved woven rush back between two upright supports and two armrests, with drop-in seat, on square tapering legs with stretcher.

41in (104cm) high

£400-600　　　　　　　　　　　　　　　**TEN**

An Edwardian Regency-style mahogany rotating adjustable cello chair.

£400-600　　　　　　　　　　　　　　　**DN**

An 18thC and later walnut chair-back settee, repairs.
c1730   *59in (150cm) wide*
£2,500-3,500   **DN**

A mid 18thC Italian sofa and four chairs, Venice area, the shaped and carved walnut seats with later seat and backrest upholstery, with some ageing and wear.
£10,000-15,000   **DOR**

A George III carved mahogany serpentine sofa, in the French Hepplewhite style, with moulded frame and cabriole legs.
c1700   *79in (200cm) wide*
£5,000-7,000   **DN**

A possibly American carved mahogany camel-back sofa.
c1800   *74in (188cm) wide*
£2,000-3,000   **SK**

Judith Picks

While Victorian style is still out of fashion, the Regency style of the early 19thC is very much in vogue. Of course, a chaise longue is not the most comfortable piece of seating furniture, but it does add an unmistakable sense of opulence and style to a room.

This piece is affordable, but does require reupholstery, which is not inexpensive. Depending how much work you want the upholsterer to do, this could easily cost £700-1,000+. It would look more dramatic with a typical Regency fabric, a stripe or a repeating pattern such as the Napoleonic bee, a laurel wreath, or Josephine's swan in gilt on a strong blue, red or green background.

A Regency mahogany and brass-strung settee, upholstered in grey and cream velvet Dralon, with reeded and turned top rail, the scrolling and turned end supports with ebony- and brass-inlaid tablets, on reeded tapering legs with castors.
86in (218cm) long
£2,000-3,000   **TEN**

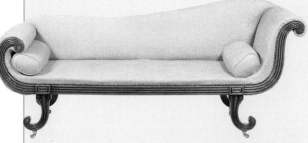

A Regency mahogany framed chaise longue, upholstered in close-nailed bottle-green floral damask, with scrolling end supports, the reeded frame with rectangular spandrels, on scrolling legs with brass caps and castors.
83in (210.5cm) long
£600-800   **TEN**

A New England Federal carved and wavy birch-inlaid mahogany sofa, refinished.
c1810-15   *71in (180cm) wide*
£1,000-1,500   **SK**

A 19thC mahogany settee, the shaped and rounded upholstered panel back continuing into downswept arms, on square, tapered legs with spade feet.

60in (152.5cm) long

£500-700   H&L

A 19thC French cream-painted canapé, upholstered in cream fruit-design silk, the moulded guilloche frame with reeded arms above a squab cushion, on stop-fluted and reeded legs.

79in (200cm) long

£3,000-4,000   TEN

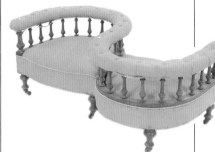

A Victorian walnut conversational settee, with turned baluster spiral supports.

56in (142cm) long

£300-400   WW

A Victorian Chesterfield settee, with later Dralon button upholstery, on turned walnut legs with later brass castors.

79in (200cm) wide

£150-250   WW

A 19thC mahogany framed and upholstered settee, leg broken.

66in (167.5cm) wide

£2,000-3,000   DN

A late 19thC George II-style mahogany and upholstered settee, covered in cream foliate-patterned fabric, on carved cabriole legs with paw feet.

84in (213cm) wide

£6,000-8,000   L&T

A late 19thC French Louis XV-style salon seating group, carved and gilded, with silk covers embroidered with birds and flowers.

Bench 83in (210cm) wide

£12,000-18,000   DOR

A late 19thC Sheraton-revival painted satinwood sofa, with padded back, seat and arms and floral-painted front rail and tapered square legs.

72in (182.5cm) wide

£1,500-2,500   DN

A French walnut settee, the moulded and carved frame upholstered with green fabric on fluted tapering legs,

c1900   56in (142cm) wide

£700-1,000   WW

An Edwardian red leather Chesterfield sofa, the overstuffed deep-buttoned back and high enclosed scroll arms over a button-upholstered seat, on square tapered legs and castors.

80in (203cm) long

£1,500-2,500   FRE

A 17thC Spanish walnut refectory table, the rectangular single plank top above an entablature frieze with four drawers, each with leaf-carved rosettes, on eight turned and bracket supports with stretchers, decorated with foliate carving.

145in (368cm) long

£20,000-30,000   L&T

One of a pair of 17thC and later carved oak refectory tables.

Possibly adapted from one larger table. Very large refectory tables are often adapted as they do not fit in today's interiors.

31.5in (80cm) high

£8,000-12,000 pair   DN

A large 17thC French oak refectory table, with a five plank top, above X-supports joined by a stretcher.

Purchased in France from an abbey by the Bethlehem Steel Corporation.

186in (472.5cm) long

£20,000-30,000   POOK

An elm and oak refectory table, the rounded three-plank top above a plain frieze, on six column gun-barrel legs with stretchers.

By repute from a monastery in Wiltshire.

119in (302cm) long

£6,000-8,000   TEN

A 17thC joined oak dining table, the three-plank rectangular top above a moulded and carved frieze, raised on gun-barrel supports united by a peripheral stretcher.

56in (143cm) long

£1,500-2,500   TEN

A 17thC oak refectory table.

During the 17thC walnut was often used for southern European refectory tables and court pieces, but oak predominated in central and northern Europe. The carving on these tables, particularly towards the beginning of the century, was bold, individual and well-executed.

29in (74cm) wide

£8,000-12,000   DN

A Charles II-style oak refectory table, the rectangular top with foldover leaves over frieze drawers, on turned legs and square block feet.

64in (162cm) long

£800-1,200   FRE

A 17thC-style oak refectory table.

85in (216cm) long

£300-400   DN

FURNITURE

An 18thC oak gate-leg table, with an oval drop-leaf top above later frieze drawer, one end tipped, both flaps with strengthening supports.

51.5in (131cm) long open
£300-400   **WW**

A Pennsylvania William & Mary walnut gate-leg table, with two demi-lune drop leaves, the frame with two drawers, on turned baluster legs.

A William and Mary walnut gate-leg table, the moulded oval top above two lateral frieze drawers, on baluster turned legs with trefoil scroll feet.

54in (138cm) long open
£2,500-3,500   **L&T**

c1740
£1,500-2,500

48in (122cm) wide
POOK

An 18thC oval oak gate-leg table, with a hinged top, with a drawer stamped with initials "I. D.", on baluster turned uprights with stretchers, with turned feet.

50.25in (127.5cm) long open
£400-600   **H&L**

A George III and later mahogany triple-pillar dining table, the reeded-edge tilt-tops on ring turned barrel stems, on reeded downswept legs, with brass caps and castors.

116in (295cm) long
£12,000-18,000   **WW**

A late George III mahogany triple-pillar dining table, with two leaf insertions, with reeded edge, on turned column supports with reeded downswept legs with brass caps and castors.

c1810   *50in (127cm) long*
£7,000-10,000   **L&T**

A mahogany triple-pedestal dining table, with one additional leaf insertion, the top and base probably associated.

c1815 and later   *28in (71cm) high*
£1,000-1,500   **DN**

A 19thC George III-style mahogany pedestal dining table, with D-ends and two leaves, with reeded edge, two baluster pedestals, on reeded outswept legs with brass cappings and castors.

100in (254cm) long
£3,500-4,500   **FRE**

An 18thC and later mahogany triangular drop-leaf table, the hinged top with re-entrant corners.

33in (85cm) long

£400-600   WW

A George III mahogany "wake" table, with two conforming D-shaped drop leaves, on plain square legs, restorations.

69in (175cm) long

£3,000-4,000   TEN

An Irish Georgian mahogany hunt table, with rounded drop-leaf sides, on square-section supports.

100in (254cm) long

£7,000-10,000   ROS

A George III mahogany drop-flap table, on square legs with brass castors.

48in (122cm) long

£450-550   H&L

Judith Picks: A Georgian Table

There are still bargains to be had. Admittedly this is a rather plain and not particularly attractive oak drop-leaf table but, look on the bright side, it is solid wood. It will last for easily another 200 years. The same cannot be said for the flat-pack MDF alternatives that will cost even more.

Due to the popularity of Scandinavian (Gustavian) furniture, many interior designers are buying up furniture such as this table and giving it a more appealing look by painting it off-white. As it has honest age, it is worth closely examining painted furniture to ensure the paint is original to the piece and not new paint that has been slightly distressed.

A late George III oak drop-leaf table, on moulded square supports, restoration.

56.5in (143.5cm) long open

£50-70   WW

A Regency mahogany drop-flap extending dining table, with moulded edge, on turned and reeded tapered legs with brass cappings and castors, with additional centre leaf.

67in (170cm) long

£600-800   **H&L**

A late George III mahogany extending dining table, with reeded edge, on six turned legs with brass caps and castors, with three additional leaves.

121in (307cm) long

£2,500-3,500   **TEN**

A Regency mahogany extending dining table, the round-cornered top on a gate-leg frame, on turned and reeded legs with castors, with three additional leaves.

104in (264cm) long

£2,500-3,500   **TEN**

A Regency mahogany extending dining table, with two hinged drop-leaves, on a centre platform support with four hipped, reeded legs with hairy-paw feet and castors, the pull-out section on plain tapering legs with toupie feet.

88in (223.5cm) long

£3,000-4,000   **TEN**

An early 19thC mahogany extending table, the D-shape ends with telescopic frames and three additional leaves, on ring-turned legs with brass caps and castors, restoration.

102in (259cm) long

£1,500-2,500   **WW**

A George IV mahogany extending dining table, in the manner of Gillows, with two additional leaf insertions.

c1825   *97in (246.5cm) long overall*

£1,500-2,500   **DN**

A George IV mahogany dining table, with moulded edge, on six ring-turned and spiral tapering legs with brass caps and castors, with six additional leaves and storage cabinet.

236in (600cm) long

£20,000-30,000   **TEN**

A late George IV mahogany extending dining table, with moulded edge, on four turned and reeded legs with brass toes and castors, with five additional leaves and storage cabinet.

170in (432cm) long extended

£12,000-18,000   **TEN**

CLOSER LOOK - AUSTRIAN REVIVAL EXTENDING TABLE

Bernhard Ludwig's workshops in Vienna undertook many important commissions in the late 19thC, including work on Peles Castle for Prince Carol of Hohenzollern Sigmaringen, who was the ruler of Romania.

Ludwig was highly regarded for his ebonised work, shown here on the mouldings.

The walnut and burr walnut veneers are of the highest quality.

A late 19thC Austrian Revival extending table, by Bernhard Ludwig, Vienna, with snail-shaped carved mounts, missing extension leaves and extra supporting leg.

This extending table comes from a dining suite which, based on the execution and the quality of the workmanship as well as the date of production, was probably made for the 1873 World Exhibition in Vienna.

The marquetry decoration on the frieze and legs is exquisite and adds credence to the idea that this was made for the World Exhibition.

c1870-5   236in (600cm) long extended
£10,000-15,000   DOR

One of a pair of mid-19thC mahogany D-end-shaped dining table end sections, with reeded edge and frieze, tapering reeded legs with brass castors, lacking extension leaves.

58in (147cm) long
£4,000-6,000 pair   H&L

A 19thC mahogany D-end extending dining table, the two rectangular centre sections each with a drop leaf and with additional leaf, on square tapered legs with spade feet.

167in (424.5cm) long extended
£5,000-7,000   H&L

A Victorian mahogany extending dining table, with four leaf insertions, with plain frieze, on reeded turned tapered legs with brass caps and castors.

c1880   153.5in (390cm) long extended
£6,000-8,000   L&T

A 19thC mahogany extending dining table, with D-ends and two extra leaves, with central column, two leaves and castors later.

96in (244cm) wide
£1,500-2,500   WW

An early 19thC Anglo-Indian carved padouk oval dining table, with a bead-moulded edge and later scalloped frieze, on carved pineapple-form support and pierced base, with four dragon feet.

100in (254cm) long
£5,000-7,000   L&T

A probably Harvard, Massachusetts Shaker cherry and pine red-painted trestle table, alterations.

c1830   78in (198cm) long
£5,000-7,000   SK

A George III mahogany and satinwood breakfast table, faults.

c1800   *61in (155cm) diam*
£2,000-2,500   **DN**

A George IV parcel-gilt and brass-mounted rosewood breakfast table, the frieze applied with anthemion leaf and scrolling vine brass banding, with trefoil platform base with brass inlaid stringing on gilt-winged animal-paw feet.

c1820   *54.25in (138cm) diam*
£12,000-18,000   **WES**

A Regency rosewood and foliate-cut brass-inlaid breakfast table.

5in (130cm) diam
£3,500-4,500   **GORL**

A George IV rosewood and satinwood parquetry breakfast table, the tilt top with radiating veneers centred by a star motif, with four hipped sabre legs with paw feet and counter-sunk castors, top and base probably associated.

c1825   *52in (132cm) diam*
£5,000-7,000   **L&T**

An early Victorian rosewood circular breakfast table, with moulded edge, on turned and lobed bulbous support with acanthus leaf-carved and scrolling cabriole legs with shell feet and brass castors.

51in (130cm) diam
£2,500-3,500   **TEN**

An early Victorian rosewood tip-top breakfast table, by Gillows of Lancaster, the circular top with a moulded bead-and-reel border above a baluster column carved with acanthus leaves and a reeded band, raised on three carved cabriole legs terminating in claw feet.

54in (138cm) diam
£8,000-10,000   **TOV**

A mid-19thC Anglo-Indian padouk breakfast table, with gadrooned edge and rosette and acanthus leaf-carved frieze, the central reeded pillar flanked by three reeded and stiff-leaf-carved scrolling uprights, on three voluted lion's paw feet.

59in (150cm) diam
£1,000-1,500   **L&T**

A large Iberian carved walnut centre table, with a pair of leaf- and flower head-carved drawers and opposing dummy drawers, on baluster-turned legs with stretchers and bun feet.

c1700   *73in (185cm) long*

£8,000-12,000   **L&T**

ESSENTIAL REFERENCE - CENTRE TABLES

Although it might be used for a variety of activities, a true centre table is essentially designed only to furnish the space in the middle of a room.

- During the 18thC the most prestigious items of furniture were placed around the side of the room. The centre table became more fashionable in the early 19thC.
- Most are circular, although other shapes are not uncommon.
- Typical early 19thC examples were of light mahogany, inlaid with Classical patterns.
- Victorian centre tables were made from walnut, mahogany and oak. They were often heavily carved and could be embellished with floral marquetry, exotic timbers, specimen marbles, porcelain plaques or paint.

A George III mahogany centre table, with plain frieze, on moulded square legs with pierced angle brackets and block feet.

c1765   *60in (153cm) wide*

£5,000-7,000   **L&T**

An early 19thC Austro-Hungarian Empire mahogany and cherry veneered table, the column support with *verde antico* decoration and gilded sphinxes, the hinged top with painted India-ink border.

This table is typical of pieces produced by the Danhauser factory.

c1800   *39in (99cm) diam*

£150,000-300,000   **DOR**

A George IV amboyna and mahogany centre table, the tilt top with radiating veneers above applied lunettes to the frieze, with turned tapering column on carved platform base on egg-and-dart carved feet, on castors.

c1825   *54in (138cm) diam*

£8,000-12,000   **DN**

An early-mid 19thC Continental rosewood and tulipwood crossbanded centre table.

      29in (73.5cm) high

£3,000-4,000   **DN**

A Philadelphia mahogany centre table, the top with radiating panels of crotch mahogany veneer tilting above a faceted standard, on triangular base with animal-paw feet, on castors.

c1830   *48in (122cm) diam*

£3,000-4,000   **POOK**

A George IV rosewood centre table, the tilt top over a tapered hexagonal column on a triform base, on raised, carved claw feet.

54in (138cm) diam

£5,000-7,000   **FRE**

A 19thC Continental carved oak centre table, the oval top with a branch-carved frieze, base modelled as a tree trunk with brass caps and castors.

44in (111.5cm) long

£3,500-4,500   **L&T**

A large 19thC carved giltwood and gesso marble-topped centre table, the shaped aprons with carved shells and foliate-scroll corners, on leaf-carved moulded cabriole legs with hairy hoof feet.

57in (145.5cm) long

£5,000-7,000   **L&T**

A 19thC early 18thC-style Italian ivory-painted and carved giltwood centre table, with an inset marble top; redecorated.

75.25in (191cm) long

£100,000-200,000   **SOTH**

A Victorian walnut, marquetry and ormolu-mounted centre table, the baluster stem and base with three carved downswept legs on lion's paw feet.

c1870   *51in (130cm) diam*

£10,000-15,000   **DN**

A late Victorian Adam-design carved mahogany serving table, with three frieze drawers, the middle drawer with an urn, griffins and foliage, on fluted tapered legs.

72in (183cm) long

£3,000-4,000   **GORL**

A French giltwood and Sèvres-style centre table, the central roundel depicting Louis XVI, on squat cabriole legs with paw feet and carved foliate swags.

31.5in (80cm) diam

£8,000-12,000   **LHA**

An early 18thC Italian carved and gilded console table, probably Rome or Florence, with later yellowish scagliola top, some restoration.

73in (185.5cm) long

£40,000-60,000   DOR

A pair of 18thC Italian overpainted and gilded console tables, with serpentine marble tops above leaf- and C-scroll carved friezes, on embellished cabriole supports terminating in hoof feet.

41in (104cm) high

£2,500-3,500   L&T

ESSENTIAL REFERENCE - NEO-CLASSICAL STYLE

The Neo-classical style developed in France in the 1750s and spread throughout Europe. It was conceived partly as a reaction against the Rococo style and partly as a result of the increased interest in the Classical style as a result of the excavations of Herculaneum (1738) and Pompeii (1748).

● Rectilinear furniture, which featured architectural forms, such as pediments on mirror frames, was common in the 1750s. A lighter style, which used grotesques, festoons, husks, ribbons and medallions, became popular in the 1760s–70s.

● Scottish architect and cabinet-maker Robert Adam was one of the leading exponents of this variation.

● In the early 19thC, the Neo-classical style developed into the more elaborate Regency style (in Britain), the relaxed Biedermeier style (in Germany), the Federal style (in the US), and the Empire style (in France, Sweden and Russia).

One of a pair of late 18thC Neo-classical giltwood console tables, on carved and openwork eagle-bases, stamped "EHC", with marble tops and red mouldings, altered, restored.

This pair of consoles is inspired by the style of the architect William Kent (1685 - 1748), who was himself strongly influenced by Italian Baroque designs.

51in (129cm) wide

£50,000-70,000 pair   DOR

A pair of George III Adam-style Spanish mahogany side tables, on fluted legs.

c1800   *39.5in (100cm) wide*

£2,000-3,000   GEOA

A pair of Italian Neo-classical parcel gilt and painted tables, one probably late 18thC Neapolitan or Tuscan, the other 20thC, each with *breche d'Alep* marble top above carved frieze, on stop-fluted legs.

57in (145cm) wide

£8,000-12,000   WES

A late 18thC and later Louis XVI-style giltwood console table, the white marble top over carved and pierced frieze, on tapered part-reeded legs with a curved undertier surmounted by an urn and floral garlands.

67.5in (171.5cm) wide

£5,000-7,000   FRE

A pair of late 18thC Italian Neo-classical walnut and parcel-gilt marble console tables, Lombardy, with original *Cipollino Marino*-veneered rectangular top, above a panelled frieze with applied foliate motifs, on square tapered legs.

c1790   *65in (165cm) wide*

£30,000-50,000   L&T

A pair of George III painted satinwood console tables, the hinged tops painted with a cluster of flowers within floral borders, the apron similarly decorated, on painted square tapering legs with spade feet.

c1790   *36in (91.5cm) wide*

£5,000-7,000 pair   **POOK**

An early 19thC Empire bronze-mounted giltwood console, the inset porphyry marble top above a frieze with applied flower heads, on tapered basket weave-carved legs headed by Egyptian terminals, with urn surmounted H-form stretcher.

39.5in (100cm) wide

£10,000-15,000   **FRE**

A Regency rosewood console table, the three-quarter gallery top over single drawer, on figural turns above plinth base and carved paw feet, with brass banding throughout.

34.75in (87.5cm) high

£3,000-4,000   **LHA**

An 18thC Italian Baroque gilded console table, Rome, carved with mermaids and decorated with masks, with a marble top.

40in (101cm) wide

£50,000-70,000   **DOR**

A French Restauration gilded console table, with marble top, marbled plinth and carved side supports.

41in (104cm) wide

£4,000-6,000   **DOR**

A late Victorian console table and mirror, the mirror within a moulded frame surmounted by scrolling anthemion plume, the grey serpentine marble table top over shaped frieze, on scrolling cabriole legs.

130in (330cm) high

£1,500-2,500   **TEN**

A pair of late 19thC Continental giltwood and gesso console tables, with *brèche d'Alep* serpentine marble tops modelled as winged monopodia terminals, on bowed support and hoof feet.

37in (94cm) high

£2,000-3,000   **WW**

An early 19thC-style giltwood and green serpentine Connemara marble-topped console table.

47in (119.5cm) wide

£700-1,000   **DN**

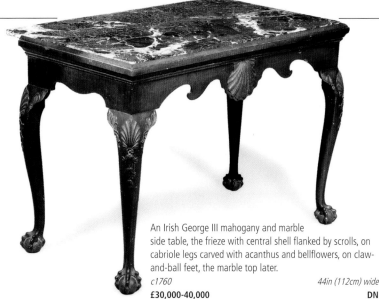

A George II walnut side table, the top with acanthus-carved edge, the frieze with central shell, on cabriole legs, each with a "green man" or "Indian" mask and scrolling acanthus, on hairy paw-and-ball feet.

c1740   *55in (140cm) wide*

£10,000-15,000   **DN**

An Irish George III mahogany and marble side table, the frieze with central shell flanked by scrolls, on cabriole legs carved with acanthus and bellflowers, on claw-and-ball feet, the marble top later.

c1760   *44in (112cm) wide*

£30,000-40,000   **DN**

A George III mahogany side table, with inlaid stringing, the drawer flame-veneered, with brass plate handles stamped "H.J".

         33in (85cm) wide

£800-1,200   **WW**

A late 18thC French overpainted serpentine side table, with gilt embellishments, the frieze with shell cartouche and beaded mouldings, on leaf-carved cabriole legs with scrolled feet.

         46in (116cm) wide

£1,500-2,500   **L&T**

A late 18thC/early 19thC kingwood, yew, mahogany and gilt metal mounted side table.

         30in (76cm) long

£2,500-3,500   **DN**

A George III Sheraton-style mahogany demi-lune side table, the top inlaid with roses and radiating satinwood stringing, the leg caps inlaid with urns, the square tapering legs and feet inlaid with ribbons and bell husks.

The demi-lune form of this table relates to table top designs by George Hepplewhite which were published by his widow in "The Cabinet-Maker & Upholsterers Guide" of 1788.

c1790   *66in (168cm) wide*

£4,000-6,000   **DN**

One of a pair of early 19thC black lacquer and gilt japanned bowfront side tables, decorated later with architectural scenes, on square tapering legs, formerly part of a dining table.

         54in (137.5cm) wide

£3,000-4,000 pair   **DN**

An Austrian Biedermeier side table, Vienna, three-sided support with black finish, with compartment and a drawer, with original gilt lock plate, the top decorated with trailing vines in India ink.

c1820   *30in (76cm) high*

£2,500-3,500   **DOR**

Judith Picks: François Linke

François Linke (1855-1946) was arguably the leading cabinetmaker of the Belle Epoque, and his influence was felt worldwide.

He was born in Pankratz in Bohemia, but moved to Paris at the age of 20, and stayed there until his death. In the mid-late 19thC the Louis XV and Louis XVI styles were revived in France, but Linke wanted to create a fresh, new style. With the help of sculptor Léon Messagé, he created a highly original series of designs, which combined the Rococo style of the Louis XV period with the new Art Nouveau style.

Linke's pieces are characterised by lavish mounts, which are often applied to comparatively simple carcases of quarter-veneered kingwood or tulipwood.

After Linke's death, one of his last foremen, Jean Bieder, acquired the business and returned to his native Switzerland with an enormous collection of Linke's casts, sketches, watercolours, glass negatives and daybooks. No furniture maker has left posterity with more comprehensive records than François Linke.

A rare inlaid kingwood lady's cylinder bureau, by François Linke, ormolu mounted and with central image of cherubs, signed "C. Guilbert", the fitted interior above two box drawers.

1910   *43.75in (111cm) wide*

£100,000-150,000   **DCB**

A late 19thC/early 20thC kingwood and satin parquetry side table, by François Linke, with ormolu mounts, and a frieze drawer, on slender cabriole legs, the lock (removed) stamped "CT LINKE SERRURERIE PARIS".

29.5in (75cm) wide

£5,000-7,000   **WW**

A pair of late 19thC-early 20thC Louis XV-style mahogany and ormolu-mounted side tables, by François Linke, with marble tops, one with drawer and extra tier, one with a drawer and cupboard, on turned tapered legs, both with "F. Linke" plaque.

30.25in (77cm) high

£1,500-2,500   **FRE**

An early 20thC mahogany gilt bronze-mounted bureau plat, by François Linke.

43.5in (110cm) long

£2,500-3,500   **DCB**

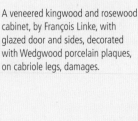

A veneered kingwood and rosewood cabinet, by François Linke, with glazed door and sides, decorated with Wedgwood porcelain plaques, on cabriole legs, damages.

26.5in (67cm) wide

£8,000-12,000   **DCB**

A Louis XVI-style mahogany and ormolu-mounted swivel desk chair, by François Linke, on turned fluted legs, headed by paterae and terminating in toupie feet, underside stamped "F. Linke".

c1900   *24.5in (62cm) high*

£4,000-6,000   **FRE**

FURNITURE

A pair of 19thC Continental painted and parcel gilt marble-topped side tables, with foliate-scrolled aprons, on shell-carved legs with shaped stretchers on claw-and-ball feet.

34in (86cm) wide

£5,000-7,000 GORL

A 19thC George II-style carved, painted and gessoed hall table, in the manner of William Kent, on cabriole legs with scrolled toes.

62in (157.5cm) long

£5,000-7,000 SK

CLOSER LOOK - DASSON SIDE TABLE

Henry Dasson established his cabinet-making workshop in the late 19thC after a brief career producing bronze artefacts and clocks in association with Godot. He specialised in the production of works for the Garde Meuble National (the national collection of France).

The parquetry-veneered top has a pierced three-quarter gallery.

The kingwood-panelled frieze drawer is opposed by a conforming dummy drawer.

The exquisite use of exotic woods and the fine detailing of the mounts are typical of Dasson's work.

This table is based on a design by Jean-Henri Riesener (1734-1806) who was a French royal ébéniste working in Paris. His work exemplified the early Neo-classical Louis XVI style.

A late 19thC Louis XVI-style mahogany, purpleheart and ormolu-mounted side table, by Henry Dasson after Jean-Henri Reisener, with drawer and dummy drawer, on square tapering legs with sabots and brass castors, twice stamped "Henry Dasson".

29in (73.5cm) high

£12,000-18,000 L&T

A Napoleon II ebonised side table, with bronze mounts, with micromosaic central scene of Cupid taking aim and a floral wreath with butterfly.

c1870 *30in (76cm) diam*

£10,000-15,000 DOR

A late 19thC Italian ebonised hardwood side table, carved in the form of a Moor bearing a bowl, with a round base.

29in (74cm) high

£7,000-10,000 DOR

A late 19thC French gilded side table, decorated with female heads, the top decorated with glass intarsia in the form of grape vines.

31in (79cm) high

£15,000-25,000 DOR

A pair of Sheraton revival satinwood and rosewood painted side tables, the tops with broad floral border, both with drawer and tapered square legs, decorated later.

c1890 *30in (76cm) high*

£2,500-3,500 DN

One of a pair of George II-style mahogany side tables, with acanthus- and shell-carved frieze, on cabriole legs with hairy paw feet.

43in (109cm) wide

£3,000-4,000 pair L&T

A late 18thC George III kingwood and satinwood marquetry occasional table, with floral marquetry top and two frieze drawers, on cabriole supports with gilt metal sabots and undertier.

31in (79cm) high

£6,000-8,000 ROS

A George IV mahogany occasional table, with four short and four dummy drawers, decorated with ebonised stringing, on turned and reeded column and reeded splay legs with brass capped feet and castors.

28.75in (73cm) high

£5,000-7,000 A&G

A William IV carved mahogany pedestal occasional table, with drawer, the top with gadrooned edge and foliage, on turned and reeded column, the foliate-carved scroll feet terminating in castors.

26.25in (66.5cm) wide

£2,000-3,000 H&L

A 19thC ebonised occasional table, with white painted and penwork leaf decoration.

19in (48cm) square

£1,000-1,500 SWO

A late 19thC French kingwood occasional table, the Carrara marble top with moulded brass border, the frieze with gilt metal leaf and scroll designs, on tapering legs with sabots.

30in (76cm) high

£1,500-2,500 A&G

A pair of late 19thC Regency-style satinwood and inlaid occasional tables, the tops inlaid with scrolling foliage, on four square tapered sabre legs with shaped stretcher.

32in (82.5cm) high

£2,000-3,000 L&T

An Edwardian quartetto nest of mahogany occasional tables, the beaded-edge tops with satinwood banding.

Largest 22in (56cm) wide

£1,000-1,500 set WW

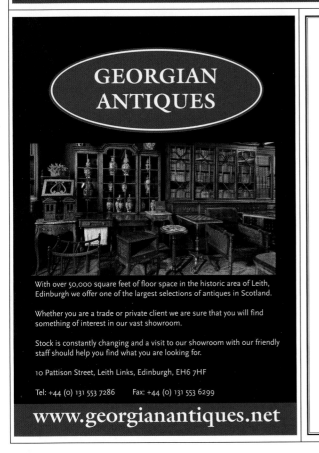

FURNITURE

ESSENTIAL REFERENCE - GILLOWS

Founded in c1727 by Robert Gillow (1704-1772), Gillows of Lancaster became the UK's leading furniture manufacturer outside London. A showroom in the capital was established in c1765, but furniture was still made in Lancaster.

- It is known for well-made Georgian, Regency and Victorian pieces in simple designs that appealed to the provincial middle classes.
- In the 1760s it began to stamp some pieces of furniture, making Gillows the first English company to adopt this practice. By the late 18thC Gillows had introduced several new furniture types, including the Davenport.
- During the 19thC it employed some of Britain's leading designers, including T. E. Collcut and B. J. Talbert.
- In 1900, Gillows merged with S.J. Waring & Sons to become Waring & Gillow.

An early 19thC mahogany library table, attributed to Gillows, with green leather writing surface, above two real and two opposing dummy drawers, on leaf- and shell-carved claw-and-ball feet with turned stretcher.

60in (152cm) wide

£7,000-10,000 **TEN**

A George III mahogany library table, the top with inset brown leather writing surface, with two short frieze drawers, on square tapered legs with castors.

c1780 *41.5in (105cm) wide*

£2,000-3,000 **FRE**

A Regency rosewood and brass-inlaid octagonal drum library table, with tooled green leather writing surface, above four real and four dummy frieze drawers, on stop-fluted sabre legs with brass caps and castors.

c1820 *39in (99cm) wide*

£7,000-10,000 **L&T**

A Regency pollard oak library table, with ebony line inlay, with two real and two dummy drawers, on panelled end supports with acanthus-carved bases on scroll feet with lacquered brass mounts.

c1820 *50in (127cm) long*

£6,000-8,000 **L&T**

A George IV rosewood library table, with inset leather writing surface, on panelled triform base with gadrooned apron and scroll feet.

c1825 *61in (154.5cm) wide*

£6,000-8,000 **L&T**

A Victorian rosewood library table, Edwards & Roberts, Wardour Street, with two short frieze drawers.

50in (127cm) long

£2,000-3,000 **GORL**

A Victorian walnut library table, Holland & Sons, the quarter veneered top with tulip wood crossbanding, with two drawers both stamped "Holland & Sons.", the legs with scroll and paterae ornament, stretchers and castors.

48in (122cm) long

£1,500-2,500 **H&L**

An 18thC mahogany architect's table, the drawer forming a table with baize-lined writing surface and compartments, the upper section with easel top and candlestands, on moulded legs with castors.

c1750 36in (92.5cm) wide

£2,500-3,500 TEN

A George III mahogany draughtsman's table, the drawer opening to a leather inset surface and sliding to reveal fitted compartments.

c1760 37in (94cm) wide

£1,000-1,500 DN

A George III mahogany artist's table, the drawer opening to reveal fitted compartmentalised interior, on split front legs.

30in (76cm) wide

£1,000-1,500 GORL

A George IV mahogany writing table, with ratchet adjustable central top section, the drawer stamped "C. HINDLEY & SONS LATE MILES & EDWARDS 134 OXFORD ST, LONDON, 20132".

c1825 41in (104cm) wide

£300-400 DN

A small William IV bird's eye maple writing table, with tooled tan leather skiver, the frieze inlaid with seaweed-style foliate scrolls, on twin pillar supports and dual splay legs with brass caps and castors.

36in (92.5cm) wide

£3,000-4,000 L&T

A small late 19thC French Louis XV-style lady's writing desk, with rosewood marquetry flowers and gilt bronze ornamental mounts, two lateral drawers and a sliding leather lined top.

28in (71cm) high

£4,000-6,000 DOR

A small late 19thC French Louis XVI-style mahogany veneered lady's writing desk, the top with gold embossed leather and rich bronze doré decoration, one frieze drawer, on conical fluted legs, restored.

£10,000-15,000 DOR

CLOSER LOOK - ORMOLU-MOUNTED MAHOGANY BUREAU PLAT

This table is unattributed, but has some elements which are reminiscent of the work of the French ébéniste Jean-Baptiste Youf, who worked for the Grand Duchess of Tuscany in the early years of the 19thC.

The "candelabra forms" flanking the drawers are based on the Classical candelabrum, which originally provided a focus or framing device for surrounding patterns and motifs.

The Classical-inspired high-quality ormolu mounts are typical Empire motifs. Pairs of mythical beasts (such as the winged lions on this table) were particularly popular.

The scrolling leaves are either laurel or olive. They symbolise either renewal, resurrection, glory and honour, or immortality, fruitfulness and plenty respectively.

An early 19thC Empire ormolu-mounted mahogany bureau plat, the central drawer with sliding leather-lined writing surface, and two leather-lined pull-out writing slides, veneered and mounted to form a centrepiece.

64.25in (164cm) wide

£40,000-60,000   SOTH

A Napoleon III ebonised ormolu- and porcelain-inset bureau plat, with two drawers above leather inset writing surface and long drawer flanked by two pairs of short drawers, on fluted tapering legs.

47.5in (121cm) wide

£1,200-1,800   LHA

A kingwood, tulipwood marquetry and gilt metal-mounted bureau plat.

c1870   *44in (112cm) wide*

£600-800   DN

A Louis XVI-style ormolu-mounted mahogany bureau plat, with gilt-tooled tan leather inset, the spring-loaded central drawer with bas-relief ormolu panel flanked by two drawers, dummy drawers to reverse, similar bas-relief plaques to sides.

c1900   *51.25in (130cm) long*

£3,000-4,000   WES

A late 19thC French Louis XV-style mahogany veneered bureau plat, with various drawers and dummy drawers, bronze doré decoration and espagnolettes (figures) to corners, with gold embossed leather writing surface.

64in (162.5cm) long

£20,000-30,000   DOR

A Charles X-style ormolu mounted mahogany bureau-plat, with gilt-tooled tan leather top above three drawers, each with applied griffins, the sides with pull-out writing surfaces, on moulded cabriole legs with paw feet.

c1900   *57.5in (146cm) long*

£4,000-6,000   WES

A Regency rosewood sofa table, with two short drawers and two opposing dummy drawers.

28in (71cm) long

£2,000-3,000   **GORL**

A George III mahogany and amboyna crossbanded sofa table, the top with kingwood banding and ebony and boxwood stringing, with two frieze drawers and two dummy drawers, with outswept legs.

c1805   *59in (150cm) wide*

£6,000-8,000   **DN**

An early 19thC probably German rosewood sofa table, the top with walnut parquetry square panels above frieze and opposing dummy drawers, on curved X-shaped supports with brass caps and castors.

70in (177cm) wide

£5,000-7,000   **L&T**

A Regency rosewood sofa and games table, the sliding leather inset top with marquetry chequer and cribbage boards to reverse, with leather backgammon board to interior, on painted and parcel gilt lyre supports with paw feet.

c1815   *39in (99cm) long*

£3,500-4,500   **DN**

A Regency pollard oak and satinwood-banded sofa table, in the manner of William Trotter, with bead-moulded edge, two real and two dummy frieze drawers, on a central column with four sabre legs with brass caps and castors.

c1820   *59in (150cm) wide*

£1,500-2,500   **L&T**

A Regency mahogany and crossbanded sofa table, in the manner of Gillows, with gilt brass cornucopia ring handles and lyre-shaped spindle-filled end supports.

c1820   *59in (150cm) wide*

£3,000-4,000   **DN**

A 19thC mahogany and inlaid sofa table, Edwards & Roberts, the hinged top crossbanded in rosewood and satinwood, strung with ebony, with four frieze drawers, on reeded splayed legs with stretcher and brass lion's claw caps and castors.

53.75in (136.5cm) long

£800-1,200   **H&L**

FURNITURE

A George III mahogany Pembroke table, with frieze drawer, on square tapering legs with hipped understretcher, block feet, brass caps and castors.

c1780   35in (90cm) long
£4,000-6,000   TEN

A George III harewood, kingwood, tulipwood and marquetry Pembroke table, the crossbanded top inlaid with central open fan panel, with drawer, on tapered square legs and block feet.

c1790   28in (71cm) high
£1,500-2,500   DN

ESSENTIAL REFERENCE - PEMBROKE TABLES

Small and typically elegant, Pembroke tables usually have one or two frieze drawers, two drop leaves supported by wooden fly-brackets, and four legs with castors.

- They were placed in the drawing room or the boudoir, and could be used for meals, cards, writing or needlework.
- According to Thomas Sheraton it takes its name "from the name of the lady who first gave orders for one of them", the Countess of Pembroke.
- Opened tables can form a rectangle, square, oval or octagon. The flaps can be rounded serpentine, or D-shaped.
- Pembroke tables were made in Britain from the mid-18thC.
- Decoration took the form of plain stringing or crossbanding, or marquetry borders. Some examples had bronze mounts.
- Late 18thC tables typically adhered to standard proportions: the side flaps equal to half the width of the central section and a third of the total height. Most had one real and one opposing dummy drawer and tapered legs that continued upwards to form the side frame of the drawer.
- Pembroke tables were still made in the 19thC, when they were typically of squat proportions.
- US examples are likely to be much more valuable, than British ones, as fewer were produced.

A Baltimore Federal inlaid mahogany Pembroke table, with moulded edge and plain inlaid skirt, the square tapering legs inlaid with thistle within oval reserves above bellflowers, within banded cuffs.

c1810   32.5in (83.5cm) long
£5,000-7,000   POOK

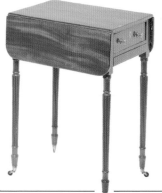

A George IV mahogany and ebony-strung Pembroke table, the single frieze drawer with fitted compartments above a shallow drawer, on reeded tapering legs with brass caps and castors.

29in (73.5cm) long
£1,000-1,500   TEN

A late 18thC Dutch marquetry Pembroke table, ornately decorated with flowers and scrolling motifs within panels, with a single frieze drawer, on square tapering legs.

29in (73.5cm) high
£1,000-1,500   A&G

A George II walnut demi-lune card table, the baize-lined hinged top enclosing a box interior, with panelled frieze and moulded girdle, on cabriole legs with pointed pad feet.

29.25in (74cm) wide

£2,000-3,000 H&L

CLOSER LOOK - GEORGE II CARD TABLE

The dished cylindrical corners held candles while the wells were for money or counters.

The figuring of the wood is excellent.

The quality of the table is shown by the quarter-veneered walnut top, which has crossbanding and chequer-banding.

The shell carving at the knees and the dainty claw-and-ball foot are further signs of quality.

A rare Philadelphia Federal satinwood veneered mahogany games table, line inlaid and with highly figured veneers inlaid with astragals, on delicate tapering legs with tapering bellflowers within line inlaid edges and banded cuffs.

c1795

43.5in (110.5cm) wide

£50,000-70,000 POOK

A George II walnut folding card table, opening to baize lined interior, with inset label to underside "Muirhead Moffatt & Co. Antiques, Glasgow".

c1750

34in (86.5cm) wide

£10,000-15,000 DN

A George III Irish mahogany serpentine card table, the foldover top with foliate-carved edge, opening to reveal baize playing surface, with gadrooned apron, on acanthus-carved cabriole legs with hairy paw feet.

c1760

36in (91.5cm) wide

£6,000-8,000 L&T

A pair of George III mahogany serpentine folding card tables, with baize-lined fold-over tops and boxwood stringing.

c1770

35in (89cm) wide

£7,000-10,000 DN

A Boston Federal mahogany and tiger maple-inlaid card table, the apron with pictorial inlays, the legs with frontal tiger maple panels outlined in stringing.

36in (91.5cm) wide

£6,000-8,000 SK

A pair of George III rosewood and yew crossbanded card tables, with line inlay, the D-shape foldover tops enclosing baize playing surface, on slender collared square legs.

c1800

36in (91.5cm) wide

£12,000-18,000 L&T

FURNITURE

A pair of Baltimore, Maryland, Hepplewhite mahogany card tables, each with a concave front with line inlays, on square tapering legs.

c1800   36in (91.5cm) wide
£3,000-4,000   POOK

One of a pair of Regency calamander and brass-mounted games tables, opening to a baize-lined playing surface, on ring-turned supports with incurved undertier on short splayed legs with brass lion's paw cappings and castors.

c1815   36in (91.5cm) wide closed
£2,500-3,500 pair   FRE

ESSENTIAL REFERENCE - CARD & GAMES TABLES

The first tables designed specifically for cards were developed in the late 17thC. They became extremely popular during the 18thC.

● Early examples were typically walnut-veneered with tapering legs – some of which swung out to support the folding top.

● During the 18thC, the fabric placed over the top became integrated into the design. From c1720 a concertina action flap-support was used as well as the swing leg. Some tables also had multiple leaves for different games.

● From the mid- to late 18thC tables were made for different games, particularly in France where square tables were made for "quadrille", circular for "brelan", and triangular for "tri". Designs became more elaborate as furniture-makers showed off their skills.

● In the late 18thC, dishings for candles or counters were omitted, and marquetry became less common.

● Gambling was banned in the Regency period, and card tables therefore became less fashionable.

A pair of early 19thC Anglo-Dutch floral marquetry swivel-top card tables, with reel-and-dart moulded edge, the interior with leaf and vine printed baize, on turned ribbed column and shaped concave quatrefoil base with claw feet.

32.5in (81.5cm) wide
£6,000-8,000   WW

A pair of Regency inlaid mahogany and ebony-lined card tables, the rear supports hingeing outward into a cruciform.

c1810   36in (91.5cm) wide
£7,000-10,000   DN

A pair of Regency rosewood games tables, the flip-tops with satinwood banded inlay concealing baize inset playing surface, on turned and spiral reeded column with foliate-carved sabre legs, brass cappings and castors.

36in (91.5cm) wide closed
£5,000-7,000   FRE

An unusual Austrian Biedermeier mahogany-veneered games table, Vienna, with nine sliding compartments.

c1830   34in (87cm) diam
£2,000-3,000   DOR

CLOSER LOOK - GEORGE II SILVER TABLE

The table is in good, honest condition. It has not been over restored. Sensitive restoration would add to the value.

Dealers and collectors like to see a piece of furniture with darker areas where dust and polish have gathered, such as around the carving and feet.

Ornate leaf carving to knees is highly defined and excellent quality.

To generalise, Irish furniture is highly desirable.

The trifid, or drake foot, is derived from Irish furniture design and was typically used on Queen Anne and early Chippendale cabriole legs.

The shell is a recurring Classical motif.

Silver tables were used for serving tea or displaying objects and therefore had galleried (or in this case) raised edging to help prevent items falling off the edge. They were designed to stand in the centre of the room and were therefore decorated on all four sides.

A George II Irish mahogany silver table.
c1750   *28in (71cm) high*
£15,000-25,000   **DN**

An 18thC New England Queen Anne carved cherrywood tray-top tea table, with applied moulded edge and scalloped apron, on angular cabriole legs with pad feet.
30.75in (77cm) wide
£5,000-7,000   **POOK**

A New England Queen Anne maple tea table, the rectangular tray top over deeply scalloped frame, on cabriole legs with pad feet.
c1765   *31.25in (79.5cm) wide*
£8,000-12,000   **POOK**

A George III mahogany silver table, the shaped top with a fret-pierced gallery above wavy frieze, on reeded square chamfered legs with pierced angle brackets and castors.
c1770   *35in (89.5cm) wide*
£3,500-4,500   **L&T**

A George III mahogany, rosewood and marquetry folding tea table, the top and interior with radiating veneers centred by a fan motif.
c1800   *36in (91.5cm) wide*
£2,500-3,500   **DN**

A pair of George IV mahogany tea tables, with a vase-turned support and four downswept legs with brass paw cappings and castors.
c1825   *36in (91.5cm) wide*
£5,000-7,000   **DN**

A Boston Queen Anne walnut and walnut veneer dressing table, the cockbeaded and string-inlaid case with long drawer and concave fan-inlaid central drawer flanked by drawers, on cabriole legs with pad feet on platforms.

c1730-50   30in (76cm) wide

£12,000-18,000   **SK**

A possibly southeastern Massachusetts Queen Anne carved cherry dressing table, with overhanging moulded top.

c1740-60   28.5in (71.5cm) high

£5,000-7,000   **SK**

A late 18thC Italian marquetry dressing table, Manifattura di Rolo, with marquetry scenes, on conical legs, with a hinged top enclosing compartments and a mirrored surface.

The town of Rolo near Modena in the province of Reggio Emilia has a strong tradition of intarsia work going back to the 17thC, and benefited, in the 18thC in particular, from an intensive program of ecclesiastical construction.

33in (85cm) wide

£8,000-10,000   **DOR**

CLOSER LOOK - GEORGE II WALNUT LOWBOY

A lowboy is an 18thC low writing or dressing table, developed from a chest on a stand with long legs.

They were mainly designed for ladies and would have one to three fitted drawers and space for a freestanding mirror.

Very early 18thC lowboys are rare and desirable.

This example is in good original condition

The inlaid concave starburst is a highly desirable feature

Pad feet on restrained cabriole legs are a typical early 18thC feature.

A George II walnut lowboy, with quarter veneered top over three drawers, the centre with inlaid concave starburst, on cabriole legs and pad feet.

26in (66cm) wide

£20,000-30,000   **GORL**

A Delaware Valley Queen Anne walnut dressing table, the rectangular top overhanging a case with four drawers, on cabriole legs with Spanish feet.

c1765   29.5in (75cm) high

£7,000-10,000   **POOK**

A Federal carved and wavy birch-inlaid mahogany two-tier dressing table, Massachusetts or New Hampshire, with single small drawer.

c1810-15   38.25in (97cm) high

£6,000-8,000   **SK**

A New York Federal carved mahogany and mahogany-veneer dressing table, with compartmented central drawer and curule legs, lacking original mirror.

c1810-20   36.75in (93cm) wide

£1,000-1,500   **SK**

An 18thC mahogany tripod table, the tilt-top, with pie-crust moulded edge, above baluster-turned stem and spiral fluted bowl, on cabriole legs, with pointed pad feet, top and base associated.

25in (63.5cm) high

£2,000-3,000 WW

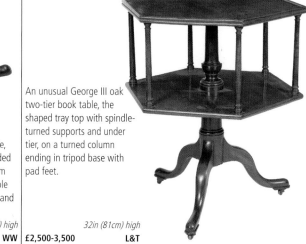

An unusual George III oak two-tier book table, the shaped tray top with spindle-turned supports and under tier, on a turned column ending in tripod base with pad feet.

32in (81cm) high

£2,500-3,500 L&T

A 19thC Italian ebony-veneered and ivory-inlaid pedestal table, in the manner of Giovanni Battista Gatti of Milan, the top inlaid with panels and friezes of Classical scenes around the Virgin Mary and putti, on turned and fluted pedestal with three scroll-hoof feet.

30in (76cm) high

£4,000-6,000 WW

A George III carved mahogany tripod table.

c1770 25in (63.5cm) high

£2,000-3,000 DN

An 18thC-style possibly Irish mahogany tripod table, the tilt-top with moulded Chippendale rim and six carved shells, on fluted column with leaf carved bowl with acanthus carved cabriole legs and claw-and-ball feet, damages.

c1900 28.75in (72cm) diam

£300-400 WW

FEET IDENTIFIER

18thC square and baluster

Mid-18thC Chippendale claw-and-ball foot

Mid-18thC UScrooked-pad foot

Mid-18thC US Queen Anne pad foot

Mid-18thC Italian Rococo stylised hoof foot

Early 19thC Regency carved lion's paw foot

Early 19thC Regency scroll foot

FURNITURE

A William IV rosewood work table, with carved paw feet.
c1830
£2,500-3,500   **GEOA**

A Regency Gillows of Lancaster mahogany drop-leaf work table, with single compartmentalised drawer above basket, on turned and reeded tapered legs with brass caps and castors.

29in (73.5cm) wide
£1,500-2,500   **GORL**

A Regency rosewood and brass marquetry work table, in the manner of George Oakley.
c1815   *30in (76cm) high*
£1,200-1,800   **DN**

A Victorian walnut octagonal work table, with a divided interior to lidded well, on associated carved rosewood tripod supports, damages and restoration.

29.5in (74cm) high
£200-300   **WW**

ESSENTIAL REFERENCE - SHAKER STYLE

The Shakers (so called because of a dance they performed in worship), or The United Society of Believers, were a religious community founded by English immigrant to America, Ann Lee in 1774. They believed furniture-making and other crafts sprang naturally from a spiritual approach to life and unintentionally left a lasting legacy in craft and design.

- Their most active period (known as the Classic Period) was c1820-c1860.
- Designs were based around three principals: function, economy and proportion. Decoration was minimal, though some items were painted. The details of the joinery work were left visible.
- Typical materials include locally available woods, such as maple, pine, cherry, birch and oak.
- The Shaker movement declined in the late 19thC, but there is still one surviving community.

A mid-19thC New England Shaker pine, cherry and birch sewing desk, with top section that lifts off the base.

42in (107cm) high
£2,500-3,500   **SK**

A Victorian rosewood and tulipwood-banded work table, with fitted interior of lidded compartments, bobbin holders and pin cushion, with C-scroll supports, the gadrooned stem with leaf-carved socle on a triform base.

The central fret-cut lid with paper label Richard Walhew, 78 Buchanan Street, Glasgow.
31in (78.5cm) high
£1,000-1,500   **TEN**

A 16thC Italian Renaissance walnut table, Bologna, with stretchers and one drawer with brass knob.

41in (104cm) long

£8,000-12,000   DOR

A George III mahogany "spider leg" table, with rectangular hinged top on turned underframing.

29in (74cm) extended

£800-1,200   H&L

A late 18thC New England stained pine and birch chair table, with rounded corner top and base and single drawer, with old red surface.

44.75in (114cm) wide

£2,500-3,500   POOK

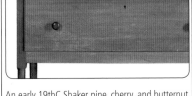

An early 19thC Shaker pine, cherry, and butternut kitchen table, possibly New Lebanon, New York, with breadboard and large thumb-moulded single drawer, on swelled legs.

66in (168cm) long

£12,000-18,000   SK

A Regency mahogany bowfront serving table, in the manner of Gillows.

The overall quality and characteristic design of this serving table strongly suggests a significant maker. The reeding of the legs would suggest Gillows, however the bold outline, lion's paw feet and distinctive carving may indicate George Smith, Thomas Hope or a contemporary.

c1815   *54in (137.5cm) wide*

£3,000-4,000   DN

A William IV mahogany serving table, in the manner of Gillows.

c1835   *91in (231cm) wide*

£3,500-4,500   DN

A large late 19thC/early 20thC pine pantry table, the rectangular planked top above plain frieze, on baluster turned legs.

118in (300cm) long

£2,500-3,500   L&T

An early 20thC 17thC-style oak draw-leaf table, with arcaded frieze, on cup and cover supports with H-stretcher, the base with initials "G.M., D.H.M".

109.25in (277cm) extended

£2,000-3,000   WW

ESSENTIAL REFERENCE - BAROQUE STYLE

The Baroque style, which was heavily influenced by early 17thC Italian painting, sculpture and architecture, was popular between c1620 and c1700.

- Furniture was typically dark and weighty, featuring architectural and sculptural elements.
- Pieces were often heavily carved with swags, double scrolls, acanthus, masks, chinoiserie (as a result of the increased trade between China and the West) and figures.
- Other popular decorative techniques included gilding, marquetry, boullework and japanning.
- By the 1730s, European taste had moved towards the lighter Rococo style developed in France.

A Charles II oak dresser.
c1680
67in (170cm) wide
£5,000-7,000
DN

A joined-oak low dresser, with three geometric moulded cushion-shaped drawers over two conforming drawers flanked by cupboard doors, on moulded plinth base and compressed bun feet.
c1690
78in (198cm) wide
£4,500-5,500
TEN

A George III joined oak low dresser, possibly Shropshire, with three drawers and two fielded panel doors below, on stile feet.
70in (178cm) wide
£3,000-4,000
TEN

An early 18thC oak low dresser, with three frieze drawers, on cabriole forelegs with pad feet.
c1740
85in (215cm) wide
£4,500-5,500
TEN

A late 18thC oak low dresser, the staged back over six long drawers, with brass drop handles, on square section cabriole forelegs.
85in (215cm) wide
£2,000-3,000
TEN

A large late Victorian pine pantry dresser, with four frieze drawers, on baluster turned legs.
120in (305cm) wide
£3,500-4,500
L&T

A large 18thC oak dresser, with moulded cornice and pierced navette fretwork frieze, the base with four long drawers, on turned uprights with wrythen slatted sides, on bracket feet.

79.5in (201cm) long

£3,000-4,000   **H&L**

A mid-18thC oak dresser, with raised three-tier delft rack above five short drawers, three short drawers to the frieze, with platform undertier, on turned and square legs.

79in (201cm) high

£3,500-4,500   **A&G**

A George III joined oak enclosed high dresser, the three fixed shelves between fluted pilasters, the base of breakfront form with four central drawers flanked by two frieze drawers and two doors, on bracket feet.

80in (202cm) wide

£6,000-8,000   **TEN**

A George III oak cottage dresser and rack, with bold pediment above two fixed shelves, the base with three drawers and arched frieze, on chamfered square legs joined by a pot board.

68in (173cm) wide

£2,000-3,000   **TEN**

A mid-19thC oak and mahogany high dresser and rack, with three graduated shelves and shaped uprights, the base with three long drawers over three central dummy drawers flanked by cupboard doors, on shaped base.

85in (214cm) wide

£2,000-3,000   **TEN**

CLOSER LOOK - HEAL'S CHESTNUT DRESSER

Heal's is a British furniture making company. It was founded in 1810, and has employed notable designers such as Mies van de Rohe, Marcel Breuer and Robin and Lucienne Day.

It has been suggested that the mark on this dresser was introduced in 1916. Very few examples of this particular mark are known to exist.

Heal's was very influenced by the Arts & Crafts movement and many pieces were shown at the Cottage Furniture Exhibition at Letchworth Garden City in 1905.

"Victorian and Edwardian Furniture and Interiors" by Jeremy Cooper includes an illustration (no. 661) of what is almost certainly this dresser.

A Heal's chestnut dresser, the bowfront with chip-carved border, above a slide and bow-fronted drawer flanked by cupboard doors with rotating handles and slides, on pot board plinth base with a maker's mark "Heal & Son, Makers London. W".

c1916

72in (183cm) wide

£10,000-15,000   **DUK**

An early 18thC Austrian Baroque hall cupboard, decorated with marquetry bands and panels, with two doors and original mounts and engraved and chased four-bar lock, restored.

87in (220cm) high

£20,000-30,000 DOR

A 17thC Flemish carved oak, walnut and ebonised kas, geometrically moulded throughout, with applied cherubs, lion masks and male torsos, with a narrow central frieze drawer, on a moulded base with fluted bun-shaped feet.

65.25in (165.5cm) wide

£4,000-6,000 H&L

A 17thC and later German oak and strapwork cupboard, inlaid with scroll and geometric motifs, with panelled doors between pilaster uprights above three arcaded panels and twelve short drawers, the lower section with breakfront frieze and two arcaded doors, on plinth base.

95in (241cm) high

£3,500-4,500 L&T

A 17thC Italian carved walnut vestry cabinet, probably Venice or Rome, partly painted in gold, with plinth drawer and two doors, with figural carvings of Saint Laurentinus and John the Baptist, together with textural cartouches, restoration.

The quality of the figures is reminiscent of the work of Italian sculptor Jacopo d'Antonio Sansovino (1486– 1570). He is best known for designing various buildings around the Piazza San Marco in Venice, such as the Zecca (public mint), the Loggetta, and the Biblioteca Marciana (public library), as well as the statues and reliefs of the Basilica of San Marco.

109in (277cm) high

£80,000-120,000 DOR

An oak and marquetry press cupboard, faults.

c1660 and later   *66in (167cm) high*

£1,800-2,200 DN

A 17thC and later oak cupboard, with two Gothic tracery carved doors and quatrefoil-carved panel, above two similarly carved drawers, and linen-fold carved door flanked by two panels.

52in (132cm) wide

£6,000-8,000 DN

An early 18thC oak tridarn, with moulded cornice and quadruple panel back, the recessed centre with two doors, the base with two bevelled short drawers above a pair of bevelled panel doors below, on block feet.

72.75in (185cm) high

£1,500-2,500   **H&L**

An early 18thC German Baroque walnut and burl walnut-veneered Frankfurter Wellenschrank, with moulded cornice and plinth, with two doors and later fitted interior.

84in (213cm) wide

£18,000-22,000   **DOR**

An 18thC Austrian Baroque walnut-veneered hall cupboard, with bird marquetry in partly burnt and engraved maple, yew and pearwood, the two doors with moulded panels.

c1740   *89in (226cm) wide*

£15,000-25,000   **DOR**

An early 19thC Pennsylvania walnut two-part Dutch cupboard.

86in (218.5cm) high

£4,000-6,000   **POOK**

A Regency oak housekeeper's clock cupboard, the moonphase dial with painted scene of a ship at sea, and cornered by painted figures of the seasons, flanked by two pairs of cupboard doors, the base with central cupboard flanked by eight drawers.

90in (229cm) wide

£7,000-10,000   **DN**

A mid-19thC Pennsylvania walnut step-back cupboard, in two parts, the upper section with shelves behind two glazed panel doors, the lower section with two recessed panel doors opening to single shelf.

£2,000-3,000   **WES**

FURNITURE

A George II walnut hanging corner cupboard, the arched door with double mouldings and feather banding, the green painted interior with three fixed shelves.

41in (105cm) high

£4,000-5,000 **TEN**

CLOSER LOOK - ITALIAN BAROQUE BOMBÉ CORNER CABINET

Venetian cabinetmakers and painters were at the peak of their skills by the mid 18thC. They were inspired by the landscape and flowers of Venice to create Italian Rococo.

They favoured lighter colour schemes, including pastel shades of pale blues, greys and off-whites. These were influenced by the fashionable furniture produced during the reign of Louis XV in France.

Venetian lacquer is perishable. To recognize a good piece from a fake one you will find an extensive network of irregular cracks, known as "craquelure". This is formed naturally with the passage of time and is impossible to remove. It is, in short, a kind of guarantee of authenticity.

Noble families in Venice maintained small, richly decorated rooms known as *casini*. Here they met their friends for conversation during the Carnival or other festive events. It is likely this corner cabinet was intended to decorate such a room.

A rare 18thC Italian Baroque bombé corner cabinet, Venice, with rocaille border and blue and white painted decoration (*lacche veneziane*) of flowers.

37in (94cm) high

£12,000-18,000 **DOR**

A Pennsylvania yellow pine two-part corner cupboard, the moulded cornice over glazed door, the base with single raised panel door and moulded base.

c1780 *81.75in (205cm) high*

£3,500-4,500 **POOK**

A late 18thC/early 19thC Dutch walnut and floral marquetry bow-fronted corner cupboard, decorated with birds and insects amidst flowers and foliage, the later ebonised stand on square section legs.

32.25in (81.5cm) wide

£600-800 **H&L**

A Middle Atlantic States Federal walnut corner cupboard, the broken arch pediment over glazed door and recessed panel cupboard door, on flared bracket feet, the case profusely inlaid with eagle, vines, paterae, etc.

c1810 *84.75in (215cm) high*

£5,000-7,000 **POOK**

A late 19thC ebonised, tortoiseshell, brass marquetry and gilt metal-mounted corner cabinet.

43in (110cm) high

£450-550 **DN**

A mahogany, satinwood and marquetry inlaid corner cabinet, the swan-neck pediment above inlaid frieze, the astragal glazed door enclosing two shelves flanked by canted glazed sides, the base with conforming frieze and marquetry decorated cupboard door.

c1890 *87in (220cm) high*

£2,000-3,000 **TEN**

A joined oak press cupboard, the later top over a carved frieze and two fielded panel doors, one carved "SLM 1684", between leaf-carved stiles, the lower section with three rectangular fielded panels, on stile feet.

59in (150cm) wide

£1,200-1,800 TEN

A George III mahogany and inlaid linen press, crossbanded and bordered with boxwood and ebony lines, fitted with sliding trays enclosed by doors, the base with two short and two long drawers, on splayed bracket feet.

49in (124cm) wide

£1,800-2,200 H&L

A late 18thC joined oak linen press, the projecting cornice above plain frieze and central panel flanked by two doors, base with three rectangular panels and two long drawers below, on stile feet.

c1780 *77in (195cm) wide*

£2,000-3,000 TEN

ESSENTIAL REFERENCE - LINEN PRESSES

The linen press (a cupboard with shelves or "presses" for storing linen) began to replace the chest in the 17thC.

- Early examples were heavy, and linear in design.
- During the mid-18thC linen presses began to be made in the highly decorative Rococo style, in fashionable light-coloured woods. The form was divided into two parts, with a series of long drawers now customarily set into the base.
- The linen presses of the late 18thC returned to more linear, architectural forms under the Neo-classical style. They featured minimal carved decoration, such as dentilled cornices and swagged garlands.
- The wardrobe (in which clothes could be hung) began to supersede the linen press in the mid-19thC.
- Many linen-presses were adapted (shelves removed and drawers cut through) to provide greater hanging space.

A late Georgian mahogany converted linen press, with flared cornice above panelled doors with oval cross-banded panels enclosing hanging rail and remaining sliding shelf, base with two short and two long drawers below, on bracket feet.

79in (200cm) high

£600-800 A&G

A late George III mahogany linen press, the dentil and blind fret cornice above two cupboard doors enclosing four sliding trays, base with two short and two long drawers, on bracket feet, restorations.

c1800 *81in (205cm)*

£1,200-1,800 TEN

A Middle Atlantic States Federal mahogany inlaid linen press, the doors enclosing four adjustable drawers, over four drawers.

c1800-10 *85in (216cm) high*

£2,500-3,500 SK

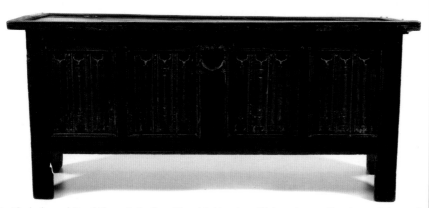

An Elizabethan oak linenfold panelled coffer, with a plain hinged moulded panel top and interior candle box and with quadruple linenfold panel front, on cut end supports.

60in (152cm) long

£4,000-6,000   **H&L**

A late 16thC panelled oak chest.

35in (89.5cm) long

£1,800-2,200   **DN**

A mid-17thC panelled oak chest, the front with relief-carved symmetrical motifs.

49in (124cm) long

£600-800   **DN**

A late 17thC South German Renaissance pine coffer, decorated with fruitwood geometric intarsia and half-profile portraits, a hinged lid with panels, claw lock, rail with drawer and handles to the sides.

73in (185cm) long

£4,000-6,000   **DOR**

A late 17thC Italian fruitwood cassone, decorated with pokerwork panels of mythological beasts within foliate scroll reserves.

27in (69cm) long

£4,000-6,000   **GORL**

A probably late 17thC Bermudan cedar six-board chest, with interior till.

44in (112cm) long

£3,000-4,000   **SK**

An 18thC Italian cedar wood chest, with relief carved panels of figures and mythological beasts, on bun feet.

51in (130cm) deep

£2,000-3,000   **GORL**

ESSENTIAL REFERENCE - TULIP MANIA

Tulips were introduced to Europe in the mid-16thC from the Ottoman Empire.

- The tulip rapidly became a coveted luxury item and status symbol in the United Provinces (now the Netherlands).
- From November 1636 to May 1637, prices reached extraordinarily high levels (some tulips sold for ten times the annual income of a skilled craftsman) before suddenly collapsing. This is arguably the first recorded speculative bubble.
- The event was popularised by Charles Mackay in "Extraordinary Popular Delusions and the Madness of Crowds" (1841). Mackay's account is now contested as many of the contemporary sources he based his conclusions on are extremely biased.

A Berks County, Pennsylvania, painted dower chest, decorated with stylised tulip vines flanked by heart-decorated ends on a green/blue ground, with two short drawers, on ogee bracket feet, dated.

1788   48.25in (123cm) long

£50,000-70,000   **POOK**

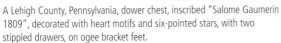

A Lehigh County, Pennsylvania, dower chest, inscribed "Salome Gaumerin 1809", decorated with heart motifs and six-pointed stars, with two stippled drawers, on ogee bracket feet.

1809   47.75in (122cm) long

£15,000-25,000   **POOK**

A Berks County, Pennsylvania pine dower chest, inscribed "LW D30 Novembre", decorated with two tombstone panels with potted flowers and columnar sides flanked by heart corners on an ochre sponged ground, dated.

1798   45.75in (118cm) long

£8,000-12,000   **POOK**

A late 17thC/early 18thC Indo-Portuguese mother-of-pearl inlaid and iron-bound hardwood coffer, with geometric patterning to top, front and sides.

25in (63.5cm) wide

£1,200-1,800   **DN**

An Italian Renaissance Revival cassone, the frieze carved with masks and foliate decoration, the body with St. Peter's third denial of Christ, angels and sleeping Roman soldiers, on dolphin feet.

64.75in (164cm) long

£12,000-18,000   **LHA**

FURNITURE

A 17thC Northern Italy Renaissance walnut chest-of-drawers, with double mouldings and four drawers, replacements.

56in (142cm) wide

£12,000-18,000   **DOR**

A late 17thC olivewood oyster-veneered chest-of-drawers, the rectangular marquetry top over two short and three long drawers, on bracket feet.

38in (96.5cm) wide

£4,000-5,000   **TEN**

A William & Mary laburnum oyster-veneered chest-of-drawers, the top inlaid with a radiating circular pattern, with two short and two long drawers, on later bracket feet.

33.5in (86cm) wide

£7,000-10,000   **GORL**

A Queen Anne walnut, ebony and boxwood strung chest-of-drawers on stand, the inlaid, quarter-veneered and crossbanded top above two short and three long drawers, on reduced stand with one long drawer, on later bun feet.

c1705   *41in (104cm) wide*

£6,000-8,000   **DN**

An early 18thC and later Italian walnut-veneered chest-of-drawers, with engraved ivory inlays, and three drawers.

34in (87cm) wide

£15,000-25,000   **DOR**

An 18thC Massachusetts child's red-painted chest-over-drawer, the lift-top on a double-arch case with drawer, on demilune cut-out ends, with turned wooden knobs.

21in (53cm) high

£2,000-3,000   **SK**

A Massachusetts Chippendale mahogany reverse serpentine chest-of-drawers, with moulded overhanging top and cockbeaded case, original brasses.

c1760-80   *31.25in (79.5cm) high*

£5,000-7,000   **SK**

A George III gentleman's mahogany serpentine dressing chest-of-drawers, the frieze drawer with compartmentalised interior and mirror, with three additional long drawers, on bracket feet.

44.5in (113cm) wide

£6,000-8,000 H&L

A Massachusetts Chippendale mahogany serpentine chest-of-drawers, with four drawers, on ogee bracket feet.

c1770 *39in (99cm) wide*

£5,000-7,000 POOK

A George III mahogany and inlaid chest-of-drawers with crossbanded and boxwood-strung top, slide and six short graduated drawers, on bracket feet.

21.75in (54.5cm) wide

£4,000-6,000 H&L

A George III mahogany serpentine chest-of-drawers, with blind fret-canted corners.

c1780 *39in (99cm) wide*

£2,000-3,000 DN

early 18thC bracket foot

Early 18thC bun foot

early 18thC flattened-ball turned foot

late 18thC ogee moulded bracket foot

early 19thC splayed bracket

A Middle Atlantic States Chippendale mahogany chest-of-drawers, with four drawers, bracket feet.

c1780 *38in (97cm) wide*

£2,000-3,000 POOK

A late 18thC mahogany serpentine chest-of-drawers, with four long graduated drawers, the canted corners decorated with acanthus leaf scrolls and reeded flat-front pilasters, on ogee bracket feet.

31in (79cm) high

£15,000-20,000 A&G

A George III satinwood, crossbanded and ebony-strung bowfront chest-of-drawers, in the manner of Gillows, the quarter-veneered top with crossbanded oval, with brushing slide and four graduated drawers, on outswept bracket feet.

c1790   *41in (104cm) wide*

£15,000-25,000   **DN**

A late 18thC Connecticut Chippendale cherry and cherry-veneer oxbow chest-of-drawers, replaced brasses, refinished.

39in (99cm) wide

£2,500-3,500   **SK**

An 18thC Indian ebony-veneered and bone-inlaid chest-of-drawers, with 12 drawers with spiral twisted handles and decorated with foliate arabesques, on later turned feet, restoration.

33in (85cm) wide

£15,000-25,000   **TOV**

A Regency black-painted and gilt bow-front chest-of-drawers, with three graduated long drawers with turned ivory handles, flanked by faux bamboo turned corner mounts, on ball feet.

43in (109cm) wide

£2,500-3,500   **GORL**

A central Massachusetts Federal inlaid cherry bowfront chest-of-drawers, with replaced wooden knobs, old refinish.

c1810   *38.5in (98cm) wide*

£1,500-2,500   **SK**

A Salem, Massachusetts, Federal carved mahogany and veneer chest-of-drawers, with carving attributed to Samuel Field McIntire, the reeded columns topped with punchwork, floral and leaf carving, with original brass.

1818   *43.5in (110cm) wide*

£4,000-6,000   **SK**

An Italian Baroque commode, Veneto, with ornamental marquetry panels in various fruit and other woods, and engraved ivory inlays, with four drawers.

c1700 · *57in (146cm) wide*
£12,000-18,000 · **DOR**

A mid-18thC German Baroque bombé commode, Dresden area, with three drawers, decorated with lozenge and cube pattern marquetry in walnut, with later mounts.

50in (127cm) wide
£8,000-12,000 · **DOR**

An 18thC French Louis XV rosewood veneer serpentine commode, with two drawers, the sides and drawer fronts with marquetry, bronze mounts and marble top.

52in (132cm) wide
£8,000-12,000 · **DOR**

CLOSER LOOK: NOËL GÉRARD

Noël Gérard ébéniste (cabinet maker) and marchand-mercier (seller) was active between 1710-1736.

He became both an ébéniste and dealer and is recorded as being established in rue du Faubourg-Saint- Antoine, Paris, in 1719.

The design of this commode, with its gently bowed form and curved canted corners and mounts, bears close similarities to commodes which have recently been attributed to Noël Gérard.

Numerous commodes, of which there were 38 examples at a cost of around 100 Livres each, are listed in Gérard's inventory of 1736. Sixteen of these were "en tombeau" and seven "à la Régence".

The red marble top, although in keeping with the piece, is not original.

His business prospered and he soon moved to the hôtel of the financier Jabach at the corner of the rue Saint-Martin in the financial and luxury goods quarter.

His illustrious clientèle included the Comte de Clermont and the fomer King of Poland, Stanislas Leczczynski.

It is also recorded that ébénistes supplied him with carcases. He stocked mounts for commodes and bronzes for his furniture designs were chased in his workshop.

A French Régence gilt-bronze-mounted brass-, tortoiseshell- and ebony-inlaid Boulle marquetry and parquetry commode, in the manner of Noël Gérard, with an associated mottled red marble top, above two short and two long drawers.

c1720 · *47in (119cm) wide*
£40,000-60,000 · **SOTH**

A Louis XV walnut serpentine-fronted commode, with crossbanded top, acanthus-carved roundels and apron, the hinged top lifting to reveal drawers, with single lower drawer, on cabriole legs.

c1760 · *52in (132cm) wide*
£6,000-8,000 · **DN**

A late 18thC Italian Neo-classical commode, by Giovanni Maffezzoli, veneered in precious woods and decorated with marquetry scenes, two *sans traverse* drawers, with green marble top, on conical legs.

Giovanni Maffezzoli (1766-1818) was born in Cremona. A pupil of the famous cabinet maker Giuseppe Maggiolini (1738-1814), he was renowned for his characteristic intarsia work.

47in (119cm) wide

£35,000-45,000   DOR

CLOSER LOOK - GEORGE III MARQUETRY COMMODE

The oval marquetry medallions are similar to those found on a group of cabinets associated with the émigré Swedish furniture-maker Christopher Fuhrlohg, who had links with Ince and Mayhew.

His influence was vital in the development of the Neo-classical style. His work demonstrates extremely skilful execution of marquetry decoration and the subtle use of woods, colour and images.

Typical features are the darker bandings framing the panels to the front, which are echoed by the stiles and tapered square legs.

Edwards & Roberts (whose stamp can be found on this commode) were among the foremost English cabinet-makers of the mid- to late 19thC.

This commode shares many features with furniture attributed to the London cabinet-making firm Ince & Mayhew.

Founded in 1845, Edwards & Roberts expanded rapidly. As well as making its own furniture inspired by 18thC prototypes, it retailed antique furniture, often applying its stamp or trade label.

A George III satinwood marquetry commode, with a central frieze drawer above a door, the drawer stamped "Edwards & Roberts".

63in (160cm) wide

£35,000-45,000   SOTH

A George III mahogany serpentine commode, in the manner of John Cobb, with three long graduated drawers, on splayed bracket feet, and with wavy apron.

c1780   *46in (116cm) wide*

£8,000-12,000   L&T

A Louis XVI kingwood, rosewood and purpleheart marble-topped commode, by Antoine Héricourt, with husk and foliate scroll gilt-bronze mounts and handles, with three banded and strung drawers, on turned tapered fluted legs with leaf cast capped feet, stamped "A. Héricourt JME".

c1780   *52in (132cm) wide*

£5,000-7,000   L&T

A late 19thC French marquetry commode, after Jean Henri Riesener, with marquetry on three sides and bronze mounts, with two doors, three drawers and marble top.

65in (165cm) wide

£20,000-30,000   DOR

A pair of Venetian-style painted bombé commodes, with faux marble tops above two long drawers, re-decorated.

c1900   *58in (147.5cm) wide*

£3,000-5,000   DN

A George II walnut chest-on-stand, the bold cornice above two short and three long feather banded and cockbeaded drawers, the stand with two deep drawers and frieze drawer, on cabriole legs with pad feet.

64in (162.5cm) high

£3,000-4,000   **TEN**

A late 18thC Southern New Hampshire Queen Anne maple carved chest-on-stand, with original brasses.

76.75in (195cm) high

£10,000-15,000   **SK**

A George II walnut and mulberry chest-on-stand.

c1735   *65in (165cm) high*

£6,000-8,000   **DN**

An Oyster Bay, Long Island, Queen Anne maple chest-on-stand, replaced brasses, refinished.

c1730-50   *65in (165cm) high*

£6,000-8,000   **SK**

A New England Queen Anne Maple and tiger maple chest-on-stand, with flat, deeply moulded cornice and valanced skirt, on cabriole legs with castors, replaced brasses, refinished.

74in (188cm) high

£3,500-4,500   **SK**

A Massachusetts William and Mary walnut veneer chest-on-stand, the drawers inlaid with crotch walnut and outlined with herringbone crossbanding, on baluster- and trumpet-turned legs with flat serpentine stretcher, on ball feet, now fitted with walnut china steps.

c1740   *62in (157cm) high*

£25,000-35,000   **POOK**

An Anglo-Indian bone-, brass- and ebony-inlaid hardwood chest-on-stand, the chest having a central bank of drawers; the stand with two drawers over bipartite deep drawer.

c1800   *49.5in (125.5cm) high*

£40,000-60,000   **WES**

FURNITURE

A William & Mary oak and walnut chest, with four graduated long drawers above three further drawers, lacking stand.

44in (111.5cm) wide

£1,500-2,500   GORL

An early 18thC walnut veneer and cross- and feather-banded chest-on-chest, with three short and three long drawers above three long drawers, on bracket feet.

69.5in (176.5cm) high

£6,000-8,000   H&L

A George II feather-banded and crossbanded burl walnut and walnut chest-on-chest, the lower section with green baize-lined pull-out writing slide.

£5,000-7,000   WES

A George III mahogany chest-on-chest, the fluted dentil cornice above two short and seven long graduated and cockbeaded drawers, between stop-fluted upper angles, with gilt metal handles, on splayed ogee bracket feet.

81in (206cm) high

£4,000-6,000   L&T

A George III mahogany chest-on-chest, the upper with dentil cornice and two short and three long drawers between fluted, canted corners, the lower with a pull-out brushing slide and three long drawers, on bracket feet.

c1780   77in (195cm) high

£3,500-4,500   TEN

ESSENTIAL REFERENCE - CHIPPENDALE STYLE

Thomas Chippendale (1718-79) was an English cabinetmaker and furniture designer.

● He began working in London c1747, and by 1753 he had a cabinetmaking workshop in St Martin's Lane.

● Chippendale worked in the Neo-classical and chinoiserie (known as Chinese Chippendale) styles. However, his most characteristic pieces are in the earlier Rococo style. Typical decoration included carved shells, foliage and trailing husks.

● In 1754 he published the first edition of his influential design book, "The Gentleman and Cabinet-Maker's Director".

● By the mid-1760s, copies had arrived in Philadelphia and inspired the American Chippendale style. This tended to be similar to its European counterpart, but less ornate. As high quality woods (such as walnut, mahogany and maple) were plentiful, veneers are uncommon.

● The term "Chippendale" is generally taken to mean "in the Chippendale style", rather than pieces made in Chippendale's own workshops. None of the latter were stamped, so authenticity can only be established by accompanying documentation.

● The Chippendale style was revived from the mid- and late 1800s into the 20thC, and is still copied today.

A Pennsylvania Chippendale walnut chest-on-chest, the broken arch bonnet with central flame finial and carved floral rosettes, with carved frieze and five short and six long drawers flanked by floral carved quarter columns, on ogee bracket feet.

c1780   94.5in (240cm) high

£25,000-35,000   POOK

A George III mahogany and brass strung chest-on-chest.
c1780   *72in (183cm) high*
£1,500-2,500   **DN**

A late 18thC New England Chippendale carved cherry chest-on-chest, with replaced brasses.
86in (218cm) high
£3,500-4,500   **SK**

A late 18thC probably Connecticut Chippendale carved cherry chest-on-chest, flanked by reeded quarter-columns, with carved top drawer, on ogee bracket feet, with original brasses.
80in (203cm) high
£4,000-6,000   **SK**

A Medfield, Massachusetts Chippendale maple tall chest, by Artemas Woodward, with original brasses, dated.
1796   *56.5in (144cm) high*
£3,500-4,500   **SK**

A William IV mahogany Wellington chest, the seven long drawers with turned-ebony bun handles.
c1835   *54in (138cm) high*
£2,000-3,000   **DN**

A Victorian walnut and gilt metal-mounted Wellington chest.
c1870   *49in (125cm) high*
£800-1,200   **DN**

WOODS

Amboyna	*Beech*	*Birch*	*Birch*
Calamander	*Cherry*	*Chestnut*	*Coromandel*
Ebony	*Elm*	*Elm (burr)*	*Flame Mahogany*
Kingwood	*Mahogany*	*Mahogany*	*Maple*
Maple (bird's eye)	*Oak (dark)*	*Oak (light)*	*Olive*
Pine	*Pine*	*Rosewood*	*Rosewood*
Satinwood	*Sycamore*	*Tiger Maple*	*Walnut*
Walnut	*Walnut (burr)*	*Yew (burr)*	*Yew*

FURNITURE

ESSENTIAL REFERENCE - SECRÉTAIRES

The secrétaire is a vertical writing cabinet with a lean-to fall-front, which lies flat against the cabinet. The fall-front conceals recessed drawers, cupboards and pigeonholes in which papers can be stored and locked away.

- An example made before c1720 might be referred to as escritoire, scriptor, scriptoire or scrutoire.
- They were often made in two parts.
- The lower section typically features a set of drawers.
- The upper section might take the form of a bookcase or a glazed display cabinet, although some secrétaire-drawers were set into chest-on-chests.
- British secrétaries often used different woods for the interior, (e.g. satinwood), and exterior (e.g. mahogany).
- The secrétaire remained a useful item of furniture and was made into the 19thC.

A Queen Anne green-japanned secrétaire-cabinet, the moulded ogee-arched top above two panelled doors enclosing seven drawers, the secrétaire drawer enclosing fitted interior, above three graduated drawers, on bulbous feet, restorations.

92in (234cm) high

£15,000-25,000 **WES**

A Queen Anne secrétaire chest-on-stand, with cushion-moulded drawer to cornice, above a fall opening to fitted interior with drawers and cupboards, on a base with two short and two long drawers.

c1710 *63in (160cm) high*

£10,000-15,000 **DN**

A Louis XVI mahogany and ormolu mounted secrétaire à abattant.

55.75in (142cm) high

£5,000-7,000 **POOK**

An early 19thC satinwood secrétaire, by Gillows, the galleried top with two open shelves flanked by cupboards, above secrétaire drawer enclosing fitted interior, above two cupboard doors, on tapering feet.

38in (97cm) wide

£6,000-8,000 **TOV**

A Victorian mahogany secrétaire wellington chest, the secrétaire two-as-one drawer with green baize-lined writing surface, drawers and pigeonholes, the moulded uprights with reeded and scrolling trusses, on platform base.

50in (127cm) high

£4,000-6,000 **TEN**

A George II walnut secrétaire bookcase, the cavetto-moulded pediment above two shaped mirror plates enclosing a fitted interior, the base with a secrétaire drawer above two long drawers, on bracket feet.

78in (198cm) high

£3,000-4,000 **TEN**

A George III mahogany and inlaid breakfront secrétaire bookcase, the central section with secrétaire drawer and cupboard enclosing three sliding trays, the adjacent cupboards with shelves and drawers.

c1810 *92in (234cm) high*

£5,000-7,000 **DN**

A Pennsylvania Chippendale walnut secretary desk and bookcase, the arched pediment flanking a flame finial over two raised panel doors, the base with fall-front and four drawers, on ogee bracket feet.

c1765 *96in (244cm) high*

£8,000-12,000 **POOK**

A Boston, Massachusetts Chippendale mahogany block front secretary bookcase, the broken arch bonnet above two scalloped panel doors with fluted pilasters, the base with a fall front and four drawers, on claw-and-ball feet.

c1765 *96in (244cm) high*

£20,000-30,000 **POOK**

A fine George III mahogany secrétaire bookcase, the fretwork-pierced swan-neck pediment above a pair of glazed doors enclosing adjustable shelves above a secrétaire drawer and cupboard doors, on bracket feet.

c1780 *103in (261cm) high*

£5,000-7,000 **L&T**

A Philadelphia classical mahogany secretary, the peaked pediment over two glazed doors and three short drawers, the base with butler's desk, on animal-paw feet.

c1825 *102in (259cm) high*

£5,000-7,000 **POOK**

A late 19thC mahogany and satinwood crossbanded inlaid secrétaire bookcase, with a pair of astragal-moulded doors above an inlaid secrétaire drawer with fitted interior above three graduated drawers, on splay feet.

91.5in (232cm) high

£1,500-2,500 **A&G**

FURNITURE

An early 18thC probably Spanish carved and painted pine bureau bookcase, the shell- and husk-carved pediment above doors and two drawers, the base with fall enclosing drawers and above two cupboard doors, on bracket feet.

94in (239cm) high

£6,000-8,000   TEN

A Queen Anne walnut bureau bookcase, with swan's neck and gilt ball finial pediment above mirror door and candle slides, the bureau interior with drawers, pigeonholes and well with sliding cover, above four drawers, on later bracket feet.

c1710   94in (239cm) high

£4,500-5,000   DN

A mid-18thC Italian black lacquered bureau cabinet, Venice, the top with a pair of doors with replaced mirror plates enclosing shelves, the flap to the bureau enclosing eight drawers and pigeonholes.

This bureau cabinet decorated with chinoiserie scenes takes its inspiration from the form of early 18thC English examples. Lacquerware inspired by Oriental models has been produced in Venice from the 16thC, but it became the height of fashion in the 18thC.

41.25in (105cm) wide

£50,000-70,000   SOTH

A small 18thC mahogany bureau cabinet, with four external drawers and a small door, two doors with mirrors, two candle holders, as well as a fall-front writing surface with interior drawers.

76in (193cm) high

£3,000-4,000   DOR

A George III mahogany bureau bookcase, the swan-neck pediment over a blind fret-carved frieze and astragal glazed doors, the base with slant front over fitted interior above three short and three long drawers, on bracket feet.

109in (277cm) high

£2,500-3,500   FRE

A George III mahogany and ebonised breakfront bookcase, with glazed upper section above central drawer and an arrangement of cupboards, on turned feet.

c1790   *91in (231cm) high*
£10,000-15,000   **DN**

A Regency rosewood, parcel gilt and gilt metal-mounted breakfront library bookcase, stamped "JAMES WINTER, 101 WARDOUR ST, SOHO, LONDON".

c1815   *89in (226cm) wide*
£5,000-7,000   **DN**

A Victorian mahogany inverted breakfront library bookcase.

c1850.   *98in (249cm) wide*
£6,000-8,000   **DN**

A Victorian mahogany breakfront bookcase, three glazed cupboards above base with two drawers over cupboard doors flanked on each side by a drawer and a cupboard, on plinth base.

c1880   *90in (228cm) high*
£12,000-18,000   **DN**

ESSENTIAL REFERENCE - BOOKCASES

The bookcase developed as a piece of library furniture in the early 18thC. Previously books had been so expensive that even the wealthiest people were unlikely to own many.

- Early 18thC examples were flat-fronted and of two sections. By the mid-1730s the form was more architectural, including broken pediments and carved decoration.
- Until c1750 solid glazing-bars were used to hold the panes of glass. Afterwards they were replaced by astragals, which could be more elaborately arranged.
- Revolving bookcases were introduced c1810.
- From the early 19thC books became substantially less expensive and demand for bookcases increased. Typical Victorian library bookcase are made of mahogany.

A late 19thC mahogany breakfront library bookcase, by S & H Jewell, with carved and applied decoration and adjustable shelves, with ivorene trade label "S & H JEWELL, 131-2 HIGH HOLBORN, LONDON WC1".

68in (173cm) wide
£1,000-1,500   **WW**

A chinoiserie painted and black-lacquer breakfront bookcase, the moulded breakfront cornice above astragal-glazed doors, the base with cupboard doors, the interior fitted for electricity.

99.5in (253cm) wide
£2,000-3,000   **FRE**

A pair of William IV rosewood library bookcases, the projecting cornice above a full-length glazed panel door enclosing adjustable shelves, on moulded plinth bases, each bearing a brass plaque verso.

108in (275cm) high

£10,000-15,000   L&T

A George III mahogany library bookcase, with pair of astragal glazed panel doors over adjustable shelves, the base with panelled cupboard with fret-carved spandrels over shelved interior, on a plinth base.

c1770   *95in (242cm) high*

£8,000-12,000   L&T

A George III mahogany bookcase, the two lancet-glazed doors over six adjustable shelves, the base with doors over central drawer and arched shaped niche, and eight drawers, on a plinth base.

87in (222cm) high

£3,500-4,500   TEN

A pair of late 19thC French Boullework open bookcases, with marquetry in brass and tortoiseshell, also with partly figural bronze mounts and maple-veneered shelves.

84in (214cm) high

£30,000-40,000   DOR

An early 19thC mahogany bookcase, with detachable cornice over three astragal-glazed doors, the central sliding, with later plush lining, base with drawers, on a plinth base.

95.5in (243cm) high

£2,500-3,500   WW

A Victorian walnut open library bookcase, the moulded dentil cornice above adjustable shelves flanked by fluted rounded corners, the base with three frieze drawers, on a plinth base.

c1880   *93in (236cm) high*

£2,500-3,500   L&T

An Edwardian satinwood, carved and painted bookcase, the two glazed doors over adjustable shelves flanked by painted columns of flowers and leaves, the crossbanded base over two cupboard doors, on toupie feet.

88in (224cm) high

£4,000-6,000   TEN

A Louis Phillippe rosewood open bookcase, the associated marble top above two adjustable shelves flanked by turned columns with gilt brass mounts.

42in (107cm) wide

£1,200-1,800   **WW**

A late Victorian mahogany open bookcase, the detachable cornice above seven adjustable shelves, with a brass plaque inscribed "S & H JEWELL, 29, 30 & 31 LITTLE QUEEN ST. HOLBORN. W.C.".

81.5in (206.5cm) high

£700-1,000   **WW**

An Edwardian walnut revolving bookcase.

34.75in (88cm) high

£500-700   **WW**

A William IV carved rosewood breakfront dwarf open bookcase, by Gillows, with adjustable shelves on fluted bun feet.

74in (187cm) wide

£8,000-12,000   **GORL**

CLOSER LOOK - FLEMISH TORTOISESHELL CABINET

Scarlet tortoiseshell is rare and desirable.

There is actually no such thing as a red tortoise. The colour is imparted by a painted red bole layer under the translucent shell.

It is flanked by columns with gilt metal Corinthian capitals.

The stand is later which detracts from the value.

The interior has a central architectural mirrored and gilt-pillared compartment enclosed by a door with a raised heart crossed with gilt metal arrows.

A 17thC Flemish scarlet tortoiseshell and ebonised architectural cabinet, on later ebonised stand, with ripple-moulded banding and gilt-metal mounts, with drawer and slide below.

Cabinet 30in (76cm) wide

£7,000-10,000   **H&L**

A spruce and oak with maple and walnut veneer cabinet-on-stand, composed of 17thC, 18thC and 19thC elements, with various pictorial inlays and bronzed flame mouldings, with numerous drawers.

71in (179cm) wide

£6,000-8,000   **DOR**

A late 17thC Flemish scarlet tortoiseshell and ebonised cabinet-on-stand, the doors enclosing an illusionist interior flanked by drawers with ripple moulding, on later parcel gilt and ebonised stand, altered.

64in (162.5cm) wide

£8,000-12,000   **GORL**

A late 17thC and later Spanish walnut vargueno on stand, with later gilded mounts, the fall revealing drawers with bone and polychrome decorated fronts, on walnut and stained beechwood stand.

49.75in (126.5cm) high

£1,000-1,500 WW

A 17thC Spanish Baroque iron-mounted walnut vargueno on 19thC stand, restoration to vargueno.

£1,800-2,200 WES

An early 18thC Dutch olive wood, rosewood, ebony and oyster-veneered cabinet-on-stand, the doors inlaid with chequer bands, floral marquetry and central medallions, enclosing shelves and drawers, the base with three drawers, on tapered supports with understretcher.

85in (215.5cm) high

£25,000-35,000 TEN

A Regency 18thC-style Chinoiserie black lacquer cabinet-on-stand, the doors enclosing an arrangement of twelve drawers around a central door with the motto "DEUM COLE REGEM SERVA" above a gryphon holding an arrowhead, fronted by cabriole legs with paw feet.

The crest and the monogram refer to Henry Cole (1808-1882), who began his career as a civil servant. Through his membership of the Society for the Encouragement of Arts, Manufacturers, and Commerce in 1845, he became involved in the organisation of the Great Exhibition in 1851. He went on to become the first director of the South Kensington Museum (now the Victoria & Albert), where a wing is named after him.

67in(170cm) high

£2,000-3,000 DN

A late 19thC French Louis XVI-style marquetry and mahogany-veneered cabinet, with bronze doré ornament and marble top, the door with porcelain inlays.

This cabinet is modelled after the work of Adam Weisweiler (1744-1820) who was a pre-eminent French master cabinetmaker (ébéniste) in the Louis XVI period, working in Paris. Weisweiler is said to have been born at Neuwied-am-Rhein, Germany, and to have received his early training in David Roentgen's workshop.

59in (151cm) high

£15,000-25,000 DOR

ESSENTIAL REFERENCE - MARQUETRY

Marquetry is a type of decorative veneer. Small pieces of coloured woods and other materials, such as ivory, mother-of-pearl and bone, are laid out in a pattern and applied to the carcase.

- It differs from inlay, in which objects are inserted into depressions in the solid base.
- It was developed by Dutch cabinetmakers in the early 16thC and introduced to Britain in the 1660s.
- Floral marquetry was popular c1660–90, with seaweed (or "arabesque") marquetry becoming more fashionable from c1690. Parquetry, a geometric variation of marquetry, was also widely used. Figurative scenes are less common, but desirable.
- Marquetry became briefly unfashionable in the early 18thC before being revived in the 1760s and 1770s.

A late 18thC Dutch walnut and marquetry display cabinet.
c1790   *82in (208cm) high*
£1,500-2,500   DN

A late 18thC Dutch walnut and floral marquetry display cabinet, the glazed door and sides enclosing shelves, the serpentine bombé base with four graduated drawers, on claw-and-ball feet.
81in (205.5cm) high
£2,500-3,500   L&T

An 18thC Dutch walnut and floral marquetry display cabinet, inlaid and crossbanded and with ebonised ground panels and spandrels, with cartouche glazed panel doors, on turned and polygonal tapered legs with undulating stretchers and pear-shaped feet.
94in (238.5cm) high
£5,000-7,000   H&L

A 19thC French kingwood and gilt metal-mounted serpentine-fronted vitrine, with glass shelves and glazed panel door, the base painted in the *Vernis Martin* manner, on cabriole legs with husk and foliate ornament and sabots.

Vernis Martin is a type of imitation Chinese lacquer made by heating oil and copal, and adding Venetian turpentine. It was named after French brothers Guillaume and Etienne-Simon Martin.
69in (175cm) high
£1,500-2,500   H&L

A pair of 19thC faux bamboo and lacquered chinoiserie cabinets, each with pagoda top, three shelves with openwork sides and galleried back, on ogee feet.
77in (198cm) high
£7,000-10,000   WW

A pair of Empire-style display cabinets, formerly 19thC bookcases, the marble top over two glazed doors enclosing two fixed shelves, with gilt cast mounts, on compressed feet.
73.5in (187cm)
£3,000-4,000   TEN

FURNITURE

A small 17thC South German softwood marquetry cabinet, decorated with an allegory of battle, restoration.

38in (97cm) wide

£5,000-7,000   **DOR**

CLOSER LOOK - PAIR OF GEORGE IV SIDE CABINETS

The flame mahogany is a good commercial colour and is well figured.

The fact that they are a pair adds considerably to the value.

The brass inlay flanked by anthemion leaves is a desirable feature.

The doors are flanked by leafage-capped scrolling-stiles, ending in animal-paw feet.

All of these are strong, Classical motifs.

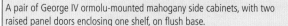

A pair of George IV ormolu-mounted mahogany side cabinets, with two raised panel doors enclosing one shelf, on flush base.

48in (122cm) wide

£12,000-18,000   **WES**

A William IV rosewood breakfront side cabinet, with later silk-backed brass grilles to the doors, enclosing adjustable shelves, on a plinth base.

75in (190cm) wide

£1,500-2,500   **WW**

A Louis XVI mahogany and ormolu-mounted demi-lune side cabinet, the moulded marble top above frieze drawer, with applied guilloche mounts, above two cupboard doors, on square tapered legs with toupie feet.

Guilloche is continuous scrolling pattern of interlacing, plaited bands. It was originally frieze ornament found on Classical architecture.

c1780   *33in (85cm) wide*

£4,500-5,500   **L&T**

An early 19thC Austrian Empire mahogany veneered side cabinet, Vienna, with applied caryatid angles, one drawer and two side doors, with gilded parnassus leaf mouldings and *verde antico* decoration on frieze and plinth, altered.

c1800-1820   *49in (124cm) wide*

£5,000-7,000   **DOR**

A Regency parcel gilt rosewood breakfront side cabinet, the later marble top above conforming case with four brass grille and cloth-panelled doors enclosing shelves, flanked by half-lobed pilasters, on flush base.

c1815   *73.25in (185.5cm) wide*

£5,000-7,000   **WES**

A George IV mahogany collector's cabinet, with slide above arrangement of 12 drawers, with sunken brass handles.

c1825   *36in (92cm) wide*

£3,000-4,000   **DN**

A George IV carved rosewood and cut-brass marquetry side cabinet, with three-quarter brass gallery above a pair of glazed doors, on reeded oviform feet.

c1825   *52in (131.5cm) wide*

£3,000-4,000   **DN**

A pair of 19thC Regency-style side cabinets, with *en grisaille* reserves on a cream ground, each with two frieze drawers above cupboard doors, flanked by spiral fluted columns, re-decorated.

39.5in (100cm) wide

£2,000-3,000 DN

A William IV rosewood folio cabinet, by John Kendell & Co, the gadrooned, inverted and hinged top above two dummy cupboard doors and one lateral door opening to a compartmented interior, on acanthus-carved bracket feet.

c1830 *54in (136.5cm) wide*

£5,000-7,000 L&T

An American Renaissance Revival porcelain-mounted, ebonised and parcel-gilt cabinet, probably New York, the stepped top applied with panels of tulipwood and burl walnut, and burl walnut panels to front and sides, on shaped plinth.

c1875-80 *55in (140cm) wide*

£3,500-4,500 SK

A Victorian burr walnut, ebonised, porcelain-inset and gilt metal-mounted inverted breakfront cabinet, with three leather inset tiers flanked by cupboards each with two shelves, formerly with a gallery.

c1870 *55in (140cm) wide*

£2,000-3,000 DN

A pair of Victorian burr walnut and marquetry pedestal cabinets.

c1870. *36in (92cm) high*

£2,500-3,500 DN

A Victorian walnut and porcelain-inset breakfront cabinet.

c1870

£2,500-3,500 DN

A 19thC Louis XV-Revival kingwood marquetry bombé cabinet, with gilt metal mounts, on paw sabots.

c1880 *51.5in (130cm) high*

£4,000-6,000 CHEF

An ebonised and painted strung side cabinet, Gillow & Co., with bevelled glass doors and sides enclosing later glass shelves, the right door stamped "GILLOW & CO 13153".

c1882-3 *40.5in (103cm) wide*

£1,000-1,500 WW

FURNITURE

A Victorian walnut, amboyna wood and inlaid credenza, with boxwood, harewood and ebonised lines and applied ebonised plaques and brass-beaded edges, the base with cupboards between fluted half columns, on plinth base.

71.25in (181cm) wide

£3,500-4,500   H&L

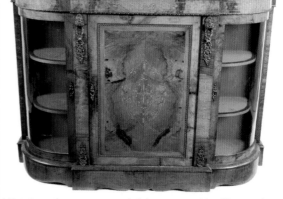

A Victorian walnut, marquetry and gilt brass-mounted breakfront credenza, the central panel door enclosing a baize-lined interior with a single shelf.

59in (150cm) wide

£2,000-3,000   WW

A late 19thC ebonised and Boulle marquetry credenza, decorated with cut-brass arabesques and gilt metal mounts, the door flanked by putti mask caryatid uprights, on splay feet.

44in (111.5cm) wide

£2,000-3,000   L&T

A Regency/George IV rosewood, Siena marble and gilt metal-mounted inverted breakfront chifonnier, the two-tier gallery with mirrored back to lower tier.

c1820   *58in (147.5cm) high*

£2,000-3,000   DN

A George IV mahogany chiffonier.

c1825   *53in (134cm) high*

£400-500   DN

A George IV rosewood chiffonier, the raised mirrored back on baluster-turned supports, above panelled doors with later mirrored panels enclosing a shelf, on plinth base.

48in (121.5cm) high

£600-800   WW

An early Victorian goncalo alves chiffonier, with bobbin-turned supports and an adjustable shelf.

Goncalo alves is a hardwood. It is sometimes referred to as zebrawood or tigerwood because of its dramatic, contrasting colours, that some compare to rosewood.

47.5in (121cm) high

£400-600   WW

FURNITURE

CLOSER LOOK - NEW YORK FEDERAL INLAID MAHOGANY SIDEBOARD

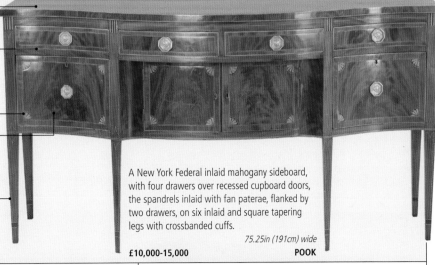

This Classically-inspired sideboard is elegant and sophisticated.

The top has a deeply serpentine front above a conforming case. This always indicates good quality.

The spandrels are delicately inlaid with fan paterae.

The flame mahogany has distinctive figuring which has been carefully chosen.

The stylishly graceful square tapering legs terminate in crossbanded cuffs.

All this points to the fact that this piece was made by a prominent cabinetmaker in New York.

A New York Federal inlaid mahogany sideboard, with four drawers over recessed cupboard doors, the spandrels inlaid with fan paterae, flanked by two drawers, on six inlaid and square tapering legs with crossbanded cuffs.

75.25in (191cm) wide

£10,000-15,000 **POOK**

A probably Philadelphia Federal curly maple D-shaped sideboard, repairs and replaced brasses.

£5,000-7,000 **WES**

A George III mahogany inlaid sideboard, the serpentine moulded top with satinwood banding over a central drawer flanked by deep drawers, on square tapered legs, on spade feet.

62in (157.5cm) wide

£3,000-4,000 **FRE**

A George III mahogany bowfront sideboard.

c1800   60in (152.5cm) wide

£1,000-2,000 **DN**

A George III mahogany and inlaid bowfronted sideboard, the top with radiating veneers, above central crossbanded drawer flanked by two drawers (each modelled as two), on square tapered legs with spade feet.

c1800   77in (195cm) wide

£4,000-6,000 **L&T**

A Regency mahogany pedestal sideboard, with three frieze drawers, between plinths with coved tops and two short drawers under, on tapered pedestals with panelled doors enclosing shelves, on carved paw feet.

85in (215.5cm) wide

£1,500-2,500 **TEN**

ESSENTIAL REFERENCE - SIDEBOARDS

The sideboard is a piece of dining furniture, designed for use as a serving table. It typically features drawers for the storage of cutlery, table linen and condiments.

- Early 18thC examples were much like pier tables, with wooden or marble tops above friezes.
- The later 18thC form of a sideboard (featuring drawers and cupboards) was designed in the early 1760s by Robert Adam.
- Late 18thC sideboards typically had six tapering legs and relied on the figuring of the timber for decoration. They were frequently mounted with a brass gallery.
- The pedestal sideboard was introduced in the Regency period by Thomas Sheraton.
- From the late 18thC, sideboards were typically designed en suite with other dining furniture, and could incorporate knife boxes, plate-warmers and wine coolers.

A William IV mahogany breakfront pedestal sideboard, the gallery back with carved anthemion and C-scrolls, the base with frieze drawer flanked by cupboard doors and leaf-carved trusses.

90in (228.5cm) wide
£1,000-2,000   TEN

A George IV mahogany breakfront sideboard, each cellaret drawer opening with a revolving action.

c1825   *72in (182.5cm) wide*
£1,500-2,500   DN

A 19thC black and gold Strawberry Hill Gothic sideboard, with marble top.
c1860   *72.5in (184cm) wide*
£2,000-2,500   RMAA

A late 19thC Adam-style carved mahogany pedestal sideboard, with frieze drawer on turned and fluted tapered legs, the tapering pedestals with ebony lines, one with drawer, the other with cellaret, both with cupboards, on carved lion's claw feet.

91.75in (233cm) wide
£1,200-1,800   H&L

A late 19thC mahogany and boxwood strung breakfront sideboard, the brass gallery above two frieze drawers and two reeded tambour doors, flanked by quarter-veneered cupboard doors, between reeded columns, on six reeded legs.

79in (200cm) wide
£2,000-3,000   TEN

A Sheraton Revival painted satinwood and rosewood banded sideboard, the four doors painted with reserves depicting Classical maidens and flowers, on painted square tapering legs.
c1900   *60in (152.5cm) wide*
£4,000-6,000   FRE

A George III mahogany bowfront commode, with cut-out side handles above the tambour slide and pull-out drawer below, raised on moulded square legs.

29in (73.5cm) high

£500-700   **A&G**

A late George III mahogany pot cupboard, with pierced handgrips on square tapering legs.

32.75in (84cm) high

£500-700   **WW**

A George III mahogany tray-top night commode.

c1780

£600-800   **DN**

One of a pair of late George III mahogany bedside cupboards, by Gillows of Lancaster, each three-quarter gallery above a bowfront door, on reeded tapering legs.

c1805   *31in (81cm) high*

£6,000-8,000 pair   **DN**

A Victorian mahogany pot cupboard, the inset marble top above a fluted body.

29.25in (74cm) high

£200-300   **WW**

One of a pair of early 20thC carved oak and green marble-mounted bedside cupboards.

32in (81cm) high

£250-350 pair   **DN**

A late 19thC Dutch mahogany and marquetry pot cupboard, with frieze drawer above door enclosing two shelves, cracks.

32in (81cm) high

£500-700   **WW**

One of a pair of late 19thC Continental marble-topped bedside cupboards, with frieze drawer above panelled door.

28.5in (72cm) high

£800-1,200 pair   **WW**

FURNITURE

A rare small Charles II walnut desk, with two gate-legs, the interior with six drawers and a well, on bobbin-turned and block legs with turned feet.

24in (61cm) wide

£10,000-15,000   TOV

An 18thC New England Queen Anne tiger maple child's desk on frame, base later.

36in (91cm) high

£1,200-1,800   SK

A George I walnut kneehole desk, with long drawer above six short drawers, three further drawers within kneehole, on bracket feet.

The arrangement of three drawers within the kneehole of this desk is an unusual feature. The majority of kneehole desks of this form and period are fitted with a central cupboard door.

c1720   *30in (76cm) high*

£4,000-6,000   DN

ESSENTIAL REFERENCE - BOULLEWORK

An intricate form of marquetry in which brass is inlaid into a dark background of tortoiseshell or ebony.

- **It takes its name from French cabinetmaker and bronze worker, André-Charles Boulle (1642-1732), who lived and worked in the Louvre for Louis XIV. When the royal residence moved to Versailles, Boulle redesigned many of the interior fittings and much of the furniture.**
- **Boulle was not the only cabinet-maker developing this technique in the late 17thC/early 18thC. Jean Bérain is another notable example. Their work can be difficult to distinguish, but Bérain usually incorporated swirling scrolls (arabesques) alongside figural images, and his designs often have a more fanciful element than Boulle's.**
- **Boullework furniture, such as tables and chests, was often made in pairs.**
- **The process of cutting out the materials for one set of designs, the première-partie, also produced an opposing set, the contre-partie.**
- **It was much imitated by 19thC European furniture makers.**

A small 18thC French Boullework desk, with marquetry of engraved brass and tortoiseshell, one door and seven drawers.

33in (85cm) wide

£7,000-10,000   DOR

A George III mahogany and satinwood crossbanded partners' desk, the top with hinged easel fitting, with three panelled doors on the opposing side. *c1800*   *49in (124.5cm) wide*

£4,000-6,000   DN

An unusual George III mahogany serpentine desk, the shaped crossbanded top above seven short drawers and recessed cupboard with two panelled doors, opening to reveal a shelved interior, on moulded plinth base. *c1760*   *71in (180cm) wide*

£5,000-7,000   L&T

A 19thC Continental cream-lacquered serpentine desk, decorated with European figures in Chinese landscapes and birds, with seven drawers on cabriole legs.

45in (114.5cm) wide

£1,500-2,500   GORL

An exhibition quality folding campaign desk, retailed by Jenners of Edinburgh.

A probably New Hampshire Federal cherry wavy birch and mahogany veneer inlaid desk/bookcase, the upper section with hinged doors over eight drawers with bird's-eye maple diamonds and compartments, the lower with four cockbeaded drawers and fold-out writing surface.

c1800-10   59in (150cm) high

£3,000-4,000   SK

c1900

£3,000-3,500   GEOA

A Victorian burr walnut pedestal desk, with an inset leather writing surface above three frieze drawers, the pedestal supports each with four further graduated drawers, on a plinth base with castors.

c1860   60in (152cm) wide

£5,000-7,000   L&T

An American "standard grade" Wooton desk, Indianapolis, Indiana, with Renaissance Revival gilt and burl veneered exterior and ebonised and bird's eye maple interior.

Patented 1874   66in (167cm) high

£4,000-6,000   POOK

A late Victorian walnut partners' desk, with inset dark blue writing surface, each pedestal with conforming cupboard doors and four short and two long drawers, on plinth bases.

c1890   98in (249cm) wide

£6,000-8,000   TEN

A late 19thC French brass inlaid and ebonised bureau Mazarin, with marquetry of partly engraved brass and mother-of-pearl, with seven drawers and door, on conical legs.

40in (102cm) wide

£12,000-18,000   DOR

FURNITURE

Millers Compares: Kidney Desks

With furniture it is always worth considering the quality of manufacture – whether hand- or machine-made. If a piece was made by a master craftsman, it would have taken longer to make, it would have cost more at the time and will almost certainly be worth more – sometimes considerably more – now. Always look for good proportion and elegance. Stand back from a piece and appraise it. The colour of the wood is very important. Good patination will lift the value – refinishing will reduce it.

This desk has excellent shape, proportion, good colour and fine detailing. It is in good, clean condition.

It is inlaid and well-painted with floral swags and Classical motifs.

It is in the desirable Sheraton Revival tradition.

A late 19thC George III-style mahogany, inlaid and painted kidney desk, in the manner of Edwards & Roberts, with leather inset to top.

52in (134cm) wide

£5,000-7,000   **DN**

Although a pleasant shape this does not have the colour and sophistication of the first desk.

The shape feels slightly "pinched".

It is in need of restoration.

An Edwardian mahogany and satinwood banded kidney desk, in the manner of Edwards & Roberts. *c1910*

48in (122cm) wide

£800-1,200   **PC**

An early 20thC French Neo-classical mahogany-veneered roll-top desk, with filigree bronze mounts, seven external drawers, roll top and four interior drawers and a slide with embossed leather surface.

59in (150cm) wide

£15,000-25,000   **DOR**

An Edwardian mahogany and marquetry pedestal desk, by Edwards & Roberts, with inset leather writing surface, above three frieze drawers, the pedestal supports each with three drawers, on shaped plinth bases, stamped "Edwards & Roberts". *c1910*

48in (122cm) wide

£1,200-1,800   **L&T**

An Edwardian Sheraton-style harewood, satinwood-banded and ebony-strung lady's cylinder writing desk, with burr walnut and red leather writing table, with fitted interior, frieze drawer above two doors flanked by reeded columns, on squat legs with brass caps and castors.

43in (109.5cm) wide

£5,000-6,000   **TEN**

An early 20thC walnut writing desk, by Whytock & Reid, the top with matched burr veneers and gallery, the ogee frieze with two drawers, on cabriole legs with lappet-carved capitals and pointed pad feet.

c1930

53in (135cm) wide

£3,000-4,000   **L&T**

A japanned bureau, decorated with stylised Oriental landscapes in red and gilding, on a black lacquer ground, with fitted interior, the base with two short and two long graduated drawers, on square bracket feet.

c1700   *40in (102cm) wide*
£2,500-3,500   **TEN**

An early 18thC walnut veneer, inlaid and cross- and feather-banded bureau, bordered with boxwood, ebony and chequer feather-strung lines, with fitted interior, the base with two short and three long drawers, on ogee bracket feet.

38.5in (98cm) wide
£1,000-1,500   **H&L**

A Queen Anne walnut bureau, the fitted interior with drawers and pigeonholes, central cupboard and well section, above two short and two long drawers, on ogee bracket feet.

c1710   *39in (99cm) high*
£3,000-4,000   **DN**

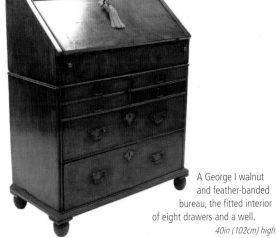

A George I walnut and feather-banded bureau, the fitted interior of eight drawers and a well.

40in (102cm) high
£2,000-3,000   **GORL**

CLOSER LOOK - GEORGE I FEATHER-BANDED BUREAU

The spectacular mulberry and walnut feather banding, with great patination, make this a desirable bureau.

Rather than use inlays, they chose to emphasise the decorative features in the wood itself.

The brass hardware (handles etc) is original.

Due to the war with France, British cabinetmakers developed their own styles, rather than following French fashions.

It has a well-fitted interior.

A George I mulberry and walnut feather-banded bureau, the interior fitted with an arrangement of drawers and cupboards above a well.

c1720   *39in (99cm) high*
£10,000-15,000   **DN**

FURNITURE

A George I cross- and feather-banded fruitwood bureau, the hinged fall revealing pigeonholes, drawers and a well with slide, above two short and two long drawers, on later bracket feet.

30.75in (78cm) wide

£2,000-3,000   **WW**

A small George I walnut bureau.

c1720   *37in (94cm) high*

£2,500-3,500   **DN**

An early 18thC Venetian Baroque walnut veneered serpentine bureau, with ebony contouring, also with engraved floral and figural ivory inlays, with five external drawers, a sloped writing surface, and six restored interior drawers.

48in (123.5cm) wide

£20,000-30,000   **DOR**

An 18thC Dutch walnut and floral marquetry bombé bureau, with graduated fitted interior containing drawers, pigeonholes and central cupboard, well with sliding cover, the case with two small and three long drawers, between shaped and canted angles, on splayed front feet.

46.75in (118.5cm) wide

£5,000-7,000   **H&L**

A George II walnut and feather-banded bureau, with fitted interior of pigeonholes and drawers above a sliding well, with two short and two long drawers, on later bracket feet.

39in (99cm) wide

£4,000-5,000   **TEN**

A mid-18thC yew wood bureau, the burr yew quarter-veneered fall enclosing fitted interior of pigeonholes above sliding well, the base with two short and three long drawers, on turnip feet.

42in (106.5cm) wide

£2,000-3,000   **TEN**

A George III mahogany and satinwood crossbanded bureau on stand, the fall enclosing fitted interior.

44in (111.5cm) wide

£1,500-2,500   **GORL**

A late George III mahogany bureau, with later marquetry and stringing, the interior with central cupboard door, drawers and pigeonholes.

42.25in (107.5cm) high

£600-800   **WW**

A North Shore, Massachusetts, Chippendale carved mahogany oxbow desk, with original brasses.

c1760-80   *43in (109cm) high*

£7,000-10,000   **SK**

CLOSER LOOK - PENNSYLVANIA SLANT-FRONT DESK

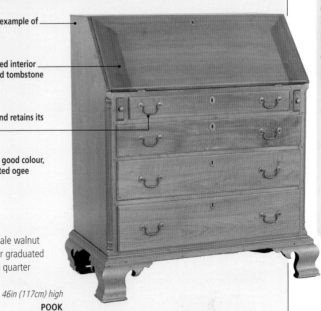

This piece is a good quality example of the form.

The fall-front encloses a fitted interior with serpentine drawers and tombstone panel prospect door.

It is in excellent condition and retains its original brass hardware.

It is desirable because of its good colour, small size and boldly executed ogee bracket feet.

A Pennsylvania Chippendale walnut slant-front desk, with four graduated drawers flanked by fluted quarter columns.

c1770   *46in (117cm) high*

£4,000-6,000   **POOK**

A mid-late 18thC possibly Pennsylvania Chippendale blue- and yellow-painted cherry slant-front desk, the interior painted yellow, with old brasses.

40.5in (103cm) high

£3,500-4,500   **SK**

A Massachusetts Chippendale mahogany block-front desk, the fall-front enclosing a fitted interior with fan-carved prospect door over case with four drawers and bracket feet.

c1770   *41.75in (106cm) high*

£4,000-6,000   **POOK**

A Connecticut River Valley Chippendale cherry slant-front desk, the fall-front with a carved six-petal flower enclosing fitted interior with carved drawers, one initialled "TH", above a case with four graduated drawers, on bracket feet.

42.75in (108.5cm) high

£5,000-7,000   **POOK**

A Boston Chippendale carved mahogany block-front slant-lid desk, the lid enclosing drawers with baluster-turned facades, and three valanced compartments, a blocked drawer and three concave blocked drawers, the topmost with carved shell, on bracket feet.

c1760-80   *43.75in (111cm) high*

£15,000-25,000   **SK**

A Victorian ebonised and burr walnut bonheur du jour, with recessed mirror flanked by two cupboards with brass gallery, the three central drawers above a red and gilt writing surface, and a shaped frieze drawer, on cabriole legs with brass foliate mounts and sabots.

50in (127cm) wide

£700-1,000   **TEN**

A late 19thC/early 20thC kingwood, rosewood, porcelain- and gilt metal-mounted bonheur du jour.

63in (160cm) high

£2,000-3,000   **DN**

A pair of late Victorian walnut, ebonised and floral marquetry bonheur du jours, with pierced brass gallery above mirror cupboard door and six drawers, oval red skiver above frieze drawer, on cabriole legs with brass foliate mounts and sabots.

47in (119.5cm) high

£6,000-8,000 pair   **TEN**

A Regency mahogany library davenport, the hinged writing slope with green leather skiver, with fitted compartments and drawers, four drawers to side, and conforming deep drawers to base, on compressed turned feet with recessed castors.

c1820   *37in (95cm) high*

£1,200-1,800   **TEN**

A Victorian walnut davenport, with an inkwell drawer and four further drawers, on wooden castors, damages and restoration.

33in (85cm) high

£500-700   **WW**

A Gothic Revival oak davenport.

30in (76cm) high

£700-900   **RMAA**

A Victorian walnut and brass-mounted davenport, the pierced brass gallery above mechanical rise with pigeonholes, the writing slope with leather skiver, flanked by seven sham drawers and three short drawers with brass locks, on a shaped base with brass egg-and-dart mounts, compressed feet and castors.

c1870   *29in (73.5cm) high*

£2,000-3,000   **TEN**

ESSENTIAL REFERENCE - CANTERBURIES

A canterbury is a small stand with slatted racks or divisions. There are two versions listed in Sheraton's "The Cabinet Maker's Dictionary": the music canterbury and the supper canterbury.

- Canterburies were made from the late 18thC. The first may have been designed for an Archbishop of Canterbury.
- The music canterbury is generally rectangular, with racks to hold sheet music (now often used to store magazines). Most examples have castors so they can be easily moved, and are short enough to be stored beneath a grand piano.
- The significantly taller supper canterbury is a round tray set above racks to hold cutlery. It stood beside a dining table, and was used, like a dumb waiter, at informal parties where servants were not in attendance. Supper canterburies typically have splayed legs and castors.

A William IV rosewood canterbury, after Loudon, with three divisions and lyre ends, with a frieze drawer and brass castors.

21.5in (54.5cm) high

£1,200-1,800　　　　WW

A late George III mahogany canterbury, the four concave-shaped dividers between turned uprights, the single drawer with small knob handles, on turned, tapering legs with brass caps and castors.

23in (58.5cm) wide

£1,200-1,800　　　　TEN

An early Victorian rosewood canterbury, the five concave-shaped dividers with ring-turned supports and profile-cut uprights, the single drawer above plain frieze, on turned baluster legs with brass caps and castors.

22in (56cm) wide

£2,000-3,000　　　　TEN

A late 19thC Louis XVI-style French amboyna, ebonised and marquetry supper canterbury, the top centred by marquetry musical trophies.

31in (79cm) high

£1,500-2,000　　　　DN

A late 19thC mahogany lyre-form canterbury, with scrolling supports with turned supports, the platform stretcher on scroll feet and castors.

19in (48cm) high

£400-600　　　　WW

An early 18thC walnut and floral marquetry cushion-framed mirror, the surround with scrolling foliage and flower heads in ebony and sycamore and with anthemion spandrels.

26.5in (67.5cm) high

£2,000-3,000   **H&L**

CLOSER LOOK - GEORGE III MIRROR

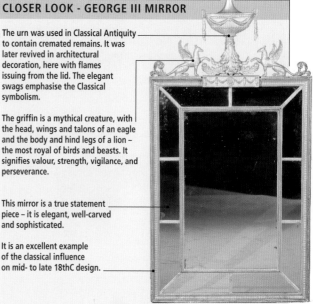

The urn was used in Classical Antiquity to contain cremated remains. It was later revived in architectural decoration, here with flames issuing from the lid. The elegant swags emphasise the Classical symbolism.

The griffin is a mythical creature, with the head, wings and talons of an eagle and the body and hind legs of a lion – the most royal of birds and beasts. It signifies valour, strength, vigilance, and perseverance.

This mirror is a true statement piece – it is elegant, well-carved and sophisticated.

It is an excellent example of the classical influence on mid- to late 18thC design.

A George III giltwood mirror, with mirrored border surmounted by a flaming urn pediment flanked by griffins.

80in (203cm) high

£15,000-25,000   **WES**

A Queen Anne eglomisé mirror, the panel depicting figures in a garden set within lacquered frame with chinoiserie decoration.

33.25in (85.5cm) high

£3,000-4,000   **LHA**

A George II giltwood and gesso pier glass, with ho ho bird cresting within a Rococo carved and pierced frame with icicle-carved corners above trailing leafy vines and flower heads with shaped pendant.

43in (110cm) high

£7,000-10,000   **L&T**

A Georgian lacquered and parcel gilt mirror, the shaped crest and surround with Chinoiserie decoration.

63in (160cm) high

£4,000-6,000   **LHA**

One of a pair of 18thC Italian Baroque gilded mirrors, Veneto, in ornamented and pierced wooden frames, plates later.

55in (140cm) high

£10,000-15,000 pair   **DOR**

A Federal inlaid and parcel-gilt mahogany mirror, John Elliot & Sons, Philadelphia, repairs.

c1804-10   *44.5in (113cm) high*

£1,000-1,500   **SK**

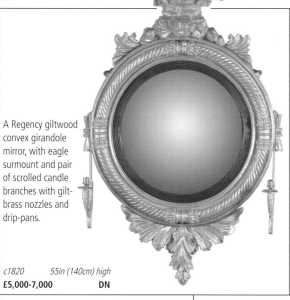

A Regency giltwood convex girandole mirror, with eagle surmount and pair of scrolled candle branches with gilt-brass nozzles and drip-pans.

c1820 55in (140cm) high
£5,000-7,000 DN

A pair of early 19thC Italian walnut and parcel-gilt wall mirrors.

29in (73.5cm) high
£2,500-3,500 DN

A 19thC Florentine carved and limed wood wall mirror, the ornate relief-carved frame with high-relief mask spandrals and an egg-and-dart moulded edge.

56in (142.5cm) high
£2,500-3,500 L&T

A 19thC gilt composition wall mirror, the leaf-cast frame surmounted by foliate scrolls and birds, the cartouche-shaped plume with a floral swag below three tiered shelves with spiral turned supports.

56in (142.5cm) high
£700-1,000 TEN

A pair of 19thC gilt and composition three-branch girandoles, the oval bevelled glass plates within a beaded slip, the moulded frame headed by scrolling foliate and shell plumes.

39in (99cm) high
£2,000-3,000 TEN

A 19thC French carved walnut overmantel mirror, the scroll leafage-carved frame with basket of flowers and a central shell-and-leaf cresting above a cartouche with a carved profile of a Roman emperor.

51in (129.5cm) high
£1,000-1,500 WW

A 19thC giltwood convex mirror, re-gilded.

22.25in (56.5cm) diam
£300-400 WW

A 19thC George III-style carved giltwood overmantel mirror, with ho ho bird cresting.

54in (137cm) wide
£5,000-7,000 DN

A 19thC Italian polychrome and painted cartouche-shaped Venetian wall mirror, the plate etched with a dancing harlequin.

36.5in (92.5cm) high

£800-1,200　　　**WW**

An Italian Renaissance Revival giltwood and gesso tabernacle frame, the broken pediment with flaming urn finials.

27in (68.5cm) high

£1,500-2,500　　　**WW**

A late 19thC Rococo-style gilt and gesso cartouche-shaped wall mirror, with acanthus leaf scrolling frame and two pairs of moulded brackets, winged serpent supports centred by foliate scrolling plume.

59in (150cm) wide

£2,500-3,500　　　**TEN**

A late 19thC mahogany and parcel-gilt wall mirror, with bevelled plate, the ribboned tied cresting with trailing husks.

48.5in (122cm) high

£1,000-1,500　　　**WW**

A late 19thC Neo-classical-style carved limewood wall mirror, the scale-carved frame surmounted by an ornate relief-carved arched pediment centred by a ram's mask motif.

77in (195cm) high

£1,500-2,500　　　**L&T**

A late 19thC Italian giltwood and gesso wall mirror, with bevelled plate and shaped radiating sun crest.

42.5in (108cm) high

£1,000-1,500　　　**WW**

A Victorian giltwood and gesso wall mirror, the oval bevelled plate to a beaded edge and an egg-and-dart outer frame, with a scrolling leaf and flower surmount and a conforming pendant base, damages and restoration.

49in (124cm) high

£500-700　　　**WW**

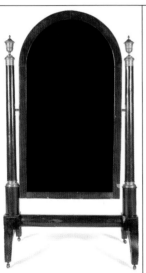

An Empire mahogany cheval mirror, the frame capped with gilt bronze urn form finials.

68in (172cm) high

£1,200-1,800   LHA

A George IV mahogany cheval mirror, on ring-turned stretchered supports with moulded scroll supports, brass caps and castors, damages.

56.5in (144cm) high

£800-1,200   WW

ESSENTIAL REFERENCE - DRESSING TABLE MIRRORS

Free-standing dressing table mirrors were made from the late 17thC. They were initially made of silver or silver-gilt and designed to match a lady's dressing set.

● By the early 18thC, sturdier, dressing table mirrors were made in the fashionable woods of the period. These typically featured a plinth base with drawers and a rectangular mirror plate. The most sophisticated, such as the example on the right, had serpentine bases.

● Oval dressing mirrors were popular from the 1770s until the British Regency/American Federal period when rectangular plates were again popular. Decoration was often limited to baluster-turning on the upright supports.

An early 18thC walnut toilet mirror, the later plate in shaped swing frame on a stepped serpentine-front box base, on later feet.

27in (68.5cm) high

£300-400   WW

A late Victorian mahogany cheval mirror, with moulded frame between scrolling leaf carved uprights joined by turned stretcher above S-scrolls centred by a silk floral pad, on castors.

59in (150cm) high

£1,500-2,500   TEN

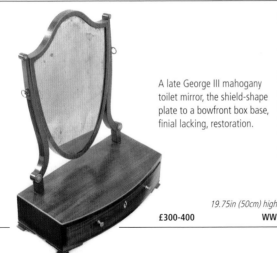

A late George III mahogany toilet mirror, the shield-shape plate to a bowfront box base, finial lacking, restoration.

19.75in (50cm) high

£300-400   WW

An early 19thC mahogany dressing table mirror, with a serpentine box base, replacements and restoration.

21.25in (54cm) wide

£300-400   WW

A Victorian mahogany circular toilet mirror, on marble inset base and ceramic bun feet.

29.5in (74.5cm) high

£400-600   WW

A French amaranth, tulipwood and gilt metal-mounted étagère, stamped "G Durand".

An étagère is a set of free-standing shelves (in two or three tiers), supported by corner posts or uprights. It is similar to a dumb water and whatnot and was used either for serving food or to display collections. Some have a removable top tier, which could be used as a tray.

c1880   *31in (79cm) high*

£3,000-4,000   **DN**

An American Rococo Revival carved rosewood étagère, possibly by Alexander Roux, the serpentine frame carved in high relief with roses, foliage, and C-scrolls, with mirrored back.

c1860   *113in (287cm) high*

£18,000-22,000   **SK**

An Edwardian rosewood and ivory marquetry oval étagère, three small drawers decorated with scrolling foliage, the side panels decorated with arabesque designs, on cabriole legs united by galleried undertier.

19.25in (49cm) wide

£2,000-3,000   **H&L**

An early 20thC Louis XV-style rosewood and ormolu-mounted étagère, with two graduated quarter-veneer serpentine-shaped tiers, on slender square cabriole legs with sabots.

53in (134.5cm) high

£800-1,200   **L&T**

A George II mahogany three-tier dumb waiter, the dished, moulded rotating tiers on tapered column supports, the triform cabriole-leg base with pad feet.

43in (109cm) high

£800-1,200   **L&T**

A George III mahogany three-tier dumb waiter, with three dished shelves, carved and turned baluster base and supports, on cabriole legs with pad feet.

42in (106cm) high

£5,000-7,000   **SWO**

A Regency mahogany dumb waiter, with two circular drop-leaf tiers, on a ring turned and reeded baluster stem, panelled tripod supports, brass caps and castors.

42in (106cm) high

£2,000-3,000   **WW**

ESSENTIAL REFERENCE - TEAPOYS

The teapoy (from the Sanskrit for "three feet") is often a small tripod stand topped by a lockable wooden box. It was used to store and mix tea in the drawing room.

- The top box typically contained tea caddies, a glass mixing bowl or a combination of both.
- The teapoy was popular during the early to mid-19thC.
- Early teapoys were elaborately decorated with lacquer, penwork or brass-inlay on rosewood, and these are desirable. From 1820 most were relatively plain, except for Tunbridgeware examples.
- Some teapoys have been converted into work boxes, which decreases the value and desirability.

A mid-19thC rosewood teapoy, with fluting and column ornament, hinged lid and loose interior boxes.

35in (90cm) high

£4,000-5,000   **DOR**

A Regency rosewood and cut brass marquetry teapoy and sewing table ensuite, each decorated in première- and contra-partie boullework, engraving and pen-work, the teapoy with four lidded canisters and two apertures, the sewing table with lift-out tray.

It is likely these pieces were made within the circle of French-trained cabinet maker Louis Constantin Le Gaigneur (active 1814-1821), who was almost exclusively patronised by the Prince Regent and his intimates. The decoration to the teapoy and sewing table comprise première-partie, a panel of rosewood inlaid with brass, and contra-partie, a sheet of brass inlaid with rosewood.

c1815   *31in (79cm) high*

£20,000-25,000   **DN**

A William IV rosewood teapoy, the top lifting to become a stationary tier.

c1835   *37in (94cm) high*

£1,000-1,500   **DN**

A William IV burr elm teapoy, the panelled sarcophagus-form top with applied ripple mouldings, opening to fitted interior, on turned and acanthus-carved column support, with cartouche base and paw feet, on castors.

31in (79cm) high

£1,000-1,500   **L&T**

A Victorian lacquered and chinoiserie-decorated teapoy, with three fitted canisters, the stand with turned stem and downswept legs, on claw-and-ball feet.

c1860   *33in (84cm) high*

£350-450   **DN**

FURNITURE

A George III mahogany and crossbanded cellaret, opening to a divided interior with divisions for eight bottles.

c1800 *28in (71cm) high*
£500-700 **DN**

A George III mahogany and brass-bound wine cooler, lead-lined.

c1770 *30in (76cm) wide*
£1,000-1,500 **DN**

A George III mahogany and brass-bound octagonal wine cooler, with lead-lined interior, brass loop handles and a brass spigot below, on a moulded stand with fluted tapering legs.

29in (73.5cm) wide
£4,000-6,000 **TEN**

A George III mahogany oval wine cellaret, the cavetto-moulded cover enclosing a metal liner, on stand with splayed and chamfered legs headed by scrolled angle frets, on castors.

28in (71cm) high
£5,000-7,000 **L&T**

A George III Chippendale mahogany and brass bound wine cooler, with two lion mask drop handles, and lead-lined interior, on four cabriole legs with pad feet and recessed castors.

24in (61cm) wide
£10,000-15,000 **TEN**

A George III mahogany and marquetry oval wine cooler, with lozenge and floral marquetry motifs, with scroll handles and tap to underside, on triangular- and square-section tapering legs, inlaid to simulate fluting, with castors.

c1780 *28in (71cm) wide*
£4,000-6,000 **DN**

A George III mahogany and crossbanded octagonal wine cooler, repairs.

c1800 *28in (71cm) high*
£400-600 **DN**

Judith Picks: Wine Coolers

Wine coolers, also known as cellarets and even, if you are very grand, gardevin have been an essential piece of furniture since the 18thC, although examples were made as early as the 15thC.

They were made in silver, porcelain or wood, but from the mid-18thC the most typical were lead-lined examples with a hexagonal or oval body with vertical sections of mahogany held together by two or three brass bands.

During the early 19thC lidded cellarets of sarcophagus form dominated the Regency pattern books. As with this example, many had great lion's paw feet and lion-mask ring handles and were larger and could be locked.

These are still useful today and can be found at many price points. Perfect to chill that rather delightful bottle of white burgundy or – with this fine example – a whole case.

A Regency mahogany sarcophagus-form wine cooler, with lead-lined interior, the tapering body between canted sides, on claw-and-ball feet.

28in (71cm) wide

£1,700-2,000   TEN

An early 19thC mahogany and rosewood crossbanded gardevin, in the manner of Gillows of Lancaster, with fitted interior, bottle and decanter divisions, and lion-mask ring handles, on turned and reeded tapering legs with brass castors.

25.5in (65cm) high

£2,000-3,000   A&G

A Regency rosewood and mahogany cellaret, the hinged top enclosing compartmentalised interior.

29in (73.5cm) wide

£1,000-1,500   GORL

A Victorian carved oak ogee sarcophagus-form cellaret, with half-reeded sides and projecting scroll and husk decorated corbels, with metal lined interior, on splayed block feet.

34.25in (87cm) long

£1,200-1,800   H&L

A 19thC and later Irish-style yew and brass-bound cellaret, with a paper-lined interior for six bottles.

24in (61cm) high

£500-700   WW

FURNITURE

A late 19thC French marquetry and gilt metal mounted jardinière, the removable top opening to a metal liner.

30in (76cm) high

£450-550   DN

A pair of late 19thC French jardinières, decorated in Boulle marquetry with brass and partly coloured and engraved lacquer.

33in (84cm) high

£8,000-12,000   DOR

A late 19thC French veneer and marquetry jardinière, with a removable lid and lead liner, and figural bronze doré decoration.

43in (110cm) high

£6,000-8,000   DOR

A late 19thC Anglo-Indian carved hardwood jardinière, supported by stylised exotic birds on trefoil base.

35in (90cm) diam

£800-1,200   GORL

An Edwardian mahogany jardinière stand, with a lift-out brass liner.

28.5in (72cm) high

£250-350   WW

A Neo-classical carved giltwood torchère, with laurel wreath and animal-skull carved frieze, on fluted turned legs with triform stretcher and urn finial, terminating in bellflower- and acanthus-carved scroll feet, lacks marble top.

c1800   *49in (124.5cm) high*

£1,000-1,500   L&T

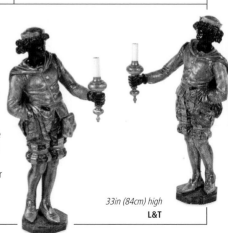

A pair of 19thC 18thC-Venetian-style gilt and polychrome lacquer blackamoor torchères, each figure holding aloft a single lamp, on octagonal plinth bases, fitted for electricity.

33in (84cm) high

£8,000-12,000   L&T

A pair of Victorian Regency-style parcel gilt mahogany tripod torchère stands, with three slender ram-headed supports (with triform undertier) terminating in ram's feet, curved stretchers on ball feet.

c1900   *39in (99cm) high*

£2,500-3,500   **L&T**

A George III mahogany butler's tray, with serpentine sides, on folding stand with turned legs.

28in (71cm) wide

£800-1,200   **GORB**

A George III mahogany butler's tray.

c1770   *31in (79cm) wide*

£500-700   **DN**

A late Regency papier-mâché tray, with gilt decoration of floral sprays, insects and a bird.

30.25in (77cm) wide

A pair of George III-style giltwood torchères, the hexagonal fret-pierced galleried tops on stop-fluted turned column supports, with acanthus-carved cabriole scroll tripod bases.

53in (134.5cm) high

£2,500-3,500   **L&T**

£1,000-1,500   **WW**

A William IV mahogany campaign butler's table, the tray lifting to reveal a hinged top and screw fitting for turned leg, on turned X-frame united by stretchers.

c1835   *32in (81cm) high*

£1,500-2,000   **DN**

A 19thC mahogany oval tray, with satinwood centre, tulipwood crossbanding, chequerbanding, within radiating bands of various specimen woods, and further crossbanding, with brass handles.

33in (84cm) wide

£400-600   **DN**

One of a pair of Georgian mahogany washstands, with raised backs and side panels, each with plain frieze, on square tapering legs.

41.5in (105.5cm) high

£1,500-2,500 pair **A&G**

A Napoleon III pedestal, with floral and figural bronze mounts and still life relief in semi-precious stones, with a shaped marble top.

51in (129cm) high

£8,000-12,000 **DOR**

ESSENTIAL REFERENCE - BLACK FOREST FURNITURE

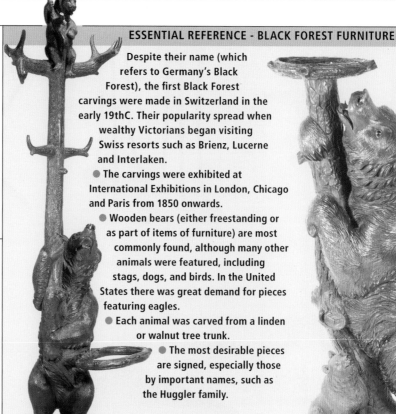

Despite their name (which refers to Germany's Black Forest), the first Black Forest carvings were made in Switzerland in the early 19thC. Their popularity spread when wealthy Victorians began visiting Swiss resorts such as Brienz, Lucerne and Interlaken.

● The carvings were exhibited at International Exhibitions in London, Chicago and Paris from 1850 onwards.

● Wooden bears (either freestanding or as part of items of furniture) are most commonly found, although many other animals were featured, including stags, dogs, and birds. In the United States there was great demand for pieces featuring eagles.

● Each animal was carved from a linden or walnut tree trunk.

● The most desirable pieces are signed, especially those by important names, such as the Huggler family.

A Black Forest carved and stained wood hall stand, with removable metal drip tray.

c1900 *81in (206cm) high*

£2,500-3,500 **DN**

A late 19thC Black Forest carved softwood climbing bear and cub torchère, both naturalistically carved beside a tree trunk.

49in (124.5cm) high

£3,000-4,000 **CAPE**

A George III mahogany kettle stand, the fluted frieze with brushing slide, on square tapering stop fluted legs with shaped X-stretcher and spade feet.

c1785 *28in (71cm) high*

£4,000-6,000 **L&T**

A late Victorian walnut duet stand, with two lyre-shaped rests with hinged ratchet easels, the sliding brass pole above a turned locking handle, on three leaf carved cabriole legs.

52in (132cm) high

£1,500-2,500 **TEN**

An Austrian revival style walnut and oak wool container, Constantin Drbal, with hinged lid and decorated with embossed leather and brass ornamental nails.

The firm Constantin Drbal, was a royal and imperial purveyor, sculptor and specialist in cut furniture and leather work.

c1880/90 *26in (67cm) high*

£3,000-4,000 **DOR**

A mahogany easel stand, the pediment with carved roundel flanked by scrolling dolphin brackets, the leaf-carved frieze above three uprights with an adjustable channel support, the lower section with hinged panel relief carved with Classical motifs and putto.

c1900 *83in (211cm) high*

£600-800 **TEN**

ESSENTIAL REFERENCE - SCREENS

Screens originated in China in around 2ndC AD. They were known in Europe from at least the Middle Ages.

- They were developed to help block draughts, separate interior spaces, and shield people from the direct heat of fires.
- The quality of decoration and materials (wood, leather and decorative cloths) reflected the owner's social standing.
- The folding screen is the oldest type. Smaller more portable screens were developed in the 18thC. These included two popular types of firescreen: the polescreen, which had a movable panel that could be used to protect a person's face from the heat of a fire, and the cheval screen, which had a fixed panel, often inset with tapestry or needlework.
- In the 19thC some screens were decorated with cut-out coloured prints (scraps).
- The increasing introduction of enclosed fires, electricity and central heating made the screen almost redundant.

A large early Victorian carved rosewood firescreen, the pierced surmount above a floral tapestry panel, on stretchered scroll supports with brass castors.

63.75in (162cm) high

£800-1,200   WW

A Victorian rosewood tapestry screen, with a gros and petit point panel, surmounted by a pierced foliate carved cresting and flanked by twin spiral turned pilasters, on carved cabriole legs with ceramic castors.

77in (195.5cm) high

£2,000-3,000   L&T

A large Victorian mahogany fire screen, with open-twist supports to the acanthus-detailed frame, and needlework panel to either side.

53in (134.5cm) high

£300-400   FLD

A George III-style mahogany and tapestry work screen, with pierced cresting and needlework inset depicting a vase of flowers above a Greek key frieze, on acanthus- and scroll-carved supports.

c1900   *64in (163cm) high*

£1,000-1,500   DN

A late 18thC Dutch leather eight-fold screen, decorated with Chinoiserie figures in landscapes, flowers and vases, probably reduced in height.

104in (264cm) high

£7,000-10,000   DN

A Louis XV-style painted three-panel floor screen, decorated with a rural scenes of a young couple in 18thC dress, reverse with floral bouquets.

65in (165cm) high

£1,000-1,500   FRE

A late Victorian four-fold découpage screen, covered with lithographically printed scraps, with cast gilt brass handles.

71in (180cm) high

£800-1,200   WW

FURNITURE

A probably South Carolina Federal ebonised and satinwood inlaid mahogany tester bedstead, the footposts with rice carving and vertical ebonised and satinwood line inlay surmounted by water leaf-carved capitals, on heavy spade feet.
c1790
£2,500-3,500   **WES**

A probably 19thC gilt and gesso four-poster bed, the domed top with gilt beaded and scrolling brackets and oval medallion of Classical figures, with pink and blue gathered silk drapes and pink button-back headboard, with two leaf cast and fluted upright posts.
122in (310cm) high
£6,000-8,000   **TEN**

A late 19thC/early 20thC Indian carved hardwood and ebonised four poster bed.
84in (213cm) high
£1,500-2,500   **DN**

A Victorian walnut bedroom suite, comprising a bed, chest with mirror and side table.
Headboard 104in (264cm) high
£3,000-4,000   **LHA**

An early 20thC French bedroom set, comprising a double bed, pair of night stands, dresser with mirror and armoire.
Armoire 92in (234cm) high
£1,200-1,800 set   **DRA**

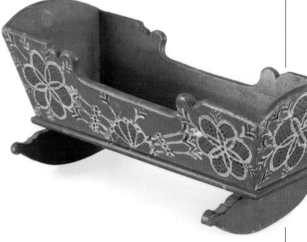

A Lancaster County, Pennsylvania painted poplar doll cradle, by the Compass Artist, with blue and white pinwheel decoration on salmon ground.
c1800   *16.5in (42cm) long*
£25,000-35,000   **POOK**

An early 19thC Italian rosewood prie-dieu, with four graduated drawers and pull-out candle slides (one missing).

A prie-dieu is a type of prayer desk primarily intended for private devotional use. Typical examples have a sloping shelf for books, and a cushioned pad on which to kneel.

34.25in (87cm) high

£500-700   WW

A 19thC mahogany dog basket, the three galleried sides above a loose cushion seat, on squat cabriole legs.

27in (69cm) wide

£1,000-1,500   L&T

A Regency mahogany bidet.

c1815   *21in (53cm) wide*

£200-300   DN

A pair of Chippendale-style giltwood brackets, their shaped demi-lune shelves supported by carved ho ho birds on foliate C-scrolls.

17.5in (44cm) high

£400-600   FRE

A set of late Regency painted and leather-mounted bed steps, with three green leather-inset treads, the top step fitted with a drawer enclosing a bidet, the second drawer sliding forward to a chamber pot.

c1830   *24in (61cm) high*

£1,500-2,500   SK

A Renaissance Revival coal scuttle, with carved bust finials and griffin masks and floral motifs throughout, with drop front opening and cast iron shovel.

27.75in (70cm) high

£500-700   LHA

A set of George III mahogany library steps, of typical A-frame form with nine rungs.

67in (170cm) high

£2,500-3,500   L&T

A set of George III-style mahogany library steps.

£300-400   DN

BOXES

A George III oval papier-mâché tea caddy, painted with figures and buildings in landscapes, with an inner lid.

Similar caddies have been attributed to Henry Clay, who patented his process of laminated panels made from pasted paper sheets in 1772. The business was eventually taken over by Jennens and Bettridge in 1816.

5in (12cm) high

£3,000-4,000   SWO

A George III oval tortoiseshell tea caddy, with a Sheffield plate ring handle, the vacant interior with traces of foil.

5.5in (14cm) wide

£1,000-1,500   WW

A George III harewood and marquetry oval tea caddy, with boxwood edging, with divided interior with traces of foil.

5.75in (14.5cm) wide

£800-1,200   WW

A George III tortoiseshell and silver decagonal tea caddy, the silver stringing with engraved decoration, front with silver plaque, missing interior lid.

5in (12cm) high

£1,500-2,500   ROS

A George III mahogany tea caddy, inlaid with ivory, rosewood, satinwood and boxwood, the inside lid with geometric engraving, and signed "M Milner 1780".

1780   *5.25in (13cm) wide*

£2,000-2,500   SWO

A late George III parquetry tea caddy, with oval panels, faux fluting and dots with banding and stringing in various woods, some stained, with brass handle and later lined interior.

Parquetry is a geometric variation of marquetry (a decorative veneer made up of small pieces of inlaid wood). It was used most widely in the 17thC and 18thC.

5.5in (14cm) wide

£700-1,000   WW

ESSENTIAL REFERENCE - THE HISTORY OF TEA

Tea was introduced to England from China sometime in the middle of the 17thC. Although there are earlier references of its use by traders in China, it was not until 1657 that we have the first account of its sale in England.

- In the late 17thC Charles II (who grew up in Holland) and Queen Catherine of Braganza were known to be tea drinkers. The aristocracy soon followed suit.
- Wooden tea caddies were made early in the 18thC, but were not introduced in any numbers as a home accessory until the second half of the century. The word caddy derives from the Malay "kati", a measure of weight about three-fifths of a kilogramme.
- In the 18thC and 19thC tea caddies were the ultimate status symbols because tea was prohibitively expensive. In fact, it was so valuable that the upper middle classes gave their used tea (called "slop" – think of slop bowl) as a gift to their servants. Caddies were kept locked to prevent theft. To preserve the freshness of the tea, the interior compartments were lined with lead –in this period no one knew lead was highly toxic.

- The high price of tea led to the 1773 Boston Tea Party in America, where the Colonists protested the high taxes on the commodity.
- After 1784, tea caddies gradually became larger following William Pitt's Commutation Act which removed most of the tea tax. An emergent middle class could start to take tea for the first time as the average price dropped by three shillings a pound. Tea was just beginning to become a national drink and more people could try the taste of Chinese Bohea, Green or Hyson tea.

A George III inlaid rosewood oval tea caddy, inlaid with fan medallions, with decorated lidded compartment.

6in (15cm) wide

£600-800   H&L

A late 18thC George III painted lead tea caddy in the form of a house, the interior bereft (back panel later replaced entirely with pine).

9in (23cm) high

£1,000-1,500   DN

A Regency tortoiseshell bow-front tea caddy, with pewter stringing and two silver plaques, one initialled "W.M.C.", on plated ball feet, with a twin-lidded and lined interior, with coral handles, damages.

7.25in (18.5cm) wide

£3,000-4,000   WW

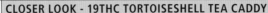

CLOSER LOOK - 19THC TORTOISESHELL TEA CADDY

Green tortoiseshell is the rarest colour, followed by blond, then red and finally sable.

There is no such thing as a green tortoise. The colour is imparted by a painted green layer under the translucent shell.

The silver finial, stringing, feet and lock are further signs of opulence.

Even though this caddy is in need of expensive restoration, its rarity and desirability contribute to its high price.

A 19thC green-stained tortoiseshell twin-division tea caddy, with domed lid, ball finial and feet.

7in (18cm) wide

£7,000-10,000   ROS

A late Regency tortoiseshell tea caddy, with pewter stringing and basket weave panels, the interior with a lid, on plated ball feet, restoration.

5in (12.5cm) high

£1,500-2,500   WW

A late Regency tortoiseshell pagoda-form tea caddy, with double-well lidded interior, the cover with silver plaque, on silvered metal ball feet.

c1820   *7.5in (19cm) wide*

£1,500-2,500   FRE

An early Victorian japanned bombé-form tea caddy, decorated with oriental figures, the interior with a pair of hinged canisters, on stamped gilt brass paw feet.

12.75in (32.5cm) wide

£1,500-2,500   WW

A Victorian tartan ware tea caddy, the cover painted with the "Burns Monument," with a divided interior, on brass ball feet.

10in (25.5cm) wide

£2,500-3,500   WW

A Victorian tortoiseshell and mother-of-pearl sarcophagus-form tea caddy, inlaid with flowers emblematic of Great Britain, base with handwritten paper label dated "21st October 1868".

7in (18cm) wide

£3,500-4,500   SWO

A 19thC Vizagapatam sandalwood and ivory tea caddy, decorated with pierced and lac decorated ivory mounts and panels featuring figures, a cat and a monkey, the interior with a similar panel inscribed "In Memory of the christening at Kylassa 28th Oct 1879," lead-lined.

10in (25.5cm) wide

£800-1,200   WW

A late 17thC silkwork and petit point textile work box, decorated with figures, a farmstead, animals and flowers, with fitted interior, on gilt fluted bun feet, in glass box with mahogany base and bun feet, carcass later.

12.5in (32cm) wide

£2,500-3,000   GORL

An early 19thC French pierced-ivory and brass-backed work box, lid decorated with flowers and a man and a woman, with paper-lined interior.

11.5in (29cm) wide

£700-1,000   WW

A Regency rosewood and ivory-inlaid sewing box, the compartments with ivory, tortoiseshell and ebony lids, the inner lid inlaid with ivory.

15.25in (39cm) wide

£600-800   LHA

A mid-19thC Anglo-Indian sarcophagus-form work box, with a fluted base and fitted interior, on bun feet.

13.5in (34cm) wide

£1,200-1,800   GORL

A mid-19thC Anglo-Indian ivory and sandalwood work box, Vizagapatam, with sloped covers flanking the swing handle, decorated with tendrils of ivy and horn-inlaid rims.

8in (19.5cm) wide

£1,500-2,500   L&T

ESSENTIAL REFERENCE - VIZAGAPATAM

Vizagapatam is a town on the southeastern coast of India. The British Empire took control in 1668, eventually taking control of India's entire eastern seaboard by the 18thC.
- Fine inlaid pieces that combined British and Indian sensibilities were being made in Vizagapatam by the mid-18thC for local merchants. Forms were almost exclusively Western, with Western and Indian inspired decoration.
- From the early 19thC Vizagapatam pieces were exported to Europe, and were displayed at the Great Exhibition in London in 1851.
- The Vizagapatam workshops declined in the late 19thC and early 20thC as demand waned.

An early 19thC Vizagapatam ivory-veneered and metal-mounted sarcophagus-form workbox, decorated with bands of scrolling and trailing foliage, with lidded and open compartments and accessories, with drawer below, on lion's claw feet.

11in (28cm) wide

£3,000-4,000   H&L

A 19thC French satinwood and cut-steel sarcophagus-form sewing necessaire, the lid with mirror, the interior with velvet lined lift-out tray fitted with mother-of-pearl and gilt metal-mounted utensils, some replacements.

9.75in (25cm) wide

£900-1,200   WW

A 19thC Vizagapatam sandalwood and porcupine quill work box, lac-decorated with ivory and horn, with lidded compartments containing horn accessories, on ribbed horn feet, damages.

12.75in (32.5cm) wide

£1,500-2,500   WW

An Anglo-Indian coromandel work box, inlaid with specimen wood radiating segments and lac-decorated bone foliage, with a compartmented lidded tray and another with specimen wood covers, repairs.

16.25in (41.5cm) wide

£600-800   WW

A 17thC Flemish ebony and ivory inlaid table cabinet, the external doors decorated with nobles and equestrian figures, the interior with central door decorated with ivory panel of a Classical female and nine small drawers with ivory figural landscape views, on bun feet.

27.5in (70cm) wide

£3,500-4,500   FRE

A 17thC oak spice cabinet, the panelled door with painted decoration, enclosing six drawers, with alterations.

13in (33.5cm) wide

£1,500-2,500   SWO

A late 17thC/early 18thC Indian rosewood and ivory inlaid table cabinet, the fall enclosing a symmetrical arrangement of ivory-inlaid drawers.

20in (51cm) wide

£1,000-2,000   TEN

A late 17thC Flemish ebonised table cabinet, with ivory panels of Romanesque soldiers, trophies and stylised pastoral landscapes, over seven drawers and small cupboard enclosing a further six drawers.

18in (45.5cm) wide

£3,500-4,500   GORL

An 18thC Indo-Portugese tortoiseshell and ivory table cabinet, with white metal mounts, escutcheon and side handles, with a hinged fall revealing six drawers, the central drawer with secret drawer behind, repairs.

8.25in (21cm) wide

£8,000-12,000   WW

An 18thC Piedmontese walnut and marquetry table cabinet, with brass mounts and inlaid ivory, the interior with cupboard and drawers, on later table stand.

24in (61cm) wide

£2,000-3,000   L&T

A late 18thC Indo-Portuguese table cabinet, with tortoiseshell, ivory and green-stained ivory decoration and marquetry bands, enclosing nine drawers.

10in (25cm) wide

£5,000-7,000   GORL

A George III carved mahogany table cabinet, the dentil cornice above foliate-carved frieze and two doors carved with oval acanthus wreaths, over fitted interior with four drawers, on moulded plinth base.

c1780   *25in (63.5cm) wide*

£1,000-2,000   L&T

A North European marquetry and satinwood table cabinet, with central cupboard surrounded by 13 small doors, with twin carrying handles.

30in (76cm) wide

£3,000-4,000   DUK

BOXES

A Vizagapatam step-form ivory table cabinet, engraved with trailing leaves and flowers, the drawers lined in cedar with silver handles and escutcheons, brass carrying handles, on bracket feet.

c1790-1800   *23in (58.5cm) wide*

£3,500-4,500   SWO

A late 18thC/early 19thC Indo-Portuguese ivory- and tortoiseshell-mounted table cabinet, with fall front enclosing ten drawers, on stud feet.

9in (23cm) wide

£1,500-2,500   GORB

A Regency bird's eye maple collector's cabinet, with ebony stringing, the cover revealing a fixed tray top above six graduated drawers enclosed by two doors, on brass ball feet.

14in (36cm) wide

£1,000-2,000   CHEF

CLOSER LOOK - 18THC TABLE CABINET

Cabinets of this design are thought to have been made for Dutch East India Company officials in either Batavia (now Jakarta) or Sri Lanka.

The metal fittings and the unusual drawer construction are both typical of the form.

The design was presumably derived from contemporary Japanese and Chinese lacquer cabinets.

A late 18thC teak and brass-bound table cabinet, the two doors enclosing an arrangement of ten drawers with brass drop handles, on bracket feet with shaped apron.

24in (61cm) wide

£2,000-3,000   TEN

A 19thC late-17thC-style ebonised Antwerp table cabinet, applied with ormolu figures and columns, and Vienna enamel plaques decorated with Classical scenes, the interior panels with Dutch landscape scenes, incomplete.

Table cabinets originated in late 15thC Italy as the demand grew for a place in which the wealthy could display curiosities or store confidential documents. In the 17thC they developed into more monumental, decorative items. They were often made to sit on a specially designed table or stand. Antwerp became an important centre of manufacture. The woods used and their purpose varied greatly. Ebony was highly prized.

21in (53.5cm) wide

£5,000-6,000   ROS

A 19thC Viennese enamel and ebonised table cabinet, with painted panels of mythological scenes and gilt-metal mounts, single drawer below twin door cabinet of three drawers and further drawer above, with an urn surmount, on a bracket foot platform, repairs.

9in (23cm) wide

£4,500-5,500   WW

A 19thC Italian Baroque-style engraved bone and ebonised wood table cabinet, damages.

£800-1,200   WES

A 19thC Italian ebonised and marquetry table cabinet, with box top, the central figural door enclosing three drawers, three further drawers to either side, base with long drawer.

16.5in (42cm) high

£300-400   WW

A possibly German painted writing box, painted with six stylised cartouches of foliage and scrolls on a dark ground within red and white borders, the sides with fruit and foliage, with iron handles, interior with pigeon holes, dated.

1585   *17in (43cm) wide*

£3,000-4,000   SWO

A James I oak desk box, the moulded top with gouged initials "A. K.", the front reeded and fluted and with a central iron locking plate, with narrow interior compartment.

21.25in (54cm) wide

£800-1,200   H&L

An Indo-Portugese table desk, with inlaid design of cherubs, flower-filled urns, and the Virgin and Child, the interior with drawers.

17.75in (45cm) wide

£2,000-3,000   LC

Judith Picks: Writing Slope

Now, I am definitely not going to give up my iPad or my laptop. I am no Luddite. But give me my old Parker 51, some Quink ink, good quality writing paper and a fine 19thC writing slope. Luxury!

This top-quality writing slope is in excellent condition, has good provenance, and is not inexpensive (but still worth it). But just look at the other writing slopes on this page – very affordable and just in need of a little TLC. A bargain every one.

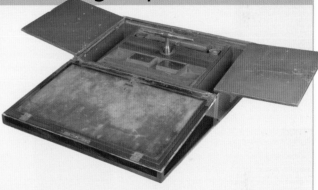

An early 19thC mahogany and brass-bound writing slope, with hinged velvet lined slope and pair of hinged panels revealing lift-out trays, the brass lock stamped "J.BRAMAH PATENT" with crown, with two brass plaques one with family crests, the other inscribed "Sir Theophilus Lee, G.C.H. G.C.C., The Elms, Bedhampton," parts missing.

Sir Theophilus Lee was the second cousin of the Duke of Wellington.

20.75in (53cm) wide

£2,500-3,500   WW

An early 19thC coromandel writing slope, by Starr and Hurry, Cornhill, with fitted satinwood extending interior, with pierced brass mounts.

15in (38cm) wide

£600-800   BELL

A George IV brass-bound rosewood writing slope, profusely brass inlaid, with a side drawer and recessed handles, the lock stamped "Thompson, Birmingham".

20in (51cm) wide

£600-800   SWO

A Victorian brass-inlaid amboyna writing slope.

19.25in (49cm) wide

£600-800   GORL

A 19th century French burrwood and rosewood writing slope, the fitted interior with short drawers, letter racks and inkwells, above velvet-lined writing surface, with gilt metal mounts, marked "Guide a Paris".

17in (43cm) wide

£600-800   DUK

BOXES

An Anglo-Indian rosewood and ivory dressing box, inlaid inside and out with engraved ivory foliate ornament, the fitted interior with rectangular dressing mirror to the lid, single drawer to front, on bracket feet.

The superb quality and high level of detail of the inlay help to make this box valuable. Rather than being flat in appearance, the leaves and flowers are further engraved and stained to give a sense of depth and perspective.

17in (43cm) wide

£5,000-7,000   H&L

A Belgian travelling dressing set, by Sergeni and Aine, in a mahogany brass-bound and strung case with elaborate scroll cartouche to lid, the green velvet- and watered silk-lined interior with faceted glass jars, bottles and boxes all with engraved silver covers, and lift-out tray with ivory manicure set.

19in (48cm) wide

£600-800   L&T

A Regency satinwood campaign toilet box, the cover with a leather pocket with easel mirror, with cut-glass bottles and boxes and lift-out tray of bone-handled tools, mounts hallmarked London, maker "R.B".

1816   *15in (38cm) wide*

£2,000-3,000   WW

A Victorian silver-mounted gentleman's travelling dressing set, the silver with mark of James Vickery, London, 1868, in a fitted coromandel box by S. Mordan & Co, including a gilt metal-mounted mirror, 14 glass boxes and jars, a beaker, a tray of manicure implements, a spoon, and a mother-of-pearl mirror, two items lacking.

£2,000-2,500   BELL

A Victorian coromandel and gilt-brass toilet box, by Charles Asprey & Son, the interior with brass-framed mirror flanked by candle sconces, with watered-silk linings and secret drawers, plush- and leather-lined with satinwood veneered sides and underside, with push-button releases, cut-glass bottles with silver covers, two ivory-handled pens, a pencil, an ivory-backed hand mirror, the silver hallmarked for London and monogrammed "CAA".

1879   *14.5in (37cm) wide*

£10,000-15,000   WW

A late George III flame mahogany decanter box, with strung edges and ebonised mouldings, with six gilt-painted decanters, lobed stoppers mainly associated, with key.

10in (25.5cm) wide

£800-1,200   L&T

A mid-19thC Victorian burl walnut, rosewood and brass inlay liqueur box, the serpentine top centred by a brass cartouche, with four etched and cut-glass decanters and matching glasses, on bun feet.

12.75in (32.5cm) wide

£600-800   FRE

A Victorian brass-mounted coromandel decanter case, with hinged lid and two doors enclosing three cut-glass decanters and stoppers, and two (formerly eight) glasses.

12.5in (32cm) wide

£600-800   GORB

A late 19thC French ebonised, kingwood banded and mother-of-pearl liqueur box, the lid inlaid with stylised silver-metal mounts and central oval, with four decanters and 16 etched glasses within a gilt metal stand, on bun feet.

13in (33.5cm) wide

£600-800   L&T

A pair of George III mahogany casket-form cutlery boxes, with fluted corners, formerly with fitted interiors, inlay of a later date, with gadrooned knops and baize-lined interiors, on brass claw-and-ball feet.

16in (41cm) high

£2,000-3,000   L&T

A pair of George III mahogany and inlaid serpentine-fronted knife boxes, with chequer feather-strung lines, with brass mounts and handles, the fitted interiors complete with a set of steel and bark-textured ivory-handled cutlery with plated terminals and engraved lion rampant armorials.

15.25in (39cm) high

£3,500-4,500   H&L

A pair of George III mahogany serpentine knife boxes, chevron-line inlaid, the lids with inlaid floral urn oval, over fitted slotted interior.

15in (38cm) high

£3,000-4,000   L&T

ESSENTIAL REFERENCE - KNIFE BOXES

Knife boxes are decorative cases with fitted, slotted interiors for storing cutlery.

- **They were usually supplied as a pair.**
- **They were introduced in the reign of George II and the basic form (with serpentine front as seen below) remained largely unchanged until the 1780s when vase-form knife boxes were introduced. Early examples were often covered in shagreen or silk-velvet. From 1760s mahogany or veneered knife boxes were popular.**
- **Decoration became increasingly lavish under George III; crossbanding and feather banding were typical.**
- **In the early 19thC knife-boxes and cutlery urns became largely redundant as sideboards increasingly had fitted drawers for cutlery.**

A George III mahogany veneered serpentine-form knife box, the lid with central satinwood inlaid bat's wing patera, and with chevron stringing throughout, with original internal knife rack, containing green-stained ivory-handled cutlery.

c1780   *Table knives 11in (28cm) long*

£1,500-2,500   TEN

A pair of George III satinwood cutlery urns, the domed covers carved with a band of acanthus leaves and acorn finials, with stepped interior of apertures.

c1790   *25in (63.5cm) high*

£5,000-7,000   DN

A pair of Hepplewhite-style mahogany knife boxes, each with an urn inlaid lid and serpentine front.

c1800   *14.25in (36.5cm) high*

£2,000-3,000   POOK

A pair of mahogany, rosewood and boxwood strung tapering knife boxes, narrowly crossbanded, the stepped lids with sphere finials, the interior with apertures for 12 items of cutlery, on sphere feet.

c1825   *18in (45.5cm) high*

£2,500-3,500 pair   TEN

A matched pair of mid-late 19thC George III-style possibly American Federal mahogany knife urns.

25in (63.5cm) high

£2,000-3,000   DN

A 14thC European oak reliquary box, with gilt-copper mounts, the lid inlaid with metal embossed with symbols of the evangelists, the sides with stylised floral decoration, traces of old paintwork.

For more information on reliquaries see p.359.

6in (15cm) wide

£6,000-8,000   DOR

A mid-17thC German ebonised, fruitwood, boxwood and marquetry Eger box, the lid with a traveller on horseback, the interior with Salome.

Eger cabinets and boxes were carved in low relief and constructed from different coloured woods. Flat intarsia (marquetry used to create depth) typically used mahogany, walnut and maple, with boxwood with elm or ash. Poplar and burr walnut were used for the relief.

14in (36cm) wide

£2,000-3,000   SWO

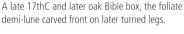

A late 17thC and later oak Bible box, the foliate demi-lune carved front on later turned legs.

26.5in (67cm) wide

£250-350   WW

A probably 18thC Anglo-Indian rosewood and ivory inlaid butterfly-form jewellery box, opening to reveal a number of similar boxes each similarly inlaid with floral patterns.

In addition to its obvious quality and excellent state of preservation, the value of the box (probably made in the Vizagapatum region in the the late 18thC) is due to its unusual shape and many inner boxes.

14in (36cm) wide

£35,000-45,000   LAW

An early 18thC probably Low Countries joined oak box, the canted lid carved in relief with leaves, the front panel depicting a religious scene above a single drawer heavily carved with foliage, the interior with a small candle box.

22in (56cm) wide

£500-700   TEN

A New England mahogany pipe box, with a lollipop-shaped hanger and single drawer, with old dark finish.

c1800   *19in (48cm) high*

£2,500-3,500   POOK

An early 19thC Italian pietra dura and gilt-bronze mounted casket, the lid with panels of flora tied by ribbons, the sides with fruit and foliage within gilt metal borders, flanked by lion masks issuing fruit and fauna, on hairy paw lion feet, rear panel blank.

12in (30.5cm) wide overall

£18,000-22,000   SWO

An early 19thC Lancaster County, Pennsylvania box, painted by the Compass Artist, with red and white stylised floral decoration on a blue ground.

12.75in (32.5cm) wide

£30,000-40,000 POOK

An early 19thC Anglo-Indian penworked ivory-veneered sandalwood dome-topped casket, with stylised foliate borders and floral motifs, on bracket feet.

17in (43cm) wide

£3,500-4,500   **DN**

An early 19thC Worcester County, Massachusetts, painted rectangular box, the black ground with red and gold Neo-classical elements, with brass bail pull on top, and wallpaper lining.

24in (61cm) wide

£1,500-2,500   **SK**

A Lancaster County, Pennsylvania painted pine trinket box, by Jonas Weber (1810-1876), inscribed "Hannah S. Ressler", the lid and sides with floral decoration, the front with a large white house, all on a dark green/blue ground.

This box was sold with a group of Ressler ephemera to include a journal by Hannah Ressler detailing an excursion from Lancaster County, Pennsylvania, to Ohio in 1848.

1848   *10.25in (26cm) wide*

£30,000-40,000   **POOK**

ESSENTIAL REFERENCE - PENNSYLVANIA DUTCH

German immigrants contributed to the increase in quality and quantity of American folk art during the 18thC and early 19thC. They took the name "Deitsch" (from the German word "Deutsch"), which gradually corrupted and became "Dutch" i.e. Pennsylvania Dutch. Some immigrant painters came from the Telemark region of Norway, and had trained in the "rosmaling" (rose painting) technique.

- **Painting was a revered skill amongst this community, as it could transform an everyday object into a piece of art.**
- **Small trinket boxes, known as "Schmückkästchen", were traditional gifts. Red, blue and blue-green ground colours were applied directly to the bare wood, then overlaid with stylised patterns. Chests were also decorated in this style.**
- **Dower chests (in which brides would stow household items that formed their dowry) were originally painted with European motifs, such as hearts, tulips and birds, with later examples including American symbols.**

A 19thC tortoiseshell jewellery box, the cushion-shaped top inset with rectangular white metal cartouche and pewter banded lines.

14in (36cm) wide

£1,500-2,500   **H&L**

A 19thC tortoiseshell box and cover, applied with silver panels and spandrels, with cash, scrolls, auspicious emblems and figures beneath a pine tree, the escutcheon formed as a butterfly, damages.

7in (18cm) wide

£2,000-2,500   **WW**

A Lancaster County, Pennsylvania painted pine dresser box, by Jonas Weber (1810-1876), painted "Sarah Weidman", the front decorated with a house with yellow trees, the lid and sides with stylised flowers, all on a black ground, dated.

One of the finest examples by Weber in existence.

1847   *10.25in (26cm) wide*

£60,000-80,000   **POOK**

A late 19thC French amboyna crossbanded and brass marquetry table top cigar case, the fitted interior with four grooved slides and a drawer, with label for "GUILLAUME".

11in (28cm) wide

£200-300   **DN**

CARVINGS

A 16thC Flemish carved boxwood carving of the Virgin and Child.

12.25in (31cm) high

£5,000-7,000 LC

An Austrian carved limewood figure of St. Barbara, Tyrol, with traces of later polychrome paintwork, restoration.

c1500 *22in (56cm) high*

£6,000-8,000 DOR

A German carved limewood group of the Madonna and Child, the reverse hollowed-out, traces of paintwork, new crown.

c1510-20 *27in (68cm) high*

£15,000-25,000 DOR

A 16thC German carved wooden group of the Virgin and Child with St Anne, feautring Anne standing with infant Jesus, with Mary as a young girl to her left, reverse hollowed-out, with later paintwork.

37in (94cm) high

£8,000-12,000 DOR

A pair of Austrian Renaissance carvings of flying angels, Tyrol, polychrome painted and gilded.

c1620-40 *24in (61cm) high*

£6,000-8,000 DOR

A Renaissance carved wooden angel's head and wings, the reverse slightly hollowed-out, polychrome painted, restoration.

c1620-40 *12in (30.5cm) wide*

£500-700 DOR

A 17thC/18thC possibly German carved walnut figure of a lion, on carved plinth base.

24.5in (62cm) high

£700-1,000 FRE

A late 17thC carved limewood figure group of St Joseph with the Infant Jesus, attributed to Johann Josef Schwanthaler, (1681-1743), the reverse hollowed, polychrome painted, restoration.

This sculpture comes with a certificate of authenticity from the Schwanthaler expert Peter Kössl.

57in (145cm) high

£8,000-12,000 DOR

A large 18thC/19thC Continental carving of Madonna and Child, each figure fitted with glass eyes, on hexagonal base.

36in (91.5cm) high

£1,200-1,800 FRE

A pair of 18thC Austrian carved wood figures of St Isidor and St Notburga, Tyrol, pencil notations on the bases.

St Isidor (c1070-1130) is the Spanish Catholic patron saint of farmers. St Notburga of Eben (c1265-1313) is one of the Tyrol's most revered saints and patron saint of farm workers and servant girls. She is often depicted with a sickle representing divine approbation. In rural Austria and Bavaria the two saints were sometimes venerated together.

24in (61cm) high

£3,000-4,000 WW

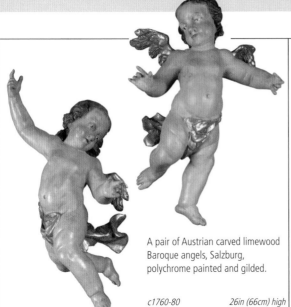

A pair of Austrian carved limewood Baroque angels, Salzburg, polychrome painted and gilded.

c1760-80   26in (66cm) high

£3,000-4,000   DOR

A 19thC Neapolitan crèche figure group, featuring carved and polychrome decorated figures of the Madonna holding Christ on her lap, attended by two saints.

20.5in (52cm) high

£1,200-1,800   FRE

A Scandinavian carved wood mangle board, with horse handle to monogrammed initials, animals, a figure on horseback and a lady, the facetted sides carved "ANO 1780, DEN20 OCTOBER, MDCCLXXX, K P D K R".

1780   28.25in (72cm) long

£1,500-2,500   WW

A pair of Austrian carved pine Crib Horses, by Johann Giner the Elder, Hall in Tyrol, polychrome painted and gilded, glass eyes, fabric bridle straps and metal stirrups, damages.

c1780-1800   11in (28cm) high

£7,000-10,000   DOR

A pair of Austrian carved wood Crib Horses, by Johann Giner the Elder, Hall in Tyrol, polychrome painted and gilded, with glass eyes and fabric bridle, some signs of age.

c1780-1800   10in (25.5cm) high

£6,000-8,000   DOR

One of a pair of Italian carved and gilded limewood figures of Spring and Summer, standing on tripod socles decorated with acanthus leaves, each with a bouquet of flowers, a sheaf of wheat as candlestick.

c1800   61in (155cm) high

£25,000-35,000 pair   DOR

A large early 19thC American carved giltwood pilot house eagle, on a Corinthian capital.

28in (71cm) high

£5,000-7,000   POOK

A large carved figure of a standing rooster, by Wilhelm Schimmel (Cumberland Valley, Pennsylvania, 1817-1890), painted in shades of yellow, red, and black.

7in (18cm) high

£10,000-15,000   POOK

THE CLOCKS & BAROMETERS MARKET

The trends we talked about in the last edition of "Antiques Handbook & Price Guide" have continued. Good-quality clocks, in original condition, and by important makers are still doing very well. London makers have always tended to be the most sought-after, but there has been one substantive change in the last year: many skilled provincial clockmakers are beginning to fetch comparable prices.

Thirty years ago the clock and barometer market was dominated by purists, with most good clocks selling to a handful of dealers and collectors. The market was for good clocks in un-restored condition. However, there is a new group of buyers entering the market who are interested in the aesthetics of a clock, and will accept sensitive restoration, especially when it comes to early clocks.

Paul Archard of Derek Roberts Antiques says that "Smaller clocks, for example carriage clocks and small bracket clocks, which fit in well with modern houses, have been popular and in particular English carriage clocks have been strong. "

Paul also points out that the longcase clock market has continued to display two distinct trends. The most desirable 17thC and early 18thC examples by well-known makers "have held ground". Meanwhile, mid-to late 18thC and 19thC large mahogany clocks have proved difficult to sell.

Tremendous excitement was aroused at Rosebery's of West Norwood, London, England, in March 2011, with the discovery of an unsigned lantern clock consigned "in the rough". It was recognised as being from the so-called First Period of lantern clockmaking, and was probably made around 1610-20. The clock displayed many Jacobean features, putting the clock near in date to the first true lantern clocks, those signed by Robert Harvey c1602-15. Such a rarity was always going to create a buzz in the saleroom. The generous layer of dust and dirt, showing it had not been cleaned for over a century, added to its authenticity! It sold for £29,000. This was a good, honest example, but there are many fake lantern clocks, so if in doubt buy from a specialist dealer or auction house.

Skeleton clocks have proved popular, particularly if the clock has unusual features. Such was the case with an exhibition standard 2ft 1in (63.5cm) eight-day clock of c1860 sold at Christie's, London, in March 2011. It had many special features: it was quarter-chiming and striking, with a year-long calendar and a four-train musical movement with 24 bells and seven gongs. Although unsigned, it sold for £110,000.

Barometers have been slow sellers unless by a top name including Daniel Quare or John Patrick. Unusual features help, and in general good-quality 18thC examples are selling better than 19thC. Dealers report that they are finding some younger buyers, so the market may well improve.

Above: A French mantel clock. See page 287.

Far Left A planetarium, by Jan Felkl & Son. See page 306.

A George I brass-mounted ebonised table clock, "Simon DeCharmes, London", the ten-pillar triple-fusée movement chiming the quarters on eight bells, and striking the hours on a further bell, the break-arch dial with calendar and false bob aperture, signed.

c1720   27in (68.5cm) high
£10,000-13,000   **DN**

An ebonised table clock, "William Wheatley, London", the arch with strike/silent selection, the substantial triple fusée movement with verge escapement, quarter chiming and repeating with eight hammers striking a nest of eight bells, and a further hammer striking a bell for the hours, movement secured by brackets, movement backplate fully engraved with foliate scroll work, bob pendulum, signed.

c1750   23in (58cm) high
£12,000-14,000   **TEN**

CLOSER LOOK - GEORGE I BRACKET CLOCK

The case is surmounted by a revolving moon-phase globe driven by a vertical pillar and a series of cogs from the movement. This is an unusual way of depicting phases of the moon.

Knowing the correct moon phase was important because trips on horseback or by coach were far less safe on a dark night. Crops could also be harvested by the light of the moon.

The trefoil-shaped chapter ring is extremely rare. The spandrels are engraved with figures emblematic of the seasons.

The shape of the chapter ring means that there must be special arrangements for the single hour hand. This is achieved by spring loading.

An unusual George I clock, "Richard Glynne, London", the subsidiary dial with twin rings, one showing minutes and the other lunar dates for the phases of the moon, with Arabic numerals (hands missing), with an eight-day single-train fusée movement.

Richard Glynne (1681-1755), was apprenticed to Henry Wynne in 1696 in the Clockmakers' Company, of which he became a freeman in 1705; he became Steward of the Company in 1725. He worked first at the sign of the Atlas and Hercules (1712-16) in Cheapside, and subsequently (1718-29) opposite Salisbury Court in Fleet Street, London. At the same time, he also made a variety of scientific instruments. All are of high quality, with clean, well-executed engraving uncluttered by unnecessary decoration.

c1720-25   25.25in (64cm) high
£30,000-40,000   **ECGW**

An ebonised striking bracket clock, with pull repeat, signed "Wm Skeggs, London", with matted dial centre with mock pendulum aperture, date aperture and signed, the arch with strike/silent selection, twin-fusée movement with verge escapement and striking on a bell, bob pendulum.

c1760   20in (51cm) high
£4,000-5,000   **TEN**

A Louis XV Boulle pendulum clock, signed "Beauvarlet à Paris", signed oblong spring-motion anchor escapement, staff pendulum with simple pendulum bob, spring suspension, eight-day movement, quarter-hour striking mechanism on three bells, Boulle casing decorated with tortoiseshell, mother of pearl and lacquer, glazed bronze doré doors depicting Ceres flanked by two putti, figural finial depicting Ariadne on the panther.

1746-58   56in (142cm) high
£14,000-16,000   **DOR**

A Louis XV Boulle pendulum clock, signed "Gosselin Paris", oblong spring-motion, anchor escapement, eight-day movement, quarter-hour striking mechanism on three bells, the Boulle casing decorated with marquetry, glazed to the sides, finial depicting Aurora seated on a cloud.

Gosselin was an important watch- and clock-making dynasty in Paris in the 18thC and 19thC.

1746-58   45in (114.5cm)
£7,000-9,000   **DOR**

A mahogany and brass-lined inverted bell-top striking clock, "John Ellicott, London", the two-train gut-fusée eight-day bell striking movement retains its original verge escapement and trip repeat, the backplate is engraved with relics from a ruined Greek temple and the central one is engraved "Ellicott, London".

John Ellicott (1706-1772) invented a compensated pendulum and developed the use of the cylinder escapement. Ellicott was a Fellow of, and on the Council of, the Royal Society, and was Clockmaker to the King. His son, Edward, joined the business in 1758 and from this time the majority of their clocks were usually signed "Ellicott", but occasionally "John Ellicott & Son".

c1770   *15.5in (39.5cm) high*
£15,000-17,000   **DR**

A George III mahogany striking bracket clock, "Isaac Fox, London", the arch with strike/silent selection, matted dial centre with date aperture and signed, twin-fusée movement converted to verge escapement and striking on a bell, with later block feet.

Isaac Fox is recorded as working in London from 1772-1794, and Isaac Jnr is recorded working c1778.
c1775   *20in (51cm) high*
£6,000-8,000   **TEN**

A Regency mahogany hour-repeating bracket clock, "Thomas Howard, London", with arched case and painted Roman dial, twin-fusée movement with engraved backplate striking upon a bell, signed.

15in (38cm) high
£3,000-4,000   **GORL**

A 19thC French boullework, ebonised and ormolu-mounted bracket clock and bracket, with a twin-train eight-day movement striking on a bell, the stepped domed cresting with a seated female warrior figure, stamped "HPA" to rear.

60in (153cm) high overall
£6,000-7,000   **L&T**

A 19thC French Louis XV-style brown ormolu-mounted Boullework bracket clock, with Cupid finial and gilt dial with enamelled tablet numerals.

c1860   *26in (66cm) high*
£3,000-4,000   **GORL**

A French Régence striking Boullework bracket clock, with bracket, signed "Roquelon A Paris", with twin-barrel movement, anchor escapement, numbered outside countwheel striking on a top-mounted bell for the half-hour strike and for the hours.

Clock 34in (86cm) high
£3,000-4,000   **TEN**

A mahogany striking bracket clock, "William Lancaster, Plymouth Dock", dial centre with mock pendulum and date aperture, twin-fusée movement with verge escapement and striking on a bell, later seatboard and case.

c1790   *21in (53cm) high*
£2,000-3,000   **TEN**

ESSENTIAL REFERENCE - JOHN KNIBB

John Knibb was born in 1650 and was apprenticed to his older brother, Joseph, in Oxford c1664.

- When Joseph moved to London in 1670 John took over the Oxford workshop, gaining the Freedom of the city in 1673.
- Clocks by either Joseph or John Knibb are rare.
- The rarity and the delicacy of their movements and the finesse of the case designs make clocks by the Knibbs extremely sought after.
- John Knibb became Mayor of Oxford in 1700.
- He continued in business until his death in 1722.

A Queen Anne ebonised eight-day longcase clock, by "John Knibb, Oxford", the fully-latched five-finned pillar inside countwheel bell-striking movement with separate shaped-cock for the pallet arbor and backplate cut for the pallets, brass dial with calendar aperture.

95in (241cm) high

£25,000-30,000   **DN**

A late 17thC walnut eight-day longcase clock, "Henry Mountlow, London", the five-finned pillar inside countwheel bell-striking movement, the dial with ringed winding holes and calendar aperture, case with later veneers.

Mountlow is thought to have worked into the first decade of the 18thC.

77in (195cm) high

£5,500-6,500   **DN**

A late 17thC walnut and floral marquetry longcase clock, "Andrew Broun, Edinburgh", the anchor escapement striking the hours on a bell, the dial with "boyes and crownes" spandrels, the Roman dial with subsidiary Arabic chapters, calendar aperture, seconds dial and ringed winding holes.

93in (236cm) high

£7,000-8,000   **L&T**

A marquetry longcase clock, "Nathaniel Pyne, London", month-going twin weight-driven movement with latched pillars, five-wheel-going train, anchor escapement and outside countwheel striking on a bell, restored.

Pyne was a Member of the Clockmakers' Company from 1677.

c1690   *80in (203cm) high*

£12,000-14,000   **TEN**

A late 17thC walnut and floral marquetry month-going longcase clock, the dial signed "Joseph Knibb Londini Fecit", the twin-train movement with recoil escapement striking the hours on a bell, with date aperture, movement significantly adapted.

93in (236cm) high

£15,000-20,000   **L&T**

A George I month-going walnut longcase clock, "John Crucefix", London, the dial with sword-hilt half-hour markers, the matted centre with subsidiary second dial and date aperture, the bell striking five-pillar movement with anchor escapement.

90in (229cm) high

£8,000-12,000   **L&T**

ESSENTIAL REFERENCE - THOMAS TOMPION

Thomas Tompion (1639-1751) has often been referred to as the "father of English clockmaking".

- His early clocks demonstrate a close working relationship with the Fromanteel, East and Knibb workshops.
- He received many Royal commissions, firstly from Charles II, for whom Tompion is known to have made one of the earliest balance-spring watches in 1676, and later William III.
- Tompion introduced serial numbering in c1682.
- In 1711 he became a partner of George Graham, who inherited the business after his death and continued to maintain the same standards.

A William and Mary eight-day longcase clock, signed "Tho: Tompion, Londini fecit", in a mulberry-veneered case, number 253, the fully-latched five-knopped and finned pillar inside countwheel bell-striking movement with anchor escapement, bolt-and-shutter maintaining power and long crutch, dial with subsidiary seconds dial and calendar aperture with pin-hole adjustment, on a later skirt, restoration.

Eight-day longcase clocks by Tompion are relatively rare, with only ten known surviving examples.

c1695   *80in (203cm) high*

£50,000-60,000   **DN**

An early 18thC Dutch eight-day musical longcase clock, "Pieter Kloch, Amsterdam", with seaweed marquetry-decorated walnut case, the dial with six-tune selector in the arch, movement playing on eight bells, the trunk door inset with a silvered-plate mercury thermometer, the hood applied with giltwood figures of Atlas and angels.

101in (257cm) high

£9,000-11,000　　　　GORL

CLOSER LOOK - MUSICAL CLOCK

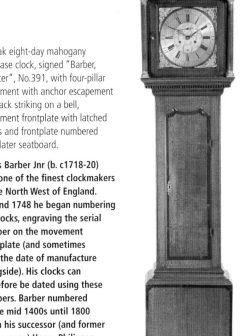

The arch has a finely painted rolling moon disc for lunar scale.

The silvered arched plaque has 12 tunes: "This Great World's a Trouble", "From Me To Thee", "O Lovely Charmer", "A Young Virgin of 15", "The Dame of Honour", "The Happy Clown", "The King Enjoys His Own", "The 103 Psalm", "The 113 Psalm", "Lilli Bule Ro", "Ormonds March", "The Shady Bowers".

The arched pediment has finely pierced frets and side movement-viewing windows and gilt-painted columns with brass capitals.

The later stipple engraving of a Classical scene (depicting three figures within a woodland background) is slightly at odds with the overall chinoiserie decoration.

The gilt-decorated skirting is of a later date.

A rare musical japanned longcase clock, the 13in (33.5cm) brass dial signed "Thomas Estwick, London", the seven-pillar triple-weight-driven movement with anchor escapement, playing a selection of 12 tunes on the half hour with 25 hammers striking 13 bells, and a further hammer striking a larger bell for the hours.

c1740　　　　*94in (239cm) high*

£12,000-18,000　　　　TEN

An early walnut eight-day striking longcase clock, the brass dial with plaque signed "Benj. Gray, London", the eight-day weight-driven movement strikes the hour on a bell and with many early features including a latched fifth pillar.

Benjamin Gray (1676-1764) was appointed Watchmaker in Ordinary to King George II. He took his friend Justin Vulliamy into partnership in 1743 and Justin married Benjamin's daughter Mary in 1746. After Gray's death the Royal Warrant was extended to the partnership at 74 Pall Mall, later re-numbered 68, which remained the headquarters of the Vulliamy business for three generations.

c1725　　　　*81in (206cm) high*

£25,000-30,000　　　　DR

A walnut eight-day longcase clock, signed "Saml Harris, London", engraved arch with rolling moonphase, later hands, five-pillar movement with anchor escapement and inside countwheel striking on a bell, later seatboard.

c1730　　　　*88in (223.5cm) high*

£4,500-5,500　　　　TEN

A George III Irish mahogany eight-day longcase clock, "David Gordon, Dublin", the four-pillar inside countwheel bell-striking movement with nameplate, some old repairs.

c1750　　　　*88in (223.5cm) high*

£3,000-4,000　　　　DN

An oak eight-day mahogany longcase clock, signed "Barber, Winster", No.391, with four-pillar movement with anchor escapement and rack striking on a bell, movement frontplate with latched pillars and frontplate numbered 391, later seatboard.

Jonas Barber Jnr (b. c1718-20) was one of the finest clockmakers in the North West of England. Around 1748 he began numbering his clocks, engraving the serial number on the movement frontplate (and sometimes with the date of manufacture alongside). His clocks can therefore be dated using these numbers. Barber numbered to the mid 1400s until 1800 when his successor (and former journeyman) Henry Philipson continued the system.

c1760　　　　*81in (206cm) high*

£7,000-8,000　　　　TEN

A mahogany longcase clock, signed "Abrm. Coles, London", with date aperture above six o'clock, the eight-day weight-driven movement has recoil anchor escapement and strikes the hours on a bell.

Abraham Coles was apprenticed to Henry Home, London, on the 5th September 1768 for seven years at £50. He was a Freeman of the Worshipful Clockmakers' Company from 1775 to 1781 when he was declared bankrupt.

c1780   *95in (241cm) high*
£8,000-10,000   **DR**

A late George III mahogany longcase clock, signed "Vulliamy, London", eight-day five-pillar movement, striking on a bell, the dial with subsidiary seconds dial and pierced date aperture, with "N/S" lever above 60, wooden shaft pendulum, two weights and a crank winding key.

86in (218.5cm) high
£50,000-70,000   **WW**

CLOSER LOOK - 8-DAY CLOCK

The pagoda case has good figuration and colour.

The arch has an unusual rocking ship automation, in front of a painted background scene, which is an extremely desirable feature.

The moulded, arched trunk door is flanked by stop brass fluted pilasters with brass capitals.

William Coe is recorded working in Cambridge c1795.

A mahogany eight-day longcase clock, signed "Coe, Cambridge", the dial with date aperture, subsidiary seconds, with five-pillar movement with anchor escapement and rack striking on a bell, later seatboard.

c1790   *108in (274cm) high*
£7,000-8,000   **TEN**

ESSENTIAL REFERENCE - JOSIAH EMERY

Josiah Emery (1725-1796) was born in Geneva, Switzerland, and settled in England where he became a key figure in English clockmaking.

- **He worked on Mudge's lever escapement and combined it with Arnold's double-S balance.**
- **He made many fine watches and clocks and submitted four timekeepers to the Board of Longitude for trial between 1792 and 1796.**
- **He was made an Honorary Freeman of the Clockmakers' Company in 1781, a distinction rarely given, which means that he must have kept his Swiss nationality.**

A mahogany eight-day striking longcase clock, "Josiah Emery, London", the eight-day weight-driven movement strikes the hours on a bell and the central fifth pillar is latched.

c1780   *87in (221cm) high*
£18,000-22,000   **DR**

A mahogany eight-day longcase clock, signed "Thos Wiggan, Bristol", with later swan's neck pediment, the arch with rolling moonphase and on arched silvered plaque marked "High Water At Bristol Key", four-pillar movement with anchor escapement and rack striking on a bell.

c1780   *96in (244cm) high*
£5,000-6,000   **TEN**

A Dutch mahogany longcase clock, signed "Klaas Johs, Andriese. Groun", with moonphase below chapter ring with a painted biblical scene, twin weight-driven movement with anchor escapement, quarter striking with two hammers onto two bells, and a further hammer striking a bell for the alarm.

c1780   *97in (247cm) high*
£5,000-7,000   **TEN**

An 18thC French ormolu-mounted ebonised and pewter marquetry longcase clock, with armorial over the squared brass dial with silvered Roman chapter ring, subsidiary seconds and date aperture.

98in (249cm) high
£13,000-15,000   **GORL**

An unusual small mahogany eight-day longcase clock, signed "Jno Thwaites, Clerkenwell, London", No.2393, with five-pillar movement with anchor escapement and rack striking on a bell.

c1800 81in (206cm) high

£5,000-6,000 TEN

A mahogany eight-day longcase clock, signed "Wm Bickerstaff, Liverpool", dial with painted scene, the arch with rolling moonphase, four-pillar movement with attached falseplate stamped "Wilson", deadbeat escapement and rack striking on a bell.

William Bickerstaff is recorded working in Liverpool 1790-1829.

c1800 102in (259cm) high

£7,000-8,000 TEN

An unusual Scottish mahogany column eight-day longcase clock, "R. Stewart, Glasgow", with painted dial, four-pillar movement with anchor escapement and rack striking on a bell, later seatboard.

c1850 80in (203cm) high

£4,000-5,000 TEN

A Louis XVI-style ormolu-mounted mahogany, amaranth and tulipwood Regulateur De Parquet, after the model by Jean-Henri Riesener, the dial signed"'LA CASA BARBOLLA, HABANA", movement signed "SAMUEL MARTI', PARIS".

c1890 88.5in (225cm) high

£20,000-25,000 RTC

A late 19thC carved oak tall-case clock, "R. J. Horner", with nine-tube three-weight movement with Whittington and Westminster chimes, the case adorned with griffins and female figures.

120in (305cm) high

£50,000-70,000 POOK

A mahogany chiming longcase clock, signed "Jos Farrer, Pontefract", the arch with Cambridge/Westminster selections, the triple weight-driven movement with deadbeat escapement, chiming eight hammers striking on to eight tubular bells and a further hammer.

c1890 93in (236cm) high

£3,500-4,500 TEN

A Victorian mahogany longcase clock, "Peter Claire, Manchester", with brass moonphase dial, the three-train eight-day movement with anchor escapement and striking on two bells.

c1900 99in (252cm) high

£7,000-8,000 L&T

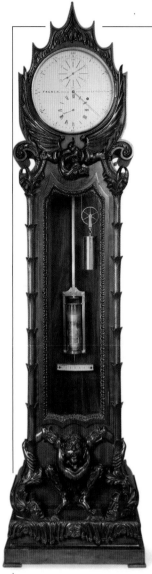

A mid-19thC rosewood longcase regulator, "D. McGregor & Co. Glasgow and Greenock", the four-pillar rack and coiled-gong striking movement with deadbeat escapement, Harrison's maintaining power and wooden rod pendulum with brass-cased cylindrical bob.

A D.W. McGregor is recorded working in Glasgow c1848.

73in (185.5cm) high

£3,000-4,000   DN

A rare 19thC French walnut-cased regulator, with a jewelled pin wheel escapement, with subsidiary dials for month, moon and date, and the signs of the Zodiac, four parts of the day, the planets and the seasons, all titled in Latin, the steel pendulum with a twin canister mercury bob.

84.5in (214.5cm) high

£12,000-14,000   WW

A mahogany floor-standing regulator, "Thomas Baxter, London", the eight-day movement having maintaining power and a dead-beat escapement, the dial engraved with the maker's name.

83in (210.5cm) high

£4,500-5,500   H&L

A Regency mahogany longcase regulator, the dial inscribed "French, Royal Exchange, London", the brass six-pillar jewelled movement with six-spoke wheelwork, deadbeat escapement with jewelled pallets, escape wheel arbor and pallet arbor, and maintaining power, all enclosed by screwed brass dust shutters, the base carved in high relief with a squatting imp.

Frenchman Santiago James Moore was a renowned maker of fine clocks, pocket and marine chronometers and barometers. He was admitted to the Clockmakers' Company in 1810 and worked from premises at Sweeting's Alley, Royal Exchange, London, (c1808-38) and Cornhill, Royal Exchange (c1839-42).

79in (200cm) high

£30,000-35,000   TOV

A mahogany regulator, signed "Thos Cowham, 4 Engine St, Hull", with painted dial, subsidiary seconds, aperture for hour indication and single minute hand, single weight-driven movement with deadbeat escapement, maintaining power.

Thomas Cowham is recorded working in Hull 1846-51.

74in (188cm) high

£4,000-5,000   TEN

An unusual Vienna-style walnut longcase timepiece, the circular enamel Roman dial with centre seconds, with bimetallic pendulum.

81in (206cm) high

£3,500-4,500   A&G

A mahogany longcase regulator, signed "J.Highley, Sheerness", with five-pillar single weight-driven movement with deadbeat escapement, with Harrison's maintaining power, with mercury tube pendulum with circular rating disc.

John Highley is recorded in Sheerness 1861-1874.

c1870   *72in (182.5cm) high*

£6,000-7,000   TEN

An Empire ormolu-mounted mantel clock, "Armingaud, Paris", the urn-form case flanked by ormolu figures of cranes, the enamel dial surmounted by a putto in a chariot led by doves, the base with musical trophies.

c1810   *17in (43cm) high*

£3,000-4,000   **FRE**

An early 19thC French Empire ormolu mantel clock, the case depicting Aurora, driving the chariot of Helios pulled by a pair of winged horses.

Clock 19in (48cm) high

£4,500-5,500   **L&T**

CLOSER LOOK - ORMOLU CLOCK

This highly desirable clock shows the western front of Rheims Cathedral.

The face and eight-day works are signed "H. Marc à Paris".

The effect is further enhanced by coloured glass inserts to the windows.

The rose window serves as the dial.

A mid-19thC Louis Philippe ormolu clock.

18.75in (47cm) high

£5,000-6,000   **FRE**

A French gilt and patinated-bronze mantel clock, surmounted by robed female lyre player, with eight-day time and strike movement with silk suspension and countwheel striking.

c1810   *25in (63.5cm) high*

£3,000-4,000   **LHA**

A French Restauration gilt-bronze figural mantel clock, the movement signed "LV", with silk-thread suspension, countwheel striking on bell.

16in (41cm) high

£4,000-5,000   **RTC**

A Viennese Neo-classical palais bronze mantel clock, signed "Georg Kramer fecit Wien MDCCCXXIV", with spring-motion, anchor escapement, eight-day movement, Viennese 4/4 hour striking mechanism, the clock supported by two kneeling temple servants, with Satyr finial and two doves stretched on a ram.

1824   *35in (90cm) high*

£15,000-17,000   **DOR**

An Austrian Biedermeier bronze clock, with round spring-motion, one-day movement, Viennese 4/4 hour striking mechanism, the unusual bronze doré housing in the French style with a young girl holding a bird's nest, and a dog on a lead.

c1830-50   *15in (38cm) high*

£4,000-5,000   **DOR**

An American cast iron "Continental" Blinking Eye timepiece, "Bradley & Hubbard, West Meriden, Connecticut", decorated with polychrome enamel, with paper dial.

c1860   *16in (41cm) high*

£1,800-2,200   **SK**

A 19thC Louis XVI-style ormolu- and Sèvres porcelain-mounted figural clock, decorated with a portrait of Louis XVI, the base set with two robed, classical maidens, with eight-day time and strike movement.

34in (87cm) high

£20,000-25,000   **LHA**

A silvered mantel clock, the enamelled blue panels with applied gem stones and gilt interior of two men supporting the dial, with music box at back of a figure.

9.75in (25cm) high

£2,500-3,500 LHA

A black slate mantel clock, "Achille Brocot", with visible Brocot suspension, with long duration movement, backplate stamped "AB" within a star and numbered 4486.

Achille Brocot (1817-1878) was an eminent French clockmaker who devised his own escapement and adjustable pendulum suspension.

c1870 *15in (38cm) high*

£1,000-1,500 TEN

A late 19thC French Louis XVI-style marble, gilt and patinated-bronze *cercle tournant* mantel clock, the bell-striking pendulum movement contained within a truncated pillar and driving a celestial globe, the hours on a silvered band and indicated by a bronze putto, numbered "747".

The term "cercle tournant" refers to the fact that the time is shown by a porcelain ring turning round against a pointer (here the putto's finger). Clocks of this kind were common in France from the middle to late 1700s, and were produced again in the late 19thC (as this particular clock was). Value is very dependent on the quality of the casting and gilding.

27.5in (70cm) high

£50,000-70,000 SOTH

A 19thC Black Forest clock, surmounted by a carved figure of a stag, the base with oak leaves and an exotic bird.

22.5in (57.5cm) high

£2,000-3,000 FRE

A Continental porcelain and gilt metal clock, designed a tree with two musicians and two birds.

15.75in (40cm) high

£1,800-2,200 LHA

A Louis XVI-style ormolu and Sèvres-style porcelain figural clock, the dial marked "A. Paris", flanked by two putti above the plaque decorated with two girls in a landscape, the movement by "Raingo Frères".

20in (51cm) high

£4,000-6,000 LHA

A 19thC French white marble and gilt-brass mantel clock, the dial marked "Mesnil a Paris", with a twin-train cylinder movement striking on a bell.

21in (53cm) high

£1,500-2,000 L&T

A French Neo-classical column clock, Henry Dasson, with round horizontal brass plate spring motion, balance wheel escapement, eight-day movement, *cercle tournant* display with enamel cartouches.

1891 *23in (58.5cm) high*

£3,000-4,000 DOR

A French Neo-classical ormolu and ivory "Prudentia" mantel clock, Parisian Pendulum works, with eight-day movement, half-hour striking mechanism on bells, the Allegory of Wisdom seated with a mirror and a snake.

c1900 *14in (36cm) high*

£6,000-8,000 DOR

A crown-wheel and verge-striking lantern clock, signed "Hen. Hotham, at Ye Black Spread Eagle", with alarm, the replaced side doors with glazed "wings", the three-train movement has crown wheel and original verge escapement.

Henry Hotham born c1652, apprenticed March 1664-65 to John Pennock (Thro' N. Payne) until 1672. Freeman of the Clockmakers Company April 1673.
c1680　　　*15.5in (39cm) high*
£6,000-8,000　　　　DR

A 17thC brass striking lantern clock, dial plate inscribed "Peter Closon Neer Holburn Bridge, Londini", with two-train movement with verge escapement and oscillating balance wheel beneath top-mounted bell, countwheel striking on a bell, both weights missing.
　　　　　15in (38cm) high
£1,800-2,200　　　　TEN

A Queen Anne brass lantern clock, "John Lindley, Nayland", the posted countwheel bell-striking movement with anchor escapement.

John Lindley appears to be unrecorded, however the construction of the movement using tapered arbors, and the style of the engraving to the dial centre (with curved script signature) suggests a date within the first 20 years of the 18thC and can be directly compared to the work of other Suffolk makers such as William Rayment of Stowmarket.
　　　　　15in (38cm) high
£4,000-5,000　　　　DN

A petite sonnerie carriage clock, with day, date, alarm and repeat, the dial with subsidiaries for day, date and alarm, the eight-day movement strikes the quarters on two bells and has a strike/silent lever in the base.
c1860　　　*5.5in (14cm) high*
£7,000-9,000　　　　DR

A grande sonnerie striking and repeating carriage clock with alarm, "Drocourt, Paris", the eight-day movement with silvered platform lever escapement and a bimetallic balance wheel, with original numbered winding key and a travel case.
c1885　　　*5.75in (14.5cm) high*
£5,000-6,000　　　　DR

CLOSER LOOK - SERIES II CARRIAGE CLOCK

Jean-Paul Garnier (1801-1869) is now recognised as the founder of the Paris carriage clock industry.

Some of his early training was as a pupil of Antide Janvier.

During his time at the clockmaking school he probably worked for the house of Lepine, with whom he remained for five years.

He is particularly noted for the invention of the chaffcutter escapement which was simple, reliable and easy to produce.

A petite sonnerie carriage clock with alarm, "Dent, Paris", the eight-day movement strikes the hours and quarters on two bells and repeats grande sonnerie.

The firm of Dent, as well as manufacturing its own clocks and being at the forefront of the production of turret clocks, regulators and similar clocks, retailed clocks by other makers. A number of high-quality French carriage clocks, almost certainly made by the best makers of the time, have the signature "Dent, Paris" on the dial.
c1855　　　*5in (12.5cm) high*
£5,000-6,000　　　　DR

A Series II striking and repeating carriage clock, the porcelain dial and chaffcutter platform signed "Paul Garnier Hger de la Marine à Paris", the case numbered 3007.
c1860　　　*6.5in (16cm) high*
£10,000-12,000　　　　DR

A 17thC German bronze table clock, with a chain-driven fusée movement with balance verge escapement.

5in (12.5cm) wide

£10,000-12,000   LHA

A George III mahogany table clock, "Mat.s Nicolason, London", with massive triple-fusée movement, converted to anchor escapement, quarter-chiming with eight hammers striking eight bells, and two further hammers striking two bells.

c1790   *24in (61cm) high*

£7,000-9,000   TEN

A George III gilt-brass mounted ebonised quarter-chiming table clock, "John Coleman, London", the six-pillar triple-fusée movement chiming the quarters on eight bells and striking the hour on a further bell, with verge escapement.

John Coleman is recorded as working from Tottenham Court Road, London, in 1781-4. He specialised in highly decorative musical and chiming clocks, mainly for export to China.

c1780   *17.5in (44cm) high*

£20,000-25,000   DN

A Westminster Cathedral chiming skeleton clock, "Maugham, Beverley", with triple-chain-driven fusée movement and anchor escapement, six spoke wheels, chiming the quarters on eight bells and striking the hour on a large gong, with twin mercury-tubed pendulum.

c1885   *24in (61cm) high*

£13,000-15,000   TEN

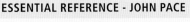

ESSENTIAL REFERENCE - JOHN PACE

John Pace (1783-1867) was born in London and worked in Abbeygate Street, Bury St Edmunds, Suffolk, from 1804-1857.

● **He was a deeply religious man who was a member of the Society of Friends (Quakers).**

● **He worked very closely with Benjamin Parker and many of Pace's clocks are signed with both names. Pace was probably the designer and retailer and Parker, a gunsmith by trade, was the clockmaker.**

● **In 1833 he patented a night timepiece (No. 6506).**

● **He exhibited at the Great Exhibition in 1851, where he described himself as an inventor, designer and manufacturer. He also mentions in detail his three-year duration and pyramidical skeleton clocks.**

● **In 1857 he moved to Chelmsford, Essex, where he remained until his death.**

A skeleton timepiece, "John Pace, Bury St. Edmunds", retailed by Robert Ladd, Cambridge, the eight-day timepiece train-mounted on the solid cast-brass back plate, all of the wheels have five tapered crossings, including the hour wheel, in oval glass dome.

c1840   *Dome 11.25in (28.5cm) high*

£4,500-5,500   DR

A rosewood-veneered acorn clock, Forestville Manufacturing Company, Bristol, Connecticut, with painted zinc dial, reverse-painted and transfer-decorated floral tablet, with eight-day time and strike fusée movement.

An acorn clock is a form of early 19thC mantel clock. The upper part of the case shaped with a double ogee curve to resemble an acorn.

c1850   *19.5in (49.5cm) high*

£8,000-12,000   SK

A late 19thC Louis XV-style French bronze and alabaster clock garniture, the clock with Samuel Marti two-train half-striking movement, with a pair of six-light figural candelabra, on stems formed as Classical maidens.

£8,000-12,000 SK

A late 19thC Louis XV-style gilt and patinated bronze clock garniture.

Clock 16.5in (42cm) high

£2,500-3,500 FRE

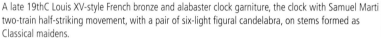

A 19thC Jacob Petit porcelain clock garniture, comprising a clock and a pair of flanking urns.

Clock 16.25in (41.5cm) high

£3,000-4,000 FRE

A French faience chinoiserie clock garniture, "J Vieillard & Co, Bordeaux", the bell-striking movement numbered 93941, and a pair of flanking vases with elephantine side handles and painted with lion rampant crests, each piece with impressed mark and numbered "857".

c1880 *Clock 16in (41cm) high*

£1,000-1,500 TEN

A late 19thC Louis XV-style ormolu and marble clock garniture.

Clock 17in (43cm) high

£3,000-4,000 L&T

An early 20thC French "Japonisme" gilt metal-mounted porcelain clock garniture.

Clock 21in (53cm) high

£1,000-1,500 FRE

A Continental Empire-style composite malachite clock garniture, with ormolu mounts, the clock with eight-day movement striking on a single bell.

£2,500-3,500 ROS

An early 20thC Tiffany & Co. Louis XV-style ormolu clock garniture, the works stamped "Tiffany & Co.", the candelabra centred by a putto with five scrolling candle arms.

Clock 25.25in (64cm) high

£4,000-5,000 FRE

A George III gilt and japanned "Act Of Parliament" clock, Robert Lumpkins, the trunk decorated with chinoiserie hunting scenes.

In 1797 Parliament introduced a British clock tax, taxing all types of clocks and watches. Many public buildings such as taverns and shops installed clocks on their premises. So unpopular was the tax that it was repealed in less than a year, thus explaining why genuine "Act of Parliament" clocks are extremely rare.

69in (175cm) high
£10,000-12,000   **SHAP**

A giltwood cartel clock, "Richard Grove, London", the eight-day duration fusée movement having a verge escapement, the dial signed, the case in the form of Rococo and Oriental design surmounted by an eagle.

32in (81cm) high
£7,000-9,000   **H&L**

A rare George III black-japanned tavern clock, "Joseph Gurney, Bristol", the five-pillar rack and bell-striking movement with five-wheel trains, the dial with pierced brass hands, shuttered winding holes and minute outer track within moulded surround, with concave-topped trunk door decorated in raised polychrome and gilt with figural chinoiserie landscape, with original oval weights and pendulum.

Joseph Gurney is recorded as working from 6 Bridge Street and Corn Street, Bristol 1783-98. Two-train tavern clocks are very rare and the current example appears to have survived in relatively original condition, retaining its original finish to the case. A tavern timepiece by Gurney is in the Bristol City Museum collection.

c1790   *58in (147cm) high*
£13,000-15,000   **DN**

A striking mahogany drop-dial wall clock, "Gibson, Royal Exchange, London", the convex dial with original painted background, the two-train eight-day gut-fusée movement with shaped plates and rack striking on a bell.

There is a Gibson recorded as working from Royal Exchange in 1818, and John Gibson is noted as working from Sweetings Alley, which is adjacent to Royal Exchange, from 1806 to 1824.

c1820   *23in (59.5cm) long*
£6,000-8,000   **DR**

A 19thC English tortoiseshell wall clock, "Robert Shaw, Manchester".

29in (73.5cm) high
£3,000-4,000   **FRE**

A gilt metal cartel wall timepiece with pull repeat, "Tavernier, A Paris", the single barrel movement with pull repeat with two hammers striking on to a bell.

c1870   *12in (30.5cm) high*
£1,200-1,800   **TEN**

A Victorian painted metal wall timepiece, "P. Wehrle, Cambridge", with iron wall mounting bracket, the skeleton plates with deadbeat escapement, five spoked wheels, replacement gut line, wooden rod pendulum, winding handle, various weights, dated.

1883   *42in (106.5cm) wide*
£2,000-3,000   **CHEF**

A Scottish inlaid mahogany eight-day wall timepiece, "C. Lunan, Aberdeen", four-pillar weight-driven movement with anchor escapement and bolt-and-shutter maintaining power.

Charles Lunan is recorded as working in Aberdeen 1760-1816. The relatively simple but purposeful nature of the movement housed in a fine quality, well-detailed case suggests that it was made for a discerning client to be used as a functional timepiece within a relatively sophisticated interior.

c1800   *44in (111.5cm) high*
£2,500-3,500   **DN**

An Austrian long-duration grande sonnerie striking mahogany and boxwood-strung Laterndluhr wall clock, "Anton Liszt, Vienna", the movement with deadbeat escapement, strikes the quarters on two gongs.

Anton Liszt was a sworn apprentice to the Imperial Royal Master and, once qualified, held a number of appointments both to the Royal Family and the State. He was once thought to be the brother of the composer, however it is now believed he was first cousin. He was a noted maker who, because of his connection to the composer and to the Court, had entrées into many of the best families in Vienna. This explains why many of his clocks are of the finest quality with embellishments not often found on clocks by other makers. In particular he is noted for producing clocks of two weeks duration. He is recorded as working between 1828 and 1868.

c1830   *43in (109cm) long*
£20,000-25,000   **DR**

An eight-day mahogany Dachluhr wall clock, "Joseph Elsner, Vienna", the enamelled dial with fired-in signature, "Joseph Elsner Grahem'scher Gang".

c1830   *34in (86cm) long*
£8,000-12,000   **DR**

An eight-day mahogany Dachluhr, with boxwood stringing, with an eight-day weight-driven movement and deadbeat escapement.

The dial was fired by Mosslinger, who was one of the better enamellers during this period.

c1840   *34in (86cm) long*
£6,000-8,000   **DR**

A Biedermeier rosewood grande sonnerie wall clock, "Juventious és Fia, Pesten", with metal cresting and mounts, the eight-day grande sonnerie movement with strike/silent.

c1850   *42.5in (108cm) long*
£5,000-7,000   **DR**

A late 19thC East Anglian mahogany drop-dial wall clock, the three-day silvered dial movement with an anchor escapement, the dial inscribed "Smith, Norwich".

52in (132cm) high
£1,800-2,200   **SWO**

A mahogany earth-driven electric wall clock, marked "No.139, Bentleys, Patent 19044/10 MFcd, Leicester", mounted with a brass-cased coil oscillating over a fixed iron bar, the rod mounted with switch gear.

Percival Arthur Bentley filed his patent No.19044 for earth-driven clocks on 13th August 1910. It is thought that only 70 were ever manufactured due to the outbreak of WWI.

c1910   *65in (165cm) high*
£10,000-12,000   **TEN**

A fusée verge pocket watch, the movement signed "T. Tompion E Banger, London", no. 3494, with pierced engraved circular balance cock, silver regulating dial over large square baluster pillars, within a silver gilt repoussé case decorated with figures and Cupids within foliate scroll borders.

c1704-5   2in (5cm) diam

£3,000-4,000   GHOU

A silver pair-cased verge pocket watch, "John Buschman, London", with gilt fusée movement, verge escapement, winged balance cock, Egyptian pillars with pierced galleries, regulator disc, barrel with worm and wheel gearing between the plates.

John Buschman (Bushman) was born c1661 in Hagen, Germany. He was made a Freeman of the Clockmakers' Company in 1692, and is believed to have worked until 1725.

c1705   2.25in (5.5cm) diam

£3,500-4,500   TEN

A George II gold pair-cased verge pocket watch, the verge movement by "Sam Atkins, London", numbered 1134, with turned pillars, and pierced and engraved balance cock with diamond end-stone, the outer case chased with a nude seated beneath a tree.

1746

£1,500-2,500   AH

An 18thC silver pair-cased fusée cylinder-repeating pocket watch, the plunge repeat movement signed "Geo Graham, London no. 923", the movement with round pillars, pierced engraved balance cock and silver regulating dial, striking on a bell to the inner case.

1747   2in (5cm) diam

£3,500-4,500   GHOU

A gold pair-cased open-faced pocket watch, signed on the backplate "Nathl Eagle, London 7706", the gilt fusée movement with a verge escapement, with a three-colour gilt chatelaine, with pendant swivels as fitted, later case.

c1760   2in (5cm) diam

£2,000-3,000   BELL

An 18ct gold gentleman's pocket watch, "J. S Huber, London, No. 505", with quarter hour repeater, gilt verge escapement movement via chain and fusée, key wind-up, open-work verge cock, silver regulator plate, two hammers on bell, with additional metal outer casing with leather.

c1780-90   2.5n (6.5cm) diam

£10,000-15,000   DOR

A late 18thC two-toned gold pocket watch, with enamel, diamonds, verge escapement.

       1.75in (4.5cm) diam

£3,000-4,000   DOR

A French open-faced gold and enamel pocket watch, signed "Romilly Paris", ref: 5343, the verge fusée movement with cylindrical pillars, pierced and engraved balance cock, the brass balance with an undersprung flat hairspring.

c1850   2.25in (5.5cm) diam

£1,500-2,000   DN

An 18ct gold hunting cased gentleman's pocket watch, the fusée lever movement detailed "E.I.Dent, Watch Maker To The Queen, London No 15531", with an 18ct gold bar link watch Albert chain, fitted with a swivel, a T-bar and with two boltrings, also a watch key.

1854

£1,500-2,000   BELL

WATCHES

Judith Picks: Good Provenance

Interesting provenance is so important. An item which once belonged to someone as fascinating as Sir Henry Layard is likely to have an increased value.

Born in Paris, he worked in England for his uncle, before leaving for Ceylon in 1839. After long travels, chiefly in Persia, he returned to Constantinople in 1842, where he made the acquaintance of Sir Stratford Canning, the British Ambassador, who employed him in various unofficial diplomatic missions in European Turkey. In 1845, Layard left to explore the ruins of Assyria (with which his name is chiefly associated) where he discovered the world famous Cyrus cylinder (dating from 539-530 BC).

Subsequently he turned to politics. First elected as a Liberal MP in 1852, he was in and out of office until 1869. He served as the Under-Secretary for Foreign Affairs and First Commissioner of Works and on the Privy Council 1868-69. In 1877 he was appointed as Ambassador at Constantinople, where he remained until 1880, when he finally retired from public life. In 1878, on the occasion of the Berlin Congress, he was appointed a Knight Grand Cross of the Order of the Bath.

Layard retired to Venice, where he devoted much of his time to collecting paintings of the Venetian school, and to writing on Italian art. His collection of Venetian paintings was donated to the nation.

An Ottoman Royal presentation gold watch, keyless wind, with skeleton movement, with dials for lunar calendar, day, month, seconds, with presentation inscriptions including "Presented to Sir Henry Layard by the Sultan 1879".

Dial 2in (5cm) diam

£30,000-40,000 **L&T**

A 19thC Swiss 18ct gold-cased open-face keywind gentleman's pocket watch, with guilloche dial, with 9ct gold Albert chain.

£500-600 **CAPE**

An 18ct gold full-hunting cased keyless lever pocket watch, signed "Thos Russell & Son", London, No.77388, frosted gilt-finished lever movement, blued overcoil hairspring, bimetallic balance.

1882 *2in (5cm) wide*

£1,000-1,500 **TEN**

A large gold pocket watch, partly gilt and bronzed, with nickel-plated cylinder movement, and windows for moon phase and calendar, in travel case.

c1900 *2.75in (7cm) diam*

£1,200-1,800 **DOR**

An 18ct gold half-hunting cased lever pocket watch, signed "S.Smith & Son, 9 Strand, Watchmakers to the Admiralty, London", the 15-jewel lever movement with overcoil hairspring, case with London import mark, hallmark rubbed, with 18ct gold chain.

c1910 *2in (5cm) wide*

£2,000-3,000 **TEN**

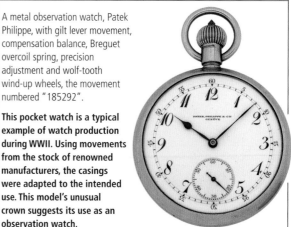

An Illinois Bunn Special pocket watch, railroad grade, with 21 jewels, 14 wg face, motor barrel, 60 hours, serial no. 5282442, model no. 173.

The 16-size Bunn Special is probably the most collected, and most researched, of the Illinois pocket watches. Of these 16-size Bunns, the most highly sought-after are the 60-hour movements made after Hamilton took over Illinois production in 1928.

2in (5cm) diam

£800-1,200 **DRA**

A metal observation watch, Patek Philippe, with gilt lever movement, compensation balance, Breguet overcoil spring, precision adjustment and wolf-tooth wind-up wheels, the movement numbered "185292".

This pocket watch is a typical example of watch production during WWII. Using movements from the stock of renowned manufacturers, the casings were adapted to the intended use. This model's unusual crown suggests its use as an observation watch.

Movement c1917 Case c1940 *2in (5cm) diam*

£3,000-4,000 **DOR**

A Martin Braun 18ct rose gold automatic "Eos" wristwatch, retrograde indicator for sunrise/ sunset and equation of time, sapphire crystal case back affixed with seven screws, Cal. 2892 A2 ETA 21 jewel movement with module MAB2, black crocodile strap, 18ct yellow gold buckle, case back stamp "Martin Braun EOS Ref. 42/032 18k".

£3,000-4,000　　　　　**LHA**

A Breuguet 18ct gold ref. 3130 wristwatch, No. 4110, retrograde power reserve indication, aperture for moonphase, 37 jewel cal. 502 rhodium plated straight line lever escapement movement with *fausses- cote* decoration, with black crocodile strap, 18ct gold stamped original deployant clasp, stamped "Automatic Ref. 3130 Breuguet 4110 K hallmarks".

With original box, papers and additional Breguet brown crocodile strap.

£8,000-12,000　　　　　**LHA**

A Breitling stainless steel chronograph wristwatch, Geneva, Navitimer, ref: 806, (Calibre 178) 17-jewel lever movement, 30-minute and 12-hour registers, case with back numbered "1343719", buttons in the band to operate chronograph hand, with original instruction booklet.

c1965　　　　*1.75in (4.5cm) wide*

£2,000-3,000　　　　　**TEN**

A Cartier lady's steel and gold quartz "Panthere" wristwatch, with quartz movement, and secret Cartier signature at 10 o'clock, numbered 1"057917 003306", the Cartier steel and gold bracelet with concealed double-deployant clasp.

c1990　　　　*1in (2.5cm) wide*

£1,200-1,800　　　　　**TEN**

A Cartier "Tank Americaine" wristwatch, calibre 077, 25 jewels, secret signature at VII, sweep centre seconds, case in 18ct white gold, pavé-set diamond sides, diamond- set crown, 18ct white gold Cartier bracelet, case, dial and movement signed.

1.5in (4cm) long

£8,000-12,000　　　　　**LHA**

A Corum stainless steel automatic calendar centre seconds wristwatch, model "GMT, Officially Certified Chronometer", with 24-hour indication, self-winding lever movement, bezel depicting the capital cities around the world, Corum strap with a steel double-deployant clasp.

c2007　　　　*1.75in (4.5cm) wide*

£1,000-1,500　　　　　**TEN**

A Roger Dubuis 18ct white gold "GMT" dual time zone mechanical wristwatch, limited edition of 28, with sapphire crystal case back, bespoke Calibre RD 9847 movement, oversized black alligator strap, original stamped 18ct white gold buckle, stamped "Roger Dubuis Geneve 17/28".

£6,000-8,000　　　　　**LHA**

An Ebel gentleman's 18ct gold wristwatch with chronograph, with 30 seconds and 60 seconds recording dials and date aperture, automatic movement, numbered "64101112 8134901", with 18ct gold band with deployant clasp.

£6,000-7,000　　　　　**WW**

A Jaeger LeCoultre 18ct gold "Reverso" wristwatch, with quartz movement, case with sliding central section to reverse to a plain polished back, numbered "140 105 1N" and "1621530", maker's buckle, with Jaeger LeCoultre boxes and guarantee booklet.

c1991　　　　*1.5in (4cm) long*

£1,500-2,000　　　　　**TEN**

A Jaeger LeCoultre lady's 18ct gold wristwatch, calibre 840 17-jewel lever movement, case numbered "975" with London import mark, with Jaeger LeCoultre 18ct gold textured integral bracelet.

c1973　　　　*1in (2.5cm) wide*

£2,000-3,000　　　　　**TEN**

A rare giant-sized World War II German Luftwaffe Aviator's "B-Uhr" wristwatch, A Lange & Sohne, numbered "214550", bimetallic balance with blued overcoil hairspring (balance staff broken), nickel silver plated case numbered "214550", band of the case numbered "FI 23882".

A. Lange & Sohne developed this model c1940 for Luftwaffe pilots. The German Air Ministry recognised the need for an accurate observer's watch to navigate and assist crews on long-range flying missions. The watches are known as B-Uhrs (Beobachtungsuhr or observer's watch). From 1941 onwards they were classified with an FI number which stands for flight and control, the 23 stands for navigation and followed by the three digit DVL number. It is arguably the most desirable WWII German aviator's watch on the market today.

c1941   2.25in (5.5cm) wide

£3,500-4,500   **TEN**

A Longines 18ct gold "Flagship" wristwatch, calibre 30L, 17-jewel lever movement, case numbered "6847 1 261".

c1960   1.5in (4cm) wide

£650-750   **TEN**

A Frank Muller PVD coated stainless steel "Casablanca No. 250" wristwatch, self-winding, decorated lever movement, blued screws, platinum rotor, reference no. "8880CDTNR", with case, and certificate enclosed.

£6,000-7,000   **DOR**

An Omega Ranchero stainless steel gentleman's wristwatch, partly red-gold plated lever movement, calibre 267, Breguet overcoil spring, the movement numbered "17038591", the casing numbered "29901".

c1961

£1,000-1,500   **DOR**

An Omega "Speedmaster Racing" stainless steel limited edition automatic calendar chronograph wristwatch, limited edition 05078/11111, calibre 1152, with self-winding lever movement, back with engraved Michael Schumacher signature and "World Champion 2001", the Omega stainless steel bracelet with concealed deployant clasp.

c2001   1.5in (4cm) wide

£1,200-1,800   **TEN**

An Omega "Seamaster" stainless steel automatic calendar centre seconds wristwatch, Professional Chronometer, 300m/1000ft, self-winding lever movement with quick date change, screw-down winding crown, helium valve positioned at ten, screw back with seamaster monogram, the Omega stainless steel bracelet with deployant clasp.

c2005   1.75in (4.5cm) wide

£1,500-2,000   **TEN**

A Patek Philippe 18ct gold wristwatch, the back with 18-jewel movement, the openwork flexible bracelet initialled "CB" to closure, movement number "1321291", case number "2759220", reference number "3844/2".

7in (18cm) long

£3,000-4,000   **IMC**

A Patek Philippe lady's 18ct gold wristwatch, ref "4106/1", 20-jewel lever movement numbered "996416", adjusted to heat, cold, isochronism and five positions, gyromax balance, with London import mark, stamped "Patek Philippe" and numbered "2676600", with Patek Philippe 18ct gold integral bracelet.

1969   1in (2.5cm) wide

£2,000-3,000   **TEN**

A Rolex 18ct gold "Precision" wristwatch, 17-jewel lever movement, blued overcoil hairspring, inside case back stamped "RWC" and with Glasgow import marks, numbered "893 9320", with Rolex strap and gilt buckle.
1957   *1.5in (4cm) wide*
£1,500-2,000   **TEN**

A Rolex stainless steel and 18ct gold "Submariner" wristwatch, with sweep second hand, 27-jewel calibre 3035 movement, two-tone Oysterlock bracelet, deployment clasp with safety, style number "R16613360B9315", serial number "U898510".
£3,500-4,500   **LHA**

A Rolex "Prince Cellini" 18ct gold wrist watch, with decorated lever movement, calibre 7040-1, "Clou de Paris", dial, reference no. "5440", the casing numbered "D756683".

c2007
£8,000-12,000   **DOR**

A Rolex Datejust 18ct gold automatic gentleman's wristwatch, with a row of diamonds framing the face, set with small, round single-cut diamonds to the dial, numbered "6339199", with original box.
7in (18cm) long
£12,000-18,000   **IMC**

A Rolex steel Oyster Perpetual "Submariner" gentleman's wristwatch, 200m, centre seconds with additional strap parts and an associated Rolex box.
£4,000-5,000   **WW**

A Schaffhausen International Watch Co. stainless steel automatic centre seconds "Ingenieur" wristwatch, with calibre 852, 21-jewel self-winding lever movement, numbered "1299021", case numbered "1364893".
c1965   *1.5in (4cm) wide*
£2,200-2,800   **TEN**

A IWC Schaffhausen "Da Vinci Rattrabanten" 18ct gold gentleman's wristwatch, with perpetual calendar and trailing hand chronograph, calibre "79251", reference no. "3751", the casing numbered "2624694", covered folding fastening, with case, manual, certificate, ownership certificate, warranty card, year slider and leather strap with gold fastening.

This particular Da Vinci is a chronograph with three push pieces. Intermediate time is measured using a second covered second hand.
c2000
£12,000-18,000   **DOR**

A Universal Geneve "Uni-Compax" 18ct gold gentleman's wristwatch, the lever movement with stop function via wheel, calibre "285", the casing numbered "1604941".
c1950-60
£1,500-2,000   **DOR**

A Vacheron & Constantin 18ct gold triple calendar wristwatch, calibre "V 485", 17-jewel lever movement, numbered "463412" and "302465", with 18ct gold buckle.
c1950   *1.5in (4cm) wide*
£7,000-8,000   **TEN**

BAROMETERS

ESSENTIAL REFERENCE - BAROMETERS

The barometer is an instrument for measuring changes in atmospheric pressure.

- Invented by the Italian philosopher and mathematician Evangelista Torricelli in 1643-4, it became popular in the 17thC as a result of the discovery of the connection between alterations in the pressure of the air and the weather.
- Barometers made in the late 17th and early 18thC are very rare and desirable, particularly by notable makers such as Daniel Quare (1649-1724).
- The most common type of barometer in the 18thC was the stick barometer. Early designs followed clock fashions, with later pieces following furniture fashions.

- The similar angle (or signpost) barometer was introduced in the 1670s, but was never widely popular.
- Wheel barometers became widespread in the late 18thC and continued throughout the 19thC.
- The aneroid ("liquid-free") barometer, which was accurate and easily portable, became popular in the 19thC. It was invented in 1843 by French engineer Lucien Vidie (1805-1866). Pocket versions were produced from c1860.
- The style of the case, the maker, and the quality of materials are the main indicators of price.
- To avoid damaging the fragile glass tubes and spilling mercury, barometers should always be kept upright and never tipped or laid flat.

A George III bow-fronted mahogany stick barometer, "Dollond, London", the silvered register plate with maker's name and a thermometer, the base with an urn cistern cover with inlaid vertical bars on each side.

39in (100cm) high

£3,000-4,000   SWO

A Georgian walnut stick barometer, the ivory register plate signed "Callaghan, 23a New Bond Street, London".

38in (96.5cm) high

£2,500-3,500   LC

A rare George III mahogany angle barometer frame, "R. Fourdrinier Sculpt. and Fred. Omphalius Inv.", the paper label inscribed "A Perpetual Regulation Of Time", with subsidiary crescent for High Water, London Bridge, The Fix D Feasts, Zodiac Signs, Calendar and Days Of The Month, the cresting with a hygrometer.

37.5in (95cm) high

£18,000-22,000   LC

A late 18thC mahogany stick barometer, George Adams, the architectural cresting centred by a brass urn finial over a waisted feather-banded trunk, the one-piece silver dial signed in an arch "George Adams, 60 Fleet Street, London, Instrument Maker to His Majesty".

George Adams was one of the most eminent instrument-makers of the 18thC, holding the appointment of "Mathematical Instrument-Maker to the Prince of Wales"(later George III). He was father of George Adams, The Younger, and Dudley Adams. George Adams Senior and Junior worked at the same address and received the Royal Patent. It is therefore difficult in many cases to assign authorship with confidence.

40in (102cm) high

£2,000-2,500   SWO

A rare George III mahogany cistern-tube stick barometer, "Hannah Adams, London".

Hannah Adams inherited the business on the death of her esteemed husband George in August 1795. She continued the business until the summer of 1796, when the stock in trade of the business was sold to William Jones.

c1796   *38in (96.5cm) high*

£1,500-2,000   DN

A George III mahogany cistern tube stick barometer, "Hannah Adams, Fleet Street, London", with vernier scale calibrated in inches and signed.

c1796   *38in (96.5cm) high*

£1,500-2,500   DN

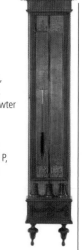

A Dutch carved mahogany "bakbarometer", "P. Wast & Zoon, Amsterdam", pewter plates inscribed "Barometer, Thermometer en Contralleur Door P, Wast en Zoon te Amsterdam".

c1800   *50.25in (127.5cm) high*

£1,500-2,000   RTC

A George III mahogany mountain stick barometer, the silvered dial inscribed "A. Adie, Edinburgh" and marked "27-31".

38.5in (97.5cm) high

£2,500-3,500   WW

A mahogany bow-front stick barometer, silvered register plate signed "J Spelzini, 91 Leather Lane, Holborn".

37.5in (95cm) high

£2,500-3,500   LC

A Dutch mahogany barometer, with two silvered register plates, one signed "A. Reballio, Rottero".

46in (117cm) high

£1,200-1,800   LC

A rosewood bow-front stick barometer, "T. Underhill, Old Mill Gate, Manchester", with a concealed mercury tube, twin vernier ivory dial signed.

T. Underhill is recorded Manchester 1830-1850.

c1840   *39in (100cm) high*

£2,500-3,500   TEN

A rosewood stick barometer, the ivory register plate signed "G. Lidston, Dartmouth".

36.5in (93cm) high

£2,000-3,000   LC

A mahogany bow-fronted stick barometer, with single vernier silvered dial signed "Dollond, London", ebony inlay, concealed tube and hygrometer.

c1840   *39in (100cm) high*

£5,500-6,500   TEN

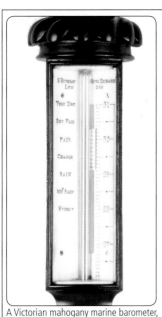

A Victorian mahogany marine barometer, with ivory vernier register signed "S. BITHRAY, ROYAL EXCHANGE, LONDON", lacking mercury and glazing.

Stephen Bithray is recorded as working from 29 Royal Exchange, London 1827-43.

c1840   37in (94cm) high
£4,000-5,000   **DN**

A rosewood and mother-of-pearl inlaid ship's stick barometer, "A Reballio & Zoon, Rotterdam", central gimbal missing.

c1850   37in (94cm) high
£1,500-2,500   **TEN**

A Victorian rosewood mercury cistern-tube stick barometer, signed "BROOKS, Ludgate Street, London", with applied mercury thermometer.

41in (104cm) high
£700-800   **DN**

A rosewood ship's barometer, "Thomas Bennett, Cork", with concealed mercury tube with angled ivory single vernier dial.

c1860   36in (91.5cm) high
£1,200-1,800   **TEN**

A Regency mahogany mercury wheel barometer with timepiece, the dial fronting a single fusée circular four-pillar movement with tic-tac escapement and signed "Holmden, London", with spirit level signed "L. STAMPA, Kirby Str't, Hatton Garden, London".

L. Stampa is recorded as working c1800-20 and he appears to have specialised in larger wheel barometers incorporating timepieces. John George Holmden is recorded as working in London 1807-40.

A George III satinwood banjo barometer, "P Borbon & Co, Edinburgh".

42in (107cm) high
£1,000-1,500   **L&T**

A George III inlaid mahogany mercury wheel barometer, "Joseph Lepori & Co., London".

c1810   39in (100cm) high
£500-600   **DN**

50in (127cm) high
£2,500-3,500   **DN**

A Regency mahogany mercury wheel barometer, "C. Negrini, Tenterden", with short duration timepiece movement .

Negrini is recorded as working in Tenterden, Kent, c1820-40.

43in (109cm) high

£600-700   DN

A William IV carved giltwood barometer, "D. Guggiari, Pelham Street, Nottingham", with silvered dials and small circular convex mirror.

41in (104cm) high

£500-700   ECGW

A mahogany 10in (25.5cm) wheel barometer, "Joseph Pini, London".

Joseph Pini is recorded working at 23 Brooke Street, London, 1838-48.

c1840   42in (106.5cm) high

£700-900   TEN

A 19thC mahogany cased banjo barometer, "P.Guarnerio, Huntingdon", with damp/dry dial, thermometer, and level.

39in (100cm) high

£600-700   ECGW

A mahogany wheel barometer, "Francis Pinney, Stamford".

Francis Pinney is recorded in Stamford 1844-68.

c1850   37in (95cm) high

£800-1,200   TEN

A Victorian Scottish mother-of-pearl, brass- and pewter-inlaid rosewood mercury wheel barometer, "D. McGregor, Greenock and Glasgow".

D. McGregor & Co. are recorded as working in Glasgow from 1856. The firm had branches in Greenock and Liverpool.

c1860   41in (104cm) high

£800-1,200   DN

A walnut wheel barometer, "Thomas Cooke, York", with unusual rack and pinion adjustment.

Thomas Cooke is recorded working in York 1837-68.

c1860   41in (104cm) high

£800-1,200   TEN

A rosewood 12in (30.5cm) wheel barometer, signed "E S Comberbach, Blackburn".

c1870   44in (112cm) high

£400-600   TEN

A French Louis XV-style gilt-brass mounted kingwood wheel barometer, "Ronquetti, Paris", the aneroid mechanism with 7.5in (19cm) eight-piece enamelled circular register calibrated in barometric inches and annotated in French, with address and inscription.

c1900   44in (112cm) high

£1,500-2,000   DN

BAROMETERS

A mahogany and brass-mounted aneroid barometer, "Negretti & Zambra", No. R/3706, the case said to be from "H. M. S. Empress".
17in (43cm) high
£400-500   CGW

A late 19thC carved walnut aneroid wall barometer.
25in (63.5cm) high
£250-300   DN

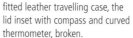

A pocket aneroid barometer, in a fitted leather travelling case, the lid inset with compass and curved thermometer, broken.
£200-250   WW

A brass oak-cased bulkhead type aneroid barometer, inscribed "John Barker & Co Ltd, Kensington".
£150-250   WW

A pocket aneroid barometer, "Negretti & Zambra", numbered "3368".
1913   *2in (5cm) diam*
£500-700   WW

A Victorian two-day marine chronometer, dial inscribed "T.Cotterell & Co. eleve de Parkinson & Frodsham, Change Alley".
c1840   *6.75in (17cm) high*
£3,000-4,000   GORL

A mid-19thC brass inlaid rosewood cased two-day marine chronometer, dials signed "HUNT & ROSKELL", London, numbered 12214, the four-pillar full-plate movement with Harrison's maintaining power, Earnshaw-type spring detent escapement.
8in (20cm) high
£2,500-3,500   DN

A two-day marine chronometer, the silvered dial signed "Gabriel, 24 Bishopsgate St, Within, London, no. 101", the spotted movement with spring detent escapement.
c1875   *Bezel 4.75in (12cm) diam*
£2,500-3,500   WW

A late 19thC brass-bound rosewood-cased two-day marine chronometer, "John Bliss & Co., New York", with movement attributed to Victor Kullberg, London, with reversed fusée, Harrison's maintaining power, and Earnshaw-type spring detent escapement.

John Bliss Snr worked as a jeweller in New York before he went into partnership with English watchmaker Edward Creighton in 1835. Bliss & Creighton worked in Manhattan, making and supplying Instruments and marine chronometers until 1853. They were the first makers in the USA to build chronometers from scratch. John Bliss later took his son as partner forming the firm, John Bliss & Son (later John Bliss & Co.) The firm closed in 1956.
8in (20cm) high
£1,500-2,500   DN

A rare eight-day amboyna-veneered mantel chronometer, silvered dial signed "Venner Time Switches Ltd" and numbered 598, the plated movement with substantial ringed pillars, the large horizontal platform with spring detent escapement countersunk into the plates, the back with two electrical connections.

Venner would have ordered this chronometer from Mercers, and Vaudrey Mercer records it as made in 1925.
11.5in (29cm) high
£5,000-7,000   WW

A George II Culpeper-type microscope, in style of Matthew Loft, with shaped specimen stage applied with rotating ten-hole specimen plate and centred with an oculus, with drawer containing five objective lenses and an ivory specimen canister to apron.

The slender diamond-section one-piece supports with turned feet and lozenge-shaped fixing plates are features normally associated with instruments from Loft's workshop.

c1740   *16in (40.5cm) high*

£6,000-8,000   **DN**

An early 19thC brass Cuff-type compound microscope, applied with pivoted piano-concave mirror, the apron drawer with six objectives, specimen clamp and other accessories, with figured mahogany pyramid-shaped box.

Instrument 14in (36cm) high unextended

£2,500-3,500   **DN**

ESSENTIAL REFERENCE - PETER DOLLOND

Peter Dollond (1730-1820) was the son of John Dollond, a Huguenot silk weaver. He started a business as an optician at the age of 20 in 1750.

- **He was joined by his father in 1752 (died 1761) and his brother, John (died 1804).**
- **Peter Dollond was appointed optician to George III and the Duke of York. His workshop was renowned for producing high-quality instruments, which were used by Nelson and Captain Cook among others.**
- **He is credited with the invention of the triple achromatic lens in 1763, which is still widely used today.**
- **After Peter's death, the family business was continued by his nephew, George Huggins, who subsequently changed his surname to Dollond.**

An early 19thC lacquered brass "Jones's Most Improved" pattern-compound microscope, Peter Dollond, the sighting tube with rotating six-lens objective plate, the folding tripod base signed "Dollond * London", in fitted mahogany box with accessories including frog-plate, brass slider, bull's eye lens, apron.

The design of this microscope was originally conceived by George Adams II in the latter years of the 18th century, however after his death in 1795, his stock and rights were bought by the brothers William and Samuel Jones who modified the design slightly and marketed it as their own.

Instrument 18in (45cm) high assembled

£3,500-4,500   **DN**

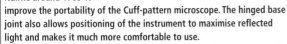

An early 19thC brass Cuff-type compound chest microscope, with pivoted substage piano-concave mirror, the mahogany box containing six objectives, subject forceps, substage cone, seven small bone sliders and other accessories.

The design of this microscope was conceived by Edward Nairne around 1765 to improve the portability of the Cuff-pattern microscope. The hinged base joint also allows positioning of the instrument to maximise reflected light and makes it much more comfortable to use.

Instrument 15in (38cm) high assembled

£2,000-3,000   **DN**

A Victorian lacquered brass monocular compound microscope, "Newton & Co., London", in original mahogany box, with four cased objective lenses, bull's eye mirror on stand and other accessories.

Instrument 14in (36cm) high

£500-600   **DN**

A Victorian lacquered brass binocular compound microscope, base signed "BAKER, 244 High Holborn, London", in original mahogany box with presentation label, containing cased objective lens and some prepared slides.

17in (43cm) high

£350-450   **DN**

A lacquered brass binocular microscope, R & J Beck, No.17880, with rack and pinion, fine focusing, in mahogany case fitted with various accessories.

Case 17in (43cm) wide

£2,500-3,500   **AH**

SCIENTIFIC INSTRUMENTS

A George III lacquered-brass portable reflector telescope.

There is a similar telescope by Walkins in the National Maritime Museum, Greenwich.

c1780   *29in (74cm) long*

£4,000-5,000   SWO

A 3in (7.5cm) library refracting telescope, "Buff & Buff, Boston, Massachusetts", engraved on viewing end "Utschneider und fraunhofer in Munchen", with two additional ocular lenses, both marked "Day Power", and an additional eyepiece marked "Astronomical Power", in walnut carrying case.

28.5in (73cm) high

£3,500-4,500   SK

A Victorian lacquered brass 2.5in (6.5cm) refracting telescope, the tube with single rack-and-pinion adjusted draw and starfinder, in original mahogany box.

c1860   *28in (72cm) long closed*

£500-600   DN

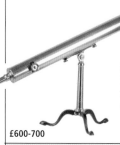

A 19thC lacquered-brass three-inch refracting telescope, "Henry Crouch, London", the tube with single rack-and-pinion adjusted draw and signature, in original pine box.

52in (132cm) long closed

£600-700   DN

ESSENTIAL REFERENCE - BAROGRAPHS

Barographs are used to record alterations in atmospheric pressure over a set period of time.

● **They were developed in the 19thC. The first examples were the mercury type, although barographs with aneroid mechanisms are more commonly seen today.**

● **Typical barographs are set in a glass-fronted wooden case with an aneroid mechanism consisting of a set of bellows that expand and contract. The bellows are linked to a pen or stylus, which records barometer readings on successive days onto a paper chart mounted on to a metal drum that slowly revolves by clockwork.**

An early 20thC oak barograph, "Perry & Co., Bournemouth", with eight-part vacuum chamber within lacquered-brass armature operating inked pointer for the clockwork-driven rotating paper-scale lined drum.

15in (38cm) wide

£600-800   DN

An early 20thC "The Dial" mahogany cased barograph, "A & N C.S. Ltd".

16.25in (41cm) wide

£1,200-1,800   GORL

A Negretti & Zambra mahogany-cased barograph, bearing the maker's metal plate reference no. R/35330, in glazed case.

13.5in (34cm) wide

£400-500   GHOU

A barograph, "Tycos, Short & Mason, London", with eight-tier vacuum and single recording arm, in oak case, with dated presentation brass plaque.

1926   *14.25in (36cm) wide*

£1,800-2,200   AH

An American wheel cutting engine, probably Connecticut, the dovetailed chestnut and cherry frame with 15.5in (39.5cm) diam, two-part brass index plate with numerous divisions including 30, 48, 56, 60, 62, 64, 72, 78, 80, 84, 96, 98 and 118 and inner rings with 6, 7, 8 and 10, adjustable cutter frame with wooden handled crank and cutter arbor.

Connecticut clock makers Daniel Burnap and John Avery used nearly identical machines. The John Avery machine is in the J. Cheney Wells collection at Old Sturbridge Village, Massachusetts.

c1780   *23in (58.5cm) long*

£10,000-15,000   **SK**

A late 18thC brass and steel fusée engine, possibly by John Wyke, with open brass frame and multiple adjustments, the tool slide bears marked "I WYKE".

Trade catalogues of the time show similar engines, these include Wyke's catalogue which shows it in Plate 60.

9.25in (23.5cm) long

£2,000-3,000   **SK**

A brass fusée engine, the vice-held machine engraved on cutter frame "Ferdinand Berthoud Fecit", with hand crank-threaded advance, knurled thumb screws and locking screws for main components, mounted on a walnut display block.

Ferdinand Berthoud (1727-1807) settled in Paris at age 19 and flourished as a watchmaker and author of horological works. This tool remains one of the few examples signed by this pre-eminent maker.

c1780   *8in (20cm) long*

£15,000-20,000   **SK**

A German brass and steel wheel cutting engine, by Christian Grunsteidel, the vice-held belt driven engine with 9.75in (25cm) dividing plate, with forty-three division rows marked "13-365", the steel indexing arm with finger loop, pivoting cutter frame.

1798   *13in (33.5cm) long*

£1,500-2,500   **SK**

An early 19thC French rose engine, from the Shop of A. L. Breguet, Paris, the 14 rosettes with 12 designed for slide following, 15.5in (39cm) brass drive wheel with 400, 300, 240, 192, 60 and additional divisions with steel spring-loaded detent, rubber follower mounted at the side of the headstock with wooden handled tension adjustment, 9.5in (24cm) diam headstock with dove-tailed slides and index attachment, 25in (63.5cm) diam drive wheel to rotate the headstock, on original walnut bench.

The slide rest is a probable replacement done by the House of Breguet in the late 19thC to modernise the machine.

48in (122cm) long

£30,000-40,000   **SK**

A 19thC Swiss brass and steel fusée engine, with wood turning handle, pivoting cutter and ferrule, gnurled thumbscrews for tightening and adjusting, and an indexed steel plate for setting the cutter lead.

14.25in (36.5cm) long

£4,000-5,000   **SK**

A late 19thC Swiss brass, iron and steel wheel cutting engine, with 6.5in (16cm) diam brass index plate with approximately 22 rows of divisions including 108, 160, 174, 180, 192, 240, 300 and 360, hand wheel-powered cutter presently set up for annular wheels.

18in (45.5cm) high

£3,000-4,000   **SK**

A rare celestial globe, by Johann Elert Bode and Johann Georg Franz.

1804   *12in (30.5cm) diam*

£5,000-6,000   DOR

An early 19thC 18in (45.5cm) terrestrial library globe, by Charles Smith and Son, London, on mahogany tripod stand, with 12 hand-coloured gores heavily annotated with states, cities, topographical features and voyages of discovery.

41in (104cm) high

£6,000-7,000   DN

A pair of early 19thC 12in (30.5cm) library globes, by Donaldson of Edinburgh, the terrestrial with additions from 1834, restorations.

1830   *38in (96.5cm) high*

£18,000-22,000   TEN

An Edwardian 18in (46cm) terrestrial globe, by W. & A.K. Johnson, Edinburgh & London, dated.

This good quality globe is in the style of Georgian library globes.

1907   *41in (104cm) high*

£6,000-7,000   GORL

Judith Picks: An Orrey

John Davies was born in Tetbury, Gloucestershire, in 1839. He was apprenticed to a watchmaker in London, however his interest in scientific instruments was such that he designed and made several one-off examples for his own use.

It is particularly interesting to note that the two moons orbiting Mars (Phobos and Deimos) were not officially discovered until 1877 by the American astronomer Asaph Hall Sn'r. This suggests that the bodies around the sphere representing Mars on this example must have been incorporated during later design stages.

A Victorian lacquered brass and mahogany orrery, the mounted ring divided for the months of the year annotated with signs of the Zodiac and figures relating to the actual distance of the earth from the sun in miles every two months, two of the five crossings signed John Davies, London, the centre with silvered Solar sphere (or optional candle), rotated via a crank, engaging with the contrate wheel beneath, which is mounted with arm applied with an angled terrestrial globe pivoted on a further pulley to allow controlled rotation during its motion around the sun, the baseboard further applied with distant sphere representing Mars, with two moons, and an extensive series of original annotated watercolour drawings relating to every aspect of the design and construction of the instrument, many dated December 1867.

c1870   *31in (79cm) long*

£10,000-15,000   DN

A rare early 19thC brass armillary sphere, made by (Johann Bernhard) Bauer or J. G. Klingersche Kunsthandlung Nuremberg, the engraved sphere partially stamped, the wood stand showing the months, days, compass directions, and the zodiac.

5.5in (14cm) diam

£6,000-8,000   DOR

A planetarium, by Jan Felkl & Son, showing the planets Mercury, Venus, Mars, and the Earth and its moon, the Sun symbolised by a candle with reflector, zodiac plate with pointer and compass rose, the globe and zodiac disc in Hungarian.

c1900   *Earth orbit 32in (82.5cm) diam*

£8,000-12,000   DOR

ESSENTIAL REFERENCE - NICOLE FRÈRES

Generally acknowledged as the "Rolls Royce" of music box makers, Nicole Frères was established in 1815 in Geneva, Switzerland. It had multiple warehouses in London from the mid-19thC.

- From 1840 to 1865 Nicole Frères made various large six- and eight-air musical boxes. Some had one long comb, others had a piano-forte arrangement of the combs. The largest boxes usually played operatic arias or oratorio music.
- Cases were often quite plain and only just large enough to contain the movement; some had inlaid lids.
- Nicole Frères closed its factories in 1895. Two former Swiss mechanics and the London agent continued to trade as Nicole Frères, carrying out repairs and selling replacement parts.

A Swiss Mermod Frères six-air interchangeable Ideal Piccolo cylinder music box, serial no. 44664, nickel-plated single-comb movement with Jacot's Patented Safety Check, zither attachment and three 11in (28cm) cylinders.

Box 30.5in (77.5cm) long

£2,500-3,500 SK

A Swiss Nicole Frères interchangeable cylinder music box, in a marquetry-decorated case, with bells and drums in sight, with six 16in (40.5cm) cylinders, on a conforming desk.

53in (134.5cm) wide

£6,000-8,000 LHA

A Swiss walnut, parquetry and ebonised music box, with gilt cylinder and six bells and central drum, under glazed door.

26in (66cm) long

£3,000-4,000 FRE

A Swiss interchangeable cylinder music box, in a marquetry and mother-of-pearl inset case, playing eight airs on three 13in (33.5cm) cylinders, the case with a drawer.

37in (94cm) wide

£3,500-4,500 LHA

A music box, with a crank wind 11in (28cm) barrel, with tune indicator (1-8), with zither attachment to the comb, numbered 0637, the case missing the tune sheet,

21.5in (54.5cm) wide

£600-800 WW

A bells-in-sight cylinder music box, the 9.25in (23.5cm) cylinder playing eight airs, the bells struck by seated Chinamen, with label "Repaired Keith, Prowse & Co., manufacturers, 48 Cheapside, London", in a walnut case.

18.75in (47.5cm) wide

£2,500-3,500 LC

MUSIC BOXES

ESSENTIAL REFERENCE - REGINA MUSIC BOXES

In 1889 Gustave Brachhausen and Paul Reissner left the Symphonion Music Box Company and their native Germany to make music boxes in the US. A steeply increased tariff on goods imported to the US in 1890 made it more cost-effective to set up shop there, rather than export from Germany.

● The Regina Music Box company was officially incorporated in 1894, and became the best-known American manufacturer.

● The company's innovations included the introduction of stronger spring-wound motors (which could play for a longer time before rewinding) and the placement of the machine's sounding board on the top to increase volume.

● Regina produced more than 100,000 music boxes between 1892 and 1920. However, only a relatively small number survived the scrap metal drives of two World Wars.

A 15.5in (39.5cm) Regina Corona automatic changer music box, the dual comb 12 disc auto-change mechanism with 26 discs.

c1900   *68in (173cm) high*

£8,000-12,000   **SK**

A Regina Sublima upright music box, with 16 discs.

c1900   *65.25in (166cm) high*

£5,000-6,000   **POOK**

A 15in (38cm) Regina auto disc-changer, with carved crest with clock in the centre, with double comb mechanism with speed control and banjo attachment, with approximately 40 discs and key.

69in (175cm) high

£20,000-30,000   **JDJ**

A Continental walnut Street Piano with Jazz Band Automata, with 16 hammers and nest of three bells, the lower section with pinned wooden barrel and worm gear which rotates the barrel and activates the eight automata figures playing in a jazz band (lacking one figure) while the operator turns the wooden handled crank.

c1880   *31.75in (80.5cm) high*

£5,000-7,000   **SK**

A 19thC Swiss rosewood and inlaid music box-on-stand, the single cylinder playing eight airs with drum and bells with gilt bird strikes, bearing retailer's label of "James Smith & Son, Liverpool".

39in (99cm) high

£1,500-2,500   **FRE**

A Mira console disc music box, with 53 discs.

c1910   *42in (106.5cm) high*

£5,000-6,000   **POOK**

A rare Caille New Century upright slot machine with music, with cast-iron trim, a six-way coin head, a twelve-tune cylinder, in an oak cabinet with nickel plated cast iron coin head.

The cylinder, changing with each play or playing the same tune over and over, was often added to circumvent gambling laws. One was paying to hear the music with the gambling aspect as a bonus.

68in (173cm) high

£25,000-35,000   **JDJ**

A rare 18thC painted wood and cut-paper ship diorama, inscribed "A. Walker Invt et Fecit, 1763", in a glazed and moulded frame.

As well as being a rare Georgian piece, this diorama is well executed with plenty of realistic detail, and is in excellent condition.

1763   *23.25in (59cm) wide*

£9,000-11,000   **WW**

A 19thC painted wooden marine diorama, of a clipper in full sail with other sailing vessels and a lighthouse in the background, within an ebonised and gilded moulded section frame, some damage.

54in (138cm) long

£2,000-3,000   **TOV**

A diorama of the sidewheel steamship "Chicago", with American flag, ensign, owner's pennant, and ship's pennant, the hull with green and red striping marked "U.S. MAIL", the foreground with small models of dory and coastal schooner.

c1860   *41in (104cm) wide*

£3,000-4,000   **JDJ**

ESSENTIAL REFERENCE - PRISONER-OF-WAR WORK

Most prisoner-of-war work was made by French prisoners of war in England during the Napoleonic wars (c1800-15). Imprisoned in "hulks" (decommissioned ships) off the coast of Plymouth, Portsmouth and other towns, the sailors would often combine their skills to make models from the limited materials available.

- The creation of such pieces allowed officers to pass the time (as they were not expected to work) and could later be sold.
- Typical items include compendiums, ship models and jewellery boxes carved from bone.
- Straw was also used. It was coloured and woven into pictorial panels and laid onto boxes.

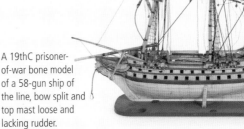

A 19thC prisoner-of-war bone model of a 58-gun ship of the line, bow split and top mast loose and lacking rudder.

21in (53cm) long

£4,500-5,500   **CAPE**

ESSENTIAL REFERENCE - SCRIMSHAW

Scrimshaw is a folk art in which the bone, teeth and tusks of whales, walruses and other marine animals are turned into decorative objects, such as novelties, keepsakes and tools. It was popular with 19thC craftsmen of coastal towns and ports, but particularly with sailors on whaling voyages.

- The surface was smoothed to provide a flat background for a design pricked out with a needle. The dots were then joined together using black ink, soot or tar, to create an image, often of a whaling scene.
- Many replicas have been made, often in resin. These are usually heavier than originals and can have a milkier, shinier finish without the natural veining of the tooth or ivory.

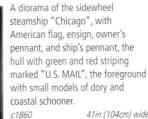

A mid-19thC engraved whale's tooth, the reverse showing a fashionably dressed woman and her two daughters, the obverse depicting a lady and a gentleman, both sides heightened with red and blue.

5.5in (14cm) long

£3,000-4,000   **SK**

A 19thC ship model of the British frigate class warship "Lydia", with fully detailed rigging and cannons.

This was displayed at the Imperial War Museum in London until 1940, when it was sold to support the war effort against Germany.

56in (142cm) long

£10,000-15,000   **POOK**

A ship-builder's model of the "S. S. Nerissa", by Hugh MacMillan, Greenock, in a glass cabinet on a black painted stand.

The "Nerissa" was built in 1926 and served various cargo and passenger routes until WWII when she was sunk off Ireland by a German submarine on 30th April 1941. Only 84 of her 290 passengers and crew were saved.

84in (213cm) long

£8,000-12,000   **SK**

A mid-19thC scrimshaw cow horn, inscribed "Henry Henderson Plumber Glasgow, 1852", engraved with various ships, buildings, emblems and initials and dates of the Henderson family, Glasgow crest and motto.

13in (33.5cm) long

£800-1,200   **L&T**

A 19thC ship's bell, cast with "F.J Penn & Company 1854", and a relief wreath, within the words "Gedenkt Te Sterven".

15in (38cm) high

£400-500   SWO

A ship's brass bell, deeply engraved "HMS Bulwark" and broad arrow, cracked and no clapper.

"HMS Bulwark" was an aircraft-carrier commissioned at Belfast in 1954. It took part in the Suez landings in 1956, Middle East Crisis in 1958, Kuwait Crisis 1961, Borneo Operations 1964 and was scrapped in 1984.

13in (33.5cm) high

£1,000-1,500   W&W

A bronze bell for "H.M. Submarine E'25", marked "commissioned 23/08/1915", with crown top and original striker.

The submarine was de-commissioned in December 1921.

8.5in (21.5cm) high

£2,500-3,500   GORL

A pair of copper and brass ship's lanterns, with convex lenses.

16in (40.5cm) high

£200-300   CHT

A German brass ship's binnacle, compass by C. Plath, Hamburg, stamped with eagle and Swastika emblem, the letter "M" and "1237", with brass mounting ring.

12in (30.5cm) diam

£800-1,200   BELL

A diving helmet, made of copper and brass.

c1940   *22in (56cm) high*

£1,600-1,800   DOR

A ship's binnacle, by "Sestrel" Henry Browne and Son, type 89521, compass no 2944N, the cylindrical oak frame surmounted by the copper compass top with glass windows and two copper handles, a spirit level contained in a brass case, compass No 2944N.

54in (137cm) high

£1,200-1,800   L&T

An early 20thC brass-mounted mahogany ship's wheel.

40.25in (102cm) diam

£400-500   GORL

A sand picture in a glass bottle, portraying a paddlewheeler flying an American flag and "FROM A. CLEMENS/Artist/McGregor, Ia./1888," the reverse with a calling card inscribed "G.T. SEAL" with flowers.

Andrew Clemens (1857-1894) was born in Dubuque, Iowa, and became deaf and mute at the age of five. He earned his livelihood by painstakingly arranging coloured sand to make pictures in glass bottles. The sand came from the naturally coloured sandstone in the Pictured Rocks area of Iowa. He worked in McGregor, Iowa, and briefly exhibited his work at South Side Museum in Chicago, Illinois. He died in 1894 at the age of 37.

1888   *8.5in (21cm) high*

£12,000-18,000   SK

THE METALWARE MARKET

One of the main influences on the silver market is the price of silver, which has risen 88% since 2001. This year has been a good one for antique silver, in particular.

People have seen that, while enjoying owning a piece of silver, it is also proving to be a good investment. As one collector said recently, it was better than having money in the bank.

High-end silver has seen some amazing prices, fuelled to a certain extent by the real shortage of good things on the market. Alastair Dickenson, an Antiques Roadshow colleague and silver specialist, says that prices in the collectors market for anything rare and unusual are extraordinary. In April 2011, Lawrences of Crewkerne, Somerset, England, sold a rare Victorian vinaigrette in the shape of a skull, by Henry William Dee, hallmarked London 1871, which had been estimated at £3,000–4,000. It made £7,800. At the same sale a rare early Victorian "castle top" vinaigrette of the University Church of St. Mary the Virgin by Nathaniel Mills, hallmarked 1843, estimated at £800–1,200, made £6,600.

Alastair has suggested that, with more access to the internet, more private people are bidding direct and possibly against each other. It may take some time for some of these record prices to be surpassed.

People often ask me what is a good area to buy in. One answer is Georgian flatware, which, in inflation-adjusted terms, is actually cheaper today than it was 25 years ago. A West End retailer will charge you around £13,000 for a modern service. Yet a full Georgian set, weighing 154 ounces, sold recently for £800 at Woolley and Wallis in Salisbury, Wiltshire, England. The metal itself has an intrinsic value of more than £800 (melt it down and that's what you'd get on the spot market), so the purchaser paid nothing for the antiquity and craft of the knives, spoons and forks. That seems to be a bargain, particularly given that nothing stays unfashionable forever.

The collectors' market for silver spoons is also very lively. At the top end of the market, a London spoon of c1500 can go for as much as £25,000. For the smaller investor, tea caddy spoons can go for under £100.

A pair of William III silver candlesticks, Richard Syng, London, the octagonal bases and conforming knops with gadrooned borders, beneath stop-fluted columns, with unmarked detachable nozzles.

1698   *9in (23cm) high 25.2oz*

£7,000-10,000   **TEN**

A pair of Queen Anne Britannia silver octagonal candlesticks, Nathaniel Lock, London, with drum pattern nozzle, tapered and knopped stems, on spreading octagonal bases.

1712   *7.5in (19cm) high 21oz*

£6,000-8,000   **A&G**

A George I Britannia silver faceted octagonal candlestick, Thomas Merry I, London, engraved with crest and "I" over "I*M".

1716   *7.5in (19cm) high 11.5oz*

£3,500-4,500   **DN**

A pair of Georgian silver candlesticks, Paul de Lamerie, with typical engraving with alternating panels of lattice and bellflowers.

See p333 for more on Paul de Lamerie.

1716-17   *6.5in (16cm) high 25oz*

£20,000-30,000   **POOK**

One of a pair of George II cast silver candlesticks, Hugh Arnett & Edward Pocock, London, with turned urn-shaped sconces on knopped tapering stems and hexagonal bases, with later nozzles.

1727   *6.25in (15.5cm) high*

£3,000-4,000 pair   **TOV**

Judith Picks

When looking at any antique there are various aspects to consider – apart from "do you like the object?" and "would you want to own it?" Silver and gold have been rising rapidly in value, partly due to the poor performance of stocks and shares and the public's nervousness about banks and pension funds.

These silver candlesticks have many other attributes, apart from their weight (an impressive 31oz each) to tempt the buyer. They are excellent early 18thC examples by a good maker, Balthazar Friedrich Behrens (1701-1760), but most importantly they have excellent royal provenance.

These sticks are part of a set of 72 candlesticks delivered c1735 to Herrenhausen, the Hanover palace of George II of Great Britain and Elector of Hanover (who reigned 1727-1760).

They retained their royal connection by descent in the Royal family of Great Britain and Hanover until the death of King William IV in 1837. At this point the two kingdoms became separate under different monarchs. Thence the candlesticks passed by descent to William's grandson, the Duke of Brunswick (1845-1923).

Finally, following the death of George Frederick's son, Ernest Augustus, in 1923 a considerable part of the Hanover silver, both German and English, was purchased by the Viennese dealer Gluckselig.

One of a pair of German silver Royal table candlesticks, Balthazar Friedrich Behrens, with shaped square bases and knopped octagonal baluster column, leaf clasped, engraved with Royal Coat of Arms and "GII" cypher to nozzles.

c1735   9in (23cm) high 31oz each

£50,000-70,000 pair   L&T

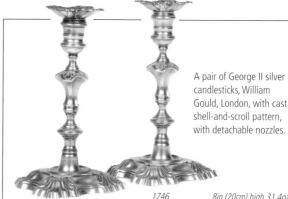

A pair of George II silver candlesticks, William Gould, London, with cast shell-and-scroll pattern, with detachable nozzles.

1746   8in (20cm) high 31.4oz

£2,000-3,000   TEN

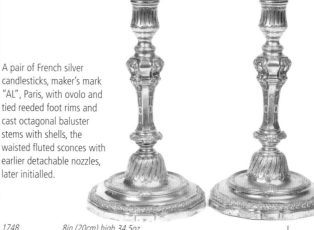

A pair of French silver candlesticks, maker's mark "AL", Paris, with ovolo and tied reeded foot rims and cast octagonal baluster stems with shells, the waisted fluted sconces with earlier detachable nozzles, later initialled.

1748   8in (20cm) high 34.5oz

£12,000-18,000   TEN

A pair of mid-18thC silver Baroque candlesticks, maker's mark "AH".

7.5in (19cm) high 25oz

£6,000-8,000   DOR

A pair of George II silver candlesticks, William Grundy, London, with urn-shaped sconces on fluted and foliate-knopped stems and scroll-cornered square bases.

1755   8in (20cm) high

£2,000-3,000   TOV

A pair of George II silver candlesticks, John Quantock, London, with shell capitals and knopped stems, on raised shaped square bases with shell motifs, underside numbered "No.1" and "No.3".

1757   9in (23cm) high 34oz

£2,500-3,500   WW

A George III silver cast candlestick, Parker and Wakelin, London, with gadrooned borders, spool-shaped capital, on square bases, engraved with armorial.

1767   9in (23cm) high 16oz

£800-1,200   WW

A pair of mid-18thC cast-silver caryatid candlesticks, probably James Warren, Dublin, the elongated drip pans with masks and scroll decoration, on triangular scroll bases, with masks, shells and foliate decoration, crested.

c1755   11.5in (29cm) high 50oz

£7,000-10,000   **WW**

A pair of George II Masonic silver Corinthian column-form candlesticks, possibly Frederick Vonham, London, with gadrooned bobeches, on waisted square foot engraved with Masonic emblems and devices.

1759   13.5in (34cm) high

£4,000-6,000   **FRE**

A pair of George III cast-silver candlesticks, Jonathan Alleine, London, on stepped square bases with gadroon and scroll decoration, with spool-shaped capitals, detachable fluted drip pans.

1769   10in (25.5cm) high 40oz

£5,000-7,000   **WW**

Two of a set of four English silver candlesticks, John Carter.

c1769   10.25in (26cm) high 70.5oz

£10,000-15,000 set   **POOK**

A matched set of four Georgian silver candlesticks, two Wakelin and Taylor (c1791-1792), two Wakelin and Garrard (1813-1814), all with the same engraved armorial.

The company currently known as Garrard & Co. was founded by George Wickes in 1735. Two apprentices, John Parker and Edward Wakelin, took over in 1760 after Wickes's retirement, and were replaced by John Wakelin and William Taylor in 1776. Robert Garrard became a partner in the company in 1792 following the death of Taylor, and became sole partner in 1802. Queen Victoria appointed Garrard as Crown Jewellers in 1843, a position it retained until 2007.

12.25in (31cm) high

£10,000-15,000   **POOK**

A pair of Austrian Late Empire silver candlesticks, Alois Nepomuk Würth, Vienna.

1817   9in (23cm) high 20oz

£2,500-3,500   **DOR**

A set of four German silver floral-moulded candlesticks, Humbert and Sohn, Berlin.

1847-1850   10in (25.5cm) high 41oz

£4,000-6,000 set   **DOR**

A pair of late 19thC Italian silver candlesticks, weighted, with mis-struck hallmark.

10in (25.5cm) high

£800-1,200   **DOR**

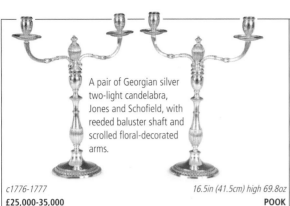

A pair of Georgian silver two-light candelabra, Jones and Schofield, with reeded baluster shaft and scrolled floral-decorated arms.

c1776-1777   16.5in (41.5cm) high 69.8oz
£25,000-35,000   POOK

A pair of Belgian silver candelabra, maker's mark "BN", Lüttich (Liege).

1789-1809 16in (40.5cm) high 95oz
£5,000-7,000   DOR

A pair of German silver seven-light candelabra, after Christian Erich Ingermann, one with maker's mark "Mau Dresden", with moulded rocailles and grape decoration.

1888   21in (53cm) high 277oz
£15,000-25,000   DOR

A pair of Rococo Revival silver candelabra, one J. C. Klinkosch, Vienna (1872-1922), the other by Robert Garrard, London (1875) with elaborate floral decoration and sculpted putto.

29in (73.5cm) high 583lb
£50,000-70,000   DOR

Two of a matched set of four George III silver candelabrum, William Pitts & Joseph Preedy, London, the branch tops with lilies and buds, with detachable reeded nozzles (one lacking), the bases with laurel band, engraved with the Camden coat of arms, loaded.

Candlesticks 1790 and 1794   22in (55.5cm) high 178oz
£40,000-60,000 set   DN

A pair of late 19thC German Neo-classical silver four-light candelabra, J.D. Schleissner and Sons, Hanau, the acanthus-embossed capital with Classical figure bearing a candle socket, impressed on foot rim "13/NH" within a shield, weighted.

50.75in (52.7cm) high
£1,000-1,500   WES

A pair of 20thC Italian silver seven-light candelabra, Nardi, Milan, with seven foliate-cast scrolling candle arms, on stepped square base and short scroll feet, stamped "lavorez a mano", "925" and "Italy"; one stamped "NARDI".

24in (61cm) high, 460oz
£6,000-8,000   FRE

A sterling silver two-handled cup, maker's mark "EG", London, with leaf decoration, later marked "HW/WG/1749".
1680   *3.15in (7.5cm) high 4.3oz*
£1,000-1,500   **LHA**

A Charles II silver tankard, maker's mark "GS", London, with scroll handle and reeded stepped cover with cast scroll thumb piece, later engraved with armorial and crested.

1679   *7in (18cm) high 37.1oz*
£5,000-7,000   **TEN**

A William and Mary Scottish silver "thistle" mug, Andrew Law II, Edinburgh, assay master John Borthwick, with moulded S-scroll handle, two moulded girdles and a lobed base, engraved "B" over "IB" over an earlier set.
1694   *3.75in (9.5cm) high 7oz*
£8,000-10,000   **DN**

A William III silver tankard, Thomas Jenkins, London, later chased with putti and lion, with scroll handle and chased domed cover with cast lion thumb piece, crested.

1698   *8in (20cm) high 39.4oz*
£2,500-3,500   **TEN**

A William III silver cup and cover, James Chadwick, London, the later domed fluted cover with ribbed turned finial, the body with wrythen lobes and beaded scroll handles, on wrythen spreading foot.
1699   *9in (23cm) high 24oz*
£1,500-2,500   **L&T**

A rare Queen Anne gilt Britannia silver two-handled privy seal cup, engraved with the coat of arms of the Privy Council of Queen Anne and "The last Privey Seale w,,ch belonge'd to England before the Union of Great Brittaine w,,ch tooke place the first of May, 1707", verso with crest of the Earl of Oxford within a garter, with scrollwork handle.
4.5in (11.5cm) high 14.5oz
£6,000-8,000   **A&G**

A Massachusetts silver tankard, John Coney, Boston, the flat lid with cast mask and dolphin thumb piece and later hinged spout lid over a tapered cylindrical body with engraved armorial.
c1710   *7.25in (18.5cm) high 32oz*
£10,000-15,000   **POOK**

A German silver and parcel-gilt cup, Philipp Stenglin, Augsburg, the rim decorated with strapwork.

4in (10cm) high 4.3oz

£2,000-3,000   DOR

An English silver caudle cup, bearing the touch of William Twell.

c1711-1712   *3in (7.5cm) high 5.1oz*

£700-1,000   POOK

An early George II silver tankard, John Gamon, London, with large scroll handle and a volute thumb piece, the body engraved with a contemporary coat of arms.

1727   *7.5in (19cm) high 31oz*

£3,000-4,000   WW

A rare pair of mid-18thC Scottish provincial silver tumbler cups, J. Glen, Glasgow, with plain sides and domed bases, marked "IG", "S", "IG", and with Glasgow town mark.

c1740   *3in (7.5cm) diam 3.3oz*

£3,000-4,000   L&T

A pair of George II silver tumbler cups, Thomas Cooke II and Richard Gurney, London, with gilded bowls.

c1754   *2.25in (5.5cm) high 3oz*

£1,000-1,500   WW

A George II silver vase-form cup and cover, Ayme Videau, London, engraved with crest and armorials of Godfrey, with chased floral swags, twin scroll handles, the cover with clasped finial.

1753   *15in (38cm) high 66oz*

£3,000-4,000   L&T

A George IV sterling silver tankard, Philip Rundell, London, the hinged lid with putti finial and a double scroll handle, the body with a continuous repoussé scene of Classical figures.

1821   *13.5in (34.5cm) high 69oz*

£3,000-4,000   FRE

A Victorian silver Gothic Revival chalice, John Hardman and Co, Birmingham, with a gilded interior and applied panels of chased decoration on matted background, with gem-set knopped stem, on raised hexafoil base with religious symbols.

John Hardman and Co. first collaborated with A.W.N. Pugin in 1838, and then continued to produce the majority of his silver designs until his death in 1852. His influence stayed with the firm and it continued to make churchplate and domestic items in the Gothic taste.

1869   8in (20cm) high 17oz
£2,000-3,000   WW

A George IV silver-gilt presentation cup and cover, Benjamin Smith II, London, the foot chased with oak leaves, the body with applied bands of acanthus leaves and cast openwork vine leaf and ovolo-moulded rim, also cast and applied with racehorses, with presentation inscription.

1828   18in (45.5cm) high 125oz
£5,000-7,000   TEN

A Victorian silver two-handled presentational cup, Frederick Elkington, Birmingham, with pierced oak leaf and acorn cast handles, rim with etched horseshoes over floral sprigs and repoussé horse race, the reverse with inscription, on etched and egg-and-dart cast circular foot.

This trophy was awarded to the winner of the Merchant's Cup at the Royal Calcutta Turf Club in 1875. The club was founded in 1795 and, for the next century, rivalled well-known British racetracks, the races being followed and results reported across the British Commonwealth.

1875   12.75in (32.5cm) high 105oz
£4,000-6,000   FRE

A British Royal silver presentation cup, cover and salver, presented to Admiral Charles H Davis, U.S.N., S Garrard, London, the cup with mermaid finial, and four panels depicting North, South East and West, the base with dolphins, the salver with Art Nouveau style ribbon border and six panels of winged messengers, the centre with the Royal Arms and inscription,.

1903/4   20in (52cm) high 195oz
£25,000-35,000   L&T

A fine Victorian silver-gilt stirrup cup in the form of a hound's head, James Barclay Hennell, with chased and engraved detail, with engraved number "6" to interior.

1879   6in (15cm) long 10.75oz
£10,000-15,000   A&G

A Victorian silver windmill cup, Soloman Nyburg & Co, the inverted bell-shaped cup chased with rural scenes, surmounted with a windmill, the reverse applied with a figure upon a ladder and a flared tube, with London import marks.

1892   19in (48cm) high 59.7oz
£2,000-3,000   TEN

A 19thC German silver wager cup, Nereshimer, Hanau, modelled as a standing lady holding a cup over her head, the sides embossed with foliate scrolls and masks.

10in (25.5cm) high 12oz
£600-800   FRE

METALWARE

Judith Picks: George I teapot

Apple-shaped teapots are always rare, but to find one of such an early date (1721-22) is extremely unusual, and something to get excited about. An earlier example, also by Colin MacKenzie (1715-16), is recorded in the National Museum of Scotland collection. This teapot is one of the earliest Scottish teapots of any form available to collectors.

From extant examples, this form of teapot only seems to have lasted in Scotland for a short time –from c1714 to 1730 – before the more commonly seen spherical, bullet-shaped teapot became the standard.

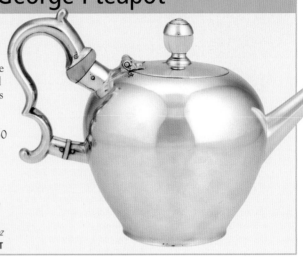

A rare George I Scottish silver apple-shaped teapot, Colin MacKenzie, Edinburgh, assay Master Edward Penman, with muscular handle with ivory insulators, with ivory bun finial on stepped mount and with silver cap.
1721/22   *6in (15cm) high 20.5oz*
£10,000-15,000   **L&T**

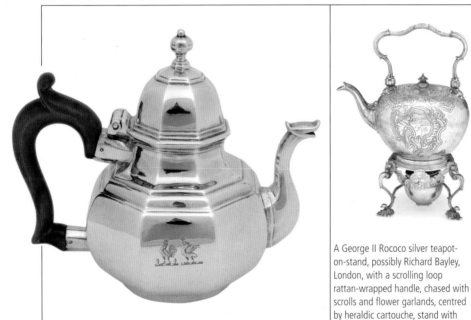

A George I silver octagonal teapot, Richard Green, London, with a faceted spout, engraved on one side with two crests.
1718   *6in (15cm) high 17.5oz*
£9,000-11,000   **LC**

A George II Rococo silver teapot-on-stand, possibly Richard Bayley, London, with a scrolling loop rattan-wrapped handle, chased with scrolls and flower garlands, centred by heraldic cartouche, stand with cast floral swags on scroll and shell cast feet.
1742   *13.25in (34cm) high, 62oz*
£1,500-2,500   **FRE**

A Scottish provincial silver inverted-pear shape teapot, James Glen, Glasgow, with scrolling foliate decoration mask detail to handle and bird's head for the spout, on circular stepped foot.
c1743   *24oz*
£2,500-3,500   **L&T**

An English silver ovoid teapot, William Shaw II & William Priest, London, on stepped circular base with wood handle and finial.
1756   *45in (12.5cm) high 11.9oz*
£500-700   **LHA**

An 18thC silver teapot, Richard Morton & Co, Sheffield.
c1773-4   *4.75in (12cm) high 11.5oz*
£2,000-3,000   **POOK**

A George III silver teapot, possibly John Swift, London, embossed with floral sprays and later eagle and motto crests, with eagle-head spout and eagle finial, on domed base.
1774
£600-800 WES

An Irish silver barrel-form teapot, Michael Homer, Dublin, with engraved decoration, ebonised finial and wood handle.
c1785 *4.5in (11.5cm) high 6.9oz*
£800-1,200 LHA

A rare George III silver oval-form teapot, Peter and Jonathan Bateman, London, with bright-cut decoration, scroll handle, flush hinged domed cover.
1790 *11in (28cm) long 12oz*
£2,000-3,000 WW

A George III silver teapot, Peter and Ann Bateman, London, the fluted ovoid body engraved with armorial crest surmounted by an eagle.
1797
£400-600 WES

A George III Irish silver teapot, probably James Stamp, Dublin, embossed with a band of Vitruvian scrolls beneath floral capped gadrooned border, on paw feet, crested.
1817 *6.25in (15.5cm) high 28oz*
£500-700 CAPE

A silver teapot, maker's mark "IW", London, with foliate decoration, with floral finial, the handle with ivory insulators.
1835 *10.25in (26cm) high 33.3oz*
£1,000-1,500 LHA

A Scottish Victorian silver teapot with burner, maker's mark "CR & S", Edinburgh, with moulded blossoms and rocailles, fixed bow handle with bone insulation.
1857-58 *13in (33.5cm) high 48oz*
£3,500-4,500 DOR

A George III silver two-handled tea urn, Robert Sharp, London, with part-fluted decoration, leaf-capped reeded loop handles, base with four bracket feet, with a later wooden tap, engraved with armorial and presentation inscription.
1792 *22in (56cm) high 117oz*
£3,000-4,000 WW

A George III tea urn, Thomas Ellerton & Richard Sibley I, London, the four lion's paw columns rising to a part-lobed body with presentation inscription and lion-mask handles, the domed cover with acorn finial, the waisted square base on four ball feet.
1803 *17.5in (44.5cm) high 125oz*
£3,500-4,500 TEN

A Queen Anne silver octagonal coffee pot, Thomas Folkingham, London, with moulded base, high domed cover and knop finial, the body later decorated with chased motifs and crested.
1711   *9.25in (23.5cm) high 30oz*
£4,000-6,000   **LC**

A George II silver coffee pot, by Edward Pocock, London, with scroll handle, faceted spout, domed hinged cover and bell-shaped finial, on a raised circular foot.
1733   *8in (20.5cm) high 20oz*
£2,000-3,000   **WW**

A George II silver pear-form coffee pot, Pezé Pilleau, London, embossed with flowers and C-scrolls, engraved with rampant lion crests, with floral bouquet finial, handle broken.
1757
£1,500-2,500   **WES**

A George III silver coffee pot, Whipham & Wright, London, the foliate chased baluster body with wood scroll handle, leaf-capped spout, with cast pine cone finial, later inscribed "RO to TBPF".
1763   *11in (28cm) high 31.9oz*
£700-1,000   **TEN**

An early George III Scottish silver coffee pot, Ebenezer Oliphant, Edinburgh, Assay Master Dougal Ged, with chased borders of flower heads, fruit and scroll decoration, with reeded foot, the S-scroll wooden handle with scroll capped terminals.

Ebenezer Oliphant was the maker of the travelling canteen given to Prince Charles Edward Stewart (Bonnie Prince Charlie), which is rightly considered one of the finest examples of mid-18thC Scottish silver. Many other contemporary silversmiths did not allow their political leanings to interfere with possible commissions, whereas Oliphant's list of patrons make it likely he was one of the few true Jacobite silversmiths.
1741/2   *11in (28cm) high 30oz*
£10,000-15,000   **L&T**

A George III silver baluster-form coffee pot, Charles Wright, London, with gadrooned foot, leaf-capped spout and wrythen acorn finial, engraved with an armorial and crested, with wood scroll handle.
1772   *11in (28cm) high 30.2oz*
£1,000-1,500   **TEN**

A Philadelphia silver coffee pot, Joseph and Nathaniel Richardson, with engraved monogram for Mordecai and Hannah Lewis, the reverse with 20thC monogram for their descendant, with foliate ornament on spout, the base with gadrooned band, with double scroll handle.
c1780   *12.5in (32cm) high, 34.2oz*
£10,000-15,000   **POOK**

A French Empire silver-gilt coffee pot, Jean Nicolas Boulanger, Paris, neck with palmette band, the spout in the form of an eagle's head.
1798-1809   *13in (33.5cm) high 40oz*
£4,000-6,000   **DOR**

A William IV four-piece silver tea and coffee set, Spooner, Clowes & Co, Birmingham, of lobed baluster form with cast foliate bracket feet, insulated leaf-capped scroll handles and domed covers with cast flower finials.

1837   *Coffee pot 9in (23cm) high 102oz*
£1,500-2,500   **TEN**

A Victorian four-piece silver tea and coffee service, John Samuel Hunt, London, each piece of compressed cushion form with vertical panels chased with trellis and formalised strapwork, crested.

1858   *Coffee pot 8in (20cm) high 69oz*
£1,000-1,500   **TEN**

A mid-19thC American silver tea and coffee service, Ball, Black & Co., decorated with Chinoiserie scenes, the coffee pot and teapot with ivory insulators.

                          Coffee pot 12in (30.5cm) high 99.6oz
£2,500-3,500   **LHA**

A silver "Francis I" tea and coffee service, Reed & Barton, including kettle-on-stand with burner, waste bowl and tray, each piece of baluster form, chased with fruit, flowers and foliage, with cornucopia around cartouches.

Pattern introduced 1906   *Kettle 14in (36cm) high 345oz*
£20,000-30,000   **FRE**

An Austrian six-part silver tea and coffee service, designed by Hans Bolek, made by Franz Schlesinger, Vienna, with fluted ivory handles and finials, the bulbous quatrefoil bodies decorated with beading.

c1910   *Teapot 7.25in (18.5cm) high 168oz*
£10,000-15,000   **DOR**

A silver tea and coffee set, EBS Ltd., London, retailed by Gebrüder Friedländer, including hot water pot with burner and tray, with some gadrooned decoration, the handle with bone insulation.

1913   *Hot water pot 12in (30.5cm) high 237oz*
£5,000-7,000   **DOR**

A French Régence-style silver tea and coffee service, Henri Lapparra, Paris, all pyriform with engraved and chased decoration and surmounted by bud finials, with carved ivory scroll handles.

c1925   *Coffeepot 9.5in (24cm) high 154oz*
£4,000-6,000   **FRE**

METALWARE

A George I Irish silver baluster covered jug, Thomas Bolton, Dublin, engraved with an armorial and "The Gift of Mrs Susanna Hall to Mrs Eleonor Stannard 1752" within a Baroque cartouche, handle replaced.

1719   *39.25oz*

£20,000-30,000   **DN**

A George I silver beer jug, William Spackman, London, with large scroll handle, domed circular foot and engraved coat of arms.

1725   *7.75in (19.5cm) high 27.25oz*

£8,000-12,000   **LC**

A late 18thC Philadelphia silver creamer, bearing the touch of Richard Humphreys.

5.5in (14cm) high 3.6oz

£1,500-2,500   **POOK**

Judith Picks

William Henry Wills and Charles Dickens began their long association in 1846, when Wills became sub-editor to Dickens on the "Daily News". Wills went on to become one of Dickens's closest friends in later life.

This jug is the subject of a letter from Dickens to Wills, dated 5th April 1862: "My Dear Wills: A little packet will come to you to-day from Hunt and Roskell's: almost at the same time, I think, as this note. The packet will contain a Claret Jug. I hope it is a pretty thing in itself for your table, and I know that you and Mrs. Wills will like it none the worse because it comes from me. It is not made of perishable material, and is so far expressive of our friendship. I have had your name and mine set upon it, in token of our many years of mutual reliance and trustfulness. It will never be so full of wine, as it is to-day of affectionate regard. Ever faithfully yours, Charles Dickens.".

Again provenance is everything! Dickens's close friendship with Henry Wills and its mention in this charming letter adds a great deal of value to the piece.

A Victorian silver claret jug, in the form of a Greek askos, John Samuel Hunt, Hunt & Roskell, London, the rim applied with two goats flanking a leaf-capped scroll handle above an applied cherub, handle inscribed "William Henry Wills from Charles Dickens".

1859   *8in (20cm) high*

£10,000-15,000   **TOV**

A William IV Rococo Revival silver cream jug, Joseph Angell Snr and Joseph Angell Jr, with foliate decoration, with wavy edge scroll border, the handle with a mask terminal, spout with mermaid mask, on three dolphin feet.

5in (12.5cm) high 8oz

£800-1,200   **WW**

A large Victorian silver wine jug, Hunt & Roskell, London, with moulded grape leaf and grape decoration, with a chariot and mythological figures, the handle with a grotesque, with gilt interior, the socket lid with cork.

1844-45   *15in (38cm) high 60oz*

£4,000-6,000   **DOR**

A Victorian silver claret jug, Turner Simpson, London, with leaf-capped bifurcated scroll handle and recessed flush-fitting cover, chased throughout with foliate rinceaux on a matted ground, the neck with oval cartouche.

1866   *14in (36cm) high 32.3oz*

£1,500-2,500   **TEN**

An American silver wine jug, Gorham Mfg. Co., Providence, Rhode Island, with a cast leaf lyre-form handle, decorated with repoussé Bacchanalian motifs, the underside of the body and top of the foot with acanthus leaves, lozenge border.

c1875   *14.25in (36.5cm) high 80oz*

£10,000-15,000   **FRE**

A pair of George II silver sauce boats, William Peaston, London, with gadrooned rims and acanthus-cast scroll handles, with later engraved heraldic shields, on shell-cast scrolling feet.
1746   *8.25in (21cm) long 19oz*
£1,200-1,800   **FRE**

A late George II silver sauce boat, David Mowden, London, with a shaped rim, a flying scroll handle, pad feet and later embossed with flowers and scrolls.
1755   *5.25in (13.5cm) high*
£100-150   **DN**

A George II silver oval sauce boat, Fuller White, London, with a leaf-lapped flying-scroll handle, an everted shaped rim, on three stepped pad feet.
1751   *6in (15cm) long 5.5oz*
£250-350   **DN**

A pair of George II silver sauce boats, possibly William Grundy, London, with gadroon borders and leaf-capped scroll handles, on shell and scroll feet, monogrammed.
1757   *8in (20cm) long 29oz*
£2,000-3,000   **SWO**

A George II Scottish silver sauce boat, maker's mark "W.S", Edinburgh, assay master Hugh Gordon, with everted scalloped rim, wide spout and engraved crest, on shell terminal scroll and hoof feet, with S-scroll handle and acanthus cap.
1757-58   *8in (20cm) wide 9oz*
£800-1,200   **L&T**

A pair of silver sauce boats, possibly by Dorothy Mills, London, with fluted sides and gadrooned borders, decorated with scrolls and shells, the marks rubbed, alterations.
1765
£1,500-2,500   **BELL**

A pair of George III tripod helmet silver sauce boats, maker's mark "WC", London, with acanthus-sheathed flying C-scroll handle, the legs with shells at the knees and pad feet.
1775   *7in (18cm) long 19.5oz*
£1,500-2,500   **TEN**

A pair of Philadelphia silver sauce boats, Thomas Fletcher.
c1820   *7.75in (19.5cm) high 49.1oz*
£10,000-15,000   **POOK**

A pair of Edwardian silver sauce boats, Carrington & Co, London, with gadroon borders, on shell-capped hoof feet with leaf-capped scroll handles.
1909   *6.5in (16cm) long 15oz*
£300-400   **SWO**

A pair of George II silver ogee-form tea caddies, possibly Samuel Taylor, London, chased and engraved with flowers and foliage, the crest with three rose motifs impaling two birds over a third bird, other crest with a Turkish figure and motto.

1747   *6in (15cm) high, 10oz*

£1,500-2,500   **L&T**

A George II silver tea caddy, Augustine Courtauld, London, with moulded borders, decorated with asymmetrical reserves of flat-chased husks, scrollwork and matting.

1741 3.5in (9cm) high 12.5oz

£1,200-1,800   **LC**

A late 18thC German silver oval bombe-form tea caddy, maker's mark "WGH", with a swing finial, the base initialled "C.C.P.L.".

5.5in (14cm) wide 10oz

£1,000-1,500   **LC**

A George III silver tea caddy, maker's mark overstruck, "T", London, engraved with floral swags and wrigglework borders, with leaf and bud finial.

1779   *4in (10cm) high 13oz*

£2,000-3,000   **SWO**

A George III silver tea caddy, maker's mark "IL", London, with armorial engraving.

1783-84   *5in (12.5cm) high 19oz*

£1,800-2,200   **DOR**

CLOSER LOOK - GEORGE III SILVER TEA CADDY

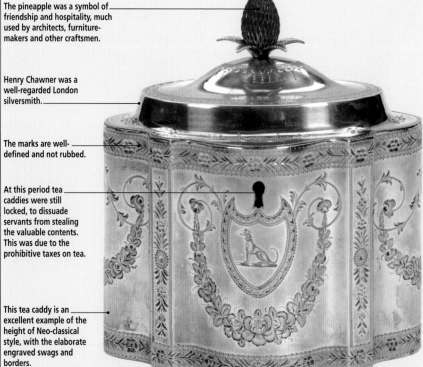

The pineapple was a symbol of friendship and hospitality, much used by architects, furniture-makers and other craftsmen.

Henry Chawner was a well-regarded London silversmith.

The marks are well-defined and not rubbed.

At this period tea caddies were still locked, to dissuade servants from stealing the valuable contents. This was due to the prohibitive taxes on tea.

This tea caddy is an excellent example of the height of Neo-classical style, with the elaborate engraved swags and borders.

A George III silver tea caddy, Henry Chawner, London, with domed cover and green-stained ivory pineapple finial, engraved with classical swags and borders, crested.

1786   *6in (15cm) high 11.25oz*

£2,000-3,000   **TEN**

A Saxony silver caddy, maker's mark Gaw(?), Halle a. Saale, assayer "Tremolierstich".
c1820   *5in (12.5cm) wide 21oz*
£1,500-2,500   **DOR**

A 19thC Ottoman silver tea caddy, assayer's mark "Tremolierstich".
5.5in (14cm) high 16oz
£1,500-2,500   **DOR**

A late Empire Bavarian (now Czech Republic) silver caddy, maker's mark "FK", Brno, with gilt interior.
1820   *5in (12.5cm) wide 15oz*
£1,800-2,200   **DOR**

A George III silver filigree caddy spoon, with a scalloped bowl and graduated roundels up the stem, oval cartouche, initialled, unmarked.
c1800   *3.5in (9cm) long*
£70-100   **WW**

A George III silver caddy spoon, Josiah Snatt, London, with a fluted bowl.
1806
£50-70   **WW**

A George III silver caddy spoon, John Lawrence, Birmingham, with a bifurcated stem and a raised scroll motif in the bowl.
1809
£300-400   **WW**

A George III silver caddy spoon, Joseph Taylor, Birmingham, with a filigree shell-shaped bowl, and bifurcated handle.
1809   *3in (7.5cm) long*
£1,000-1,500   **WW**

A George III silver caddy spoon, Samuel Pemberton, Birmingham, with repeating border of engraved stylised leaves.
1810
£200-300   **WW**

A George III caddy spoon, Timothy Renou, London, with a part-fluted acorn bowl, and a "Fiddle" pattern stem with a pointed top section.
1812
£300-400   **WW**

An early 19thC Scottish provincial silver "Fiddle" pattern caddy spoon, maker's mark "I&GH", Paisley, the terminal with script initials.
c1820   *3.25in (8.5cm) long 0.3oz*
£700-900   **WW**

A George IV silver "Fiddle" pattern caddy spoon, George Burrows, London, with a shovel bowl, engraved foliate decoration.
1823   *4in (10cm) long*
£200-300   **WW**

An early 19thC Scottish provincial silver caddy spoon, John Macrae, Inverness, with fluted shell bowl, the terminal with script initials.
c1830   *3.5in (9cm) long 0.3oz*
£1,000-1,500   **WW**

An early 19thC Scottish provincial silver caddy spoon, George Sanster, Aberdeen, the shaped handle engraved with a crest.
c1840   *4in (10cm) long 0.6oz*
£500-700   **WW**

A Victorian silver floral caddy spoon, Hilliard & Thomason, Birmingham, the tendril stem with an applied leaf and two small florets, petalled bowl.
c1850
£100-150   **WW**

A Scottish provincial silver caddy spoon, William Robb, Edinburgh, the heart-shaped bowl with embossed view of Balmoral castle, the thistle handle with lion rampant within crowned shield as finial.
1918   *3.25in (8.5cm) long 0.6oz*
£250-350   **L&T**

A James I silver St. Peter apostle spoon, John Quick, Barnstaple, the gilt figure with a spoked nimbus and large key emblem, the back of the bowl pricked "IB" over "TM" over "1666".

c1620   *7.5in (19cm) long 1.5oz*
£3,500-4,500   **LC**

A rare Commonwealth/Charles II silver seal-top spoon, probably Norwich, with double-baluster gilt terminal, the top pricked "IE" over "1650" over "IE", struck with the marks "ST" or "TS" (monogram) and a fleur de lys on the back of the stam, and feline mask in bowl.

1655-1665   *6.5in (16cm) long 1.5oz*
£3,500-4,500   **LC**

A Charles II provincial silver trefid spoon, John Peard I, Barnstaple, the front of the stem with an engraved line to each side, later pricked "1699" over "T*D" over "M&C".

c1600-80   *7.75in (19.5cm) long 2oz*
£1,200-1,800   **DN**

A rare Charles II Scottish silver trefid spoon, Alexander Reid, Edinburgh, assay master John Borthwick, engraved on the back of stem "AH" over "ES", traces of gilding.

1681   *8in (20cm) long 1.5oz*
£8,000-10,000   **DN**

A rare James II provincial silver lace-back trefid spoon and matched three-prong fork, Fordington/Crewkerne, both struck with barbed roses, and decorated with pineapples, the spoon back pricked "G.V." over "S.G." over "1687".

1687   Spoon 7.5in (19cm) long 2.35oz
£5,000-7,000   **DN**

A William and Mary silver trefid spoon, Lawrence Coles, London, with engraved foliage, the back with a vacant oval cartouche, in a contemporary black shagreen case, silver dot piqued with a cypher "RA" and "1690".

1689   *7.75in (19.5cm) long 1.95oz*
£8,000-12,000   **DN**

A rare Queen Anne English provincial silver trefid spoon, Eli Bilton I, Newcastle, with beaded rat-tail, the top of the back of the stem engraved "H" over "TE".

1703   *8.5in (21.5cm) long 1.95oz*
£2,500-3,500   **DN**

A William and Mary silver-gilt trefid spoon, Thomas Issod, London, with formal foliate engraving to each side, the border engraved with formal acanthus leaf work.

1689   *9in (23cm) long, 2.4oz*
£10,000-12,000   **DN**

A George II silver "Hanoverian" pattern serving ladle, Samuel Hitchcock, London, with plain rat-tail, the reverse of the terminal engraved with a crest.

1720   *14in (36cm) long 8oz*
£1,500-2,500   **WW**

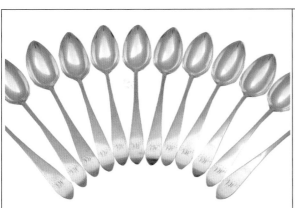

A set of twelve silver "Old English Point" pattern tablespoons, Thomas Davie, Greenock, the terminal script engraved "MA".

c1805 — 9in (23cm) long 26oz
£2,500-3,500 — WW

A rare "Fiddle" pattern teaspoon, Alexander Glenny, initials "WSD".

Alexander Glenny's work is among the rarest of all 19thC provincial silversmiths.

c1840
£5,000-7,000 — WW

A rare silver "Old English" pattern dessert spoon, John and Patrick Riach, script initial "L".

c1840 — 0.9oz
£4,000-6,000 — WW

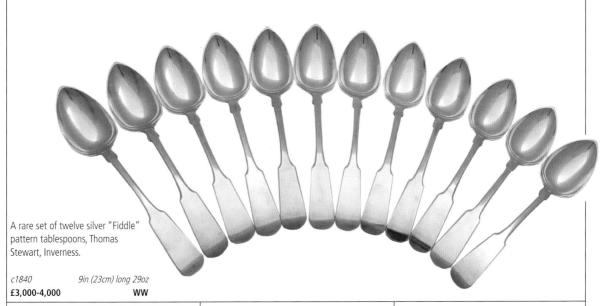

A rare set of twelve silver "Fiddle" pattern tablespoons, Thomas Stewart, Inverness.

c1840 — 9in (23cm) long 29oz
£3,000-4,000 — WW

A pair of George III "sprung" serving tongs, Messrs. Eley, Fearn & Chawner, London, with corrugated grips.

1813 — 5.5oz
£200-300 — LC

A pair of Victorian silver "Fiddle, Thread and Shell" pattern asparagus tongs, The Lias Brothers, London, the blades with pierced scroll decoration.

1842 — 10in (25.5cm) long
£250-350 — WW

A pair of Victorian cast-silver macabre sugar tongs, the sprung pivot in the form of a skull, with red and green eyes, the arms and grips inset-formed as bones.

3in (7.5cm) long 1.1oz
£400-600 — WW

METALWARE

CLOSER LOOK - GEORGE II SILVER OVAL TUREEN

The arms are those of Henry Fane of Wormsley, Watlington, Oxfordshire, MP for Lyme Regis (1757-1777) and his first wife Charlotte, daughter of Nicholas Rowe, the celebrated poet and dramatist.

The Garrard ledgers, held at the Victoria & Albert Museum in London show the following entry in George Wickes's accounts, "Henry Fane August 4th 1737 'Turreen & cover' (sic) 131ozs . 10; cost £55.0s.0d.".

The castings of the handles on this tureen had been used by Wickes on a tureen for Lord North in 1735.

Another tureen, made for Frederick, Prince of Wales in 1743, employed the same cast handles and lion masks and paw feet.

Similar handle and feet castings were later used by Paul de Lamerie on a tureen of 1751.

A George II silver oval tureen and cover, George Wickes, London, applied with cast armorials of Fane and Rowe within cartouches, the cast scroll handle with stylised lion-mask, paw and leaf decoration, the handles cast as bull's heads, on lion-mask and claw-and-ball capped feet.

1737   *16.5in (42cm) long 129.7oz*

£25,000-35,000   **DN**

A pair of George III silver vegetable dishes and covers, William Laver, London, with reeded rims and twin loop handles, crested.

1789   *15in (38cm) long 61.8oz*

£2,000-3,000   **TEN**

An early 19thC silver tureen, Robert Hennell, with engraved crest inscribed "Prudenter Qui Sedulo", on gadrooned border and animal paw feet.

c1815   *8.5in (21.5cm) high 87.8oz*

£3,000-4,000   **POOK**

A set of four George IV silver entrée dishes and covers, Philip Rundell, London, with shell and foliate-scroll borders, and lion rampant handles, engraved with a coat of arms and the presentation inscription, losses.

1822   *12.25in (31cm) long 350oz*

£50,000-70,000   **WW**

A German silver ornamental tureen, Gebrüder Gerike, Berlin, assayer's mark "Tremolierstich", with two sculpted St Mark's lion supports, gadrooned rim, lion finial and mythical beast handles, gilt interior.

c1830   *17in (43cm) high 234oz*

£18,000-22,000   **DOR**

One of a pair of very rare sterling silver entrée dishes, John S. Hunt for Hunt & Roskell, London, with lids and Sheffield plate warming bases.

This represents the marriage of an heraldic heiress. Note the two crests, one for Amherst and the other for Pitt on the reverse side, and also on the chafing dish.

1845-46   *15in (38cm) wide 158oz*

£10,000-15,000 pair   **DS**

A silver serving tureen, Moore for Tiffany & Co., the curved handles ending in bifurcate scrolls and flat leaves, the cover with tooled ovolo band, body with geometric and beaded rims, monogrammed.

1854-70   *12.25in (31cm) high 72oz*

£4,000-6,000   **SK**

A silver stag-head soup tureen, retailed by Shreve, Stanwood & Co., Boston, with beaded accenting, leaftip and beaded rims, with cast stag-head handles, engraved "EAF", the ring-form handle topped by a hops finial centred by stag's head, on trumpet foot.

1860-69   *18.5in (47cm) wide 85oz*

£7,000-10,000   SK

A Victorian silver two-handled soup tureen and cover, James Garrard, London, with beaded borders and scroll handles, domed pull-off cover, with a liner, on leaf-capped four scroll feet, with presentation inscription.

1886   *15in (38cm) long 110oz*

£3,000-4,000   WW

A late 19thC French silver tureen and underplate, "A.AUCOC, Paris", with cast foliate decoration and foliate handles, with blossom finial.

16.75in (42.5cm) long 124oz

£2,000-3,000   FRE

ESSENTIAL REFERENCE - PAUL STORR

Paul Storr was England's most celebrated 19thC silversmith, though his talents lay in brilliantly realising the designs of others, rather than purely as a designer.
- He was apprenticed to the Swedish-born Neo-classical master, Andrew Fogelberg in Soho, London.
- He entered his first mark while in a brief partnership with William Frisbee 1792-1796.
- By 1807, styled as Storr and Co. he produced a substantial number of pieces for the Royal Goldsmiths, Rundell, Bridge & Rundell. In 1811 he formed a sub-partnership with them. He made many pieces of elaborate silverware for the company in the Neo-classical and Rococo styles, for a variety of noble patrons, including the Prince Regent.

- Storr left Rundell, Bridge & Rundell in 1819, having used his time with them to make alliances with some of the most eminent sculptors and artist-craftsmen of the period (including John Flaxman).
- In 1822 he went into partnership with John Mortimer, who had retail premises in New Bond Street. He recruited various talented craftsmen who had previously worked for Rundell, as well as his nephew, John Hunt, as a chaser.
- Storr retired in 1838, but the firm continued under the name Mortimer and Hunt, becoming Hunt & Roskell from 1842.

A set of four George III silver sauce tureens and covers, Paul Storr, London, applied with trailing oak leaves and acorns, the handles modelled as branches, with lion rampant finials, on acanthus leaf shell-scroll bracket feet, engraved with two armorials, with silver liners, numbered 5, 6,7 and 8.

1816   *10.25in (26cm) long 256oz*

£100,000-150,000   WW

METALWARE

A large Augsburg silver-gilt salver, Erhard Warnberger, assayer's mark "Tremolierstich", with a chased ruin in a landscape and three figures, the rim with embossed Baroque fruit and birds.

A large salver of excellent workmanship by the renowned Augsburg master Erhard I. Warnberger.

1680   *26in (66cm) wide 37oz*
£50,000-70,000   **DOR**

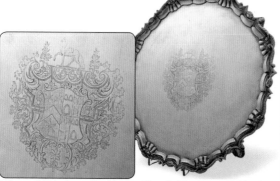

A George II Irish silver salver, Matthew West, Dublin, the moulded border with masks, shells and scroll motifs, the centre engraved with an armorial, on four heavy scroll-and-pad feet.
1736   *15.5in (39cm) diam 72oz*
£5,000-7,000   **WW**

A George III silver armorial tray, Ebenezer Coker, London, with beaded rim, the border chased with Rococo scrolls, flowers and shells, around (later engraved) armorial, on four claw-and-ball feet.
1767   *119oz*
£2,500-3,500   **TEN**

A George II silver footed salver, Chas. Hatfield, London, with armorial engraving.
1730-31   *15in (38cm) long 64oz*
£2,500-3,500   **DOR**

A George III silver circular table salver, Parker & Wakelin, London, the edge with alternating gadroon and shell-and-leaf scroll, with Rococo-engraved band incorporating scenes of the elements, with a central engraved armorial, on cast open-work scroll feet.
1760   *27.5in (70cm) diam 240.45oz*
£25,000-35,000   **DN**

A George III silver-gilt salver, James Scott, Dublin, applied with a pierced die-stamped trailing vine border, the centre engraved with an armorial, on three satyr-mask feet.
1808   *11in (28cm) diam 30oz*
£8,000-12,000   **WW**

A George III silver circular salver, John Scofield, London, with beaded border, on tripod feet moulded with anthemion, engraved with a crest.
1780   7in (18cm) wide 10.15oz
£400-500   DN

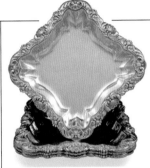

A set of four George IV silver serving dishes, Philip Rundell, London with shell and foliate-scroll border, engraved "A.D. 1821, Presented to Henry Russell Esq. Late Resident at the Court of Hyderabad by the British Officers serving with the Berar Division of the Nizams Army in token of their respect regard and Esteem".
1822   10in (25.5cm) wide 130oz
£10,000-15,000   WW

An early 19thC American silver footed tray, Taylor & Hinsdale, New York , with a central cartouche, inscribed "M. Willett", the border engraved.

This plate was purchased with the money granted to Col. Marinus Willett by Congress for his Revolutionary services. He quickly gained fame as a Sons of Liberty member when he seized arms from the British as they attempted to flee New York City. Later he helped defend Peekskill and Fort Stanwix and was one of the founding members of the Society of the Cincinnati.
20.25in (51.5cm) wide 85.5oz
£3,500-4,500   POOK

An early Victorian silver salver, Robert Hennell II, London, the cast border with C-scrolls, flowers and foliage on an engraved diaper ground, on three acanthus and rocaille panel feet, engraving erased verso.
1837   18.5in (47.5cm) wide 93.75oz
£1,500-2,500   DN

A Victorian silver circular salver, Daniel & Charles Houle, London, engraved with a band of leaves and shells, the raised border with a cartouche, quatrefoil and scroll rim, on four cast cartouche feet.
1850   16.5in (42cm) diam 67.25oz
£1,000-1,500   DN

A Victorian three-part silver plateau, Robert Garrard London, with rounded end pieces flanking rectangular centre section, each section with central rounded horizontal band with overlapping leaftip flanked by pierced quatrefoil scalloped upper rim, and lower rim with partially reeded openwork flutes and stylised husk flowers, the end sections with a single toupee foot accented with leaftips and topped by a patera boss, the centre section and the centre edge of one end section with four further legs with patera bosses, the silver and mirror mounted on mahogany, edge of centre section stamped "R.S. Garrard Panton St London".
1871   69in (175cm) long
£15,000-20,000   SK

A large American sterling silver fish serving tray, Ball, Black & Co., with a cast rim of foliage, two scroll handles to the sides cast with fish.
c1860   31.5in (80cm) wide 79oz
£3,000-4,000   FRE

A late Victorian large silver circular salver, by William Gibson & John Langman, London, with a Chippendale border, centrally engraved with the crest of Fane, on six cast scroll feet.

The crest is the generic arms of the head of the Fane family.
1897   26in (66cm) diam 202.35oz
£4,500-5,000   DN

An Edwardian sterling silver gallery tray, Henry Atkin, Sheffield, of oval form with a shaped pierced gallery and open hand-holds around a foliate-engraved surface centred by a monogram, on ball feet.
1903   25in (63.5cm) wide 112oz
£2,500-3,500   FRE

A George II silver basket, Francis Crimp, London, of pinched lozenge form with a rope-twist rim and swing handle above vertical wire-work sides, monogrammed.

1759　　*12in (30.5cm) long 27oz*
£4,000-6,000　　　　**FRE**

A George III silver cake basket, Edward Aldridge, London, the basket with wrythen panels pierced with alternating patterns beneath a cast foliate gadrooned openwork rim, with openwork trellis-pattern swing handle with gadrooned borders.

1767　　*15in (38cm) long 31.5oz*
£1,000-1,500　　　　**TEN**

A Pennsylvania silver cake basket, Harvey Lewis, Philadelphia, with pierced shell and "wing" swing handle with owner's initials "MSR", chased with rosettes, shells and leaves, on machined foot.

c1815　　*10.25in (26cm) diam 33oz*
£25,000-35,000　　　　**FRE**

A George III silver basket, probably Kirkby for Waterhouse & Co, Sheffield, the foliate-chased bowl with everted reeded acanthus cast foliate rim, with acanthus-capped swing handle, engraved with armorial, on collet gadrooned foot.

1818　　*13in (33.5cm) long 40oz*
£600-800　　　　**TEN**

A George IV Irish silver swing-handled basket, William Nowlan, Dublin, with embossed foliate scroll and bird decoration on matted background, the pierced foliate scroll swing handle with caryatid supports, on raised shaped foot.

1828　　*13in (33.5cm) diam 48oz*
£1,800-2,200　　　　**WW**

An Edwardian silver basket, Charles Stuart Harris, London, with pierced decoration and embossed with rosettes and swags, beaded border, on four shell feet.

1902　　*14in (36cm) long 50oz*
£2,500-3,500　　　　**WW**

An Edwardian silver-gilt sugar basket, John Henry Rawlings, London, the pierced body with swag and bow decoration and floral detailed swing handle, red glass liner, with matched silver-gilt sifter spoon.

1909
£400-600　　　　**FLD**

A William III Britannia silver Monteith, John Leach, London, with eight scroll panels, the gadrooned wavy rim with applied cherub masks, lion mask and drop handles, on a spreading foot.

1700   *12in (30.5cm) diam 61oz*

£15,000-25,000   **L&T**

A George I silver sugar bowl and cover, John Gibbons, London.

1724   *4.5in (11.5cm) diam 6.6oz*

£2,500-3,500   **POOK**

Judith Picks

Paul de Lamerie is THE name in silver-making, due to his flair for design, but also – like Paul Storr after him – his ability as a businessman. De Lamerie sold much of his incredible silver from his own workshop and also used the best retailers.

Most pieces by this great maker fetch high prices, but these strawberry dishes are even more desirable due to their use of Britannia silver – an alloy of silver that contains significantly more silver than sterling silver. It was introduced in 1697 as a result of the Great Recoinage of 1696, which attempted to make silver coins less valuable than silver items of the same weight. It failed, and sterling was reintroduced in 1720. As a result, Britannia pieces are comparatively rare, as well as being made of more precious metal than sterling ones.

The arms in the centre of the dishes are Vane impaling Fitzroy, for Henry Vane (c1705-1758) eldest son of Gilbert, 2nd Baron Barnard whom he succeeded in 1753. Walpole wrote of him "Whenever he was drunk he told all he knew, and when he was sober, more than he knew" (George II, vol.i, p.117).

An 18thC Channel Islands silver twin-handled christening bowl, maker's mark "GS", Jersey, with twin scroll handles engraved "A*D*S*C".

c1730-79   *5in (12.5cm) wide 2.5oz*

£2,500-3,500   **DN**

A pair of George II Britannia silver strawberry dishes, Paul de Lamerie, London, with pie-crust edge and ribbed panels engraved alternately with foliate strapwork and diaper, one engraved with crest, the centres engraved with coats of arms.

9.75in (25cm) diam 30oz

£30,000-40,000   **SOTH**

A silver punch bowl, Dominick & Haff, retailed by Frank Herschede, with foliate-and-scroll cast rim, decorated with a band of blossoms centred by cartouches, with a silver plated ladle.

1900   *11.5in (29cm) diam 52oz*

£1,000-1,500   **FRE**

A George III silver cruet frame, W. Burwash & R. Sibley, London, with eight cut-glass bottles with silver mounts.

1808-09   *9in (23cm) high 40oz*
£3,000-4,000   **DOR**

A Regency silver cruet stand, William Southey, London, with eight bottles, the stem with lion's head and leaf-cast loop handle, the tray with out-scrolled foliate handles and a gadrooned rim with shells, on paw feet.

1812   *14.5in (37cm) long 52oz*
£5,000-7,000   **FRE**

A pair of Victorian silver and parcel-gilt cruet frames, in the form of a sculpted fruit vendor and flower vendor, R. & S. Garrard, London.

1870-71   *6.75in (17cm) high 35oz*
£5,000-7,000   **DOR**

A set of four George III silver salt cellars, Paul Storr, London, applied with oak leaves and acorns, the handles as branches, on acanthus leaf shell-scroll bracket feet, with gilded interiors, engraved with crests, numbered 5, 6,7, and 8.

1816   *5.5in (14cm) wide 44oz*
£15,000-25,000   **WW**

A pair of New Orleans coin silver salts, marked "A. Rasch N. Orleans", with frosted glass liners.

c1830   *4in (10cm) wide 7.7oz*
£3,500-4,500 pair   **POOK**

A French silver cruet frame, maker's mark "LR", Paris, with replaced colourless glass bottles with stoppers, with monogram.

1819-1838   *12in (230.5cm) high 24oz*
£1,500-2,500   **DOR**

A William & Mary lighthouse-form caster, maker's mark a mallet device, London, with gadrooned foot and cover and original inner sleeve, engraved with later armorial.

1690   *7in (18cm) high 11.8oz*
£1,200-1,800   **TEN**

A set of three early George II silver casters, Thomas Cooke II & Richard Gurney, London, with bell finials, scroll-and-trellis pierced cover panels, central girdles and on moulded bases, engraved with a crest.

1729   *Tallest 7in (18cm) high 17.25oz*
£2,500-3,500   **DN**

A pair of late 18thC Dutch silver sugar casters, maker's mark "I*S", Amsterdam marks, with applied cut-card and cast figures above and below, centre with coat of arms, vacant cartouches and lion supporters, the covers with three pierced panels.

10in (25.5cm) high 17oz each
£1,000-1,500   **L&T**

A Victorian silver novelty cockerell pepper pot, Walter Thornhill, London.

1883   *4.5in (11.5cm) long 4.5oz*

£800-900   **WW**

An Edwardian silver wren pepper pot, William Hornby, London, with pull-off cover.

1906   *1.5in (4cm) high*

£200-300   **WW**

A novelty silver dog pepper pot, maker's mark worn, London modelled as a standing Samoyed dog, pull-off pierced head.

1909   *4in (10cm) long 6oz*

£800-1,000   **WW**

A pair of silver owl pepperettes, Atkins Bros, Sheffield, set with green glass eyes.

1913   *2.25in (5.5cm) high 3.6oz*

£600-700   **DN**

A novelty silver dog pepper pot, Sebastian Garrard, London, modelled as a seated mastif, pull-off pierced cover.

1922   *2.5in (5.5cm) high 3.5oz*

£1,200-1,400   **WW**

A late 19thC Continental novelty silver elephant pepperette, import marks for Edinburgh.

1931   *2.75in (7cm) high*

£600-700   **L&T**

A pair of Continental novelty silver figural pepperettes, modelled as man and woman, 800 standard.

11oz

£300-400   **GORL**

A pair of Edwardian duck-shaped silver salts, maker's mark "C & N", Birmingham, with inlaid glass eyes and ruby glass liners, in fitted case.

1905   *3.75in (9.5cm) long*

£400-600   **CAPE**

A Victorian novelty pepperette modelled as a standing frog, James Barclay Hennell, London.

1881   *4.5in (11.5cm) high 6oz*

£4,000-5,000   **TEN**

METALWARE

ESSENTIAL REFERENCE - RUNDELL, BRIDGE & RUNDELL

Philip Rundell (1743-1827) arrived in London in c1768 and began working as a shopman to silversmiths Theed and Picket. In 1772 he acquired sole ownership of the business.

- In 1788 he took John Bridge into partnership. The firm was initially styled Rundell & Bridge, becoming known as Rundell, Bridge and Rundell after Philip's nephew Edmund was made a partner in 1805.
- In 1797 Rundell & Bridge was appointed Goldsmith and Jeweller to King George III and the Royal Family.
- By 1806 it employed 1,000 people. The firm gave many important commissions to independent silversmiths, such as Paul Storr and Benjamin Smith.
- William Theed joined the partnership in 1808 (staying until his death in 1817), and Storr in 1811 (withdrawing in 1819).
- The firm specialised in large presentation plate, which was popular during the last years of the Napoleonic wars.
- Rundell's work, particularly during the Regency period, is characterised by outstanding craftsmanship and design.
- The firm closed in 1842, and many moulds were sold.

One of a pair of George III silver wine coolers, liners and rims, Digby Scott and Benjamin Smith for Rundell, Bridge & Rundell, London, with scrolling grape vines and masks above engraved coats of arms, handles terminating in masks.
1806
12.25in (31.5cm) high 220oz
£50,000-70,000 pair   SOTH

A George II silver escutcheon wine label, Sandilands Drinkwater, London, with a chased vine border, incised "PORT", with maker's mark and lion passant only.
c1740
£400-500   WW

A George III silver wine label, Hester Bateman, London, with a feather edge and a oval cartouche surmount, crested incised "MADEIRA", with maker's mark and lion passant only.
1780
£300-400   WW

A silver "BRANDY" label, William Jamieson, Aberdeen, with canted corners, reeded borders.
c1830   *1.75in (4.5cm) long 0.3oz*
£250-350   WW

A Victorian canted silver wine label, W.R. Sobey, London, incised and filled "MARSALA".
1869
£80-100   WW

A rare George III silver "EAU D'OR" wine label, by Joseph Willmore, Birmingham, decorated with putti, grapevine and a Bacchus mask.
1814   *2.25in (5.5cm) long*
£450-550   WW

One of a pair of George III silver wine coasters, Robert Hennell, with beaded rims, pierced with fluted and scroll-work bands, urn roundels and crested cartouche, turned wood bases.
4.75in (12cm) diam
£500-600 pair   AH

A pair of George III Neo-classical silver wine bottle coasters, maker's mark "TH", London, with leaftip cast narrow flange, the friezes with repoussé figurative panels depicting Cupid and maidens, with turned satinwood inset bases.
1805   *6in (15cm) diam*
£1,500-2,500 pair   TEN

A William IV silver wine coaster, Barber, Cattles and North York, with a turned wooden base and a gadrooned border.

The date letter is partially worn.

c1831   *6.25in (15.5cm) diam*
£250-350   WW

A pair of early-Victorian Irish silver wine coasters, James Moore, Dublin, embossed with figures, windmills, animals, and buildings amongst trees, the wooden bases set with central silver button, crested.
1843   *6in (15cm) diam*
£5,000-7,000   WW

An Austrian Biedermeier silver figure of a cat, maker's mark "Schiffer", Vienna, head as the hinged lid, with colourless glass liner, weighted.

Franz Schiffer was a renowned Viennese silversmith.

1856   *4.75in (12cm) high*
£4,000-5,000   DOR

CLOSER LOOK - GEORGE IV VASE

This is a silver-gilt presentation vase of exceptional quality and made by one of the best firms of silversmiths in the country.

It was presented to Sir Henry Russell, (1783-1852) who, while staying in India, organised what was called the "Russell Brigade", a brigade of 4,000 of the Nizam's irregular cavalry under British Officers.

The unusual decoration on either side of the vase tells the story of the British cavalry officers and Indian soldiers.

The designs were produced by Thomas Stothard following consultation with the sculptor, Sir Henry Chantrey. He based the shape on a plate from Piranesi with an additional tiger on the lid (now missing), and elephant's heads on the pedestals. He also insisted that the serpent handles should be modelled from life, rather than the using the imaginary serpents shown in Piranesi.

Giovanni Battista Piranesi was an Italian artist who produced books of etchings featuring sites in Rome.

The vase and stand are extremely heavy at 546oz.

A George IV silver-gilt presentation vase and stand, Philip Rundell for Rundell, Bridge and Rundell, London.

1823   *28.25in (71.5cm) high 546oz*
£120,000-180,000   WW

A 19thC Spanish Colonial silver sheep censer, with movable bow handle, socket lids.

11in (28cm) long 95oz
£2,500-3,500   DOR

A 19thC silver and parcel gilt figure of a leaping stag, with detachable head, the weighted base plate decorated with a moulded hunting scene.

9in (23cm) high
£18,000-22,000   DOR

A George III and later silver épergne, base and top, by Thomas Pitts, with central William IV additions by Joseph Craddock, London, with four cast candle branches, and four lower branches supporting (missing) glass dishes.

1761 and 1830   *18.5in (47cm) high 193.85oz*
£12,000-18,000   DN

A Victorian épergne and stand, Stephen Smith, London, four-bowl stand modelled as an oak tree with boy on horseback and cow beneath, with presentation inscription to Hugh Miller, on three acanthus and anthemion bracket feet, stand applied with trailing vines.

1865   *31in (79cm) high 147oz*
£8,000-12,000   TEN

An early 20thC silver model of a Portuguese sailing ship, sculpted in the round, with Portuguese hallmark, on later wooden base.

15in (38cm) high 47oz
£5,000-6,000   DOR

A rare William III silver heart-shaped nutmeg grater, possibly by Thomas Ker, Edinburgh, with twin hinged covers, stand-away hinges and a suspensory ring, decorated with bands and borders of repeating geometric designs, silver grater maker's mark only.

c1700   *1.5in (4cm) long, 1.25oz*
£4,000-5,000   **LC**

An 18thC silver nutmeg grater, Samuel Meriton, with chased scroll decoration, the screw-off cover opens to reveal the grater, on circular foot.

c1770   *2in (5cm) high*
£800-1,000   **WW**

A George III silver nutmeg grater, maker's mark "IP", London, with hinged cover and base, bright-cut engraved borders and cartouche inscribed "IM to MW 1779 and JC Obt 3d Moth 6 1834, AET 90".

c1779   *2in (5cm) long*
£600-700   **TEN**

A George III silver cylindrical nutmeg grater, Samuel Pemberton, Birmingham, the domed cover revealing the steel grater, with pricked and line decoration, engraved with a script monogram.

1816   *1.25in (3.5cm) high*
£350-450   **DN**

A George IV kitchen nutmeg grater, John Reily, London, with a mounted, blued-steel body, a foliate shell handle, a recess and a flush-hinged base engraved with two crests.

1825   *4in (10cm) high*
£1,500-2,000   **LC**

A rare Victorian silver nutmeg grater, in the form of a strawberry, Hilliard & Thomason, Birmingham, with part polished & part matt texturing, hinging open to reveal a hinged grater.

1856   *1.5in (4cm) long*
£7,000-8,000   **LC**

An Edwardian novelty silver pincushion, modelled as a standing pug dog, Grey & Co, Birmingham.

1904   *2.75in (7cm) long*
£800-1,200   **GORL**

A silver statue of an Irish Guard's drummer, Carrington and Co, London on a wooden plinth applied with an enamelled badge of the Irish Guard's Regiment, with wooden case.

1913

     7.75in (45cm) high on plinth 58oz
£5,000-7,000   **WW**

An Edwardian silver novelty pincushion, in the form of a Chinese pheasant S. Mordan & Co, Chester, on a textured base, loaded.

1905   *4in (10cm) long*
£250-350   **WW**

An Edwardian novelty silver pincushion, modelled as a bull, Cohen & Charles, Birmingham.

1906   *2.5in (6.5cm) long*
£500-600   **GORL**

A rare Edwardian novelty silver kangaroo pincushion, K and F, Birmingham, modelled in a sitting position.

c1907   *2in (5cm) high*
£800-1,200   **WW**

One of a pair of George III Sheffield plate campana-form wine coolers, Matthew Boulton, with egg-and-dart borders and acanthus leaf decoration, circular rubbed-in silver shields to sides, engraved with the arms of Fane, with mask handles.

c1810   *10.25in (26cm) high*

£5,000-7,000 pair   **DN**

A pair of 19thC silver-plated dolphin-form vessels, on naturalistic wave-form bases.

8.25in (21cm) long

£600-800   **LHA**

A Victorian electroplate three-piece candelabra garniture, Elkington & Co., Birmingham, the triform bases with coats of arms, the vine- and leaf-wrapped scroll stem with putti, detachable scroll branches and alternate fruit basket fitting for centre of six-light piece.

Tallest 29.5in (74.5cm) high

£8,000-12,000   **SOTH**

A Victorian silver-plated centrepiece, probably by Elkington, the shallow circular dish with chased acanthus and foliate scrolls and beaded border, on Gothic-arched central column with Classical figures, on a stepped base.

19in (48cm) high

£1,000-1,500   **L&T**

A pair of William IV Rococo Revival Sheffield plate campana-form wine coolers, with armorials below the detachable shaped rims, with rocaille scroll handles and feet, with liners.

c1830   *11in (28cm) high*

£2,000-3,000   **L&T**

A large Italian Neo-classical silver-plated centrepiece, Fratelli Broggi, the base with seated Classical figures, with the etched dished glass tier surmounted by an urn issuing a central stemmed glass dish.

31.5in (80cm) high

£1,500-2,500   **FRE**

A Continental silver-plated centrepiece, maker's mark "B&G", with winged victory over the circular bowl, the base mounted with four putti with festoons.

27.5in (70cm) high

£2,000-3,000   **LHA**

METALWARE

A 17thC Dutch brass warming pan, with a turned handle, with a stamped maker's mark.

40.5in (103cm) long

£250-350 WW

A brass figural lectern in the form of an eagle, on a ringed standard, the hexagonal base over lion-form feet.

60.5in (154cm) high

£2,000-3,000 LHA

A pair of French gilt-brass cassolettes, with pierced reversible covers with butterfly and peach finial.

11.75in (30cm) high

£800-1,200 WW

A Victorian copper tea urn, with fluted domed lid, gadrooned shell-moulded rim, scroll side handles and brass tap, on four mask-headed legs, quadripartite base and ball feet.

16.5in (41.5cm) high

£150-250 AH

A 19thC copper turbot pan and cover, with inscribed initials "M C", possibly for Marlborough College.

31in (78.5cm) across handles

£300-400 WW

A 19thC Pennsylvania copper tea kettle, stamped "A. Keeney Carlisle".

10.5in (27cm) high

£300-400 POOK

A large 19thC copper saucepan and cover, with cast iron handles, impressed number "24".

10in (25.5cm) diam

£150-250 GORL

A pair of 18thC Continental pewter Passover plates, engraved with the star of David surrounded by floriform decoration and Hebrew to edge, stamped with different makers' marks.

9.5in (24cm) diam

£400-600 LHA

A pair of pewter chalices, Peter Young, New York, the tulip bowls on baluster-turned stems, stepped and incised on domed foot.

1772-1800   *8.5in (21.5cm) high*

£8,000-12,000 FRE

A 19thC pewter gallon measure, with scroll handle.

11in (28cm) high

£300-400 L&T

One of a pair of Regency tôleware chestnut urns and covers, with lion's head and ring handles.

13in (33.5cm) high

£800-1,200 pair SWO

A 19thC Pennsylvania tôle coffee pot, with vibrant floral and foliate swag decoration.

10.25in (26cm) high

£10,000-15,000 POOK

THE GLASS MARKET

In general, the glass market has been rather quiet over the last year. Prices for good glass are rising, but not spectacularly. We're waiting for a new generation of antique glass buyers. Jeanette Hayhurst, of antiqueglass-london.com, confirms that there is still great interest in, and enthusiasm for, rare early drinking glasses and good-quality engraved glass. Collectors are still on the hunt for early 18thC heavy baluster drinking glasses. Good quality examples in excellent condition are something of a rarity, and will always attract top prices. Collectors are also always on the lookout for glass that exhibits a high level of craftsmanship, for example excellent examples of air-, colour- and mercury-twists in a fragile stem. These pieces demonstrate glass craftsmanship at its best. They were made in small numbers and were expensive at the time, and are consequently sought-after today.

Victorian rummers are popular and, in my view, under-priced. They are best bought singly. Decanters are extremely under-priced. You can still buy a Georgian decanter for £200-250. Compare that to a new decanter, which is most likely mass-produced and worth virtually nothing as soon as you've left the store. To fetch top prices

antique decanters should always have their original stopper. Check that the design and decoration fit that of the decanter. Examine the proportion – it should "look" right – and lastly make sure the stopper fits the neck properly. Some decanters are numbered on the decanter and the stopper – check that the numbers correspond.

Paperweights made by the great French factories Clichy, Baccarat and St. Louis, are still in demand and rare examples with unusual features will attract top prices. Some good paperweights were made in England by Walsh-Walsh and Bacchus. Look out, too, for Scottish paperweights, particularly by Paul Ysart, and American paperweights by the Boston & Sandwich, New England, and Pairpoint Glass companies.

Mid- to late 19thC Bohemian glass has a strong collecting base, but the condition and craftsmanship must be of top quality. Low- to medium-quality will not sell unless it is very cheap. Engraving must be very detailed and cutting deep. The subject should be realistic and powerful.

In a tough market, condition is paramount. Damage reduces the value of glass considerably. Repairs are costly and can spoil the proportion of a piece.

A miniature wine glass, the funnel bowl on a triple annulated knop and inverted acorn stem, with folded circular foot.

c1730   4in (10cm) high
£600-800   TEN

A wine glass, the round funnel bowl engraved with Baroque border, the stem with flattened annular knop over a ball knop, on a teared inverted baluster with basal knop.

A heavy baluster wine glass, the funnel bowl with solid base with tear, on a teared inverted baluster stem, with folded foot.

c1710   6in (15cm) high
£1,500-2,500   TEN

A wine glass, the bell bowl with single air bubble in the solid base, with a drop knop over a teared inverted baluster basal knop, domed foot.

c1730   7in (18cm) high
£1,200-1,800   TEN

c1730   6in (15cm) high
£1,500-2,500   TEN

GLASS

A composite-stem wine glass, the bell bowl engraved with a carnation, over double-series opaque-twist stem comprising a pair of heavy tapes around a corkscrew, on beaded base.

c1750   7in (18cm) high
£1,000-1,500   TEN

A wine glass, the round funnel bowl engraved with a rose, bud and leaves, with shoulder-and-centre-knopped multiple spiral air-twist stem.

c1750   6in (15cm) high
£600-800   TEN

CLOSER LOOK - BEILBY ENAMELLED WINE GLASS

William Beilby (1740–1819) and his sister Mary (1749-97) were British glassworkers known to have produced outstanding enamelled glass during the second half of the 18thC. The Beilbys worked in Newcastle upon Tyne from 1757 to 1778.

In 1761 Beilby became possibly the first man in England, to fire enamels into glass, so that they became virtually part of the glass itself. The bowl is well enamelled in white with fruiting vines and leaves, in the Beilby style.

The double-series opaque-twist stem comprising a pair of heavy spiral threads outside a multi-ply corkscrew points to a date between 1755-80. A composite stem such as this is a reliable indicator of quality.

The Beilbys did not manufacture glass, they decorated glass from the local glasshouses.

A probably Beilby enamelled wine glass, with ogee bowl.

c1765   6in (15cm) high
£2,500-3,500   TEN

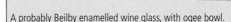

A Newcastle light baluster wine glass, Dutch-engraved with a coat of arms (possibly that of William of Orange), on a flattened knop, teared knop and bubble-inclusion baluster stem.

c1755   7in (18cm) high
£1,500-2,500   TEN

A Newcastle light baluster wine glass, Dutch-engraved with a family drinking around a table, inscribed "T Goet Sycses Opd Veriaering", on a triple annulated ring knop, teared inverted baluster and basal knop stem.

c1755   8in (20cm) high
£4,000-6,000   TEN

An air-twist wine glass, the round funnel bowl moulded with vertical ribs, upon a cable air twist stem.

c1765   7in (18cm) high
£500-700   TEN

A late 18thC Continental colour-twist stem wine glass, the double-series mixed twist comprising a pair of heavy opaque spiral threads and a pair of red tapes around a central opaque gauze.

     7in (18cm) high
£600-800   TEN

An early 19thC rummer, etched and engraved with an Irish harp supported by birds and verso with initials "AC", the short plain stem with blade shoulder knop and conical foot, marked under the foot "Dun (sic) by George Murray".
c1800 *6in (15cm) high*
£600-800 **H&L**

A large Masonic ceremonial rummer, wheel-cut with initials "J.E.I.", with a pair of pillars and mason's tools, sun and moon motifs, crossed keys, the all-seeing eye and a ladder framing the initials "C.H.F.".
c1800-20 *7in (18cm) high*
£250-350 **H&L**

A commemorative glass goblet, with coat of arms for the Cinque Ports and the date 1st August 1799 in gilt decoration, on square foot.

This goblet was probably made to celebrate the Royal Review at Mote Park, Maidstone, on 1st August 1799, where George III and Prime Minister William Pitt met over 3,000 of the Kent Volunteers, who were defending the area against Napoleon.
1799 *6in (15cm) high*
£1,500-2,500 **WW**

A rare Napoleonic commemorative glass rinser, engraved with Colchester coat-of-arms encircled with the inscription "Loyal Colchester Volunteers", with initials "C.A.C" above husk swags, dated.
1797 *5in (12.5cm) diam*
£400-600 **WW**

An Austrian Biedermeier white alabaster and rosé overlay glass ewer, Mayerhofer & Klinkosch, with silver mount and hinged lid.
1848 *11in (28cm) high*
£1,000-1,500 **DOR**

A Victorian cut-glass and silver-mounted claret jug, Charles Boyton, London, the glass hobnail-cut, with lion rampant and shield thumbpiece, and vine stock S-scroll handle, the broad collar repoussé with Bacchic masks and fruiting vines.
1897 *11in (28cm) high*
£1,000-1,500 **TEN**

A pair of French cut-glass wine jugs, the silver mounts with gilt interior and no hallmarks.
c1900 *7.25in (18.5cm) high*
£1,200-1,800 **DOR**

A pair of mid-19thC Bristol blue glass decanters, the twisted necks continuing to reeded bodies and a flattened base, with brass ring stoppers, one marked "Brandy" the other "Rum".
13in (33cm) high
£1,500-2,500 **FRE**

GLASS

A pair of Regency cut-glass pedestal bowls, the everted rims with diamond patterning between bands of fluting, the knopped stem on square lemon-squeezer base.

8in (20cm) high

£800-1,200   L&T

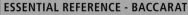
The Baccarat glassworks were founded in 1764 at Saint-Anne, Baccarat, Lorraine, France. The company was the largest French producer of fine glassware during the 19thC.

● From c1846 to c1849 Baccarat produced the carpet-ground millefiori paperweights for which it is well known.

● As well as paperweights, 19thC pieces include cut-glass tablewares and vases, and opaline vases.

● Most pieces were decorated at Baccarat, though some were worked on by glasscutters at independent firms, such as the Escalier de Cristal.

● Baccarat won its first gold medal at the 1855 World's Fair in Paris, for which it designed two huge matching candelabra measuring 17ft (5.25m) high.

● Notable artists included François de Fontenay (1810-1884).

● The factory is still in operation today under the name Compagnie des Cristalleries de Baccarat.

A probably Baccarat ormolu and cut-glass mounted pedestal jar and cover, the body and base deeply slice-cut with repeat anthemion motifs, on a petalled wirework collar from three scroll legs with ram-mask feet, on engine-turned plinth.

c1830-40   14in (36cm) high

£1,500-2,500   TEN

A large mid-19thC Clichy glass latticino amphora vase, with blue and white even striations, on metal stand.

15in (38cm) high

£1,200-1,800   WW

A Baccarat cranberry glass punch bowl, with etched and gilt flowering ivy decoration, on a gilt bronze stand with feet in the form of oak branches, leaves and acorns.

9in (23cm) high overall

£1,500-2,500   LHA

A Stiegel-style blown cobalt blue master salt, with diamond pattern over flute with applied petal foot.

3.5in (8.5cm) high

£800-1,200   POOK

A mid-19thC Sandwich Glass panelled violet tulip vase.

9.75in (25cm) high

£1,200-1,800   POOK

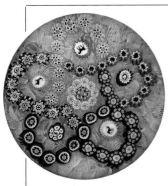

A Baccarat millefiori paperweight, with animal silhouette canes, on an "upset muslin" ground.

3in (7.5cm) diam

£6,000-8,000　　　　　　DCP

A Baccarat double clematis paperweight, with a millefiori garland on "upset muslin" ground.

"Upset muslin" is the term given to a background which is made up of various short sections of canes containing white spirals that have been heated and melted together.

c1850　　　　　　3in (7.5cm) diam

£2,000-3,000　　　　　　DCP

CLOSER LOOK - BACCARAT PAPERWEIGHT

Baccarat was one of the three main French producers of paperweights in the 19thC, along with St. Louis and Clichy.

One of the canes on the side is signed within the cane "B1848", which is a desirable feature.

This weight has a typical Baccarat carpet-ground.

"Gridel" canes (canes featuring tiny animals - a feature unique to Baccarat) were named after a boy whose paper cut-outs inspired his uncle, a Baccarat executive, to try something similar in glass.

Unusually there are nine Gridel canes including two butterflies, goat, dog, horse, two roosters, elephant and deer. There is also a rare flower silhouette cane.

A rare Baccarat carpet-ground paperweight, with Gridel canes, signed.

3in (7.5cm) diam

£8,000-12,000　　　　　　JDJ

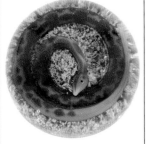

A rare Baccarat coiled green and brown snake paperweight, set on a rock ground.

3in (7.5cm) diam

£3,000-4,000　　　　　　JDJ

A Clichy paperweight, with six circlets of millefiori canes, on an opaque red ground.

3in (7.5cm) diam

£5,000-7,000　　　　　　JDJ

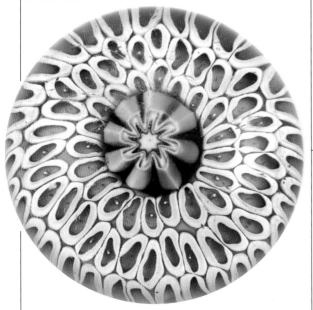

A rare Clichy honeycomb paperweight, with white honeycombs over an opaque red ground and one large central green millefiori cane.

3in (7.5cm) diam

£7,000-10,000　　　　　　JDJ

A mid-19thC St. Louis millefiori garland paperweight, with pink and white cane outer ring centered by a pink and green floret, on white latticino ground.

2.5in (6.5cm) diam

£180-220　　　　　　FRE

A 19thC Boston & Sandwich Glass Co. poinsettia paperweight, in clear glass.

3in (7.5cm) diam

£350-450　　　　　　FRE

An Austrian Gottlob Mohn glass beaker, with gilt banding, painted in transparent technique with a bay scene, inscribed below "Meersburg am Bodensee", signed "G. Mohn fec. 1813".

1813   *4in (10cm) high*

£15,000-25,000   DOR

ESSENTIAL REFERENCE - LITHYALIN

Lithyalin, a polished opaque glass that resembled hardstones, was patented in 1829 by Freidrich Egermann (1777-1864).

● **It may have been inspired by the opaque glass, such as Hyalith (1819), produced by Count Georg Franz August Langueval von Buquoy in southern Bohemia.**

● **Strong colours, particularly red and brown-ochre, are typical of Lithyalin glass. Dark-green, blue and purple are more unusual. The surface was brushed with metal oxides to resemble veining and marbling.**

● **Pieces were typically cut and polished, and sometimes gilded or enamelled.**

● **Lithyalin was used predominantly for decorative items, such as vases, beakers and scent bottles.**

● **It was also produced at Harrach Glassworks in the Czech Republic, and Hautin & Co. in France. Such pieces are difficult to distinguish from those by Egermann, but may be slightly lighter in colour.**

A Lithyalin marbled glass scent bottle, with stopper, the brown-ochre marbling with gilt edging, gilt leaf festoons and horizontal cut grooves.

c1837   *5in (12.5cm) high*

£1,000-1,500   DOR

An Austrian Kothgasser-Ranftbecher beaker, with silver yellow-stained band and gilt leaf border, decorated with a polychrome stable boy from a princely estate with horse on a grass base, reverse with gilt monogram "J. W.", silver-yellow 16-pointed star in base.

c1825   *4.25in (11.5cm) high*

£12,000-18,000   DOR

A Bohemian Zwischengilt glass beaker, decorated with a bear hunt, with silver acanthus leaf borders and a horseman, a beater, a hunter with a spear and a musket, hunting dogs and a bear in a gilt etched forest landscape, base with hunting dog and fleeing deer, leaf tendrils, gilt etched frame to medallion on red glass ground.

c1740   *3in (7.5cm) high*

£10,000-15,000   DOR

A Bohemian "Memories of Hayda 1852" Lithyalin glass beaker, by Friedrich Egermann, with dark red, brown, turquoise and blue marbling, and gilt rim, with engraved gilt dedication.

1852

£2,500-3,500   DOR

A Hyalith glass flacon with stopper, with wide gilt edging, gilt criss-cross band, ten oval gilt medallions with gilt painted flowers and foliage.

c1837   *3.5in (9.5cm) high*

£1,500-2,500   DOR

A Bohemian Count Buquoy (Georgental) Glassworks black Hyalith tête-à-tête tea service, decorated with handpainted gilt motifs including Chinese people, a pagoda, leaves, animals, birds, butterflies and insects in an Oriental landscape, and within a double line-and-star border, restoration.

c1830

£8,000-12,000   FIS

A late 17thC German drinking glass, copper-wheel and diamond-point engraved with a battle scene by Hermann Schwinger, the scene with soldiers on horseback firing pistols in a forest clearing, on late 19thC tin base with embossed foliate motifs, the base of the bowl with diamond point inscription reading "H.Schwinger Cristall Schneider zu Nürnberg".

This incredibly realistic and detailed scene also includes clouds of gun smoke, which have been delicately engraved using a diamond point.

£12,000-15,000   FIS

A pair of 19thC Bohemian glass lidded goblets, etched with stags in a landscape, with spike-topped covers, on faceted, lobed bases.

13.5in (34cm) high

£800-1,200   LHA

A mid-late 19thC Bohemian ruby overlay glass goblet, engraved with Napoleon I on horseback, with grenadiers and French troops, with smooth knop.

This scene presumably depicts Napoleon's retreat from Russia.

7.5in (19cm) high

£1,200-1,800   DOR

A pair of late 19thC Bohemian red-cut-to-clear table lustres, each with a flared urn top depicting stags in landscapes, hung with prisms, on a shaped column support and circular foot.

12in (30.5cm) high

£200-300   FRE

A mid-19thC Bohemian footed goblet, the clear glass body cased with rosalin, with cobalt blue and white enamel overlay cut with flowering branches and leaves, further cut decoration to socle, on spherical base.

5in (12.5cm) high

£600-800   DOR

A late 19thC Bohemian lidded goblet, decorated with symbols of friendship, the red-glazed body with engraved border and decoration, medallions with symbols and dedication, "May health, happiness and joy bless your days".

11in (28cm) high

£400-500   DOR

A mid-19thC German spa beaker, the colourless waisted body overlaid with yellow flashing, with low-relief cut panels showing a copper-wheel engraved scenes of Aachen, surrounded by cut scrolling foliate and lattice designs.

c1860

£400-600   FIS

A pair of Bohemian chalice-form enamel and gilt portrait vases, decorated with portraits of ladies.

10.5in (27cm) high

£1,200-1,800   **LHA**

A pair of 19thC Bohemian enamel and gilt glass lustres, decorated with portraits of ladies and flowers, hung with cut lead crystal lustres.

11.5in (29cm) high

£2,500-3,500   **LHA**

A mid-late 19thC Bohemian green alabaster glass goblet, with gilt rims, and gold- and silver-painted foliate and floral tendrils and rocailles, on faceted base and foot.

5.5in (14cm) high

£350-450   **DOR**

A late 19thC Bohemian opaque, pink and blue glass pedestal vase and cover, reserved with gilt, blue, green and white scrolled foliage and shells.

27in (68.5cm) high

£12,000-18,000   **L&T**

A mid-19thC Bohemian Josephinenhütte glassworks lidded bowl, the green body cased in white and cut through to form frames surrounding handpainted polychrome enamelled vignettes of anthropomorphic animals in domestic or woodland scenes, and bunches of flowers, the borders gilded with scrolling foliate designs.

The scene pictured depicts two foxes, a wolf and a monkey with a spell book entitled "Spell Claims". The scene on the reverse takes place in a cave with a bear with a sceptre and crown handing an envelope marked " The Brown King at Brown home" to a tomcat. On the ground lies a letter stating "Improved Draft Constitution, the King is ready to share, Brown shall be King, the prison sentence ceases, the only punishment is death.". These scenes allude to the German Revolution of 1848/49 and can be traced back to Johann Wolfgang Goethe's 1793 epic "Reineke Fuchs". It is possible that the scenes refer to the parable of the Roman consul, Menenius Agrippa's "The Revolution in the Animal Kingdom".

13in (33.5cm) high

£2,000-3,000   **FIS**

A pair of Italian carved limewood flambeaux angels, each holding a cornucopia as a candlestick, polychrome painted and gilded, replaced drip trays.

c1600   *24in (61cm) high*
£2,500-3,500   **DOR**

A pair of early 18thC Spanish painted candlesticks, the baluster-turned stems on a spreading circular base with bracket feet.

29in (74cm) high
£500-700   **L&T**

A pair of early 18thC brass petal-base candlesticks.

9in (23cm) high
£400-600   **SWO**

A pair of George I brass candlesticks, the sockets with broad drip-pan rims, on knopped, waisted and hexagonal section shafts and hexagonal bases.

c1720   *9in (23cm) high*
£350-450   **DN**

A pair of 18thC brass ejector candlesticks, on petal bases.

7in (18cm) high
£250-350   **SWO**

A pair of George II brass candlesticks, the sockets above inverted baluster and ball-knopped stems, on domed bases.

c1760   *6.75in (17cm) high*
£200-300   **DN**

A pair of George III mahogany candlesticks, with stop-fluted columns, the tops with gilt-brass mounts and cast-leaf sconces.

13in (33.5cm) high
£600-800   **SWO**

A pair of Neo-classical bronze figural candelabra, after Jean-Jacques Pradier, cast by Suisse Frères.

26in (66cm) high
£1,000-1,500   **SWO**

A pair of Regency bronze and parcel-gilt candelabra, the composite upward-tapering reeded columns each on three paw feet and a triform base.

21in (53cm) high

£2,500-3,500   SWO

A pair of 19thC French gilt candelabra, with four scrolled branches and five sconces, on urn-shaped columns and square plinths with applied motifs.

24in (61cm) high

£1,500-2,500   SWO

A pair of Regency/George IV brass twin-light candelabra, each with foliate-cast sockets and drip pans on foliate-cast branches rising from behind recumbent hounds, on rectangular bases.

c1820   *11in (28cm) wide*

£500-700   DN

A pair of 19thC bronze and ormolu candlesticks, after a design by Thomas Abbott, modelled as cranes on a rocky base holding aloft a Rococo sconce.

16in (40cm) high

£1,000-1,500   A&G

A pair of 19thC French Neo-classical ormolu figural candelabra, the acanthus scroll branches supported by an urn beside a Classical maiden, signed "F. Barbedienne", on white marble canted square bases with applied beaded and berried leaf bands, drilled.

20in (51cm) high

£500-700   TOV

A pair of Louis XV-style bronze and ormolu three-branch candelabra, the stem cast with a putto riding a dolphin.

17in (43cm) high

£400-600   GORL

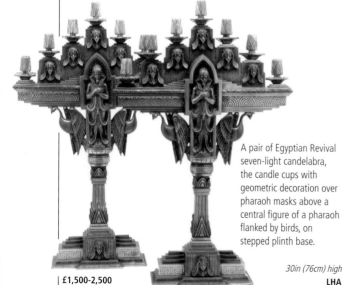

A pair of Egyptian Revival seven-light candelabra, the candle cups with geometric decoration over pharaoh masks above a central figure of a pharaoh flanked by birds, on stepped plinth base.

30in (76cm) high

£1,500-2,500   LHA

A pair of Charles X gilt and patinated bronze candelabra, each with one stiff and four scrolling candlearms, on lion's paw supports and a triform base.

19.5in (50cm) high

£1,000-1,500   FRE

One of a pair of 19thC Empire-style gilded and patinated bronze figural candelabra, each with a winged angel standing atop a raised pedestal base.

36.5in (92.5cm)

£15,000-25,000 pair   SK

A pair of 19thC French ormolu candelabra, each modelled as a lady holding rose briar twin branches, on circular bases with wheat and baskets of fruit and flowers.

17.75in (45cm) high

£1,200-1,800   WW

A pair of Victorian Gothic Revival brass altar sticks, each spiral column with ruby and clear glass cabochons, on circular bases and bun feet, converted to electricity.

30in (76cm) high

£1,000-1,500   GORL

A pair of 19thC Louis XV-style ormolu candlesticks, Henry Dasson, Paris, each with a foliate bobeche over a stem with entwined putti and Rococo scrolls, on shaped circular base, signed and dated.

1888   *14.25in (37cm) high*

£1,000-1,500   FRE

A pair of late 19thC Louis XV-style gilt and patinated bronze candelabra, with figural stems from which issue four outscrolling branches, on moulded rouge marble bases with cast paw feet.

24in (61cm) high

£2,500-3,500   L&T

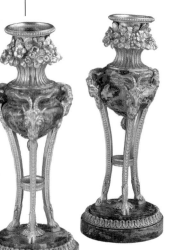

A pair of late 19thC French lapis lazuli and ormolu-mounted candlesticks, Maison Millet, with ram's head monopodia triform supports with an urn issuing fruit and flowers, with detachable nozzles, stamped "MILLET", repairs.

Established by T. Millet in 1853, the Maison Millet specialised in "meubles et bronzes d'art, genre ancien et moderne" and was awarded medals at many of the late 19thC Universal Exhibitions. An auction of the firm's inventory was held in 1906 and it finally ceased trading in 1918.

7in (18cm) high

£800-1,200   WW

A pair of late 19thC Louis XV-style parcel-gilt and patinated bronze eight-light candelabra, candle arms emanating from a central flower-filled cornucopia raised by black-patinated cherubs, the bases with Vitruvian scroll and leaf-tip bands.

37.25in (94.5cm) high

£8,000-12,000   SK

A pair of late 19thC ormolu six-light candelabra, decorated with birds, fox masks, hunting horns, acorns, oak leaves and tassels, on concave-sided triangular marble bases.

29in (73.5cm) high

£1,500-2,500   CHT

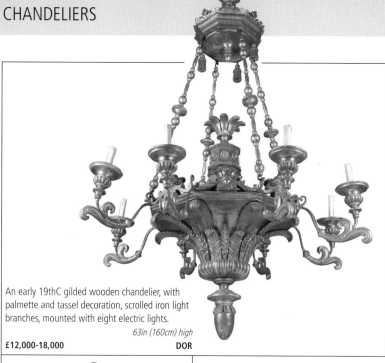

An early 19thC gilded wooden chandelier, with palmette and tassel decoration, scrolled iron light branches, mounted with eight electric lights.

63in (160cm) high

£12,000-18,000　　　　DOR

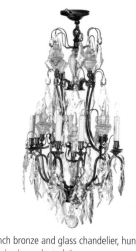

A French bronze and glass chandelier, hung with prisms in six graduated tiers.

34in (86.6cm) high

£2,000-3,000　　　　LHA

A Sèvres-style gilt-metal-mounted eight-light chandelier, the baluster form standard decorated with figures in landscapes, issuing S-scroll candle arms ending in floral decorated cups.

36.5in (93cm) high

£700-1,000　　　　LHA

A pair of French Régence-style ormolu chandeliers, Paris, each with a central orb cast with rosettes within a diaper pattern and with six scroll branches.

c1900　　　　*28in (71cm) high*

£20,000-30,000　　　　SOTH

An early 20thC salon chandelier, the bronze shaft with entwined leaves, mounted with 20 electric lights on three tiers.

47in (119cm) high

£3,000-4,000　　　　DOR

An early 20thC painted glass and bronze chandelier, with putti and laurel tendrils and festoons of flowers, mounted with ten electric lights.

51in (130cm) high

£8,000-12,000　　　　DOR

A George III Chippendale-style cast-brass entrance hall lantern, formerly with glass panes, the leaf-cast knop issuing six scrolling uprights with trailing graduated husks, the later faux chain gasolier mount with original leaf-cast rose stamped "ABERCROMBIE".

22in (56cm) high
£3,500-4,500   L&T

A George III Chippendale-style cast-brass hall lantern, the rocaille crestings on chased and pounced ribbon-tied acanthus leaf uprights, the later fixed faux chain gasolier mount with original leaf-cast rose stamped "ABERCROMBIE", formerly with glass panels.

22in (56cm) high
£2,500-3,500   L&T

A Victorian brass hall lantern, with leaded stained glass panels.

34in (87cm) high
£300-400   WW

A large late 19thC Belgian brass hall lantern, D. J. Meert, Bruxelles, with a trellis domed corona with scrolling caryatid supports, the hexagonal sides enclosing a hanging six-light candelabra, above an ornate openwork scroll apron.

57in (146cm) high
£3,500-4,500   L&T

A Victorian brass and glazed wall lantern, the bevelled panes beneath a corona cast with fleurs de lys, suspended from a scrolling and foliate cast bracket, the backplate cast with a maiden's mask.

c1880   22in (56cm) high
£1,000-1,500   DN

One of a pair of George III bell-form hall lanterns, with cylindrical glass shades and circular glass smoke-shade suspended by chains, later fitted for electricity.

29in (73.5cm) high
£1,500-2,500 pair   L&T

An early 20thC Louis XIV-style gilt metal and glazed hall lantern, the green glazed arched sides with foliate-cast mounts, with five supports rising to a ceiling fitment.

29in (73.5cm) high
£700-900   DN

LIGHTING

A pair of Neo-classical ormolu four-light sconces.

12in (30.5cm) high

£1,200-1,800   LHA

One of a pair of Restauration ormolu and patinated bronze four-light wall appliqués, the foliate-cast sockets on scrolling branches held aloft by cherubs, issuing from foliate-cast brackets, fitted for electricity.

c1830   *Lamp 19in (48cm) high*

£5,000-7,000 pair   DN

A Victorian brass and glass-shaded gas wall appliqué, the stem cast as gryphon, the circular backplate with further mouldings, refitted for electricity, later green glass shade.

c1875   *13in (33cm) high*

£600-800   DN

A pair of ormolu and floral porcelain mounted wall lights, both stamped Mottheau, Paris.

Maison Mottheau et Fils was a well-known Parisian company specialising in lighting fixtures. It exhibited at the Paris Exposition Universelle in 1900.

20in (51cm) high

£1,000-1,500   WW

A set of four French ormolu three-branch wall appliqués, with anthemion, female and satyr mask vase silhouette backplates with three S-scroll branches supporting campana nozzles cast with lambrequins and strapwork.

c1900   *19in (48cm) high*

£2,000-3,000 set   TEN

An early 20thC American Neo-classical bronze three-light sconce, attributed to Caldwell, centred with a Bacchanalian mask issuing the oval ring.

14.5in (37cm) wide

£1,000-1,500   LHA

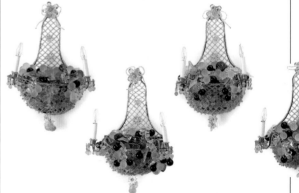

A set of four 20thC Continental glass-beaded basket-form wall lights, with coloured and frosted glass fruit, against a ribbon-tied glass bead lattice backplate, each with two scrolled candlearms.

23in (59cm) high

£1,200-1,800   FRE

A pair of 19thC Derbyshire spar urns, now mounted as table lamps.

Urn 14in (36cm) high

£3,500-4,500   POOK

A pair of late Victorian brass and cut-glass mounted columnar oil lamps, with etched opaque glass spherical shades, with burners above a faceted and dished reservoir, the Corinthian capitals on reeded shafts and stepped bases.

36in (91.5cm) high overall

£600-800   DN

A pair of late 19thC Empire-style brass Argand lamps, the urn forms with entwined reeded handles and fruiting grapevine rim, mounted with frosted and etched colourless glass tulip-shaped shades.

20in (51cm) high

£700-1,000   SK

ESSENTIAL REFERENCE - LAMPS

The fuel source in 18thC oil lamps was controlled by an adjustable metal tube, surrounded by a glass chimney.

- Gas lighting was sold commercially from 1792, but did not become widespread until the early/mid-19thC.
- Gas was superseded by electricity by the late 19thC. At this point many gas fittings were converted for electricity.
- Lighting is typically found in the dominant style of the period. The arrival of electricity heralded the beginning of designer lighting. Louis Comfort Tiffany's famous leaded-glass lamps were among the first examples of the genre (see pp566-7).
- Quality is very important when determining a lamp's desirability. Large, highly worked pieces produced by craftsmen, made from good materials were valuable when made and are likely to still be valuable today.

A late 19thC oil lamp, with six-panel lithophane shade, three decorated with children, two with maidens and one with a stag and a dog, with cut glass reservoir and stand.

14.5in (37cm) high

£450-550   GORL

A patinated metal-mounted electrotype figural table lamp, after Mayer, the three electrical sockets in flowers rising from an urn held by a boy, on a circular marble base.

Nicolas Mayer (1852-1929) was a French bronze sculptor.

c1900   *38in (96.5cm) high*

£700-1,000   DN

A pair of Louis XVI-style marble and gilt-bronze cassolettes, mounted as lamps, on monopodial supports with mask mounts connected with foliate swags, on circular marble bases.

13.75in (35.5cm) high

£1,500-2,500   LHA

A pair of Empire-style gilt metal mounted opalescent glass urns, with swan-form handles, mounted as lamps.

Urns 18in (45.5cm) high

£1,200-1,800   LHA

JEWELLERY

A 15thC European golden ring, engraved with the initial "P" between branches.

2.5in (6.5cm) wide 0.2oz (5.23g)

£2,000-3,000   G&M

A medieval ring, of gilded copper alloy, with a cruciform symbol within a rope border, two letter "T"s.

£300-400   TEN

A mid-16thC French Renaissance gold and onyx cameo brooch, carved in high relief with "The Judgement of Paris", above the letter "A".

A very similar French cameo of this date is in the Kunsthistorisches Museum, Vienna. The inclusion of a letter is rare, and may be a carver's signature or the owner's initial.

1.5in (4cm) wide

£2,000-3,000   DN

A 16thC gold posy ring, with regular square indentations throughout, engraved to the inside "I LYVE IN HOPE X X", with a cruciform symbol.

£1,000-1,500   TEN

A large Scottish annular brass brooch, with pierced and engraved Celtic knotwork bosses and with foliate detail between, with integral swing pin.

This is a particularly finely executed example of this type of brass brooch with good definition and fine details.

6in (15cm) diam

£1,800-2,200   L&T

An early 17thC Greek Orthodox cross pendant, set with fancy-cut foil-backed emeralds and pearl accents, losses.

From the Russian Imperial Exhibit and Sale of items from the Hammer Collection. Accompanied by two letters, one from Russian Imperial Exhibit dated January 21, 1933 describing the pendant, and an exhibition tag. All of these trace the cross to the collection of Grand Duchess Tatiana, daughter of Nicholas II.

2.5in (6.5cm) long

£5,000-7,000   SK

Reliquaries

A reliquary is a casket or vessel designed to hold sacred objects or the relics of a saint. They are customarily found in churches, but other examples were made to be worn, as Catholics believed they conferred protective powers to their wearers. Early examples of personal reliquaries (dating from the Middle Ages) were relatively plain, but later pieces were more ostentatious. They were typically made from precious metals, and were often very richly wrought, for example with gemstones and enamelling. Many took the shape of the relic contained within.

A 17thC gold cruciform pendant, set with crudely cut diamonds.

1.5in (4cm) high

£1,000-1,500   WW

A late 17thC gold-mounted floral brooch, set with emeralds and decorated in green, black and white enamel.

3in (7.5cm) high

£2,000-3,000   WW

A late 17thC northern European silver reliquary, chased with Biblical scenes and foliate decoration, the hinged covers open to reveal pierced scroll section, the inside engraved with diagrams of the sections and their related Saints.

1.5in (4cm) long 1.2oz

£4,500-5,500   WW

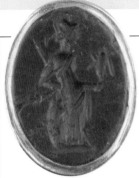

A rare Georgian Scottish gold-mounted signet ring, collet-set with an oval-cut bloodstone incised with a Classical figural intaglio.

While Scottish goldsmiths and jewellers must have made large numbers of gold rings during the 18thC, only a tiny proportion survive and any Scottish ring is rare. This example, with George III marks, is of particular interest. The much earlier intaglio set to the head shows the great interest in the historical and archaeological in Scotland.

£1,200-1,500   L&T

An 18thC silver plaid brooch, with engraved Celtic knot bosses and beast work, with integral swing pin, the reverse with traces of original engraved initials.

3.75in (9.5cm) diam

£1,500-2,500   L&T

A small George III diamond brooch, the blue guilloche enamel plaque star-set with a diamond and set in silver and gold, within a diamond surround.

0.5in (1.5cm) wide

£600-800   WW

A George III diamond-set foliate brooch, set in silver and gold, with closed back mount, possibly later converted.

£2,500-3,500   WW

A George III two-stone ring, set with a pear-shaped emerald and diamond in silver and gold, with closed back mount.

£1,000-1,500   WW

A George III moss agate and diamond plaque ring, the closed-back mount engraved with fluted, scrolling decoration and with bifurcated shoulders to the shank, one diamond missing, in case by Heming.

£2,000-3,000   WW

Judith Picks: Nelson

More than 200 years after the Battle of Trafalgar, the British still love Nelson. They also love a good story of intrigue and romance, and this locket seems to represent all of that perfectly. The initial, the anchor and the date (the battle of the Nile) suggest that the pale-coloured hair belonged to Nelson himself. That might be exciting enough on its own, but the hair must have been mounted after 1798, but before 1799 when King Ferdinand of Naples made Nelson the Duke of Bronte, after which he invariably used the initials "NB" rather than just "N". It was in this period that Nelson first met Emma, Lady Hamilton, and began their famous love affair. This promotes the romantic probability that the auburn coloured hair on the reverse of the locket belonged to Emma – it certainly appears to match the other known example of Emma's hair, a lock mounted behind a miniature of her carried by Nelson to his death at Trafalgar. This locket is a completely unique relic of an enduring love affair, and as such justifies its high value.

A late 18thC double-sided gold locket, with hair in stylised bow, with seed pearls, anchor and initial "N" and "1st Aug. 1798", mounted reverse with a spray of auburn hair set with seed pearls.

1798   *3.25in (8.5cm) high*

£50,000-70,000   WW

A George III diamond and garnet brooch pendant, centred with a cluster of cushion-shaped diamonds within garnet surround and diamond-set scroll frame, set in silver on gold, with closed-back mount.

1.5in (4cm) wide

£1,000-1,500   WW

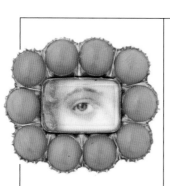

A yellow-gold and coral lover's eye brooch, containing 10 round coral cabochons surrounding a portrait.

c1830   *1in (2.5cm) long*
£1,000-1,500   **LHA**

A gold Jewish wedding ring, of traditional design, incorporating a pointed architectural motif, flanked by mask- and scroll-decorated shoulders, with traces of enamelled decoration.

0.4oz
£20,000-30,000   **L&T**

A rare mid-19thC gold bracelet, decorated with enamel, old-cut diamonds and opals, socket fastening.

7in (18cm) long
Total diamond weight 0.40ct
£3,500-4,500   **DOR**

A gold and enamel armlet, set with Baroque pearls and with engraved dedication "a ma soeur, 10 Fevrier 1851", with variable socket fastening.

1.34oz
£2,500-3,500   **DOR**

A Victorian amethyst rivière necklace, set in gold cut-down collets, with detachable amethyst-set gold cruciform pendant with brooch mount, in box.

15.75in (40cm) long.
£3,500-4,500   **WW**

A cased set of three Victorian diamond brooches, set in silver and gold, the principal brooch of scroll design, with detachable brooch fitting and pendant loop, the other pair of brooches probably converted from earrings, in fitted case by Joseph Johnson of Dublin.

£7,000-10,000   **WW**

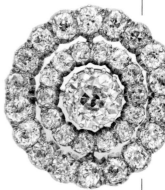

A Victorian diamond-set brooch/pendant, the central claw-set old-European-cut diamond within two borders of graduated similarly cut diamonds.

3in (7.5cm) diam
principal diamond 2.38ct
£5,500-6,500   **L&T**

A 19thC coral bandeau, mounted with graduated coral branches and boules, on a gilt-metal adjustable frame.

7.5in (19cm) wide
£1,000-1,500   **WW**

A Victorian gold hinged bangle, with elaborate engraved scroll work and presentation inscription, set with blue stones, in fitted case.

1870
£600-800   **WW**

A Victorian diamond and emerald fleur de lys brooch, the mainly rose-cut diamonds set in white claws, with a band of five calibré cut emeralds in yellow claw settings, in a fitted case.

1.5in (4cm) long
diamond weight 3.5ct
£3,000-4,000   **TEN**

ESSENTIAL REFERENCE - JOHN BROGDEN

John Brogden was a Victorian jeweller, who worked between 1842 and 1885. His designs were inspired by archaeological (particularly ancient Egyptian) and Renaissance objects.

● He was apprenticed to a London firm of watch- and clockmakers. In 1842 he became a partner in the London jewellery firm of Watherston and Brogden (est. 1798). He took over the firm in 1864 and ran it under his own name until 1880.

● Brogden won awards at various exhibitions in Paris and London from the 1850s to the 1870s. His work was praised by Castellani (the Italian jeweller who initiated the archaelogical revival movement that Brogden worked in) at the 1878 International Exhibition in Paris.

One of a pair of Victorian scarab cuff links, by John Brogden, with green enamel decoration, chased underbodies and ruby eyes, signed "JB" twice.

Scarab 0.5in (1.5cm) long

£5,500-6,500 pair　　　　WW

A late Victorian gold and opal cameo archaeological brooch, by John Brogden, the opal cameo carved with a Classical god on a red guilloche enamel ground within rope twist gold mount with glazed locket back, on a gold tubular ridged bar, signed "Brogden", in original red velvet fitted box.

c1870

£2,000-3,000　　　　　　DN

A Victorian diamond cluster brooch, the old-cut diamonds set in a star formation within a detachable blue enamelled frame.

1.75in (4.5cm) wide
diamond weight 3.25ct

£1,000-1,500　　　TEN

A Victorian diamond crescent brooch, two rows of graduated old-cut diamonds are spaced by tiny diamonds, in white claw settings, on a yellow mount.

1.25in (3.5cm) long
diamond weight 4.5ct

£2,000-3,000　　　TEN

A Victorian emerald, half pearl and enamel brooch, the open-work domed mount of half pearls with blue and red enamel scrolls between, above a rope twist border.

c1880　　　*1.25in (3.5cm) long*

£1,800-2,200　　　　DN

A Holbeinesque pendant, set with a cabochon ruby surrounded by enamel quatrefoil motifs within enamelled flowers, set with oval chrysoberyls, a cluster of four square chrysoberyls suspended from the base, the reverse scroll-engraved with a locket centre containing hair.

3in (7.5cm) long

£3,000-4,000　　　TEN

Judith Picks

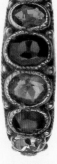

The language of stones was used in 19thC jewellery to convey messages of love. Stones were arranged so that their initials spelled out names or more often words, such as DEAREST: diamond, emerald, amethyst, ruby, emerald, sapphire, topaz; and REGARD: ruby, emerald, garnet, amethyst, ruby, diamond.

A Victorian "DEAREST" ring, set in gold, engraved "my dearest love".

£1,500-2,500　WW

A Victorian "REGARD" ring, set in gold, with two turquoise-centred florettes to the shoulders.

£1,000-1,500　　　WW

A Victorian graduated oval-shaped amethyst rivière necklace and earrings, set in gilt-metal collet mounts, the earrings with screw fittings.

£650-750   WW

A Victorian diamond five-stone ring, the graduated old-cut diamonds spaced by pairs of tiny diamonds, in yellow claw settings, on a carved mount to a plain polished shank.

diamond weight 4.75ct

£8,000-12,000   TEN

A Victorian diamond and seed pearl star brooch, set with old-cut diamonds and split and seed pearls.

1in (2.5cm) diam

£800-1,200   TEN

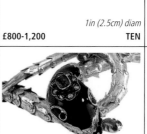

A Victorian diamond- and sapphire-set bee pendant, set with circular-cut diamonds and an oval-shaped sapphire, set in silver and gold.

1in (2.5cm) long

£1,800-2,200   WW

A late Victorian diamond crescent brooch, the graduated old-brilliant-cut diamonds claw-set in open-backed collets above a pierced galleried mount, mounted in gold backed silver.

c1890   *1.5in (4cm) diam*
diamond weight 4.6ct

£4,000-6,000   DN

A late Victorian shell-shaped diamond brooch/pendant, set with cushion-shaped old-cut diamonds, mounted in gold backed silver.

c1890   *2.25in (5.5cm) long*
diamond weight 5ct

£2,000-3,000   DN

A late 19thC gold serpent bracelet, enamelled and set with diamonds, emeralds, green tinted chalcedony and synthetic corundum, alterations.

9in (23cm) long 1.2oz

£1,500-2,500   DOR

A late Victorian pearl and diamond pendant brooch, with bow top, wreath and heart-shaped surmount, set with old brilliant-cut and rose-cut diamonds, mounted in gold backed silver.

1.5in (4cm) long

£2,000-3,000   DN

A late Victorian diamond and tourmaline pendant brooch, in original leather case.

2in (5cm) long

£3,000-4,000   GORL

A pair of 19thC European Renaissance-style gold, enamel and stone-set figural saint brooches, in velvet-lined fitted leather case.

2in (5cm) high

£4,000-6,000   SK

A Victorian amethyst and diamond pendant, the large amethyst wrapped with diamonds in the shape of a snake with emerald eyes, with baroque pearl suspended from its tail.

2.5in (6.5cm) long
diamond weight 0.7ct

£2,000-3,000   TEN

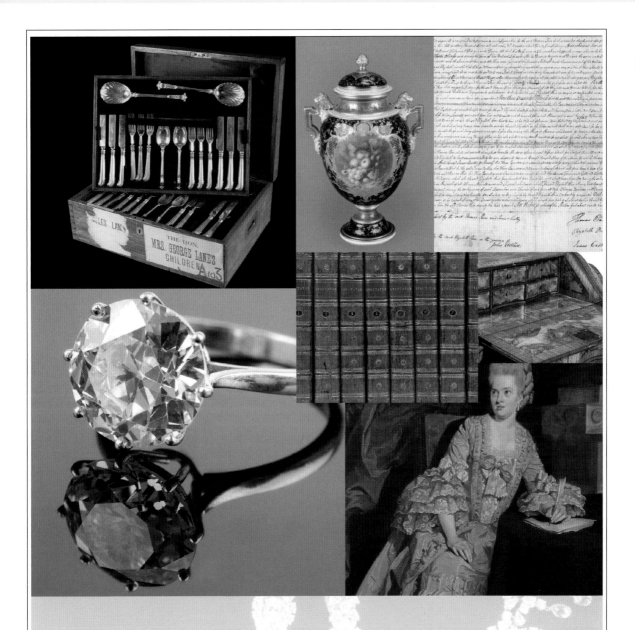

Judith Picks: Lalique jewellery

I had known, and loved, Lalique art glass for many years before I discovered that René Lalique had crafted exquisite jewellery much earlier. I was further enchanted by visiting the collection in the Gulbenkian Museum in Lisbon, Portgual, last year. The story of this artist/jeweller is fascinating.

In 1872, when he was 12, he entered the College Turgot where he started drawing and sketching. Following the death of his father two years later, Lalique began working as an apprentice to the goldsmith Louis Aucoc in Paris, and attended evening classes at the École des Arts Décoratifs. In 1876 he moved to London to attend Sydenham Art College.

On returning to France, he worked as a freelance artist, designing jewellery for Cartier, Boucheron and other jewellers. In 1885 he opened his own business and designed and made his own jewellery and other glass pieces. By 1890, Lalique was recognized as one of France's foremost Art Nouveau jewellery designers, creating innovative pieces for Samuel Bing's new Paris shop, Maison de l'Art Nouveau. The artist-jeweller became the absolute master of the Art Nouveau jewel, in which he blended symbolism and naturalism with long-abandoned techniques and materials.

Unfortunately, as you can see on this page, such artistry does not come cheap!

An Art Nouveau gold dragonfly pendant, by René Lalique, the four dragonflies grouped around a central opal, with plique-à-jour enamel wings and set with diamonds, twice signed "LALIQUE", with associated gold chain mounted with opal beads, in fitted box.

3.75in (9.5cm) wide

£50,000-70,000　　　　　　　　**WW**

An Art Nouveau gold and enamel brooch, by René Lalique; depicting four dancing nymphs joined with ribbons, on green enamel ground, signed "LALIQUE" with French control mark.

2.5in (6.5cm) wide

£15,000-25,000　　　　　　　　**WW**

An Art Nouveau enamel pansy *plaque de coul* dog collar centrepiece, by René Lalique, the cream-coloured pansy with blue centre detail, pavé-set with graduated circular-cut diamonds set in gold, signed "LALIQUE".

The style of the pansy and the use of cloissoné cells to form the plique-à-jour enamel flower were inspired by Japanese designs – a favourite of René Lalique.

2.5in (6.5cm) wide

£50,000-70,000　　　　　　　　**WW**

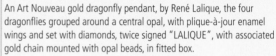

An early 20thC French Art Nouveau horn clematis pendant, by Georges Pierre, on a brown silk ribbon, signed verso "GIP".

4in (10cm) long

£800-1,200　　　　　　　　**SHAP**

A Jugendstil silver, citrine and marcasite pendant necklace, probably Phorzheim, the pendant bezel-set with a citrine among stylised leaves and scrolling wirework tendrils, suspending a cascade of graduating drops and fringe with bead terminals, with marcasite highlights.

4.25in (11cm) long

£3,500-4,500　　　　　　　　**SK**

An Art Nouveau silver-gilt and opal buckle, by Gorham, the elaborate scrolling form with bud motifs, bezel-set with opal cabochons, and suspending a drop, with maker's marks.

4.5in (11cm) long

£1,500-2,500　　　　　　　　**SK**

An Edwardian gold, ruby and diamond dress ring, with central oblong-cut ruby flanked by bands of brilliant-cut diamonds.

£2,500-3,500   GORL

An Edwardian gold and diamond flower head pendant brooch, in Hunt & Roskell case.

1.5in (4cm) diam
diamond weight 5ct

£7,000-10,000   GORL

An Edwardian diamond, emerald and pearl necklace, the old brilliant-cut diamond drop in a millegrain collet suspended from an emerald and old-cut diamond cluster connection, attached to a graduated pearl necklace with ruby and rose-cut diamond cluster clasp.

c1910   *14in (36cm) long Drop 1.93ct*

£10,000-15,000   DN

A Belle Époque pendant necklace, mounted with two pearls and a lozenge set with calibre cut sapphires among diamond and demantoid garnet foliage, set in platinum and gold.

£7,000-10,000   WW

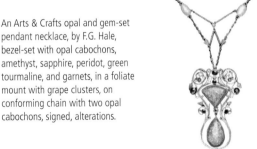

A French Arts and Crafts enamelled gold necklace, in the manner of Carlo Giuliano, with ornate scroll links, each set with a brilliant-cut diamond and white opal, on fine-link chain.

18in (45.5cm) long

£2,500-3,500   GORL

An Arts and Crafts turquoise, blue enamel and gold brooch, by Jessie King, attributed to Liberty & Co, with wirework surround with translucent enamelled jewelling and turquoises at points.

1.25in (3.5cm) wide

£1,000-1,500   DN

An Arts and Crafts silver and moonstone necklace, attributed to Frances Thalia How and Jean Milne, the shield-shaped pendant with a festoon of cabochons below, the open-work two-row links to stone-set panels, in original fitted case.

17in (43cm) long

£5,000-7,000   DN

An Arts and Crafts turquoise and pearl-mounted brooch, by Mürrle, Bennett & Co., signed.

1.5in (4cm) wide

£600-800   WW

An Arts and Crafts silver pendant, by Mürrle, Bennett & Co., mounted with two amethysts and three pearls, signed, on a fine-link silver neck chain.

£1,000-1,500   WW

An Arts & Crafts opal and gem-set pendant necklace, by F.G. Hale, bezel-set with opal cabochons, amethyst, sapphire, peridot, green tourmaline, and garnets, in a foliate mount with grape clusters, on conforming chain with two opal cabochons, signed, alterations.

£12,000-18,000   SK

An Art Deco diamond and emerald ring, set in platinum, control mark probably French.

£1,500-2,500   WW

An Art Deco 18ct white gold and diamond double clip, set with baguette- and brilliant-cut diamonds.

2.25in (5.5cm) wide

£4,500-5,500   GORL

An Art Deco sapphire and diamond brooch, centred with a rectangular shaped sapphire and millegrain set with eight cut diamonds and two circular-cut diamonds.

2.25in (5.5cm) wide

£3,000-4,000   LC

An Art Deco diamond necklace, converting into four bracelets or necklaces of different lengths, set with circular and baguette-cut diamonds in platinum.

Each bracelet 7.25in (18.5cm) long

£30,000-40,000   WW

An Art Deco platinum, diamond and onyx necklace, the old European- and single-cut diamonds with rectangular mixed cut onyx accents.

16in (40cm) long diamond weight 15.85ct

£7,000-10,000   LHA

An Art Deco platinum, spinel and diamond brooch, bead-set with old-European, transitional, and old-mine-cut diamonds, with central cushion-cut spinel and cushion- and circular-cut spinel highlights.

1.5in (4cm) long
total diamond weight 4.43ct

£3,500-4,500   SK

An Art Deco sapphire and diamond plaque brooch, centred with an emerald-cut sapphire with smaller sapphires and diamonds, set in white gold, one sapphire missing.

£2,000-3,000   WW

A pair of French Art Deco platinum and white gold "cube" cufflinks, decorated with black enamel and diamonds.

£1,200-1,800   WW

An Art Deco platinum, diamond and jade brooch, Lacloche Frères, mounted with two jade discs and diamonds within black enamel border, signed to reverse.

2in (5cm) wide

£3,500-4,500   WW

A George III scroll-design silver necklace, set with white and blue pastes, with artificial pearl drop.

£400-600   WW

A Victorian gilt metal necklace, set with white paste stones.

£450-550   WW

A 19thC Continental gold filigree cross pendant, set with pink paste, in fitted leather case.

2.5in (6.5cm) long

£800-1,200   GORL

A 19thC French silver *tremblante* flower brooch, set with clear paste.

1.75in (4.5cm) diam

£500-700   GORL

An Edwardian paste-set brooch, set with blue and white paste stones.

£200-300   WW

An Arts and Crafts silver necklace, brooch and earrings set, by Arthur & Georgie Gaskin, the foil-backed faceted green pastes in rubover settings on floral and bead frames, brooch signed "G".

Necklace 15in (38cm) long

£3,500-4,500   TEN

An Arts and Crafts silver pendant, Arthur & Georgie Gaskin, the foil-backed faceted green stones in rubover setting on scrolling wirework frame, signed "G".

Pendant 3in (7.5cm) long

£1,500-2,000   TEN

An American Arts and Crafts silver peacock brooch, set with paste stones and decorated with polychrome enamel, marked "240" and "sterling".

c1910   *2.25in (5.5cm) wide*

£350-450   WW

An Arts and Crafts brooch, by Dorrie Nossiter, set with faceted and cabochon stones, set in silver with gold beads and leaf motifs.

1.25in (3.5cm) long

£300-400   TEN

An Arts and Crafts pendant, attributed to Jessie King for Liberty & Co, with a panel of enamelled stylised leaf motifs, topped and finished by stones.

2in (5cm)

£500-700   TEN

A 1950s/1960s Chanel goldtone Byzantine necklace, probably by Robert Goossens, with an oversized faux pearl link flanked by rhinestones, stamped "Chanel".

£1,000-1,500   **LHA**

A Chanel cream lucite Maltese Cross cuff, with red, green and pink poured glass, stamped "Chanel".

£1,000-1,500   **LHA**

A mid-1940s Coro gold-plated monkey Duette brooch, with red, green and clear crystals.

£250-350   **PC**

A mid-1950s Dior unicorn brooch, by Mitchell Maer, in rhodium-plate, pavé-set with clear rhinestones.

2.5in (6.25cm) high
£150-200   **PC**

A Dior wreath brooch and earrings, in silver tone metal with gold metal decoration, prong-set with clear rhinestones, marked "ChrDior 1959".

1959   Brooch 2.5in (6.5cm) high
£300-400   **PC**

A 1960s/1970s Stanley Hagler pink brooch, featuring a cluster of flowerheads in moulded glass and glass beads and pink rhinestones.

3.5in (9cm) wide
£140-160   **CRIS**

A 1960s Stanley Hagler cobalt blue glass necklace and earrings set.

Earrings 1in (2.5cm) diam
£350-450   **CRIS**

A 1950s Har Oriental head pendant bracelet, with silver-plated chain and Lucite head, decorated with jade glass cabouchons and small aurora borealis crystal rhinestones.

Bracelet 7in (18cm) long
£100-120   **CRIS**

Judith Picks: Sungod Brooch

This "Sungod" brooch by Joseff of Hollywood is one of my favourite pieces of costume jewellery – along with the similar "Moon with Ruff" brooch. Luckily I (or should I say my husband) bought this from our friends in Cristobal, London about 10 years ago. He paid under £100 for each brooch. The "Sungod" will now sell for £400-500. The much rarer "Moon with Ruff", if you can find it, would be closer to £1,000.

A Miriam Haskell two-strand faux pearl necklace, with floral pendant of pink, blue and red glass beads, seed pearls, clear rose montées and amethyst poured-glass leaves.

c1960   *14in (36cm) long*

£1,500-2,000   **PC**

A late 1940s Joseff of Hollywood Sungod brooch, with suspended rhinestone eyes, marked "Joseff" on round plate to reverse, with original patina.

£400-500   **PC**

A 1950s Miriam Haskell rose pink bracelet, with gold-plated ivy leaves and diamanté on clasp.

£200-250   **CRIS**

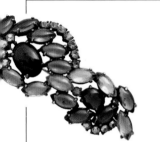

A 1950s Schiaparelli brooch, in gilt metal, prong-set with green and blue glass stones and small aurora borealis rhinestone highlights.

3.5in (9cm) long

£300-400   **PC**

A 1930s Trifari articulated enamel and diamanté windmill brooch, designed by Alfred Philippe, with central faux ruby cabochon.

2.5in (6.5cm) high

£850-950   **CRIS**

A Trifari first edition sterling silver crown brooch, prong-set with several large glass cabochon and glue-set rhinestones.

1944

£300-400   **PC**

JEWELLERY

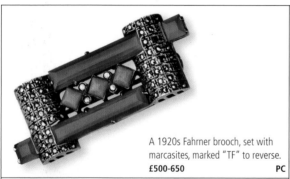

A 1920s Fahrner brooch, set with marcasites, marked "TF" to reverse.
£500-650 PC

A 1950s Coppolo e Toppo red Venetian glass bead bow necklace, bracelet and earrings set, marked "Made in Italy by Coppolo e Toppo".

This appears to be an extremely high price for costume jewellery pieces, however, this is justified by the fact that this is a complete set made from exceptional poured-glass beads.
£2,000-2,500 CRIS

ESSENTIAL REFERENCE - ROY LICHTENSTEIN

Roy Lichtenstein (1923–1997) was a leading figure in the American Pop Art movement, along with Andy Warhol, Jasper Johns and James Rosenquist.

● His work was based on popular advertising and old-fashioned comic strips, typically featuring thick outlines, bright colours and Lichtenstein's hallmark "Benday" dots (an old printing process). It often parodied its subject in a humorous manner.

● Lichtenstein's most famous work is arguably "Whaam!" (1963), which shows a fighter aircraft firing a rocket into an enemy plane.

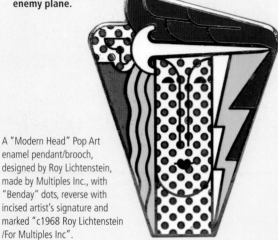

A "Modern Head" Pop Art enamel pendant/brooch, designed by Roy Lichtenstein, made by Multiples Inc., with "Benday" dots, reverse with incised artist's signature and marked "c1968 Roy Lichtenstein /For Multiples Inc".
1968 *3in (7.5cm)*
£2,500-3,000 SK

A Maison Gripoix pâte-de-verre leaf necklace, with faux pearl accents.

Founded in Paris in the 1870s, Maison Gripoix began to create costume jewellery by making copies of Sarah Bernhardt's fine Art Nouveau pieces. The house soon began to create looks for numerous couturiers, from Chanel and Worth in the 1920s, to Christian Dior in the 1940s, and Yves St. Laurent in the 1980s. In the 1990s, the house began to produce its distinct Histoire de Verre line, which incorporates foliate motifs and faux pearls.
21in (53cm) long
£700-1,000 SK

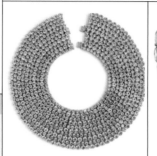

A 1950s Hattie Carnegie clear chaton-cut rhinestone Cleopatra collar.
9.5in (24cm) diam
£800-1,200 GUK

An Yves Saint Laurent rhinestone and black velvet necklace, with a removable black velvet choker collar, stamped "Yves Saint Laurent".
£800-1,200 LHA

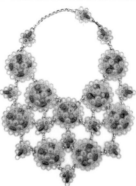

A Kenneth Jay Lane bib necklace, set with turquoise, coral and emerald glass in a floral motif, stamped "KJL".
£400-600 LHA

A 1990s Karl Lagerfeld pastries runway necklace, designed by Ugo Correani, signed "U. Correani" on metal plaque.
£1,000-1,500 SK

ESSENTIAL READING:

Costume Jewellery, Judith Miller: *Miller's* (2010) **£25**

A gold-mounted chalcedony and enamel vinaigrette, with an overall mask of pierced scrolls and flowers, the rim with narrow white enamel band marked "Gage D'Amour et D'Amite", the foot with hinged compartment.

c1750   *1.5in (4cm) high*

£1,000-1,500   **TEN**

A George III silver vinaigrette, Matthew Linwood, Birmingham, the cover engraved with a portrait of Lord Nelson, the grille stamped with his ship "The Victory" and "Trafalgar, Oct 21 1805".

1805   *1.25in (3.5cm) long*

£2,000-3,000   **TEN**

A George IV silver gilt engine-turned vinaigrette, possibly Isaac Rowley, London, with a mounted oval micromosaic plaque of a Dutch tulip-collecting scene, with cast scrolling border and a cast thumbpiece.

1821   *1.75in (4.5cm) long*

£8,000-12,000   **ROS**

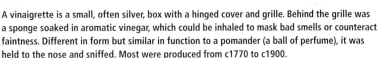

A Victorian silver and enamel porcelain vinaigrette, Edward Edwards, London, with engine-turned sides and a pierced foliate grille, the cover inset with a porcelain plaque depicting a cherub and a butterfly.

1838   *2in (5cm) long*

£5,000-7,000   **TEN**

A Victorian silver castle-top vinaigrette, Nathaniel Mills, London, the cover with low-relief view of Newstead Abbey, the sides and base engine-turned with blank cartouche.

A vinaigrette is a small, often silver, box with a hinged cover and grille. Behind the grille was a sponge soaked in aromatic vinegar, which could be inhaled to mask bad smells or counteract faintness. Different in form but similar in function to a pomander (a ball of perfume), it was held to the nose and sniffed. Most were produced from c1770 to c1900.

1850   *1.5in (4cm) long*

£1,500-2,500   **H&L**

A Victorian silver castle-top vinaigrette, Nathaniel Mills, Birmingham, engraved with a view of Bath Abbey against a radial-engraved ground.

1851   *1.75in (4.5cm) wide*

£2,500-3,500   **TEN**

A late 18thC Scottish gold-mounted hardstone vinaigrette, the scalloped mounts with foliate engraving and beaded borders, the hinged cover with cabochon rock crystal, opening to reveal a hinged, pierced and engraved grille.

3in (7.5cm) high

£2,000-3,000   **L&T**

An early Victorian silver castle-top card case, Nathaniel Mills, Birmingham, chased with views of Windsor and Kenilworth castles, on a scroll-pierced ground, in a leather-covered case.

1838   *4in (10cm) high*
£1,200-1,800   **DN**

A rare silver castle-top card case, maker's mark "L&W", embossed with a scene of Battle Abbey, Sussex, with foliate and floral scrolls and lattice work surround, the reverse with floral scrolls and cartouche inscribed "FWB to MBH".

                                             1.8oz
£1,500-2,500   **L&T**

A Victorian silver castle-top card case, Joseph Wilmore, Birmingham, chased with a view of St Paul's Cathedral and St George's Chapel, Windsor, amongst crisply chased and carved flowers and fruits.

1842   *4in (10cm) high*
£800-1,200   **TEN**

A Victorian silver castle-top card case, Nathaniel Mills, Birmingham, with a view of St Paul's Cathedral in relief, flanked by scrolling foliage, vacant cartouche to reverse.

1843   *3.5in (9cm) long*
£1,200-1,800   **WW**

A Victorian silver card case, Samson Mordan & Co, London, engraved with boats by a seaside town, the reverse with sailing boats passing a country house, within scrolling foliate background, with vacant shield-shape cartouche.

1844   *4in (10cm) high*
£700-1,000   **SWO**

A Victorian silver-gilt castle-top card case, Nathaniel Mills, Birmingham, depicting a view of Warwick Castle in high relief, flanked by chased scrolls.

1845   *3.5in (9cm) high 2oz*
£700-1,000   **WW**

A Victorian silver castle-top card case, Nathaniel Mills, Birmingham, with a landscape view of the Crystal Palace, bordered by foliate scroll decoration, the reverse with vacant cartouche.

1850   *4in (10cm) high 2.3oz*
£1,500-2,500   **WW**

A Victorian silver castle-top card case, by David Pettifer, Birmingham, embossed with a scene of Windsor Castle, with foliate scroll decoration on matted background, the reverse initialled.

1853   *4in (10cm) long 2.8oz*
£700-900   **WW**

A rare Victorian silver castle-top card case, Aston and Son, Birmingham, embossed with a view of Queens College, Cork, in high relief, flanked by chased scrolls, the reverse cartouche inscribed "Midy".

1859   *4in (10cm) high 2.25oz*
£1,500-2,500   **WW**

A tortoiseshell eglomisé and mother-of-pearl card case, depicting Robert Mills' original design for the Washington Monument, a spray of mother-of-pearl flowers to verso.

The Mills design of 1836 was modified and the Washington Monument completed in 1886.

c1840   3.75in (9.5cm) high

£200-300   FRE

A Chinese export carved ivory card case, depicting Napoleon's house and tomb, both with integral basal title plaques.

c1850   4in (10cm) high

£500-700   TEN

A Victorian mother-of-pearl and abalone card case, the hinged cover with an applied vacant plaque.

4.25in (11cm) high

£200-300   WW

A mid-19thC Chinese Canton ivory card case, carved in high relief to the front with peonies and chrysanthemums on a key-work ground, the reverse with figures amongst pavilions.

4.5in (11.5cm) high

£2,000-3,000   DN

A tartanware visiting card case, in Stuart tartan, depicting a seated couple, with lift-off cover.

Tartanware was made primarily by the Mauchlineware manufacturer J. & J. Smith from the early 19thC. As Scotland became a fashionable holiday destination from the 1850s, demand for this souvenir ware boomed.

4in (10cm)

£100-150   AH

CLOSER LOOK - CARVED IVORY CARD CASE

The case has many important auspicious symbols. The dragon is a symbol of male vigour and fertility, as well as the Emperor. The phoenix is commonly seen alongside a dragon, symbolising the Empress.

It is meticulously carved, with exceptional three-dimensional village scenes.

The figures are animated and expressive, showing the work of a highly skilled carver.

The bat is one of the symbols for good luck. Often five bats are shown, representing the Five Blessings: a long life, riches, health, love of virtue and a natural death.

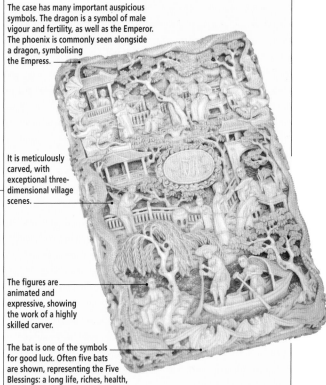

A Chinese late Qing dynasty carved ivory card case, both sides carved with a village scene, with the eight immortals to the sides, the corners with dragons, bats and phoenix, carved monogram to centre.

4.25in (11cm) high

£5,000-7,000   FRE

A late 19thC Chinese export wood card case, carved with figures in a courtyard amid pine and willow trees.

4.25in (11cm) high

£350-450   IMC

A late 19thC Japanese Shibayama ivory, lacquer and inlay card case, decorated with birds, bats and insects.

4.75in (12cm) high

£2,000-3,000   FRE

ESSENTIAL REFERENCE - SNUFF

Snuff has been known in Europe since the 16thC, when it is recorded that Catherine de Medici's headaches were cured with powdered tobacco. It became common in Britain in the early 18thC after large quantities were seized from captured Spanish ships.

- Small gold and silver snuff boxes, engraved, studded with precious stones, or decorated with Staffordshire enamels, were made, as were carved treen (wood) examples.
- Large snuff mulls were designed to stand on a table for communal use.

A French rectangular gold snuff box, maker's mark "CIP", Paris, with machine-engraved ground bordered by chased floral scrolls on a matted ground.

c1840   *3in (7.5cm) wide 4.2oz*

£3,500-4,500   **TEN**

A George I gold snuffbox, chased and engraved with a dog chasing wildfowl within a scroll-bordered frame flanked by strapwork, the base with narrow border worked with similar hunting scenes.

c1720   *2.75in (7cm) long 2.83oz*

£5,000-7,000   **TEN**

A French gold and enamel snuffbox, with central scroll-edged enamel panel depicting a pastoral scene within a frame of engraved and chased scrolls against blue enamel, cushion-moulded borders, engraved "750".

c1900   *3.25in (8.5cm) wide 3.4oz*

£2,000-3,000   **TEN**

A Queen Anne Britannia silver oval tobacco box, William Fleming, London, with reeded borders, the cover engraved with an armorial and crest within a foliate scroll cartouche.

1707   *4in (10cm) long 12oz*

£8,000-12,000   **WW**

A Louis XV silver and enamel snuffbox, with gilt interior, Paris, with green enamelled Rococo decoration.

c1770   *2.5in (6.5cm) 3.25oz*

£2,000-3,000   **DOR**

A George IV Irish silver-gilt table snuff box, chased with repeating floral and foliate patterns with shamrock to cover, with inset panel of petrified wood, the interior with hinged compartment and engraved coat of arms, with maker's name "GARDNER", losses.

1825   *3.25in (8.5cm) long 7oz*

£3,000-4,000   **WW**

A Victorian silver snuff box, Alfred Taylor, Birmingham, engraved with a view of St Botolph's Church, Boston.

1856   *2.75in (7cm) long 2.5oz*

£1,200-1,800   **TEN**

A mid-18thC French gold and enamelled table snuff box, maker's mark "EC " below a crowned fleur de lys, with "jewelled" borders, foliate decoration and oval portrait medallions with wreath borders, on blue enamelled ground.

2.5in (6.5cm) wide

£6,000-8,000   **GORL**

A Bilston enamel rectangular snuff box, decorated with a young man flying a kite to amuse his female companion, the sides with panels of flowers, some restoration.

c1780   *2.75in (7cm) wide*

£400-600   **WW**

A late 18thC French gold mounted tortoiseshell snuff box, maker's mark "P.G.", the mounts with chased foliate decoration, with an oval plaque painted with two young ladies.

3.25in (8.5cm) wide

£2,500-3,500   **WW**

An early 19thC tortoiseshell and horn circular snuff box, the cover and base with inset gouache views of Vesuvius erupting during the day and night, with gilt metal borders.

3.25in (8.5cm) diam

£1,500-2,500   **WW**

A mother-of-pearl, tortoiseshell and piqué work snuff box, J.R. Pearce, London, the tortoiseshell panels with gilt and silver trailing foliage, the cover with applied plaque engraved with a lion crest, with foil-lined interior and stained bone spoon.

2.25in (5.5cm) wide

£2,500-3,500   **WW**

ESSENTIAL REFERENCE - STOBWASSER

The German japanner Johann Heinrich Stobwasser (1740–1829) founded his factory in Brunswick in 1763. A subsidiary factory in Berlin was run by his brother-in-law Jean Guérin from 1772.

- The company is notable for producing intricately and finely painted papier-mâché snuff boxes.
- These were often decorated with mythological scenes after Old Masters, as well as portraits, landscapes, and sentimental scenes.
- Boxes nearly always bore the Stobwasser name, which was later combined with those who carried on the business into the mid-19thC.
- Some larger objects, such as commodes, were also produced.
- The company closed after World War I.

A 19thC papier mâché snuff box, painted with a scene of party guests fleeing a ghostly apparition, with gilt lacquered interior.

4in (10cm) diam

£400-600   **H&L**

A 19thC German Stobwasser lacquer snuff box, painted with "Cheval effragant L'apres Vernet", depicting a gentleman with a white horse, the base inscribed in red script "Stobwasser Fabrik....5825".

4in (10cm) diam

£1,200-1,800   **TOV**

A German Stobwasser papier-mâché snuff box, with a portrait of Maria Stuart, titled in red script to the underside of the cover, with indistinct maker's mark and "15118" to base interior.

c1870   *4in (10cm) diam*

£700-1,000   **TOV**

OBJETS DE VERTU

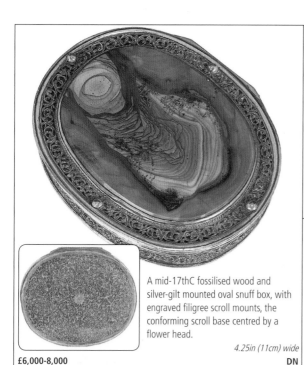

A mid-17thC fossilised wood and silver-gilt mounted oval snuff box, with engraved filigree scroll mounts, the conforming scroll base centred by a flower head.

4.25in (11cm) wide

£6,000-8,000   DN

A mid-18thC gilt-metal mounted Meissen porcelain snuff box, decorated with *fête champêtre* vignettes, on a moulded geometric ground.

3.25in (8.5cm) wide

£1,500-2,500   GORL

An 18thC French silver-mounted St Cloud porcelain snuff box, modelled as a shoe, with hinged lid and decorated with floral sprays.

4in (10cm) long

£1,000-1,500   GORL

A mid-late 18thC German agate snuffbox, Berlin, mounted with silver.

3in (7.5cm) wide

£2,500-3,500   DOR

A late 18th century ivory and ebony banded baluster snuff mull, with wooden base, with applied plaque engraved with initials, with ivory snuff spoon with turned handle and simple pierced bowl.

2.75in (7cm) high

£1,500-2,500   L&T

A George III ivory and gold mounted navette-form snuff box, the cover with bright-cut gold borders around an *en grisaille* miniature of two Classical figures.

c1800   *4in (10cm) long*

£400-600   TEN

A George III stained ivory tobacco box, inscribed "A Token of Respect from Josh. Septs. Ovenden, to Mr. Philp. Ovenden, 1st Jan 1812".

1812   *3.5in (9cm) diam*

£450-550   GORL

An early 19thC Chinese carved tortoiseshell snuff box, decorated with figures and pavilions, a florette band and a diaper base, the inside cover later inset with a portrait of British frigate.

3.75in (9.5cm) wide

£350-450   DN

A George III satin birch snuff box, the lid decorated with a printed scene of an interior, the sides and base with penwork detailing.

5in (12.5cm) wide

£500-700   **GORL**

A late 18thC French carved coquilla nut snuff box, modelled as an animal and decorated on each side with two figures and flowers.

The coquilla nut is the thick-shelled seed of a Brazilian feather-leaved palm, which can be polished and used for decorative carving or turning.

3.75in (9.5cm) long

£200-300   **GORL**

An 18thC French carved coquilla nut snuff box, decorated in high relief with figures, flowers and foliage.

3.5in (9cm) long

£150-250   **GORL**

An 18thC carved treen snuff box, modelled as a monkey's head, with applied bead eyes and bone teeth, with a hinged cover.

2in (5cm) long

£250-350   **WW**

An early 19thC French snuff box, with printed design possibly to commemorate the Treaty of Luneville in 1801.

3.25in (8.5cm)

£200-300   **GORL**

An early 19thC French pollard elm snuff box, with tortoiseshell lining, carved with a scene of Napoleon's army retreating across the Elster.

3.25in (8.5cm)

£250-350   **GORL**

An early 19thC burr birch snuff box, inset with a portrait miniature of a lady, with a gilt metal border, to a tortoiseshell-lined interior.

3.25in (8.5cm) diam

£350-450   **WW**

A Victorian Scottish treen snuff box, the integral hinged cover painted with a fisherman, on a diaper body, the interior with traces of foil.

3.25in (8cm) wide

£250-300   **WW**

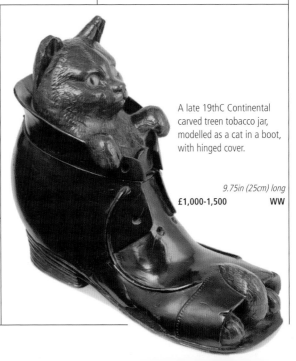

A late 19thC Continental carved treen tobacco jar, modelled as a cat in a boot, with hinged cover.

9.75in (25cm) long

£1,000-1,500   **WW**

CLOSER LOOK - TREEN GOBLET

The exquisitely chased silver mounts have royal provenance, and are headed by the crown finial.

This is a rare and important silver-mounted English treen lidded goblet.

The treen cup has a deep patina.

The condition is excellent for its age.

A large early 17thC lidded silver-mounted treen goblet, maker's mark "IR", with crown finial, the interior engraved with the coat of arms of King Charles I, "Regi et Patriae Fidelis Anno Domini 1625", and "The gift of Richard Hawkins of Marcham in Berkshire Esquire".

21in (53cm) high

£8,000-12,000 DOR

A George I silver mounted lignum vitae quaich, of segmental construction, with cane banding and inset Queen Anne coin base.

6in (15cm) diam

£450-550 GORL

A late 18thC Pennsylvania maple treen sugar bowl.

With a plaque inscribed "Made by Cornelius Weygandt 1713-1799 Bequeathed by his Great gr. gr. grand daughter Mrs. Sallie E. Weygandt Garnier January 31 1896 to his Great gr. gr. grandson Ethan Allan Weaver".

6.5in (16cm) high

£450-550 POOK

An 18thC turned shallow treen salt, with a waisted foot.

4in (10cm) diam

£400-500 WW

An 18thC turned treen salt, with an everted rim, on a waisted stem foot.

3.75in (9.5cm) diam

£400-500 WW

An 18thC turned lignum vitae pounce pot, with a threaded and pierced top.

The wood lignum vitae is extremely strong, tough and dense. As well as these small treen objects, it is typically used for cricket balls and lawn bowls, croquet mallets and British police truncheons.

4in (10cm) high

£400-500 WW

A late 18thC lignum vitae mortar and pestle, with ring-turned decoration.

Mortar 9in (23cm) long

£2,000-3,000 SWO

An early 19thC lignum vitae treen cup and cover with reeded banding.

9in (23cm) high

£250-350 WW

An early 19thC turned lignum vitae goblet, with moulded rim and knopped stem, on a welled spreading foot, damages.

4.5in (11.5cm) high

£200-300 WW

An early 19thC New York State burl ash bowl.

10.5in (27cm) diam

£500-700 POOK

An early 18thC carved treen pipe tamper, modelled as a griffin holding a shield, on an inverted stepped plinth.

4.5in (11.5cm) high

£400-500   WW

An 18thC carved treen pipe tamper, with a seated fox surmount.

4.25in (11cm) high

£180-220   WW

An 18thC carved treen pipe tamper, with a squirrel surmount sitting on a lift-up cage containing two chickens.

4.25in (11cm) high

£200-300   WW

An early 19thC carved oak pipe tamper, modelled as a clenched fist with oak bough to the terminal.

2.25in (5.5cm) long

£400-600   WW

A 19thC ivory miniature globe, in a lignum vitae case with domed lid, the etched ivory ball marked with the continents and major seas.

4in (10cm) high

£1,000-1,500   FRE

A mid 19thC Newton's terrestrial globe, in treen acorn case, the globe rotating on axis pins within the cup of the acorn.

Globe 2.25in (5.5cm) diam

£2,000-3,000   CHEF

An early 19thC Welsh carved fruitwood love spoon, the handle with chip carved decoration and pierced cross, wheel and heart motifs.

12.5in (32cm) high

£800-1,200   WW

A 19thC Welsh treen double love spoon, the handle with chip-carved decoration, mirror and pierced decoration.

14.5in (37cm) long

£800-1,200   WW

A late 18thC French carved boxwood scent bottle and stopper, decorated with two male busts, birds and foliage.

4.5in (11.5cm) long

£400-600   GORL

A 19th Century novelty treen inkwell, in the form of a boot, with rising cover.

6.75in (17cm) long

£150-250   A&H

A mid 17thC turned lignum vitae pill box and cover.

£600-800   **WW**

CLOSER LOOK - TREEN AUTOMATON

This is a particularly complex and rare automaton, showing 22 different activities.

All actions are driven by wood gears and pulleys.

Folk art is highly sought after.

Although quite a late example, and not by a known carver, the complexity adds to the desirability.

A late 19thC carved wood folk art automaton, with five tiers.

64in (162.5cm) wide

£6,000-8,000   **POOK**

An 18thC treen straw splitter, with inset brass cutters, stamped "J. AUSTIN", on a faceted base.

The straw splitter was invented in the late 17thC. It was used to cut straw into a number of different pieces, which could then be braided, flattened and sold to straw-hat manufacturers.

4.25in (11cm) long

£200-300   **WW**

A late 18thC turned sycamore muffineer, with a threaded pierced cover.

5.75in (14.5cm) high

£200-300   **WW**

A George III turned lignum vitae coffee grinder, with an iron and turned-wood crank handle, repairs.

11in (28cm) high

£1,000-1,500   **WW**

A Regency turned lignum vitae door stop, with a brass ring handle.

7.25in (18.5cm) high

£600-800   **WW**

An early 19thC turned lignum pestle.

This pestle comes from the W. J. Shepherd collection, which was sold by Sotheby's in November 1983. This was the most famous sale of treen objects of all time, and in such cases the collection name itself provides additional provenance.

11.5in (29cm) high

£200-300   **WW**

A late 19thC treen lignum vitae miniature cruet, the stand with five turned casters.

4in (10cm) high

£200-300   **LC**

A 19thC Chester, Connecticut, treen inkwell, bearing the label of S. Silliman & Co.

4.25in (11cm) wide

£200-300   **POOK**

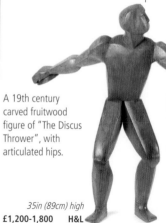

A 19th century carved fruitwood figure of "The Discus Thrower", with articulated hips.

35in (89cm) high

£1,200-1,800   **H&L**

A Victorian silver vesta case, Sampson Mordan & Co, London, enamelled with a mounted lifeguard, the reverse monogrammed, with suspensory ring.

1890   2.25in (5.5cm) long 1oz

£2,500-3,500   WW

A Victorian silver vesta case, Sampson Mordan & Co, London, enamelled with the changing of the guard.

Sampson Mordan & Co. were known for high-quality small silver and gold objects, particularly propelling pencils. Vesta cases by the company are sought-after, particularly in novelty shapes or enamelled with motifs. The sentry box shaped vesta case (see right) is more commonly found. This more detailed example is very rare.

1891   1.75in (4.5cm) long 1.5oz

£3,000-4,000   WW

A Victorian Coldstream Guard enamelled vesta case, Sampson Mordan & Co, with arched enamelled depiction of a guard full length, verso inscribed "The Sergeant Major from HG 1898", registered number "38283" stamped to cover, engraved with retailer's name.

Sold with photocopies of photographs of the Sergeant Major: Sergeant Major Alfred Best (later promoted) born Yorkshire 1865. He fought in the Boer War where he won the Distinguished Conduct Medal.

1895   2.5in (6.5cm) high

£2,000-3,000   TEN

A gold cigarette case and matching vesta case, Cartier, London, 1932, with linear decoration, the thumbpieces set with eight cut diamonds, each signed "Cartier London", with Cartier gold-mounted black leather notebook, and gold fluted pencil.

Cigarette case 3in (7.5cm) 4oz

£1,500-2,500   DN

A silver cigarette case, presented by Ayn Rand to her lover Nathaniel Branden, the lid engraved reproducing in outline the jacket design for "Who is Ayn Rand" by Nathaniel and Barbar Branden, the interior of the lid engraved "June 18, 1962", hallmarked 220.

The relationship between the philosopher and author, Ayn Rand and her much younger acolyte, Nathaniel Branden, was to cause a major scandal among Rand's followers. Beginning as an eager fan writing fan mail to the author, Branden eventually joined her inner circle and what began as an intense intellectual relationship progressed to a physical one. The affair was kept secret from most of Rand's close followers, but had to be endured by both Rand's husband and Branden's wife, both of whom the lovers told of their ongoing liaison. Branden's honesty didn't extend to his next affair, in which he was effectively cheating on both Rand and his wife. When this came to light, it caused an irreparable break with Rand, who went from holding Branden as the living ideal of her philosophies, her "perfect man", to equally intense vilification of him. "June 18, 1962" is likely the publication date of Branden's book or the party held in celebration shortly afterwards. This is a unique and very personal Rand artefact demonstrating the tangled web of the Brandens and the philosopher.

3.75in (9.5cm) high

£8,000-12,000   BLNY

A Victorian silver vesta case, London, with later soft-enamelled panel of a terrier, maker's marks rubbed.

1886   2.25in (5.5cm)

£200-300   GORL

An unusual Edwardian silver and enamel vesta case, maker's mark "W.H.S.", Birmingham, with an oval enamel panel depicting a golfer.

1905   1.75in (4.5cm) high

£1,500-2,500   A&G

A German Art Deco nickel-plated smoker's compendium, in the form of a stylised aeroplane with detachable wing cigarette cases, cigar cutter prop, vesta holder turret, undercarriage pipe rest, lift-out cockpit ashtrays and a hinged cover on the fuselage for cigars, with gilt interior.

Provenance: Property of James William Dell (c1880-1968), who served with the British National Antarctic Expedition as able seaman on board "Discovery" 1901-1904 lead by Robert Falcon Scott, and as boatswain and electrician on board "Quest" on the Shackleton-Rowett Antarctic Expedition 1921-22, lead by Sir Ernest Henry Shackleton.

1925-30   9.5in (24cm) long

£1,000-1,500   LC

A George III provincial silver inkstand, Robert Cattle and James Barber, York, on paw feet with shell and gadroon borders, with two mounted cut-glass cylindrical bottles and a Georgian silver-mounted cut-glass rectangular box.

1812   *10in (25.5cm) wide 17oz*

£1,500-2,500   SWO

A Louis Philippe gilt, patinated-bronze and marmo Siena-mounted desk set, comprising inkstand with urn-shaped well and hinged lid, a pair of candlesticks en suite and a letter clip, all with engine-milled decoration and Vitruvian scroll banding.

c1835   *Ink stand 4.5in (11.5cm) high*

£500-700   DN

A 19thC probably Italian rouge marble inkstand, with an oval depression flanked by metal inkwell and pounce pot, and carved below with a shell dish, on three bun feet.

10in (25.5cm) wide

£1,000-1,500   L&T

ESSENTIAL REFERENCE - THE GRAND TOUR

The Grand Tour was a journey around the major cities of Europe undertaken by wealthy ladies and gentlemen to complete their education in the Arts. The ultimate goal was Italy, regarded as the centre of art, architecture and learning.

- The concept developed in the late 16thC/early 17thC, but was most popular in the 18thC, between the excavations of Herculaneum (1738) and Pompeii (1748), and the Napoleonic Wars (1803-1815).
- Collecting art and antiquities became one of the main functions of the Tour. Back home these collections had a powerful impact on the development of Classically inspired architecture and design. The Palladian style evolved in the early 18thC, and the lighter Neo-classical style was popular in the late 18thC.

RIGHT: A late 19thC Grand Tour gilt bronze and Siena marble inkstand, the campana-shaped well with three compartments and satyr-mask handles, on a rectangular marble base with pen well.

9in (23cm) wide

£350-450   L&T

LEFT: A 19thC Grand Tour marble inkstand, set with portrait cameos, the interior with three gilt-edged glass inkpots and three quill holders.

6in (15cm) diam

£1,000-1,500   ROS

A late 19thC Louis XV-style patinated metal and ormolu inkstand, after Georges Van De Voords, the seated putto beside a flaming torch above C-scroll base with two lidded inkpots, signed "Van de Voords" and stamped "484 BB".

16in (40.5cm) long

£1,000-1,500   FRE

A Victorian Treasury silver inkstand, Elkington & Co, London, with double hinged compartments, one with twin inkwells, the other for pens, with two hinged scroll handles, on squat bun feet.

1899   *10in (25.5cm) wide 68oz*

£1,000-1,500   L&T

A silver inkstand, Carrington & Co., London, with hinged compartments, two with glass ink pots, on bracket feet, with ring handles to sides.

8.25in (21cm) long 42oz

£1,200-1,800   FRE

An 18thC Battersea enamel sewing case, decorated with panels of courting couples, landscapes and flower sprays, on a white gilt jewelled ground, containing sewing implements including a thimble, pencil, scissors and tweezers, damages.

3in (7.5cm)

£600-800   WW

A South Staffordshire enamel étui, painted with scenes of courting couples within Rococo panels of raised enamel, containing various sewing implements including scissors, pencil and bodkin.

c1780   *4in (10cm) high*

£1,800-2,200   WW

A rare English enamel box/ bonbonnière, formed as a large pink rose, with metal-mounted hinged cover.

c1760-70   *1.75in (4.5cm)*

£2,000-3,000   WW

A late 18thC enamel egg-shaped box and cover, decorated with flower sprays and raised foliate sprigs on a pale yellow ground, some restoration.

2in (5cm) long

£400-600   WW

A pair of 19thC French silver enamelled urns, decorated with scenes of courting couples to one side, verso with trophies representing the Arts on a cobalt ground with further gilt decoration.

7.75in (19.5cm) high

£2,500-3,500   LHA

A 19thC Viennese enamel tureen, the cover and foot with reserves after Woewerman against a floral ground, the cobalt body enamelled with floral garlands and mounted with scroll handles, with gilt portrait finial.

11in (28cm) wide

£3,500-4,500   FRE

A late 19thC French "Japonisme" ormolu and cloisonné enamel inkstand, F. Barbedienne, decorated with arabesques in reds, greens and browns, "F. Barbedienne" foundry mark to lid rim.

6.25in (15.5cm) high

£1,200-1,800   FRE

A late 19thC/early 20thC Austro-Hungarian enamelled bell pull, with swing handle and push-piece, in translucent mauve with bands of white guilloche enamel, gold leaf foliate swags and laurel bands.

3in (7.5cm) high

£700-900   SWO

A late 19thC Continental enamelled gilt-metal jewellery box, with ecru and gilt foliate C-scrolls on an olive green enamel ground, with a berried finial, the ropework rim opening to silk-lined interior, on ball feet.

8in (20cm) long

£1,000-1,500   FRE

OBJETS DE VERTU

CLOSER LOOK - SILVER-MOUNTED IVORY MORTAR

This is an extremely rare and early silver-mounted ivory mortar. The mortar dates from 1480-1550.

Turned ivory objects, though mentioned in Tudor inventories, are rare survivals seldom found outside the Royal household.

In size, though not in splendour, the only other extant example is the Howard Grace Cup mounted in 1525 (and earlier) now in the collections of the Victoria & Albert Museum in London.

The fine quality of this piece is shown in the three cast-shell silver feet rising to a circular ring mount chased with fruit amidst strapwork between raised indented borders beneath a stylised acanthus rim.

An Elizabeth I silver-mounted turned ivory mortar, maker's mark "EE" struck four times, London, the mortar probably South German.

Silver c1570-1600   *5in (12.5cm) high*

£6,000-8,000   TEN

A pair of Austrian ivory portrait busts of Kaiser Leopold I and Empress Eleonore Magdalena, with metal mounts and verso with gilded straps, on later wooden socles.

c1700   *6.5in (16.5cm) high*

£8,000-12,000   DOR

A 17thC/18thC Indian carved ivory figure of a lion, probably Mughal, on a rectangular plinth supported on short columns over a second plinth with traces of original gilt scrollwork, on ball feet.

6.75in (17cm) long

£4,000-6,000   FRE

A 17thC and later German Baroque bone and ivory table cabinet, probably Augsburg, carved with shells, scrolls, fruiting garlands and Classical figures, with cupboards, drawers, and a hidden column of further drawers, on ball feet.

20in (51cm) high

£25,000-30,000   FRE

An 18thC French carved ivory snuff rasp, with a shell terminal above a figure of Diana, with an iron rasp and a screw hinge to the back panel decorated with a lady holding a lamp above Cupid, damages.

7.5in (19cm) high

£1,200-1,800   WW

A pair of early 19thC South Indian carved ivory figures of Shiva and Parvati, wearing elaborately folded dhotis.

Shiva 9in (23cm) high

£1,500-2,500   SWO

An early 19thC possibly French carved ivory bodkin case and cover, decorated with cartouches depicting figures in rustic settings, within scroll borders.

6in (15cm) long

£800-1,200   H&L

One of a rare pair of 19thC French ivory mirrors, Dieppe, embellished with heraldic shields, standing lions, cherubs with musical instruments and eagles on a background of leaves and flowers, the central shield marked "Montjoye St. Denys".

c1820-1830   *33in (85cm) high*

£8,000-12,000 pair   **DS**

A 19thC carved ivory triptych panel, carved in relief with an Egyptian scene in a palace, highlighted in colours, and framed within shaped arched panels.

8in (20cm) high

£800-1,200   **ROS**

A 19thC European carved ivory cup-on-stand, carved with Classical female figures on the backs of mythical beasts, the turned column with foliate, beaded and bulbous decoration to a foliate-banded circular base.

5in (12.5cm) high

£1,000-1,500   **ROS**

A mid-19thC American mahogany and whalebone yarn swift sewing stand, the turned ivory yarn-holder and axis spoke with red and black sealing wax, expanding panbone slats, the lower shaft with brass thread holders topped with ivory finials, mounted on a mahogany case.

24.5in (62.5cm) high

£9,000-11,000   **SK**

A French carved ivory casket, Dieppe, the side panels depicting different mythological scenes, including Jupiter and Europa, within acanthus leaf and strapwork spandrels with scroll-and-shell-carved arched hinged handle, on acanthus leaf and paw feet.

c1850   *7.25in (18.5cm) wide*

£4,000-6,000   **TEN**

A 19thC Continental finely carved Rococo-style ivory cheval mirror, the bevelled oval plate within a conforming frame surmounted with a torch and quiver crest, surrounded by three cherubs on a naturalistic, floral base.

8.25in (21cm) wide

£8,000-10,000   **LHA**

A German Historicism period silver-gilt-mounted ivory tankard, carved with putti playing music, the base and hinged lid with mask and grape decoration, the handle with a female half-figure, with apocryphal hallmark.

c1870   *9in (23cm) high*

£12,000-15,000   **DOR**

A late 19thC German ivory and silver-mounted tankard, the lid carved as man with centaurs, the handle with a winged female bust, the body carved with a continuous Bacchanalian scene, the silver with repoussé satyr masks on scrolling foliate ground, with crescent and crown marks.

15.5in (39cm) high

£15,000-20,000   **LHA**

ESSENTIAL REFERENCE - DIEPPE

Ivory has been carved in the French costal town of Dieppe since the early Renaissance period.

- During the early 19thC much ivory was imported from the French Territories in Africa to Dieppe.
- Most of the items that were made at Dieppe were small, such as brush handles or the hinged figures on this page. These were primarily made for the tourist trade.
- Very occasionally a wealthy client would commission a major work, such as the mirrors on p383.
- Dieppe ivory is almost never signed.
- The nearby Château Musée opened in 1906. Much of its collection is dedicated to ivory carvings.

A 19thC Dieppe carved and paste-set ivory triptych figure of a young Norman queen, possibly Eleanor of Aquitaine, opening to reveal revellers in garden setting.

8in (20cm) high

£3,000-4,000   RTC

A mid 19thC French carved ivory triptych figure of Elizabeth I, possibly Dieppe, opening to reveal three scenes of Elizabeth signing the order of judgment against Mary Queen of Scots, inscribed "a reine Elizabeth signe le jugement a mort de Marie Stuart".

3.25in (8.5cm) high

£1,000-1,500   FRE

A carved ivory pedestal bust of Oliver Cromwell, by Matthew Noble, on a concave-sided rectangular plinth inscribed "Cromwell born 23 April 1599 died 3 Sep 1659", signed and dated.

Renowned Victorian sculptor Matthew Noble (1818-1876) exhibited regularly at the Royal Academy from 1845 until his death in 1876. His works in London include statues of Peel and Derby in Parliament Square, Franklin in Waterloo Place, and monuments in Westminster Abbey and St Paul's Cathedral. Some of his pieces were reproduced as parian ware by Copeland (see p19).

1860   *5in (12cm) high*

£2,000-3,000   TEN

A mid-late 19thC German carved ivory, silver and rock crystal figure of a flower seller, probably Hanau, on tapered silver-gilt stem over ovoid rock crystal base mounted with silver-gilt flower swags, on four ball feet.

9in (23cm) high

£4,500-5,500   SK

A mid-late 19thC ivory statuette of Ludwig XIV.

8in (20cm) high

£6,000-8,000   DOR

A late 19thC European carved ivory group of a shepherd and shepherdess playing around a dovecote, on an ebonised plinth below a glass dome.

Ivory 5in (12.5cm) high

£1,200-1,800   SWO

A 17thC English School oil-on-copper portrait miniature of a lady, with indistinct inscription in gilt "AETATE SUI....AO 20....159..".

2.5in (6.5cm) diam

£10,000-12,000   **SWO**

A 17thC Flemish School oil-on-copper portrait miniature of a man, said to be the artist Annibale Carracci, inscribed verso, in 19thC engraved gilt-metal mount.

Image 1.75in (4.5cm) wide

£2,500-3,500   **SWO**

A 17thC oil-on-copper portrait miniature of a man, said to be the artist Nicholas Poussin, of the circle of Gonzalez Coques (Flemish, 1618-1684), inscribed verso, in 19thC engraved gilt-metal mount.

Image 2in (5cm) wide

£4,500-5,500   **SWO**

An English School portrait miniature of a gentleman, initialled "JS 1766", in gilt-metal leaf-edged frame with plaited hair locket to the reverse.

1.25in (3.5cm) wide

£2,500-3,500   **TEN**

A watercolour-on-ivory portrait miniature of Benjamin Franklin, attributed to Daniel Nikolaus Chodowiecki, (German, 1726-1801), in gilt frame.

4in (10cm) high

£2,500-3,500   **FRE**

A watercolour-on-ivory portrait miniature of a young woman, by Thomas Hazlehurst (British, 1740-1821), initialled lower left.

3.5in (9cm) high

£1,000-1,500   **POOK**

A portrait miniature of a lady, attributed to George Engleheart (1752-1829), initialled "E", the reverse with seed-pearl-trimmed hair locket within a guilloche enamel machine-turned blue glass-covered border, in gold metal frame.

c1790   *3.25in (8.5cm) high*

£2,500-3,500   **TEN**

A portrait miniature of a gentleman, attributed to Charles Shirreff (b.1750), in gold metal closed-back frame with vase-form suspension loop.

c1790   *2.5in (6.5cm) high*

£700-1,000   **TEN**

A watercolour-on-ivory miniature memorial, possibly by Samuel Folwell, with figures flanking a tomb, the reverse with braid of hair and engraved: "My Dear I am going to him who gave me to you L.S. Died Feb 14, 1799 Aged 25 yrs".

1799   *1.75in (4.5cm)*

£2,500-3,500   **POOK**

An ivory portrait miniature of Prince Charles Edward Stuart (Bonnie Prince Charlie), after Robert Strange, the prince in full dress with blue sash and order of the garter, with blue Balmoral bonnet and white cockade, in black japanned frame with gilt border and mount.

Sir Robert Strange (1721-92) was an Edinburgh artist and ardent Jacobite.

2.5in (6.5cm) high

£1,800-2,200   **L&T**

OBJETS DE VERTU

One of a pair of French watercolour-and gouache-on-ivory portrait miniatures of Napoleon and Marie Louise, each full figure in presentation dress, in gilt metal frames.

5.25in (13cm) high

£2,000-3,000 pair   **FRE**

An enamelled copper portrait miniature of George Washington, by William Russell Birch after Gilbert Stuart, signed, in an oval gilt-brass bezel.

William Birch was born in Warwickshire, England, in 1755. He learned the basics of enamelling as an apprentice to a London goldsmith, and later introduced the technique to America following his emigration in 1794. His most notable enamel portraits were approximately 60 portrait miniatures of George Washington, of which this is one.

£25,000-35,000   **SK**

CLOSER LOOK - MINIATURE OF WASHINGTON

Robert Field was a portrait painter, miniature painter and engraver who enjoyed success in his time, but whose work fell into relative obscurity following his early death aged 40.

He was one of the four most highly sought-after American miniaturists in his time.

Martha Washington commissioned Field in 1800 to paint some miniatures as mementoes for friends and family, to commemorate the General and President on the one-year anniversary of his death.

The lock of Washington's hair makes it irresistible to collectors.

The miniature has exemplary provenance.

A watercolour-on-ivory portrait miniature of George Washington, by Robert Field (c1769-1819), signed and dated, in gilt-brass locket, reverse with a woven lock of Washington's hair overlaid with "GW" cypher in gilt foil.

c1801   *2.75in (7cm) high*

£200,000-300,000   **SK**

An early 19thC English School oil-on-ivory portrait miniature of a gentleman, in gold hair-back frame.

2.75in (7cm) high

£2,000-3,000   **GORL**

An ivory portrait miniature of Lord Henry Stuart Darnley, after Van Loo, inscribed "Vanloo" to lower left-hand edge, in oval gold frame with suspension loop, verso inscribed "Lord Henry Stuart Darnley King of Scotland".

Henry Stuart, 1st Duke of Albany (1545–1565), styled Lord Darnley before 1565, was the first cousin and second husband of Mary, Queen of Scots. He was the father of her son King James VI, who succeeded Queen Elizabeth I as King James I of England.

Image 2.75in (7cm) high

£2,500-3,500   **L&T**

A painted ivory portrait miniature of Mary Queen of Scots, signed "EM", in gilt-metal frame, with gilt tooled-leather display case.

Image 3in (7.5cm) high

£2,000-3,000   **L&T**

A silhouette of a family, by W. Seville, with artist's stamp.

17in (43cm) wide

£700-1,000   **LHA**

A silhouette of a family, with polychrome decoration throughout.

16.5in (42cm) wide

£800-1,200   **LHA**

A French gold and amethyst hand seal, modelled with four stylised satyr heads, on fluted stem with four paw feet, with a plain matrix, marked to base "Kern Paris 607".

3.5in (9cm) high
£1,000-1,500   **WW**

A George II gold and hardstone fob seal in the form of Aphrodite, with diamond-studded collar, the fluted base inset with a carnelian carved as a woman's head.

c1750   *1.25in (3.5cm) high*
£800-1,200   **TEN**

A 19thC gold-mounted citrine-coloured glass hand seal, the waisted cylindrical handle with fluted decoration, the mount with foliate decoration, the matrix engraved with an armorial.

2.25in (5.5cm) long
£500-700   **WW**

An Austrian agate bowl, with enamelled silver-gilt mount, by Hermann Böhm, with Vienna greyhound hallmark.

1872-1922   *3in (7.5cm) diam*
£550-650   **DOR**

An Italian micromosaic of a lady in a turban, by Gioacchino Barberi after Dolci or Terbruggen, in fitted Morocco leather case with maker's label to reverse.

c1820-40   *1.75in (4.5cm) high*
£5,000-6,000   **TEN**

A mid-18thC gold-mounted agate needle case, the mounts chased with scrolls and flowering foliage, champlêve enamelled in white with "L'amitie vous l'ofere" over bright orange agate.

c1765   *3.25in (8.5cm) long*
£1,200-1,800   **DN**

A George III gold-mounted agate nécessaire, the gold cagework mounts chased with rocaille, foliage, scroll and bird motifs, with white enamelled band with the gold inscription "Rien Nest Trop Bon Pour Ce Qu'on Aime", with garnet-set thumbpiece.

2.25in (5.5cm) high
£4,500-5,500   **TOV**

A George III papier-mâché boat-form double coaster, decorated with gilt grapevines.

c1800   *15.5in (39cm) long*
£550-650   **LHA**

A Swiss silver-gilt and enamelled singing bird box, the hinged lid painted with an Alpine landscape, the box with floral ornamental enamelling, bird with polychrome plumage.

c1880   *3.5in (9cm) wide*
£6,000-8,000   **DOR**

A Swiss silver and enamelled singing bird box, London import marks for H.C.F. Ltd, London, painted with Watteauesque lovers, with chevron engine-turned guilloche blue enamel canted angles, on in-swept short feet.

1928   *41in (105cm) wide*
£9,000-11,000   **TEN**

OBJETS DE VERTU

A Russian silver, enamel and cabochon-inlaid kovsch, Cyrillic, with mark "I Ch".

c1891   *8in (20cm) diam 14oz*
£3,000-5,000   **POOK**

A Russian silver-gilt and enamelled kovsch, maker's mark "C. E. Bolin", Moscow, with some cloisonné decoration, some translucent enamel on engraved ground, with Kokoschnik hallmark.

1896-1908   *6.5in (16cm) long 5.2oz*
£6,000-8,000   **DOR**

A Russian silver-gilt and shaded cloisonné enamel kovsch, 6th Artel Moscow, in the form of a cockerel, decorated with scrolling flowerheads on cream and pale-green grounds, the rim with a geometric pattern, rope-twist borders.

1910   *6.5in (16cm) long*
£20,000-30,000   **L&T**

An early 20thC Russian cloisonné and shaded enamel kovsch, maker's mark "HA", decorated with stylised floral panels and turquoise beaded borders, gilt-wash interior, with purity mark "88".

88 refers to 88 zolotniks. The zolotnik was used in Russia as early as the 11thC to denote the weight of gold coin, and later came to represent the purity of silver. 88 zolotniks has the equivalent millesimal fineness of 916 (91.66% pure silver and 8.34% copper or other metal), slightly under that of sterling silver, which has a millesimal fineness of 925.

11.25in (28.5cm) long
£45,000-55,000   **FRE**

A silver-gilt and cloisonné cup and saucer, Nikolaj V. Alekseev, Moscow, with floral ornamental enamelling.

1898-1908   *3in (7.5cm) high 9oz*
£4,000-6,000   **DOR**

A Russian silver and enamel tankard, M. Ovchinnikov.

c1900   *7.5in (19cm) high 33oz*
£3,500-4,500   **POOK**

A Russian silver-gilt and shaded cloisonné enamel tea-glass holder, 6th Artel, Moscow, decorated with a sirin and stylised polychrome foliage on blue, cream and green ground, the foot and handle with scroll and geometric motifs.

1908-1917   *4.25in (11cm) high*
£18,000-22,000   **L&T**

An early 20thC Russian silver and shaded enamel covered chalice, Ivan Khlebnikov, the body decorated with stylised flowers, the foot depicting firebirds and floral panels, with bird finial, with purity mark "88".

15in (38cm) high
£150,000-200,000   **FRE**

A Russian silver and enamel box, Khlebnikov, St Petersburg, with foliate border and ruby-inset thumbpiece, with gilt interior.

1899-1908

£1,200-1,800   TEN

A Russian silver-gilt and shaded cloisonné enamel tea-caddy, Pavel Ovchinnikov, Moscow, the chamfered angles decorated with palm leaves, the sides with floral sprays within stylised palm leaves, the borders with blue geometric decoration, maker's mark and Imperial Warrant.

1908-1917   *3.75in (9.5cm) high*

£15,000-20,000   L&T

A Russian silver-gilt and cloisonné enamel card case, Feodor Rückert, Moscow, decorated with the Queen of Clubs and the Jack of Spades, within stylised formal foliate borders and ropetwist borders, the base engraved "Dec 25th 1901", with scratched number "2415".

c1890   *3.75in (9.5cm) high*

£80,000-120,000   L&T

A Russian silver-gilt and shaded cloisonné enamel bowl, Fedor Rückert, Moscow, with six lobes decorated inside and out with stylised floral sprays alternating with exotic wading birds on pale blue and cream-coloured grounds, the moss-green rim with filigree, the centre enamelled with the Stork and the Fox from Krylov's fable.

1896-1908   *3.75in (9.5cm) diam*

£25,000-30,000   L&T

A Russian silver-gilt and shaded cloisonné enamel tazza, Orest Kurliukov, the bowl decorated with shaped roundels supporting stylised floral scrolls, the central roundel within a border of white and turquoise pellets.

c1890   *10.5in (27cm) wide*

£40,000-60,000   L&T

A pair of Russian silver-gilt and enamel oil and vinegar cruets, maker's mark "ZA", with matching under tray.

c1908-1917   *Cruets 12.5in (32cm) high 35.6oz*

£3,000-4,000   POOK

A Russian silver-gilt and shaded cloisonné tea-set, Fedor Rückert, Kurliukov, Moscow, decorated with falconer, gryphons, and stags within floral scrolls, the teapot and milk jug with the initials of F. Rückert, over-struck with the maker's mark of Orest Kurliukov, the sugar bowl with maker's mark of Orest Kurliukov, with a similar pair of sugar-tongs, maker's mark "P.Sh".

1899-1908   *Teapot 6.5in (16cm) high*

£200,000-250,000   L&T

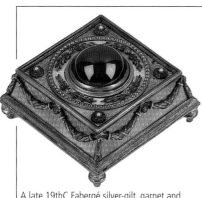

A late 19thC Fabergé silver-gilt, garnet and enamel square bell push, workmaster Michael Perchin, Moscow, with a cabochon garnet push-piece on a white translucent guilloche enamel ground with foliate sprays, the sides with laurel swags and small ruby cabochons on a light green enamel ground.

1.75in (4.5cm) wide

£25,000-30,000   **DN**

A Fabergé gold, jade and diamond cigarette case, workmaster Henrik Wigstrom, with diamond-set release and enamelled band, with original Russian fitted wood case.

1896-1908   *4in (10cm) wide*

£25,000-30,000   **LHA**

A Fabergé emerald crystal, silver, enamel, carnelian, and stone-set seal, workmaster Michael Perchin, St. Petersburg, the pearl-coloured basse taille enamelled base with silver water lilies, set with red stone cabochon and six rose-cut diamond mélée, with carved carnelian seal for G.G. Kuznetsov.

c1890   *2.75in (7cm) long*

£60,000-70,000   **SK**

A Fabergé cloisonné and silver-gilt tea strainer, Moscow.

c1890   6.25in (15.5cm) long 3.7oz

£4,000-6,000   **DOR**

A Fabergé silver-gilt and shaded cloisonné enamel kovsch, Moscow, the rim enamelled with a band of vine scrolls on a stippled ground, the handle with a shaded enamel flower head centred with a cabochon sapphire, marked with Imperial Warrant.

1899-1908   *4in (10cm) long*

£15,000-25,000   **L&T**

A Russian silver-gilt and cloisonné enamel tea caddy, workmaster Fedor Rückert, the sides with birds on blue and brown grounds, the lower border with geometric motifs, the cork stopper with silver-gilt mount applied with a hinged openwork handle, with purity mark "91".

4.75in (12cm) high

£300,000-400,000   **L&T**

A Fabergé gold-mounted yellow guilloche enamel scent bottle, workmaster Michael Perchin, with purity mark "56", with foliate border.

Michael Perchin (1860-1903) was arguably the most important of Fabergé's head workmasters, working from 1886 until 1903. Drawing inspiration from the collection of 18thC French enamelled objects in the Hermitage, Perchin produced pieces in a variety of styles, notably Renaissance, Rococo Revival and Neo-classical.

1.75in (4.5cm) long

£10,000-15,000   **L&T**

A small Fabergé silver-gilt and shaded cloisonné enamel kovsch, workmaster Fedor Rückert, Moscow, enamelled in the Old Russian style in blue, ochre, and grey with stylised elongated handle, with purity mark "88" with Imperial Warrant.

1908-1917   *3.25in (8.5cm) high*

£30,000-40,000   **L&T**

A Fabergé silver-gilt and shaded cloisonné enamel pill box, workmaster Fedor Rückert, Moscow, enamelled with stylised foliage and geometric motifs in muted tones of blue, green and brown.

1908-1917   *2.25in (5.5cm) wide*

£12,000-18,000   **L&T**

A Fabergé silver gem-set kovsch, workmaster Karl Gustav Hjalmar Armfelt, St Petersburg, with everted tab handle and cockerel's head prow, inset with garnet and green cabochon stones amongst hooked strapwork.
c1899-1903   *6in (15cm) high*
£15,000-20,000   **TEN**

A Fabergé silver-mounted standing mirror, workmaster Julius Rappoport, Moscow, the rim with palmettes and beaded trim, decorated with laurel festoons and medallion with bow, with purity mark "88".
1894   *24in (61cm) high*
£50,000-60,000   **DOR**

A Fabergé silver photograph frame, maker's mark "AN", containing a photograph of Queen Alexandra of Britain, the reverse inscribed "Christmas 1904, with purity mark "88", in fitted holly wood box with accompanying paperwork.
c1900   *3.5in (9cm) high*
£8,000-12,000   **FRE**

A set of four Fabergé silver-gilt covered bowls, workmaster Anders Nevalainen, applied with ribbon-tied swags, and acanthus leaves, with ball finials, with Imperial Warrant, and purity mark "88".
c1900   *3in (7.5cm) diam*
£8,000-12,000 set   **L&T**

A Fabergé silver tea and coffee service, work master Alexander Wäkevä, St. Petersburg, with parcel-gilt interior, the pot handles with bone insulation, engraved monogram, purity mark "88".
1908-1917.   *coffee pot 7.25in (18.5cm) high 48oz*
£10,000-15,000   **DOR**

A Fabergé silver swing-handled basket, workmaster Stefan Wäkeva, Moscow, the rim repoussé and chased with a band of cornucopia on a stippled ground.
1908-1917   *8.75in (22cm) long*
£7,000-10,000   **L&T**

A Fabergé silver bowl, Moscow, the centre with Imperial double eagle and inscribed "Krieg 1914", with purity mark "88", company mark "K. Fabergé".
1908-1917   *4.25in (11cm) diam 5.4oz*
£8,000-12,000   **DOR**

A Fabergé silver-mounted sandstone match-holder and striker, workmaster Julius Rappoport, St Petersburg, with a Neo-classical mount, the side with panels of pierced anthemion leaves and scrolls, the apex with a silver-lined match-holder.

Julius Rappoport (1864-1916) trained in Berlin and opened his own workshop in St Petersburg in 1883, quickly becoming one of Fabergé's most important suppliers of silver objects. He often used nature as an inspiration.
c1890   *4.75in (12cm) high*
£12,000-18,000   **L&T**

A Fabergé gold and cornelian revolving seal, workmaster Erik Kollin, St Petersburg, the gold mount in Scythian style with ribbed terminals, the swivelling matrix engraved on one side with an elaborate Russian armorial, the other with an open padlock and the date "20 March 1895".
c1900   *10.000-15.000*

A Fabergé copper and brass glass holder, with overlaid Russian double-eagle and the inscription "War 1914/1915 K. Fabergé".

These base metal objects were made by Fabergé for the benefit of the Russian Fund for War Widows and Orphans. They were sold at the same price as the silver objects and the profit was donated to this fund.
1915   *3.25in (8.5cm) high*
£4,000-5,000   **DOR**

A rare 17thC Russian silver and parcel-gilt bowl, Charka of Semen Bogdanovich Nesterow, the rim with an engraving in Cyrillic.

c1650   6.5in (16cm) long 5.3oz
£25,000-35,000   DOR

A Russian silver and parcel-gilt lidded tankard, maker's mark "Ja. S.", Moscow, the body with three medallions containing portraits of rulers (possibly Tsar Peter II and Tsarina Elisabeth), the hinged lid decorated with engraved scenes.

1741-1749   6in (15cm) high, 20oz
£25,000-35,000   DOR

Four Russian and French silver candlesticks from the service of the Tsarina Catherine II, two Robert-Joseph Auguste, Paris, one Johan Henrik Blom, St. Petersburg, one without hallmark, all with engraved inventory number and with year letter "E".

Catherine the Great commissioned this famous dinner service from the renowned Paris master Robert-Joseph Auguste (1725-1805). It was later added to over the course of the years, with many additions being the work of the renowned St. Petersburg goldsmith Johan Henrik Blom (d.1805).

1768/69   19in (48cm) high 300.8oz
£200,000-300,000   DOR

A Russian silver lidded goblet, Carl Tegelsten, St. Petersburg, set with gemstone cabochons, with gilt interior, hallmark Pawel Dmitrijew.

1851   12in (30.5cm) high 28oz
£8,000-12,000   DOR

A Russian silver hot water jug, Nichols & Plinke, St Petersburg, with semi-gadroon ornament, and scale-edged handle.

c1866-70   11in (28cm) high 38oz
£2,000-3,000   TEN

A rare Russian silver cuspidor, Sazikov, St Petersburg, with engine-turned ground and two cartouches, one engraved with a crossed leaf clasped "P", the other with armorials and crest, glass liner, with Imperial warrant mark.

1871   4.5in (11.5cm) diam 17oz
£1,500-2,500   L&T

A Russian Imperial presentation silver and parcel-gilt punch set, Mikhail Grachev, presented to Rear Admiral Charles Henry Davis, U.S.N., the bowl as a stylised Viking longship with 12 kovsch-shaped punch cups, with a punch ladle with geometric designs.

1905   Bowl 21in (53cm) wide, 235oz
£70,000-100,000   L&T

A Russian Imperial Manufactory porcelain plate, the gilt chevron rim with small, colourful, painted flowering branches and bouquet of flowers, underglaze blue mark from the reign of Tsarina Catherine II.

1762-1796　　　*10in (25.5cm) diam*

£1,200-1,800　　　DOR

A Russian porcelain figure of a young woman, by Francis Gardner, Moscow, on a scroll-moulded base, damages.

8in (20cm) high

£2,000-3,000　　　BE

A late 19thC Russian porcelain egg, decorated with the bust of "Saint Tsarina Helena", the burnished gilt body with matt gilt borders, the reverse with star and aureole.

Helena Drepane (257-336) was the mother of Constantine the Great. Legend attributes the finding of the Holy Cross to her.

4in (10cm) high

£5,000-7,000　　　DOR

A 17thC Russian icon, Ukraine, depicting the protection of the Mother of God, in two registers, painted on a gold ground.

c1686　　　*43in (109cm) high*

£2,000-3,000　　　SWO

A Russian icon, divided into four parts, showing the Entry into Jerusalem, the Transfiguration, the Dormition of the Virgin, and a Bishop saint, within a silver-gilt frame, rizla-engraved and chased with flowers, some over-painting.

c1800　　　*12.5in (32cm) high*

£1,500-2,500　　　TEN

A Russian painted wood and silver gilt oklad icon, Andrej Kowalskij, Moscow, with some enamelling.

1847　　　*12in (30.5cm) high*

£2,000-3,000　　　DOR

An early 19thC Russian bone wedding casket, probably Archangel, with pierced, engraved and lac decoration, with panel dated "1827", the sides with initials, the main body with a divided interior, on disc feet.

1827　　　*10.25in (26cm) wide*

£1,000-1,500　　　WW

An early 19thC Russian nephrite and jasper vase, with applied band of leaves carved from revna jasper, on a spreading foot, damages.

Russian nephrite, a calcium magnesium silicate form of jade, is found in Siberia and mined near Lake Baikal. Revna jasper, a rare grey and green veined jasper, is found in the Ural mountains not far from the Imperial Lapidary workshops in Kolyvan which were established in 1786 and produced decorative items including urns, fireplaces etc for the Imperial court. Nephrite was favoured by the Russian Imperial family at the end of the 19thC.

16.75in (42cm) high

£7,000-10,000　　　WW

A Russian agate figure of a rhinoceros, Avenir I. Soumin, St. Petersburg, with ruby eyes, in original wooden case.

c1900　　　*3.5in (9cm) long*

£12,000-18,000　　　DOR

A George III white statuary marble and marmo Siena inverted-breakfront chimneypiece, with central tablet with relief carved swagged and fluted urn, the ends with urns above Siena marble inset jambs and plinth, alterations.

This style of chimneypiece, designed with fluted decoration inset with marmo Siena, or in other cases marmo Brocatello, was favoured in the late 18thC as more decorative types of marble became readily available.

c1780   *71in (180cm) wide*
£5,000-7,000   **DN**

A large oak reredos, carved with foliage and Gothic designs.

c1890   *140.75in (357.5cm) wide*
£6,000-7,000   **RMAA**

A large 19thC carved oak overmantel, constructed from 17thC elements, with lozenge frieze divided by acanthus-carved corbels, to a coat of arms surmounted by three helmets and beasts, flanked by guilloche-decorated arches with figures.

79in (200cm) wide
£1,800-2,200   **WW**

An Art Nouveau cast iron fireplace, mounted with 16 tiles decorated with irises.

39in (99cm) wide
£500-700   **GORL**

Judith Picks: Christopher Dresser

I think, quite simply, Christopher Dresser's designs were a century ahead of their time and beautifully combine form and function. One of the first independent industrial designers, Dresser (1834-1904) was at the forefront of design reform in 19thC Britain, and embraced modern manufacturing in metalware, furniture, wallpaper, textiles, ceramics and glass. He believed that industrial design would allow ordinary people to have well-made, attractive objects at a reasonable cost.

In 1847 he won a place at the newly established Government School of Design where he specialised in botanical studies. By 1868 he had a number of roles: designer, advisor to manufacturers, author and teacher. His early designs for wallpapers, fabrics and ceramics for manufacturers such as Minton and Wedgwood were inspired by his botanical studies. He was also fascinated by Japanese culture. In 1876 he became the first European designer commissioned to visit Japan, which had reopened its borders in 1854.

Much of Dresser's most influential work was produced from the late 1870s onwards, when he worked for smaller firms which allowed him greater control. He designed silver and electroplate for Hukin & Heath, Birmingham and James Dixon & Sons, Sheffield; brass and copper for Benham & Froud; and "japanned" metal for Richard Perry, Wolverhampton. In 1879 he was appointed Art Director at the Linthorpe pottery, near Middlesbrough. When Linthorpe closed in 1889, its moulds were acquired by a rival, Ault Pottery in Derbyshire, for whom Dresser produced new designs from 1893. He also designed "Clutha" (cloud) art glass for the James Couper, Glasgow, which was sold by Liberty in the 1890s.

Dresser continued to run his studio and produced designs for another 11 years until his death in 1904.

A cast iron fireplace, attributed to Christopher Dresser, with zigzag detailing and stylised-pattern tiles attributed to Minton.

40in (102cm) wide
£2,000-3,000   **DN**

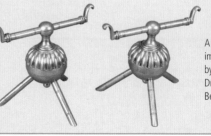

A pair of brass fire implement rests, by Christopher Dresser for Benham & Froud.

7in (18cm) high
£300-500   **DN**

A George II brass, steel and cast iron fire grate, the bow-front basket to flaming finials and shell-capped supports.

26in (66cm) wide

£1,500-2,500   WW

A George III steel and cast iron fire grate, possibly formerly the property of the Duke of Wellington, the arched back above downswept sides and polished serpentine front, surmounted by urn-shaped finials, on tapering forelegs.

Supplied with a letter of provenance from an antiques dealer dated 1966: "As far as I know, the fire grate along with another was purchased from J.A.S.A. Lewis & Son... Both came from secondary rooms at Apsley House, when surplus furniture and fittings were sold before the house was converted to a museum in 1935".

30.5in (77cm) wide

£2,500-3,500   CAPE

A George III brass and cast iron fire grate, the serpentine apron pierced and engraved with scrolling cornucopia, on column supports.

28.5in (72cm) high

£800-1,200   WW

A George III engraved brass and cast iron fire grate.

c1780   *33in (85cm) wide*

£2,500-3,500   DN

A Regency cast iron and steel fire basket, the stepped base with a drawer, and two brass fenders.

20in (51cm) high

£1,000-1,500   WW

A Regency cast iron fire grate, the back detached.

c1815   *36in (91cm) high*

£1,800-2,200   DN

A mid-19thC cast iron and brass-mounted fire grate, in the manner of Richard Bridgens, with arched backplate and bow-fronted, railed basket, the octagonal openwork standards with knopped finials.

40in (102cm) wide

£1,500-2,500   DN

A 19thC George III-style brass and iron fire basket, with bulbous urn-shaped finials standing on fluted column legs with plinth feet.

36in (91.5cm) high

£3,500-4,500   DN

A 19thC brass and iron fire grate, the sides with trellis moulding, the ogee-shaped canopy with foliate scrolls, the raised serpentine bracket with urn finials, on dragon monopodia.

33.5in (86cm) high

£1,000-1,500   AH

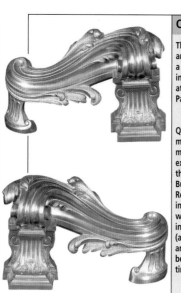

A pair of early 19thC foliate-cast gilt-bronze andirons, with later billet bars.

15.75in (40cm) wide

£300-500   DN

CLOSER LOOK - VICTORIAN CHINOISERIE-STYLE GILT-BRASS DRAGON ANDIRONS

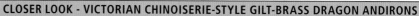

The dragons on these andirons are identical to a pair on a fender now in the Banqueting room at George IV's Royal Pavilion, Brighton.

Queen Victoria had moved some of the more elaborate and exotic fittings from the Pavilion to Buckingham Palace. Replacements, inspired by the originals, were commissioned in 1850. The fender (and potentially these andirons) may have been acquired at this time.

The style and quality suggests William or Mark Feetham as possible makers.

The firm was established in 1805, and became one of the most respected London ironmongers. This was due in part to the design flair of Edward Sayer, who joined as an apprentice in 1821.

A pair of Victorian Chinoiserie-style gilt-brass dragon andirons.

c1850   *19in (48cm) wide*

£10,000-15,000   SOTH

A pair of 20thC brass andirons, in the form of a horse-drawn plough with handler, on stepped rectangular base and splay feet.

12in (30.5cm) long

£100-150   DA&H

A pair of large late 19thC Continental bronze andirons, each with a cherub over a mask flanked by cast satyrs, above a central lion mask flanked by putti and swags, on a shaped base.

40.5in (103cm) high

£2,000-3,000   FRE

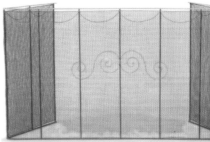

A pair of brass double urn andirons, with chain pattern connectors, on oblong steel bases.

12in (30.5cm) wide

£350-450   A&G

A set of three 19thC polished steel fire irons, with brass finials.

30in (76cm) long

£1,200-1,800   WW

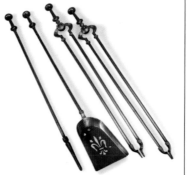

A set of four late Victorian copper fire tools, comprising shovel, poker and two pairs of tongs, the tapering grips all with bun finial.

Shovel 26in (66cm) long

£400-600   DN

A George III brass and wire folding fire screen.

c1790   *54in (137.5cm) wide*

£1,000-1,500   POOK

A Bilston Foundaries cast iron garden bench, designed by Edward Bawden, with elaborate geometric pierced back and slatted seat, on standard legs.

48in (122cm) wide

£2,000-3,000   GORL

A French cast iron bench, the pierced back with circular and oval roundels, centred with a dog and foliage, with wooden splats.

50in (127cm) long

£1,000-1,500   SWO

A German Black Forest carved bench, the two upright supports modelled as bears holding a rectangular shaped seat, the back support with a central carved bear among trees and carved flower heads.

61in (155cm) wide

£1,000-1,500   TEN

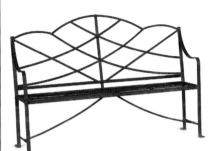
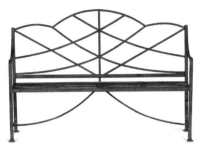

A pair of George III painted cast iron garden benches, each with a serpentine crest rail and claw feet.

c1800   53in (135cm) long

£10,000-15,000   POOK

ESSENTIAL REFERENCE - COALBROOKDALE

Established in 1708 in Shropshire, England, the Coalbrookdale iron foundry initially produced utilitarian ironwork. From the late 18thC it also began to produce decorative grates, stoves, and garden furniture, including the benches for which it is best known today. The decoration of these often included nasturtium leaves, horse chestnut leaves, ferns and lily of the valley.

● Benches were available in a range of sizes, from single seats to 72in (183cm) benches, with either iron or wooden seats. Two paint finishes were available (green or chocolate brown) as was a bronzed finish.
● Many pieces were exported to the US and Europe.
● The firm is still operating today.

A George III painted cast iron garden bench with a tripartite back and frontal claw feet.

c1810   51.5in (131cm) long

£3,500-4,500   POOK

A Coalbrookdale Indian-style cast iron garden bench, the back rest with single arch with trefoil and radiating strapwork, flanked by foliate panels, with scrolled armrests, on hoof feet.

This design, No.90929, was registered and patented by the Coalbrookdale Foundry on 28th April 1853 and appears as No.20 in the castings catalogue.

72in (183cm) wide

£2,000-3,000   AH

An early 19thC carved marble garden seat, decorated with an urn, Pliny doves and acanthus leaves, on scroll stands and plinth bases.

77in (195cm) wide

£8,000-12,000   GORL

A pair of late 19thC cast iron whippet figures.

39in (99cm) wide

£2,000-3,000 **POOK**

A set of four 20thC bronze garden statues of the Four Seasons, modelled as female figures, on leaf-cast scroll plinths.

74in (187cm) high

£6,000-7,000 **GORL**

An early 19thC Derbyshire Blue John spar urn on stand, a raised band to the shoulder, the body with deep purple inclusions, on a mainly white/amber body, on a Derbyshire spar, white and black marble-mounted base.

Blue John is a hardstone – specifically a variety of fluorspar. It has a translucent appearance and is banded in violet-blue and yellow. It takes its name from a corruption of the French bleu-jaune. It was mined in the Castleton area of Derbyshire (The Blue John Mines) and reached the height of its popularity in the 1760s.

13in (33.5cm) high

£4,000-5,000 **TEN**

A cast stone garden figure of a young woman, on a rectangular plinth, with some ageing and weathering.

c1900 *76.5in (194cm) high*

£10,000-15,000 **DOR**

A pair of early 19thC Derbyshire Blue John spar pedestal urns and covers, with acorn finials, the bodies with deep purple, amber and yellow inclusions and veining, on white marble stems and feet, on black marble plinths.

10in (25.5cm) high

£5,000-7,000 **TEN**

A 19thC Italian carved marble fountain base, carved as a large shell supported by a child satyr and a putto upon a naturalistic base with integral foliate- and shell-carved circular base.

47in (119.5cm) high

£15,000-25,000 **FRE**

A pair of 19thC Italian marble campana-form urns, with lotus leaf-carved sides, on a socle foot.

36in (91.5cm) high

£6,000-7,000 **L&T**

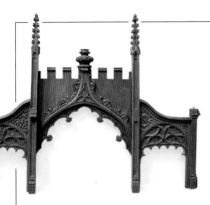

A Gothic Revival oak triple arch.
c1890
102in (259cm) wide
£600-800   RMAA

A wrought iron balustrade, with oak bookrest.
137.5in (349cm) long
£700-900   RMAA

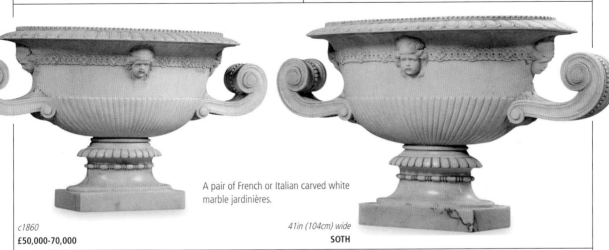

A pair of French or Italian carved white marble jardinières.
c1860
£50,000-70,000

41in (104cm) wide
SOTH

A late 19thC American copper and wood banner and lyre weather vane, with remains of black paint and areas of verdigris, bullet hole repairs.

107in (272cm) long

£8,000-12,000 SK

A late 19thC American moulded copper cow weather vane, on a copper rod, the weathered verdigris surface with traces of earlier gilding, including stand.

36.5in (93cm) long

£10,000-15,000 SK

A small late 19thC American moulded gilt-copper pig weather vane, with stand, old regilding.

13.25in (34cm) wide

£4,000-6,000 SK

A late 19thC American moulded copper gamecock weather vane, on a copper sphere and arrow, with stand, weathered gilt surface.

21in (53cm) long

£2,000-3,000 SK

A late 19thC American gilt "Blackhawk" running horse weather vane, on copper rod, weathered gilt on yellow sized surface, with stand.

22.75in (58cm) long

£2,000-3,000 SK

A late 19thC/early 20thC American leaping stag weather vane, attributed to the Thomas W. Jones Company, New York City, with zinc ears and antlers, in a verdigris patina, with later wood stand.

£8,000-12,000 JDJ

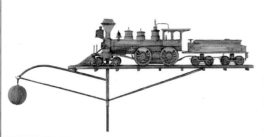

A 20thC Baldwin American-type copper weathervane of a locomotive.

91in (231cm) long

£5,000-7,000 POOK

A late 19thC American A. E. Jewell Co. "Blackhawk" weather vane, with original gilded surfaces with verdigris patina, modelled with cast head and ears, with custom stand.

24in (61cm) long

£8,000-10,000 JDJ

An early 20thC American moulded sheet copper "setter" dog weather vane, with weathered gilt surface, on copper rod, including stand.

33in (85cm) long

£5,000-7,000 SK

A carved and painted counter-top cigar store sailor figure, holding three cigars in one hand, with a barrel inscribed "WE SELL TOBACCO" and a leafy plant beside him on carved base with incised lettering "CIGARS," repairs.

35in (90cm) high

£3,000-4,000   **SK**

A painted cast iron figure of George Washington.

c1900   *36.5in (94cm) high*

£3,000-4,000   **POOK**

A late 19thC French painted doll shop trade sign, one side painted with a fashionable doll and advertising "Paris Bebes," the reverse similarly inscribed.

20.25in (52cm) wide

£1,500-2,500   **SK**

A late 19thC carved and painted cigar store Indian, holding a bundle of cigars in one hand and to his chest, on original carved tapered wooden base, old repainted surface.

69.5in (176cm) high

£1,200-1,800   **SK**

A carved and painted cigar store figure of Punch, on a hewn base.

70in (177cm) high

£1,000-1,500   **FRE**

A carved and painted cigar store Indian, the standing female figure with full feather headdress, holding dagger to her chest the other raised in striking position, on rectangular plinth base.

65in (165cm) high

£1,500-2,500   **LHA**

A mid-late 19thC cigar store Indian, probably from the shop of Samuel A. Robb, New York, holding packet of cigars and a blue package in right hand, knife in left, on painted box base.

55in (140cm) high

£10,000-15,000   **JDJ**

An Afghan carpet.

187in (475cm) long

£1,500-2,000   DN

An Afshar carpet, the indigo field with two stepped medallions surrounded by tribal and geometric devices framed by spandrels and narrow ivory borders.

113in (288cm) long

£1,500-2,500   TEN

An early 20thC Bakhtiyari carpet, the red field with central ivory and indigo star medallion, indigo spandrels, within ivory tree-and-hill border between red bands.

203in (515cm)

£1,800-2,200   L&T

A late 19thC Bakshaish carpet.

178in (452cm) long

£800-1,200   FRE

An early 20thC Bidjar rug, the blue ground with millefleur field within a rosette and trellising vine guard border on red ground.

£1,200-1,800   WES

A Bidjar blue-ground carpet.

240in (610cm) long

£600-700   CHEF

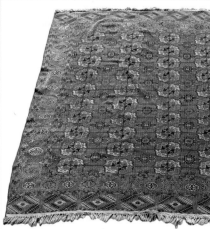

A Bokhara carpet, with brick-red field.

121in (308cm) long

£2,500-3,500   DN

A Fereghan rug, with elongated centre medallion on ivory field with all-over flowering vines, within triple scrolling borders.

119.5in (304cm) long

£9,000-11,000   LHA

A Fereghan Sarouk rug, the salmon ovoid medallion with olive-brown branches with celadon, soft blue and rose flower heads on a blue field within a faded salmon border.

c1880   *81in (205cm) long*

£3,000-4,000   RTC

A late 19thC Fereghan Sarouk carpet.

139in (353cm) long

£5,000-7,000   FRE

A Hamadan carpet.

c1920   *1117in (2837cm) long*
£4,000-5,000   **FRE**

A Heriz carpet, with flowers and leaves on a red ground, with one wide and two narrow borders.

c1900   *161in (409cm) long*
£2,000-3,000   **DN**

A room-sized Heriz rug, with a central yellow and red medallion on an ivory field with salmon corners within blue and red borders.

c1900   *144in (366cm) long*
£18,000-22,000   **POOK**

A Heriz carpet.

c1920   *128in (325cm) long*
£2,000-3,000   **FRE**

A late 19thC Heriz carpet, cut and reduced in size.

                          187in (475cm) long
£2,000-3,000   **FRE**

A pictorial Isfahan rug, the cream field depicting a garden scene with birds and flowering plants enclosed by borders of scrolling floral vines and indigo guard stripes, silk highlights and woven on silk.

                          79in (200cm) long
£1,500-2,500   **TEN**

An Isfahan rug.

122in (311cm) long
£3,000-4,000   **DN**

One of a pair of Karaja runners, the indigo fields with geometric stellar and flower head medallions, enclosed by main green and rose meander arrowhead borders.

Larger 191in (484cm) long
£6,000-7,000 pair   **H&L**

A late 19thC Kashan Mohtashem rug.

                    78in (198cm) long
£4,500-4,500   **FRE**

A Kashan pictorial rug.

c1930   *80in (203cm) long*
£800-1,200   **FRE**

TEXTILES

A late 19thC Kashan Motashem rug.

78in (198cm) long

£4,500-5,500   **FRE**

A Kashan pictorial rug.

c1930   *80in (203cm) long*

£800-1,200   **FRE**

A late 19thC/early 20thC Kashan Kurk carpet, the indigo field with all-over palmette and scrolling foliate vine pattern, within scrolling foliate vine border, between indigo and red bands.

220in (558cm) long

£18,000-22,000   **L&T**

ESSENTIAL REFERENCE - KASHAN

Following the Safavid conquest of Persia in 1501, Sha Tahmasp I established royal carpet-weaving workshops. This was the beginning of the classic age of Persian carpets, which lasted until the 18thC. The four great centres of 16thC and 17thC production were Kashan, Kerman, Isfahan and Tabriz.

● Kashan was the centre of silk carpet weaving in the 16thC. Pieces with hunting motifs and medallion and spandrel designs have been copied in more recent times.

● Very few rugs were produced in the 18thC, but weaving was reintroduced in the late 19thC by merchants hoping to emulate the success of the Tabriz workshops. Typical pieces featured curvilinear designs in jewel-like colours and with a high knot count.

● Fine late 19thC/early 20thC Kashan rugs are often loosely referred to using the terms "Kurk" (soft quality wool) or "Motashem" (possibly the name of a master weaver from the city).

A late 19thC Kashan Motashem carpet.

204in (518cm) long

£15,000-25,000   **FRE**

A large Kashan Souaf sand ground Tree of Life rug.

118in (300cm) long

£4,000-5,000   **CHEF**

A mid-20thC Kerman Laver rug, the blue ground with floral spray field within a complementary guard border on blue ground.

£1,500-2,500   **WES**

A Kerman Lavar Tree of Life rug, the domed ivory field with exotic birds, deer and hyena surrounding multiple trees, within multiple borders.

219in (556cm) long

£7,000-10,000   **LHA**

A late 19thC Kermanshah carpet.

157in (399cm) long
£1,800-2,200 FRE

A Khamseh rug, the deep indigo field with three ivory stepped medallions containing chickens, the field with further tribal motifs enclosed by ivory stepped borders and rosette guard stripes.

113in (287cm) long
£1,000-1,500 TEN

A Kurdish runner, the brick-red field with a column of polychrome octagons flanked by "Memling" guls and tribal motifs enclosed by narrow borders of meandering vines and zoomorphic devices.

164in (416cm)
£1,200-1,800 TEN

A late 19thC Kurdish runner.

A mid-19thC Kurdish rug.

105in (267cm) long
£1,500-2,000 FRE

69in (175cm) long
£1,500-2,000 FRE

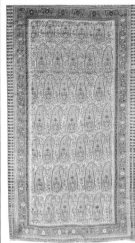

A Mahal Carpet.
c1900 118in (300cm) long
£1,500-2,500 FRE

A mid-20thC Mashad carpet.
121in (307cm) long
£2,000-3,000 FRE

A late 19thC Qashqa'i runner, inscribed.
140in (356cm) long
£4,000-5,000 FRE

A Qashqa'i gallery carpet, the ivory field with large boteh design with floral cores within a madder border, all drawn in saffron, cornflower and midnight-blue, celadon-green and chocolate-brown.
c1900 116in (295cm) long
£2,000-3,000 RTC

A modern Qum silk rug, the deep blue field surrounding a cream ground medallion, within a pale teal and ruby-red border.

51in (129cm) long

£1,500-2,000   RTC

A modern Qum silk meditation rug, the beige ground with dragons, animals and birds in a landscape within an animal, bird and trellising vine guard border on red ground.

£600-700   WES

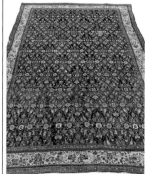

A Senneh carpet.

c1900   *267in (678cm) long*

£3,000-4,000   FRE

A late 19thC Senneh rug, with coloured silk warps.

80in (203cm) long

£8,000-12,000   FRE

A Serapi carpet, with a central navy medallion on a red field with ivory corners.

c1900   *810in (2057cm) long*

£1,000-1,500   POOK

A Serapi runner, the camel field with four extended diamond and arrowhead medallions, within an interlocking main border and multiple minor borders.

193in (490cm) long

£1,000-1,500   TEN

A Sultanabad carpet.

173in (439cm) long

£7,000-8,000   DN

A late 19thC/early 20thC Tabriz carpet, the red field with central blue and red medallion suspending pendants, blue spandrels, various hunting animals, within rust-red cartouche and rosette border, the cartouches containing script, between blue bands.

135in (343cm) long

£3,500-4,500   L&T

A Tabriz carpet.

c1940   *264in (671cm) long*

£12,000-18,000   FRE

A late 19thC/early 20thC Tabriz carpet, the pink field with all-over palmette and floral pattern, within ivory palmette and vine border between green and brown bands.

150in (381cm) long

£2,500-3,500   L&T

A Tabriz wool carpet, with overall panel design on a coral field.

c1910   *141in (358cm) long*

£4,000-5,000   LHA

A late 19thC Ziegler carpet, Sultanabad district.

129in (328cm) long

£3,000-4,000   FRE

A late 19thC Ziegler carpet, Sultanabad, the rust-red field with palmette and large curling leaf pattern, within cream turtle palmette border between bands.

122in (310cm) long

£6,500-7,500   L&T

ESSENTIAL REFERENCE - ZIEGLER CARPETS

Responding to the needs of European clients, the British/Swiss firm Ziegler & Co. set up carpet making workshops in c1885 in Sultanabad, north-west Persia to produce traditional designs adapted for the Western market.

- Terracotta- or ivory-coloured fields are common, surrounded by pale or dark blue borders.
- Typical Zielger carpets feature large-scale motifs in a vine lattice. These features are usually combined with an overall repeat pattern within large borders.
- A particularly Western innovation was the use of human figures as the main pictorial element of a design.
- Ziegler carpets are not finely woven, but tend to use lustrous fine-quality wool. They are very collectable today.

A late 19thC Ziegler carpet, Sultanabad, the ivory field with indigo medallion issuing four diagonal large red floral shoots, indigo spandrels, within indigo palmette and vine border between red bands.

224in (570cm) long

£45,000-55,000   L&T

A late 19thC Ziegler carpet, Sultanabad, the ivory field with indigo medallion issuing four diagonal floral shoots, camel spandrels, within rust-red palmette and vine border between blue bands.

185in (470cm) long

£50,000-60,000   L&T

A large Persian part-silk carpet, with a field of large and small flower heads with foliage, on a beige ground with touches of red and five-row conforming border.

172in (437cm) long

£2,000-3,000   GORB

A Persian carpet, with mother-and-child design on an ivory field with dark navy border.

c1900   *96in (244cm) long*

£7,000-10,000   POOK

A Persian wool and silk carpet, with elaborate centre medallion with fig and urn decoration and multiple borders.

c1900   *1108in (2814cm) long*

£12,000-18,000   LHA

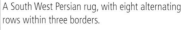

A South West Persian rug, with eight alternating rows within three borders.

£800-1,200   DN

A late 19thC Chelaberd rug.

80in (203cm) long

£2,000-3,000   FRE

A Chelaberd long rug, inscribed indistinctly and dated in part 137.

125in (318cm) long

£2,500-3,500   FRE

A Karabagh long rug.

c1900   *116in (295cm) long*

£800-1,200   FRE

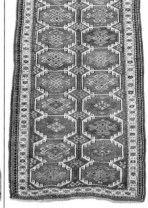

A late 19thC Karabagh rug.

102in (259cm) long

£2,500-3,500   FRE

A mid-19thC Karabagh Kasim Ushag rug.

93in (236cm) long

£2,500-3,500   FRE

A late 19thC/early 20thC Kazak Chajli long rug, the red field with three octagonal indigo and cream medallions, hooked lozenges between, within cream polychrome octagon border between bands.

108in (275cm) long

£4,000-5,000   L&T

A Kazak Eagle throw rug, with three medallions on a red field with ivory border.

c1900   *84in (213cm) long*

£3,500-4,500   POOK

A Kazak Bordjalou double niche prayer rug, inscribed and dated "1320" (1902).

1902   *100in (254cm) long*

£3,000-4,000   FRE

A mid-19thC Kazak Bordjalou rug.

88in (224cm) long

£1,000-1,500   FRE

A Kazak Cloudband throw rug, with three medallions on a red field with ivory border.

c1900   *510in (1295cm) long*

£2,000-3,000   POOK

A late 19thC Kuba Konagkend runner.

123in (312cm) long

£5,000-6,000   **FRE**

A Kuba rug, with an all-over design of blue-green and burgundy on a beige field within a Kufic border.

c1900   *66in (168cm) long*

£900-1,100   **RTC**

A Kuba Seychour rug.

c1900   *79in (201cm) long*

£800-1,200   **FRE**

A Seychour rug, the cornflower blue and ivory bird's head border surrounds four repeating St. Andrew's cross medallions in black, rust-red, olive-green and blue on an ivory field, damages.

c1880   *98in (249cm) long*

£350-450   **RTC**

A Shirvan long rug, dated 1289 (1873).

1873   *108in (275cm) long*

£5,000-6,000   **FRE**

A Shirvan prayer rug, the ivory field with all-over geometric floral design outlined in madder within a latched border of navy-blue, saffron, madder and black, dated 1333 (1916).

1916   *71in (180cm) long*

£1,200-1,800   **RTC**

A Shirvan carpet, with repeating medallions on a navy field with ivory border.

c1900   *52in (132cm) long*

£1,500-2,500   **POOK**

A Caucasian runner, with a diagonal stripe field and multiple borders.

c1900   *104in (264cm) long*

£2,000-3,000   **POOK**

A Caucasian blue-ground runner, signed.

210in (533cm) long

£1,800-2,200   **CHEF**

A late 19thC Caucasian rug, with geometrics on a yellow field, with ivory border.

57in (145cm) long

£1,800-2,200   **POOK**

A Caucasian long rug, with repeating medallions and multiple borders.

c1900   *124in (315cm) long*

£1,500-2,500   **POOK**

An early 20thC Caucasian runner, with medallions on a red field with multiple borders.

32in (81cm) long

£1,500-2,500   **POOK**

A mid-19thC Bergama rug.

87in (221cm) long

£4,000-5,000 **FRE**

A 19thC Bergama rug.

75in (191cm) long

£5,000-6,000 **FRE**

A Beshir runner, the Herati field centred by a large octagon, framed by similar spandrels and compartmented borders of stellar motifs.

167in (425cm) long

£1,500-2,000 **TEN**

An early Hereke silk prayer rug, the field decorated with urns issuing flowers and birds within multiple foliate borders, with Arabic inscriptions.

65in (165cm) long

£40,000-50,000 **LHA**

A mid-19thC Saryk Turkoman ensi, with magenta silk highlights.

70in (178cm) long

£2,000-3,000 **FRE**

A mid-19thC Tekke Turkoman torba.

36in (91cm) long

£3,000-4,000 **FRE**

A Tekke Turkoman carpet.

c1920 *126in (320cm) long*

£550-650 **WW**

A Turkoman Salor rug, with geometric pattern on a dark-red field and double diamond end borders.

c1925 *104in (264cm) long*

£1,500-2,500 **POOK**

A late 19thC Ushak carpet, the light blue field with all-over palmette, scroll and foliate pattern, within red palmette and hooked lozenge border between bands.

201in (510cm) long

£7,000-8,000 **L&T**

A 19thC Ushak rug.

62in (157cm) long

£8,000-12,000 **FRE**

A late 19thC Ushak carpet, the slate-grey field with ivory and orange lozenge medallion, within ivory rosette and palmette border between orange and lemon bands.

238in (605cm) long

£15,000-25,000   L&T

A late 19thC/early 20thC Ushak carpet, the blue field with all-over tree pattern, within ochre palmette and foliate border between green and red bands.

189in (480cm) long

£2,000-3,000   L&T

An Ushak carpet, pale indigo field with an all-over lattice design of large palmettes and stylised flower heads enclosed by narrow soft madder borders of stylised vines.

104in (264cm) long

£1,500-2,500   TEN

A late 19thC Peking rug, with an arabesque medallion in typical shades of blue.

c1900   *68in (173cm) long*

£200-300   RTC

A room-sized Peking rug, with a dragon on a black ground, reduced width.

c1935   *146in (371cm) long*

£3,000-4,000   POOK

A French Aubusson-style woven carpet, in red, cream and ivory tones, decorated with floral sprays throughout.

209in (530cm) long

£2,500-3,500   DN

A room-sized Indian Agra rug, with central medallion on a teal field with red border.

c1900   *124in (315cm) long*

£3,000-4,000   POOK

A 19thC Indian Agra carpet, with a geometric design on a red ground with one wide and seven narrow borders.

232in (590cm) long

£1,500-2,500   DN

TEXTILES

A room-sized Indian Agra rug, with overall floral design on a maroon field with green border.

c1900   *114in (290cm) long*
£3,500-4,500   **POOK**

An Indian carpet, the ivory field with a floral sprays emanating from vase forms surrounding large palmettes of turquoise, navy blue and pink, within a deep rose border.

c1900   *148in (376cm) long*
£2,000-3,000   **RTC**

An Indian Agra carpet, with overall floral pattern on a lime-green field with rust border.

c1880   *1110in (2819cm) long*
£30,000-40,000   **POOK**

An Indian Larestan carpet.

Provenance: Lehman Brothers Collection, New York.

c1900   *1111in (2822cm) long*
£3,000-4,000   **FRE**

A late 19thC Indian Amritsar carpet, the ivory field with all-over Mughal flower and tree pattern, within similar blue border between burgundy bands (worn).

214in (543cm) long
£7,000-9,000   **L&T**

A 20thC Tibetan flatweave runner, the field with red and black "tiger" pattern.

87in (220cm) long
£500-600   **L&T**

An American hooked rug, with horse and pinwheel flowers.

c1900   *52in (132cm) long*
£6,000-7,000   **POOK**

An American hooked rug, depicting a dog in a floral landscape.

c1920   *54in (137cm) long*
£1,500-2,500   **POOK**

An American hooked rug, depicting a fox eating berries.

c1900   *38in (97cm) long*
£1,500-2,500   **POOK**

An American red quilted "lindsey woolsey" bedcover, inscribed "Elizabeth Northrop Age 19 1829".

Whole cloth quilts comprised of linen warp and wool weft are often referred to as "linsey-woolsey". The term is derived from the Middle English word "lynsey" a corruption of "Lindsay," the village in England where the cloth was first made. It was one of the first fabrics used in American quilts. The term is commonly used today to describe heavy, quilted bedcovers, and can refer to any coarse cotton or linen fabric woven with wool.

97in (246cm) long

£5,000-6,000 **POOK**

BRITISH PATCHWORK

The earliest known examples of British patchwork were made c1708. 18thC pieces were often mosaic patterns made up of patches joined one-by-one (unlike American pieces, made up of patterned blocks), and often had large central motifs. Early 19thC patchwork typically featured repeated motifs, such as stars. "Crazy" patchwork quilts (scraps of fabric arranged randomly) were popular from c1870 to the early 20thC.

An early Victorian patchwork quilt, made from coloured silks and linens.

86in (219cm) long

£500-600 **DN**

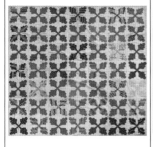

A Dauphin County, Pennsylvania, oak leaf appliqué quilt cover, dated.

1847 *88in (224cm) long*

£700-1,000 **POOK**

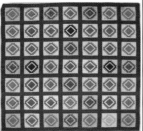

A 19thC American pieced grid-pattern quilt.

106in (269cm) long

£800-1,200 **POOK**

A 19thC American appliqué tulip quilt, signed "Mary A. Penney".

85in (216cm) long

£1,000-1,500 **POOK**

A 19thC American appliqué quilt, with four floral sprays within a vine border.

79in (201cm) long

£800-1,200 **POOK**

A 19thC American appliqué tulip-pattern quilt, with vine border.

94in (239cm) long

£1,000-1,500 **POOK**

A Lancaster County, Pennsylvania, yellow lilies pieced and appliqué quilt, initialled "JMW 1851".

90in (229cm) long

£2,500-3,500 **POOK**

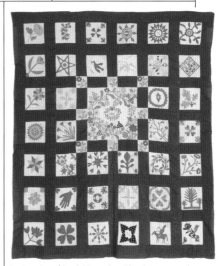

An American friendship quilt, with a large central floral wreath.

c1870 *91in (231cm) long*

£2,000-3,000 **POOK**

TEXTILES

Judith Picks: 19thC album quilt

Many hours would have been spent developing this intricately appliquéd pieced-cotton design. Roller-printed chintz furnishing fabric was cut out to provide decorative flower, bird and spray designs, heightened by pieces of printed cotton dress fabric arranged in "compass star" and leaf forms. The scalloped border, created from the same lighter-weight dress fabric, provided the final finishing touches.

This particular quilt bears 58 signatures from prominent men and women of New York, Philadelphia, Newport and New Jersey families, many of whom were related by marriage and business. The album quilt served as a tangible statement of these important connections.

One signature, that of Sarah Morrell, Philadelphia, may indicate the same woman associated with a famous album quilt, referred to as the Sarah Morrell Album Quilt, in the collection of the Museum of American Folk Art, New York. The quilts share similarly worked diamond-edged squares enclosing chintz floral pieces.

An appliquéd album quilt, by Rachel A. Allen, New Egypt, bearing signatures of members of the Wain, Allen, Shinn, Brick, Oliphant, Newbold, Biddle and Morrell families.
1844
£2,500-3,500   FRE

An American Mennonite pieced quilt, with geometric patterns, with sawtooth borders.
c1900   80in (203cm) long
£3,500-4,500   POOK

An American crazy quilt, the satin and velvet patches heightened with embroidered and appliquéd devices, with teal velvet border, corner block signed and dated "FH Gen 1885".
1885   64in (163cm) wide
£550-650   FRE

A late 19thC Lancaster County, Pennsylvania, friendship sampler quilt, made by members from the Hostetter, Bollinger, Fry, Dutt, and Snyder families.
88in (224cm) long
£3,000-4,000   POOK

An early 20thC American pieced and appliquéd wool quilt, centred with a red square with five appliquéd black cat figures with glass button eyes, three tulips, and a leaf, surrounded by concentric square borders with geometric, all-over quilting in a shell pattern.
82in (208cm) long
£3,500-4,500   SK

An early 20thC Lancaster County, Pennsylvania, polished cotton sampler quilt, signed "Mrs. Harry Sensenig, Bareville, Lancaster Co. PA".
91in (231cm) wide
£700-1,000   POOK

An Amish bar quilt, dated.
1928   80in (203cm) long
£1,800-2,200   POOK

A 16thC Flemish Classical mythological figural tapestry, Brussels, woven within an elaborate four-sided border with fruit and foliage around central husk stem with scrolling vase motifs corners, on brown ground.

125in (317.5cm) long

£50,000-60,000   **SOTH**

A Flemish verdure tapestry, worked with large birds amongst the flowering tree branches, over a woodland pool flanked by flowering water plants including flag iris, and a view to a distant castle.

c1650-1700   *96in (244cm) wide*

£2,500-3,500   **TEN**

A late 17thC/early 18thC French wool tapestry fragment, depicting foot soldiers, possibly Swiss Guards, before a battlefield.

115in (292cm) high

£3,000-4,000   **SK**

A Continental wool tapestry, depicting the triumph of Alexander the Great, the king on a chariot surrounded by troops and musicians, set within a scrolling foliate border.

177.5in (451cm) wide

£15,000-20,000   **LHA**

A 17thC wool tapestry, attributed to the Mortlake Factory, depicting a forest scene with birds in trees and in a stream, within a scrolling foliate border, centred with an armorial crest.

ESSENTIAL REFERENCE - THE GOBELINS TAPESTRY FACTORY

Established in Paris, France, c1662 by Jean-Baptiste Colbert and Charles Le Brun, the Gobelins Tapestry Factory initially made furnishings for Louis XIV.

- Over 800 artists, weavers, dyers and apprentices were employed under Le Brun.
- In the late 17thC, artistic originality stagnated and royal spending was curtailed due to war with the Netherlands. All but one workshop closed in 1694.
- When the factory reopened in 1699 tapestries were produced in a lighter style.
- Tapestries *à Alentours* (panels with elaborate floral surrounds) were popular in the early 18thC.
- In 1939, the factory moved to Aubusson. Artists such as Gromaire, Picasso and Mira produced cartoons for monumental hangings for state buildings.
- The factory is still operational today.

The Mortlake works made use of the weaving skills of immigrant Flemish workers. These workers were highly skilled in depicting natural textures and effects such as flesh and water. It was at the height of its fame and production in the 17thC when this tapestry was made.

158in (401cm) high

£6,000-7,000   **LHA**

A French wool tapestry, attributed to Gobelins Workshop, depicting Cupid surrounded by figures in a wooded landscape, within a repeating leaf and shell border.

117in (297cm) wide

£8,000-12,000   **LHA**

A Continental wool tapestry, depicting two figures in a pastoral setting with sheep, pigs, a cow and dogs, with trees and a village in the background, within a foliate border.

112in (284cm) high

£8,000-12,000   **LHA**

TEXTILES

A Brussels wool tapestry, by U. Leyniers, depicting peasants at work in a village, with a tower and a windmill in the background, signed lower right "U. Leyniers", set within a scrolling vine border.

The signature is that of Urban Leyniers. He and Daniel III Leyniers were in partnership between 1729 and 1745. They manufactured a number of series of tapestries including those of The Triumphs of the Gods, Telemachus and the Teniers subjects – loosely inspired by the pastoral paintings of David Teniers the Younger (1610–1690).

124.75in (317cm) high

£15,000-25,000　　　　　　　　　　　　　　**LHA**

A Continental wool tapestry, depicting a peasant revelry with characters playing various games, drinking and smoking in a village landscape, set within a scrolling foliate border.

85.5in (217cm) wide

£3,000-4,000　　　　　　　　　　　　　　**LHA**

An 18thC Flemish wool tapestry, depicting exotic birds in a wooded landscape.

88in (223.5cm) high

£2,000-3,000　　　　　**POOK**

An 18thC Aubusson tapestry panel, depicting an exotic bird perched in a tree.

94in (239cm) high

£1,200-1,800　　　　　**TEN**

A Continental wool tapestry, depicting figures in Renaissance costumes standing in a garden with a village in the background, set within a border, with cotton backing.

84.5in (215cm) wide

£3,500-4,500　　　　　**LHA**

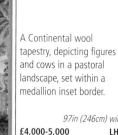

An 18thC Flemish verdure tapestry fragment, worked in hues of blue, green, brown and ivory, depicting a view of a medieval town through a lush forest, within an olive-green and light brown double border.

£2,500-3,500　　　　　**WES**

A Continental wool tapestry, depicting figures and cows in a pastoral landscape, set within a medallion inset border.

97in (246cm) wide

£4,000-5,000　　　**LHA**

A Continental wool tapestry, depicting figures in a wooded landscape as Cupid looks on, with a village in the background.

84.75in (215cm) wide with border

£5,000-6,000　　　　　**LHA**

A small 18thC silk-on-linen pictorial needlework, depicting an oak tree flanked by flowering trees, a pond, and an assortment of animals and birds, losses, in a period giltwood frame.

12.5in (32cm) wide

£1,500-2,500   SK

A Pennsylvania silk and paint-on-silk pictorial needlepoint, attributed to the Folwell School, depicting two lovers in a pastoral landscape, the background with a cottage and three men working in a field.

According to family tradition, the schoolgirl who worked this piece was Kathryn Myers, b.1778.

c1805   *24.25in (61.5cm) wide*

£5,000-6,000   POOK

A late 18thC Chester County silk embroidery and lace picture, by Hannah Brinton, with a border of blossoming vines enclosing a flower filled urn.

16.5in (41.5cm) wide

£10,000-12,000   POOK

An early 19thC George Washington memorial silk-on-silk needlework, by Mary Guild, Miss Remington's School, Hallowell, Maine, inscribed on the glass, with metallic threads, pencil, paint and ink, framed.

19in (48cm) wide

£20,000-25,000   FRE

An early 19thC silk, chenille and paint-on-silk needlework picture, Folwell School, Philadelphia, depicting "The Cottagers," framed.

24.5in (62cm) wide

£2,000-3,000   FRE

An early 19th century silk and needlework picture, depicting a girl seated next to a dog with a lake scene behind, with a *verre eglomisé* mount and gilt frame.

16.5in (41.5cm) wide

£400-500   WW

An early 19thC silkwork panel, the central oval depicting a shepherdess above a ribbon-tied garland and a clover and acorn surround.

18.25in (46cm) high

£150-250   WW

TEXTILES

A silk and chenille-on-silk needlework mourning picture, depicting a young girl in front of a weeping willow and lake with swans, eglomisé mount inscribed "M.A. Pray in her 13th month daughter of J & C Pray Worked by her sister C. Pray, 1823", heightened with watercolour on silk ground, in gilt frame.

The needlework exhibits characteristics of Maine memorials in its use of oversized flowers in the foreground and river with swans in the background.

1823   *37.75in (96cm) wide*

£30,000-40,000   **FRE**

An embroidered silk thanka, depicting Buddha beneath a tree bearing peaches, flanked by two attendants, and above four Bodhisattva, with dragon and emblem borders, and with text in different scripts.

36in (91.5cm) high

£2,000-3,000   **IMC**

A Flemish Medieval-style embroidered panel, depicting a woodland hunting scene with a river and a castle beyond.

69in (175cm) wide

£800-1,200   **WW**

An early 18thC woolwork panel, depicting a man and a woman, three angels seated at a table beneath a tree beyond, and stone-and-brick mansion, with long and short stitches on a cream canvas ground, in later frame.

19in (48cm) wide

£2,000-3,000   **TOV**

One of a pair of early 18thC probably Flemish woolwork panels, depicting foliage, with later tassel edges, later mounted.

27in (68.5cm) high

£600-800 pair   **DN**

A woolwork panel, depicting three figures, two dogs and a tree in front of a country house in cross-stitch, in later ogee-moulded tortoiseshell-veneered frame.

c1750   *31in (79cm) high*

£1,500-2,500   **TEN**

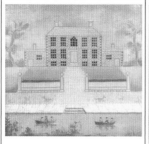

A late 18thC/early 19thC needlework and painted picture, depicting a country house with a river in front, two rowing boats and animals, framed.

16in (40.5cm) wide

£1,000-1,500   **DN**

A wool-on-linen memorial needlework, by Letitia Laise, in memory of her mother Ann, framed.

1844   *16.5in (42cm) wide*

£1,000-1,500   **POOK**

A Victorian woolwork panel, depicting the paddle steamer HMS Victoria and Albert.

22in (56cm) wide

£450-550   **GORL**

A Victorian woolwork panel, depicting "HMS Bombay on fire, December 22nd 1864", framed.

1864   *20.5in (52cm) wide*

£700-800   **GORL**

A Newport, Rhode Island, silk-on-linen needlework sampler, by Rebeca Willbor, worked with "Rebeca/Willbor born/jenauary 13/& made thiS in/ November 5/in NewPort/RhodiSland/1773", enclosed on three sides with urns issuing a naturalistic flowering border centred at the top with a large bird, in original wood frame.

This sampler is similar in style to a group of samplers stitched in the mid-late 18thC by girls in the Newport, Rhode Island area. The typical style includes horizontal bands of pictorial motifs (often strawberries) and inscriptions, with wide floral borders along the sides and a cartouche at the bottom containing the needleworker's name, birth date, and the date of the sampler. There is generally a bird in the top border, or people and animals.

1773   *15.5in (39.5cm) high*

£8,000-12,000   **SK**

A band-pattern silk-on-linen needlework sampler, by Sarah Baker, with bands of embroidered flowers, leaves and acorns, over two bands of alphabets and upper case inscription "SARAH BAKER 1664", in a later wood frame.

1664   *31.75in (81.5cm) long*

£6,000-7,000   **SK**

A George II needlework sampler, by Elizabeth Peace, worked with religious text within a floral surround, coloured chevron borders, alphabets and numbers.

The colours and level of detail are excellent, and the zigzag pattern is unusual.

1736   *17in (43cm)*

£4,000-5,000   **GORL**

A Newport, Rhode Island, silk-on-linen needlework sampler, by Rebecca Westgate, worked with a house flanked by trees, flowers, animals, and birds, and inscriptions, in a later wood frame.

1777   *17.5in (44.5cm) high*

£3,500-4,500   **SK**

A silk-on-linen sampler, by Rachel Aston, worked with alphabet and verse within a stylised strawberry border, dated.

1786   *16.5in (42cm) high*

£2,500-3,500   **POOK**

A George III Scottish sampler, worked with verse, surrounded by crests and foliage in reserves, above a house surrounded by further foliage, framed and glazed.

19in (48cm) high

£1,500-2,500   **DN**

A Reading, Pennsylvania silk-on-linen sampler, by Mary Hiester, worked with verse over bands of flowers and thistle, dated.

1795   *19.5in (49.5cm) high*

£4,000-5,000   **POOK**

A George III Canadian needlework sampler, by Esther Bourdon Lippincott, Montreal, worked with a Biblical verse, flowers, figures and animals within a floral border, dated.

1800   *15.5in (39cm) high*

£1,200-1,800   **GORL**

A George III needlework sampler, by Elizabeth Stephens, worked with St Paul's Cathedral and animals, flowers and angels within a floral border, dated, framed.

1810   *21in (53cm) high*

£1,200-1,800   **GORL**

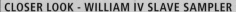

TEXTILES

An early 19thC wool and thread on canvas needlework sampler, by Anna Martha Brooks, aged seven, worked in petit point with a country house in a stylised garden with figures and animals, within an undulating floral border, in an ebonised frame, faults.

1827   *15in (38cm) high*

£1,500-2,500   **TOV**

CLOSER LOOK - WILLIAM IV SLAVE SAMPLER

Samplers depicting slaves are very rare, and this example is also in excellent condition.

Josiah Wedgwood became an important member of the Society for the Abolition of the Slave Trade in 1787. As well as actively promoting the movement amongst his influential friends and business colleagues, he produced and distributed slavery medallions at his own expense.

This sampler reads
" Though thousand foes our paths attend, Yet God shall be our stay, Ten thousand angels he can send, To drive our foes away.".

The design of a kneeling, shackled slave and the more common words "Am I not a Man and a Brother", was devised by Wedgwood's senior craftsman William Hackwood.

It was produced on brooches, necklace pendants, and inset into items such as snuffboxes.

A William IV slave sampler, worked with a kneeling Negro slave in shackles above a verse, initialled "EN" and dated.

1831   *15in (38cm) diam*

£6,000-7,000   **GORL**

A Reading, Pennsylvania, silk-on-linen sampler, by Harriet Arnold, worked with potted flowers above a brick house flanked by pine trees, within a strawberry vine border.

1828   *17in (43cm) high*

£10,000-15,000   **POOK**

A 19thC needlework sampler, by Mary Eleanor Story, aged nine, worked with "The Menai Bridge, Nr Bangor, Caernarvonshire", with boats and figures, the bottom panel with bridge measurements, in a maple frame.

Designed by Thomas Telford, and the first modern suspension bridge in the world, the Menai Bridge was finished in 1826. It would have been a wonder of modern construction when this sampler was made. Samplers featuring such industrial, architectural features are very rare.

22in (56cm) long

£5,500-6,500   **H&L**

A silk-on-linen needlework sampler, by Eliza Bower, worked with a pious verse enclosed by peonies tied with blue ribbon, within a foliate border, and the dedication "Respectfully presented to Richard F. and Maria Bower by their affectionate daughter, Eliza Bower', framed.

c1830   *17.5in (44.5cm) wide*

£2,000-3,000   **FRE**

An American silk-on-linen sampler, by Sarah Miller at Mrs. Robins school, worked with two central brick buildings surrounded by swans, doves, and flowers.

1841   *18in (46cm) wide*

£5,000-6,000   **POOK**

A 17thC European beadwork panel, decorated throughout with geometric flowers and foliage, initialled and dated on the silk backing "MH".
1671   10.5in (27cm) high
£300-400   GORL

A late 18thC printed linen panel, inscribed, "J. Laughton Sculpt" titled "The Aviary or Bird Fancyers Recreation".
26in (66cm) wide
£600-700   POOK

One of a pair of early 19thC felt pictures, by George Smart, of applied felt, cloth and leather on watercolour paper background, one of a postman leading a donkey, the other of an old woman with a basket of game, framed, with original maker's label verso.
1833   16in (40.5cm) wide
£1,800-2,200 pair   GORL

A Victorian heart-shaped sweetheart's cushion, worked with numerous glass beads, two religious panels and a New Year's good luck panel.
10.5in (26.5cm) wide
£100-150   GORL

A Persian Qashqa'i bagface cushion, with faded red latched medallion on a deep teal field.
29in (74cm) wide
£300-400   RTC

An American embroidered wool, silk, and cotton needlework huswif, with five embroidered black wool pockets of black wool fabric, bound with red and yellow silk, lined with floral printed cotton, dated.

The roll-up/huswif/housewife is an oblong pouch for needles and pins, etc, which could be rolled up and carried in the larger pocket that 18thC and 19thC women wore under their skirts.
1836   29in (74cm) long
£1,500-2,000   SK

A Pennsylvania watercolour on silk pocket, inscribed "R.S. Bellows", dated.
1844   7.75in (19.5cm) high
£300-400   POOK

A 19thC silk Masonic apron, for the Bernville Lodge, with printed symbols, and "No. 122.".
15.75in (40cm) wide
£200-300   POOK

A school girl sample book, "Specimens of Needlework", of Letitia Mercer, Derrylee School, Northern Ireland, with examples of patchwork, button holes, darning, silk-on-linen samplers, doll dresses, pen wipes, (in total approximately 50 pieces).
c1863
£2,500-3,500   POOK

An early 19thC mother-of-pearl and gilt pierced brisé fan, painted to one side with a central cartouche of Classical figures, flanked by further vignettes of figures and landscapes, within borders of birds and scrolls, in glazed and gilded case.

10in (25.5cm) long

£1,500-2,500   TOV

A 19thC printed and hand-highlighted fan, decorated with figures playing blind man's buff, with painted end blades and floral highlights, in gilt painted frame.

£300-400   MAR

A 19th Century ivory and silk fan, painted with courtiers in a garden, in a gilt glazed fan case, with plaque to interior "September 3rd 1850 to Mary A Mitchell with her husbands love; a souvenir of Eugenie, Empress of the French to whom this fan formerly belonged".

Case 26in (66cm) wide

£500-600   H&L

A 19thC cockade fan, the paper leaf decorated with flower heads and trailing foliage, the ivory guards with gilt floral decoration.

18in (45.5cm) long

£350-450   H&L

A 19thC Chinese brisé fan, the silver lacquer silk painted with figures and flowers, with box.

8in (20cm) wide

£1,500-2,500   LC

A 19thC Chinese gilt and ivory brisé fan, painted with three panels, one containing figures, the others landscapes, carved with flowers and animals, damages.

£800-1,200   WW

A late 19thC Chinese carved ivory brisé fan, carved and pierced with figures, birds and an ox amidst pine, pagodas, flowers and foliage.

7in (18cm) long

£1,500-2,500   TOV

A late 19thC Cantonese lacquered fan of a thousand faces, decorated with figures outside a pavilion, each with a painted ivory face, in original box.

22.5in (57cm) wide

£300-400   GORL

A late 19thC Cantonese carved sandalwood fan of a thousand faces, decorated with figures around pavilions, with painted ivory faces, in lacquered box.

20in (51cm) wide

£300-400   GORL

A Cantonese export ivory brisé fan, with French verse to the leaf "Si vous aimez ce qu j'aime vous vous aimerez vous meme", the guards carved with multiple flower heads and birds.

6in (15cm) long

£500-600   H&L

A French floral silk brocade gown, with fitted lace up bodice, lace and ruching at the train, sleevelets and stomacher.
c1760
£1,200-1,800 LHA

A George III brocade silk gentleman's court waistcoat, with silver and applied spangle braiding.
£300-500 TOV

A George III green and ivory chiné silk frock coat.
c1790
£800-1,200 TOV

ESSENTIAL REFERENCE - 18THC MENSWEAR

For most of the 18thC, aristocratic men's clothing was made from brightly coloured fabrics, such as velvet and floral brocades. Colours became more muted after the French Revolution (1789-99). Dark-coloured tailcoats and pale breeches (intended to give the impression of nudity) were common.

- All 18thC mensware is rare today, but everyday wear is extremely difficult to find, as only expensive, decorative items were preserved.
- Waistcoats survive in comparatively large numbers.
- Early 18thC pieces might be decorated with embroidery, metal lace, and bullion fringe.
- By c1765 waistcoats were shorter, often made of light silks, embroidered or trimmed with lace. By the 1790s waistcoats were mostly plain, and reached only to the waist.

A late 18thC gentleman's three-piece green corded, silk effect and embroidered court suit, comprising breeches, a silk embroidered waistcoat, with mandarin collar and two slanted pockets, and a long tail coat with extensive floral decoration, and later lace cuffs, finished with embroidered buttons throughout.
£3,500-4,500 DN

A pair of Queen Victoria's wool and lacework ivory-topped black stockings, with openwork "VR" initials beneath a coronet.
c1838
£600-800 L&T

A probably 19thC dark green silk gentleman's costume, comprising of trousers, waistcoat and coat, waistcoat with silver silk embroidery.

£600-800 LHA

An early 20thC Lord and Taylor equestrian suit, comprising a jacket, attached waistcoat and jodhpurs, labelled "Lord and Taylor".
£80-120 LHA

Judith Picks: Royal dress

There's nothing like a touch of royalty to add a frisson to a sale – particularly in a royal wedding year.

The rather unglamorous and revealing dress Catherine Middleton modelled at a St Andrews charity event (where she may well have caught the eye of a prince) sold for an incredible sum of £65,000 in early 2011!

This example of the late Queen Mother's wedding dress was one of three prototypes and was the basis for the final design. (The actual dress would, if it ever came on the market, be worth a great deal more). It is interesting that Lady Elizabeth Bowes-Lyon chose a very fashionable "flapper-style" dress rather than a traditional wedding gown.

With all the interest in the "King's Speech" and the wedding of Prince William and Catherine Middleton, Royal memorabilia is on a roll.

A Handley Seymour prototype for the Queen Mother's wedding dress, of Medieval style, in ivory crêpe de chine applied with cloth of silver and pearl studded bands, with a silver and tulle train, a bobbin lace veil, scraps of silk and satin, a wreath of orange blossom and an unrelated petticoat, with related printed publications.

1923

£4,000-5,000 DN

A Chanel blue lace evening dress, with a fitted bodice, full skirt with ruffled hemline, labelled "Chanel/4161".

1958 *Bust 36in (91.5cm)*

£2,500-3,500 LHA

A Christian Dior ribbed silk cocoon coat, with oversized black beaded buttons, labelled "Christian Dior/102610" from the autumn 1959 collection.

1959 *Bust 34in (86cm)*

£1,800-2,200 LHA

A Norman Norell mint green mermaid gown, full length with all-over sequins atop jersey, labelled "Norman Norell for Bonwit Teller".

£1,500-2,500 LHA

A 1960s Pierre Cardin ivory knit dress, with multiple seams leading into circular panels at hemline, labelled "Pierre Cardin".

£1,200-1,800 LHA

An Andy Warhol "Souper Dress", coloured screenprint on paper, titled on original label at collar, with care instructions.

c1965 *38in (96.5cm) long*

£2,000-3,000 DRA

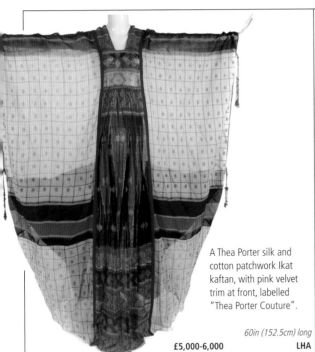

A Thea Porter silk and cotton patchwork Ikat kaftan, with pink velvet trim at front, labelled "Thea Porter Couture".

60in (152.5cm) long
£5,000-6,000   LHA

A 1970s Yves Saint Laurent khaki "Safari" suit, the tunic with a lace-up front, labelled "Saint Laurent".

Size 38
£4,000-5,000   LHA

A Gianni Versace graphic print sequin cocktail dress, labelled "Versus".

Size 40
£800-1,200   LHA

A Gianni Versace black bondage top, with rhinestone-encrusted buckles, labelled "Gianni Versace Couture".

Bust 34in (86cm)
£2,000-3,000   LHA

A 1970s Halston white jersey evening kaftan, with rhinestone detailing at V-neck, labelled "Halston".

£2,000-3,000   LHA

A 1980s Christian Dior cream chiffon gown, with gypsy-style bodice with embroidered flowers and butterflies, with ruffled panels cascading down sides of skirt, labelled "Christian Dior/1565".

£2,500-3,500   LHA

A 1980s Christian Lacroix floral "Valentine" outfit, with a sweetheart neckline and heart-shaped flower detail, together with a matching pencil skirt, labelled "Christian Lacroix".

£800-1,200   LHA

A 1980s Yves Saint Laurent pink leather bolero jacket, with a broad multicolour cabochon rhinestone trim to the lapels, labelled "Yves Saint Laurent".

Size 38
£500-700   LHA

An Issey Miyake purple pleated minidress, with twisted voluminous "paper lantern" sleeves, abstract neckline, sewn using only one seam, labelled "Issey Miyake".

size small
£1,000-1,300   LHA

TEXTILES

A Cartier yellow gold, emerald, onyx and diamond-accented cloth purse, the gold stamped "Cartier 14Kt" and serial number "17806", the purse interior signed "Cartier".

c1950

£4,000-5,000   **LHA**

A Chanel black lambskin quilted bag, with gold tone chain handles, with gold tone logo closure, zip top with tassel pull, lined in leather, stamped "Chanel".

13.5in (34cm) wide

£2,000-3,000   **LHA**

A Chanel grey suede bag, with chain link handles, logo at front, zipper closure, stamped "Chanel".

12in (30.5cm) wide

£700-900   **LHA**

A Gucci red leather bag, with bamboo handles, stamped "Gucci".

13.5in (34cm) wide

£500-700   **LHA**

A Hermès brown leather Kelly bag, with gold hardware, matching shoulder strap, lock and key sheath, stamped "Hermès Paris".

2001   *14in (36cm) wide*

£2,500-3,500   **LHA**

A Hermès black leather Birkin bag, with gold hardware, lock and key sheath, stamped "Hermès".

2005   *10in (25.5cm) wide*

£3,500-4,500   **LHA**

A Hermès brown leather Kelly bag, with a matching strap, with palladium hardware, lock and key sheath, stamped "Hermès".

A Hermès blue Brighton crocodile Birkin bag, with palladium hardware, lock and key sheath, stamped "Hermès".

2008   *14in (36cm) wide*

£20,000-25,000   **LHA**

2003   *14in (36cm) wide*

£4,000-5,000   **LHA**

An Anne Marie of Paris black suede "Telephone" bag, the dial reading "Patricia Chicago MI2-3137", stamped "Anne Marie/Paris".

7in (18cm) high

£700-900   LHA

A Judith Leiber "Stained Glass" dog minaudiere handbag, with a hidden chain shoulder strap, stamped "Judith Leiber".

A minaudiere is a small ornamental case for a woman's cosmetics, jewellery, or personal items that is often carried as a handbag.

4in (10cm) high

£1,000-1,500   LHA

A Moschino "Fudge the Fashionistas, Let them Eat Cake" handbag, in a chocolate covered bolide style, with brown leather appliqué atop off-white leather, stamped "Moschino".

1996   *14in (36cm) high*

£1,000-1,500   LHA

A crocodile suitcase, with a pocketed fabric interior, and leather lining with trade label for "CUTHBERTSON & HARPER, CALCUTTA", with English lever locks and key.

20in (51cm) wide

£250-350   WW

A crocodile Gladstone travelling bag, with leather-lined interior with a pocket, fitted with an easel ivorene mirror, scissors, penknife, file, button hook, and tweezers, and board mounted with alarm clock and other implements, on five stud feet.

13.25in (33.5cm) wide

£1,000-1,500   WW

A crocodile Gladstone bag, stamped in gilt "MADE BY H. GREAVES, NEW ST, BIRMINGHAM," the front stamped with initials "E.R.", the lock stamped "GREAVES LTD BIRMINGHAM", with five brass stud feet.

14.25in (36.5cm) wide

£800-1,200   WW

A crocodile hat box, with brass buckles and lock stamped "Y & T", with leather and silk tiered interior, the underside stamped "1468", with four brass stud feet.

16in (40.5cm) high

£2,000-3,000   WW

Two crocodile suitcases, made in India.
c1860

£2,000-2,500   GEOA

A Louis Vuitton travelling trunk, decorated with overall typical monogram design, with paper label, indistinctly numbered "155411", lacking interior tray.

32in (81cm) long

£3,500-4,500   TOV

A Louis Vuitton trunk, No 195153, with leather edges and lift-out tray.

32in (81cm) wide

£1,500-2,500   SWO

A pair of child's black leather and suede button boots.

The scalloped edging was popular after c1867.
c1870
£200-500   BZ

A pair of 19thC brown satin slippers with raised gold-coloured embroidery.

c1880
£100-200   BZ

A pair of green velvet slippers, the uppers extravagantly embroidered with metal thread.

c1880
£200-500   BZ

A pair of blue velvet slippers, embroidered with raised chenille flowers and with gold heels.
c1880
£200-500   BZ

A pair of brown leather shoes with Louis heels, decorated with beads and embroidery.

c1880
£200-500   BZ

A pair of cream satin shoes, decorated with pearl beads and lined with leather.

c1880
£200-500   BZ

A pair of 19thC pink silk wedding shoes, with Louis heels and rosette detail, marked "Hook Knowles Co Ltd Makers to the Royal Family, 66 & 65 New Bond Street London".
£50-80   LDY

A pair of brown satin shoes, with ornamental buckles set with cut steel stones.
c1890
£200-500   BZ

A pair of black glacé leather shoes, decorated with gold embroidery and silk bows, marked "Joseph Box Regent Street".
c1890
£200-500   BZ

A pair of black leather laced boots.

The pointed toes gave the illusion of a longer and thinner foot. This elegant style began in France in the late 1880s, as a reaction to concerns over the narrowness of shoes. A high instep was said to add to the attractiveness of the shoe and its wearer. This more comfortable style was popular into the early 20thC.
c1900
£200-500   BZ

A pair of black leather laced shoes with Louis heels.
c1900
£200-500   BZ

A pair of c1910s/20s leather boots with press stud fastenings, with original tag and fabric straps.
c1900
£200-300   CANS

A pair of 1920s snakeskin and black leather shoes, marked "Lennards".
£50-100   CANS

A pair of Turkish-inspired mules, red suede and gold leather uppers on red heels, marked "Harrods Ltd, London".

The Turkish style was popular towards the end of the 19thC and again in the 1930s and 1940s when it was used by Salvatore Ferragamo.
c1940
£200-500   BZ

A pair of evening shoes handmade for the future Queen Elizabeth II, black suede with gold leather trim. These shoes were a wedding present made for the princess by Latvian displaced persons living in Germany.
1947
£1,000-1,500   BZ

A 1970s pair of Terry de Havilland "Zebedee" sandals, metallic red and blue leather with "spring" heels.
1979
£200-500   RELL

A pair of 1980s Alaia black suede court shoes, with velvet and braid floral decoration.
£200-500   RELL

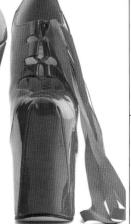

A pair of 1990s Vivienne Westwood super-elevated court shoes, red patent leather.
£1,000-1,500   PC

A pair of Gianni Versace black leather Medusa boots, with gold lace-up style Medusa emblems at front, stamped "Gianni Versace".
£600-800   LHA

Barratt, John, "The Coniston Copper Mines Letters of John Barratt, 1823-1834", manuscript letter copy book, bound in half Morocco by Bernard C. Middleton.

Although copper has been mined at Coniston since as early as 1800BC, it was on a very small scale. In the 1830s John Barratt opened up the mines on an industrial scale, new deep shafts were sunk and the use of gunpowder brought about significant growth. The workforce rapidly increased from 20 men in 1820 to 600. A railway line was opened in 1859 to carry the ore which had previously been boated down the lake.

£4,000-5,000   TEN

CLOSER LOOK - DANTE'S "DIVINA COMMEDIA"

Changes were made to this edition during printing, and several quires were re-set and the anchor device added. This first issue is without the Aldine anchor device, with the uncorrected "Alaghieri" on the reverse of the subtitle and quires a-c in the first setting.

This edition (along with editions of Petrach) was carefully worked on by Pietro Bembo (1470-1547) at the house of Ricano. Striving for uniformity of language and spelling, Bembo chose to imitate 14thC literary Florentine consistently, eliminating contamination by contemporary language and Latin that had become standard in the 15thC. Bembo's editing makes this a key work in the attempt to reform and sophisticate the Italian language.

It has an impeccable provenance. It was acquired by Joseph Smith, British Consul in Venice (1744-1760). He was patron of Canaletto and a passionate collector of art and books and manuscripts.

The Irish Tighe family (including Mary Tighe, the poet and an acquaintance of Keats) acquired this volume from the British Consul while on the Grand Tour.

It is in excellent condition for its age.

Dante [Dante Alighieri], [Divina Commedia] "Le Terze Rime", first Aldine edition, first issue, front free endpaper with 1981 Tighe family biro presentation inscription, engraved bookplate of consul Joseph Smith, with 18thC vellum over boards.
1502
£10,000-15,000   BLO

Bell, John, "Travels from St. Petersburg in Russia to diverse parts of Asia", first edition, published by Robert and Andrew Foulis, with folding map, bound in contemporary calf gilt, red labels.
1763
£1,500-2,000   L&T

"The Holie Bible", first edition of the Douai Old Testament, in two volumes, largely translated by Gregory Martin, titles within typographic borders, bound in 19thC polished calf, re-backed, preserving original gilt backstrips.
1609-1610
£2,500-3,500   BLO

Chippendale, Thomas, "The Gentleman and Cabinet Maker's Director", printed for the author, slip-bound in leather over original binding.
1754
£5,000-7,000   POOK

Doyle, Sir Arthur Conan, "The Hound of the Baskervilles", first edition, published by George Newnes, half-title and 16 plates by Sidney Paget, original pictorial cloth, gilt, spine slightly faded.
1902
£2,000-3,000   BLO

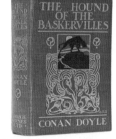

Dickens, Charles, "A Christmas Carol", first edition, first issue, hand-coloured etched frontispiece and three plates by John Leech, lacks contents leaf, bookplate on front pastedown, original pink/brown cloth, in Morocco-backed marbled-board drop-back box.
1843
£2,000-3,000   BLO

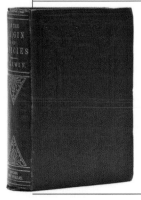

Darwin, Charles, "On the Origin of Species", fifth edition, published by John Murray, original blind-stamped cloth, with 32pp publisher's catalogue at end, slightly foxed and browned, various ink marks.

"On the Origin of Species" was originally published in 1859 and rapidly sold out. This edition (the fifth) is the first to feature the phrase "survival of the fittest", which had been coined by Herbert Spencer in "Principles of Biology" (1864).
1869
£2,500-3,000   BLO

Finaughty, William, "Recollections of William Finaughty Elephant Hunter, 1864-1875", first edition, one of 250 copies, privately printed in Philadelphia, with original buckram-backed boards, original paper labels.
1916
£1,500-2,500   BLO

Grahame, Kenneth, "The Wind in the Willows", first edition, published by Methuen, frontispiece by W. Graham Robertson, with original pictorial cloth, tissue guard, small inscription to front free endpaper, spine ends frayed, corners bumped.
1908
£1,500-2,500　　　　　BLO

Kipling, Rudyard, "The Jungle Book" and "The Second Jungle Book", first editions, frontispiece and illustrations by J. L.Kipling and others, original blue gilt pictorial cloth, rubbed at extremities.
1894-95
£1,500-2,000　　　　　BLO

Miller, Patrick, "The Elevation, Section, Plan, and Views, of a Triple Vessel, and of Wheels...", first edition, published by William Scott, Edinburgh, Adam Smith's copy with his book label on front pastedown.

An industrial work by an enthusiastic amateur engineer (regarded as the inventor of practical steam navigation), belonging to one of the leading figures of the Scottish Enlightenment, the philosopher and social scientist, Adam Smith. One of a number of presentation copies bound for Miller by William Scott. Another edition was published in the same year, with parallel French and English titles and text.
1787
£5,000-6,000　　　　　BLO

Necker, Jacques, "Mémoire présenté au Roi par M. Necker, concernant l'établissement des Administrations Provinciales", manuscript fair copy signed by the author, stitched with pink ribbon, with rare printed text (1781).

Jacques Necker (1732-1804) was finance minister to Louis XVI. This is one of the few manuscript fair copies of this sensitive document submitted secretly to Louis XVI and other high-ranking officials. In it, Necker criticised the existing tax-gathering systems and called for reforms. In May 1781 his enemies obtained a copy and published it.
1778 and 1781
£10,000-15,000　　　　　BLO

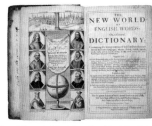

Phillips, Edward, "The New World of English Words; or, a General Dictionary...", first edition, published by E. Tyler for Nath. Brooke, with engraved additional title, re-backed to style with gilt spine in compartments and red Morocco label, browned, damages.

Compiled by the nephew of John Milton, this dictionary was attacked by Thomas Blount who had published his own dictionary, "Glossographia" two years previously and whose sales had dropped as a result of the appearance of this work.
1658
£1,500-2,000　　　　　BLO

Sclater, Philip Lutley and Oldfield, Thomas, "The Book of Antelopes", in four volumes, published by Nissen, with 100 hand-coloured lithographed plates by J. Smit after Joseph Wolf, in contemporary half green Morocco, spine faded.
1894-1900
£5,000-6,000　　　　　BLO

Stevenson, Robert Louis, "A Child's Garden of Verses", first edition, published by Longman's & Co., with original cloth in modern cloth drop-back box.
1885
£4,000-5,000　　　　　BLO

Stoker, Bram, "Dracula", first edition, first issue, published by Archibald Constable, inscribed from the author to Mrs W.S. Gilbert on front fly-leaf, with original yellow cloth, in black buckram drop-back box.

This is a rare edition, with no advertisements as issued and printed on slightly thicker stock. The inscription reads "To Mrs. W.S. Gilbert with Bram Stoker's very warm regards, 12/7/97". Mrs Gilbert (wife of William Schwenck Gilbert, of Gilbert & Sullivan fame), was a friend of Stoker. At the time of the book's publication, rumours were circulating about Gilbert and Stoker's wife, Florence, as they often socialised together.
1897
£35,000-45,000　　　　　BLO

Wilde, Oscar, "Lady Windermere's Fan: A Play About a Good Woman," first edition, one of 500 copies, 14pp advertisements, bookplate of Lily Antrobus, with original salmon cloth with gilt decorations by Charles Shannon.
1893
£1,000-1,500　　　　　BLO

Barrie, J.M., "Peter and Wendy", first edition, published by Hodder & Stoughton, frontispiece, pictorial title and 11 plates by F.D. Bedford, with original green gilt pictorial cloth and dust jacket.

J.M. Barrie's classic children's book, was extended and developed in response to the success of the play "Peter Pan" (1904) and the novel "Peter Pan in Kensington Gardens" (1906). This edition features the first inclusion of Peter's visit to Wendy Darling when she has grown up and married. It is rare in such good condition.
1911
£3,500-4,500 BLO

Christie, Agatha, "The Murder on the Links", first edition, published by The Bodley Head, with 8pp advertisements, original orange cloth, one corner with minor bump.
1923
£4,000-5,000 BLO

Du Maurier, Daphne, "Rebecca", first edition, published by Victor Gollancz, first edition with presentation inscription on visiting card affixed to front endpaper, original black cloth gilt and dustwrapper, minor creasing.
1938
£2,000-3,000 L&T

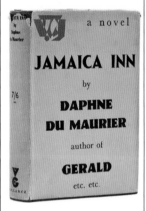

Du Maurier, Daphne, "Jamaica Inn", first edition, published by Victor Gollancz, signed on front free endpaper, original cloth, dust jacket torn, spine slightly browned.
1936
£4,000-5,000 BLO

Eliot, T.S., "The Waste Land", true first edition, number 482 of 1,000, published by Boni and Liveright, with original flexible black cloth cover, lacking dust jacket, rubbing to boards.

With the word "mountain" spelled correctly on line 339 (p. 41).
1922
£2,000-3,000 LHA

Eliot, T.S., "Prufrock, and Other Observations," published by The Egoist, in original stiff buff paper wrappers lettered in black, in custom cloth-backed chemise and slipcase by J.A.S. Macdonald, NY, some wear to extremities.

One of 500 copies of the first edition of Eliot's first work.
1917
£5,500-6,500 LHA

Fleming, Ian, "Moonraker", first edition, published by Jonathan Cape, with original boards, dust jacket, small ink name on front free endpaper, slightly dulled at spine, a few minor marks on lower panel.

Issue with "shoo" on p.10 (the scarcer of the two issues) and printed on the slightly thinner paper stock.
1955
£3,500-4,500 BLO

Fleming, Ian, "From Russia, With Love", first edition, signed and inscribed to Geoffrey Boothroyd on front free endpaper, with original boards, dustjacket, rubbed at edges, worn at corners.

The inscription reads, "To Geoffrey Boothroyd/ Herewith appointed/ 'Armourer' to J. Bond./ from/ Ian Fleming", relating to Boothroyd's role of adviser to Fleming concerning Bond's guns. The dust jacket by Richard Chopping features a specially-adapted Smith & Wesson and on the inside flap notes "modified by, and the property of, Geoffrey Boothroyd".
1957
£15,000-20,000 BLO

Greene, Graham, "Journey Without Maps", first edition, published by Heinemann, with un-clipped dust jacket, book society wrap around, and yellow cloth.
1936
£5,000-6,000 GORL

Greene, Graham, "The Lawless Roads", first edition, published by Longman, with un-clipped dust jacket, red cloth with lettering in gold.
1939
£2,000-3,000 GORL

James, P.D., "Cover Her Face", first edition, published by Faber and Faber, the dust jacket by Charles Mozley, with original cloth, very minor sunning, edge wear with a few small closed tears.

James' first novel is rare, particularly in good condition, as many copies seemingly went directly to public libraries.

1962

£2,000-3,000   BLO

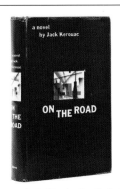

Kerouac, Jack, "On the Road", first edition, published by Viking Press, with the bookplate of Dutch book collector A.S.A. Struik on front pastedown, ink inscription on front free endpaper, original black cloth and dust jacket, a few small closed nicks, slight edge rubbing.

"On the Road" is a key work in the Beat Generation canon.

1957

£1,500-2,500   BLO

Lewis, C.S., "The Silver Chair", first edition, published by Geoffrey Bles, frontispiece, illustrations and map endpapers by Pauline Baynes, small ink name to head of front free endpaper, original boards and dust jacket, restoration.

An attractive example of one of the rarer Narnia titles.

1953

£2,000-3,000   BLO

Plath, Sylvia [Victoria Lucas], "The Bell Jar", first edition, published by Heinemann, original boards and dust jacket, fraying to spine ends.

"The Bell Jar" is Sylvia Plath's only novel. Originally published in the UK under the pseudonym Victoria Lucas, it was first published under Plath's name in 1967. It was not published in the USA until 1971.

1963

£1,500-2,500   BLO

Judith Picks: George Orwell

As a student at Edinburgh University in the late 1960s, I wrote one of my main essays on Eric Blair – better known as George Orwell. I bought second-hand copies at James Thin bookshop of "Down and Out in Paris and London", "1984" and "Keep the Aspidistra Flying". I remember looking longingly at first editions, one signed by "Eric Blair" himself, but as an impoverished student there was no way I could afford £100-200 for them. At the time this was upsetting, as I found the idea that Orwell had actually signed the books made them more special. But looking at this page – perhaps I should have taken out a loan! Those "second hand books" would have made an excellent investment. These copies are all in excellent condition, with original dust jackets and "Down and Out" has a particularly good inscription. It is always worth looking at old books in jumble sales, charity shops and car boot sales. You never know what you may find!

Orwell, George, "Down and Out in Paris and London", first edition, published by Victor Gollancz, signed by the author, "with the nations kind regards to Mr L. P. Moore, without who's kind assistance this book would never have been published - Eric Blair, 24.12.32", with dust jacket.

1933

£100,000-120,000   GORL

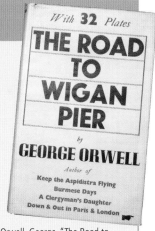

Orwell, George, "Keep The Aspidistra Flying", first edition, published by Victor Gollancz, with dust jacket and "Compton Mackenzie writes" review wrap, with original blue cloth.

1936

£13,000-15,000   GORL

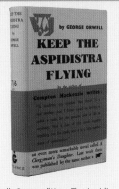

Orwell, George, "The Road to Wigan Pier", first edition, published by Victor Gollancz, with original dust jacket and blue cloth.

1937

£11,000-13,000   GORL

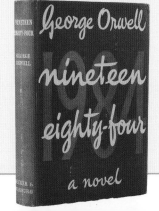

Orwell, George, "Nineteen Eighty-Four", first edition, published by Secker and Warburg, with original unclipped dust jacket and green cloth.

1949

£5,000-6,000   GORL

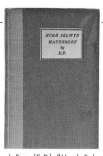

Pound, Ezra [E.P.], "Hugh Selwyn Mauberley", first edition, second state, 170 of 200 copies, published by Ovid Press, with Wiston Old Rectory book label on front paste-down, original cloth-backed boards, upper cover, uncut and unopened.

With inverted "p" for a "d" in "age-old" in line 16, p.12.
1920
£1,200-1,800   BLO

Powell, Anthony, "From a View to a Death", first edition, with contemporary dedication on front free endpaper to John Wyndham, original cloth, dust jacket by Misha Black, slight spotting, edge-wear and creasing, spine browned.

1933
£3,000-4,000   BLO

Rowling, J.K., "Harry Potter and the Philosopher's Stone, uncorrected proof copy, published by Bloomsbury, full number line, original white and yellow paper wrappers, creases, dustmarks to covers, small ink circle on half title.

With incorrect printing of J.A. Rowling on title.
1997
£2,000-3,000   L&T

Rowling, J.K., "Harry Potter and the Philosopher's Stone", first edition, original pictorial boards, minor bump, minor rubbing to extreme corner-tips.

This is the true first edition of the first Harry Potter book, one of a very small hardback print run (500 according to the publisher), largely intended for public libraries. Many are, therefore, extremely damaged, making this near-mint condition example extremely desirable.
1997
£15,000-20,000   BLO

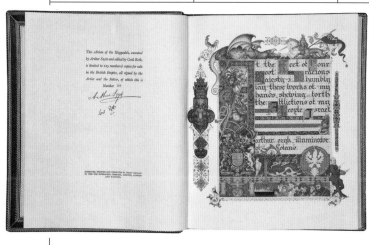

Szyk, Arthur, "The Haggadah", first edition, number 43 of 125, edited by Cecil Roth, published by Beaconsfield Press, English & Hebrew printed in russet and black, signed by the author/artist and the editor, printed on vellum with illustrated silk doublures, in original blue crushed gilt pictorial Morocco by Sangorski & Sutcliffe, and drop-back box.

A magnificent deluxe version of one of the most important books in the canon of the Jewish faith, a prayer book designed to integrate the whole family but especially the children, hence the importance of the illustrations.
1939
£25,000-30,000   BLO

Tolkien, J.R.R., "The Hobbit", first American edition, published by Houghton Mifflin, Boston, with map endpapers and illustrations by Tolkien, original blue-lettered and orange-stamped tan cloth in dust jacket.
1938
£8,000-10,000   BLNY

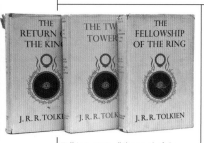

Tolkien, J.R.R., "The Lord of the Rings," 3 vol., first editions, first impressions, with maps, ink name dated on front free endpaper of first 2 vol., damage to dust jackets.

Vol.III third state with sagging text and printed '4' on p.49.
1954-55
£4,000-5,000   BLO

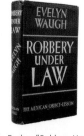

Waugh, Evelyn, "Robbery Under Law", first edition, published by Chapman & Hall, signed on the free end paper, "John Balfom, with kind regards and thanks from Evelyn Waugh", un-clipped dust jacket and original blue cloth.
1939
£3,000-4,000   GORL

Wodehouse, P.G., "The Pothunters", first edition, first issue, published by Adam & Charles Black, signed on front free endpaper, with 10 plates by R. Noel Pocock, with original blue cloth, rubbed at edges with some minor marking.
1902
£3,500-4,500   BLO

Woolf, Virginia, "The Waves", first edition, published by Hogarth Press, with original purple cloth and dust jacket by Vanessa Bell.
1931
£2,500-3,500   BLO

Allen, Joseph, "Geography Bewitched - Bonny Scotia," a caricature map card of Scotland, based on the caricature map by Bowles and Carver.

c1820   *5.5in (14cm) high*

£400-500   **JPOT**

ESSENTIAL REFERENCE - AARON ARROWSMITH

Aaron Arrowsmith (1750–1823) was an British cartographer, who lived and worked in London. He specialised in producing large-scale and up-to-date individual maps.

- During his early career he worked for John Cary and William Faden.
- In 1790 he became famous for his large chart of the world on Mercator projection (a type of mapping that represents lines of constant course as straight segments).
- In c1810 he became Hydrographer to the Prince of Wales (later George IV).
- After his death the business was taken over by his sons Aaron and Samuel, until around 1839 when it passed to his nephew John.

Arrowsmith, Aaron, "Map Of The World On A Globular Projection Exhibiting Particularly The Nautical Researches Of Capn. James Cook…", two sheets, the title with portrait of Cook flanked by Victory, Britannia and navigational instruments, engraved by J. Puke. Published 1794, this edition 1799.

1799   *73.5in (187cm) wide*

£16,000-18,000   **JPOT**

Arrowsmith, Aaron, "This improved Map of India compiled from all the latest & most authentic materials", one engraved map on nine sheets, hand-coloured, with index map.

In a note below the dedication Arrowsmith thanks the Duke of Wellington, Col. Allan, Genl. Kyd, Sir John Malcolm, Sir James Mackintosh, Dr. Buchanan, Mr Sydenham and the Court of Directors for their assistance in the production of this map.

1816   *96in (244cm) long*

£10,000-12,000   **L&T**

H. Bowles & S. Carver, "Bowles's Two-Sheet Plan Of The Cities Of London & Westminster", on two uncut sheets joined.

This map illustrates the expanding urbanisation of the capital in all directions at this time. Recent developments include, in the northwest, the cricket ground at Lisson Grove (Lord's predecessor) and the development of streets around Edgware Road, as well as developments at Tottenham Court Road, Oxford Street and today's Marylebone Road. Sloane Street and Square become recognisable and the market gardens of Southwark are becoming built-up. This is not recorded in James L Howgego's "Printed Maps of London, 1553-1850".

1796-1800   *37in (94cm) wide*

£1,000-1,500   **JPOT**

Cary, John, "New and Accurate Plan of London and Westminster, the Borough of Southwark and parts Adjacent… with an Alphabetical List of…500 of the most considerable Streets…", engraved with full original hand-colouring, linen-backed, folding into marbled slipcase.

1816   *59in (150cm) wide*

£2,500-3,000   **BLO**

Cellarius, Andreas, "Haemisphaerii Borealis Coeli et Terrae Sphaerica Scenographia," a hand-coloured engraved celestial map, published by J. Janssonius, Amsterdam, some chips and tears.

c1660-1666   *19.75in (50cm) wide*

£2,000-2,500   **FRE**

De Leth, A. & H., "Carte Nouvelle De La Mer Du Sud …", showing the Pacific and discoveries there, with large insets and vignettes, on two sheets.

The map is based on Nicolas De Fer's (1645-1720) very rare map of 1713.

1740   *37in (95cm) long*

£13,000-15,000   **JPOT**

CLOSER LOOK - RARE BATTLE OF YORKTOWN MAP

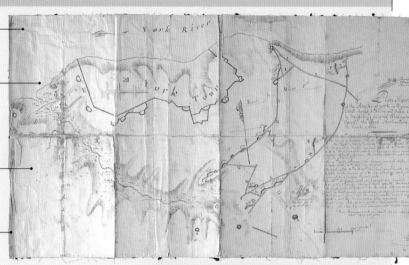

The Battle of Yorktown saw the combined American and French forces overwhelming the British, leading to their ultimate surrender on October 19, 1781, to General George Washington.

Ten days after the battle Lieutenant Colonel Jean Baptiste Gouvion (who was personally praised by Washington as having the "energy and precision which constitutes the great engineer") prepared this detailed map. The actual drafting was presumably the work of a draftsman in the engineer unit.

A similar map (labelled "Washington's Official Map of Yorktown") is held in the National Archives in Annapolis, Maryland. This example, although smaller, is in much better condition. It retains the original red and yellow colourings.

It is likely this map was either made for Washington himself, or his aide de camp, Tobias Lear.

Gouvion, Colonel Jean Baptiste, a rare battle of Yorktown map, showing the area of the siege works and the British defences across the river at Gloucester, on three sheets with black ink, with yellow and red colouring showing the American/French and British forces respectively.

24in (61cm) wide

£700,000-900,000 JDJ

Gibson, John, "Atlas Minimus Illustratus", revised, corrected, and improved by E. Bowen, published by T. Carnan and F. Newbery, with engraved frontispiece and 52 maps, red Morocco gilt covers.

1774

£2,000-2,500 LC

Godson, William, an 18thC uncoloured copperplate map of Winchester, Hampshire, engraved by R. Benning, with vignettes of important local buildings and text detailing "The Most Remarkable Events That Have Happen'd To The City…".

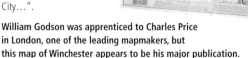

William Godson was apprenticed to Charles Price in London, one of the leading mapmakers, but this map of Winchester appears to be his major publication.

1750 *49.25in (125cm) wide*

£3,000-3,500 JPOT

Haines & Co., "A New And Correct Plan Of The Cities Of London & Westminster", titled in a garlanded cartouche at upper left, with inset views of landmarks, on canvas, minor repairs.

Haines & Co., unlike most other map publishers, is known only for large, two-sheet map publications intended as "wall-maps", and its work is consequently very rare.

1796 *41in (104cm) wide*

£2,000-2,500 JPOT

Homann, J.B., "Planiglobii Terrestris cum utroq Hemisphærio Cælesti; Asiae Recentissima Delineatio; Europa Christiani Orbis Domina; Totius Africae; Totius Americae", Nuremberg, five engraved maps with original hand-colouring.

c1720 *Each 23in (58.5cm) wide*

£2,000-3,000 set BLO

Hondius, Jodocus [Joost de Hondt], "Septentrio America", a hand-coloured double-page engraved map.

19in (49.5cm) wide

£1,500-2,000 DN

Moll, Herman, "A New And Correct Map Of The World, Laid Down According To The Newest Discoveries, And From The Most Exact Observations," with dedication to George II and celestial diagrams, minor repairs.

The map shows a precise depiction of California as an island, despite Moll's claims of being based on the "newest observations", and illustrates partial coastlines in the Pacific. One of the best-known and most sought-after British large-scale maps.

1709-c1715 *38.5in (98cm) wide*

£4,000-5,000 JPOT

Speed, John, "Northumberland", published by Sudbury and Humble, a county map with inset plans of Berwick and Newcastle, with column of coats of arms and panel of Roman remains, with extensive hand-colouring, dated 1610 but 1627.

1627 *20in (51cm) wide*

£500-600 BLO

CLOSER LOOK - MAP OF NORTH AMERICA AND CANADA

The map is signed (bottom left) by John Thornton (1641-1708) who worked for the English East India Company and the Hudson Bay Company.

The Hudson Bay Company used Thornton's maps to illustrate its claims over domain in North America. This map features a red boundary line running through Lake Mistassini just below 60 degrees north latitude. At the time this map was made the French were insisting the boundary ran across James Bay at 52 degrees north, and they owned everything south of it.

Much detail is given to the small settlements on the coast of Newfoundland. This makes it possible this map was actually a special commission for a patron with an interest in the fishing business.

Thornton, John, a manuscript map of North America and Canada, hand-coloured map on vellum marked "made by John Thornton at the Signe of the Platt in the Minories Anno".

1699 *26.5in (67.5cm) wide*

£200,000-250,000 LAW

Wallis, J., "London And Westminster In The Reign Of Queen Elizabeth ... 1563", an 18thC interpretation of the Ralph Agas/George Vertue map of Elizabethan London, on two joined sheets, minor restoration.

London is shown from Southwark with Shakespeare's Globe visible. London Bridge is the only bridge to cross the Thames at this time. The City walls are clearly visible and there is not a great deal of settlement outside the safety of these walls. The hills of Highgate and Hampstead are distant, rural villages.

40.5in (103cm) wide

£800-1,000 JPOT

Charles I, autograph letter to the Privy Council in Scotland, announcing his determination to stamp out "the practise of exorbitant and unsufferable usury," one page.

Countersigned by the Master of Requests, James Galloway, afterwards Lord Dunkeld, who had been appointed to receive the "legal forfeits" of Scottish usurers. In May the Scottish Privy Council agreed to levy fines for usury.

1632
£1,500-2,000   **L&T**

Washington, George, autograph letter to his nephew George Augustine Washington, four pages.

This rare letter shows Washington considering family issues. He writes that his nephew can expect to inherit a significant parcel of land, since "if Mrs. Washington should survive me there is a moral certainty of my dying without issue, and should I be the longest liver, the matter in my opinion is almost as certain; for whilst I retain the reasoning faculties I shall never marry a girl; and it is not probable that I should have children by a woman of an age suitable to my own, should I be disposed to enter into a second marriage.".
1786
£70,000-90,000   **JDJ**

Darwin, Charles, autographed letter to an unnamed correspondent, three pages, sent from "1 Carlton Terrace, Southampton. Aug. 21".

Letter reads, "Dear Sir, Severe illness in my family on a journey has prevented me from sooner thanking you for your very obliging note. I did not receive the specimen, which followed me from place to place, until it was quite withered; but the monstrosity is a common one. I should not expect this fusion of two flowers to be inherited, but it would be worth trial; nor indeed should I expect that the flower would set seed, but both these points would be worth ascertaining. Such facts, as I have collected, lead me quite to disbelieve in "jump of any size", but I know no objection to them on any other score...".
1826
£4,000-5,000   **LC**

Bonaparte, Napoleon, autograph letter, one page, sent from Paris, March 22, framed with engraved portrait.

To Monsieur Mollien, acknowledging the receipt of the report on the expenses of the Army of Italy, but questioning the existence of three pay offices.
1806
£800-1,200   **FRE**

An Abraham Lincoln signed photograph, by Thomas Le Mere at Brady's gallery, Washington, D.C., signed by Lincoln below the image.

One of 24 photo images (of the 119 known photos) of Lincoln standing.

1863   *4in (10cm) high*
£50,000-70,000

An original photograph of Anna Pavlova (and male partner), by Edward Steichen, silver print, with Steichen's signature at lower right.

c1920   *10in (25.5cm) high*
£1,200-1,800   **FRE**

Dulac, Edmund, "Dreamland", original drawing and watercolour for Edgar Allan Poe's "The Bells and Other Poems" (1912), signed and dated lower left corner, framed and glazed.
1912
£5,000-6,000   **BLNY**

A Queen Anne wooden lady doll, with gesso-over-wood painted head, shoulders and hands, brown glass eyes and human hair wig, wearing apricot silk dress with embroidered linen apron and straw hat, holding miniature rag doll, restored.

c1750   15.5in (39cm) high

£7,000-8,000   SK

A late 18thC German wooden gentleman doll, gesso-over-wood painted shoulder-head, hands and legs, with brown painted hair, in original soldier's dress uniform with gilded paper trim.

5in (12.5cm) high

£3,500-4,500   SK

CLOSER LOOK - GERMAN DOLL

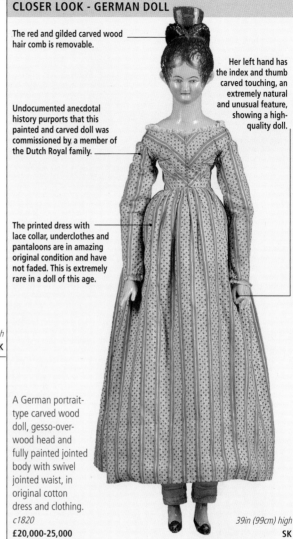

The red and gilded carved wood hair comb is removable.

Her left hand has the index and thumb carved touching, an extremely natural and unusual feature, showing a high-quality doll.

Undocumented anecdotal history purports that this painted and carved doll was commissioned by a member of the Dutch Royal family.

The printed dress with lace collar, underclothes and pantaloons are in amazing original condition and have not faded. This is extremely rare in a doll of this age.

A German portrait-type carved wood doll, gesso-over-wood head and fully painted jointed body with swivel jointed waist, in original cotton dress and clothing.

c1820   39in (99cm) high

£20,000-25,000   SK

An early 19thC folk art cloth lady doll, with hand-embroidered features, applied nose, human hair wig, in printed cotton dress with white cotton undergarments, missing one shoe.

For a doll of this age, it is incredible that the original fabric is in such good condition, and retains its vibrant colour.

25in (63.5cm) high

£7,000-8,000   SK

An early Austrian Grödnertal wood lady doll, gessoed and painted shoulder-head, black painted hair, with peg-jointed body and limbs, in gauze dress with lace trim and amber-coloured beaded necklace, with satin satchel.

c1820   7in (18cm) high

£1,200-1,800   SK

Seven early Grödnertal-type wooden dolls in a Victorian domed vignette, with a papier-mâché faux landscape and tree limbs, containing seven wood dolls, all with gessoed and painted shoulder-heads, peg-jointed bodies and limbs, in original costumes.

c1820   Dome 18in (45.5cm) high

£6,000-7,000   SK

A large Austrian Grödnertal wooden lady doll, with carved hair and jointed limbs at shoulders, elbows, hips and knees, in red and black printed gauze dress and cotton under-slip, replaced lower legs.

c1820   32in (81cm) high

£3,500-4,500   SK

A rare German papier-mâché doll, attributed to Lowenthal & Comp., cloth body with papier-mâché arms and head, with painted features and black glass eyes, in Vierlande provincial costume and matching cloth bonnet with attached human hair braids.

c1840   13.5in (34cm) high

£3,000-4,000   SK

TOYS AND DOLLS

A German papier-mâché doll, with cloth body and kid hands, painted features and black glass eyes, in blue patterned off-the-shoulder dress with a complementary floral apron.

c1840   *29in (74cm) high*

£1,200-1,800   SK

A German KPM porcelain lady doll, with painted and moulded features with blue eyes, kid body with glazed porcelain arms, in cotton and lace dress and brown leather shoes.

c1845   *17in (43cm) high*

£4,000-5,000   SK

A rare German KPM porcelain lady doll, with painted and moulded features, with human hair wig, cloth body with kid arms, in cream silk velvet dress with green satin trim and underskirt, matching hat, lace under-blouse, and brown high-button boots.

This KPM porcelain doll's wig makes her extremely rare. Her ball head has seven pierced holes.

c1845   *17in (43cm) high*

£3,500-4,500   SK

A German papier-mâché Scottish Highlander doll, with rare moulded helmet and painted features, cloth body with painted cloth arms and black boots, in authentic red wool and wool plaid Scottish costume.

c1850   *16in (40.5cm) high*

£2,500-3,500   SK

A German papier-mâché Kris Kringle doll, the overstuffed cloth body with kid hands, in wool plaid costume with blue fur trim, black leather shoes, and paper-covered muslin cone hat with fur and dated Christmas die cut, hung with around 55 toys.

This doll comes with a handwritten note reading: "Kris Kringle sends greeting through Cousin Anna to the children, and wishes them a Merry Christmas & Happy New Year – Christmas Eve 1852.".

1852   *22in (56cm) high*

£9,000-11,000   SK

A small Philadelphia Ludwig Greiner child doll, with papier-mâché shoulder-head and cloth body with kid arms, in silk dress with jacket and ermine cape, missing one shoe.

c1860   *8.5in (21.5cm) high*

£1,500-2,000   SK

A Rhode Island Izannah Walker painted cloth child doll, with oil-painted stockinette head and shoulders, the muslin body with oil painted limbs, in cream cotton dress and under-blouse.

c1860   *18in (45.5cm) high*

£8,000-12,000   SK

An unusual German Frozen Charlotte squeak toy, with china head and lower torso with jointed arms, cloth-covered torso contains squeaker mechanism, unusual black curly moulded hair and painted features.

c1880   *4.5in (11.5cm) high*

£2,000-2,500   SK

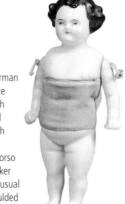

An American calico black folk doll, with oil-painted face and features, fur hat and cotton and lace outfit with velvet sash.

c1880   *12.5in (32cm) high*

£200-250   BEJ

An unusual Martha Chase "Black Mammy" cloth character doll, with moulded features, black caracul wig and red bandana, sateen body with painted arms and legs, wearing white cotton dress with floral apron.

Caracul is also called Persian lamb.

c1910   26in (66cm) high
£4,000-5,000   **SK**

A rare Martha Chase "Mr Micawber" character doll, the stockinette head with moulded and painted features, sateen body with original label, painted stockinette limbs, wearing original tuxedo, top hat, spats and black leather shoes.

Mr. Micawber is a character from "David Copperfield" by Charles Dickens.

c1920   15.5in (39cm) high
£3,000-4,000   **SK**

A Cuno & Otto "Admiral Winfield Scott Schley" bisque portrait doll, socket head incised "17 SC", on a five-piece jointed composition body with moulded black boots and painted white gloves, wearing a wool admiral's full dress uniform and matching hat.

c1900   8in (20cm) high
£800-1,200   **SK**

An early Francois Gaultier bisque fashion doll, with brown stationary glass eyes, blonde human hair wig and gusseted French kid body, wearing original embroidered wool costume, brown leather shoes and a matching hat.

c1870   14in (36cm) high
£2,000-3,000   **SK**

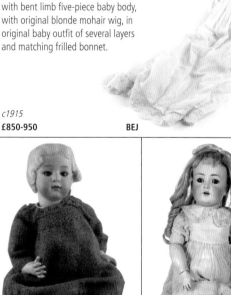

A Hertel and Schwab bisque character baby doll, mould 152, with bent limb five-piece baby body, with original blonde mohair wig, in original baby outfit of several layers and matching frilled bonnet.

c1915
£850-950   **BEJ**

A Jumeau Bebe "Elizabeth" bisque portrait doll, with blue paperweight eyes, brown human hair wig, head incised "10", jointed composition body marked "Jumeau", wearing aqua cotton dress with silk bonnet and parasol with original Au Nain Blue store label, original signed brown leather shoes.

c1880   23in (58cm) high
£15,000-20,000   **SK**

A Gebruder Heubach bisque doll, mould no.4, with sleeping eyes and jointed composition body.

11in (28cm) high
£550-650   **GORL**

A Kämmer & Rheinhardt "Mein Liebling" bisque girl doll, with blue glass flirty eyes, blonde mohair wig, joined composition limbs and body, wearing pale blue muslin dress, marked "K*R Simon & Halbig 117n".

20in (51cm) high
£1,200-1,800   **AH**

A Kestner bisque character girl doll, with brown painted eyes, light brown mohair wig, on a fully jointed composition body, wearing pink cotton checked dress and black leather shoes, incised "K/Made in Germany/14/208".

A Kämmer & Rheinhardt bisque Scottish boy doll, with blue painted eyes, blond mohair wig, fully jointed composition body, wearing original kilt and hat with matching socks and black leather shoes, incised "K*R 112/43".

c1910   16.5in (42cm) high
£6,000-8,000   **SK**

A Kestner bisque fashion doll, with fixed blue paperweight glass eyes, light brown mohair wig, stuffed kid body and limbs, with bisque hands, in cream lace and blue velvet dress with gold appliqué, marked "J".

                    17in (43cm) high
£350-450   **AH**

c1910   23.5in (60cm) high
£25,000-30,000   **SK**

LEFT: A late Käthe Kruse girl doll, with plastic head, blonde mohair wig, cotton body and limbs, wearing original blue and white polka dot dress and underwear, cream chinchilla fabric coat, crocheted hat, white socks, leather shoes and original label.

                    18in (45.5cm) high
£500-600   **SK**

RIGHT: A Käthe Kruse boy doll, with weighted head, oil-painted features, cloth body with stitched hands and separate thumb, wearing original yellow and white cotton romper suit, black socks and kid shoes, numbered "90774" on left sole, in maker's paper-covered box with labels.

c1914
£4,000-5,000   **SK**

An Armand Marseille bisque Oriental baby doll, with brown glass sleeping eyes, moulded hair, composition bent-limbed body, marked "353/4K".

                    15in (38cm) high
£800-1,200   **AH**

An Armand Marseille bisque Scottish boy character doll, with blond mohair wig, on a fully jointed composition body, wearing a Scottish costume with matching black hat and leather shoes, head incised "Made in Germany/A 6 M".

c1910   19in (48cm) high
£11,000-13,000   **SK**

A Rohmer porcelain fashion lady doll, with swivel head, shoulder plate and glazed porcelain arms, blonde sheepskin wig, gusseted all-kid body with jointed knees and signed "Rohmer", wearing printed cotton dress, silk bonnet and white leather boots.

c1865   17.5in (44cm) high
£3,500-4,500   **SK**

A J.B. Shepherd cloth baby doll, with moulded and painted stockinette shoulder-head, lower arms and legs, wearing printed cotton dress and white cotton and lace apron.

c1900   21in (53cm) high
£2,500-3,500   **SK**

A Simon & Halbig bisque lady doll, with moulded blonde hair, blue painted eyes, cloth body with bisque head, arms and lower legs, painted grey button-up boots, wearing patterned organza dress with aqua satin trim.

c1880   *8in (20cm) high*

£1,200-1,800   **SK**

A Simon & Halbig bisque doll, mould 939, with fixed eyes, pierced ears and jointed composition body.

14.5in (37cm) high

£600-700   **GORL**

A Steiner clockwork walking doll, with Schilling bisque head, original period clothes and characteristic Steiner tinplate boots.

The body of the doll has been opened to repair the mechanism, which reduces the value marginally.

12.75in (32.5cm) high

£3,000-4,000   **MTB**

A Chinese Ming-Ming baby "pot"-head character doll, in original outfit.

c1930   *10in (25.5cm) high*

£200-250   **BEJ**

A 1930s child's fur muff with celluloid doll head, in mint condition.

Although made for a child, this is a nice accessory for a slightly larger doll to hold and so is of interest to doll and costume collectors.

8in (20cm) wide

£200-250   **BEJ**

A late Georgian painted wood three-story dolls' house, divided into three distinct sections with hinged locking doors, the interior with nine rooms, some with vintage wallpapers or painted-over papers, as well as some pictures or wall hangings.

The trio of faux front doors (disproportionately small relative to the large windows) is a common feature of English dolls' houses of this vintage.

40in (102cm) high

£7,000-8,000   **SK**

A Victorian box-back dolls' house, the single-piece front with portico door and balustraded first floor, enclosing four rooms with some furniture and fittings.

23in (58cm) high

£800-1,000   **GORB**

An early 20thC George III-design dolls' house, with single-piece front enclosing two rooms.

19in (48cm) high

£600-800   **GORB**

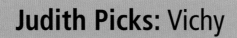

Judith Picks: Vichy

I think the fascination with automata stems from a childhood wonder at all things magical.

Of all of the automata I have seen, this gymnast by Vichy is among the most impressive. The engineering sophistication is astounding.

The sequence begins with the gymnast standing, poised, between the two chairs. At the drop of the coin, he raises the chair in his right hand waist-high, flexing his wrist so that the hand and chair are outstretched. He then lowers the chair to the ground and, with his hand still grasping the top rail for support raises his body into a handstand position, tilting the chair so that only its back two legs are resting on the stage. When his body is at ninety-degrees from the base, he raises the chair into the air, once again flexing from the right wrist so that the chair is horizontal and his entire weight rests in his left hand while simultaneously raising his head as if to survey the crowd, until body and chair are held in perfect alignment, before gracefully lowering himself back to a standing position. As a finale, he stretches his hand to release the chair, raising his free arm in the air, and bowing his head for applause.

It is one of the only 19thC automaton capable of catching and lifting an independent object as part of its routine. It is not surprising that Vichy is rated so highly.

A Vichy automaton of a Moroccan Harpist, with papier-mâché head, bone teeth, paperweight eyes with articulated lids, black mohair wig beneath satin turban, the going-barrel movement playing two airs and causing the figure to move her arms and incline her head, wearing silk costume and elaborate jewellery.

29in (73.5cm) high

£9,000-11,000   **SK**

A rare Vichy coin-operated automaton gymnast with two chairs, with papier-mâché head, brown glass eyes, on panelled oak base with coin-slot, large going-barrel motor driving five cams and four-air cartel cylinder movement, in the original spangled gold satin theatrical costume.

Vichy's Gymnast was one of the firm's largest and most elaborate automata. This example is one of the few in original costume, and the only known with coin-operated mechanism.

35.5in (90cm) high

£70,000-90,000   **SK**

A Vichy drunkard on park bench automaton, with papier-mâché head, auburn mohair wig, brown glass eyes with articulated lids, with articulated leather lower lip, the going-barrel movement causing the figure to raise the bottle and move drunkenly, accompanied by two airs, in wool suit, pleated shirt, felt hat and leather shoes, with "Vichy" key and "acorn" stop/start.

19in (48cm) high

£25,000-30,000   **SK**

A Vichy musical automaton of a Flamenco guitar player, the bisque head with fixed blue glass eyes, brown wig with long plait, "pearl" bonnet, wearing red silk jacket and grey skirt with gilded floral cut card motifs, on a wheeled key-wind stop/start musical mechanism causing her hand and head to move, with original key, original case.

c1890   *19.25in (49cm) high*

£4,500-5,500   **TEN**

A Vichy monkey harpist automaton, with papier-mâché head, amber glass eyes with articulated lids, articulated jaw and upper lip, bone teeth, with wood and gilt-brass harp with lion's head capital, in original silk outfit, felt tricorn hat and white wig, with "acorn" stop/start and iron key stamped "GV".

This monkey-person in 18thC dress mimics the court musicians, who wore monkey masks while performing.

17.5in (44.5cm) high

£10,000-15,000   **SK**

A French "Mephistopheles" bisque automaton head and arms, incised "L.B. Depose", set under dome together with his bisque hands holding miniature playing cards, hands repainted.

This type of head is typically seen on a standing Lambert automata.

c1880   *Head 4in (10cm) high*

£1,500-2,000   **SK**

A rare Adolf Müller automaton of a black footman with gong, articulated glass eyes and leather eyelids, the long-duration going-barrel movement with five cams causing the figure to roll his eyes as he beats the gong, wearing original silk and velvet costume, with key stamped "A. Steuart".

Müller's work is often associated with Vichy's. They were contemporaries working in different countries, trying to capture opposing sides of the automata market.

34in (87cm) high

£12,000-14,000   **SK**

A large Roullet & Decamps female magician automaton, with brown-tinted bisque Jumeau flange head stamped "Depose Tete Jumeau 10", brown paperweight glass eyes, brown human hair wig, composition hands, the table top mounted with two overturned silver paper-covered flowerpots, and a gold-foiled die, opening to a mohair-covered monkey head, a bisque child's face with hands, and a bisque clown with painted face, figure redressed in antique fabrics.

c1890   *28in (71cm) high*

£50,000-60,000   **SK**

A 19thC French magician automaton, wearing lace costume and holding a ring beside a table with a head in a box, on a rectangular velvet plinth base.

19.5in (49.5cm) high

£4,500-5,500   **LHA**

A French automaton singing bird in cage, of typical domed form.

12in (30.5cm) high

£600-700   **LHA**

A 19thC French painted papier-mâché model of a bulldog, with articulated head and growler.

13.5in (34cm) high

£1,200-1,800   **GORL**

A large 19thC Pennsylvania carved and painted trick box, decorated with a philphlot on a green ground, the box opening to reveal a leaping dog with two mechanical couples in an erotic embrace.

10.25in (26cm) wide

£5,000-7,000   **POOK**

A rare cast iron "Park" still bank, painted in green, red and white trim, brown roof, embossed "Park Bank" on façade.

4in (10cm) high

£3,500-4,500   BER

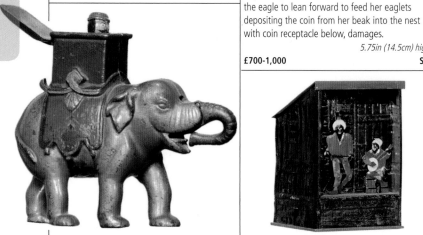

A painted cast-iron eagle and eaglets mechanical bank, by J.&E. Stevens Co., Cromwell, Connecticut, "Pat Jan 23 1883', activated by placing a coin into the eagle's beak and depressing the snake-form lever, which causes the eagle to lean forward to feed her eaglets depositing the coin from her beak into the nest with coin receptacle below, damages.

5.75in (14.5cm) high

£700-1,000   SK

A cast-iron mechanical cabin bank, by J.&E. Stevens Co., Cromwell, Connecticut, activated by placing a coin on the roof just above the door and pulling the handle on the right side of the bank, which causes the figure's feet to swing up and knock the coin into the bank, paint wear.

c1885   *3.75in (9.5cm) high*

£1,200-1,800   SK

A painted cast-iron elephant Howdah mechanical bank, by Enterprise Mfg. Co., Philadelphia, Pennsylvania, activated by placing a coin in the elephant's mouth and depressing the lever, the elephant eats the coin by pushing it into his mouth with his trunk while a small wooden man pops up from the howdah.

c1884   *5.5in (14cm) high*

£400-500   SK

A painted tin mechanical "Weedens Plantation Darkey Savings Bank", by Weeden Mfg. Co., New Bedford, Massachusetts, activated by winding the mechanism on the side of the bank and dropping a coin in the slot, the dancer begins to dance as the banjo player strums his instrument, manufacturer's paper label.

c1888   *5.5in (14cm) high*

£1,500-2,000   SK

A painted cast-iron "Teddy and The Bear" mechanical bank, by J. & E. Stevens Co., Cromwell, Connecticut, activated by sliding a piece on the rifle back into position and pushing the bear down into the tree, then placing a coin in front of the sliding piece and pressing the base lever, Teddy lowers his head and shoots the coin into the stump and the bear pops up, paint wear.

c1907   *9.25in (23.5cm) high*

£1,500-2,000   SK

A rare policeman safe bank, by J.M. Harper, depicting a Keystone cop standing guard in front of vault safe, with replaced screw.

c1907   *5.25in (13cm) high*

£4,000-5,000   BER

A rare early 20thC cast-iron "Mama Katzenjammer" mechanical bank, by Kenton, Ohio, with her sons Hans and Fritz, activated by placing a coin in the slot, which makes her eyes roll up, with rare original coin trap.

Mama Katzenjammer is a character from the American comic strip, "The Katzenjammer Kids", about two unruly boys, Hans and Fritz. It was created by the German immigrant Rudolph Dirks and drawn by Harold H. Knerr 1912-1949.

6.5in (16cm) high

£10,000-15,000   JDJ

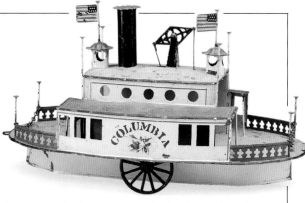

A rare 1880s Althof Bergmann "Columbia" ferry boat, with cast-iron wheels simulating the paddle wheels, a working walking beam and dual pilot houses with American flags on top of the cabin area (replaced flags).

13.5in (34.5cm) long

£25,000-35,000　　　　　　　　　　　　　　JDJ

A rare Althof Bergmann clockwork Santa sleigh with goats.

Only three examples of this toy are currently known, of which this is the example in the best condition.

20in (51cm) long

£100,000-200,000　　　　　　　　　　　JDJ

A French Citroën C4 Sedan, in bright red with maroon roof, with running boards, opening driver's door, nickel grille and dummy lights, clockwork inoperative.

£600-800　　　　　　　　　　　　　　　　BER

A George Brown clockwork "Broadway & 5th Avenue" omnibus, the bombe-shaped body heavily stencilled and labelled "BROADWAY & 5TH AVENUE" with white horses, and oversized driver.

13in (33.5cm) long

£25,000-35,000　　　　　　　　　　　　　　JDJ

A French Citroën clockwork C4 Semi Truck & Trailer, tractor in red and black pulling blue trailer, rubber tyres, opening door, embossed seating, body rear doors opens.

19in (48cm) long

£800-1,200　　　　　　　　　　　　　　　　BER

A Gunthermann clockwork limousine, lithographed cream and black with black and gold lining and red wheels, with opening doors, chauffeur, scuttle-mounted lamps and pressed tinplate spoked wheels.

14in (36cm) long

£2,000-2,500　　　　　　　　　　　　　　TOV

A Lehmann clockwork horseless carriage and driver, No.545, the tinplate body printed "OHO".

1906-16　　　　　*4in (10cm) long*

£350-450　　　　　　　　　　　　　AH

A Bing clockwork De Dion two-seater, in light green with red lining, adjustable front axle steering wheel, hand brake, and central gilded headlamp with cast yellow spoked wheels with white rubber tyres.

c1907　　　　　　　*8in (20cm) long*

£800-1,000　　　　　　　　　　　　TOV

An early 20thC German "Blériot" wind-up lithographed tinplate aeroplane, distributed by Einco, with celluloid propellers, in original box.

Einco was the trade name used by Eisenmann & Co., a toy import company based in London. Founded in the late 19thC by brothers Josef and Gabriel Eisenmann, the company had an office in Germany and distributed bisque dolls, teddy bears and other toys.

18in (46cm) long

£4,000-5,000　　　　　　　　　　　　SK

TOYS AND DOLLS

ESSENTIAL REFERENCE - STEIFF

Steiff GmbH was founded in 1880 in Giengen, Germany by seamstress Margarete Steiff.

- Steiff's first animals with moveable limbs were made in 1903. One of these was a teddy bear called 55PB.
- The trademark "button in ear" was designed in 1904, as a way of distinguishing Steiff products. Early buttons were embossed with an elephant. Buttons from 1905 onward bore the word "Steiff".
- Production ceased during World War II, resuming in 1947.
- In the 1950s, some pre-War models were slightly modified and produced again. In 1980, the factory started producing replicas of its old models, sometimes in limited editions for collectors.

LEFT AND CENTRE: An early Steiff officer and his wife, the officer with shoe-button eyes, the woman with glass eyes, both with original button.

Officer 22in (56cm) high

£4,500-5,500 pair   JDJ

LEFT OF CENTRE: An early Steiff black coachman's attendant, with side-glancing glass eyes, original Steiff button.

16in (40.5cm) high

£4,500-5,500   JDJ

RIGHT OF CENTRE: An early Steiff blacksmith, with shoe-button eyes, original Steiff button.

20in (51cm) high

£2,500-3,500   JDJ

RIGHT: An early Steiff coachman, with glass eyes, and original Steiff button.

21in (53cm) high

£4,000-5,000   JDJ

A Steiff white mohair teddy bear, with brown and black glass eyes, brown stitched nose, mouth and claws, swivel head, jointed elongated limbs with felt pads, hump and button-in-ear.

c1920   16in (40.5cm) high

£1,000-1,500   SAS

RIGHT: A large Steiff mohair teddy bear, with shoe-button eyes, light brown embroidered nose and claws, swivel joints, cream-coloured felt pads, long limbs and pronounced hump, with underscored "F" button-in-ear, some damage.

c1905

£5,500-6,500   SK

ON SHOULDER: A small Steiff white mohair teddy bear, black shoe-button eyes, light brown embroidered nose and claws, swivel joints, long limbs and cream-coloured felt pads, with underscored "F" button in ear, damage.

White mohair bears are generally more collectable than brown bears, as they are rarer and far less likely to survive in good order.

c1905   10in (25.5cm) high

£2,000-3,000   SK

A Steiff bear-on-wheels, with jointed head, ear button, burlap fur.

1900-10

£1,500-2,000   PC

A Steiff white mohair teddy bear, with black boot-button eyes, brown stitched nose, mouth and claws, swivel head, jointed elongated limbs with felt pads, hump and plain button-in-ear.

1908   16in (40.5cm) high

£2,500-3,000   SAS

A brown Steiff bear, with green ribbon and button in ear.

This bear is unusual in this colour.

c1920   18in (45.5cm) high

£2,000-2,500   TBW

A 1920s Steiff two-tone plush teddy bear, with rare "startled" eyes, stitched muzzle and two replaced pads, with button to ear.

18in (45.5cm) high

£4,500-5,500   GORL

A Steiff blonde teddy bear, with button-in-ear, and remnant of a tag.

1927-34   11.75in (30cm)

£1,000-1,500   TBW

An early 20thC Bing mohair teddy bear, with boot-button eyes.

c1910   *21in (53cm) high*
£1,000-1,200   **PC**

A 1930s Chiltern Hugmee gold plush teddy bear, with glass eyes, stitched muzzle and velvet pads.

21in (53cm)
£300-400   **GORL**

A large Farnell gold mohair teddy bear, with replacement orange and black eyes, pronounced muzzle, black nose, mouth, webbed hand claws and feet claws, swivel head, elongated limbs with cloth pads, heavy restoration.

30in (76cm) high
£400-500   **SAS**

A large 1930s Chiltern Winter Skater teddy bear, wearing hooded jacket and muffler, with label on foot "Chilton Toys, Anurge Pets, Institute of Hygiene".

This bear was almost certainly made for a shop display.

27in (68.5cm) high
£1,200-1,800   **LC**

A table model kaleidoscope, "C.C. Bush & Co., Prov., RI Patent Reissued Nov. 11, 1873", with leatherette wrapping and brass trim, on turned wood base..

13.25in (33.5cm) high

£1,800-2,200   JDJ

CLOSER LOOK - MAGIC LANTERN

The magic lantern, an early type of image projector, was developed by Dutch physicist Christian Huygens in the late 1650s. During the 18thC and 19thC they were taken around the country by travelling entertainers and mediums, who would use them to "summon" demons or spirits.

Magic lanterns are collected as examples of pre-cinema moving image.

This example is clearly of high quality and would have been very expensive in its day. Cheaper lanterns, designed for children, were made out of tinplate.

Original magic lanterns were gas powered, and many were subsequently converted to electricity, which can decrease value and desirability. This example is in complete condition and has all its original lenses.

W.C. (William Charles) Hughes was originally a stage entertainer, before he became an optician and lantern-manufacturer in 1879. In 1884 he patented an improved choreutoscope, a special mechanical lantern slide used to produce moving images.

A Victorian mahogany and gilt lacquered-brass biunial magic lantern projector, W.C. Hughes, the lacquered brass fittings and lens mounts with numerous adjustments and two self centring R. Beard's slides, with maker's plaque beneath a japanned-metal chimney.

Biunial magic lanterns (with two lenses) are relatively rare. Triunial lanterns are even rarer.

26in (66cm) high

£2,500-3,000   TOV

A Cantonese red and white ivory chess set.

King 4.25in (11cm) high

£800-1,200   LC

A rare Schoenhut St. Clair Dairy Co. milk wagon, complete with driver, milk crate, and horse, in near mint condition.

During the 1920s and early 1930s, the Schoenhut Toy Co. of Philadelphia, Pennsylvania, produced several different milk and bread wagons. This is the only known example of this milk wagon and is therefore likely to have been a special order.

23in (58.5cm) long

£7,000-8,000   JDJ

A large German hand-painted Noah's Ark, with over 200 animals in the early Erzgebirge style, some overpainting and damage to animals.

The more animals with the ark, the higher the value. The animals were often carved by people who hadn't seen live examples.

£25,000-35,000   BER

A Beeson O gauge electric 3-rail 2-4-0 no.790 Hardwicke locomotive and six-wheel tender, in L.N.W.R. black livery.

One of a batch of six produced in nickel silver between 1964 and 1966.

£8,000-10,000 TEN

A Beeson O gauge electric 3-rail 0-4-4 No.440 tank locomotive, in Caledonian dark blue livery.

£8,000-10,000 TEN

A Beeson O gauge electric 3-rail 0-4-4 no.1342 tank locomotive, in Midland fully lined red livery.

£3,500-4,500 TEN

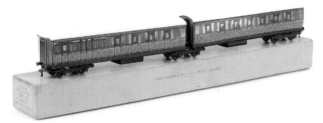

A Hornby O gauge 20v electric 4-6-2 locomotive no. 6201 "Princess Elizabeth", finished in L.M.S. maroon livery, and matching six-wheeled tender, within original red-lined display box, minor damages.

£2,000-2,500 TOV

A rare Hornby O gauge G.W. "GUNPOWDER VAN", in grey with "GW", red cross and "G.P.V." to van sides, in near mint condition, in good condition box with "GW" label to one end.

£2,000-2,500 VEC

A Hornby Dublo 3-rail D2 post-war Gresley L.N.E.R. articulated coach set, complete with centre bogie and corridor connection, in near-mint condition, in very good condition box, dated "5/48".

£1,500-2,000 VEC

A Hornby O gauge special tender 4-4-0 clockwork locomotive, "County of Bedford", RN 3821, in lined G.W.R. green livery, with Great Western and crest to tender sides, black nameplates, "GC-VGC".

£500-600 W&W

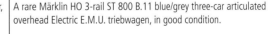

A rare Märklin HO 3-rail pre-War R800 0-4-0 black locomotive and tender, with "R800" and "Märklin" to cab-sides, in excellent condition, in very good condition original box.

£800-1,200 VEC

A rare Märklin HO 3-rail ST 800 B.11 blue/grey three-car articulated overhead Electric E.M.U. triebwagen, in good condition.

£2,000-3,000 VEC

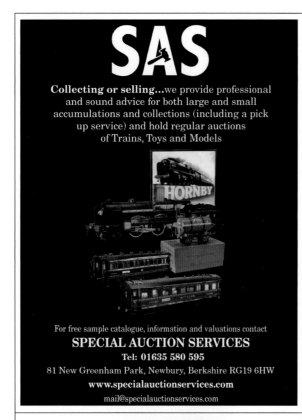

A 3.5in (9cm) gauge 4-4-0 coal fired live-steam L.M.S. locomotive and tender, "Ethel Annie", with traditional fittings, cased, in display cabinet with track.

31in (79cm) long

£1,200-1,800   CHT

A 5.5in (14cm) gauge 0-6-0 live-steam pannier tank engine, No.7400, with forward and reverse, pressure gauge, whistle, sprung buffers, and other traditional fittings.

31in (79cm) long

£1,400-1,600   CHT

A 5.5in (14cm) gauge 4-1-1 coal-fired live-steam G.N.R. livery Stirling Single-style engine and tender, No 772, with forward reverse, pressure gauge, sprung buffers, and other traditional fittings.

49in (124.5cm) long

£2,500-3,500   CHT

A 1/16-scale live-steam model Boston and Albany "402" locomotive, by Everett W. Clem, Shrewsbury, Massachusetts, with one cylinder, one gallon tank capacity, 3.5in (9cm) gauge, working blueprints, early photographs and publication material.

This model burned anthracite screenings, produced 100 pounds of steam pressure and achieved a top speed of ten miles per hour. The "402", with over 1,000 separate parts, was made by Mr Clem over a four year period and 2,000 hours of labour. Based on a 176-tonne prototype, the 200-pound model is shown in photographs hauling a flatbed car with ten passengers around a track in North Bellingham, Massachusetts, about 1950.

1945   *42in (107cm) long*

£5,500-6,500   SK

A scratch-built 5in (13cm) gauge live-steam 2-4-0 G.W.R. tank locomotive, based on the metro design by Martin Evans, finished in green G.W.R livery with cast "970" number plate, with maker's plaque "Built by C.N. Foster, Shipley 1981", on a piece of display track.

31.5in (80cm) long

£3,000-4,000   TEN

A scratch-built 5in (13cm) gauge live-steam model of a 4-2-2 G.N.R. stirling single no. 5 locomotive and tender, finished in green G.N.R. livery, with brass makers plaque "No. 5 Maker William Longstaff 1969", on a piece of display track, in glazed case.

62.5in (159cm) long

£6,500-7,500   TEN

A 2.5in (6.5cm) live-steam "Piddler" 0-4-0 locomotive.

£350-450   SWO

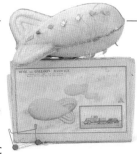

A rare Minic 76M Barrage balloon set, comprising an assembled Buckram-style fabric balloon, a six-wheel Lorry with winch and four-wheel trailer, both in camouflage finish, in good condition original box with instruction leaflet.

£3,000-4,000   VEC

A Radiguet ocean liner, with copper finish and black hull, wooden decking, tin cabin, three stacks, two masts, clockwork driven, some restoration.

19in (48cm) long

£8,000-10,000   BER

A coal-fired live-steam traction engine, with chain-link worm-and-peg steering, whistle, pressure gauge, forward and reverse gear, brass-band boiler, green and black livery.

23in (58cm) long

£1,000-1,500   CHT

A 4'- scale fowler A9 single-cylinder agricultural traction engine, single cylinder with Stephensons link-valve gear, driving two-speed gear set to single-drive rear axle, fly wheel-driven regulator for valve chest, cylinder with displacement and ratchet lubrications, axle-driven cable drum and drive shaft-locking pins, chain-link steering to front with leaf springs to axle, complete with tools, driver's seat, engineering drawings, Pressure Test Certificate for 2009, working pressure 100lbs/square inch, 4' stroke.

71in (180cm) long

£14,000-16,000   AH

A 2in- (5cm-) scale Fowler Showman's live-steam traction engine with crane, "IRIS", canopy inscribed "The Pride of Yorkshire", finished in maroon livery, with cream, with chimney extension, yellow spoked wheels, maker's plaque "John Fowler & Co Leeds".

43in (109cm) long

£10,000-15,000   TEN

A 2in- (5cm-) scale Burrell showman's live-steam traction engine with crane, "Thetford Town", after the design by Ronald H. Clark, in maroon and black livery, the double-cranked compound engine with double gearing, with chimney extension, maker's brass plaque to both sides "Chas Burrell & Sons Ltd, Manufacturers, Thetford, England, No. 4085".

69.75in (177cm) long

£10,000-15,000   TEN

A 1in- (2.5cm-) scale freelance showman's scenic live-steam traction engine, "Vulcan", reg. no. "BJ 4789", in maroon livery, canopy inscribed "R.B and S. Ellse Mech, Engineering, Doncaster", with crane attachment and chimney extension, yellow spoked metal wheels with rubber tyres.

26.75in (68cm) long

£3,500-4,500   TEN

A Durham and North Yorkshire 2in- (5cm-) scale live-steam two-speed traction engine, built by J. Hepwood, Boroughbridge, with three shafts, flywheel, cast aluminium wheel rims, working pressure 100psi, steel boiler, on wooden display stand.

30.75in (78cm) long

£4,000-5,000   TEN

Judith Picks

For me, one of the most exciting moments of the "BBC Sports Relief Antiques Roadshow" was when I was asked to value the gold medal José Mourinho won for leading Chelsea Football Club to the League title in the 2005-06 season. He had hurled it to delighted fans celebrating Chelsea's 3-0 win over Manchester United and the fan who caught it subsequently sold it at Bonhams for £21,600. An amazing price for a very recent medal, but fans are fans and it is Chelsea after all.

This medal has far greater age and heritage. The inaugural match of the now famous Football Association Challenge Cup (F.A. Cup) in 1872 was won by the Wanderers F.C. The triumphant players were all presented with an inscribed gold medal, but this is the only example known to have survived. Although it almost didn't. In the 1950s the vendor's grandfather, a jeweller, bought the medal as part of a consignment of scrap gold. A keen football fan, he fortunately recognised the importance of the medal and saved it from its intended destination of the melting pot. Phew!

A rare gold winner's medal from the inaugural Football Association Challenge Cup final of 1872, by William Joseph Taylor of London, with a band of laurel, the reverse with "FOOTBALL ASSOCIATION CHALLENGE CUP, 1872".

1in (2.5cm) diam

£70,000-90,000   **GBA**

A 9ct gold medal, awarded to Stanley Matthews on September 19th 1934 for playing for the Football League v Ireland at Belfast.

Matthews was aged 19 and scored in the match, which the England Football League won 6-1. Just ten days later he won his first Cap playing for England against Wales.

£1,200-1,800   **LT**

An F.A. Cup 9ct gold winner's medal, awarded to Danny Blanchflower of Tottenham Hotspur, inscribed "1961-62", and "THE FOOTBALL ASSOCIATION, CHALLENGE CUP, WINNERS, TOTTENHAM HOTSPUR F.C., D. BLANCHFLOWER", with later pierced scrolling frame and suspension loop.

Robert Dennis "Danny" Blanchflower (1926-1993) became one of the most influential and respected players of his generation, captaining both Tottenham Hotspur and his national side, Northern Ireland. The 1962 F.A. Cup match was played at Wembley on 5th May 1962, with Spurs defeating Burnley 3-1. Blanchflower scored his side's third and decisive goal from the penalty spot in the 80th minute.

£18,000-22,000   **GBA**

An early woollen, button-up white England shirt, worn by John Goodall, with embroidered three lions cloth badge.

This is believed to be John Goodall's England debut shirt worn in the match v Scotland at Hampden Park 17th March 1888. Goodall scored one of the goals in England's 5-0 win. This is one of the earliest England shirts ever to be offered at auction.

£5,000-6,000   **GBA**

A red long-sleeved, button-up England no. 5 shirt, worn by Jim Taylor in the 1951 match v Argentina at Wembley Stadium, with embroidered three lions cloth badge inscribed "ARGENTINA".

This match was the first time the England red shirt was used, because the team's white shirts were too similar to Argentina's pale blue and white.

1950-51

£10,000-12,000   **GBA**

A red long-sleeved, crew-neck England No. 4 jersey, worn by Nobby Stiles in the 1966 World Cup final, with embroidered three lions badge.

One of the enduring images of the 1966 World Cup final was Nobby Stiles' impromptu celebratory jig on the Wembley pitch, wearing this shirt, and holding the Jules Rimet Trophy aloft in one hand and his dentures in the other.

£90,000-110,000   **GBA**

A purple England v Scotland international cap, worn by John Goodall 1888-1895, inscribed in silver wire "1888-89-91-92-94-95", with full page plate of Goodall extracted from "Famous Footballers" wearing the cap.
£3,000-4,000 GBA

A white England v Ireland international cap, worn by John Goodall 1894-1897, inscribed in silver wire "1894-95-96-97".
£4,000-5,000 GBA

A rare England v Wales international programme, played at Arsenal 15th March 1920.
£3,500-4,500 GBA

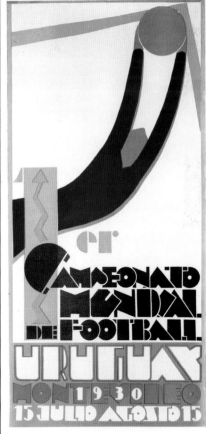

A programme for the first international match played at Wembley England v Scotland 12th April 1924.
£3,500-4,500 GBA

An England v Belgium international programme played at West Bromwich Albion 8th December 1924.
£2,000-2,500 GBA

A rare and previously unrecorded public notice, served by the Magistrates of Alnwick in Northumberland in 1821 cautioning inhabitants that the playing of football in the streets is an offence against the laws, printed by J. Graham, Alnwick, dated February 22nd 1821.
£2,000-2,500 GBA

"The Northern Football Annual 1876", edited by the author of "Football In The North", published by E. Hulton & Co., re-bound by R. Riviere & Son Ltd, with original paper wrappers preserved.

This extremely rare annual was the first to focus on football in the North of England. It was presumably not a commercial success, as it did not continue.
1876
£6,000-7,000 GBA

An official 1930 World Cup poster, designed by Guillermo Laborde, printed by Olivera y Fernandez, Montevideo, linen-backed.

Guillermo Laborde (1886-1940) was originally on the panel that had been formed to select the winner of a competition to design the official poster for the first World Cup in 1930. He later resigned as he wished to enter the competition himself.
1930 *31in (79cm) high*
£5,500-6,500 GBA

An autographed cricket bat, signed by the 1934 Australian and fifteen English county teams.

This bat is an almost complete record of the 1934 English cricketing summer, lacking only the Glamorgan & Leicestershire county teams.

£700-900   GBA

A 19thC autographed Sammy Woods cricket bat, by Odd & Son, Croydon, with the initials "S M J W", the face with approximately 22 ink signatures including the Test players S.M.J. Woods, W.G. Grace, A.E. Stoddart.

"Sammy" Woods is one of only five cricketers to have represented Australia and England at Test cricket, making three appearances for each country.

£3,000-4,000   GBA

A rare gold medal, awarded to Harry Charlwood on the first official Test Match, 15th March 1877 at the Melbourne Cricket Ground between Australia and England, the obverse engraved with crossed cricket bats, stumps and a ball.

£12,000-15,000   GBA

An Australian "Baggy Green" cricket cap and green and gold neck tie, worn by Colin McCool in the Australian "Invincibles" tour of England in 1948.

Colin McCool was born in Paddington, Sydney, 9th December 1916. The right-hand bat and leg break googly bowler played in 14 Tests for Australia, top-scoring with 104 not out and with a best bowling analysis of 5 for 41.

£5,000-6,000   GBA

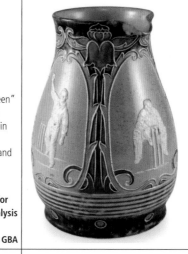

A 19thC Doulton Lambeth stoneware cricketing jug, decorated with three panels showing a bowler, wicket keeper and batsman.

8in (20cm) high

£150-200   GORB

A Doulton Lambeth cricket tyg, the handles modelled as cricket bat trophies, with three applied scenes of bowlers and batsmen beneath silver plated rim, printed marks and dated.

1881   *6in (15cm) high*

£250-350   GORL

"John Wisden's Cricketers' Almanack For 1919," edited by Sydney H. Pardon, published by John Wisden & Co. with original brown cloth gilt.

£3,500-4,500   GBA

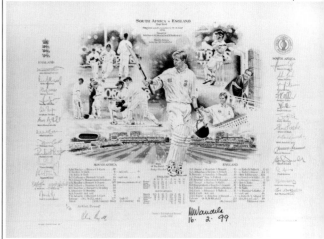

A signed artist's proof print of the 1998 South African cricket team in England, after a painting by Richard Ryall, numbered "1 of 8 Artist's Proof", signed by both teams, the artist and Nelson Mandela, dated in his hand "16th February 1999".

30.25in (76.5cm) wide

£1,500-2,000   GBA

A curved-faced sand iron, used by American champion Bobby Jones and later used as a trophy club by the Oxford University Golf Club, retailed by Ernest Sales of Sunningdale, with illegal curved face, and presentation plate.

£6,000-7,000 GBA

A Tom Morris longnose playclub, the scared fruitwood head stamped "T. Morris", horn inserts to sole, lead counterweight, with hickory shaft.

£1,200-1,800 L&T

A Charles Ashford "Skibbie" combination wood, with hickory shaft.

£1,500-2,500 L&T

An Edward M. Fitzjohn anti-shank brass adjustable putter, the rectangular face marked with a target, with hickory shaft.

£1,500-2,000 L&T

A George Strath of Troon long-nosed putter, with beech head, hickory shaft, repairs.
1885

£3,000-4,000 GBA

LEFT: A feathery golf ball, in reasonably good condition.
c1850

£1,800-2,200 GBA

RIGHT: A Haskell patent bramble-pattern rubber-core golf ball, some paint loss.
c1900

£450-550 GBA

A Doulton Lambeth salt-glazed stoneware golfing mug, sprigged in white with golfers, with impressed marks.

6in (15cm) high

£800-1,200 DN

An early 20thC novelty silver hat pin holder, maker's mark "EFB", Birmingham, modelled as a golf bag with leather handle.
1912 *5.25in (13cm) high 3.7oz*

£600-700 TEN

A Fruitland Nurseries, August, Georgia, Gardeners Catalogue, "Fall 1934-Spring '35".

The land occupied by the Fruitland Nurseries was sold to Bobby Jones and became Augusta National Golf Club. Today the holes are named after plants grown at the nurseries.

£1,000-1,500 L&T

A "Golf De La Soukra Tunis" poster, printed by Imprimerie de Vaugrard, Paris.

A joint effort between the French Railway and the Tunisian Tourist Authority to lure French golfers to the "bigger fields and vast open spaces" of Tunisia.

1932 *39in (99cm) high*

£3,000-4,000 SWA

A William IV Irish silver "Tarporley Hunt" trophy cup, James le Bass, Dublin, embossed with Classical figures in horse-drawn chariots, with two engraved cartouches reading "Tarporley Hunt 1858," and "Won by James Platt's Welsh Heiress".

1832-33   11.5in (29cm) high 55oz
£3,000-4,000   ECGW

An oak jockey scale, by Allen & Hanburys Ltd, London, the U arms over a solid seat, flanked by a lidded beam scale, on wheeled frame.

c1980   39in (99cm) wide
£1,000-1,500   TEN

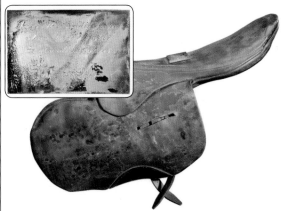

The "Arkle" saddle, used by Pat Taaffe, set with a metal plaque inscribed "THIS IS THE SADDLE I USED WHEN I RODE "ARKLE" TO WIN ALL HIS RACES", and engraved with Taaffe's signature.

Arkle is universally regarded as being the greatest steeplechaser of all time. His Timeform rating of 212 has never been eclipsed. The saddle comes with a 1970s letter from Neil Durden-Smith, then Secretary of the Anglo-American Sporting Club, authenticating the saddle.

£12,000-18,000   GBA

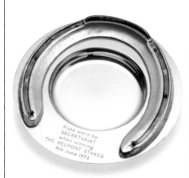

A racing plate worn by Secretariat when winning The Belmont Stakes 7th June 1973, mounted on a silver ashtray, Garrard's, London, inscribed "PLATE WORN BY SECRETARIAT, WHEN WINNING THE BELMONT STAKES, 9TH JUNE 1973".

£2,500-3,000   GBA

A rare official match programme for the England v France rugby game at Twickenham in 1911.

£2,000-2,500   GBA

A large Copeland stoneware jug, with rugby scenes moulded in white raised relief between grassy borders on a green ground.

7in (18cm) high
£300-350   GBA

A Babe Ruth autographed baseball, inscribed "To Billy from Babe Ruth" on an official American League ball stamped "William Harridge, Pres".

"Billy" was the nephew of the editor of "Sporting News," Armond Van Pelt, who had Babe Ruth sign this baseball during a radio interview in the 1930s.

2.75in (7cm) diam
£4,000-5,000   DRA

A green Ireland No.13 international rugby union shirt, worn in 1979, 1980 and 1982.

£250-350   GBA

An early 4.5in (11.5cm) brass and wood fishing reel, with an ivory handle, stamped "A & G Wilson Edinburgh, Fishing Rod and Tackle Makers to his late RHPA".

£450-550   LC

An African Baule carved wood female figure, with bent knees, hands to the abdomen, scarification patterns on the face and lower back, incised coiffure, dark patina.

11.5in (29cm) high

£1,200-1,800   SK

An African Baule carved wood female figure, with hands to the abdomen, scarification marks on the face and body, elaborate coiffure, dark patina, insect damage.

15in (38cm) high

£1,000-1,500   SK

An early 20thC African Dan passport mask, Ivory Coast, with excised geometric design around the eyes and protruding mouth, accented with kaolin, deep, well-handled patina, mounted on a custom display stand.

6in (15cm) high

£1,000-1,500   DRA

An early 20thC African Senufo carved wood Kpelie Janus mask, Ivory Coast, with elaborate facial regalia and stylised finial, on display stand.

Images of duality among the tribes of this region often refer to the link between the world of the living and the spirit realm. The moral portrayed is that humans are inextricably connected to the souls of their forebears.

12in (30cm) high

£1,200-1,800   DRA

An early 20thC African Bamana carved wood figural medicine container, Mali, the lid featuring a classic female ancestor with elaborate headdress and elongated facial features, on star-shaped base, with slight erosion and signs of ritual use.

23in (58cm) high

£1,200-1,800   DRA

An African Bamana antelope headdress, Mali, with incised decoration, on metal plate stand.

58.25in (147.5cm) high

£350-450   WW

An African Dogon mask, Mali, with pointed head and horns, triangular eye sockets and notched nose, pierced edge.

14.5in (37cm) high

£300-400   WW

An African Dogon Satimbe mask, Mali, with stylised anamorphic face, mounted with a standing figure with arms outstretched and flattened face.

39in (99cm) high

£500-600   RTC

A rare early 20thC African Mumuye abstract mask, Nigeria, accented with red clay, with over-sized eyes and flat snout, well-weathered with signs of heavy use, on custom display stand.

14.5in (37cm) long

£3,000-4,000   **DRA**

A rare early 20thC African Tiv ilborivungu cult fetish ritual staff, Nigeria, with carved wood male head featuring inlaid glass eyes, scarification of tears, and human hair woven in braids, over a femur bone wrapped with beads, on metal display stand.

The traditional use of these objects from the only documented cannibal cult in Africa relates to the legend of a Tiv ancestor known as Poor. According to local legend, his thigh bone was removed so that his memory would be perpetuated. Over time, the original artefact was lost, and was substituted with relics (Imborivungu).

7in (18cm) high

£1,500-2,500   **DRA**

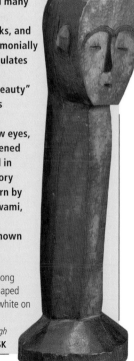

An early 20thC African Ibo carved wood helmet mask, Nigeria, the superstructure featuring ancestors and avian images, with raised scarification on kaolin-covered face and remnants of traditional costume, some losses, on metal display stand, without costume.

This mask and costume represent the spirit of a young deceased maiden, thought of as a protective entity.

22in (56cm) high

£1,200-1,800   **DRA**

An African Urhobo carved wood male figure, Nigeria, the seated figure with flaring torso, extended arms with hands each holding an implement, the stylised head with scarification, wearing European-style hat, necklace, and detailed waistband, wood loss.

42in (107cm) high

£6,000-8,000   **SK**

An African Jekri Itsekri paddle, Nigeria, the teardrop-shape blade pierced with crocodiles and incised decoration with a part-pierced shaft and conforming handles, losses.

62.25in (158cm) long

£300-400   **WW**

ESSENTIAL REFERENCE - WAREGA ART

The Warega (or Lega) began to migrate from Uganda to the Congo in the 16thC. They were fierce warriors, and they assimilated many cultures along the way.

● Almost all their art (limited to masks, and wood or ivory figures) is used ceremonially by the "Bwami" society, which regulates nearly all aspects of Warega life.

● The Warega do not consider the "beauty" of an object to be relevant, only its mystical success.

● Masks are typically flat with narrow eyes, a long flat nose, and a partially opened mouth. They may be plain, covered in kaolin, or decorated with spots. Ivory masks are rare and can only be worn by members of the highest level of Bwami, known as "Kendi".

● Small, roughly carved statuettes known as "ikenga" are also made.

An African Warega carved wood head, with long faceted neck, the stylised head with heart-shaped face, traces of red pigment on one side and white on the opposite, pyro-engraved detail.

21.5in (54cm) high

£14,000-16,000   **SK**

An African carved wood fetish figure, Kongo, with one hand to the hips, the other raised to throw a spear (missing), with inlaid mirror eyes, dark patina, throwing arm broken and re-attached.

11.25in (28.5cm) high

£4,000-5,000   **SK**

ESSENTIAL REFERENCE - FANG BYERI FIGURES

The Fang tribes are spread over a vast area of equatorial Africa, mainly in the rainforest of Gabon.

- Fang statuary can be divided into three main groups: heads on long necks, half-figures and full figures, standing or seated. Simply carved, they manage to exhibit a high degree of sophistication in the coordination of bulbous forms.
- The Fang practice a cult devoted to ancestor lineages, the "byeri", who protect them from the dead and offer help in day-to-day life.
- The guardian figures were placed on top of a byeri box (reliquary) in which the bones of ancestors were kept.
- With large heads, long bodies, and short extremities, Fang byeri figures have the proportions of a newborn. This emphasises the group's continuity with its ancestors and with the three classes of the society: the "not-yet-born", the living, and the dead.
- From 1930 onwards, traditional Fang religion and art underwent a drastic transformation and Byeri figures were no longer made.

An African Fang carved wood male figure, the cylindrical torso supported by muscular legs and rounded hips, the round head with pointed teeth, protruding ears, and inlaid glass eyes, honey-coloured patina.

14.5in (37cm) high

£12,000-14,000 SK

An early 20thC African Punu maiden spirit mask, Gabon, with incised coiffure, accented with red pigment on forehead band, and several layers of kaolin clay, on metal display stand.

11.5in (29cm) high

£2,000-3,000 DRA

An early 20thC African Aakan colonial figural comb, Ghana, topped by a Colonialist wearing a coat and hat, linear pattern to base, with lustrous patina, on display stand.

6.75in (17cm) high

£1,000-1,500 DRA

An African Kota wood and metal reliquary figure, Gabon, with oval head framed by crescent-shaped flanges, the heart-shaped face with metal pointed teeth, the neck and front covered with stapled brass and copper sheeting, old tag on reverse reads "Babamba, Gaboon".

19.5in (49.5cm) high

£20,000-25,000 SK

A rare African Mbole carved wood mask, with narrow pierced eyes, narrow nose with central indentation, the forehead with grooved and painted stripes, remnant white pigment and pyro-engraved details, old repair and old tags on reverse.

14in (36cm) high

£60,000-80,000 SK

An African Shona carved wood headrest, the stylised form with pyro-engraved detail, repairs.

7.5in (19cm) wide

£2,500-3,500 SK

An African carved wood female figure, Tanzania, on a round base with hands to the wide hips, square shoulders, dark patina, cracks.

12in (30.5cm) high

£1,000-1,500 SK

An African Yoruba carved wood equestrian figure, the male figure on a diminutive stylised horse and holding a snake in one hand that extends to the horse's head, traces of blue and red pigments, insect damage.

20.25in (51.5cm) high

£1,200-1,800 SK

An Inuit stone and ivory "Bible Study" group, by Ennutsiak, E7-603, from Iqaluit.

Ennutsiak (1896-1967) was an early pioneer of Inuit sculpture. A complex and detailed work, the subject matter of this piece is unusual as it shows how Western religion began to infiltrate Inuit society.

c1955   *5.5in (14cm) long*
£12,000-18,000   **WAD**

CLOSER LOOK - "DANCING POLAR BEAR"

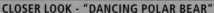

Pauta Saila is the best-known sculptor of polar bears, with examples being highly sought-after, particularly in large sizes such as this one.

Known as "nanuk", the powerful polar bear is both feared and revered by the Inuit. The hunters believed if they killed a bear they would take its spirit; if the bear killed the hunter it would also be empowered by the spirit of the hunter.

Dancing bears standing on one leg are Saila's trademark form, and poke gentle fun at the creature.

Heavily stylised and almost modern, the form is heavy yet balanced, and manages to evoke the power and strength of the bear.

An Inuit stone and ivory "Dancing Polar Bear" figure, by Pauta Saila (1916-2009), E7-990, from Cape Dorset, signed in syllabics.

c1980   *18in (45.5cm) high*
£25,000-35,000   **WAD**

An Inuit antler "Mother with Child in her Amaut" figure, by Luke Iksiktaaryuk (1909-1977), E2-45, from Baker Lake.

c1967   *7.5in (19cm) high*
£15,000-20,000   **WAD**

An Inuit stone "Mother Embracing Child" figure, by Johnny Inukpuk (1911-2007), E9-904, Inukjuak.

c1970   *14.5in (37cm) high*
£6,000-8,000   **WAD**

An Inuit stone "Mother Cradling Child" figure, by Osuitok Ipeelee (1923-2005), E7-1154, from Cape Dorset.

c1960   *8.5in (21.5cm) high*
£14,000-16,000   **WAD**

An Inuit stone and antler "Caribou" figure, by Shorty Killiktee (1949-), E7-308, Cape Dorset.

1991   *31in (79cm) high*
£6,500-7,500   **WAD**

An Inuit stone "Transformation" figure, by Andy Miki (1918-1983), E1-436, from Arviat, signed in syllabics.

6.5in (16cm) high
£7,000-10,000   **WAD**

An Inuit stone "Hooded Figure", by John Pangnark (1920-1980), E1-104, from Arviat.

7.25in (18.5cm) high
£9,000-11,000   **WAD**

An Inuit stone and bone "Shaman with Cross" figure, by Charlie Ugyuk (1931-1998), E4-341, from Spence Bay.

23in (58cm) high

£18,000-22,000   WAD

An Inuit stone and antler "Shaman Transforming into Musk Ox" figure, by Judas Ullulaq (1937-1998), E4-342, from Gjoa Haven.

This piece was described by Judas (through an interpreter) as a Shaman whose animal skin parka is infested with worms – one of which is entering the shaman's ear. This induces the transformation into a musk ox and is the cause of his grimace.

12in (30.5cm) high

£9,000-11,000   WAD

CLOSER LOOK - "MOTHER NURSING HER CHILD"

Smiler (1921-1986) is considered one of the earliest and most accomplished Inuit artists of the 1950s, and worked with pioneer James Houston.

The handling of the mouth, with its inlaid carved ivory teeth, and the eyes, with soap highlights, is typical of the sensitivity of Smiler's work.

The heavy, rounded form, the style of the legs and the wide coat collar are other typical features of his work.

This sculpture was acquired by Sir Norman Hartnell, the Queen's dressmaker, during a visit to Canada in the 1950s.

An Inuit stone, ivory- and soapstone-inlaid "Mother Nursing Her Child" figure, by Isa Smiler, E9-706, from Inukjuak.

c1950   *9.5in (24cm) high*

£30,000-40,000   WAD

An Inuit stone, antler and bone "Ikaliyuk" (Fish-maker) figure, by Judas Ullulaq (1937-1998), E4-342, from Gjoa Haven, with fish chopper (not shown).

The legend of Qiviuq, the wanderer, is well known in the Netsilik region. The figure depicted here is the fish-maker whom Qiviuq meets at the edge of a large body of water that he wishes to cross. The fish-maker chops wood and the chips fall into the water to become fish. He creates a giant fish for Qiviuq, that Qiviuq rides upon to cross the water.

1994   *13.25in (33.5cm) high*

£12,000-14,000   WAD

An Inuit stone "Woman" figure, by an unidentified artist, from Cape Dorset.

c1950   *6.5in (16.5cm) high*

£6,000-8,000   WAD

An Inuit limited edition "Hare Spirits" skin stencil print, 7/50, by Kenojuak Ashevak (1927-), E7-1035, Cape Dorset.

1960   *Framed 23.5in (60cm) wide*

£8,000-10,000   WAD

An Inuit limited edition stone-cut "Bird Humans" print, 13/50, by Kenojak Ashevak (1927-), E7-1035, from Cape Dorset.

1960   *Framed 28in (71cm) wide*

£6,000-8,000   WAD

An Inuit limited edition "Two Bears Hunting" stone block print, 20/50, by Niviaxie (1908-1959), E7-1077, from Cape Dorset.

1959   *Framed 21in (53cm) wide*

£12,000-14,000   WAD

A rare mid-19thC Northwest Coast Chilkat dance blanket, hand-woven cedar bark and mountain goat hair dyed with natural pigments, decorated with highly stylised clan symbols and animal forms.

with fringe 64in (162.5cm) long

£15,000-20,000   DRA

A late 19thC/early 20thC Northwest Coast Haida carved wood miniature face mask, painted in red, black and green, damages, on display stand.

It has been suggested that this mask may have originally been part of a totem pole or house facade.

5.25in (13cm) high

£1,500-2,000   DRA

A 19thC Northwest Haida coast carved argillite pipe, the stylised openwork carving with one human/bear and multiple avian forms.

6.5in (16cm) long

£8,000-10,000   SK

A late 19thC Northwest Coast Haida carved wood totem pole, the cedar form with elaborate openwork featuring a whale, beaver, wolf, human and avian form.

16in (40.5cm) high

£6,000-8,000   SK

A 19thC Northwest Coast Kwakwaka'wakw carved cedar Tsonqua mask, with sunken eyes and cheeks, projecting ovoid mouth, old repair to lips, painted black with red–brown details, patina of use, wood loss.

In Kwakwaka'wakw mythology Dzunukwa (also Tsonoqua) is the "wild woman of the forest". She is venerated as a bringer of wealth, but is also greatly feared by children, because she is also known as an ogress who steals children and carries them home in her basket to eat.

18.25in (46cm) high

£18,000-22,000   SK

A 19thC Northwest Coast Kwakwaka'wakw carved wood figure, with flat back and two holes for attachment, with hands to the chest and lower abdomen, the large stylised head with traces of black and red pigments, dark patina, wood loss.

This figure is most likely to be a shaman's figure.

34in (86cm) high

£5,000-6,000   SK

A late 19thC Northwest Coast Haida carved wood canoe model, painted with totemic designs in red, black, and green–blue, with two unusual maskettes attached to the upper prows, one original, the other carved by Northwest Coast authority Steve Brown.

36in (91.5cm) long

£7,500-8,500   SK

A pair of late 19thC Northwest Coast Tlingit painted leggings, fringed on three sides and painted with classic form–line animal imagery in black and red pigments, brass thimble danglers.

12.5in (32cm) long

£18,000-22,000   SK

A late 19thC Northwest Coast Tlingit beaded cloth "Octopus" bag, the trade cloth form with eight bifurcated tabs off the bottom, partially beaded on the front with multicoloured abstract floral devices, bead loss.

21in (53cm) long

£2,500-3,500   SK

A Northwest baleen lidded basket, the ivory knop in the shape of a bear attacking a seal, with ivory plaque to base marked "227 Omnik, Pt. Hope Alaska".

4in (10cm) diam

£1,200-1,800   **SK**

A late 19thC Northwest Coast kerf bentwood box, decorated with abstract animal images using commercial paint, old tag on bottom reads "Hudson Bay Fur Co. Curio Department, Seattle Wash", patina of use.

9.5in (24cm) high

£1,200-1,800   **SK**

An early 20thC Northwest Coast carved wood bowl in the form of a beaver, with abalone eyes and nostrils, remnant seed beads in the tail, repaired foot.

16in (40.5cm) long

£4,000-6,000   **SK**

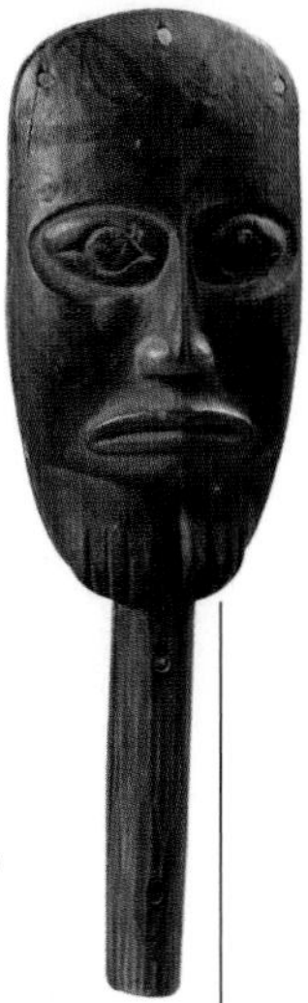

A late 19thC Northwest coast polychrome carved wood shaman's rattle, one side carved in the form of a stylised face with paws and painted animal ears, verso painted with a stylised figure below similar animal ears, red, green and black pigments, dark patina, repairs.

8.25in (21cm) high

£10,000-15,000   **SK**

A late 19thC Northwest Coast polychrome carved wood totem pole, hollow back, with various stylised animal and bird figures.

23in (58.5cm) high

£2,000-3,000   **SK**

A Northwest Coast carved and painted totem pole, with various stylised human and animal figures.

c1920   42in (106.5cm) high

£3,500-4,500   **POOK**

A California Yokuts polychrome pictorial coiled basketry bowl, woven with human figures and stacked triangle pattern, with small bird feathers at rim.

c1900   10.5in (27cm) diam

£4,500-5,500   **POOK**

A California Yokuts coiled rattlesnake basketry seed jar, woven with a band of human figures holding hands above three diamond "rattlesnake bands".

c1900   6.75in (17cm) high

£10,000-15,000   **POOK**

An early 20thC Iroquois/Seneca carved wood false face mask, New York, with strong downward mouth, bulging cylindrical eyes, red paint, and black horse hair, interior shows wear consistent with ritual use.

This mask was worn in healing ceremonies.

12in (30.5cm) high

£2,000-3,000   **DRA**

A rare pair of mid-19thC Northeast beaded hide and cloth moccasins, Penobscot, the puckered vamps and cuffs covered with red and blue trade cloth and silk appliqué work, with white bead edging and double C-scroll pattern to vamps, silk edging to cuffs.

10in (25.5cm) long

£6,000-7,000   **SK**

A late 19thC Northwest Tahltan beaded cloth and hide bandolier bag, British Columbia, the cloth strap faced with red trade cloth and partially beaded, the hide pouch beaded with multicoloured concentric design and abstract animal head devices, minor bead loss.

31.5in (80cm) long

£10,000-15,000 SK

A late 19thC Central Plains Lakota beaded hide cradle, the rawhide tab with multicoloured geometric designs, the body with bold multicoloured eight-point cross and geometric devices on a white ground, minor losses.

29in (73.5cm) long

£10,000-15,000 SK

A late 19thC Central Plains Lakota beaded-hide and cloth cradle, the hide top-half and flap beaded with multicoloured geometric designs on light blue background, lined with calico, with cream-coloured flannel bottom.

Overall 39in (99cm) long

£3,000-4,000 SK

A late 19thC Central Plains Lakota beaded and quilled hide pipe bag, roll-beaded at the opening, the central panel with multicoloured hourglass devices on a light blue background, multicoloured quilled rawhide slats and fringe from the bottom.

35in (89cm) long

£2,500-3,500 SK

A rare late 19thC Central Plains Lakota beaded hide horse neck cover, with multicoloured seed beads on both sides, the strip at the top with projecting horn-like devices, with two sets American flags, three Morning Stars, and other geometric devices, on dark blue background, bead loss.

48in (122cm) long

£4,000-5,000 SK

An 1870s Central Plains Lakota beaded and quilled buffalo hide rifle scabbard, fringed at mouth and barrel, red trade cloth edging, remnant quilled stripes, the beaded panels with hourglass and cross devices on a light blue ground, minor losses.

40in (101.5cm) long

£15,000-20,000 SK

A late 19thC Northern Plains/Plateau beaded hide knife sheath, the front beaded with a cross device and a multicoloured diagonal stripe pattern, with roll-beaded carrying strap and roll-beaded fringe, with old butcher's knife.

9.5in (24cm) long

£4,500-5,500 SK

A mid-19thC Plains painted buffalo hide robe, painted on the flesh side with a central sun symbol flanked by elaborate feather abstractions, and with geometric border, in red, blue, green and yellow, damaged.

85in (216cm) long

£6,000-8,000 SK

A late 19thC Central Plains Cheyenne beaded buffalo hide Possible bag, beaded on the front, sides, and flap with multicoloured geometric devices on a barred background, tin cones with red-dyed horsehair from the sides and flap.

22in (56cm) long

£2,500-3,500 SK

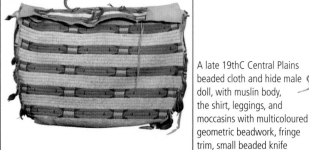

A late 19thC Central Plains beaded cloth and hide male doll, with muslin body, the shirt, leggings, and moccasins with multicoloured geometric beadwork, fringe trim, small beaded knife sheath, red face paint.

14in (36cm) high

£2,500-3,500 SK

A Southwest Hopi painted and carved cottonwood Kachina doll.

Kachina dolls are made by the Hopi tribe of north-eastern Arizona, and related tribes. The carved wooden figurines represent helper deities and were used to teach children about tribal religious beliefs and spiritual ancestry. As well as being painted, many were decorated with specially sewn clothing. They are still made today, but this very rare example dates from the 19thC or before and retains nearly all of its original painted finish.

Provenance: From the collection of a Mid-Atlantic Historical Museum.

10.5in (27cm) high

£18,000-22,000 FRE

An early 20thC Southwest Apache coiled basketry bowl, the shallow form with concentric stepped triangle pattern.

9.25in (23.5cm) diam

£500-700 SK

A late 19thC Southwest Zuni polychrome pottery olla, the high-shoulder form with classic stylised volute and medallion pattern, ladle wear at rim.

9.75in (25cm) high

£3,000-4,000 SK

A 1920s Southwest Navajo pictorial weaving, woven in a natural-colour homespun wool.

64in (162.5cm) long

£1,200-1,800 SK

A Southwest Zuni turquoise tab necklace, with two pairs of jaclaw.

c1920 *19in (48cm) long*

£1,500-2,000 SK

A Southwest Santa Clara carved and polished blackware wedding jar, the double-spouted form with a deeply cared Avanyu pattern, signed "Pablita, Santa Clare, Pueblo".

10in (25.5cm) high

£200-300 SK

A Southwest Pima coiled basketry bowl, with flat bottom and shallow flared sides, decorated with 16 standing human figures, damages.

c1900 *19in (48cm) diam*

£250-350 SK

A Southwest Acoma polychrome pottery olla, painted with heartline deer, bird, foliate devices, with two-colour rainbow frame line, orange, red–brown and dark brown on a cream–coloured ground.

c1900 *13in (33.5cm) high*

£7,000-8,000 SK

TRIBAL ART

A large Pre-Columbian Mexican terracotta "Admiral-form" shaman figural vessel, Colima, with stylised shell necklace, traditional top-knot, horn hat and spout, with rare Pre-Columbian indigenous repair, with dendrite deposits.

The shaman tomb guardian protected the deceased in the afterlife. The restoration shows particular care for the piece, or for the deceased.

200 BC-250AD   *16.5in (42cm) high*
£6,000-8,000   DRA

A Pre-Columbian Mexican redware dog, Colima, with tail spout, incised eyes, mouth and nose, and negative-resist design, with dendrite deposits.

200BC-250AD   *14in (36cm) long*
£5,000-6,000   DRA

A Pre-Columbian Mexican chinesco painted female figural idol, Nayarit, kneeling with one arm to her abdomen, the other under her breast, adorned with incised plated hair, a nose ring, painted and negative-resist designs, restoration.

200BC-250AD   *10.5in (27cm) high*
£5,000-6,000   DRA

A large Pre-Columbian Mexican Mixtec carved volcanic stone female idol, the figure wearing a headdress, with hand to breast, archaic face with heart-shaped brow and ear spools, on display stand.

800-1,500AD   *25in (63cm) high*
£3,000-4,000   DRA

A Pre-Columbian Mexican Veracruz stone hacha, with nose ring and ornate head gear, original pigment.

This unusual image is of a sacrificial victim relating to the Mesoamerican ball game.

550-800AD   *8.25in (21cm) high*
£2,000-3,000   DRA

A Pre-Columbian Mexican carved limestone male figure, Huastec, with hands to the chest, characteristic depression at centre of chest, with elaborate headdress and draped collar, damages and repairs.

1200-1500   *51in (129.5cm) high*
£18,000-22,000   SK

A Pre-Columbian Mayan carved jade plaque, carved on one side with a seated male figure wearing an elaborate headdress and ornamentation, pierced in five places for attachment, restoration.

500-800AD   *4.5in (11.5cm) high*
£2,000-3,000   SK

A late 19thC Mexican Saltillo poncho-style serape, woven in one piece, with central serrated diamond on an overall zigzag pattern, brown, light blue, and cream colours, minor stains.

77in (195.5cm) long
£1,800-2,200   SK

A 19thC New Mexican retablo, possibly by The Quill Pen Santero, tempera and gesso on a hand-adzed five-sided panel, depicting the Virgin Mary flanked by large candles, with an image of a crescent moon at her feet.

11in (28cm) high
£12,000-14,000   SK

A 19thC New Zealand Maori carved wood canoe bailer, scoop partially edged with scroll design, the unusual double handle with bird-head finials sharing a common mouth, patina of use.

Provenance: Collected by Rev. Alfred Fairbrother, Baptist minister to the Maoris, 1882-85.

21in (53cm) long

£3,000-4,000   SK

A 19thC New Zealand Maori carved wood male figure, with arms projecting behind the back, the three-fingered hands clasping a protruding abdomen, with squat legs, with deeply carved tattoo designs, haliotis shell inlay eyes, dark patina.

Provenance: Collected by Rev. Alfred Fairbrother, Baptist minister to the Maoris, 1882-85.

30in (76cm) high

£22,000-24,000   SK

A rare 19thC Easter Island/Rapa Nui mo'ai kavakava figure, eyes accented with shell and obsidian.

The name "mo'ai kavakava", given to small wooden figures of stooped and emaciated men, is formed from "mo'ai" (the name given to the monumental monolithic human figures found on Easter Island) and the word "kavakava" meaning ribs. These figures are believed to be representations of ancestors, and were worn around the necks of the men who took part in ritual dances.

24.75in (63cm) high

£5,000-6,000   DRA

A mid-20thC Papua New Guinea carved wood Waksuk female idol, the elongated figure with abstract facial features and incised scarification, red pigment accenting the face, on metal display stand.

54in (137cm) high

£2,000-3,000   DRA

A Moungalaulau Tongan ironwood paddle club, incised with linear decoration, the end with a carved loop, stamped "GBGB 1840", on steel stand.

42.5in (108cm) long

£4,000-5,000   LHA

A large mid-19thC Hawaiian koa wood calabash, with early round stand (not shown), various native repairs.

16.5in (42cm) diam

£9,000-11,000   SK

A rare 19thC Micronesian root club, Gilbert Island, naturally formed spiral staff with woven-cane handle, reddish patina, minor losses, on metal display stand.

28in (71cm) high

£1,200-1,800   DRA

A 19thC Polynesian Maori carved wood treasure box, with incised scroll designs, stylised Tiki figure on one end and Tiki head on the other, dark rich patina, with stand.

16.5in (42cm) long

£8,000-12,000   SK

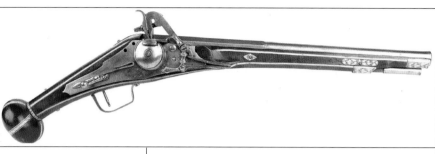

A German Augsburg 28-bore wheel-lock holster pistol, struck with a fir-cone barrelsmith's mark and stamped head within shield, the full walnut stock inset with bone stringing, with two engraved staghorn plaques and side plates.

c1640   25in (63.5cm) long

£15,000-20,000   L&T

A pair of .700 calibre Irish flintlock yeomanry pistols, by Powell, Dublin, regulation full stocks carved with an apron moulding about the tangs, brass mounts of regulation type comprising moulded side-plates, spurred pommels engraved with expanded flower heads, with ramrods.

c1750   18in (45.5cm) long

£5,500-6,500   TDM

A pair of George III silver-mounted flintlock pistols, by Joseph Griffin, London, barrels and locks with maker's mark, stained walnut stocks, carved shells around the tang, silver by "I.K", London, with ramrods.

1769

£5,000-6,000   WW

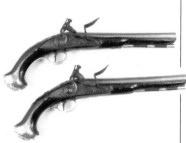

A cased pair of 54-bore silver-mounted flintlock travelling pistols, by Joyner, London, box-lock actions engraved with scrollwork with figured walnut butts inlaid with silver wire, the engraved steel trigger-guards with a Rococo flower, in a mid-19thC case with accessories.

1779   9.25in (23.5cm) long

£3,000-4,000   TDM

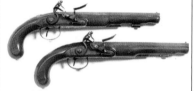

A pair of flintlock duelling pistols, by Gill & Knubley, London, with inscribed octagonal barrels, proof-marked, full walnut stock, chased action, and trigger guard with acorn bracket, flattened bag-shaped grip with shell, carved upper section, and plain silver cartouche.

c1785   14.5in (37cm) long

£3,000-4,000   AH

An 18th century French flintlock pistol, by Le Maire, steel lockplate inscribed Le Maire and with silver relief-moulded pommel, silver trigger guard and wooden ramrod.

17in (43.5cm) long

£4,000-5,000   BELL

A late 18thC flintlock holster pistol, the circular barrel engraved "D. Egg London", the lockplate also engraved "D. Egg" and "GR" crown, with smooth walnut grip, brass trigger guard, pommel and mounts (lacking flint plate).

the barrel 5in (12.5cm) long

£500-600   BELL

A rare garniture of French flintlock pistols, by Nicholas Noel Boutet, Versailles, comprising a matched pair of officer's pistols and a matched pair of flintlock pocket or muff pistols, mounted with carved walnut, metal engraved with various motifs, including Medusa head and foliage, in original case.

c1798

£80,000-100,000   JDJ

An Irish long sea service pistol, with a brass barrel inscribed "DUBLIN CASTLE," and stamped ordnance marks, the lock stamped "TOWER" and "GR" crowned, with a walnut stock with brass mounts and a belt clip.

c1800   20in (51cm) long

£4,000-5,000   WW

ARMS, ARMOUR & MILITARIA

A cased pair of French 80-bore pin-fire target pistols, by "F. Claudin A Paris", the signed barrels rifled with 12 grooves and engraved with foliage at the breech, fluted walnut butt carved with panels of scrolling foliage, and engraved steel mounts, with accessories.

c1860   15.5in (39.5cm) long
£6,000-7,000   **TDM**

A cased pair of 38-bore percussion duelling pistols, by Samuel Nock, London, figured walnut half-stocks with slender chequered butts, engraved steel mounts comprising blued trigger-guards decorated with serpents and foliage, with silver escutcheons, horn fore-end caps, in case with accessories.

c1833   15.75in (40cm) long
£7,000-8,000   **TDM**

A pair of 18-bore flintlock duelling pistols, by Jover, London, the octagonal sighted barrels signed "Jover London", inlaid with gold, stamped with barrelsmith's mark, mounts engraved with flowers, with silver escutcheons, with original ramrods.

c1805-10   15.25in (38.5cm) long
£9,000-11,000   **TDM**

A 40-bore flintlock duelling pistol, by Joseph Manton, London, the scratch-rifled twist octagonal barrel fitted with silver fore-sight, recessed patent breech inlaid with a platinum line, breech tang decorated with a trophy-of-arms, with engraved steel mounts, silver escutcheon engraved with the owner's initial, horn fore-end cap, and associate ramrod.

1810   14.5in (37cm) long
£4,000-5,000   **TDM**

A 19thC possibly Japanese miniature pistol, the octagonal barrel with gilt floral decoration, the wooden stock with similar decoration.

3in (7.5cm) long
£600-700   **CHT**

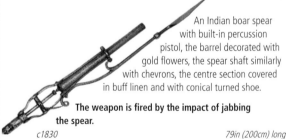

A rare cased set of French Boutet flintlock pistols, bearing the personal cartouche of Noel Boutet, barrels inlaid with gold, the carved walnut stocks with burnished steel furniture and inlays, with original ramrods.

£300,000-400,000   **JDJ**

An early 19thC cased pair of duelling pistols, by Bennett & Lacy, London, gold line at breechs, well figured walnut tapering half-stocks with blank silver escutcheon, fore-end caps, silver barrel bolt escutcheons, fine chequered butts, engraved trigger-guards with pineapple finials, in original mahogany case with accessories.

£5,500-6,500   **L&T**

An Indian boar spear with built-in percussion pistol, the barrel decorated with gold flowers, the spear shaft similarly with chevrons, the centre section covered in buff linen and with conical turned shoe. **The weapon is fired by the impact of jabbing the spear.**

c1830   79in (200cm) long
£3,000-4,000   **L&T**

A French combination double-barrel percussion pistol, with barrels either side of dagger blade, with bone grips, barrel signed "Devisme a Paris, 34-bore".

c1830   16in (40.5cm) long
£1,500-2,500   **L&T**

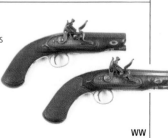

A pair of Regency silver-mounted overcoat travelling flintlock pistols, by Brander & Potts, octagonal barrels inscribed "0 MINORIE'S LONDON," the locks engraved with trophies, with walnut stocks, and engraved trigger guard by Moses Brent, London, with ramrods.

1817
£3,500-4,500   **WW**

CLOSER LOOK - RARE ENGRAVED AND GOLD-INLAID REVOLVER

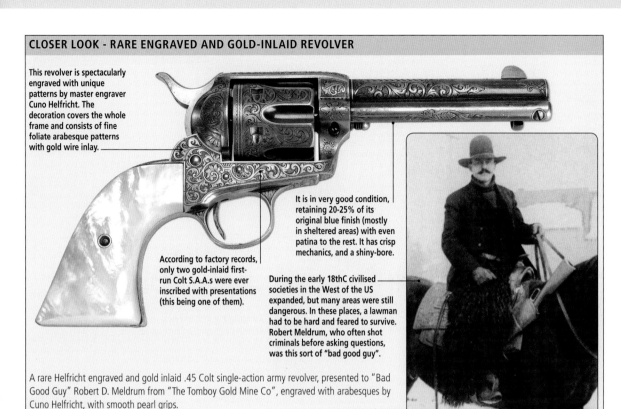

This revolver is spectacularly engraved with unique patterns by master engraver Cuno Helfricht. The decoration covers the whole frame and consists of fine foliate arabesque patterns with gold wire inlay.

According to factory records, only two gold-inlaid first-run Colt S.A.A.s were ever inscribed with presentations (this being one of them).

It is in very good condition, retaining 20-25% of its original blue finish (mostly in sheltered areas) with even patina to the rest. It has crisp mechanics, and a shiny-bore.

During the early 18thC civilised societies in the West of the US expanded, but many areas were still dangerous. In these places, a lawman had to be hard and feared to survive. Robert Meldrum, who often shot criminals before asking questions, was this sort of "bad good guy".

A rare Helfricht engraved and gold inlaid .45 Colt single-action army revolver, presented to "Bad Good Guy" Robert D. Meldrum from "The Tomboy Gold Mine Co", engraved with arabesques by Cuno Helfricht, with smooth pearl grips.

£150,000-250,000   JDJ

A Remington .44 calibre revolver, with bone slab-sided butt, barrel engraved "patented Sept 14 1858 E Remington and Sons lion New York USA", with brass trigger guard and frame.

35in (14cm) long

£1,500-2,500   L&T

A Tucker & Sherrard State of Texas Confederate .44 calibre revolver, serial no. 81.

This gun was a war souvenir of a 28th Maine soldier. Tucker & Sherrard had a contract for pistols with the State of Texas in 1862. There is controversy over how many guns were delivered, but among astute collectors and historians, the only model of this gun considered truly Confederate-used is this configuration with the low, straight hammer spur and square-back trigger guard. Some earlier texts have referred to this gun as a "Mormon dragoon".

£50,000-60,000   JDJ

A W. Tranter double-action .54-bore percussion revolver, No.196405, the blued octagonal barrel with London proof marks, frame inscribed "John Hayton Grahams Town", five shot cylinder, action chased overall with leaves, chequered walnut grips.

c1864   *13in (33.5cm) long*

£1,000-1,500   AH

A Remington 1858 patent .44 calibre "New Model" revolver, with blued octagonal barrel and six-shot cylinder, integral ejector rod, brass trigger guard and walnut grips.

c1865   *14.5in (37cm) long*

£1,800-2,200   AH

A Rogers & Spencer .44 calibre revolver, no.3311, with blued octagonal barrel and six-shot cylinder, integral ejector rod, walnut grips.

c1865   *14in (36cm) long*

£600-800   AH

A large 8-bore flintlock wall gun, plain lock signed "J Frazer", with large iron flange (wall hook), walnut fullstock with brass furniture and large brass foresight.

c1750   *73in (185.5cm) long*

£1,500-2,000   L&T

A flintlock coaching blunderbuss, by Mewis & Co, with brass bell-ended barrel, Birmingham proof marks, top-mounted spring-loaded steel bayonet, full walnut stock with ram in brass pipes, engraved steel action with maker's name, brass side bracket engraved "DONCASTER & YORK NO.10".

c1780-90   *30in (76cm) long*

£3,000-4,000   AH

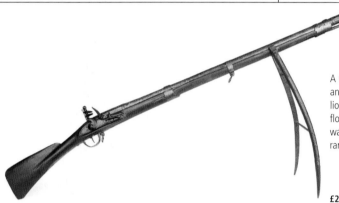

A rare Indian 12-bore flintlock gun, the English lock signed and dated "Debenham 1784" and with East India Company lion, the two-stage Indian barrel with inlaid gold scrolls, flower heads and foliage, brass furniture, full plain stained walnut stock with unusual forked bipod stand, with original ramrod.

54in (137.5cm) long

£2,000-3,000   L&T

A military 11-bore flintlock musket, the lock plate engraved with East India Company lion, ringed cock, patent cock screw, regulation barrel, London Gunmakers view and proof marks, walnut stock with chequered grip scrolled trigger guard.

c1800   *56in (142cm) long*

£1,000-1,500   L&T

A Bohemian 20-bore wheel-lock sporting rifle, the plain lock and cock overlaid with fine cut brass formed and engraved in tulip heads and foliate scrolls, the barrel struck with lion mark and an intertwined cypher "SF", with carved walnut stock, with fore-end of horn.

c1690   *48in (121cm) long*

£5,500-6,500   L&T

An English 12-bore percussion double-barrel big-game rifle, the locks with safety slides signed "Westley Richards" folding leaf sight, two grooved rifling, walnut half-stock with chequered grip and patch box.

c1850   *37in (94cm) long*

£2,500-3,500   L&T

A Pennsylvania flintlock .45 calibre long rifle, by Melchoir Fordney, Lancaster, with relief-carved tiger maple full stock with ornate brass furniture with German silver thumbrest, set triggers and octagonal barrel, the lock stamped "R. & W.C. Biddle, Philadelphia".

42.5in (108.5cm) long

£12,000-18,000   POOK

An English percussion cased single-barrel rifle, signed Manton, serial no. 10210, engraved with foliate scroll decoration, barrel tang with lion's head engraved with foliate scrolls, silver escutcheons, with accessories.

c1831   *46in (117cm) long*

£4,500-5,500   L&T

A Scottish cased percussion large-bore big-game rifle, signed "Thomas Kennedy Kilmarnock Rifle Maker To His Royal Highness Prince Albert", decorated with gold lines and stars, chequered walnut half-stock with engraved steel barrel bolt escutcheons, horn tipped fore-end, with accessories.

c1850   *51in (129.5cm) long*

£6,000-8,000   L&T

Judith Picks: Roosevelt's shotgun

Knowing he wasn't going to run for a second term as President of the US, Theodore Roosevelt began planning a major hunting safari in early 1908. The media kept the world informed of his intentions, and this prompted various manufacturers to write to the President, including Ansley H. Fox, President of the A. H. Fox Gun Company.

Initially Roosevelt declined Fox's offer of a shotgun, but in September 1908 he changed his mind and accepted. This created a difficult situation for Fox's craftsmen as the expedition was scheduled to leave in six months. Fortunately, the company had plans to exhibit two "F" grade shotguns at the Grand American Handicap in the spring of 1909. One of these, no. 13292, was part-finished and could be delivered in time to President Roosevelt, who was delighted with it. In February 1909 he wrote to Mr Fox, saying "I really think it is the most beautiful gun I have ever seen.".

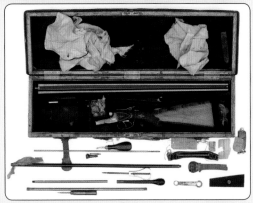

An A. H. Fox "F" grade 2ga calibre shotgun, marked "MADE EXPRESSLY FOR HON. THEODORE ROOSEVELT" serial no. 13292, frame engraved with foliate arabesque scrolls and oak leaves, with gold setter to the sides, hinge pin inlaid with four gold diamonds, engraved with various vignettes, mounted with French walnut, in oak and leather trunk case.
£500,000-700,000   **JDJ**

A very early Henry .44 calibre lever-action repeating rifle, serial no. "516", the octagonal barrel with integral magazine, half-moon German silver front sight, no provision on barrel for rear sight, top flat of barrel in small letters "HENRY'S PATENT. OCT. 16, 1860 / MANUFACT'D BY THE NEW HAVEN ARMS. CO. NEW HAVEN. CT", mounted with walnut, brass buttplate.
1860
£80,000-100,000   **JDJ**

A Henry .44 calibre Winchester model 66 lever-action rifle, serial no. "84012", the gold-plated fittings heavily engraved with arabesques and various motifs, including eagles' heads, by Conrad Ulrich, mounted with crotch, flame grain walnut.
£70,000-90,000   **JDJ**

A rare Winchester first model "One of the Hundred" .44 calibre lever-action rifle, serial no. 19675, with 24.25in (61.5cm) octagonal barrel, full magazine, with mortised thumb print dust cover and single set trigger, engraved with foliate arabesque scrolls, top flat engraved "One of the Hundred" and with fleur-de-lys.

Records at the Buffalo Bill Historical Center, Cody Firearms Museum, Cody, WY, show that only eight of these rare rifles were ever produced.
1873
£250,000-350,000   **JDJ**

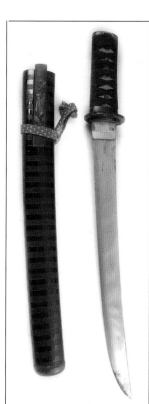

A Japanese tanto, with a long blade, signed tang, gilt bronze tsuba, bound sharkskin handle, in a striped lacquer scabbard.

Blade 13in (33cm) long

£1,000-1,500 WW

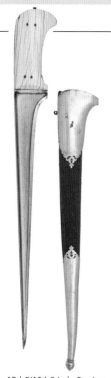

A late 18thC/19thC Indo-Persian pesh-kabz, with reinforced blade of finely watered steel and gold overlaid tang, the grip fitted with a pair of shaped ivory grip-scales, in original velvet-covered scabbard with gilt-copper locket and chape.

18in (46cm) long

£2,500-3,000 TDM

CLOSER LOOK - HIGHLAND DIRK

The wooden handle is finely carved with a basket weave design with added carved studs and applied shoulder mounts. These are evidence that this is a high-quality dirk.

The parallel mounting of the knife and fork (Highlander's eating utensils) is a feature that was only seen on dirks for a very short time (perhaps as short as 20 years).

While it is assumed that provincial silversmiths were involved in the manufacture of dirks, it is very rare to find marked period examples (only two other marked Inverness dirks are known). It was not until the early Victorian period that dirks were more regularly marked.

The blade is marked for London bladesmith Jeffries. This suggests the blade could have been part of the earlier outfitting of Highland Regiments by George III and recycled as part of this dirk.

A rare mid-18thC Scottish provincial mounted Highland dirk, by Robert Anderson, marked "RA", "camel", "INS", the pommel cap with scalloped mount and engraved "John MacDonald" in script, the single fullered blade marked "GR" with crown above and "Jeffries" below, with knife and fork similarly carved.

19in (48cm) long

£6,000-7,000 L&T

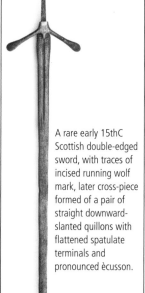

A rare early 15thC Scottish double-edged sword, with traces of incised running wolf mark, later cross-piece formed of a pair of straight downward-slanted quillons with flattened spatulate terminals and pronounced ècusson.

Blade 30.75in (78cm) long

£3,000-4,000 TDM

An Italian folding ranseur, the triple blades hinged so the head can be folded down, the curved side blades folding inwards.

c1600 *104in (264cm) long*

£4,500-5,500 L&T

A late 19thC 16thC-Saxon-style etched rapier, stamped with a circular mark, rectangular ricasso and grip etched with scrolling leafy tendrils and flower heads on each side, iron hilt including a pair of straight quillons of hollow-diamond section, with a grip of twisted wire.

This sword is probably the work of the notorious forger Anton Konrad of Dresden. It is almost certainly inspired by the silver-mounted rapier of Christian II, Elector of Saxony, preserved in the Germanisches National Museum, Berlin.

Blade 33.75in (85.5cm) long

£2,500-3,500 TDM

An American Civil War presentation sword, to Brevet Brigadier General Andrew Denison, the hilt in the form of Lady Liberty, the Clauberg double edged blade etched with various patriotic motifs, the silver coloured scabbard with three relief carved mounts.

Blade 34in (86.5cm) long

£35,000-40,000 JDJ

A rare mid-17thC Scottish basket-hilted broadsword, the earlier possibly Spanish blade bears the mark "Sahagom" the mark of the Spanish swordsmith, with original leather-covered wooden scabbard.

Overall 34.5in (87.5cm) long

£4,500-5,500   L&T

A mid-18thC Highland basket-hilted backsword, with double fullered blade.

Blade 34.5in (87.5cm) long

£1,200-1,800   W&W

A late 18thC Perthshire Highlanders basket-hilted backsword, the basket pierced with thistles and engraved with thistle leaves, with star of the Order of the Thistle, "116" and "Nemo Me Impune Lacessit".

The blade is very similar to the blades on swords issued earlier to the Highland Regiments and marked Jeffreys or Drury. This sword can be dated incredibly precisely. The 116th Regiment of Foot (Perthshire Highlanders) was raised in January 1794 and sent to serve in Ireland. It received its official number (116) in January 1795 and was disbanded in September 1795.

1795   *Overall 37.25in (95cm) long*

£2,500-3,500   L&T

An early 19thC Scottish basket-hilted broadsword, the side plates and knuckle-plate are pierced with holes and the shields are pierced with hearts and holes, the black leather scabbard with three silver mounts heavily embossed with thistles.

Overall 39.5in (100cm) long

£1,800-2,200   L&T

A late 18thC/19thC Turkish kilig, with engraved brass vertically re-curved crosspiece, horn grip inset with brass and steel nails, in original wooden scabbard with velvet covering and chape repoussé.

24.75in (63cm) long

£2,500-3,000   TDM

An 18thC/19thC Japanese Shinshinto Edo wakizashi, the scabbard (saya) of roiro lacquer fitted with matching shibuichi kurikata, koiguchi, kojiri and fichi-kashira, each inlaid in iro-e takazogan of a dancing man and flowers, a pair of gold menuki of a sinuous coiled dragons in pursuit of a fiery pearl wrapped with blue silk cord.

£800-1,200   WES

A Civil War Confederate Nashville Plow Works C. Sharp & Hamilton cavalry sabre.

Blade 33.25in (84.5cm) long

£3,500-4,500   POOK

A Victorian officer's regimental-pattern mameluke-hilted dress sword of the 18th Hussars, by Hawkes & Co London, Manufacturers to the Queen, etched with crowned "VR" cypher, regimental badge with motto and battle honours "Peninsula" and "Waterloo".

Blade 30.5in (77cm) long

£2,500-3,000   W&W

A 19thC German engraved cowhorn powder flask, with curved flattened body, decorated on the inner face with a pattern of concentric circles, on the outer with a pair of half sunbursts and a fleur-de-lys and the date "1606" in a central medallion, steel mounts comprising nozzle with spring cut-off, basal cap and belt hook.

11.5in (29cm) long

£600-700   TDM

A Scottish flattened cowhorn powder flask, decorated with a crown, flower heads, initials "AET + DC" and the dates 1696 and 1765, with plain brass base cover, front suspension ring on a shaped brass collar.

15in (38cm) long

£2,000-3,000   L&T

CLOSER LOOK - SCRIMSHAW POWDER HORN

By the late 18thC American scrimshaw horns had evolved into a form of sophisticated Folk Art. This horn is notable for its comparatively early date – very few other examples are known.

It is very similar in design and decorative motifs to a named and dated horn made by Jacob Curtis of Maine in 1723. It is likely due to this similarity, and the relative scarcity of these types of horn, that Curtis made this example.

Curtis volunteered in His Majesty's Service 1722-1725 in Col. John Wheelwright's command. In 1724 this command famously massacred the inhabitants of the village of Abenaki headed by Jesuit missionary Father Rasle. Curtis may have accompanied this expedition.

"P.D." probably refers to another member of Wheelwright's command: Phillip Durrell Jr., who may have carried it during the attack on Abenaki.

A rare early 18thC American scrimshaw powder horn, Maine, with inscribed decoration including repeating wampum, with branded owner's initials "PD", dated.

1724   *11in (28cm) long*

£15,000-20,000   JDJ

A rare early 18thC silver-mounted pocket ram's horn powder flask, the silver with an engraved inscription, "Dunblain fight Nov. 13th 1715 Kings Gen: D Argile. Prenders & Mar Inv:At:Def: by Erl of Sur lnd: Prs:in: Takn: by Gen: Cartr: & Wills Pretender:Erl:Mar & ye rest of ye Party run away from Perth. M. CadogenYr Kings Gen. Jan 30th1715/6", the silver nozzle and end with incised line turning.

The engraving refers to the aftermath of the Battle of Sheriffmuir, fought North of Dunblane in 1715. It was part of an unsuccessful Jacobite Rising, led by the Earl of Mar, to regain the Stuart crown from the Hanoverian King George I, whose army was led by the Duke of Argyll.

5.5in (14cm) long

£3,500-4,500   L&T

An engraved powder horn, inscribed "Jonathan Conant", decorated with animals, stars, etc.

1749   *11.5in (29cm) long*

£2,000-2,500   POOK

A decorated ox bone powder horn, engraved with fleur-de-lys, a crescent moon and Greek key pattern, the nozzle platform cut with starburst decoration, the steel top chiselled with sunburst decoration, spring loaded cut-off valve.

c1760   *17.5in (44cm) high*

£600-700   L&T

An 18thC/19thC Indian silver-mounted brass powder horn, the body delicately decorated with foliage, on stand.

7in (18cm) long

£500-600   WW

An early 19thC powder horn, with incised decoration including the badge of the 90th Perthshire Volunteers, together with Egypt battle honours, thistles and roses, Masonic symbols, and dove of peace.

14in (36cm) long

£1,200-1,800   L&T

A Military General Service medal, 1793-1814, with clasp "Toulouse", awarded to George Hill, 10th Hussars.

£1,000-1,500   WW

A Waterloo 1815 medal, awarded to Thomas Broad, 2nd Batt, 3rd Reg Guards.

The 2nd Battalion 3rd Foot Guards played an important part in the Waterloo campaign. They marched 27 miles in 15 hours to join the action at Quatre Bras on the 16th June. On the 18th June the regiment (with companies of Coldstream and First Guards) was placed on a ridge behind Hougoumont. The Duke of Wellington claimed, "The success off the Battle of Waterloo turned on the closing of the gates of the Hougoumont" after the epic defence of this strategic point where 30,000 French troops failed to take and maintain control.

£3,000-4,000   W&W

A pair of medals, awarded to Corp James Hooper, 28th Regiment foot, comprising Military General Service Medal 1847, with six clasps for "Corunna", "Talavera", "Busaco", "Albuhera", "Vittoria", and "Toulouse", and Waterloo 1815 medal.

£5,000-6,000   TEN

A pair of medals, awarded to Sergeant William Bird 4th Light Dragoons, comprising Ghuznee 1839 medal, and Army Long Service and Good Conduct Medal, first Type, awarded 1851, together with a photocopy of his discharge papers.

£1,500-2,000   TEN

A South Africa 1854 medal, awarded to R. Ward, 12th Regt, once lacquered.

£500-600   WW

A pair of medals, awarded to "300. PTE.H.McCAFFERY. 80TH FOOT.", comprising an India General Service 1854 medal, with "Perak" clasp, and a South Africa 1879 medal, with "1878-9" clasp.

£1,200-1,800   TEN

A Victoria, Empress of India silver medal, G. G. Adams, with swivel suspension bar, in fitted case.

£500-600   WW

A pair of medals, awarded to "837 Tpr J Mace 1st Life Guards", comprising Egypt 1882 medal, with "Tel el Kebir" clasp and Khedive's Star 1882 NVF medal.

£300-400   W&W

A George V Distinguished Service Medal, awarded to Edward Williams ERA 3/Class, HMS Bellerophon for services at Jutland.

£600-800   CHT

A George V War-end medal, awarded to "302727 Sjt. H[ugh] W. Hodges. 5 London. R.".

£350-450   WW

An 18thC silver Royalist badge, with the Royal Arms on one side and King Charles I's portrait on the other.

c1745 *1.75in (4.5cm) high*

£500-600 LC

An OR's cast oval shoulder belt plate of The 79th (Cameron Highlanders) Regt badge, with crown, "79 Regt or" and "Cameron Highlanders" around edge, with a letter from the Regimental Museum, Fort George.

c1806-15 *2.75in (7cm) high*

£1,000-1,500 W&W

An unusual early 19thC officer's shoulder belt plate, traces of gilt, bearing silver-plated anchor and castle.

3.5in (9cm) high

£500-600 W&W

An officers' silver-plated and gilt 1829 (Bell-top) shako plate of The Honourable Artillery Company, with gilt grenade with crowned "VR" on the ball, on silver plated crowned rayed star.

This badge was worn 1837-1844.

£650-850 W&W

An other ranks' brass 1829 (bell-topped) shako plate of The 99th Regiment, "99" within crowned, rayed star.

£400-500 W&W

A rare officers' gilt and silver-plated 1829 (bell-top) shako plate of The 44th (East Essex) Regiment, "44" within pierced battle-honour scrolls and laurel wreath on silver plated cut star, all on crowned ray star.

£500-700 W&W

A Russian Crimea period grenadier OR's brass fur cap plate, die-struck crowned double-headed eagle with sword and orb, stylized "N" to central shield, a grenade in each lower corner.

9in (23cm) high

£200-300 W&W

A piper's pre-1881 WM plaid brooch of The 79th (Cameron Highlanders), stamped "B" and "25".

£180-220 W&W

A Devonshire Regiment brass helmet plate, with silver mounts.

£300-400 TEN

A Sixth Dragoon Guards (Carabiniers) regimental brooch, set with old-cut diamonds, calibre sapphires and a cabochon ruby.

£1,000-1,500 ECGW

A gold, enamel and rose-cut diamond Royal Artillery badge brooch, the field gun with rose-cut diamond wheel, blue enamel motto and red enamel crown, stamped "15c".

0.5in (1.5cm) wide

£300-400 DN

An English pikeman's pot helmet, with low raised moulded comb and down-turned rim, with rear plume holder, ear defences missing.

c1580 · 8in (20cm) long
£1,000-1,500 · **L&T**

An English funery close helmet, the two-piece visor with sighting slots, rolled and rope edging, with patinated black background and gilded decoration, of foliate scrolls, the low comb with plume holder.

c1590 · 12in (30.5cm) high
£2,500-3,000 · **L&T**

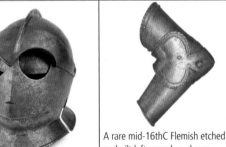

A Burgonet Savoyard death's-head type helmet, with double visor, the top section with hooded eye brows with rope moulding, low roped comb with hook and eye latch.

11in (28cm) high
£3,500-4,500 · **L&T**

A rare mid-16thC Flemish etched and gilt left-armed vambrace for the tilt, the main edges with inward turns roped with pairs of chiselled lines and accompanied by narrow bands of etched and gilt symmetrical running foliage.

A vambrace is a "tubular" or "gutter" defence for the forearm.

£4,000-5,000 · **TDM**

A German Augsburg narrow *anime cuirass*, decorated articulated breast plate, each lame shaped and filed on the top edge with ogees and cusps, engraved with the cross of the Knights of St John.

c1590 · 20in (51cm) high
£9,000-11,000 · **L&T**

A Lieutenant-General's full dress coatee, with gold embroidered loops arranged in threes, gilt-metal general officer's buttons, and detached gold round-cord epaulette and aiguillette.

This pattern of coatee was worn in Full Dress and Dress by Lieutenant-Generals 1811-28. Its original owner George Vaughan Hart held that rank 1811-25, but the style in which the tails are sewn back may indicate that this coatee was made early in the period.

£7,000-8,000 · **TDM**

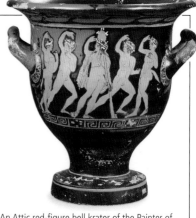

A 14thC/13thC BC Minoan oinochoe with dark brown painting showing tunas, some tiny parts of the painting missing, otherwise intact, with TL-analysis.

9in (23cm) high

£20,000-30,000   G&M

A 14thC/13thC BC three-handled Minoan krater, with dark brown painting of water birds, small parts of the painting have flaked off, tiny fragments are missing, with TL-analysis.

8in (20cm) high

£20,000-30,000   G&M

An Attic red-figure bell krater of the Painter of Louvre G 508, Thiasos with young Dionysos, four satyrs and three youths, intact.

390-370BC   *13in (33.5cm) high*

£4,000-5,000   G&M

A large Attic black-figure lekythos of the Gela Painter, displays two maenads riding on bulls, over-painting.

500-490 BC   *13in (33.5cm) high*

£5,000-7,000   G&M

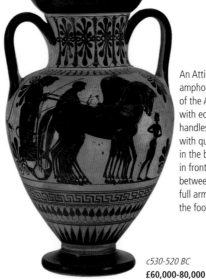

An Attic black-figured amphora, in the manner of the Antimenes Painter, with echinus foot and triple handles, the body painted with quadriga, woman in the background, youth in front, verso with fight between two warriors in full armour, a graffito under the foot.

c530-520 BC   *16in (40.5cm) high*

£60,000-80,000   SOTH

A 19th dynasty Egyptian polychrome limestone ushabti of Djehuty-Mose (Tothmes), overseer of the cattle in the temple of Amun, holding a djed-pillar and Knot of Isis, wearing pleated shirt and kilt, a ba-bird with wings outstretched on the chest, short beard and double wig, painted in black, columns and lines of inscription on the kilt.

This ushabti (funeral figure) is one of a very small group of private ushabtis inscribed with the Khamuas formula (a magic spell to help the deceased into the domain of Osiris). It takes its name from the ushabtis of Prince Khamuas or Khaemwaset, a son of Ramesses II.

PORPHYRY SPHINX

A 1stC AD Roman Imperial green porphyry sphinx of an Egyptian Queen, probably from the reign of Domitian, with broad beaded collar and centrally divided ribbed wig with voluted curls surmounted by the vulture headdress.

This sphinx and other Egyptian sculptures were excavated in 1856-58 from a garden near the church of Santa Maria Sopra Minerva, Rome. From the 16thC similar discoveries had been made in the area, previously the site of a temple to Isis and Serapis, which had been restored and expanded in the late 1stC AD by Domitian.

37.5cm (95cm) long

£3,000,000+   SOTH

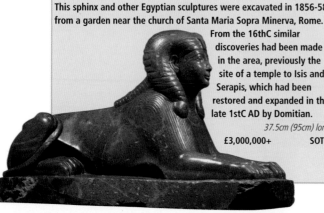

A South Arabian alabaster Sabaean head of a woman, with triangular face and long roughly worked hair, eyes inlaid in limestone, neck broken.

1stC BC-1stC AD   *12in (30.5cm) high*

£8,000-9,000   G&M

c1292-1190BC   *12.5in (32cm) high*

£800,000-1,000,000   G&M

Judith Picks: Battle of Fulford swords

A rare 11thC Anglo-Saxon iron stabbing sword, with pattern welding and blood channel, in very good condition, mounted on display stand.

These swords were dredged from the River Ouse in the 1850s, at the site of the Battle of Fulford, and were identified and conserved by York Museum in 1976. The battle took place at the village of Fulford, near York, on the 20th September 1066, when King Harald of Norway (Hardrada) and Tostig, his English ally (brother of King Harold of England) fought and defeated the Northern Earls, Edwin and Morcar. The English King Harold was holding himself in readiness for the expected Norman invasion in Sussex when he received news of this defeat and had to force-march 300 miles to reinforce the Northern army. He crushed the invaders at the Battle of Stamford Bridge, only to receive the news of the Norman invasion, whereupon he had to march south to confront the Normans at the battle of Hastings – and we all know what happened there!

22in (56cm) long

£1,200-1,800   ANDG

A rare 11thC Viking single-handed double-edged iron sword, with complete blade and tang, in very good condition excluding battle dents.

Overall 31in (79cm) long

£1,800-2,200   ANDG

A 4thC/5thC AD combat helmet, with vertical bronze strips connecting four oval bronze plates, the horizontal rim made of iron, the plates originally plated with silver, green patina, silver plates missing.

8in (20cm) high

£40,000-50,000   G&M

A 5thC BC Greek bronze Chalcidian helmet, the carinated crown with an attached appliqué depicting skylla, with small nose-guard, long eyebrow lines and a flanged neck-guard, cheek pieces and parts of the plume holders missing.

9in (23cm) high

£20,000-30,000   G&M

A 6thC BC Corinthian bronze helmet, tips of the cheek-guards and rim of the neck-guard restored, excellent condition.

11in (28cm) high

£40,000-50,000   G&M

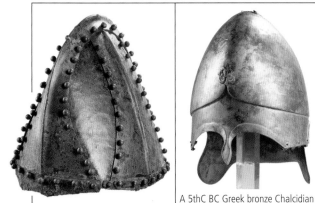

A 2ndC/3rdC AD Roman Imperial Period bluish clear glass askos with handle, thumb lift broken.

4in (10cm) high

£3,000-5,000   G&M

A 4thC AD Roman iridescent glass jug, with combed handle, repaired.

8.75in (22cm) high

£500-800   GORL

An 18thC violin, labelled "Made & Sold by John Johnson at The Harp & Crown Inn Cheapside, London, 1755", two-piece back, with two silver-mounted violin bows, case.

14in (36cm) long

£1,000-1,500　　GHOU

A German violin, probably by Joseph Klotz, labelled "Reincius Liessem Fecit Londini 1759", with bow and case.

13.75in (35.5cm) long

£2,000-2,500　　SWO

A violin, by Jean-Baptiste Colin, with a two-piece back and paper label, dated, with inlaid German bow and case.

1899　　14in (36cm) long

£1,000-1,500　　SWO

A late 19thC Mittenwald violoncello, of the Neuner & Hornsteiner School, bearing the number "10184" to the end of the fingerboard, with two-piece back.

29.25in (74cm) long

£2,500-3,000　　GHOU

A German violoncello, labelled "Atelier fur Kunstlerischen Geigenbau, Alban Voigt & Co. Sachsen & London, Anno 1902", with soft case.

30.25in (77cm) long

£3,000-5,000　　GHOU

A C.F. Martin & Co. acoustic guitar, style 1-27, no. 8199, with bound rosewood back and sides, spruce top with ebony, ivory and mother-of-pearl sound hole surrounds, bound ebony fretboard, with original coffin case.

c1898

£1,500-2,000　　GHOU

A Gibson Les Paul Standard, serial no. 91857, with painted headstock, mahogany back and neck, bound rosewood fretboard with trapezoid pearl inlay, with two-piece maple top and burst finish, non-original hard case.

This guitar is accompanied with a certificate of authenticity from Clive Brown, which also details the condition of the guitar.

1959

£100,000-150,000　　GHOU

A Fender Stratocaster, serial no. 69215, with maple neck, "clay" dots to the rosewood fretboard and well-worn Fiesta red body, with non-standard hard case.

1961

£14,000-18,000　　GHOU

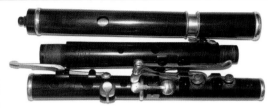

An English rosewood flute, by Rudall Carte & Co, stamped "Rudall Carte & Co, 23 Berners Street, Oxford Street, London no. 7103", with eight nickel keys on wooden blocks.
c1870
£2,000-2,500 **GHOU**

A Boosey & Hawkes Besson "700" gold lacquered four-valve tuba, with case.
£700-1,000 **GHOU**

A three-row Anglo concertina, by C. Jeffries, with 30 metal buttons on pierced metal ends, both stamped "C. Jeffries Maker", with six-fold bellows and gilt tooled-leather sides.

£5,000-7,000 **GHOU**

A Steinway & Sons mahogany boudoir grand piano forte, serial no. 209717, raised on square tapered legs and spade feet with castors.

c1921-22   *71in (180cm) long*
£7,000-9,000 **GORL**

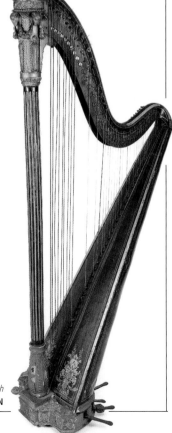

An early 19thC pedal harp, by J. Erat, Wardour Street, London, numbered 606 to signature plate, with 43 strings and five swell doors to the gilt foliate decorated faux rosewood grained sound box, the base with eight brass pedals and on paw feet, losses.

67in (170cm) high
£2,000-3,000 **DN**

DECORATIVE ARTS MARKET

As with many areas of collecting, Decorative Arts pieces have seen a rise in sales and prices of high-end items, and stagnation of mid-to-low-end goods. There have been fewer high-quality items on the market, but these have seen very healthy competition and high prices.

Wedgwood Fairyland lustre ceramics have been on a roll, whether they sell in the UK, US, Canada or Australia. Many of the serious collectors already have examples of the more common patterns and therefore prices remain quite steady. What are highly contested are the rare patterns, unusual colourways and, of particular interest, the experimental or trial pieces.

Some Doulton wares are still very buoyant, whereas other areas are quite simply unfashionable. Demand for the Royal Doulton Burslem figures has fallen dramatically, and only the prototypes, limited production and rare colourways are fetching good money. George Tinworth's desirable mice and frog figures, and Hannah Barlow's more unusual animal subjects, still have a strong collectors' interest, but there is little demand for other Doulton stoneware and faience. The colours of these pieces are considered dull.

The opposite is true of the high-flying inter-War Doulton pieces with experimental glazes – especially anything lustred or flambéd. A mid-1930s vase by Charles Noke and Harry Nixon, with experimental "Chang" glazes and modelled with a dragon, sold for £9,800 at Bonhams, London, in March 2011. The experimental-glaze figures have done much better than the Burslem figures, with a Titanium glazed version of a seated gnome HN380 reaching £5,000 at the same sale.

Moorcroft and Martin Brothers have continued to be strong in the market place. Clarice Cliff will command high prices if the pattern and shape are rare. The Ohio school, meanwhile, including Rookwood and Roseville, has had a quiet year, with few exciting pieces coming onto the market.

20thC silver has continued to sell well, particularly pieces by Charles Robert Ashbee, Archibald Knox and Omar Ramsden. In April 2011, Lawrences of Crewkerne, Somerset, England, sold a spectacular and rare silver centrepiece (356oz) from 1971 by Christopher Lawrence. It was estimated at £7,000–9,000 and sold for £21,000.

In Art Nouveau glass, it is the big names that continue to sell: Gallé, Tiffany, Loetz and Daum. Rare Art Deco Lalique is still much in demand.

Bronze and ivory figures by Demêtre Chiparus and Ferdinand Preiss have performed extremely well, but there are fakes so buyers must be cautious.

The sale of early 20thC furniture has been unspectacular – with collectors feeling that it is easier to add a piece of ceramic or glass to a collection than a cabinet or dining table.

Right: A patinated bronze and ivory "Bal Costumé" figure group, by Demêtre Chiparus. 19.25in (49cm) high £25,000-35,000 L&T

Left: A Clarice Cliff advertising plaque. See page 491.

A tall Art Nouveau Riessner, Stellmacher & Kessel figural centrepiece, by Eduard Stellmacher, featuring a standing maiden holding poppies, signed "Stellmacher", "Amphora 74", red "RSTK Turn-Teplitz", restoration and losses.

The company that later became Amphora, was founded in 1892 in Turn-Teplitz, Bohemia (now Austria/the Czech Republic) by Eduard Stellmacher, Hans and Karl Riessner, and Rudolf Kessel. It was incorporated as Riessner, Stellmacher and Kessel. The word "Amphora" consistently appeared on pieces from the late 1890s, and the firm was officially renamed "Riessner & Kessel Amphora" after the departure of Stellmacher in 1905.

26.75in (68cm) high

£1,200-1,800   DRA

A rare Art Nouveau Riessner, Stellmacher & Kessel figural maiden's head, by Eduard Stellmacher, signed "Ed. Stellmacher", and "Amphora 8021 12", restoration.

13in (33.5cm) high

£1,200-1,800   DRA

An Art Nouveau Riessner, Stellmacher & Kessel two-handled vase, decorated with a maiden, red "RSTK Turn-Teplitz, Amphora, 41 658" mark, light wear to gilt.

10.5in (27cm) high

£1,200-1,800   DRA

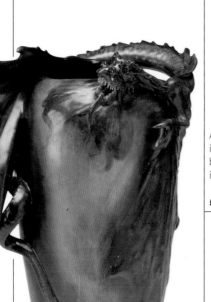

A tall rare Imperial Amphora figural vase with a dragon wrapped around the rim, circular stamp "IMPERIAL AMPHORA 4105 52, AUSTRIA" and crown, restoration to several areas.

17in (43cm) high

£5,000-6,000   DRA

A pair of Art Nouveau Amphora ewers, modelled in relief with flag iris flowers, glazed in green, buff and purple, highlighted in gilt, with impressed marks, minor damages.

17in (43cm) high

£1,200-1,800   WW

A tall Art Nouveau Amphora vase, with four lotus tendrils as handles, beneath a row of four smaller ones, stamped "AUSTRIA", crown and "39?1 45", restoration.

19in (48cm) high

£900-1,100   DRA

An Art Nouveau Amphora vase, with four floral stems as handles, above reticulated leaves, stamped "Amphora A 53 3438, 202 1268", restoration.

16.5in (42cm) high

£250-350   DRA

An Amphora bottle-shaped vase, carved with stylised trees in purple and gold, stamped "AUSTRIA 1207".

6.5in (16cm) high

£200-300   DRA

An Arequipa cabinet vase, carved with a floral band and covered in blue-grey frothy matt glaze, stamped "AREQUIPA CALIFORNIA MMKW 1624".

3.5in (9cm) high

£600-800   DRA

An Arequipa ovoid vase, deeply carved with green flower and tall leaves against a sheer brown and green ground, stamped mark, light damage.

8in (20cm) high

£2,000-3,000   DRA

An Arequipa squat vase, excised with seahorses on a carved yellow ground, the brown clay showing through, incised "M. M. T.", light damages.

5.25in (13cm) wide

£1,200-1,800   DRA

An Arequipa tapered vase, decorated in squeezebag with a band of white, yellow and brown leaves on a frothy green ground, blue ink mark, minor glaze flaking.

7.5in (19cm) high

£2,000-3,000   DRA

A large Clewell copper-clad ovoid vase, with blue-to-red patina, scratches.

14.25in (36.5cm) high

£2,500-3,000   DRA

A rare Clewell copper-clad vase, modelled around a stylised Arts and Crafts landscape, pottery body stamped "X2", with original patina, splits to copper.

13.5in (34cm) high

£2,500-3,500   DRA

A rare Chelsea Keramic Art Works pillow vase, painted by Hugh Robertson in barbotine style with a white bird on a dark ground, stamped "CHELSEA KERAMIC ART WORKS/ROBERTSON & SONS", signed "HCR".

5.25in (13cm) high

£800-1,200   DRA

A Chelsea Keramic Art Works bulbous vase, decorated by Josephine Day with an applied rose branch covered in blue-grey glaze on olive green ground, two small chips to rim, some losses to petals, stamped "CKAW" and "JD".

£450-550   DRA

A Chelsea Keramic Art Works tall burnished red clay urn, stamped "CKAW", firing split to one handle.

13in (33cm) high

£1,200-1,800   DRA

A Clarice Cliff "Appliqué Garden" bowl, with painted black "Appliqué" mark, "Bizarre" mark and facsimile signature.

c1930   *8in (20cm) diam*

£1,000-1,500   L&T

A Clarice Cliff "Appliqué Orange Lucerne" vase, shape no. 204, printed marks, painted "Appliqué", together with a black stepped glass stand.

8.75in (22cm) high

£4,000-5,000   SWO

A Clarice Cliff "Berries" conical sugar sifter, hand-painted with stylised fruit and foliage over panel ground between orange and green banding, combined "FANTASQUE" and "Bizarre" mark.

c1931   *5.5in (14cm) high*

£1,000-1,500   FLD

CLOSER LOOK - RED AUTUMN VASE

The limited use of colour is extremely striking.

It is possible that the featured colours were not a conscious choice, but a result of Cliff experimenting with a simpler colourway in 1930 before producing the multicoloured version of "Autumn" later in 1930.

In putting this pattern on shape 369, Cliff mixed a strictly Cubist shape with a flowing pattern.

Geometric shapes with many corners and edges are more prone to damage than rounded shapes. This example is in extremely good condition.

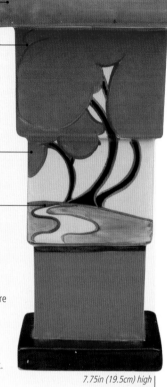

A Clarice Cliff "Red Autumn" square stepped vase, shape 369, hand-painted with a stylised tree and cottage landscape within green, red and black banding, combined "FANTASQUE" and "Bizarre" mark.

c1930   *7.75in (19.5cm) high*

£6,000-8,000   FLD

A rare Clarice Cliff "Red Carpet" wall plaque, painted in colours inside a grey rim printed mark, paper label.

12in (30.5cm) diam

£1,800-2,200   WW

A rare Clarice Cliff "Café" Bizarre vase, shape no.200, with printed factory marks.

7.5in (19cm) high

£8,000-10,000   WW

A Clarice Cliff "Castellated Circles" archaic vase, shape 374, incised "374", "Bizarre" mark and facsimile signature, hairlines.

c1930   *12in (30.5cm) high*

£1,200-1,800   L&T

A Clarice Cliff "Blue Chintz" Fantasque Bizarre conical sugar sifter, printed marks.

5.5in (14cm) high

£400-500   SWO

A Clarice Cliff "Cornwall" Bizarre Stamford tea-for-two set, comprising teapot and cover, milk jug and sugar basin, two cups, saucers and a side plate, with printed factory marks.

£4,000-5,000   WW

A Clarice Cliff "Diamonds" double-handled Lotus jug, painted with a deep band of alternate geometric panels within black, blue and yellow banding, with large "Bizarre" mark.

c1929   *11.75in (30cm) high*
£1,200-1,800   FLD

A Clarice Cliff "Blue Firs" miniature advertising plaque, hand-painted with a stylised coastal tree landscape, "Blue Firs" and script signature mark.

The plaque seems to have been created to replace the function of the miniature vases in the shape 177 series. Virtually the full pattern is included on both the plaque and the vase.

c1933   *2.25in (5.5cm) high*
£3,000-4,000   FLD

A Clarice Cliff "Forest Glen" vase, shape 360, painted with a stylised cottage landscape below a Delecia-style streaked sky, with "Bizarre" mark.

7.75in (19.5cm) high
£1,500-2,000   FLD

A rare Clarice Cliff "Honolulu" Fantasque Bizarre Conical tea-for-two set, comprising conical teapot and cover, milk jug and sugar basin, two cups, saucers and a side plate, painted in green and black, printed marks.

1933   *Teapot 4.75in (12cm) high*
£5,000-6,000   WW

A Clarice Cliff "Inspiration Knight Errant" circular charger, painted in coloured enamels, with printed and painted factory marks.

18in (45.5cm) diam
£3,500-4,500   L&T

A large Clarice Cliff "Lydiat" yo-yo vase, with printed factory marks.

18in (45.5cm) high
£1,500-2,000   L&T

A Clarice Cliff "Orange Roof Cottage" sugar sifter, painted with a stylised landscape with cottage and bridge between black and orange banding, combined "FANTASQUE" and "Bizarre" mark.

c1932   *5.5in (14cm) high*
£1,000-1,500   FLD

A Clarice Cliff "Red Roofs" Fantasque Bizarre twin-handled Lotus jug, painted in colours between orange and green bands printed mark, firing line to body.

11.75in (30cm) high
£2,000-3,000   WW

A Clarice Cliff "Sharks Teeth" conical biscuit barrel, shape 402, decorated with coloured bands and serrated motifs, printed mark "Bizarre", painted mark "Clarice Cliff".

c1930   *8in (20cm) high*
£2,500-3,500   L&T

DECORATIVE ARTS

A Clarice Cliff "Summerhouse" globe vase, shape 370, painted with a stylised garden scene with tree and summerhouse between yellow, black and orange banding, combined "FANTASQUE" and "Bizarre" mark.

c1931   *6in (15cm) high*

£2,200-2,800   **FLD**

CLOSER LOOK - CLIFF WALL PLAQUE

This plaque pushed the A.J. Wilkinson factory to its technical limits as it featured so many colours.

It was probably designed to act as a centrepiece for a special display of Clarice Cliff ware for a major retailer or at an exhibition.

The style, composition and use of many colours suggest it is a sample, by one painter. This is likely to have been Cliff herself.

The mark is completely hand-painted. The signature and word "Bizarre" closely resembles Cliff's handwriting from this period, which was more casual than the carefully done version on her backstamps.

This large plaque caused a sensation when it was "discovered" in 2007 as it had been in a private collection since the 1960s.

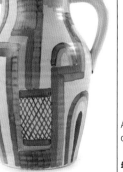

A large Clarice Cliff "Tambourine Dancer" circular wall plaque, painted with a stylised female dancer on a multicoloured abstract foliate ground over a Latona-style cream glaze, reverse painted "Bizarre by Clarice Cliff – A.J. Wilkinson Ltd, Newport Pottery Burslem".

c1932-34

£3,000-4,000   **FLD**

A Clarice Cliff "Xanthic" conical sugar sifter, painted with an abstract linear pattern in grey, orange and yellow between orange and yellow banding, with "Bizarre" mark.

5.5in (14cm) high

£1,000-1,500   **FLD**

A Clarice Cliff "Tennis" Bizarre twin-handled Lotus jug, with printed marks, paper collection label, minor firing fault.

Provenance: Sevi Guatelli Collection.

11.75in (30cm) high

£6,500-7,500   **WW**

A Clarice Cliff "Marlene" wall mask, painted in colours, with printed factory mark.

6.75in (17cm) high

£300-400   **WW**

One of a set of eight Dame Laura Knight for Clarice Cliff "Circus" dinner plates, printed and painted in gilt and coloured enamels with clowns, acrobats and performing animals, printed factory marks.

In 1934, Harrods organised an exhibition called "Modern Art for the Table", featuring ceramics and glass designed by leading artists of the day, including Paul Nash, Graham Sutherland, Eric Ravilious and Dame Laura Knight. These were produced by leading tableware manufacturers such as Clarice Cliff (A.J. Wilkinson's Ltd, and its subsidiary Newport Pottery). A year later the best pieces of this collaboration were displayed once again, this time in a high-profile exhibition at the Royal Academy, called "British Art in Industry".

Designed 1934

£3,500-4,500 set   **L&T**

A Dame Laura Knight for Clarice Cliff "Circus" teapot and cover, printed and painted in gilt and coloured enamels with clowns and acrobats, printed factory marks.

Designed 1934   *7in (18cm) high*

£2,500-3,000   **L&T**

ESSENTIAL REFERENCE - WILLIAM DE MORGAN

Initially a designer of stained glass, William de Morgan (1839-1917) began to produce tiles and other pottery items in London in 1869.

- Having trained at the Royal Academy Schools, he was an associate of William Morris, Edward Burne-Jones and Dante Gabriel Rossetti in the early 1860s.
- Patterns include stylised and grotesque flora and fauna inspired by medieval Persian, Moorish and Greek designs.
- Pieces were typically painted in ruby or copper lustre or "Persian" colours – green, black and turquoise.
- He worked for various potteries: Chelsea (1872), Merton Abbey (1882) and Sands End, Fulham (1889).

A William De Morgan copper lustre charger, the well with a serpent, the rim with a frieze of winged lions, impressed "J H Davis" mark.

12in (30.5cm) diam

£2,500-3,500   WW

A William De Morgan "Frightened Bird" double-lustre charger, painted with a large eagle beside a bird defending her nest, in shades of ruby and copper lustre on a white ground, impressed "H" mark.

14.25in (36.5cm) diam

£10,000-15,000   WW

A William De Morgan ruby lustre charger, painted with an antelope before a fruiting tree with a lizard climbing the trunk, in the foreground two scaly fish swimming in the river, highlighted in silver on a cream ground, impressed number to reverse, in half and re-stuck.

14.5in (37cm) diam

£2,500-3,500   WW

A William De Morgan "Persian" deep dish, painted by Charles Passenger, enamelled with a wide floral border and floral centre, artist signed monogram and "W.D.M. Fulham".

11.25in (28.5cm) diam

£6,000-8,000   SK

A William De Morgan charger, painted by Halsey Ricardo in ruby, with a mysterious winged portrait, flanked by hawks, above a mask and leaping fish, painted "HR" monogram.

It has been suggested that the mysterious figure is a caricature of British artist and designer Edward Burne-Jones (1833-1898).

14.5in (37cm) diam

£3,000-4,000   WW

A William De Morgan ruby lustre bottle vase, painted by Joe Juster with a frieze of leaping gazelle on a white ground, painted "Fulham JJ 2402".

10in (25.5cm) high

£5,000-6,000   WW

A William De Morgan double-lustre twin-handled vase, applied with twin angular handles, painted in ruby and copper lustre with a shoal of scaly fish.

12.25in (31cm) high

£5,000-6,000   WW

A William De Morgan double-lustre vase, painted with snails, butterflies and insects amongst foliage, in ruby, sand and copper lustre, restoration.

6.25in (15.5cm) high

£3,000-4,000   WW

A William De Morgan "Persian" tile, decorated in green and blue on a white ground with a duck, impressed marks, minor glaze frits.

6in (15cm) wide

£3,500-4,500　　　　WW

A William De Morgan Sand's End "Persian" tile panel, painted with two facing peacocks flanking a central panel of flowers and foliage, in shades of green, blue and purple on a white ground, framed marks concealed, damages.

33in (84.5cm) high

£3,500-4,500　　　　WW

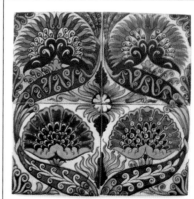

A set of four William De Morgan Sand's End "Mongolian" tiles, each painted in shades of blue and green, impressed mark.

Each 6in (15cm) wide

£2,500-3,500 set　　　　WW

Judith Picks

Prices for William De Morgan's pottery have risen dramatically over the last few years. This is totally understandable when you look at the high-quality glazes and designs. These "boxing hares", for example, immediately caught my eye.

In the wild, amorous male hares can sometimes be seen boxing over the affections of female hares. Although they can mate at any time of year, such a display is particularly associated with the month of March, when short crops make the hares easy to spot. They also leap and chase each other in March, leading to the phrase "mad as a March hare". These tiles are beautifully coloured, true to life, and have a very attractive humorous quality that appeals to collectors.

A William De Morgan Chelsea Period tile, painted with boxing hares in blue on a white ground, with impressed mark.

6in (15cm) wide

£4,000-5,000　　　　WW

A William De Morgan "Marlborough" three-tile panel, painted in shades of green and blue, marks concealed.

Each 8in (20cm) wide

£4,000-5,000 set　　　　WW

A William De Morgan "Marlborough" three-tile panel painted in shades of green, blue, yellow and aubergine, marks concealed.

This design is based on water lilies and indicates the influence of William Morris.

Each 8in (20cm) wide

£3,500-4,500 set　　　　WW

A William De Morgan Merton Abbey two-tile galleon panel, painted in shades of blue, green, aubergine and yellow with a ship before a Classical temple, impressed Merton Abbey mark, framed.

12in (30.5cm) wide

£5,000-6,000　　　　WW

A set of three William De Morgan ruby lustre tiles, each painted with a galleon at full sail, impressed mark to reverse.

Each 6in (15cm) wide

£5,000-6,000　　　　WW

A large Doulton Lambeth shouldered ovoid vase, by John Broad, decorated with a large applied scrolling Oriental dragon over an incised foliate ground, with tonal blue and green glazed finish, impressed and incised marks.

9in (23cm) high

£5,000-6,000 **FLD**

A pair of Doulton Lambeth stoneware baluster vases, by Hannah Barlow and Eliza Simmance, incised with grazing cattle, between panels of incised foliage and applied florets, in green, brown and white on a buff ground, impressed and incised marks.

16in (40.5cm) high

£2,000-3,000 **WW**

A Doulton Lambeth stoneware solifleur vase, by Florence Barlow, slip-decorated with budgerigars perched in hoops, in shades of blue, green and brown on a buff ground, the neck with mask motif, impressed and incised marks.

16in (40.5cm) high

£2,000-2,500 **WW**

A Doulton Lambeth ewer, by Mark V. Marshall and an unrecorded assistant, numbered "601", the handle and neck modelled with acanthus scrolls ending in busts, the base of the handle with a black-glazed Moorish man, body with gilt scrolls and low relief designs of foliate trails, impressed "Art Union of London Copyright".

c1895 *11in (28cm) high*

£3,500-4,500 **SK**

A pair of Doulton Lambeth stoneware vases, by Eliza Simmance, tubeline-decorated with Art Nouveau flower stems, in shades of ochre, green and blue on a mottled blue ground impressed and incised marks.

17in (43cm) high

£1,000-1,500 **WW**

A pair of late 19thC Doulton Burslem Ewers, the mottled cream body painted with summer flora and with oval cartouches of a girl bearing bulrushes and a girl bearing a potted plant, with gilt scroll handles.

9in (23cm) high

£700-900 **DA&H**

A large Doulton Burslem exhibition-quality baluster vase, decorated in underglaze blue with a scene of Classical figures, with raised gilt and enamelled foliate borders, restoration.

31.5in (80cm) high

£1,500-2,000 **GORL**

A Doulton Sung bulbous vase, by Charles Noke and F. Allen, signed "Sung Doulton England Noke F. Allen F 2.4."

28in (71cm) high

£300-400 **DRA**

A late 19thC Royal Doulton bottle-form vase, with Japanese-style gilt dragon wrapping itself around the vase in high relief, signed, with diamond-shaped registration mark.

1883 *14.25in (36.5cm) high*

£1,000-1,500 **IMC**

A pair of Royal Doulton "William Wordsworth" commemorative twin-handled vases, by Charles Noke, modelled in low relief, painted in colours, with printed marks.

Introduced in 1933, these jugs were from an open edition, meaning it is not possible to know how many were made. The quantity must have been comparatively low, as they are rare and hard to find today.

7in (18cm) high

£2,500-3,000 **WW**

DECORATIVE ARTS

A Doulton Lambeth "Play Goers" stoneware mouse group, by George Tinworth, with impressed marks, "GT" monogram, restoration.

5in (12.5cm) high

£3,500-4,500 WW

A rare large Doulton Lambeth salt-glazed stoneware figure of a monkey, by George Tinworth, on a brown glazed oval base, "GT" monogram.

c1885 *20.5in (52cm) high*

£15,000-20,000 WW

A Doulton Lambeth "In Memory of Public Library Act" stoneware frog sculpture, by George Tinworth, with impressed marks and "GT" monogram, restoration.

6in (15cm) high

£2,000-3,000 WW

A rare Doulton Lambeth "The Scrimmage" stoneware frog group, by George Tinworth, modelled as six frogs around a football, glazed blue, green and brown, with impressed mark and incised "GT" monogram.

4.75in (12cm) high

£5,000-6,000 WW

A large Royal Doulton stoneware dragon finial, designed by Gilbert Bayes, glazed in colours, minor firing faults.

Gilbert Bayes (1872-1953) was a Royal Academician, sculptor and medallist. He became particularly well-known for his architectural sculpture, his interest in colour, and his work with Royal Doulton. This extremely rare dragon was designed for use on the central pole of the York Rise housing estate in London.

27in (68.5cm) high

£12,000-14,000 WW

A Royal Doulton "Spooks" figure, HN89, potted by C.J. Noke, the two figures with red hats and a pale blue cloak, script marks "Spooks", "CJ Noke sc. Doulton" and printed Doulton mark.

7in (18cm) high

£4,000-5,000 SWO

A rare Royal Doulton "The Little Land" figure, designed by Harry Tittensor, painted in colours, printed and painted marks, impressed signature.

7.5in (19cm) high

£4,500-5,500 WW

Judith Picks: "One of the Forty"

When I am asked how I value items, I usually quote my "CARD" principle: Condition, Age, Rarity and Desirability.

These two figures, based on "Ali Baba and the Forty Thieves" were produced from c1920-1938 and were designed by Harry Tittensor. There are 14 styles with no less than 49 HN numbers, ranging from HN417 to HN1354. They are SO rare that the "Charlton Royal Doulton Figurines" catalogue quotes the one on the left as "none known to exist" and has no photograph available of the figure on the right at all!

Very often figures that were not particularly popular at the time, for whatever reason, are highly sought-after now. Although at this period people were fascinated by exoticism, it could be surmised that these figures were not particularly appealing and hence not many people bought them, and a gain adding to their desirability now. Even damaged they are valuable.

A rare large Royal Doulton "One of the Forty" figures, designed by Harry Tittensor, HN501, painted in shades of green and blue, printed and painted marks.

8in (20cm) high

£4,000-5,000 WW

A very rare Royal Doulton "One of the Forty" figure, designed by Harry Tittensor, style 14, model 313, possibly HN1354 (multicoloured), potting date "11.22(?)", printed, painted and impressed marks, cracked.

8in (20cm) high

£3,000-4,000 DN

A large Goldscheider table clock, signed on base with "Sculpture" symbol and "Friedrich Goldscheider Wein, 1437, PAEBÖLD".

c1900   27.5in (70cm) high
£2,500-3,000   WKA

A Goldscheider "Aspaia" ceramic bust, by Friedrich Goldscheider, with beige body, applied with beige, brown and golden shades, signed on base with "Sculpture" symbol, marked "Friedrich Goldscheider Wein, 3224/28/26" and "Pinotte", restored.

c1900   26in (66cm) high
£4,000-5,000   WKA

ESSENTIAL REFERENCE - GOLDSCHEIDER

Friedrich Goldscheider (1861-1922) moved from Pilsen to Vienna, Austria, in 1885, and established his factory soon afterwards.

- Early products were sculpted Art Nouveau-style pieces of red earthenware, cold-painted in imitation of Viennese bronzes. Statuary, tobacco jars, jardinières and wall masks were common.
- Goldscheider is now best-know for the Art Deco figures of fashionable women it produced after World War I. These figures accurately depicted contemporary costumes and hairstyles.
- Many were modelled by well-known artists including Josef Lorenzl and Stefan Dakon.
- The most common are dancer figures, typically depicted in scanty stage costumes.
- The factory closed in the mid-1950s.

A Goldscheider "Mondonave" "Lucréce" ceramic bust, with brown and black body, applied with beige and brown shades, signed on base "Mondonave", with "Sculpture" symbol, and "Friedrich Goldscheider Wein, 2103/45/34".

c1905   22in (56cm) high
£1,500-2,000   WKA

A Goldscheider "Mondonave" ceramic bust, set with opals, pale-coloured and black body, applied with beige and brown shades, signed on base "Mondonave", with "Sculpture" symbol, and "Friedrich Goldscheider Wein, REPRODUCTION RESERVÉ, 2580/29/13".

c1905   26in (66cm) high
£3,000-4,000   WKA

A Goldscheider wall mask, modelled as a woman with blue hair, with impressed and printed marks.

10in (25.5cm) high
£450-550   WW

A Goldscheider wall mask, model no.6429, modelled as a woman in a yellow hat, with incised and printed marks.

9in (23cm) high
£800-1,200   WW

A large Goldscheider wall mask, model no.6335, modelled as a woman in blue beret and beads, with impressed and printed marks.

11in (28cm) high
£600-800   WW

A Goldscheider wall mask, model no.7999, modelled as a stylised woman with orange hair and blue scarf, with printed and impressed marks.

9in (23cm) high
£700-800   WW

A Goldscheider "The Butterfly Girl" figure, by Lorenzl, moulded with hands aloft, on domed circular base, with printed and impressed marks, and mock "Lorenzl" signature.

13in (33.5cm) high

£1,200-1,800 **GORL**

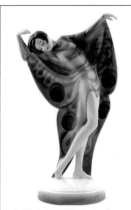

A Goldscheider "The Butterfly Dancer" figure, model no.5900, by Josef Lorenzl, spray glazed in red and grey, impressed marks, with printed marks and facsimile signature.

18in (45.5cm) high

£3,000-4,000 **WW**

A Goldscheider figure of a dancing girl, by Stefan Dakon, with her blue floral painted skirt held aloft, printed and impressed facsimile signature mark, damaged.

9in (23cm) high

£400-600 **GORL**

A Goldscheider figure of a dancing girl, model no.7053, designed by Josef Lorenzl.

16.25in (41cm) high

£1,800-2,200 **WW**

A Goldscheider figure of a tambourine dancer, model no.7699, by Stefan Dakon, with impressed and printed marks, original paper label, restoration.

16.5in (41.5cm) high

£1,200-1,800 **WW**

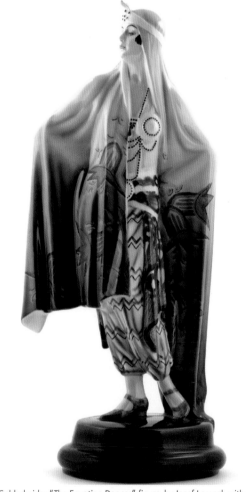

A Goldscheider figure of a woman holding a large ostrich feather fan, model no.5876, by Stefan Dakon, holding a patterned garment to her naked body, with impressed and printed marks and facsimile signature.

19in (48cm) high

£7,000-8,000 **WW**

A Goldscheider "Spanish Dancer" figure, model no.5616, by Josef Lorenzl, modelled wearing a shawl and holding a fan, impressed and printed marks, facsimile signature.

19in (48cm) high

£1,800-2,200 **WW**

A Goldscheider "The Egyptian Dancer" figure, by Josef Lorenzl, with printed and impressed marks.

18in (45.5cm) high

£7,000-8,000 **WW**

DECORATIVE ARTS

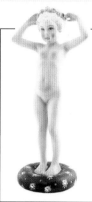

A Lenci porcelain figure modelled as a naked child with floral garland in her hair, signed "A. Jacopi".

11in (28cm) high

£1,000-1,500 BELL

A Lenci porcelain figure of a mother and child.

13in (33cm) high

£1,500-2,000 GORL

ESSENTIAL REFERENCE - LENCI

Founded in Turin, Italy, in 1919 by Enrico and Helen (Elena) König Scavini, Lenci produced dolls and from 1928, earthenware figurines and vases.

- Many of the best figurines were designed by Helen König Scavini, who had trained as an artist. Other notable artists include Gigi Chessa, Sandro Vacchetti, Giovanni Grande and Abele Jacopi.
- Lenci figurines were typically tall and thin, with characteristic Lenci pale yellow hair. Nude figures are common – the "Nudino" range is particularly sought-after today.
- Wares are typically in the bright palette of provincial northern Italy. Modelling shows a Germanic influence.
- In the 1950s, Lenci produced licensed Disney figures, including Bambi, Thumper, Peter Pan, Dumbo and Pinocchio.
- Lenci continued to produce ceramics until 1964, when the factory returned to exclusively producing dolls.
- In 1999 a limited number of ceramic pieces were recreated to celebrate the factory's 80th anniversary.

A Lenci bust of a young girl, by Helen König Scavini, her blonde hair spotted with gold and tied with gold ribbons.

11in (28cm) high

£2,000-2,500 FLD

A large Lenci wall mask, by Camillo Ghigo, with green ringlet hair adorned with wild flowers and a lizard, with painted mark and partial original paper label.

11in (28cm) long

£1,500-2,000 FLD

An Art Deco Lenci footed trumpet vase, decorated with stylised women and deer in a landscape on a turquoise ground, on circular foot, painted marks and "CH" monogram.

10.75in (27.5cm) high

£800-1,000 GORL

A 1930s Lenci "Nell" figure, by Helen König Scavini, modelled as a young lady in a black dress and red beret, seated on a bench with a small frog, with painted marks, restoration.

1933 *9in (23cm) high*

£3,000-4,000 FLD

A Lenci earthenware pedestal vase, painted with a Surrealist landscape of vehicles by a pitched big-top, beside a river, with painted marks and "LH" monogram.

11in (28cm) high

£1,200-1,800 WW

A George Jones majolica game pie dish, cover and liner, pattern no.2262, the cover moulded with fox and goose, the base with game trophies.

c1860   *10in (25.5cm) wide*
£1,000-1,500   **TEN**

A Minton majolica game pie dish and cover, the cover moulded with dead game, the base with basket work and oak leaves.

c1860   *15in (38cm) long*
£800-1,000   **TEN**

ESSENTIAL REFERENCE - GEORGE JONES MAJOLICA

George Jones (c1824-1893) worked for Minton in Stoke-on-Trent before setting up his own Trent Pottery (also in Stoke-on-Trent) in 1861. Initially the firm produced earthenware, notably majolica. It started making bone china in 1872.

● Jones's pieces were impeccably modelled and extremely well glazed.
● Naturalistic forms predominate. Animal and exotic bird figures are sought-after, as are strawberry dishes.
● It can be difficult to distinguish between George Jones's majolica and the more naturalistic Minton designs, which Jones may have worked on during his time at the factory.
● Jones's pieces have a distinctive, simulated tortoiseshell glaze on the bottom. This was copied by other British and American firms, but with inferior skill.
● Most pieces are lined with a pale pink or turquoise glaze.
● The first mark was a monogram of the initials "GJ", with "& Sons" added from December 1873, and a crescent shape from 1874. Pattern numbers and letters were painted in black onto a white thumbprint pressed into the base.
● The factory remained open until 1951.

A Minton majolica parrot, retailed by John Mortlock, Oxford Street, London, modelled after the Chinese original, base edged with repeat fleur de lys motifs in gilt, impressed "Mintons" and date, also "Mortlock/Mintons, with globe and strapwork mark.

1861   *8.5in (21.5cm) high*
£400-600   **TEN**

A possibly Minton majolica garden seat, the flat blue-glazed surface pierced for carrying, with mustard bandings, decorated with flowering branches against a pale and dark blue ground, banded base, overglaze painted "M3262" and four dots in pink script.

c1875   *17.75in (45cm) high*
£1,200-1,800   **TEN**

A George Jones majolica garden seat, moulded with herons and a bird within pond landscape of lilies and flowers on a dark blue ground, the pierced top with basket moulding.

c1875   *19in (48cm) high*
£2,000-3,000   **L&T**

A Minton majolica casserole dish, cover and liner, the knop modelled as a fly and a toadstool, on a bed of strawberry blossoms and leaves, the body modelled as a grey wall face with four ducks and a fox, the sides moulded with ivy, ferns and foliage, impressed "Mintons", year mark and "2062", lid damaged.

1876   *15.75in (40cm) wide*
£15,000-20,000   **TEN**

A pair of Wedgwood majolica ewers for water and wine, modelled with Neptune and Bacchus holding a fish and goat with seaweed and fruiting vine swags, impressed marks, date code, each incised "236".

1867   *20.5in (52cm) high*
£2,200-2,800   **SWO**

A Wedgwood majolica bust of Sir Walter Scott, in honey-treacle-coloured glaze, with impressed mark.

c1880   *19in (48cm) high*
£1,000-1,500   **SK**

A late 19thC Portuguese majolica Palissy-style dish, modelled with sea creatures and crustacea, chipped.

14.25in (36.5cm) diam
£1,500-2,500   **DN**

A Delphine Massier "Frogs in Row-Boat" majolica table centrepiece, with brown script mark "Delphine Massier Vallauris (A.M.)"
c1890   *17in (43cm) wide*
£2,000-2,500   **TEN**

An English majolica cheese bell and stand, attributed to Joseph Holdcroft, the domed cover with moulded fish against a cobalt-blue ground and surmounted by a moulded fish handle.
c1870   *10in (25.5cm) high*
£600-800   **FRE**

A Marblehead tile, incised with blue and brown fish under pale blue waves, on a speckled matt grey ground, with ship mark.

Complete with original pencil and charcoal sketch. From the collection of Arthur Baggs' daughter, Mary Trowbridge Baggs Tweet of Tolland, Connecticut.

6in (15cm) wide
£8,000-10,000   **DRA**

A Marblehead beaker-shaped vase, incised and painted with stylised trees in charcoal against a speckled dark green-blue ground, with ship mark, incised "HT".
4in (10cm) wide
£3,000-3,500   **DRA**

A Marblehead spherical vase, incised and painted by Arthur Baggs, with stylised flowers in blue and pale yellow on a speckled grey ground, with ship mark, incised "AB T".
4.75in (12cm) wide
£2,000-2,500   **DRA**

CLOSER LOOK - ROYAL WORCESTER EXHIBITION VASE

This is one of a series of vases painted with figurative subjects by Josiah Rushton, in the 1860s and 1870s, after Ruben's originals dating from 1512.

In this depiction Galatea appears surrounded by other sea creatures whose forms are somewhat inspired by Michelangelo, whereas the bright colours and decoration are supposed to be inspired by ancient Roman painting.

These vases are all huge, mainly around 30in (76cm) high. This is even taller at nearly 36in (91cm) high. The size alone is a challenge for the potter.

This urn is even more decorative than most, having been made for an exhibition, and is signed and dated 1866. Most of Rushton's wares are unmarked.

It is unusual in that it is made of earthenware decorated to such an extent with opaque majolica colours.

A Royal Worcester "Triumph of Galatea" majolica exhibition urn, by Josiah Rushton after Raphael, with Royal Worcester crown mark, inscribed "Royal Porcelain Works Worcester "signed and dated by artist.
1866   *35.75in (90.5cm) high*
£6,000-7,000   **DRA**

A Marblehead ovoid vase, carved and painted with tall trees with red fruit on an indigo ground, with ship mark.

6.5in (16cm) high
£2,000-3,000   **DRA**

A pair of Martin Brothers stoneware vases, incised with birds wading and flying amongst flag iris and bulrushes, in blue, brown and white on a buff ground incised "4-1887, R W Martin & Bros, London & Southall", restoration.

1887   *4in (36cm) high*
£1,500-2,000   **WW**

A large Martin Brothers stoneware gourd vase, glazed in mottled blue inlaid with pale blue ribs, incised "4-1897, Martin Bros London & Southall".

1897   *11in (28cm) high*
£4,000-5,000   **WW**

A Martin Brothers stoneware vase, by Walter and Edwin Martin, incised with eel, fish and jellyfish, in ochre on a veined green ground, incised "3 1901 Martin Bros, London & Southall".

1901   *6in (15cm) high*
£2,000-3,000   **WW**

A Martin Brothers stoneware vase, incised with fish, limpets and jellyfish and glazed in shades of green and brown on a blue ground, incised "5-1897 Martin Bros, London & Southall".

1897   *6in (15cm) high*
£4,000-5,000   **WW**

A Martin Brothers stoneware gourd vase, by Walter and Edwin Martin, modelled with three grotesque handles, glazed black, incised "3 1908 Martin Bros, London & Southall".

1908   *6in (15.5cm) high*
£4,000-5,000   **WW**

A pair of Martin Brothers stoneware bird vases, by Robert Wallace Martin, each modelled with anthropomorphic birds in relief inside geometric foliate borders, in shades of ochre, blue and green, one incised "3 3 83 Martin Bros, London & Southall", the other "3 3 83 R W Martin & Bros London & Southall".

1883   *12in (30.5cm) high*
£4,000-5,000   **WW**

A Martin Brothers stoneware vase, incised with monkeys stealing fruit, amongst scrolling foliage, in shades of ochre and brown, incised "10-1893 Martin Bros, London & Southall".

1893   *9in (23cm) high*
£5,000-6,000   **WW**

A Martin Brothers stoneware face jug, each side modelled with a smiling face, glazed in shades of grey, green and ochre, incised "R W Martin London & Southall".

6in (15.5cm) high
£1,500-2,500   **WW**

A Martin Brothers stoneware fish vase, incised and moulded with a scene of fantastical fish, with two swan's neck handles and a band of cattails, incised "R.W. Martin & Bros. London & Southall".

1883   *8.5in (21.5cm) high*
£5,000-6,000   **SK**

Judith Picks

I have long been fascinated by these very expressive grotesque Martin Brothers birds, and many years ago was the underbidder for a pair at an auction in Sussex (yet another of my "the one that got away" regrets!).

Twenty years ago few came on the market but, due I suppose to the record prices achieved in recent years, they seem to keep appearing. I met a vendor recently who said she was delighted to sell as she had always hated the bird and could not believe that anyone would pay in excess of £10,000 for it. What do they say about "one man's meat being another man's poison"?

A Martin Brothers stoneware bird jar and cover, modelled with downcast, smiling gaze, glazed in shades of green, blue and ochre, incised "Martin Brothers London & Southall 7-1900", on ebonised wood base.

1900   *9in (23cm) high*
£10,000-15,000   **WW**

A Martin Brothers stoneware bird jar and cover, by Robert Wallace Martin, modelled standing with puffed-up chest and alert look, glazed in shades of green and brown, incised "R W Martin & Son Southall", on an ebonised wood base.

9in (23cm) high
£9,000-11,000   **WW**

A rare Martin Brothers bird cruet set, by Robert Wallace Martin, glazed in shades of ochre, blue and green, incised "R W Martin" to base, painted "Martin Bros London & Southall" panel to back, minor restoration.

Tallest 6in (15cm) high
£9,000-11,000   **WW**

A rare Martin Brothers stoneware monkey jar and cover, by Robert Wallace Martin, modelled with toothy grin, glazed in shades of brown, incised "Martin Bros" and "Martin Bros London & Southall", minor restoration.

6in (15cm) high
£7,000-8,000   **WW**

A Martin Brothers stoneware pawn chess piece, by Robert Wallace Martin, modelled as a bust wearing armour, glazed mottled white incised "R W Martin & Bros London & Southall".

1902   *3.5in (9cm) high*
£1,500-2,000   **WW**

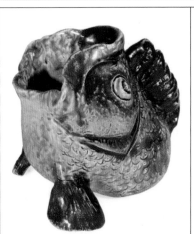

A rare Martin Brothers stoneware grotesque spoon-warmer modelled as a scaly fish, by Robert Wallace Martin, glazed in shades of green and brown, incised "Martin Bros London & Southall", restoration.

6in (15cm) high
£6,000-8,000   **WW**

A very rare Martin Brothers stoneware spoon-warmer modelled as a rodent creature, by Robert Wallace Martin, glazed in shades of brown, incised "R W Martin & Bros, London & Southall".

6in (15m) high
£30,000-40,000   **WW**

A rare Martin Brothers stoneware mantel clock, by Robert Wallace Martin, modelled with Ionic pillars and winged lion capitals, in shades of green, blue and brown, with Lund & Blockley movement incised "18 R W Martin London 12-1874".

1874   *8in (20cm) high*
£6,000-7,000   **WW**

One of a pair of Minton "Cloisonné" moonflasks, each printed in gilt and silver-gilt with Japanese flower vases, on a turquoise ground impressed marks.

8in (20cm) high

£300-400 pair   **WW**

A Minton "Cloisonné" vase, by Dr. Christopher Dresser, printed and enamelled in colours and gilt on a pink ground with geometric panels, on moulded foot, restoration.

8in (20cm) high

£700-800   **WW**

A pair of Minton "Cloisonné" vases, by Dr. Christopher Dresser, decorated with gilt and coloured enamels on a turquoise ground.

c1875   *5in (12.5cm) high*

£800-1,000 pair   **L&T**

A Minton pottery ornithological two-handled pedestal vase, by Wenceslas (William) Mussill, painted in the Barbotine technique with a blue-winged parrot and a yellow-headed parrot, signed, impressed "Minton", year cipher, gilded crown and globe mark and "England".

Wenceslas (William) Mussill, (1829-1906), a flower and bird painter, was born in Austria near Carlsbad. He was influenced by the work of John Bateman of Biddulph Grange who published the book "Mexican Orchids". In the 1870s he went to Minton where he was offered a weekly salary but refused, wishing to be paid separately for each piece. His work was only fired once.

c1880   *19in (48.5cm) high*

£2,500-3,000   **TEN**

A rare Minton porcelain Japanese gourd-form vase and cover, attributed to Dr. Christopher Dresser, with modelled silk tie, painted in the Persian manner with elaborate panels of flowers in yellow, coral and white on a red and blue panelled ground, highlighted in gilt, with printed mark.

10.5in (27cm) high

£7,500-8,500   **WW**

A Minton Secessionist five-tile panel, by John Wadsworth, tubeline decorated with stylised iris flower stems, in yellow, green and salmon pink, highlighted in gilt, impressed marks.

panel 30in (76cm) high

£1,000-1,500   **WW**

A pair of Aesthetic Movement Minton "The Seven Ages of Man" pilgrim flasks, by Henry Stacy Marks, painted with medieval figures, painted and highlighted in gilt, with date mark and impressed marks.

1876   *17in (43cm) high*

£7,000-9,000   **WW**

A pair of Aesthetic Movement Minton four-tile panels, each painted with an egret before bulrushes, painted in colours on a celadon ground, impressed marks.

32in (81cm) high

£2,500-3,000   **WW**

An Aesthetic Movement Minton charger, slip-decorated with an Egyptian dancer, the rim with bird roundels amongst foliage, in colours on a terracotta ground, impressed marks, date code.

1872   *13.5in (34cm) diam*

£700-800   **WW**

A James Macintyre twin-handled "Alhambra" vase, by William Moorcroft, painted in shades of pink and blue, highlighted in gilt, with printed factory mark.

10in (25.5cm) high

£1,000-1,500   WW

A James Macintyre & Co Florian Ware "Anemone" vase, by William Moorcroft, painted in shades of blue and green on a white ground, printed mark, painted green signature, minor restoration.

8in (20cm) high

£1,500-2,000   WW

A James Macintyre & Co. Florian Ware "Hazledene" jardiniere, by William Moorcroft, painted in shades of pale blue and green, printed, impressed marks, painted green signature, damages.

8in (20cm) high

£2,500-3,000   WW

A James Macintyre & Co. Hesperian Ware "Lilac" vase, by William Moorcroft, tubeline decorated with flower sprays in blue on a pale blue ground, highlighted with a light red printed marks, facsimile green signature.

This vase carries the unusual printed Hesperian mark for the retailers Osler, London.

11in (28cm) high

£4,000-5,000   WW

A large Moorcroft Florian "Poppy" vase, by William Moorcroft, inscribed in green "W Moorcroft Des.", with printed registration no "326471".

c1900   *12.5in (32cm) high*

£3,500-4,000   SWO

A pair of James Macintyre & Sons Florian Ware baluster vases, by William Moorcroft, painted in green and gold with panels of flowers in shades of green and blue, highlighted in gilt, printed mark, painted green monogram.

8.25in (21cm) high

£2,000-3,000   WW

BEWARE!

Although these vases are genuine, period examples, some Moorcroft patterns were reproduced as miniatures in the 1970s and are generally worth less, fetching between £70 and £250.

A James Macintyre & Co. "Poppies" miniature vase, by William Moorcroft, with Macintyre mark and "W.M."

c1905   *3.25in (8.5cm) high*

£1,000-1,500   SWO

A James Macintyre & Co "Alhambra" pattern miniature tradesman's sample ewer, by William Moorcroft, tubeline decorated in blue and salmon, highlighted in gilt, printed factory mark.

c1903   *2.5in (6.5cm) high*

£2,200-2,800   WW

A large Moorcroft Pottery "Big Poppy" flambé vase, by William Moorcroft, covered in a rich flambé glaze, with painted blue signature, dated, with paper label.

The size and the fact that this vase is dated suggest that it was produced for an exhibition.

1930 *15.5in (39cm) high*
£5,000-6,000 WW

A Moorcroft Pottery "Eventide" jar and cover, impressed factory marks, initialled in blue "W.M", traces of original printed paper label.

c1930 *6.5in (16cm) diam*
£3,000-4,000 L&T

A Moorcroft Pottery "Fish" flambé vase, by William Moorcroft, painted in colours under a flambé glaze, applied paper label, with painted blue signature.

5.5in (14cm) high
£5,000-6,000 WW

A Moorcroft Pottery "Moonlit Blue" vase, by William Moorcroft, painted in shades of blue and green on a deep blue ground, impressed marks, painted green signature.

8.5in (21.5cm) high
£2,500-3,000 WW

A Moorcroft Pottery "Pansies" baluster vase, decorated with a band of flowers on a white ground, impressed factory marks, signed in green.

c1915 *6in (15cm) high*
£1,000-1,500 L&T

A Moorcroft Pottery "Pansies" large ginger jar and cover, with William Moorcroft signature in green, impressed marks.

c1920 *11in (28cm) high*
£1,500-2,000 L&T

A Moorcroft Pottery "Pomegranate" vase, slip-trailed, with impressed and painted marks.

8.75in (22cm) high
£500-700 BE

A Moorcroft Pottery "Waratah" vase, by William Moorcroft, painted in shades of red and green on a graduated green and blue ground, with impressed marks, painted blue signature.

4in (10cm) high
£6,000-7,000 WW

A Moorcroft Pottery "Wisteria" vase, by William Moorcroft, painted in shades of pink, purple and green on a white ground, painted green signature, dated.

1913 *9in (23cm) high*
£6,000-7,000 WW

A Bernard Moore inverted baluster vase, the mottled mustard, green and blue swirled wave crests with jewelled enamelled spray, highlighted in gilt, marked in the glaze.

7.25in (18.5cm) high

£600-700 AH

A Bernard Moore high-fired ruby ovoid jar, in a prunus design, with an enamelled lacquered-brass pierced cover, painted mark.

It is possible the cover was produced by the Duchess of Sutherland's Cripples' Guild.

15in (38cm) high

£1,500-2,000 DN

A Bernard Moore ginger jar and cover, by Dora M. Billington, painted with scaly fish in ruby flambé glaze, painted mark, artist's monogram, cover in half and re-stuck.

£1,000-1,500 WW

A Bernard Moore blue-glazed figure of a monkey, with orange eyes.

2.25in (5.5cm)

£300-400 GORL

A Cantagalli Iznik pedestal bowl, painted with flowers and foliage in colours on a white ground, painted cockerel mark, damages.

Similar bowls were retailed by Morris & Co and are illustrated in the Morris & Co catalogues.

9.75in (25cm) wide

£3,500-4,500 WW

A pair of Morris & Co. "Pink & Hawthorn" tiles, designed by William Morris, painted in shades of green and yellow, later framed.

Each 5in (12.5cm) wide

£1,500-2,500 WW

ESSENTIAL REFERENCE - EDWARD BURNE-JONES

Artist and designer, Edward Burne-Jones (1833–1898) was a close friend of William Morris and worked with him on a variety of art forms.

- Along with Morris, Dante Gabriel Rossetti, Ford Madox Brown, Philip Webb, Charles Faulkner and Peter Paul Marshall, he was a founding partner in Morris, Marshall, Faulkner, and Co. (later Morris & Co.), established 1861.
- As part of Morris & Co., Burne-Jones was closely involved in the rejuvenation of English stained glass, which came to define the typical Arts and Crafts home. Many of his windows featured medieval figures.
- He came to public attention in May 1877 when many of his paintings, including "The Beguiling of Merlin" were shown in the first exhibition at the Grosvenor Gallery.
- As well as stained glass, he also designed ceramic tiles, jewellery, tapestries, mosaics and book illustration, most famously designing woodcuts for the Kelmscott Press edition of the works of Geoffrey Chaucer in 1896.
- He was made a Baronet in 1894.
- He was extremely influential among English artists of the Aesthetic movement, and French Symbolist painters.
- Deemed unfashionable for most of the 20thC, the work of Burne-Jones began to be re-evaluated in the 1970s.

A Morris & Co "Dido" two-tile panel, by Edward Burne-Jones, from "The Goode Wimmen" series, painted in colours, later frame, damages.

10.25in (26cm) high

£6,000-7,000 WW

A rare Morris & Company "Alceste" two-tile panel, by Edward Burne-Jones from "The Goode Wimmen" series, painted in colours, in later frame.

10.25in (26cm) high

£12,000-14,000 WW

An early Newcomb College mug, painted with stylised artichokes in green on a blue ground, marked "NC/JM/Q/F-49/X/triangle" and with paper label "APPROVED BY THE SOCIETY OF ARTS & CRAFTS".

1901	5.5in (14cm) wide
£500-700	DRA

An early and unusual Newcomb College experimental sang de boeuf spherical vase, by Roberta B. Kennon, decorated with blue crocuses on a blue and pink ground, marked "NC/JM/U/R.B.K. Kennon/H23(?)".

Roberta Kennon studied with Arthur Wesley Dow in Ipswich, MA, in the summer of 1902.

1902	6.25in (15.5cm) high
£900-1,100	DRA

A tall early Newcomb College vase, carved by Marie De Hoa LeBlanc, with tall pine trees, marked "NC/MHLB/AY38/JM".

1906	12.25in (31cm) high
£12,000-14,000	DRA

A Newcomb College transitional corseted vase, carved with white blossoms.

1919	7.5in (19cm) high
£1,200-1,800	DRA

A Newcomb College bowl, by Henrietta Bailey, with a band of blue flowers, "NC 259 HB IL5".

1916	8in (20cm) diam
£700-900	DRA

A Newcomb College transitional squat vessel, by Sadie Irvine, decorated with clusters of pink berries, marked "NC SI ID62".

1916	5.5in (14cm) diam
£700-900	DRA

A Newcomb College squat vessel, carved by A.F. Simpson with pink freesia blossoms on a blue ground.

1937	8in (20cm) wide
£1,200-1,800	DRA

A rare Newcomb College milk pitcher, by Sadie Irvine, decorated with sailboats on Lake Ponchartrain in blues and greens against a pink sky.

1918	4.75in (12cm) wide
£2,000-3,000	DRA

A Newcomb College vase, by Sadie Irvine, with nicotina leaves, marked "NC/SI/209/MW24".

1922	7.5in (19cm) high
£2,500-3,500	DRA

A Newcomb College vase, carved by A.F. Simpson with a moonlit bayou landscape.

1923	6.75in (17cm) high
£800-1,200	DRA

DECORATIVE ARTS

A Newcomb College cylindrical vase, carved by A.F. Simpson with a bayou scene of tall oak trees, Spanish moss, and a full moon.

8in (20cm) high

£1,500-2,000   DRA

A Newcomb College cabinet vase, carved by A.F. Simpson, with tall pines, marked "NC/JM/IJ37/AFS/367/238".

1916   4in (10cm) high

£2,000-3,000   DRA

A Newcomb College ovoid vase, carved with a windswept landscape of bending trees in blue-greens against an ivory sky.

1919   5.5in (14cm) high

£2,000-3,000   DRA

A Newcomb College vase, carved with live oak trees and Spanish moss against a vermilion sky, marked "NC/4/RA72" and with paper label.

1928   5.25in (13cm) high

£2,500-3,000   DRA

ESSENTIAL REFERENCE - NORTH DAKOTA SCHOOL

The North Dakota School of Mines was established in 1892 at the University of North Dakota. From 1909 students on the ceramics course, lead by Margaret Cable, began to make utilitarian wares, such as tiles, bricks and jugs, as well as decorative pieces, such as bowls and vases.

● Many talented instructors worked at the university, including Margaret's sister Flora Cable Huckfield, Frieda Hammers, Margaret Pachl and Julia Mattson.

● Pieces show the influence of the Arts and Crafts movement, as well as Art Nouveau and Art Deco.

● Typical decoration includes flora and fauna, farming and hunting scenes, as well as Native American motifs.

● Early pieces are marked "U.N.D.", however most pieces are stamped with the full name of the university.

● The pottery is still active today.

A North Dakota School of Mines bulbous vase, by Margaret Cable, with cut-back daffodils in light brown on a deep brown ground, with circular ink mark and "M. Cable/273".

8in (20cm) high

£2,000-3,000   DRA

A North Dakota School of Mines vase, by Julia Mattson, decorated with rodeo riders under matt brown glaze, with indigo stamp "JM 133A".

6.5in (16cm) high

£1,200-1,800   DRA

A North Dakota School of Mines bulbous vase, carved by Flora Huckfield, with large flowers under a frothy pale green and mustard glaze, incised "S Undegaard Huckfield 914", blue ink stamp.

7.5in (19cm) wide

£1,500-2,000   DRA

A North Dakota School of Mines bulbous vase, carved by Marie B. Thormodsgard with Arabian Nights scene excised in black against a caramel ground, with ink stamp "M.B.T.".

c1930   7.75in (19.5cm) high

£5,000-6,000   DRA

A large George Ohr "Joe Jefferson" mug, inscribed "Here's your good health and all your family's and may they live long and prosper, J. Jefferson", in gun-metal, green and amber speckled glaze, script signature and "3-1896".

1896   *6.25in (15.5cm) high*

£1,200-1,800   **DRA**

A small George Ohr dimpled bisque-fired clay vessel, stamped "G.E. Ohr Biloxi, Miss".

4in (10cm) high

£1,200-1,800   **DRA**

A George Ohr squat vessel, with scalloped rim, in a fine blue, green, and pink sponged glaze, with die-stamped mark.

4.25in (11cm) wide

£3,000-4,000   **DRA**

A George Ohr bisque-fired cabinet vase, with deep in-body twist, inscribed "Mud from N.O. Street 1905," with script signature and date.

1905   *3.75in (9.5cm) wide*

£2,500-3,500   **DRA**

A George Ohr cabinet vase, with folded rim and notched band covered in gunmetal brown glaze, and impressed "G.E.OHR Biloxi, Miss.".

4in (10cm) high

£1,200-1,800   **DRA**

A George Ohr bisque-fired white clay water jug, with script signature.

6in (15cm) high

£1,200-1,800   **DRA**

A George Ohr vessel, of Chinese melon shape, in gunmetal glaze over an amber ground, with script signature.

4.25in (11cm) high

£2,500-3,500   **CRA**

A George Ohr vase, with pinched rim, its asymmetrical bulbous base sponge-painted in gunmetal glaze, covered in mirrored cobalt glaze, marked "G. E. OHR, Biloxi, Miss.".

4.5in (11.5cm) high

£3,000-4,000   **DRA**

A George Ohr squat vessel, with flaring rim covered in a sponged-on brown and green glaze, stamped "GEO. E OHR BILOXI, MISS.".

2.75in (7cm) high

£900-1,100   **DRA**

A George Ohr novelty hat, with speckled gunmetal glaze on an amber ground, stamped "G. E. OHR BILOXI".

3.25in (8.5cm) high

£1,200-1,800   **DRA**

A Pewabic spherical ribbed vase, in a lustred bright blue glaze, with circular stamp mark.

7in (18cm) high

£600-800   CRA

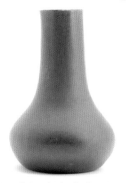

An early Pewabic bottle-shaped vase, covered in a fine leathery matt dark green and oxblood glaze, stamped "Pewabic" with leaves.

7in (18cm) high

£500-600   DRA

A rare early Pewabic crackleware plate, incised with ducks on water against an indigo and white ground, mark obscured by glaze.

9in (23cm) diam

£500-700   DRA

A Pewabic vase, covered in dripping, lustred green glaze, stamped "PEWABIC DETROIT", with paper label.

6.25in (15.5cm) high

£600-800   DRA

ESSENTIAL REFERENCE - QUIMPER

Quimper faience (tin-glazed earthenware) has been made in Loc Maria, near Quimper, France, since the early 18thC.

- **The first factory was founded by Pierre Bosquet in 1708. His daughter married, Pierre Bellevaux, originally from Nivernais, who brought with him the secrets of Nevers faience.**
- **Quimper's most famous design is the "Petit Breton", a naive representation of a Breton man and/or woman in traditional costume. It first became popular in c1870 and is still produced on souvenir wares.**
- **Faience is still made in Quimper today.**

A set of four late 19thC Quimper botanical plates, painted with a different flower or branch, painted and impressed "PB" marks for Porquier-Beau.

9in (23cm) diam

£2,500-3,500   WW

A large late 19thC Quimper marriage plate, painted with a scene of present-giving at a Breton wedding, beneath the Brittany coat of arms within a blue foliate border, "PB" monogram mark.

13.5in (34cm)

£700-1,000   WW

A Quimper coffee pot, marked "Henriot".

c1930   *10in (25.5cm) high*

£100-150   MILA

A Quimper cheese dish, with bagpipes and lid, marked "Henriot".

c1930   *11in (28cm) long*

£200-250   MILA

A rare Rookwood carved Standard glaze narrow vase, incised and painted, probably by K. Shirayamadani, with amber fish on a bottle-green ground, the surface with long drips, with flame mark and "589E/0".

1900   *8.25in (21cm) high*
£2,000-3,000   **DRA**

A Rookwood Standard glaze two-handled vase, painted by E. Nourse with yellow orchids, uncrazed, with flame mark.

1903   *5.75in (14.5cm) high*
£200-300   **DRA**

GLAZE

Founded by Maria Longworth Nichols in 1880, the Rookwood Pottery of Cincinnati, Ohio, is arguably the most important producer of American Art Pottery. This is largely due to the innovation and quality shown in its many glazes. Dates are when glazes were introduced.

Standard glaze (1884):
Translucent high gloss that gave all colours a yellow-brown hue.

Iris (1884):
Colourless glaze with the same richness and depth as the Standard. Production ceased by 1912 due to high-lead content.

Sea Green (c1885):
Used almost exclusively for seascapes and fish. Largely abandoned by 1904.

Matt glaze (c1900):
Flat and opaque with a coarse texture.

Vellum (1900):
Diffuses the painted decoration giving it an Impressionist appearance. Majority produced before 1915.

Jewel Porcelain (1915)
Rich, heavy and in simple colours.

A Rookwood Iris glaze vase, painted by Olga G. Reed, with golden blossoms, with flame mark and "II/808/O.G.R. W."

1902   *7.75in (19.5cm) high*
£800-1,200   **DRA**

A Rookwood black Iris glaze ovoid vase, painted by Sarah Sax with a holly branch against black ground, with flame mark and artist cipher.

1906   *6.25in (15.5cm) high*
£2,500-3,500   **DRA**

A Rookwood Iris glaze vase, painted by E.T. Hurley with fish swimming against celadon water, with flame mark.

1910   *8in (20cm) high*
£3,000-4,000   **DRA**

A Rookwood Sea Green glaze two-handled vase, painted by E.T. Hurley with amber day lilies on a celadon ground, with flame mark and "77A/E.T.H./G", restorations.

1898   *7.75in (19.5cm) high*
£1,500-2,000   **DRA**

A rare Rookwood Sea Green glaze ovoid vase, painted by E.T. Hurley with swimming fish, with flame mark and "II/900C/ETH".

1902   *8in (20cm) high*
£2,000-3,000   **DRA**

A Rookwood Matt glaze vase, painted by Olga G. Reed with red maple leaves on a shaded indigo ground, with flame mark and "III/7BZ/O.G.R."

1903   *11.25in (28.5cm) high*
£1,200-1,800   **DRA**

A Rookwood Vellum glaze tapered vase, painted by E.T. Hurley with a bird in flight among tall grass, with flame mark and "950D/V/ETH".

1907 9in (23cm) high
£2,000-3,000 DRA

A tall Rookwood Scenic Vellum vase, painted by E.T. Hurley with a mountainous lakeland scene, with flame mark and "XIV/ETH/2039C/V".

1914 11.75in (30cm) high
£1,500-2,000 DRA

A Rookwood Scenic Vellum glaze plaque, by Ed Diers with an autumnal landscape, mounted in period, but not necessarily original, frame, with flame mark and "XVII/V/ED".

1917 Plaque 5in (12.5cm) wide
£2,500-3,500 DRA

A Rookwood Vellum vase, painted by Ed Diers, with branches of wisteria, with flame mark and "XXV/ED/1023C/V".

1925 10.5in (27cm) high
£1,500-2,000 DRA

A large Rookwood Jewel porcelain vase, by William Hentschel, with a geometric design over a cobalt ground, with seconded mark, drilled base, with flame mark and "XV/515/WEH/X".

1915 14in (36cm) high
£500-700 DRA

A Roseville "Azurean" vase, painted by Anthony Dunleavy with a large sailboat, stamped "azurean 912 RP CO FD."

12.5in (32cm) high
£800-1,200 DRA

A Roseville green "Baneda" vase, marked "599-12".

£1,500-2,000 DRA

A Roseville red "Carnelian II" "Beehive" vase, 450-14, with black label.

This is part of the 400 series.

14in (36cm) high
£7,000-8,000 DRA

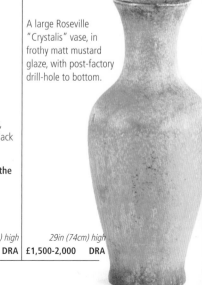

A large Roseville "Crystalis" vase, in frothy matt mustard glaze, with post-factory drill-hole to bottom.

29in (74cm) high
£1,500-2,000 DRA

A large Roseville experimental "Della Robbia" covered jar, carved and enamel-decorated by Helen Smith with clematis vines in lavenders, greens, and ivory, with "Rozane Ware" medallion, incised "H. Smith".

9in (23cm) high

£3,500-4,500   **DRA**

A Roseville "Della Robbia" bulbous vase, excised with a stylised floral pattern in celadon and green.

14in (36cm) high

£4,500-5,500   **DRA**

A Roseville "Della Robbia" five-colour bottle-shaped vase, incised and excised with flowers in shades of blue and green, with Rozane seal and artist's initials "K.D.".

11.5in (29cm) high

£4,000-5,000   **DRA**

A large Roseville "Della Robbia" vase, incised and excised with cavaliers in a forest in greens, brown and pink, with Rozane Ware seal and artist's initials "G.D.".

14in (36cm) high

£5,000-6,000   **DRA**

A Roseville "Della Robbia" vase, carved with blue and small yellow peacock feathers on a celadon and forest green ground, with "ROZANE WARE" medallion.

6.75in (17cm) high

£2,000-2,500   **DRA**

A Roseville "Blue Falline" two-handled vase, with stepped neck, with foil label.

7.25in (18.5cm) high

£800-1,200   **DRA**

A Roseville "Pauleo" floor vase, with matt green and raspberry red mottled glaze.

30in (76cm) high

£3,500-4,500   **DRA**

A large Roseville brown "Pine Cone" urn, 912-15, with impressed mark.

£800-1,200   **DRA**

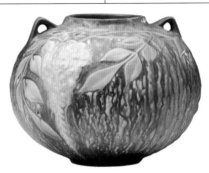

A Roseville "Blue Wisteria" bulbous vase, with foil label.

8.5in (21.5cm) high

£500-700   **DRA**

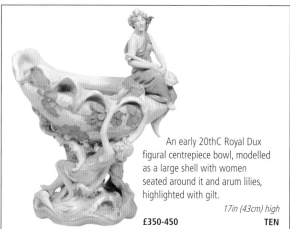

An early 20thC Royal Dux figural centrepiece bowl, modelled as a large shell with women seated around it and arum lilies, highlighted with gilt.

17in (43cm) high

£350-450   **TEN**

An early 20thC Royal Dux figural bowl, modelled as a young girl wearing a toga, gazing into a lotus-form pool, highlighted with gilt, with impressed and applied pink triangle pad mark and impressed "597".

11in (28cm) high

£200-300   **TEN**

An early 20thC Royal Dux figure of a young woman, highlighted with gilt, on canted square base, with impressed and applied pink triangle pad mark and impressed "1379".

19in (48cm) high

£700-800   **TEN**

A pair of large early 20thC Royal Dux figures of a goatherd and a shepherdess, on panelled canted square plinths, highlighted with gilt, both with impressed and applied pink triangle pad marks, impressed "1660" and "1061".

He 31in (79cm) high

£450-550   **TEN**

An early 20thC Royal Dux hunter group, comprising a father kneeling with a double barrelled percussion shotgun, and his son holding game birds, highlighted with gilt, with impressed and applied pink triangle pad mark and impressed "2385".

23in (59.5cm) high

£700-800   **TEN**

A Royal Dux figurine, depicting a fisherwoman flanked by seashells.

16.5in (41cm) high

£350-450   **LHA**

Judith Picks

Although not of the same quality as some of the finest Goldscheider figures (see p.498), this Royal Dux group is distinctly Art Deco, which is a very desirable period. It shows movement and embodies the new freedom of the 1920s, shown by the very sensual dance, the woman's haircut and the very risqué, and quite shocking, cut of the dress. Unlike a lot of the best Goldscheider figures, though, these figures are also still relatively affordable.

Most people are aware of the more standard Art Nouveau Royal Dux figures, in muted colours. Those sell well, but these Art Deco figures are often overlooked.

A Royal Dux figurine of a pair dancers, he in wide brimmed hat and short blue jacket, she in a blue clinging dress, with pink triangle mark B and "3164 AO 9504033".

9in (23cm) high

£400-600   **ECGW**

A Royal Dux "Carnival" figural group, depicting a dancing couple at a masked ball, marks on base.

19.5in (49cm) high

£250-350   **IMC**

A Royal Dux figure of two dancers, wearing exotic clothes in blue highlighted in gilt, with applied triangle and impressed marks.

The male dancer is probably modelled on Rudolf Nureyev, the Russian ballet dancer.

13in (33.5cm) high

£350-450   **WW**

ESSENTIAL REFERENCE - RUSKIN

Founded by William Howson Taylor (1876–1935) in 1901 in West Smethwick, England, Ruskin Pottery was named in honour of the Arts and Crafts champion John Ruskin.

- The pottery is well-known for its glazes. These can be divided into four categories: soufflé, lustre, crystalline and high-fired "flambé" glazes.
- The earliest, soufflé was derived from a 17th/18thC Chinese ceramic in which cobalt powder was blown onto wet glaze.
- The shiny, jewel-like lustre glaze was produced 1905-1925. The most desirable colourway is "Kingfisher blue".
- Crystalline and matt wares, which required only one firing and were therefore cheaper to produce, were made from 1922.
- The most desirable Ruskin pieces are decorated with complex, high-fired glazes. From 1903 these were applied to a fine porcelain and stoneware mix body, which could withstand the sequence of high-temperature firings.
- The pottery closed in 1935.

A Ruskin Pottery "Kingfisher Blue" lustre vase, splashed petrol lustre glaze, impressed marks, dated.

1925   *10in (25.5cm) high*

£800-1,200   WW

A Ruskin Pottery high-fired scent bottle and cover, with a transmutation glaze in magenta suffused with purplish and pale blue exploding nebula, the cover in the form of a crown, stamped "Ruskin, England", dated.

1927   *8in (20cm) high*

£1,500-2,000   SWO

A Ruskin Pottery soufflé vase, of shouldered form, covered in a pink and blue soufflé glaze, with impressed marks, dated.

1911   *7in (18cm) high*

£400-500   WW

A Ruskin Pottery high-fired vase, decorated with flambé purple and red glazes and green spatters, impressed factory mark, dated.

1906   *7in (18cm) high*

£700-800   L&T

A Ruskin Pottery high-fired vase, with a flared collar neck, decorated with tonal purple and red bloom over white ground with green mottled and spotted detail, impressed oval "West Smethwick" mark.

9in (23cm) high

£2,000-2,500   FLD

A Teco tulip vase, in green glaze, with some charcoal details, stamped "Teco".

12in (30.5cm) high

£3,500-4,500   DRA

A Teco tulip-shaped vase, in matt green glaze, stamped "Teco".

12.5in (32cm) high

£4,000-5,000   DRA

A rare Teco "Calla Lily" vase, model no. 141, in smooth green glaze, impressed "TECO" twice.

c1905   *17in (43cm) high*

£200,000-250,000   SOT

DECORATIVE ARTS

ESSENTIAL REFERENCE - VAN BRIGGLE

Artus Van Briggle (1869-1904) and his wife Anna founded their pottery in Colorado Springs, Colorado, in 1899.

- Artus had previously worked for the Rookwood Pottery.
- Van Briggle vessels are typically of organic form, either left plain or decorated with embossed patterns of stylised flowers or Native American designs.
- Pieces were decorated with rich matt glazes, derived from Chinese Ming dynasty glazes. A favourite decorative technique involved spraying coloured glazes onto clean-lined pots using an atomiser.
- Green is the most common colour, particularly on early pieces, followed by blue, then maroon. Multiple glazes on a single piece are rare, and iridescent finishes (1904) are even rarer. Most likely these were produced in a single kiln test.
- The finest pieces were produced before Artus's death, but good-quality wares were made under Anna's direction until she sold the pottery in 1912.
- The pottery is still active today.

An early Van Briggle bottle-shaped bud vase, in matt chartreuse glaze, incised "AA VANBRIGGLE/1902/III/39OE".

1902   *3.25in (8.5cm) high*
£1,000-1,500   **DRA**

A large Van Briggle vase, embossed with daisies under a frothy matt green glaze, incised "AA Van Briggle COLO SPGS 767".

1908-11   *12in (30.5cm) wide*
£5,500-6,500   **DRA**

A Van Briggle squat vessel, embossed with leaves under robin's egg blue matt glaze, marked "AA 1915".

1915   *3.5in (9cm) high*
£400-500   **DRA**

An early Van Briggle tapered vase, embossed with yucca under yellow and green glaze, marked "AA/VAN BRIGGLE/1903/III/169".

1903   *12.5in (32cm) high*
£1,500-2,000   **DRA**

An early Van Briggle vase, embossed with flowers and leaves under a feathered green-to-blue glaze, marked "AA Van Briggle 1903 III".

1903   *14in (36cm) high*
£5,000-6,000   **DRA**

A Van Briggle "Lorelei" vase, in frothy matt pink glaze, marked "AA/17/Van Briggle/1905/V".

1905   *9.75in (25cm) high*
£6,000-7,000   **DRA**

A Van Briggle bulbous vase, embossed with leaves and covered in frothy mint-green glaze, the dark red clay showing through, marked "AA Van Briggle Colo Springs 1906".

1906   *8.25in (21cm) high*
£1,200-1,800   **DRA**

A tall Van Briggle vase, in "Persian Rose" glaze, with four short handles and embossed with peacock feathers.

1919   *13.5in (34.5cm) high*
£800-1,200   **DRA**

A 1930s Van Briggle "Lorelei" vase, in "Persian Rose" glaze, with "AA VAN BRIGGLE/COLO SPGS" on "dirty" bottom, and overall crazing.

10in (25.5cm) high
£400-500   **DRA**

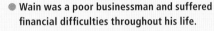

ESSENTIAL REFERENCE - LOUIS WAIN

Louis Wain (1860-1939) was the first artist to consistently depict anthropomorphic animals – largely cats – who walked upright and exhibited human facial expressions.

- He trained at the West London School of Art.
- He supported his mother and five sisters following his father's death in 1880.
- At the age of 23, he married his sister's (much older) governess, Emily Richardson. Sadly she died of cancer three years later.

- Wain was a poor businessman and suffered financial difficulties throughout his life.
- From 1917, he began to suffer from schizophrenia. In 1924 he was committed to a pauper's ward. A year later an appeal was launched on his behalf, and he was transferred to more pleasant facilities.
- As well as illustrations of cats, he also designed several Cubist-style ceramic animal figures for Austrian manufacturer, Amphora.

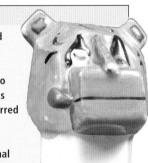

A Louis Wain "The Lucky Pig – I Charm All Your Ills Away" figure, painted green, yellow, black and red, with painted trident mark, impressed "Made in England, Rd No 638320" and painted "Louis Wain" mark.

Designed c1914   *4.75in (12cm) high*
£600-700   **TEN**

A Louis Wain model of a cat, painted in green, yellow, blue and red, with painted and printed marks including trident mark and impressed "Rd no 637134, Made in England".

Designed c1914   *5in (12.5cm) high*
£2,500-3,500   **ROS**

A Louis Wain "Haw Haw" dog model, painted in blue, green, white and orange, with painted and printed marks including trident mark and "Rd no 63831?, Made in England".

Designed c1914   *5in (12.5cm) high*
£1,200-1,800   **ROS**

A Walrath tile, matt-painted with church in landscape, on Beaver Falls blank, with raised "Beaver Falls" mark, in contemporary Arts and Crafts frame.

6in (15cm) wide
£3,500-4,500   **DRA**

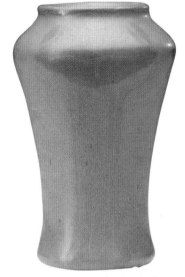

A Walrath vase, matt-painted with lemons and leaves on a brown ground, incised "Walrath Pottery".

A Walrath vase, matt-painted with stylised water lilies, incised "Walrath Pottery".

4.5in (11.5cm) high
£2,500-3,500   **DRA**

7in (18cm) high
£4,000-5,000   **DRA**

Millers Compares

These Fairyland Lustre bowls were luxury items when they were produced in the 1920s. Featuring designs by Daisy Makeig Jones (1881-1945), their magical quality intensifies the more you examine them.

The value differential of these two pieces, both beautiful in their own right, is down to pattern, rarity, strong colours and the fact that the "Geisha" pattern works extremely well on the octagonal bowl. The sumptuous decoration on the interior of the "Geisha" bowl (which is different from the exterior) is also very striking.

A Wedgwood Fairyland Lustre "Jumping Faun and Woodland Elves III" bowl, by Daisy Makeig Jones, pattern number "Z5462".

8in (20cm) diam

£1,000-1,500 SWO

A Wedgwood Fairyland Lustre "Geisha" octagonal bowl, the base with Portland vase mark, "Wedgwood Made in England" and "Z4968".

6.25in (15.5cm) diam

£5,500-6,500 JDJ

A Wedgwood Fairyland Lustre "Candlemas" vase, by Daisy Makeig-Jones, shape no. 2034, printed and painted in colours and gilt on a black lustre ground, printed and painted marks.

8.75in (22cm) high

£4,000-5,000 WW

A Wedgwood Fairyland Lustre "Torches" plaque, signed verso with Portland vase mark, "Wedgwood Made in England", "Z5331" and "j".

11in (28cm) high

£25,000-35,000 JDJ

A Wedgwood Fairyland Lustre "Candlemass" malfrey pot, base with Portland vase mark and "Wedgwood England".

10.5in (27cm) diam

£20,000-30,000 JDJ

A pair of Wedgwood Fairyland Lustre pillar vases, by Daisy Makeig-Jones, shape no.3451, with printed and painted marks.

11.75in (30cm) high

£18,000-22,000 WW

A Wedgwood Fairyland Lustre "Woodland Elves VIII – Boxing Match" bowl, possibly a trial piece, pattern "Z5125", ungilded throughout, the exterior depicting "Castle on a Road", with printed mark, hairline crack.

c1918 *10.5in (26.5cm) diam*

£1,000-1,500 SK

A Wedgwood Fairyland Lustre "Firbolg" malfrey pot, with Portland vase mark to base, "Wedgwood England" and "Z5200".

9.5in (24cm) diam

£5,000-6,000 JDJ

A Wedgwood matt green ovoid ribbed vase, by Keith Murray, with printed factory mark and facsimile signature.

8in (20cm) high

£250-350 WW

A Wedgwood matt green ribbed vase, by Keith Murray, with "KM" mark.

This is a rare shape.

c1934 *5in (12.5cm) high*

£700-800 SCG

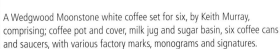

A Wedgwood Moonstone white coffee set for six, by Keith Murray, comprising; coffee pot and cover, milk jug and sugar basin, six coffee cans and saucers, with various factory marks, monograms and signatures.

Coffee pot 8in (20cm) high

£400-600 WW

A Wedgwood grey ribbed vase, by Keith Murray, with signature mark.

c1932 *8in (20cm) high*

£1,800-2,200 SCG

A Wedgwood black ribbed vase, by Keith Murray, with signature mark.

c1932 *5.5in (14cm) high*

£1,400-1,600 SCG

A Wedgwood brown vase, by Keith Murray, with signature mark.

c1932 *9in (23cm) high*

£1,200-1,600 SCG

A Wedgwood straw-yellow bowl, by Keith Murray, with "KM" mark.

c1934 *5.75in (14.5cm) diam*

£300-400 SCG

A Wedgwood "Garden" dinner service, by Eric Ravilious, printed in sepia and yellow, comprising three meat plates, three tureens, six dinner plates, six dessert plates, six side plates, six soup cups and saucers and sauce boat, printed factory marks, impressed date codes.

1952-4 *Largest meat plate 15in (38cm) wide*

£2,000-2,500 TEN

A Wedgwood George VI coronation tankard, by Eric Ravilious, with printed factory marks.

1937 *4in (10.5cm) high*

£200-300 WW

A Wedgwood George VI "Marina Green" coronation tankard, by Eric Ravilious, pattern number "CL 6225", dated.

Marina Green is the rarest of the colourways associated with this design.

1937 *4in (10cm) high*

£2,000-2,500 A&G

DECORATIVE ARTS

A rare Weller "Coppertone" double bud vase, in the form of two jumping fish, with kiln stamp.

8in (20cm) high

£2,500-3,000　　　**DRA**

A large Weller Dickensware "Canterbury Pilgrimage-Chaucer" vase, stamped "DICKENSWARE WELLER", with artist's signature "A.D. X20014".

18in (45.5cm) high

£2,000-3,000　　　**DRA**

A Weller "Eocean" vase, painted by Hester Pillsbury with pink orchids on a shaded pink ground, with incised mark and artist's mark.

15.5in (39cm) high

£1,500-2,000　　　**CRA**

A Weller "Hudson" vase, painted by McLaughlin, with pink and white hollyhocks, with incised mark and artist's signature.

11.5in (29cm) high

£800-1,200　　　**DRA**

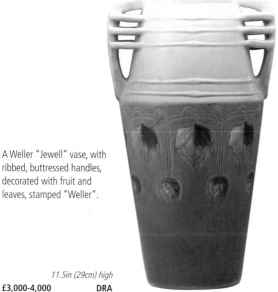

A Weller "Jewell" vase, with ribbed, buttressed handles, decorated with fruit and leaves, stamped "Weller".

11.5in (29cm) high

£3,000-4,000　　　**DRA**

A Weller "Knifewood" jardinière, with daisies and butterflies.

8.5in (21.5cm) wide

£400-500　　　**DRA**

A rare Weller Matt Green vase, the reticulated rim with poppy design.

13.75in (35.5cm) high

£1,200-1,800　　　**DRA**

A Weller "Perfecto" tall ovoid vase, decorated with tulips and swirling leaves, impressed "Weller".

12in (30.5cm) high

£1,000-1,500　　　**CRA**

A large Weller "Sicard" floor vase, with grapevine design, marked "#6 210 Sicard Weller".

25.25in (64cm) high

£3,000-4,000　　　**DRA**

A Weller "Sicard" corseted vase on three feet, decorated with stylised flowers, marked in script.

7in (18cm) high

£600-800　　　**DRA**

A rare Weller "Voile" jardinière and pedestal set.

32in (81cm) high

£800-1,200　　　**DRA**

A Wemyss medium pig figure, decorated by Joe Nekola with cabbage roses, painted mark "Wemyss Ware/ J.N./ Made in England".
Post 1930   *11in (28cm) long*
£1,500-2,000   **L&T**

A small Wemyss pig figure, decorated by Karel Nekola with cabbage roses, painted and impressed marks "Wemyss".
c1890   *6.25in (15.5cm) long*
£2,000-3,000   **L&T**

A large Wemyss ewer and basin, decorated with cabbage roses, both with impressed marks "Wemyss Ware/R. H. & S." and painted "T. Goode & Co." retailer's mark.
c1900   *basin 15.25in (38.5cm)*
£900-1,100   **L&T**

An early 20thC Wemyss medium preserve jar and cover, decorated by James Sharp with dog roses, painted and impressed marks "Wemyss".
4.5in (11.5cm) high
£500-700   **L&T**

A Wemyss heart tray, decorated with cabbage roses, impressed "Wemyss Ware/ R.H.& S.".
c1900   *10in (25.5cm) across*
£400-500   **L&T**

An early 20thC Wemyss tall mug, decorated with cabbage roses, painted and impressed marks "Wemyss".
7in (18cm) high
£200-300   **L&T**

An early 20thC Wemyss large basin, decorated with cabbage roses, impressed mark "Wemyss", painted mark "T. Goode & Co., London".
14.5in (37cm) diam
£500-700   **L&T**

An early 20thC Wemyss medium footbath, decorated with yellow roses, with "T. Goode & Co." printed retailer's mark, restored.
18.5in (47cm) long
£1,200-1,800   **L&T**

A Wemyss large basket, decorated with yellow cabbage roses, impressed mark "Wemyss", printed "T. Goode & Co." retailer's mark.
c1900   *16in (40.5cm) diam*
£1,500-2,000   **L&T**

An early 20thC Wemyss medium "Grosvenor" vase, decorated by Edwin Sandland with chrysanthemums, painted marks "Wemyss".

8in (20cm) high

£500-600   L&T

A large Wemyss cat figure, decorated by Joe Nekola with clover, painted mark "Wemyss Ware/ Made in England", restoration.

Post 1930   *12.5in (32cm) high*

£1,500-2,000   L&T

A Wemyss large pig figure, decorated by Joe Nekola with red clover, painted marks, "Nekola pinxt./ Plichta,/ London./ England".

Post 1930   *18in (45.5cm) long*

£1,500-2,500   L&T

An early 20thC Wemyss pomade and cover, decorated with daffodils, "T. Goode & Co." retailer's mark.

3.25in (8.5cm) diam

£700-800   L&T

An early 20thC Wemyss large mug, decorated with sweet peas, impressed and painted marks "Wemyss", "T. Goode & Co." retailer's mark.

5.5in (14cm) high

£300-400   L&T

A Wemyss small dog bowl, decorated with sweet peas and bearing inscription "Qui Aime Jean/ Aime Son Chien", painted and impressed mark "Wemyss", with two printed "T. Goode & Co." retailer's marks.

c1900   *6.75in (17cm) diam*

£500-600   L&T

An early 20thC Wemyss porridge dish and cover, decorated with thistles, painted marks "Wemyss/ T. Goode & Co", impressed mark "Wemyss".

6in (15cm) high

£800-1,000   L&T

An early 20thC Wemyss beaker vase, decorated with thistles, painted and impressed marks "Wemyss".

11in (28cm) high

£1,200-1,800   L&T

A Wemyss medium "Grosvenor" vase, decorated with tulips, impressed mark "Wemyss Ware R. H. & S.", "T. Goode & Co." retailer's mark.

c1900   *8in (20cm) high*

£350-450   L&T

A Wemyss small loving cup, decorated with apples, impressed mark "Wemyss Ware R. H. & S.".

c1900

£350-450   L&T

An early 20thC Wemyss large ewer, decorated with mallards, painted and indistinctly impressed marks "Wemyss".

10in (25.5cm) high

£800-1,000   L&T

An early 20thC Wemyss Earlshall mug, decorated with huntsmen and hounds in a landscape with crows flying above, impressed mark "Wemyss".

6in (15cm) high

£1,500-2,000   L&T

An early 20thC Wemyss small pig figure, decorated with green glaze, impressed mark "Wemyss".

4in (10cm) high

£450-550   L&T

Judith Picks: Wemyss

It could be due to the fact that I grew up in Scotland, or that I remember my grandmother having a Wemyss pig, but I have to confess I have a soft spot for Wemyss pottery. And it has many devotees – including the late Queen Mother and the present Prince of Wales – so I am in good company.

The value of Wemyss items is dictated by condition – many pieces have been chipped and restored; age – the early period 1882-1915 is best; the decorator – pieces by Karel Nekola are highly desirable; how rare the shape or decoration is; and, finally, how cute it is.

That brings me to this tabby cat – the alert look, the glass eyes, the particularly jaunty demeanour... even though he has a few minor restorations, his rarity and desirability make him irresistible.

A Wemyss large tabby cat figure, decorated in black, brown and pink with applied glass eyes, impressed mark "Wemyss Ware/ R.H. & S.", minor restorations.

c1900   12.5in (32cm) high

£6,000-8,000   L&T

A Wemyss large pig figure, painted in shades of black, pink and white, painted "Wemyss Made in England".

15.5in (39cm) wide

£1,800-2,200   WW

A early 20thC Wemyss small "Japan" vase, decorated with fishing boats, impressed mark "Wemyss", "T Goode & Co." retailer's mark.

6.5in (16cm) high

£600-800   L&T

A rare Wemyss garden seat, painted by Karel Nekola with dog roses and briars, a pair of blue tits, a Mrs Blackcap and two cabbage white butterflies, painted mark "Wemyss".

c1890   18in (45.5cm) high

£9,000-11,000   L&T

DECORATIVE ARTS

A late 19thC Zsolnay flambé-glazed figural vase, modelled with three frolicking bacchantes in the foreground, with borders in a deep purple lustre, with raised factory mark.

16.5in (42cm) high

£9,000-11,000 SK

An early 20thC Zsolnay figure of a bird, in Eosin glaze, seated on a branch, printed marks.

9.5in (24cm) high

£400-500 GORL

A rare Zsolnay vase, decorated with a polychrome Eosin glaze and embellished with flowering branches and ornamental bands, base with impressed mark and model no. "5996", numbered "246" and "27".

1900 *8.5in (21.5cm) high*

£3,000-4,000 DOR

ESSENTIAL REFERENCE - ZSOLNAY

In 1865, Vilmós Zsolnay purchased his brother's artisan pottery (est. 1862) in Fünfkirchen (now Pécs) in Hungary.

● **Vincse Wartha became artistic director in 1893.** Zsolnay then began to specialise in organic Art Nouveau forms.

● **These had low-relief moulding and were decorated with marbled, shaded and crystalline glazes. The most popular was the iridescent "Eosin" (introduced 1893).** It was gradually introduced in different colours, including green, red, blue and purple.

● **The factory remains open as a Hungarian State concern.**

A Zsolnay figural jug, in Eosin glaze, base with "Zsolnay/Pecs/5986" plus Fünfkirchen mark.

c1900 *17.5in (44cm) high*

£800-1,200 WKA

A large Zsolnay sculptural vase, attributed to Lajos Mack, moulded with the figure of a maiden, in Eosin glaze, with moulded factory seal and impressed number "3945".

c1900 *17in (43cm) high*

£1,500-2,000 L&T

A Zsolnay jardinière, in the form of a wave with a young woman fishing with a net, in a sang de boeuf glaze, the underside with raised five towers mark and model no. "7037".

c1902-4 *16in (40.5cm) long*

£1,200-1,800 DOR

A Zsolnay planter, in Eosin glaze, decorated with a landscape, base with Fünfhausen relief mark, unclear numbering "88/89, 110".

c1900 *12.5in (32cm) diam*

£12,000-18,000 WKA

A Zsolnay shouldered ovoid unique vase, painted in colours and gilt with a flower design, with printed mark, painted "Unique piece by Miss F Ravosz".

13in (33.5cm) high

£200-300 DN

An unusual American Encaustic Tiling Co. cabinet vase, carved and enamel-decorated with white blossoms on cobalt ground with a purple band around the rim, stamped "AETCo.", incised "GR".

This design has been attributed to Frederick Rhead, who worked at American Encaustic from 1917 to 1927. It is strongly reminiscent of his work at Arequipa.

3.25in (8.5cm) high

£1,500-2,000   DRA

One of a rare pair of large American Encaustic Tiling Co. grate tiles, decorated with putti within ribbon and foliate design, covered in matt turquoise glaze, restoration.

35.75in (91.5cm) high

£800-1,200 pair   DRA

A large Ohio State ribbed ovoid vase, by Arthur Baggs, in Persian blue glaze on a ribbed body, marked "#1 N.F.S. Copper Blue Vase, Arthur E. Baggs, Huges Hall, O.S.U.", with paper label, with handwritten note.

Arthur Baggs (1855-1947) was the director of Marblehead Pottery (see p502) from 1905 until it closed in 1936. This vase is from the collection of Arthur Baggs's daughter, Mary Trowbridge Baggs Tweet of Tolland, CT.

11in (28cm) high

£2,000-3,000   DRA

An early John Bennett vase, painted with white daffodils, signed "J. Bennett 101 Lex Ave. NY. JB/77".

This rare and early vase was made the first year Bennett set up shop on Lexington Avenue in New York.

1877   *10.5in (27cm) high*

£1,500-2,500   DRA

ESSENTIAL REFERENCE - BOCH FRÈRES

Belgium and Luxembourg were partitioned in 1839. The Boch family, which had been producing pottery in what was now Luxembourg since 1767, consequently established the Kéramis factory in La Louvière, Belgium, trading under the name Boch Frères.

- **During the 1920s and 1930s the factory began to produce large quantities of Art Deco pottery.**
- **Design was overseen by Charles Catteau (employed 1906-45). Pieces were hand-decorated in vibrant cloisonné enamels, often azure-blue and yellow, on an off-white craquelure ground.**
- **Pieces are marked with a she-wolf and/or the "Kéramis" mark. Many are impressed with Catteau's signature.**
- **The pottery was active until World War II.**

A Burmantoft's Faience Anglo-Persian vase, by Leonard King, model no. "D.125", painted with flowers in shades of blue, green and aubergine on a white ground, with impressed and painted marks, and "LK" monogram.

9in (23cm) high

£1,200-1,800   WW

A Bushey Heath Pottery Persian-style vase, by Fred Passenger, painted with stylised flower sprays in shades of blue, aubergine and green on a white ground, with printed round mark.

8in (20cm) high

£2,500-3,500   WW

A large and unusual Boch Frères charger, by Etondeur, painted with two petrols before geometric waves and stars, highlighted in gilt, with painted signature, verso with painted marks.

24.5in (62cm) diam

£2,000-3,000   WW

A Boch Frères vase, by Charles Catteau, decorated with panels of abstract birds and foliage in purple, black, green and white over an oxide-glazed ground, impressed marks.

13in (33.5cm) high

£1,000-1,500   FLD

A Boch Frères vase, attributed to Charles Catteau, pattern "D 1101", enamelled in blue, yellow and turquoise with stylised foliage panels printed marks.

9in (23cm) high

£500-700   WW

A Dedham experimental cylindrical vase, by Hugh Robertson, in a two-tone red and celadon oxblood flambé glaze, incised "Dedham Pottery HCR".

7in (18cm) high

£2,000-3,000   **DRA**

A large Dedham experimental bulbous vase, by Hugh Robertson, in a thick, dripping forest-green, celadon and brown flambé glaze, incised "Dedham BW Pottery".

7.25in (18.5cm) high

£1,500-2,000   **DRA**

A Della Robbia "Sepia" incised and painted terracotta charger, by Harold Steward Rathbone, decorated with the profile of a girl within a foliate border, verso incised and painted factory marks and "HSR/DR/-95".

1895   *14in (35.5cm) diam*

£1,000-1,500   **L&T**

A Fulper trumpet vase, in Chinese Blue flambé glaze, with vertical mark, damaged.

13in (33.5cm) high

£100-150   **DRA**

An Emile Gallé faience cat, with whimsical indigo motifs on yellow ground, and glass eyes, signed "E Gallé Nancy".

13in (33.5cm) high

£2,000-3,000   **DRA**

A Fulper cat doorstop, in Chinese Blue Flambé crystalline glaze, with vertical stamp.

9in (23cm) long

£800-1,000   **DRA**

A Charles Graham salt-glazed stoneware vase, acid-etched with parrots and butterfly on a leafy oak branch, impressed mark with patent date.

1885   *7.25in (18.5cm) high*

£2,200-2,800   **DRA**

A Grand Feu cylindrical vase, in café-au-lait crystalline glaze, stamped "BRAUCKMAN ART POTTERY" and dedicated "A Christmas Gift from Kittie Wilkinson Dec.25-1917, Los Angeles, Cal."

1917   *7in (18cm) high*

£2,000-3,000   **DRA**

A Jervis vase, decorated in the style of Grueby with full-height leaves and blossoms, in mint-green matt glaze, with incised vertical mark and "V".

7in (18cm) high

£2,000-3,000   **DRA**

An Art Deco Robert Lallemant "La Boxe" vase, depicting two boxers in a ring, stamped "T R Lallemant France".

8.5in (21.5cm) high

£1,200-1,800   DRA

A large Linthorpe Pottery vase, by Dr. Christopher Dresser, model no. "749", with impressed floret panels, glazed a running blue over green and ochre, impressed marks, with facsimile signature.

10.25in (26cm) high

£3,000-4,000   WW

A Limoges enamelled vase, by Camille Faure, relief-decorated with green icicles and pink and blue flower heads on a peacock-blue ground, signed "C. Faure-Limoges", missing base, possibly converted into a table lamp.

9.5in (24cm) high

£1,000-1,500   LOC

A Marguerite Mahood "Tudor Lady" figure, in colours of green and mauve, incised date letter "M, 1530" and "Marguerite Mahood", loss to headdress.

c1943   *9.5in (24cm) high*

£3,000-4,000   JA

An Owens Utopian bottle-shaped vase, painted by Cora McCandless with a Native American chief, deep crazing, with impressed mark and artist's initials, repairs.

15.5in (39cm) high

£1,000-1,500   DRA

A large Pilkington's vase, painted by William S. Mycock with a four-mast sailing ship, in golden lustre on a vivid red ground, with impressed and painted marks, painted cypher and date code.

1909   *11.75in (30cm) high*

£3,000-4,000   WW

A Pilkington's ovoid vase, painted by Gordon Forsyth with heraldic lions, in gold on a blue lustre ground, with impressed marks, painted artist's cipher and date mark.

1909   *8in (20cm) high*

£2,000-3,000   WW

ESSENTIAL REFERENCE - LONGWY

The Longwy pottery was founded in the late 17thC at a Carmelite convent in the Meurthe et Moselle region in France.

- It developed a unique cloisonné-style method of decoration, using saturated enamel colours and crackled glazes.
- During the 1920s and 1930s it became a well-known industrial manufacturer of ceramics, producing hand-finished Art Deco stoneware and earthenware pots.
- Some pieces were inspired by Egyptian, Greek and Roman artefacts.
- The Art Deco pieces were sold mainly through Primavera, the household department of the Parisian store Le Printemps.
- The factory is still operating today.

A Longwy Pottery jardiniere, modelled in low relief with Oriental panels and mask handles, with impressed marks.

16.25in (41cm) diam

£700-800   WW

A Longwy earthenware mantel clock, modelled as a Chinese dragon with elaborate saddle, glazed pale blue impressed marks, minor losses.

19in (48cm) high

£4,500-5,500   WW

Judith Picks: Pattern books

The predominance of some decorative motifs within certain periods can be ascribed to the popularity of pattern books, which allowed for the national and international dissemination of new forms and styles in the days before 20thC communication technology. These books were used extensively by designers, particularly those who based their work on historical styles. Two of the most influential and historically important examples are Thomas Chippendale's "The Gentleman and Cabinet-Maker's Director" (first published in 1754), and Owen Jones's "The Grammar of Ornament" (first published in 1851).

It is also possible to find an individual factory's pattern books or, as here, a large folio of colour lithographic plates relating to the Art Nouveau designs on Sèvres porcelain.

These primary sources are as important for collectors today as they were for the designers of the period, as they can be invaluable in identifying wares from different factories and dating them.

I've bought a large number of design books over the years, and have found them to be useful and great value, as if you are lucky they can be inexpensive when they come up at auction.

Sandier, Alex and Lechevallier-Chevignard, Georges, "Les Cartons de la Manufacture Nationale de Sèvres", published by Librairie Generale de L'Architecture et des Arts Decoratifs, Paris.

£150-200   **FLD**

A Sèvres Art Nouveau vase, enamelled with trailing floral decoration on pale blue ground, with black date stamp and russet circular stamp "Decoree a Sèvres 98", signed "Mimard L".

1897   *16in (40.5cm) high*

£5,000-6,000   **MACK**

A Vance Avon Faience triangular vase, decorated in squeezebag and incised with tulips on a deep blue ground, signed "M.P. 188-10D5", restoration.

The factory that became the Vance pottery was founded in Tiltonville, Ohio, in c1880. In 1900 it was acquired by several businessmen, including J. Nelson Vance, who wanted to make it a centre for the production of Art Pottery. The name changed to the Avon Faience Company in 1902. Frederick Hurten Rhead joined designer William P. Jervis in 1903. Rhead introduced a line of Art Nouveau-style ceramics often outlined with squeezed white slip, as with this example. Production finished at Tiltonville in 1905, and moved to Wheeling, West Virginia. Bodies changed from earthenware to semi-porcelain. Production finished in 1908.

9in (23cm) high

£1,500-2,500   **DRA**

An Adelaide Robineau cabinet vase, in turquoise flambé glaze, incised "AR/237/05".

5in (12.5cm) high

£2,000-3,000   **DRA**

A rare Shawsheen vase, incised with stylised flowers in matt pastel colours, signed "SAP".

5in (12.5cm) wide

£1,000-1,500   **DRA**

A University City rounded bowl, carved with a band of green squirrels on a darker green ground, incised "UC 5144".

6in (15cm) high

£2,500-3,500   **DRA**

A rare Volkmar vase, carved with deep blue trillium and swirling leaves on mottled brown and green ground, incised "V" mark, glaze fleck to high point.

8.25in (21cm) high

£1,200-1,800   **DRA**

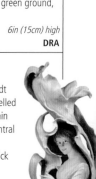

A late 19thC Volkstedt "Good Night" enamelled and moulded porcelain mantel vase, with central portrait of a maiden holding a chamberstick in high relief, with underglaze mark for "Richard Eckert & Co.", old repairs.

18.25in (46.5cm) high

£1,500-2,500   **SK**

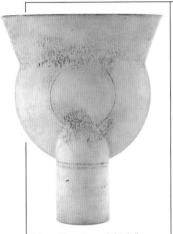

A large Hans Coper "Thistle" vase, of T-material, externally glazed in white slip, internally with manganese, with impressed seal mark.

18.5in (47cm) high

£25,000-30,000 WW

A small Hans Coper "Cup" form on drum base, each side with pressed dimples, glazed in black manganese, with impressed seal mark.

4.25in (11cm) high

£7,000-9,000 WW

ESSENTIAL REFERENCE - HANS COPER

Hans Coper (1920–1981), one of the leading figures in the 20thC Studio Pottery movement, was born in Germany. He fled to Britain in 1939, but was interned in Canada as an enemy alien. He returned to Britain in 1942.

- In 1946 he began working as an assistant in the studio of Lucie Rie, where he collaborated on her tablewares. Some pieces from this period are signed by both artists.
- Coper left to establish his own studio at Digswell House in Hertfordshire in 1958, though he and Rie continued to collaborate closely.
- He exhibited extensively, mainly in London, but also in Tokyo, Hamburg and in Holland.
- From 1960 onwards he also taught pottery at the Camberwell School of Art and the Royal College of Art, both in London.
- His non-functional pieces were thrown on a potter's wheel then altered by hand into distinctive forms, such as "Space", "Cup" and "Thistle".
- Coper's pots are typically roughly textured and coloured with oxides, particularly manganese oxide.
- He used T-material, a very refractory white clay with a high molochite content made by Morgan Refractories in Cheshire.

A Hans Coper "Spade" vase, of T-material, manganese covered in a white slip, with impressed seal mark.

8.25in (21cm) high

£15,000-20,000 WW

A Sam Haile bellied jug, slip-decorated in tenmoku over deep celadon glaze, impressed seal mark, hairline to top rim.

8in (20cm) high

£250-350 WW

A large Shoji Hamada stoneware dish, in matt off-white glaze with olive green trails poured across the well.

Two large dishes of a closely related design and size are illustrated in a contemporary photograph, showing Shoji Hamada together with Bernard Leach at Hamada's pottery in Mashiko, Japan, in 1971.

c1963 *21.75in (54.5cm) diam*

£18,000-22,000 SOTH

A Shoji Hamada stoneware water jar and cover, with four loop handles, with ash glaze to the foot, the interior tenmoku, in wooden travel box, cover applied with paper label.

9in (23cm) high

£6,000-7,000 WW

A Shigeyoshi Ichino stoneware vase, glazed to the foot, painted with simple panels of flower stems, impressed seal mark.

10in (25.5cm) high

£300-400 WW

A rare Leach Pottery stoneware vase, by Shoji Hamada, the cut-sided form with collar rim, covered to the foot with a dark tenmoku glaze speckled with blue, impressed seal marks.

5.25in (13cm) high

£4,000-5,000 WW

An early Leach Pottery earthenware vase and cover, by Bernard Leach, incised with scrolling foliate design to body and cover, glazed green/yellow, with impressed "St Ives" mark, "BL" monogram.

8in (20cm) high

£2,000-3,000   WW

A Bernard Leach earthenware vase, incised with a frieze of a scaly fish, glazed to the foot, impressed "BL" mark.

7.5in (19cm) high

£600-800   WW

A Leach Pottery tile, by Bernard Leach, painted with flowers in brown on a cream ground, painted monogram and Leach pottery mark, verso with impressed marks.

4.25in (11cm) wide

£500-600   WW

A Lucie Rie stoneware bottle vase, with flattened flaring neck, glazed in turquoise with blended spots of brown, with bronzed rim, impressed seal mark.

11in (28cm) high

£2,500-3,500   WW

A Lucie Rie porcelain flaring bowl, with dripping copper glaze over glossy deep ochre body, impressed with artist's seal.

9.25in (23.5cm) diam

£3,000-4,000   DRA

A tall Natzler bottle-shaped vase, in mottled turquoise and gunmetal matt glaze, signed "Natzler" with original inventory tag.

18.5in (47cm) high

£12,000-18,000   DRA

An early Henry Varnum Poor "Three Mile Island" glazed ceramic vase, incised "HVP 29", with Montross Gallery label to base.

1929   5.75in (14.5cm) diam

£1,200-1,800   DRA

A large Wenford Bridge potter charger, by Michael Cardew, painted to the well with a wading bird, in blue on a celadon ground, impressed seal marks.

16in (40.5cm) high

£1,000-1,500   WW

A Marguerite Wildenhain/Pond Farm four-sided stoneware vessel, with incised and impressed patterns, in celadon and mahogany glaze, incised "Wildenhain".

4in (10cm) high

£1,200-1,800   DRA

An Aesthetic Movement walnut sofa, in the manner of George Faulkner Armitage, with turned and reeded front uprights, the seat rail carved with quarter sunflowers, the rear legs with castors, reupholstered in red.

Repeated quarter sunflower friezes are typical of Armitage.

81in (205cm) wide

£350-450   DN

A Victorian Aesthetic Movement oak bookcase cabinet, in the manner of Gillows and Bruce Talbert, hinges and locks stamped "COMYN CHING & CO.", in five sections with adjustable shelves, and cupboards.

145in (368cm) long

£800-1,200   RTC

An Aesthetic Movement ebonised and gilt decorated side cabinet, in the manner of Dr. Christopher Dresser, the central doors decorated with standing cranes, flanked by glazed doors, on turned feet, with label for "T. H. Filmer & Sons".

72in (183cm) wide

£500-600   WHP

An Aesthetic Movement ash chest-of-drawers, Edwards & Roberts, with two short over three long graduated drawers on a plinth base, stamped maker's mark to drawer.

c1880   *39in (99cm) high*

£400-500   L&T

An Aesthetic Movement ebonised side cabinet, by Edward William Godwin, with two drawers above fretted supports and open undertier, above a further two drawers, with brass handles, on ringed turned tapering legs.

29in (74cm) high

£4,000-5,000   TEN

ESSENTIAL REFERENCE - LAMB OF MANCHESTER

James Lamb (1816-1903) was the leading Manchester cabinet maker of the Victorian period, and became an important figure in the Aesthetic Movement.

- **He founded a large workshop in John Dalton Street, Manchester, in 1843. The business was later moved to a large factory building in Castlefield.**
- **It became known for high-quality workmanship and materials, and innovative design.**
- **The company exhibited at the 1862 London Universal Exhibition and at the 1867 and 1878 Paris exhibitions.**
- **Lamb worked in association with important designers including Charles Bevan and Alfred Waterhouse.**
- **The company was taken over by Goodall, Lamb & Heighway in 1899.**

An Aesthetic Movement parcel-gilt and walnut library bookcase, by Lamb of Manchester, crossbanded throughout and inlaid with panels of stylised flowers, foliage, birds and motifs, the locks and drawers stamped "Lamb. Manchester".

107in (272cm) high

£12,000-18,000   H&L

An Aesthetic Movement walnut, ebony and parcel-gilt side cabinet, by Lamb of Manchester, with mirrored back over inverted breakfront frieze, over glazed door enclosing shelving lined in purple velvet, on turned feet, stamped "Lamb, Manchester 32261".

54.25in (138cm) wide

£2,000-2,500   AH

An Aesthetic Movement ebonised cabinet, attributed to Bruce Talbert for Gillows, with turned uprights and legs and decorative brass beadings, gilt highlights, amboyna inlay to the central drawer, the doors with painted panels of maidens amidst Classical swags.

The handles and hinges are identical to those used by Talbert on many other pieces he designed for Gillows.

75in (190cm) high

£1,800-2,200   DN

ESSENTIAL REFERENCE - BRUCE TALBERT

Bruce James Talbert (1838–1881) was an influential Scottish decorator and furniture designer, who worked in the Aesthetic and Gothic Revival styles.

● He trained as a carver in Dundee, and later as an architect.

● In the mid-1860s, having worked for Manchester cabinetmakers Doveston, Bird & Hull, and the wood- and metalworks, Skidmore's Art Manufacturers, Talbert moved to London. There he designed furniture for Holland & Sons's stand at the Paris Exposition Universelle of 1867. His "Pericles" Gothic sideboard was a Grand Prix winner.

● By 1868 he was designing furniture for Gillows of Lancaster and had returned to Dundee to set up a design practice.

● He published his influential book "Gothic Forms Applied to Furniture, Metal Work and Decoration for Domestic Purposes" in 1868.

● In 1869 he returned to London to work as a freelance commercial designer, assisted by a small number of pupils.

● Best known as a furniture designer, Talbert also designed metalwork for Cox & Sons, cast iron for the Colebrookdale Co., textiles for Warners, Barbone & Miller and Cowlishaw, Nichol & Co., and wallpapers for Jeffrey & Co.

An Aesthetic Movement oak and glazed standing corner cabinet, by Bruce Talbert probably for Gillow & Co.

The castellated cornice detail above the bevel glazed door is identical to the moulding on his famous "Pet" sideboard exhibited at the 1872 London International Exhibition and his "Pericles" sideboard, which was exhibited at the 1867 Paris Exhibition where it was a Grand Prix winner.

71in (180cm) high

£6,000-7,000   DN

An Anglo-Japanese ebonised "Pagoda" square centre table, the top with cusp corners and two curl-up edges, fretted supports united by an undertier, on castors.

32in (81cm) wide

£1,500-2,000   DN

An Aesthetic Movement bone-inlaid, parcel-ebonised and painted walnut cabinet, with Japanese-style arched arabesque-painted panel door, opening to two shelves, some damages.

41.5in (105.5cm) high

£1,000-1,500   WES

An Aesthetic Movement painted, parcel-gilt and ebonised pier mirror, the top panel painted with a Classical figural scene and the carved border with foliage with gilt reserve, with shaped apron with turned elements.

42.5in (108cm) high

£2,000-2,500   LHA

A Gothic Revival carved oak, embossed-leather and caned armchair, designed by John Pollard Seddon for the 1851 Great Exhibition.

43in (109cm) high

£4,000-5,000   DN

A set of six Gothic Revival oak chairs, by Edward Welby Pugin, with cantilevered pegged legs on brass ball feet to front, curved pegged back splats, red velvet seats.

Pugin designed an identical chair for The Grange, his family home in Ramsgate, in 1864.

33in (84cm) high

£2,500-3,000 set   WW

A Gothic Revival oak side table, in the manner of A.W.N. Pugin, with two drawers with brass drop handles on chamfered supports with curved brackets, linked by a stretcher.

c1860   *54in (137cm) wide*

£2,500-3,000   L&T

A 19thC Gothic Revival oak table, with single plank top, the carved frame with alternating entwined monograms and roundels, the carved octagonal supports with moulded capitals, bases and carved leaves and grapes roundels, joined by chamfered stretchers and shaped block feet.

29in (73cm) wide

£3,000-4,000   TEN

A Gothic Revival stained oak cabinet, attributed to Charles Locke Eastlake, the architectural roof with arched and turned supports.

An architectural roof is a relatively rare feature of Gothic Revival furniture. However, it can be seen in the furniture of Philip Webb, particularly in the Red House – for example, on the settle Rossetti and Burne Jones never finished painting and on the dining room dresser. It was also used by Richard Norman Shaw on his famous secrétaire bookcase exhibited at the 1862 International Exhibition, in London and was often used by William Burgess on furniture and fireplaces.

98in (249cm) high

£1,500-2,000   DN

A Gothic Revival japanned display cabinet, the castellated top above a glazed panel door over shelves, the lower section with two Gothic arched tracery panelled doors decorated with exotic birds and foliage, over fitted interior, on a plinth base.

c1880   *67in (170cm) high*

£1,200-1,800   L&T

A Victorian Gothic Revival oak cabinet bookcase, the moulded cornice above a pair of astragal-glazed cabinet doors enclosing adjustable shelves, above a pair of Gothic arch-moulded panel doors, on a plinth base.

c1880   *86in (218.5cm) high*

£2,000-2,500   DN

A Gothic Revival oak bookcase, in the manner of Richard Norman Shaw, the cornice applied with a painted panel in the manner of Henry Stacy Marks depicting a country scene, the two glazed doors headed by Gothic arches, with engraved brass strap hinges, on fluted feet.

101in (256cm) high

£3,500-4,000   H&L

A "Truth Travestied, Truth the Conqueror, Truth Jailor" triptych, by Alexander Fisher, with pencil and watercolour depictions of Arthurian figures, in a Gothic arched frame with leather roundels and painted leather panel depicting a grotesque creature, signed "AF".

36in (92cm) high

£3,500-4,000   WW

ESSENTIAL REFERENCE - ERNEST GIMSON

Ernest Gimson (1864-1919) is considered to be one of the most influential designers of the Arts and Crafts movement.

- He was founder member of the short-lived furniture company, Kenton and Co., established in 1890. Those working for the company acted as designers rather than craftsmen and explored inventive new ways of recreating traditional crafts.
- In 1893, following the collapse of Kenton & Co., Gimson and two other former members, Sidney and Ernest Barnsley, moved to Gloucestershire in the Cotswolds. The style of furniture he and the Barnsleys created there is often referred to as the "Cotswold" style.
- In 1900, Gimson set up a furniture workshop in Cirencester. He later moved to larger workshops at Daneway House.
- He was inspired by nature, Byzantine and Islamic arts, 17thC and 18thC English furniture and the Arts and Crafts tradition.
- Gimson believed that design was not something to be added once the work was finished, rather it should come from the careful use of proportion and construction, choice and knowledge of materials, and tools and techniques.

One of a pair of macassar ebony and inlaid library chairs, by Ernest Gimson, the shaped backs with cross rails with chequered stringing, with drop-in seats, on square tapering legs with H-form stretchers.

£7,000-8,000 pair   DUK

A walnut two-drawer side table, by Ernest Gimson, the top with moulded border, above two short drawers with hammered ring handles, on square legs with H-form stretcher.

40in (101.5cm) wide

£5,000-6,000   DUK

A macassar ebony library table, by Ernest Gimson, the top edged with two lines of chequered banding of satinwood and walnut, above four short drawers with silvered ring handles, on four pairs of two square tapering legs with conforming stretchers, with through tenon joints.

72in (183cm) wide

£35,000-40,000   DUK

An oak chest-of-drawers, by Ernest Gimson, the bowfronted top above two short and three long graduated drawers with hammered handles and chip-carved drawer dividers, with exposed jointing, on open plinth base.

38.5in (98cm) high

£12,000-14,000   DUK

A pair of rush-seated armchairs, by Ernest Gimson, the backs with bobbin-turned rails above flat-topped arms, rush seats and turned legs and stretchers.

48in (122cm) high

£1,500-2,000   DUK

A Limbert lamp table, no.251, with a hexagonal top over a four-sided cut-out base with long corbels, with branded mark.

17in (43cm) wide

£1,500-2,000   DRA

A Limbert Ebon-Oak plant stand, with broad apron panels inset with cane, the top supported by shaped corbels, replacements and damages.

14in (36cm) wide

£1,200-1,400   DRA

A two-door Limbert china cabinet, with plate rail and adjustable shelves, refinished, branded on back.

46in (117cm) wide

£1,800-2,200   DRA

A Limbert oval library table, no.146, with early paper label.

45in (114cm) wide

£3,000-4,000   DRA

Two of a set of six post-1955 Robert "Mouseman" Thompson oak lattice dining chairs, each with carved mouse signature.

33.5in (85cm) high

£3,000-4,000 set   **TEN**

A Robert "Mouseman" Thompson burr oak kidney-shaped table, on four octagonal legs, with carved mouse signature.

£5,000-6,000   **TEN**

A Robert "Mouseman" Thompson panelled oak wardrobe, with fitted interior, wrought-iron hinges and latch, on block feet, with carved recessed mouse signature.

47.75in (121.5cm) wide

£3,000-4,000   **TEN**

A mid-20thC Robert "Mouseman" Thompson oak sideboard, the top with adzed surface decoration and canted angles, above three central drawers, flanked by panelled cupboard doors enclosing single shelves, on facetted supports, with carved mouse signature.

73in (185cm) wide

£4,500-5,500   **L&T**

A Robert "Mouseman" Thompson oak kneehole dressing table, the canted top with a low rear gallery, with six graduated drawers, the sides and back panelled, on octagonal feet, mouse carved to left front corner.

c1950   *54in (137cm) wide*

£4,000-5,000   **L&T**

A pair of Robert "Mouseman" Thompson oak open bookcases, fitted with adjustable shelves, each with carved mouse signature.

32.75in (83cm) wide

£5,500-6,500   **TEN**

A Robert "Mouseman" Thompson carved oak pheasant, by Stan Dodds, with carved mouse signature.

Stan Dodds worked at the Mouseman workshops at Kilburn, York, from the late 1940s to the late 1980s as a master carver. Pheasants took around 80 hours to carve, each one is numbered under the green baize.

19in (48cm) long

£2,000-2,500   **TEN**

A pair of Robert "Mouseman" Thompson oak bookends, each carved as squirrels eating nuts, each with carved mouse signature.

7.75in (19.5cm) high

£3,500-4,500   **TEN**

A Robert "Mouseman" Thompson oak longcase clock, twin-weight driven, striking the hours and halves with three hammers striking three gong rods, movement backplate stamped "E. Schmeckenbecher", with carved mouse signature.

76in (193cm) high

£3,500-4,500   **TEN**

DECORATIVE ARTS

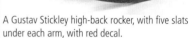

A pair of Gustav Stickley V-back armchairs, no.354 1/2 A, with red decals.

37.5in (95cm) high

£1,000-1,500   DRA

A Gustav Stickley high-back rocker, with five slats under each arm, with red decal.

38.5in (98cm) high

£1,000-1,500   DRA

An early Gustav Stickley Morris chair, no.2342, with slats to floor and webbed seat frame, with early red decal.

40in (101.5cm) high

£1,500-2,500   DRA

A rare Gustav Stickley wicker chair, with loose cushion.

33.5in (85cm) high

£1,500-2,000   DRA

A Gustav Stickley circular dining table, with cross-stretchers topped by a rounded finial, complete with two leaves.

48in (122cm) diam

£650-750   DRA

A Gustav Stickley split-pedestal dining table, with circular top, complete with four leaves, with red decal.

48in (122cm) diam

£1,500-2,000   DRA

A Gustav Stickley china cabinet, designed by Harvey Ellis, with three shelves, an arched apron and a hammered copper V-pull, original finish, key, and paper label.

Stickley hired Harvey Ellis in May 1903. Although Ellis died soon afterwards (January 1904), he had a profound effect on Gustav Stickley's furniture, as well as the design of his magazine, "The Craftsman". Lighter shapes of furniture were introduced, featuring arches and tapering legs. Stickley also began offering furniture in willow to complement his heavy oak designs.

36in (91.5cm) wide

£5,000-6,000   DRA

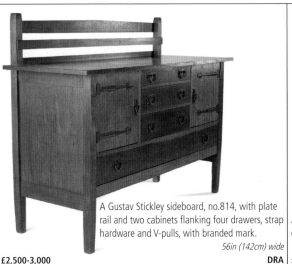

A Gustav Stickley sideboard, no.814, with plate rail and two cabinets flanking four drawers, strap hardware and V-pulls, with branded mark.

56in (142cm) wide

£2,500-3,000   **DRA**

A Gustav Stickley sideboard, no.816, with hammered copper hardware, with branded signature.

48in (122cm) wide

£2,500-3,000   **DRA**

A small Gustav Stickley double-door bookcase, with keyed through-tenon construction and hammered copper hardware, with red decal and paper label.

44.5in (113cm) wide

£2,500-3,000   **DRA**

An L. & J.G. Stickley even-arm settle, with wide back rail, tall post legs and side slat, with signed "The Work of..." decal.

72in (183cm) long

£1,000-1,500   **DRA**

An L. & J.G. Stickley magazine stand, no.45, with curved back-splash and sides.

46in (117cm) high

£1,000-1,500   **DRA**

An L. & J.G. Stickley/Onondaga two-drawer desk, with slatted sides and copper ring pulls.

42in (107cm) wide

£750-950   **DRA**

An L. & J.G. Stickley double-door china cabinet, no.728, with arched toe board and back, with "The Work of..." decal.

55in (140cm) wide

£1,500-2,500   **DRA**

A Stickley Bros. shaving mirror, on rotating stand, with metal tag and branded mark.

19.75in (50cm) high

£200-300   **DRA**

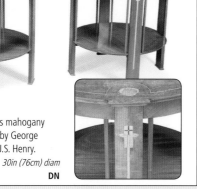

A pair of Arts and Crafts mahogany and inlaid lamp tables, by George Montague Ellwood for J.S. Henry.

30in (76cm) diam

£3,500-4,000　　　　　DN

A Liberty & Co. Athelstan oak dressing table, by Leonard Wyburd, the rectangular mirror between heart-pierced uprights, the two drawers with block and baton handles, with ivorine label.

55in (140cm) high

£600-700　　　　　DN

A rare Liberty & Co mahogany Thebes stool, with rectangular twin-seat section, on four turned legs, with remains of strung seat.

31.5in (80cm) wide

£1,500-2,000　　　　　WW

ESSENTIAL REFERENCE - MORRIS & CO.

The company that became Morris & Co. was founded in 1861 as Morris, Marshall, Faulkner & Co. William Morris (1834-1896) assumed sole control in 1875.

- **Using natural materials and traditional handcraft techniques, the company produced original ceramics, textiles, wallpaper, carpets and furniture.**
- **Rush seating is common for dining chairs. Armchairs are often upholstered with Morris & Co. fabric.**
- **Joints and hinges were used as decorative features.**
- **Copies abound, but authentic furniture is stamped "Morris & Co.".**

A Morris & Co. stained oak sideboard, by W. A. S. Benson, carved with stylised plants, with a planked back rack, three frieze drawers above a recess with a drawer under and flanked by panel doors, on turned feet, stamped mark to one drawer.

67.25in (171cm) wide

£5,000-8,000　　　　　DN

A Morris & Co walnut sideboard, by Philip Webb, with stamped marks to drawer.

59in (152cm) wide

£8,500-9,500　　　　　WW

A Morris & Co. oak centre table, by Philip Webb, with stepped moulded border, on turned splayed legs with cross stretchers and a moulded stretcher with four turned uprights on plinth bases with castors.

Philip Webb was Morris & Co.'s chief furniture designer. This piece relates to a design first produced during the early years of Morris & Co., when furniture on this scale was made to fulfil a specific commission or architectural interior. This table shows Webb's interest in medieval furniture. His furniture designs demonstrate a solidity and architectural presence with features drawn from his knowledge of early furniture from around the world. An example of this design can be seen in the long drawing room at Kelmscott House where Morris lived from 1878.

71in (180cm) wide

£6,500-7,500　　　　　DUK

ESSENTIAL REFERENCE - GORDON RUSSELL

(Sydney) Gordon Russell (1892-1980) became interested in the Arts and Crafts movement after 1904, when his family moved to the Cotswolds. He began designing furniture in this style c1914.

● He worked with E. W. Gimson and Sidney & Ernest Barnsley.

● From 1925 he designed furniture with greater simplicity, moving into more explicitly Modern furniture with an increased element of machine work in 1930.

● During World War II he developed utility furniture as chairman of the government's Utility Furniture Design Panel. This was a natural progression from the Cotswold school philosophy, which emphasised good materials, quality workmanship and simple, well-proportioned designs.

● In 1947 he became director of the Council of Industrial Design (now the Design Council).

● In 1955 he was knighted for services to design.

A large Arts and Crafts oak sideboard, the heavily moulded cornice above a mirrored back flanked by brass-inlaid panels and turned columns, the base with two central drawers, two small and two large doors, on bracket feet.
c1910   87in (221cm) high
£600-800   L&T

A George Walton oak table, the rectangular top on hexagonal legs united by stretchers, on trestle feet.
c1910   60in (152cm) long
£1,500-2,500   L&T

A Gordon Russell walnut bedside cabinet, inlaid with yew banding and having carved ebony handles and legs, the square inlaid top above a slide and open shelf, above a single panelled door enclosing a single shelf and raised on faceted baluster shaped legs.
c1930   34in (86cm) high
£800-1,200   L&T

ESSENTIAL REFERENCE - GEORGE WALTON

Scottish designer George Walton (1867-1933) was the youngest of 12 children. After the death of his father in 1873, Walton become a bank clerk, while also studying at the Glasgow School of Art.

● In 1888 he was commissioned to design the interiors of some of Miss Catherine Cranston's tea rooms. Walton gave up banking and opened his own showrooms, with the firm expanding into woodwork, furniture making and stained glass.

● In 1896 Walton and Charles Rennie Mackintosh (for whom he designed some early furniture) collaborated on further tea rooms for Miss Cranston.

● In 1897 Walton moved to London and opened a branch in York.

● He designed the Photographic Salon in the Dudley Gallery, the Eastman Exhibition in the New Gallery in Regent Street and a series of Eastman Kodak showrooms in London, Glasgow, Brussels, Milan, Vienna and Moscow, which brought him international fame. The domestic nature of his designs created a relaxed and unthreatening atmosphere in which to shop, and this was much copied.

A Scottish Arts and Crafts stained pine and pokerwork hall settle, the moulded top rail above tongue-and-groove back decorated with pokerwork and coloured paints with roses, with green-upholstered squab seat.
c1900   74in (188cm) wide
£1,500-2,000   L&T

One of a pair of limed oak small bookcases, in the style of Jean-Michel Frank, with caned shelves.
21.5in (54.5cm) wide
£2,500-3,000 pair   SDR

An Arts and Crafts four-panel window screen, carved with acorns and stylised leaves.
Each panel 6.5in (16cm) wide
£800-1,200   DRA

A George Walton oak breakfront library bookcase, with stained- and leaded-glass panels inset with copper and brass depicting plants, with maker's circular ivorine label to the rear inscribed "George Walton & Co Ltd/ Designers, Manufacturers and Decorators/ 150 & 152 Wellington St, Glasgow/ Also at London and York/ Design no.".

This bookcase may have been made for a Kodak showroom.
c1900   86in (218cm) wide
£15,000-20,000   L&T

A Harden matching double crest rail armchair and rocker, with curved arms and exposed through-tenons on front rail and long side slats under arms.

Armchair 38.5in (98cm) high

£1,800-2,200   **DRA**

A Lakeside Crafters footstool, with cut-out sides and leather drop-in seat fastened with leather straps, with decal.

22in (56cm) wide

£600-800   **DRA**

A Michigan Chair Co. spindled hall seat, with original ebonised finish, damages.

41.75in (106cm) wide

£600-800   **DRA**

A Plail Brothers barrel chair, with spindles, original finish.

30in (76cm) high

£800-1,200   **DRA**

A Brooks drop-front desk, with interior gallery, lower drawer, shelf and pair of bookcases, with original finish.

62.5in (159cm) wide

£900-1,100   **DRA**

A three-panel screen, designed by Pittsburgh architects Alden and Harlow, carved with Native American motifs, set with 36 original platinum-print photographs of Native Americans by Frank A. Rinehart, signed by the photographer.

c1901   *Centre panel 100in (254cm) high*

£120,000-180,000   **DRA**

A Roycroft column-shaped lectern, with worn original finish.

21in (53.5cm) wide

£4,000-5,000   **DRA**

A J.M. Young drop-arm settle, with 19 back slats and four slats under each arm, quadrilinear post construction.

106in (269cm) long

£2,000-2,500   **DRA**

An Arts and Crafts oak and pewter hall bench, carved with scroll foliage, Celtic knotwork, dragons, elves, fairies, angels and imps.

This bench is unattributed to any particular artist, however, it is clearly a wood carver's real tour de force and is possibly of Irish origin.

56in (142cm) wide

£1,500-2,000   **DN**

Judith Picks: Carlo Bugatti

I have admired the work of Carlo Bugatti for many years. Although very often, as here, described as an Art Nouveau designer, he was never mainstream and one of the most compelling features of his work is its originality.

Carlo Bugatti was born in Milan, Italy in 1856. Although he worked with ceramics, musical instruments, silverware, and textiles, he is best known for his furniture designs. Influenced by Gothic, Moorish and Oriental styles, Bugatti used inlays of exotic woods, copper, pewter and vellum in his designs. In the summer of 1888 his work was displayed at the Italian Exhibition at Earls Court in London, his first international show. His furniture was awarded an honorary prize at this exhibition and his characteristic furniture style began to find avid devotees around the world.

Not the most practical furniture in the world – his pieces make a strong design statement.

A Carlo Bugatti walnut armchair, with embossed copper decoration, the back covered in vellum and painted with a frieze of poppies, with studded vellum seat on crossed vellum-covered supports.
c1900   41in (104cm) high
£10,000-15,000   L&T

A Carlo Bugatti walnut and vellum desk and chair, inlaid with brass and pewter, the writing inset, chair seat and back decorated with stylised foliage and birds, reverse of seat back signed "Bugatti".
c1902   Desk 53.5in (136cm) wide
£50,000-60,000   SOTH

An Emile Gallé mother-of-pearl and fruitwood marquetry-inlaid two-drawer side table, inlaid with butterflies, morning glories, spider chrysanthemums, and other foliage, with two looped handles and two drawers, on foliate-carved legs with stretcher, signed in bottom drawer.
c1900   34.5in (87.5cm) wide
£80,000-100,000   SK

An Art Nouveau mirror-set oak hall stand, retailed by Goumain Frères, with foliage-carved frame and ormolu hooks modelled as dragonflies, the side with an inset metal maker's plaque.
90in (229cm) high
£5,000-6,000   WW

A Shapland & Petter mahogany desk, decorated with honesty plants throughout.
43in (109cm) high
£4,000-5,000   GORL

An Art Nouveau oak and inlaid glazed bookcase, in the manner of C.F.A. Voysey, with chamferred tapering columns, enclosing adjustable shelved interior.
c1910   72in (183cm) high
£2,000-2,500   LSK

An Art Nouveau mahogany fainting couch, the pierce-carved foliate frame over an upholstered back and seat raised on five legs.

58in (147cm) long

£700-900 LHA

An Art Nouveau P.E. Gane armchair, of cacateuse form, the back inlaid with a stylised plant form, with upholstered panel seat, on tapering legs linked by stretchers.

c1900

£500-600 L&T

An Art Nouveau mahogany and inlaid display cabinet, with central mirrored recess, the two base doors flanking a mother-of-pearl and marquetry floral panel, on square tapering supports, with applied trade label "D. Hibbert Cabinet Maker 273 & 275 Stamford St Ashton-U-Lyne".

48in (122cm) wide

£1,200-1,800 DN

An Art Nouveau mahogany, rosewood and inlaid display cabinet, the shaped top enclosing a mirror and recesses, shaped panel and glazed doors, on tapered supports with open plinth base, inset label "Thos. Edwards & Sons Cabinet Makers Newcastle Staffs".

60.25in (153cm) wide

£4,500-5,500 DN

An Art Nouveau inlaid-mahogany display cabinet, inlaid with flower heads and whiplash decoration, the glazed central single door mounted with pewter decoration, on tapering octagonal front legs, lock stamped "Salmon Bros London".

72in (183cm) high

£1,500-2,000 TEN

An English Art Nouveau, oak writing desk, with leaded and glazed panel and asymmetric single cupboard door, above a writing surface and two drawers, on slender supports with pad feet and stretchers.

c1910

49in (124cm) high

£550-650 L&T

An Art Nouveau inlaid mahogany display cabinet, the central door with three undulating mullions with coloured wood inlays and slender stalks, green velvet interior, flanked by open shelves and two small glass doors, on shaped legs with shelf stretcher.

51.5in (130cm) wide

£3,000-4,000 SK

A set of eight Art Deco rosewood dining chairs, comprising two armchairs and six sidechairs, with plum-colored silk upholstery.

Armchairs 39in (99cm) high

£2,000-2,500   **DRA**

One of a set of ten Art Deco elbow chairs, by Laszlo Hoenig, with tapered rectangular backs, the seats upholstered in patterned leather, on tapering legs.

£1,000-1,500 set   **A&G**

One of a pair of French Art Deco-style oak lounge chairs, with trapezoidal back with rounded top over the plank seats, the arms and skirts veneered with rounded, diagonal slats.

34.25in (87cm) high

£1,000-1,500 pair   **LHA**

A pair of French Art Deco club chairs, with beaded crest rail over the upholstered back, arms and seats set within a cornucopia-carved frame, on tapering reeded legs.

33.75in (86cm) high

£3,000-4,000   **LHA**

A pair of Art Deco lounge chairs, upholstered in golden velvet with geometeric patterned cushions, on tapered feet.

35in (89cm) high

£250-350   **DRA**

A large wrought-iron console table, by Edgar Brandt, on stepped Portor marble base, stamped "E. BRANDT, PARIS".

82in (208cm) long

£80,000-100,000   **SOTH**

A French Art Deco marble, onyx and bronze stand, the rectangular top with rounded corners, on banded, tapering legs with bronze mounts.

23.75in (60cm) high

£750-850   **LHA**

An unusual Art Deco mahogany metal-inlaid dining table, by Laszlo Hoenig, the top inset with large plate glass panel, the border with unusual inlaid polished steels spaces, on fluted tapering legs with brass caps.

£1,000-1,500   **A&G**

An Art Deco Continental burl walnut and ivory-inlaid writing table, with two frieze drawers with roundel ivory ball-form pulls, and pull-out writing slide, on tapering square section legs with ivory-tipped feet.

c1930   *43in (109cm) wide*

£8,000-10,000   **SK**

An Art Deco birch armoire, of bowfront form, with two doors flanked by half round columns.

64.5in (164cm) high

£1,000-1,500   **LHA**

An Art Deco French cherry-veneered cabinet, with long door over a drawer and a short door over four drawers, all with circular bronze pulls stamped "Lq Depose No 32147", on a plinth base.

63in (160cm) high

£1,500-2,000   **LHA**

An Art Deco French mahogany veneered bar cabinet, with a bevelled glass door above two drawers, the panelled door opening to a shelved interior, on a plinth base, with chromed hardware.

49in (125cm) wide

£2,000-2,500   **LHA**

An Art Deco French mahogany-veneered bookcase cabinet, retailed by Bedel & Cie., with symmetrical shelves, over four panelled doors with silvered hardware, on a plinth, with Bedel sticker.

115.5in (293cm) wide

£2,500-3,000   **LHA**

An Art Deco French cerused oak sideboard, with two panelled doors flanked by quarter-round shelves, on conforming plinth base.

73in (185cm) wide

£800-1,200   **LHA**

An Art Deco mahogany sideboard, by Jules Leleu, with four central drawers flanked by two large doors, with nickel hardware and feet trim.

71in (180cm) wide

£2,000-3,000   **DRA**

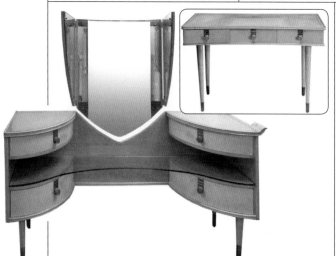

An Art Deco satinwood dressing table and side table, by Laszlo Hoenig, dressing table with shaped mirror, flanked by lights above plate-glass shelves, flanked by drawers, faced in leather with fluted Bakelite handles, side table with inset tooled-leather top above three short drawers.

Dressing table 61in (155cm) wide

£1,500-2,000   **A&G**

A French Art Deco rosewood-veneered semainier, the seven drawers with circular brass pulls surmounted with and flanked by shelves, on plinth base.

61.25in (155.5cm) high

£1,000-1,500   **LHA**

An American painted skyscraper bookcase, after Paul Frankl, the superstructure of asymmetrical form with various shelves, the base with two cabinet doors.

74in (188cm) high

£1,200-1,800   **LHA**

A Daum blown-out and enamelled "Summer" Art Glass vase, with moulded green trees framing orange and yellow landscapes, incised "Daum Nancy", with the Cross of Lorraine.

c1910   *11.25in (28.5cm) high*
£5,000-6,000   **FRE**

A Daum martelé cameo glass vase, with foliate decoration, signed "Daum Nancy", with the Cross of Lorraine.

11.5in (29cm) high
£1,500-2,000   **LHA**

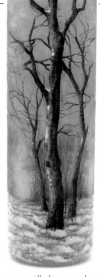

A Daum enamelled cameo glass vase, with triangular opening and a circular foot, decorated with a winter landscape, with enamelled signature "Daum Nancy", with the Cross of Lorraine.

6in (15cm) high
£3,000-4,000   **LHA**

A Daum cameo glass vase, the tapering cylindrical body in mottled orange and clear glass overlaid and acid etched with trees in a landscape and over-painted with coloured enamels, with painted mark "Daum/ Nancy".

c1900   *11in (28cm) high*
£1,500-2,000   **L&T**

A Daum footed vase, with irregular pulled rim, acid-etched with fruiting branches in deep green and red on orange and white mottled ground, marked "DAUM NANCY FRANCE" in cameo.

9.5in (24cm) high
£1,500-2,000   **DRA**

A Daum three-sided bottle vase, acid-etched with bright red poppies against a striped ground, signed "DAUM NANCY'", with the Cross of Lorraine in cameo.

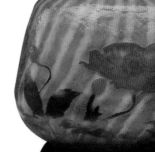

4.75in (12cm) high
£1,500-2,000   **DRA**

A Daum tapered vase, with applied and wheel-carved olives, wheel-carved branches and leaves, engraved "DAUM NANCY", with the Cross of Lorraine.

11.25in (28.5cm) high
£2,000-2,500   **DRA**

A tall Daum footed vase, wheel-carved with purple crocuses on a white martelé ground, over banded, acid-etched pedestal foot, signed "DAUM NANCY", with Cross of Lorraine.

14in (36cm) high
£2,000-2,500   **DRA**

A Daum cameo glass vase, with tall silver and green trees on an amethyst and emerald ground, signed "Daum Nancy".

12.5in (32cm) high
£1,500-2,000   **DRA**

A tall Daum cameo glass vase, decorated with a marsh scene in autumnal colours, signed "Daum Nancy France".

22in (56cm) high
£1,500-2,000   **DRA**

DECORATIVE ARTS

A miniature Daum glass vase, enamel-decorated with red sweet peas, etched "Daum Nancy", with the Cross of Lorraine.

5.5in (14cm) high

£1,500-2,000   DRA

CLOSER LOOK - DAUM VASE

Daum Frères was established in the late 19thC when brothers Jean-Louis Auguste and Jean-Antonin Daum assumed control of their father's glass factory in Nancy, Lorraine, France.

The subject matter is typical of Daum, which, like its contemporary Emile Gallé, looked primarily to nature and the local countryside for inspiration.

The finely observed botanic detail of the imagery is also characteristic of Daum, which commissioned a team of highly talented artists, including Henri Bergé, Charles Schneider and Amalric Walter, to design its glass.

The appearance of driving rain is effectively achieved by a series of acid-etched diagonal striations.

A Daum enamelled cameo glass vase, decorated with rain-swept trees, with etched signature "Daum Nancy", with the Cross of Lorraine.

4.75in (12cm) high

£7,000-8,000   LHA

A pair of Daum Nancy cameo glass bowls, with pinched rims, each with an enamelled winter scene on an orange-to-yellow mottled ground, both signed, with the Cross of Lorraine.

c1900   *5in (12.5cm) diam*

£4,000-5,000   RTC

A Daum enamelled cameo glass Prairie jug, decorated with prairie flowers and landscape, with applied, frosted glass, handle with gilt highlights, signed "Daum Nancy", with the Cross of Lorraine.

6.25in (15.5cm) high

£10,000-15,000   JDJ

A Daum enamelled cameo glass vase, the mottled glass decorated with a landscape, with enamelled "Daum Nancy", with the Cross of Lorraine, further marked "HF".

6.25in (15.5cm) high

£2,500-3,000   LHA

A narrow Daum footed vase, with padded and wheel-carved deep purple violets on pastel ground, and acid-etched green leaves and vines, silver applied to foot at a later date, engraved "DAUM NANCY", with the Cross of Lorraine.

8.25in (21cm) high

£900-1,100   DRA

A tall Daum footed vase, with acid-cut and enamelled forest scene against a white mottled ground, signed "DAUM NANCY", with the Cross of Lorraine.

15.25in (39cm) high

£3,000-4,000   DRA

A tall Daum cameo glass vase, etched with river landscape in deep burgundy on mottled amber, marked in cameo "Daum Nancy", with the Cross of Lorraine.

23.75in (60.5cm) high

£1,500-2,000   DRA

A Gallé cameo glass vase, decorated with butterflies and flowers, signed in cameo with star.

After 1904   *9.25in (23.5cm) high*
£1,500-2,000   **LHA**

A Gallé cameo glass vase, with a misty landscape in plum, olive and lemon, signed "Gallé".

10in (25.5cm) high
£1,800-2,200   **DRA**

A Gallé cameo glass vase, decorated with a mountainous lakeside landscape, with raised "Gallé" signature.

c1920   *5.25in (13cm) high*
£1,000-1,500   **DOR**

A Gallé cameo glass tapered vase, the frosted ground overlaid in purple and green and decorated with flowers and leaves, with cameo mark "Gallé" with star.

After 1904   *14.5in (37cm) high*
£1,500-2,000   **DN**

A Gallé cameo glass vase, decorated with boats by a shoreline, signed "Gallé" with star.

After 1904   *20in (51cm) high*
£2,000-2,500   **LHA**

ESSENTIAL REFERENCE - EMILE GALLÉ

Emile Gallé (1846-1904) is known for his Art Nouveau glass, furniture and ceramics.

● He set up his first glass-decorating workshop in Nancy, France, in 1873, beginning commercial production of Art Nouveau cameo glass c1899.

● Gallé cameo used up to five layers of differently coloured glass, cut by hand to create subtle colour gradations.

● By 1900, it was the largest European producer of luxury glass. At this time, increasing use was made of acid-etching on middle-range pieces.

● Gallé was strongly influenced by nature, and this can be seen in both the form and decoration of his glass.

● In 1901, Gallé established the Ecole de Nancy, based on the English Arts and Crafts guilds.

● A star next to Gallé's signature indicates a piece produced after his death.

● The factory closed in 1936.

A Gallé cameo glass bud vase, with red carnations on a yellow ground, with cameo signature.

8in (20cm) high
£1,000-1,500   **DRA**

A Gallé cameo glass vase, decorated with fruiting acers in green on a pink ground, signed.

15in (38cm) high
£1,800-2,200   **GORL**

A Gallé cameo glass vase, decorated with flowers and leaves, with vertical cameo signature.

20.5in (52cm) high
£1,200-1,800   **LHA**

A Gallé cameo glass vase, of irregular form, with fern decoration, signed on base in cameo "E. Gallé" with butterfly.

5.5in (14cm) high

£800-1,200   LHA

A Gallé cameo glass vase, decorated with flowers, signed in cameo.

7in (18cm) high

£1,500-2,000   LHA

A Gallé cameo glass vase, with a misty landscape in plum, olive and lemon, signed "Gallé".

10in (25.5cm) high

£1,800-2,200   DRA

A Gallé cameo glass vase, decorated with flowers, signed in cameo.

30in (76cm) high

£1,500-2,000   LHA

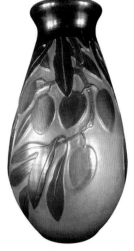

A Gallé cameo vase, decorated with olive branches.

c1900   *5in (13cm) high*

£650-750   MDM

A Gallé cameo glass oval bowl, with purple blossoms on an etched, frosted ground, with cameo signature.

11in (28cm) long

£800-1,200   DRA

A Gallé cameo "Canoe" bowl.

c1900   *8in (20.5cm) long*

£1,000-1,200   MDM

A large Gallé "Aquatic" bowl.

c1900   *7in (18cm) diam*

£1,800-2,000   MDM

A Gallé clear glass scalloped bowl, enamel-painted with dragonflies, wild flowers and garlands, signed "E. Gallé a Nancy".

7.5in (19cm) diam

£1,200-1,800   DRA

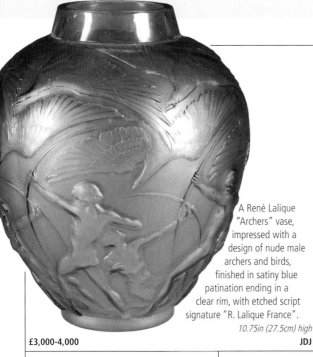

A René Lalique "Archers" vase, impressed with a design of nude male archers and birds, finished in satiny blue patination ending in a clear rim, with etched script signature "R. Lalique France".

10.75in (27.5cm) high

£3,000-4,000   JDJ

A René Lalique "Avallon" vase, of opalescent glass with green patina, engraved "R. Lalique", M p.436, no.986.

c1927   *5.75in (14.5cm) high*

£2,200-2,800   DRA

A René Lalique "Bacchus" vase, of clear and frosted glass with grey patina, stencilled "R. LALIQUE FRANCE", M p.469, no.10-922.

c1938   *6.5in (16.5cm) high*

£1,800-2,200   DRA

A René Lalique "Bresse" vase, of cased opalescent turquoise glass, stencilled "R. LALIQUE FRANCE", M p.454, no.1073.

c1931   *3.5in (9cm) high*

£2,500-3,000   DRA

A René Lalique "Chamois" vase, of amber glass with white patina, etched "R. Lalique France", M p.455, no.1075.

1931   *4.5in (11.5cm) high*

£650-750   DRA

A René Lalique "Coqs et Plumes" vase, with blue-green patina, stencilled "R. LALIQUE FRANCE", M p.445, no.1033.

c1928   *6.25in (15.5cm) high*

£1,200-1,800   DRA

A René Lalique "Dentelle" vase, of clear and frosted glass, moulded "R. Lalique", M p.426, no.943.

c1912   *7.5in (19cm) high*

£450-550   DRA

A René Lalique "Domremy" vase, of emerald green glass, engraved "R. Lalique France", M p.434, no.979.

All the "M p." numbers in this section are page references to "René Lalique 1860-1945 maître- verrier. Analyse de l'oeuvre et catalogue raisonné" by Félix Marcilhac.

c1926   *8in (20cm) high*

£4,500-5,500   DRA

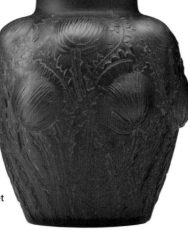

A René Lalique "Grenade" vase, of black glass with white patina, stencilled "R. LALIQUE", M p.448, no.1045.

c1930   *4.25in (11cm) high*

£2,500-3,500   DRA

A René Lalique "Gui" vase, of deep teal green glass, moulded "R. LALIQUE", M p.427, no.948.

c1920   *7in (18cm) high*
£2,500-3,500   **DRA**

A René Lalique "Moissac" vase, of yellow glass, wheel-cut 'R. LALIQUE FRANCE', M p.437, no.992.

c1927   *4.5in (11.5cm) high*
£2,000-2,500   **DRA**

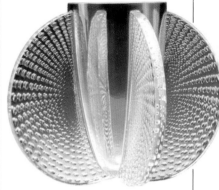

A René Lalique "Orly" vase, of clear glass, stencilled "R. LALIQUE FRANCE", M p.462, no.10-891.

c1935   *6.25in (15.5cm) high*
£2,500-3,000   **DRA**

A René Lalique "Palmes" vase, of cased yellow glass, moulded "R. LALIQUE MADE IN FRANCE", engraved "R. Lalique 952", M p.428, no.952.

c1923   *4.5in (11.5cm) high*
£1,500-2,000   **DRA**

A René Lalique "Saint-Francois" vase, of opalescent glass, stencilled "R. LALIQUE FRANCE", M p.450, no.1055.

c1930   *6.5in (16cm) high*
£2,000-2,500   **DRA**

A René Lalique "Soudan" vase, of opalescent glass with blue patina, engraved "R. Lalique, no.1016", M p.442, no.1016.

c1928   *7in (18cm) high*
£2,500-3,000   **DRA**

A René Lalique "Sauge" vase, of clear and frosted glass with green patina, engraved "R. Lalique France, no.935", M p.425, no.935.

c1923   *10in (25.5cm) high*
£1,200-1,800   **DRA**

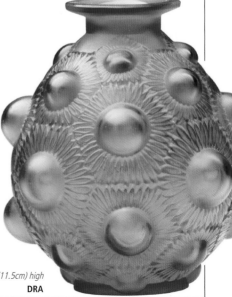

A René Lalique "Tournesols" vase, of electric blue glass, engraved "R. Lalique France no.1007", M p.440, no.1007.

c1927   *4.5in (11.5cm) high*
£2,000-2,500   **DRA**

A René Lalique "Moyenne Nue" statuette, in opalescent glass with blue patina, engraved "R. Lalique France No.830".

c1912   6in (15cm) high

£3,000-3,500   DRA

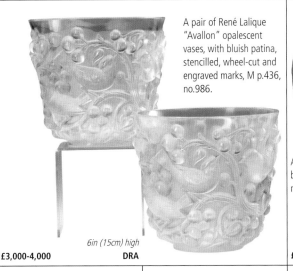

A pair of René Lalique "Avallon" opalescent vases, with bluish patina, stencilled, wheel-cut and engraved marks, M p.436, no.986.

6in (15cm) high

£3,000-4,000   DRA

A René Lalique "Eglantines" glass box and cover, sepia stained, moulded "R. Lalique" mark.

5.25in (13cm) diam

£900-1,100   DN

A René Lalique glass "Figurines et Voiles" circular box and cover, in clear glass with blue patina, with moulded mark "R LALIQUE MADE IN FRANCE".

4.25in (11cm) diam

£1,200-1,800   DN

A Lalique "Jaffa" glass punch set, in clear and frosted amber glass, comprising bowl, serving tray and six matching cups, each moulded with an overlapping leaf design, nos. "3252", "3680", and "3885".

Tray 16.5in (42cm) diam

£500-700   L&T

A René Lalique "Fleur" bowl, of clear and frosted glass with grey patina and black enamel decoration, moulded "R. LALIQUE" and engraved "France No.3100".

c1912   4.5in (11.5cm) diam

£600-800   DRA

A René Lalique "Daim" paperweight, of dark grey glass, moulded and stencilled "R. LALIQUE", M p.389, no.1168.

c1926   3in (7.5cm) high

£500-600   DRA

A René Lalique "Inseparables" clock, of clear and frosted glass, original eight-day wind-up movement, moulded "R. LALIQUE" mark.

c1926   4.75in (12cm) wide

£1,500-2,000   DRA

A mid-20thC René Lalique-style "Deux Figurines" moulded glass clock, the arched glass surround with a pair of Classically draped ladies holding a floral wreath enclosing a clock face, with an electrified illuminated base.

15.25in (39cm) high

£6,000-7,000   FRE

ESSENTIAL REFERENCE - LOETZ

The Loetz glassworks was founded in 1840 by Johann Loetz (1778-1848) in Klostermuhle, Bohemia (now Austria). After his death it was taken over by his widow Susanna and the company became known as "Loetz-Witwe" ("witwe" meaning widow in German). Much Loetz glass was exported to the US.

- Loetz's grandson, Max Ritter von Spaun (d.1909) took over in 1870, and under his direction the factory became extremely profitable.
- Iridescent glass was patented by von Spaun in 1895. It was used for organic-shaped, Art Nouveau-style pieces by notable designers, including Gustav Gurschner, Maria Kirschner and, from the Wiener Werkstätte, Josef Hoffmann, Koloman Moser, Dagobert Peche and Michael Powolny.
- Loetz collaborated with Viennese glass retailers such as E. Bakalowits Söhne.
- Marks include "Loetz/Austria" in script, or a circle encompassing two crossed arrows and four stars. Many pieces were not marked.
- The company closed in 1948.

A Loetz "Flammarion" vase, the form by Josef Hoffmann, the clear glass cased in milky white, trailed with silver bands between the layers, the lower part with light green bands pulled into flame-shaped motifs.

1910   *5.5in (14cm) high*

£4,000-5,000   **DOR**

A Loetz "Phänomen Gre 358" vase, by Josef Hoffmann for E. Bakalowits Söhne, the clear glass cased in opalescent yellow, trailed with silver-yellow bands and embellished with opalescent orange, veined silver-blue, and dark brown bands, iridescent, supported on three columns.

1900   *7in (18cm) high*

£22,000-24,000   **DOR**

A Loetz glass vase, with iridescent Papillon oil-spot decoration, etched "Loetz Austria".

6in (15cm) high

£750-850   **LHA**

A rare Loetz "Cristall" vase, by Franz Hofstötter for the 1900 Paris World Fair, the clear glass shaded blue at base, applied with carved green heart-shaped leaves and green and silver-yellow bands pulled into a wavy pattern, iridescent, with carved signature "Loetz Austria".

10in (25.5cm) high

£15,000-20,000   **DOR**

A Loetz mounted glass vase, the clear blue vase splashed with turquoise blue iridescence, in Juventa pewter mount, mount stamped "Juventa Prima Metal".

12in (30.5cm) high

£3,000-4,000   **TEN**

A tall Loetz "Luna Optisch" vase, by Robert Holubetz for E. Bakalowits Söhne, the greenish glass with blue-shaded casing, iridescent.

1901   *13in (33.5cm) high*

£3,000-4,000   **DOR**

A Loetz snake and tree trunk vase, the clear glass covered with silver-yellow specks, decorated with a green glass snake embellished with silver-yellow splashes, iridescent.

c1902   12in (30.5cm) high

£1,500-2,000   **DOR**

A Loetz vase, with a pinched trefoil rim, cranberry oil-stained colouration with yellow swirls throughout, the base signed "Loetz, Austria".

c1905   10.5in (27cm) diam

£900-1,100   **RTC**

A Loetz silver-mounted glass vase, the green-tinted body splashed with silvery blue creta Papillon colouring, the mounts as grotesque masks issuing scrolling tendrils, mounts marked "Sterling Silver", damage to silver.

c1900   9.5in (24cm) high

£1,200-1,800   **TOV**

A Loetz "Phänomen Gre 1/158" vase, of reddish cased glass trailed with silver-yellow bands divided into dotted ribs, the lower part with a silver-yellow veined serrated band, the upper embellished with silver-yellow bands, iridescent, carved "Loetz Austria".

1901/2   15in (38cm) high

£7,000-8,000   **DOR**

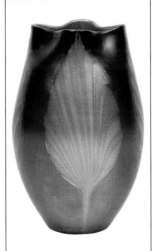

A Loetz "Phänomen" vase, the reddish-brown tinted glass cased in shaded opalescent yellow, on the outside decorated with four large applied opalescent yellow and silver-yellow striped leaves, signed "Loetz Austria".

c1901   8in (20cm) high

£4,500-5,500   **DOR**

A Loetz orange "Phänomen" glass flower vase, modelled as a single trumpet flower with two scrolling leaves, on flaring base.

            10.75in (27.5cm) high

£1,200-1,800   **WW**

A Loetz "Phänomen Gre 7624" vase, the yellow-cased glass trailed on the outside with white and brown veined bands pulled into diagonal curves, iridescence, the flaring body tapered towards the neck.

c1900   9in (23cm) high

£2,000-2,500   **DOR**

A small Loetz Witwe "Phänomen" pattern iridescent glass vase, the yellowish cased glass with silver-yellow threads divided into dotted ribs, the lower part also covered with blue and silver-yellow striped bands.

c1900   5in (12.5cm) high

£3,000-4,000   **DOR**

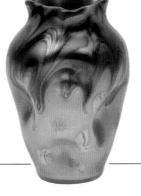

A Loetz "Phänomen Gre 2/314" iridescent glass vase, in opalescent yellow cased glass, the upper part trailed with brown and silver-blue bands, the lower half applied with veined dots, with carved "Loetz Austria".

c1902   6in (15cm) high

£4,000-5,000   **DOR**

ESSENTIAL REFERENCE - VENINI

In 1921 Paolo Venini (1895-1959) and Giacomo Cappelin set up a glassworks, Vetri Soffiati Muranesi Cappelin-Venini & C. on the Venetian island of Murano. The partnership was dissolved in 1925, and Venini established his own glassworks.

● It revived and updated many traditional Venetian techniques, as well as introducing new ones. Carlo Scarpa, artistic director from 1934-1947, introduced many hallmark Venini techniques, including the "Sommerso" technique, which created a coloured halo by casing the main body with a thin layer of colour and then a layer of clear glass.

● Venini & C. was the leading Post-War Italian glassworks.

● New forms were introduced, including the "Fazzoletto" (handkerchief) vase, developed in c1948 by Paolo Venini and Fulvio Bianconi (1915-1996), one of the company's most innovative and important designers.

● Venini & C. is still active today.

A Venini "Pezzato" glass vase, by Fulvio Bianconi, the clear glass internally decorated with large honey-coloured, black, and turquoise rectangles, the underside with three-line acid-etched factory mark "Venini Murano Italia".

c1950   *9in (23cm) high*
£7,000-8,000   **DOR**

A Venini "Pezzato Parigi" glass vase, by Fulvio Bianconi, the "pezzato" glass made of freely moulded triangular glass pieces, with incised two-line signature.

1951   *9in (23cm) high*
£6,500-7,500   **DOR**

A Venini "Pezzato" glass bowl, by Fulvio Bianconi, of fused coloured glass panels in the Parigi colourway, circular acid stamp "Venini Murano Italia", with foil label.

1950   *7.25in (18.5cm) diam*
£1,200-1,800   **DN**

A Venini "Occhi" glass vase, by Carlo Scarpa, of red, aubergine and clear glass, etched "Venini Italia" to base.

8in (20cm) high
£1,500-2,000   **WW**

A Venini "Inciso" glass vase, by Paolo Venini, the clear glass cased in orange red, carved with horizontal lines, the conical body with a slightly inverted rim, base with acid-etched circular factory mark.

13in (33.5cm) high
£1,200-1,800   **DOR**

A Venini "Pulegoso" glass vase, by Napoleone Martinuzzi, of green foam glass.

c1930   *14in (36cm) high*
£7,000-8,000   **DOR**

A large A.V.E.M. tapering glass vase, by Anzolo Fuga, with polychrome rods and murrines, and acid-etched finish.

17.5in (44cm) high

£1,200-1,800   **DRA**

A large mid-20thC Cenedese aquarium block, decorated with three stylised angel fish swimming amongst reeds.

12in (30.5cm) wide

£1,000-1,500   **FLD**

A rare Artisti Barovier black glass vase, by Giuseppe Barovier, with star-shaped aventurine murrines, signed "AB" and with crown tesserae.

7in (18cm) high

£4,000-5,000   **DRA**

A Fratelli Toso "Cattedrale" glass vase, with square murrines, red and gold foil label, marked "Made in Murano Italy".

8.75in (22cm) high

£1,500-2,000   **DRA**

A Fratelli Toso vase, designed by Pollio Perelda.

1953

£10,000-12,000   **FIS**

An Aureliano Toso "Oriente" vase, by Dino Martens, model no.5513, the clear glass internally decorated with polychrome patches, a large star motif, and meshwork patterns.

Designed 1954   *15in (38cm) high*

£5,000-6,000   **DOR**

A Seguso Vetri D'Arte "Pesce" (fish) sculpture, by Flavio Poli, in red and lemon-yellow sommerso glass.

1955–60   *17in (43cm) high*

£1,500-2,000   **DOR**

A Vistosi "Pulcino" (Little Bird), by Alexandro Pianon, of mould-blown glass with murrines, metal wire, and dark-brown painted decoration.

1962   *12in (30.5cm) high*

£3,500-4,000   **DOR**

Judith Picks: Mounted Tiffany Vase

What I love about so many antiques is that their very existence can be a pure matter of chance.

In c1897, Siegfried Bing changed the nature of his recently-opened gallery, the Maison de l'Art Nouveau. Neither the Paris press nor the French populace had particularly liked the mixture of Continental and American styles that he had previously shown. To counteract this xenophobia, Bing hired three new designers, Eugéne Gaillard, Edouard Colonna, and Georges de Feure, to create works in all media that were unified in style and more elegantly French in appearance.

One of the first assignments given to Colonna was to create silver mountings for Bing's unsold stock of Tiffany glass. As can be seen, he transformed a Tiffany vase into a precious objet d'art, in which the silver mount and the opals beautifully compliment the gentle iridescence of the Favrile glass. Very few Tiffany Favrile vases with Colonna mountings remain, but they show what an entrepreneur and a highly skilled artist can achieve.

A rare silver-mounted Tiffany "Favrile" vase, engraved "o4771", the silver mount set with five opals.

c1897

£60,000-70,000 SOT

A tall Tiffany gold "Favrile" iridescent vase, with ribbed design, marked "L.C. Tiffany-Favrile 1540-1490N".

12.25in (31cm) high

£1,000-1,500 DRA

A Tiffany gold "Favrile" bud vase, with pulled green heart-shaped leaf decoration, etched "L.C. Tiffany Favrile 1518J".

6in (15cm) high

£1,200-1,800 DRA

A Tiffany gold "Favrile" glass floriform vase, with ruffled rim over the circular foot, signed "L.C. Tiffany Favrile".

1940 *9.5in (24cm) high*

£1,200-1,800 LHA

A Tiffany "Favrile" glass vase, with engraved leaf decoration, etched on base "8667 J L.C.Tiffany-Favrile".

12in (30.5cm) high

£6,000-7,000 LHA

A Tiffany "Favrile" vase, with gold pulled-feather decoration on heat-reactive glass with a lustred pale-yellow ground, etched "L.C.Tiffany Favrile F140" and circular paper label.

9.5in (24cm) high

£1,000-1,500 DRA

A Tiffany Studios "Favrile" glass tazza, with leaf pattern and green lustre finish, etched "L.C.T. 842 Favrile".

6.5in (16cm) high

£600-800 DRA

A Tiffany "Favrile" bud vase, on enamelled base, base stamped "LOUIS C TIFFANY FURNACES INC150" liner etched "5-L. CT. Favrile".

11.75in (30cm) high

£600-800 DRA

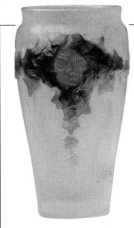

A miniature Gabriel Argy-Rousseau pâte-de-verre "Masques" vase, etched "G ARGY ROUSSEAU", stamped "5034".

4in (10cm) high

£3,500-4,500 DRA

A Gabriel Argy-Rousseau pâte-de-verre bowl, in red, purple, green and white shades, with large flowers with stems in relief all round, inscribed "G. Argy-Rousseau" and "FRANCE".

1920 *3in (7.5cm) high*

£6,000-7,000 WKA

A DeVez cameo glass vase, decorated with pine trees, signed in cameo.

23.75in (60cm) high

£650-750 LHA

MILLERS COMPARES

I have collected Monart glass for over 20 years and it is interesting to see how the collecting market has evolved. Monart Glass was manufactured from about 1922 until c1961 at Moncrieff's Glassworks, Perth, Scotland. It was developed by Salvador Ysart, a master glassmaker originally from Barcelona, Spain, and his four sons. The two vases here show what has happened to prices for Monart.

This vase is a standard shape and has typical decoration. Coloured glass powder or granules and canes were rolled (marvered) into clear or coloured blanks and then twisted into whorls, or other pulled decoration, before being covered with another layer of clear glass. Gold powder or aventurine was often included. These vases have dropped in value.

A Guild of Handicrafts rock crystal and silver-mounted vase, by Charles Robert Ashbee, with twin mythical beast scroll handles in high relief, the lightly hammered splayed foot applied to the corners with angel motifs, hallmarked London.

1902 *10in (25.5cm) high*

£3,000-4,000 L&T

A pair of Durand orange "Cluthra" glass two-handled vases, with clear applied design, both marked.

12.25in (31cm) high

£550-650 DRA

This vase, with a more interesting shape and complex, much rarer, "cloisonné" surface decoration has increased in value substantially.

A large Monart "Cloisonné" vase, shape "OD", decorated in a mottled and fissured tonal ochre and brown pattern over colourless glass.

10in (25.5cm) high

£700-1,000 FLD

A Monart beaker vase, shape "OE", with graduated green to yellow mottles with aventurine inclusions, cased in colourless glass, the base with polished pontil marks.

8in (20cm) high

£100-150 WW

An E. Michel glass vase, carved with the Three Graces to one side, verso with a cherub holding a laurel wreath on its head and a palm branch in his hand, signed "E. Michel".

11.25in (28.5cm) high

£10,000-15,000 JDJ

DECORATIVE ARTS

A large Muller Frères cameo vase, cased in magenta over cranberry over clear and acid-cut with large peony flowers in bud and full bloom, with acid-cut signature to the side.

18in (45.5cm) high

£2,500-3,000   FLD

An Orrefors "Ariel" bowl, by Edvin Öhrström, the thick glass wall with radiating burgundy and clear square patterns, signed "Orrefors Ariel No.500M Edvin Öhrström".

7.25in (18.5cm) diam

£400-500   TEN

An Orrefors "Ariel" "Girls and Dove" vase, by Edvin Öhrström, marked "ORREFORS Ariel Nr. 624 O".

1965   7.25in (18.5cm) high

£1,500-2,000   FIS

A tall Quezal "Jack-in-the-Pulpit" vase, with lustred gold blossom and purple glaze to emerald stem, incised "Quezal".

14.75in (37.5cm) high

£2,000-2,500   DRA

An H.G. Richardson striated glass ovoid vase, after a design by Dr. Christopher Dresser, with knopped neck.

8.25in (21cm) high

£300-400   WW

A Royal Flemish covered jar, with gilt decoration of cherubs fighting dragons on front and back, with dark mauve and gilt base, neck and stopper.

15.5in (39cm) high

£7,000-8,000   JDJ

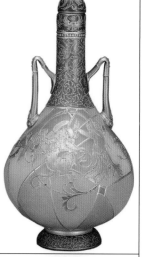

A large Schneider "Water Lily" cameo glass and enamelled vase, the body with stylised water lilies in blue on a pale blue ground.

c1925   22in (56cm) high

£1,500-2,000   FRE

A Steuben "Cluthra" vase, with flared rim and allover blue decoration, marked "Steuben".

8.25in (21cm) high

£650-750   LHA

A Steuben blue "Aurene" baluster vase, signed "Steuben Aurene 3273", drill-hole repair to base.

14.75in (37.5cm) high

£600-700   DRA

A Le Verre Français cameo glass bowl, etched with stylised blossoms in mottled cobalt and orange, etched "Le Verre Français".

8.75in (22cm) diam

£600-800 DRA

A Le Verre Français cameo glass bulbous vase, with stylised blossoms in mottled oranges, etched "Le Verre Français France" and signed "Charder".

6.75in (17cm) high

£350-450 DRA

An Amalric Walter pâte-de-verre figurine of a mouse, perched on a rock, eating a nut, signed "A WALTER NANCY".

3.5in (9cm) high

£800-1,200 DRA

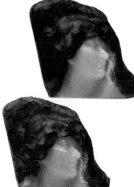

A pair of Amalric Walter figural bookends, signed "A WALTER NANCY", artist's mark "A. Finot".

4.5in (11.5cm) high

£2,500-3,000 DRA

A late 19thC Thomas Webb ivory cameo glass vase, the body double ivory-cased and cut-back with a fruiting rowan tree bough, below stiff leaf collar picked out in tonal green and brown staining, with acid-cut signature to base.

9.75in (25cm) high

£1,500-2,000 FLD

A late 19thC cameo glass vase, by Thomas Webb, the body cased in opal over cinnamon, and cut-back with a duck in flight over water lilies, all between banded borders.

7.5in (19cm) high

£900-1,200 FLD

A pair of citron cameo glass vases, attributed to Thomas Webb, decorated with white morning glories.

10in (25.5cm) high

£1,500-2,000 DRA

A Wiener Werkstätte footed glass vase, by Dagobert Peche, made by Oertel, of amethyst glass overlaid with white glass and cut with star motifs.

This is one of only 11 examples made.

1919-20 *9in (23cm) high*

£5,500-6,500 L&T

An Austrian vase, with blue iridescent exterior, the applied tears covered in silver, losses and restorations to tendrils.

6.25in (15.5cm) high

£300-500 DRA

DECORATIVE ARTS

One of a pair of 19thC Arts and Crafts English School stained and leaded glass panels, depicting a male and a female figure in 17thC costume, each bearing coat of arms.

Panels bear the arms of The Worshipful Company of Cordwainers of the City of London and The Worshipful Company of Goldsmiths.

33in (85cm) high

£2,000-2,500 pair   L&T

An Arts and Crafts window, stained and leaded glass, decorated with bacchanale and grapes, framed.

36.25in (92cm) high

£1,500-2,000   DRA

A "Gather Ye Rosebuds" stained glass panel, by Charles Edward Kempe, decorated with a woman picking a briar rose.

45.5in (115.5cm) high

£4,000-5,000   WW

A stained glass panel, by William Glasby, depicting a pre-Raphaelite maiden dreaming at the water's edge, inside a border of foliate panels, signed, in a painted wood frame.

William Glasby (1863-1941) worked at Morris & Co. between 1909-1911 and 1913-1923.

24.5in (62cm) wide

£2,000-2,500   WW

One of a set of four painted stained and leaded glass panels, after John Moyr Smith, each with four pictorial panels, based on Aesop's Fables designs for Minton, above geometric panels

c1880   *44in (112.5cm) high*

£1,800-2,200 set   L&T

A "Noah and the Dove" stained glass window panel.

25.5in (65cm) wide

£1,500-2,000   WW

A Stephen Adam & Son stained, painted and leaded glass panel, Glasgow, signed.

Stephen Adam (1846-1910) established his studio in Bath Street, Glasgow in 1870. He was responsible for much of the finest stained glass produced in the country for the next 40 years. Much of his secular glass, such as this window, was commissioned by the newly wealthy Scottish industrialists and shipping magnates.

c1900   *52in (132cm) high*

£3,000-4,000   L&T

One of four Aesthetic Movement stained glass panels, with flowers and fruit surrounded by a geometric foliate border.

24in (61cm) high

£4,500-5,500 set   WW

A rare George III opaline glass and gold-mounted scent bottle, in the form of a Negress's head, highlighted in red enamel, the neck with scalloped gold rim, the stopper inset with a diamond, in fitted case.
c1760   *2.5in (6.5cm) high*
£800-1,000   TEN

A René Lalique "Ambre" perfume bottle, for D'Orsay, raised "Lalique Ambre D'Orsay", M p.933, no.4.

For more information on M p. numbers see p551.
5in (12.5cm) high
£700-900   DRA

A René Lalique "Amphitrite" perfume bottle, of clear and frosted glass with sepia patina, engraved "R. Lalique France", moulded "Lalique", M p.335, no.514.
c1920   *3.5in (9cm) high*
£1,500-2,500   DRA

A René Lalique "Le Jade" perfume bottle, for Roger et Gallét, in green glass with grey patina, moulded "R. L. FRANCE" M p.948, no.15.
3.25in (8.5cm) high
£1,500-2,000   DRA

A René Lalique "Pan" perfume bottle, of clear and frosted glass with sepia patina, moulded "R. Lalique", engraved "Lalique", M p.332, no.504.
c1920   *5in (12.5cm) high*
£1,500-2,000   DRA

A Stourbridge cameo glass scent bottle, probably Stevens & Williams, with white overlaid on red, acid-etched and wheel-cut with flowering lotus and a butterfly, with silver-coloured metal mount and stopper, and fitted case.
c1880-90   *10in (25.5cm) long*
£1,500-2,000   H&L

A Stourbridge blue and white cameo glass and silver-mounted scent bottle, worked in low relief with flower and leaves, the silver stopper by William Thomas Wright & Frederick Davies, London.
1884   *11in (28cm) long*
£1,200-1,800   TEN

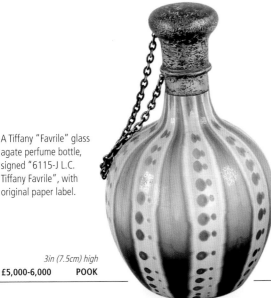

A Tiffany "Favrile" glass agate perfume bottle, signed "6115-J L.C. Tiffany Favrile", with original paper label.
3in (7.5cm) high
£5,000-6,000   POOK

ESSENTIAL REFERENCE - WEBB CAMEO GLASS

Thomas Webb & Sons was established in 1837 near Stourbridge, West Midlands, by Thomas Webb (1802–69).

- **It produced a varied range of decorative glass, including cameo.**
- **John Norwood produced the first cameo pieces in the 1870s.**
- **Most Webb cameo was designed by George Woodall in the late 19thC. The best pieces were marked "GEM CAMEO".**
- **The factory closed in 1990.**

A Webb cameo glass perfume bottle, decorated with flowers, with Webb & Sons cameo stamp, the silver lid by Sampson Mordan & Co., London.
1887   *4.5in (11.5cm) high*
£1,500-2,000   LHA

DECORATIVE ARTS

A Liberty & Co. "Cymric" silver, enamel and mother-of-pearl boudoir clock, topped by a sugar-loaf turquoise cabochon, the dial with green- and blue-enamelled bezel, over three turquoise cabochons, and two ovoid mother-of-pearl inlays, with French movement.

1904   *4.25in (11cm) high*

£8,000-10,000   **SK**

A Liberty & Co. "Tudric" pewter and copper mantel clock, model no.660, cast in low relief with a row of stylised trees, the dial copper, with stamped marks.

11.5in (29cm) high

£9,000-11,000   **WW**

A rare Liberty & Co. "Tudric" pewter architectural mantel clock, by Archibald Knox, model no.096, the face and hands set with abalone shell panels, stamped marks.

12in (30.5cm) high

£22,000-28,000   **WW**

A Tiffany Studios mantel clock, front with impressed stylised leaf design, with camel-back top and scrolled sides, finished in gold doré, marked "Tiffany Studios New York 2078", "Tiffany & Co. New York" on the dial and "Chelsea Clock Co. Boston USA" on the works.

12in (30.5cm) wide

£10,000-15,000   **JDJ**

ESSENTIAL REFERENCE - LIBERTY & CO.

Established by Arthur Lasenby Liberty (1843-1917) in 1875, London department store Liberty & Co. is known for its furniture, fabrics, jewellery and metalware.

- It initially specialised in Oriental- and Moorish-style pieces, but soon began to stock Arts and Crafts and Art Nouveau wares.
- Archibald Knox (1864-1933) began designing for Liberty in 1899, designing much of the Celtic Revival, including the "Cymric" (silver) and "Tudric" (pewter) ranges.
- Liberty & Co. is still active.

A Liberty & Co "Tudric" pewter and enamel mantel clock, by Archibald Knox, model no.0609, with cast foliate decoration, the dial inset and enamelled with berried foliage in shades of red, green and blue, stamped marks.

8.25in (21cm) high

£10,000-15,000   **WW**

A silvered wall clock, attributed to George Walton, made for Goodyers, London, the dial repoussé-decorated with foliate motifs and central turquoise enamel panel, flanked by vertical strapwork and corresponding enamel panelling.

c1900   *20in (51cm) wide*

£1,500-2,000   **L&T**

An Arts and Crafts hammered copper and pewter mantel clock, with pewter face with two-train movement signed "D.C. Co.", and a plaque moulded with "Tempus Fugit", borders with studded banding.

18in (45.5cm) high

£1,200-1,800   **SK**

An Arts and Crafts oak eight-day longcase clock, with brass-inset case inscribed "Time Flys" and leaded stained-glass trunk door, with associated chiming movement.

79in (201cm) high

£3,500-4,500   **GORL**

A rare Cartier Art Deco table clock, with one diamond rhomb, rose quartz, onyx and enamel, striped lever movement, inscribed "Geneva Clock Co.", compensation balance, Breguet overcoil spring, the movement numbered 23652, in fitted case.

c1930   *3.5in (9cm) high 13oz*
£25,000-30,000   **DOR**

An Art Deco "Limousin Cathedral" marble clock, the dial flanked by mounted gilded spelter female seated semi-nudes, with French brass eight-day movement with key.

23in (58cm) wide
£1,000-1,500   **LSK**

A Gilbert Rohde "World's Fair" burlwood and chrome desk clock, for Herman Miller, with black numeral markers, with Herman Miller metal tag, numbered 4084B.

9in (23cm) high
£1,500-2,000   **DRA**

A Herman Miller desk clock, in angular wood frame, face marked "Herman Miller".

9.75in (25cm) wide
£2,000-3,000   **DRA**

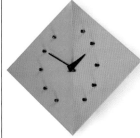

A George Nelson kite clock, for Howard Miller, in rare colour combination with black enamelled wood numeral markers and metal hands, with embossed Howard Miller mark, with foil and clear plastic labels.

21.5in (54cm) wide
£1,500-2,000   **DRA**

ESSENTIAL REFERENCE - GEORGE NELSON

Along with Charles and Ray Eames, George Nelson (1908–1986) was one of the founders of American Modernism.

- In 1945 he was made Director of Design at Herman Miller.
- He created a line of clocks for Howard Miller in 1949. The first was "Clock 4755" (Ball Clock). They were discontinued in the 1980s, but re-issued by Vitra in the 1990s.
- Nelson's great innovation was the Comprehensive Storage System or CSS (1959), the forerunner of system furniture.

A large George Nelson bentwood "Sunflower" clock, for Howard Miller, with brass accents and enamelled metal hands, with Howard Miller label.

29.75in (75.5cm) diam
£1,200-1,800   **DRA**

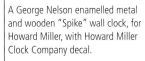

A George Nelson enamelled metal and wooden "Spike" wall clock, for Howard Miller, with Howard Miller Clock Company decal.

c1952   *18in (45.5cm) diam*
£250-350   **DRA**

A George Nelson ball clock, for Howard Miller, with enamelled metal hands and multicoloured wooden spheres radiating from brass spokes, with Howard Miller decal.

13.25in (34cm) diam
£750-850   **DRA**

ESSENTIAL REFERENCE - TIFFANY LAMPS

Louis Comfort Tiffany (1848-1933) was the son of Charles Tiffany, jewellery maker and founder of Tiffany & Co. (1837).

● He set up Louis Comfort Tiffany and Associated Artists in 1878, Tiffany Glass Co. in 1885 and Tiffany Furnaces in 1892. Lamps and bronzes were made at Tiffany Studios, which was established in 1900.

● Nature is a major inspiration in all Tiffany glass and lamps.

● Tiffany's free-blown glass was first put on sale in 1892. "Favrile", the first iridescent Art Glass range, was launched in 1894.

● In 1899 Tiffany introduced a range of lamps with leaded hemispherical glass shades. These were handmade by laying stained glass onto wooden moulds.

● The first run of lamps included "Nautilus"," Dragonfly" and "Wisteria". By 1906 there were over 125 designs, ranging from simple geometric patterns to complex depictions of flowers, foliage and insects.

● Some lamps have separate stands.

● Tiffany Studios closed in 1932. Tiffany & Co. is still active.

A Tiffany Studios three-light "Lily" table lamp, with three Favrile shades depicting green leaves on an opalescent ground, shades etched "L.C.T." on bronze base stamped "TIFFANY STUDIOS NEW YORK 28593", crack to one shade.

21in (53.5cm) high

£3,500-4,500　　DRA

A Tiffany Studios ten-light "Lily" table lamp, with Favrile glass shades, the scrolled arms and base moulded with lily pads and vines, base marked "TIFFANY STUDIOS, NEW YORK, 381", damages and replacements.

21.5in (54.5cm) high

£15,000-20,000　　SK

A Tiffany Studios "Acorn" table lamp, shade of yellow and green glass, over a converted bronze single-socket oil lamp base stamped "TIFFANY STUDIOS NEW YORK 161", shade stamped "TIFFANY STUDIOS NEW YORK".

22.25in (56cm) high

£7,000-8,000　　DRA

A Tiffany Studios "Acorn" table lamp, shade of blue, green, and yellow slag glass, over a three-arm, single-socket fluted bronze base, base and shade stamped "TIFFANY STUDIOS NEW YORK", base with "TGDCo 259".

21in (53.5cm) high

£8,000-10,000　　DRA

A rare Tiffany Studios "Grape" table lamp, shade impressed "TIFFANY STUDIOS/NEW YORK" with partially effaced number, base impressed "TIFFANY STUDIOS/NEW YORK/346".

c1902　　*26.5in (67cm) high*

£800,000-1,000,000　　SOT

A Tiffany Studios "Dragonfly" table lamp, the green and amber shade with oval amber jewels and red cabochon eyes, with pierced metal overlay at wings, shade marked "TIFFANY STUDIOS NEW YORK 1495", on green patinated-bronze turtle-shell base, stamped "TIFFANY STUDIOS NEW YORK 587".

c1910　　*26in (66cm) high*

£90,000-110,000　　SK

A Tiffany Studios "Elaborate Peony" table lamp, shade with striated patterns of red and lavender peonies among foliage, stamped "TIFFANY STUDIOS NEW YORK 1903", the base of tree-form, stamped "TIFFANY STUDIOS NEW YORK, 553".

c1910　　*33in (85cm) high*

£250,000-300,000　　SK

A Tiffany Studios "Favrile" glass and bronze table lamp, the slightly ribbed shade with pulled decoration, signed "L.C.T. Favrile", mounted in a harp base, stamped "TIFFANY STUDIOS NEW YORK 419".

13.25in (34cm) high

£4,500-5,500   **LHA**

A Tiffany Studios ormolu desk lamp, with domed shade on a two-socket, fluted base, stamped "TIFFANY STUDIOS NEW YORK 817".

18.25in (46cm) high

£1,000-1,500   **DRA**

A Tiffany Studios desk lamp, with gold pulled-feather glass shade over single-socket bronze base, base stamped "TIFFANY STUDIOS NEW YORK 273G1".

13.25in (34cm) high

£2,000-3,000   **DRA**

A Tiffany Studios double-arm bronze student lamp, with applied, curled rope-like designs.

30.5in (77cm) high

£1,200-1,800   **DRA**

A Tiffany Studios three-legged bronze candlestick, with blown green glass, complete with snuffer on hook, stamped "TIFFANY STUDIOS NEW YORK 1212", original patina.

10in (25.5cm) high

£3,000-4,000   **DRA**

A Tiffany Studios four-stemmed bronze candlestick, with gold "Favrile" glass shade on removable bobeche, stamped "TIFFANY STUDIOS NEW YORK 1201", shade etched "L.C.T. Favrile", original patina.

17.75in (45cm) high

£2,000-2,500   **DRA**

A Tiffany Studios bronze floriform candlestick, with blown-in green glass, complete with bobeche, with new patina, stamped "TIFFANY STUDIOS NEW YORK 91100".

20in (51cm) high

£1,500-2,000   **DRA**

A pair of Tiffany Studios doré bronze candlesticks, with candle cup held in three prongs on four wide ribbed legs terminating in paw feet on shaped base, both marked "TIFFANY STUDIOS NEW YORK 1201".

11.5in (29cm) high

£1,500-2,500   **SK**

A Tiffany Studios bronze candlestick, with root base, stamped "TIFFANY STUDIOS NEW YORK", re-patinated.

12.75in (32.5cm) high

£2,000-2,500   **DRA**

A pair of Tiffany Studios gold doré candlesticks, embossed with flames, stamped "TIFFANY STUDIOS NEW YORK", original patina.

9.25in (23.5cm) high

£3,000-4,000   **DRA**

A Handel table lamp, with an oversized leaded glass shade with pink rose border against a yellow ground, over a three-socket trumpet-shaped base, marked "Handel".

26.5in (67cm) high

£4,000-5,000   **DRA**

A Handel table lamp, the faceted shade of caramel slag glass with a band of applied oak leaves, over a three-socket base decorated with tall leaves and buds, base stamped "Handel".

24in (61cm) high

£2,000-3,000   **DRA**

A Handel table lamp, the iridised hemispherical shade obverse-painted with an autumnal landscape and birds in flight, on three-socket fluted base, shade signed "Handel 6953 R" and stamped "Handel PAT'D. NO. 979664", base stamped "Handel".

23.5in (59.5cm) high

£5,000-6,000   **DRA**

A Handel table lamp, with a panelled glass shade in the "Cattail" pattern, over a three-socket bulbous base, shade stamped "HANDEL PAT'D NO.", replacements.

24.5in (62cm) high

£5,000-6,000   **DRA**

A Handel table lamp, with a chipped-glass shade reverse-painted with Greek ruins, over a three-socket base in the Asian taste, shade stamped and signed "Handel 6004", original patina.

24in (61cm) high

£5,000-6,000   **DRA**

A Handel table lamp, the acid-etched shade reverse-painted by F. Gubisch, shade signed "HANDEL LAMPS", patent number, and "Handel 7122 Gubisch".

24in (61cm) high

£5,000-6,000   **DRA**

A rare Handel table lamp, the acid-etched shade reverse-painted with a lakeside landscape at dusk, painted by F. Gubisch, on three-socket "Teroma" base obverse-painted with a river landscape, shade stamped "Handel Lamps" with patent, base signed "F. Gubisch".

23.5in (59.5cm) high

£6,500-7,500   **DRA**

A Handel table lamp, the chipped-ice shade reverse- and obverse-painted with tall green reeds painted on the exterior against a yellow ground, over a three-socket tree-trunk base, shade signed "O.S. Patents no. 979864 Handel. #5351", base stamped "Handel".

23.25in (59cm) diam

£7,000-8,000   **DRA**

ESSENTIAL REFERENCE - DARD HUNTER

William Joseph "Dard" Hunter (1883-1966) was born in Ohio, USA. In 1904 he applied for what was initially a summer position with the Roycrofters, a community of craftsmen following the teachings of William Morris in East Aurora, New York.

- He visited Vienna in 1908. Roycroft design consequently began to incorporate geometric patterns and stylised figures inspired by the Wiener Werkstätte.

- Hunter's designs for books, leather, glass, metal, pottery, jewellery, and furniture, helped distinguish Roycroft pieces from other American Arts and Crafts products.

- In 1910 he left the Roycrofters and returned to Vienna, where he took courses in lithography, book decoration, and letter design.

- In 1912, having lived briefly in England, he moved to Marlborough, New York. There he built a paper mill where he could manufacture paper using entirely 17thC techniques. Papermaking and printing subsequently became a life-long passion.

A Roycroft flaring shade, designed by Dard Hunter, of bright green and purple leaded slag glass, break to one glass piece on outer edge, stamped Orb & Cross mark.

18in (45.5cm) wide

£7,000-8,000　　　　**DRA**

A Roycroft hammered copper helmet-shade lamp, with Orb & Cross mark.

16.25in (41cm) high

£1,200-1,800　　　　**DRA**

A Roycroft brass-washed hammered copper table lamp, no.914, with riveted strap base and Steuben "Aurene" shade, stamped with middle period Orb & Cross mark.

14.75in (37.5cm) high

£3,000-4,000　　　　**DRA**

A Roycroft hammered copper and mica helmet-shade table lamp, with Orb & Cross mark.

14.5in (37cm) high

£1,500-2,500　　　　**DRA**

A pair of rare Roycroft brass-washed hammered-copper candlesticks, with factory modifications to make them into candle lamps.

Metal 15.5in (39cm) high

£3,000-4,000　　　　**DRA**

A Roycroft wall sconce, designed by Dard Hunter, with cylindrical shade of leaded glass in bright green and purple, with wall cap.

8.5in (47cm) high

£6,000-7,000　　　　**DRA**

A Susse Frères "Danseuse au Cothurne" patinated and gilded bronze figural lamp, from the cycle "Le jeu de l'écharpe", designed by Agathon Leonard, on marbled stone base, signed and stamped with foundry mark.

1898   18in (45.5cm) high

£22,000-24,000   DOR

CLOSER LOOK - "LOIE FULLER" LAMP

Established in 1860, Siot-Decauville was one of the best-known Parisian art foundries of the 19thC. It specialised in bronze reproductions of works by the renowned artists of the time, including Jean-Louis Meissonier, Jean A. Mercie, Laurent Marqueste, and François-Raoul Larche.

An American ex-patriot, Loie Fuller found fame as a regular performer at the Folies Bergère in Paris, where she captivated audiences with her innovative choreographic creations such as the "Fire Dance".

Her radical style and beauty attracted the attention of many of the most celebrated artists of the day, including Henri de Toulouse-Lautrec, Auguste Rodin and François-Raoul Larche. She became the embodiment of the Art Nouveau movement, and is symbolized in many important images of early 20th century Paris.

Larche (1860-1912) studied sculpture under François Jouffroy and Jean-Alexandre-Joseph Falguière at the École des Beaux Arts. Although his life and career were brief, his work was acclaimed at the 1900 Paris Exposition Universelle and he was awarded the gold medal for sculpture.

A Siot-Decauville "Loie Fuller" figural lamp, by François-Raoul Larche, inscribed "Raoul Larche" with foundry mark.

c1900   17.5in (44cm) high

£15,000-20,000   LHA

A Loetz "Phänomen Gre 85/3890" table lamp, by Kolomon Moser for E. Bakalowits Söhne, the clear glass cased in opalescent yellow, on the outside trailed with silver-yellow bands and a silver-blue and violet striped garland, on a Pest silver base decorated with beading, with import marks, and maker's mark.

1900   11in (28cm) high

£9,000-11,000   DOR

A Daum Nancy cameo glass and wrought-iron table lamp, the shade depicting ships on a green and orange ground, on three wrought-iron supports and hammered collar, above overlaid glass base depicting a rural landscape, on domed iron base, signed "Daum Nancy" and with the Cross of Lorraine.

c1915   17.5in (44cm) high

£3,000-4,000   FRE

A Gallé cameo glass table lamp, decorated with clematis in shades of brown against a pink ground, signed to shade and base.

17in (43cm) high

£3,000-4,000   GORL

A Gallé cameo glass desk lamp, the trumpet shade decorated with violets in blue on a blush ground, on arching bronze base modelled with a fairy and whiplash curls, signed.

16in (40.5cm) high

£3,000-4,000   GORL

A René Lalique "Camaret" (Quatre Rangées e Poissons) table lamp, of clear and frosted glass with peach patina, with wheel-carved signature "R Lalique France no. 1010", the lamp Marcilhac no. 2167, the vase Marcilhac no. 1010.

1928   11.5in (29cm) high

£60,000-70,000   SOTH

A Secessionist brass inlaid rosewood lamp, attributed to Erhald & Sons, the shade set with mother-of-pearl and amber-coloured glass border, on a circular column and swept base.

£600-700   GORL

A Royal Dux figural lamp, modelled as a maiden standing among poppies and leafage, and holding a small Vaseline glass light shade, applied and impressed pink triangle pad mark and "1197".

c1910   32in (81cm) high

£2,000-3,000   TEN

An Art Nouveau silvered bronze, carved ivory, shell and iridescent glass table lamp, in the form of a carved ivory nude sprite reclining on a leaf above a polished nautilus shell enclosing a single light, topped by floriform light with iridescent flaring shade.

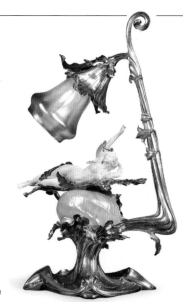

22.25in (56.5cm) high

£5,500-6,500   SK

An Art Nouveau brass oil lamp, by George Leleu, the domed shade set with glass cabochons above a green glass reservoir, on stand cast and pierced with holly, signed.

22in (56cm) high

£1,000-1,500   GORL

A Schneider "Pheasant" lamp, with leaded glass body, the head, tail and feet in cast bronze, impressed "Charles Schneider".

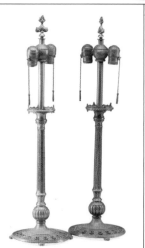

24in (61cm) long

£1,800-2,200   JDJ

One of a pair of American Art Nouveau cast-metal and Quezal glass figural candlesticks, each with a feather-pulled shade in tones of gold and green, the base in the form of a woodland nymph.

19.75in (49.5cm)

£15,000-20,000 pair   SK

A bronze table lamp base, by Oscar Bach, decorated with a hunting scene, under verdigris patina, signed "Oscar Bach".

26in (66cm) high

£2,000-2,500   DRA

A pair of bronze table lamp bases, by Oscar Bach, each with two sockets and pierced base, both marked with Oscar Bach metal tags.

28in (71cm) high

£1,500-2,000   DRA

An Art Deco cast-metal figural lamp, the frosted-glass diffuser decorated with repeating concentric circles supported by a female nude figure on circular stepped base.

40.5in (103cm) high

£750-850   LHA

A Kosmos Brenner "Rainbow Satin" miniature lamp, the rainbow mother-of-pearl satin glass raindrop pattern lamp with nickel-plated brass collar, the brass burner marked "Patent Reform Kosmos Brenner Achill Fischel Ohligs".

12in (30.5cm) high

£4,000-5,000   JDJ

ESSENTIAL REFERENCE - W.A.S. BENSON

In 1880 William Arthur Smith Benson (1854-1924) established a workshop in London to produce turned metalware. By 1882 he also had a foundry and showroom in Kensington.

● He worked primarily in brass and copper. Unlike other Arts and Crafts metalworkers, he often used machine-made parts in his work. He designed useful, functional pieces with contemporary life in mind.

● Common decorative motifs include flower blossoms, buds and foliage.

● He provided most of the lighting used in interiors designed by William Morris, who had initially encouraged him to start his business.

● After Morris' death in 1896, Benson became the director of Morris & Co.

One of a pair of brass and copper wall candelabra, by W.A.S. Benson, each with curved wall bracket, suspending a square- and circular-section column with spherical spacer and moulded finial, and issuing three curved branches with broad drip-trays and three prongs for candles.

c1900   *22in (56cm) high*

£4,000-5,000 pair   L&T

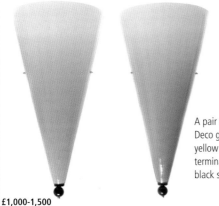

A pair of French Art Deco glass sconces, the yellow conical shades terminating with a black spherical finial.

38.5in (97cm) high

£1,000-1,500   LHA

A Daum Art Deco acid-etched chandelier, the domed diffuser decorated with scrolls on a chipped-ice ground, the central standard with internal gilt decoration, signed "Daum Nancy France", with the Cross of Lorraine.

35in (89cm) high

£6,500-7,500   LHA

A Morgan Colt iron eight-socket candlelight chandelier, with cut-out figures.

27.75in (70cm) diam

£2,000-2,500   DRA

A Muller Frères cameo glass chandelier, with orange and brown mottled glass bowl and shades, in a wrought-iron frame with fruiting vines, shades marked "Muller Frères Luneville".

Muller Frères was established in Luneville, France in 1895. During the Art Nouveau period, it became one of the pre-eminent glass studios in France. It closed in 1933.

47in (119.5cm) high

£800-1,000   DRA

A 1930s Volmer aluminium and black laminate floor lamp, by Donald Desky, with drum-shaped paper shade.

Shade 18in (46cm) diam

£1,000-1,500   DRA

A Liberty & Co. copper wall mirror, by Archibald Knox, the frame repoussé-decorated with intertwined tendrils and Celtic knots, and set with four turquoise Ruskin pottery roundels.

c1900 *37in (93cm) high*

£5,000-6,000 **L&T**

A Liberty & Co. "Cymric" silver and enamel mirror, by Jessie M. King, silver hallmarked Birmingham, cast in low relief with flowers and foliage panels on a green and blue enamel ground, stamped marks.

1907 *13.75in (35.5cm) high*

£5,000-6,000 **WW**

A Liberty & Co. "Tudric" pewter vase, by Archibald Knox, with three buttressed legs and embossed with honesty leaves, stamped "made in England 09 7".

c1905 *11.5in (29cm) high*

£700-800 **DRA**

A Liberty & Co. "Cymric" silver and glass claret jug, by Archibald Knox, model no.2088, cast in low relief with Celtic entrelac panels, set with turquoise stones, stamped marks, silver hallmarked Birmingham.

1903 *12.5in (32cm) high*

£10,000-12,000 **WW**

A Liberty & Co. "Tudric" pewter and glass claret jug, by Archibald Knox, model no.0308, cast in low relief with berried, whiplash stems, with stamped marks.

12.25in (31cm) high

£3,000-4,000 **WW**

A Liberty & Co. "Cymric" silver four-piece tea and coffee service, by Archibald Knox, model no.5208, engraved with a crest, silver hallmarked Birmingham.

1902 *Coffee pot 7in (18cm) high 24oz*

£1,800-2,200 **DN**

A Liberty & Co "Cymric" silver christening cup, by Oliver Baker, mounted with a band of Mexican opals, the handle surmounted with a turquoise cabochon stamped marks, "L & Co", hallmarked Birmingham.

1900 *3.25in (8.5cm) high*

£1,000-1,500 **WW**

A pair of Liberty & Co. "Tudric" pewter candlesticks, by Archibald Knox, each circular sconce supported by three shaped supports, the circular base with cast foliate decoration, underside stamped "0223, Tudric".

c1905 *9in (23cm) high*

£3,000-4,000 **L&T**

A set of six Liberty & Co "Cymric" silver and enamel cake forks, by Archibald Knox, enamelled in blue and green with honesty terminals, in fitted case, stamped marks, silver hallmarked Birmingham.

1902

£600-800 **WW**

A Tiffany & Co. silver water jug, with hand-hammered finish, and applied handle.

1877   *8in (20cm) high 26.9oz*

£3,500-4,500   **LHA**

A Tiffany & Co. silver-gilt water jug, with all-over woven pattern, and dual serpent applied handle.

7.75in (19.5cm) high 31.9oz

£3,500-4,500   **LHA**

An Aesthetic Movement Tiffany & Co. silver and mixed metal jug, with hammered surface, decorated as a pool with three copper carp and two copper and brass dragonflies above, with various marks, base monogrammed and dated "Xmas 1880".

Provenance: This jug was given as a Christmas present to a member of the Young family, who were friends with the Tiffany family. It has been in their family ever since.

1880   *7.25in (18.5cm) high 27oz*

£35,000-40,000   **SK**

A pair of Tiffany & Co. brass ewers, with incised Classical decoration, stamp marked.

14.5in (37cm) high

£250-350   **DRA**

A Tiffany & Co. silver tankard, with flat lid with pierced thumbpiece, with two horizontal applied bands of rocaille C-scroll cartouches with flower heads and diapering, lid engraved with presentation monograms.

1875-91   *8.25in (21cm) high 33oz*

£1,200-1,800   **SK**

A Tiffany & Co. silver centre-bowl, pattern no.4383, with ruffled rim over the two tiger-form handles, the whole cast with ferns and flowers.

1875   *14.75in (37.5cm) wide 43oz*

£6,500-7,500   **LHA**

A Tiffany & Co. silver chamberstick, of handled heart form having floral repoussé-decoration, with conical snuffer.

1886   *10.5in (27cm) long 7.6oz*

£300-400   **LHA**

A Tiffany Studios "Grapevine" bronze and slag glass desk set, including a pen tray, rocker blotter, stamp box, inkwell, and blotter ends, all pieces stamped "Tiffany Studios New York".

£900-1,100   **POOK**

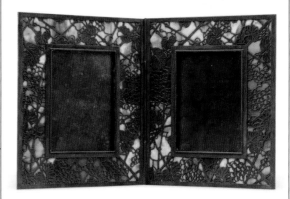

A Tiffany Studios "Grapevine" bronze and slag glass double picture frame, set with striated and mottled green glass with bronze overlay of grapevines, both parts signed "Tiffany Studios New York", no."5" and "6".

15in (38cm) high

£5,000-6,000   **JDJ**

ESSENTIAL REFERENCE - GEORG JENSEN

Georg Jensen (1866-1935) was one of the most important silversmiths of the 20thC. He adhered to the principals of the Arts and Crafts movement.

● From 1880 he trained as a goldsmith in Copenhagen.
● He studied sculpture at the Royal Academy of Fine Arts, Copenhagen, graduating in 1892.
● In 1898 he started a small porcelain factory, which failed.
● He then travelled extensively in France and Italy.
● From 1901 he worked as a silversmith with the master Mogens Ballin.
● He opened his own silver and jewellery workshop in 1904.
● In 1907, he began his association with the painter Johan Rohde (1856-1935), with whom he evolved the simple, striking style that was to make him famous.
● Jensen's tea wares typically have graceful curves, decorated finials and elongated handles.
● His vessels often have the famous Jensen satiny surface, produced by annealing the piece, immersing it in sulphuric acid, and then buffing it, allowing slight oxidisation to remain.
● Some of the early silver, and most of the early jewellery is Art Nouveau in style.
● By the end of the 1920's he had retail outlets in New York, Paris, London, Berlin and Stockholm.
● Many of his designs are still produced today. The Georg Jensen company now has branches all over the world.

A four-piece Georg Jensen "Magnolia Blossom" silver and ivory tea and coffee service, each with applied stylised blossom finials, all with stamped marks, numbered "2D".

c1925-32   *Coffee pot 7.5in (19cm) high*
£6,000-7,000   L&T

A pair of Georg Jensen silver sugar bowls, the overhead handle with moulded blossoms to the bases, the undersides with maker's marks and silver hallmarks, model no. "235 A".

1945-77   *3in (7.5cm) high 6.5oz*
£3,500-4,500   DOR

A Georg Jensen silver "Blossom" gravy boat and ladle, both monogrammed, marked "Dessin GI 825 S Sterling Denmark 177", with Georg Jensen crown mark, ladle marked "141 GI Denmark Sterling".

1925-32   *Gravy boat 8.25in (21cm) long*
£2,000-2,500   DRA

A Georg Jensen silver bowl, with leaf and berry stem.

10in (25.5cm) diam 38.4oz
£3,500-4,500   POOK

A Georg Jensen silver "Blossom" cream pitcher and covered sugar bowl, both stamped "Georg Jensen Denmark Sterling".

Cream pitcher 3.75in (9.5cm) high
£700-900   DRA

A Georg Jensen silver and amber-mounted box, on a foliate-form stand above hand-chased leaf decoration, the body of square lobed form raised on citron feet.

c1930   *5.25in (13cm) high*
    12.9oz
£4,500-5,500   LHA

A Georg Jensen silver tea service, designed by Georg Jensen, with ivory handles.

1925-1932
Teapot 7in (18cm) high
£1,200-1,800   LHA

A Roycroft hammered copper cylindrical vase, by Walter Jennings, with silver overlay, with Orb & Cross and Jennings two-dot mark.

6.5in (16cm) high

£1,500-2,000   DRA

A Roycroft hammered copper vase, with collared and riveted base, with Orb & Cross mark.

11in (28cm) high

£2,000-2,500   DRA

A Roycroft hammered copper "American Beauty" vase, stamped Orb & Cross mark, mild wear to original patina.

1910-15   21in (53cm) high

£1,500-2,000   DRA

A Roycroft copper "Ali Baba" vase, covered in a fine and unusual verdigris patina, with Orb & Cross mark.

16in (40.5cm) high

£1,200-1,800   DRA

A Roycroft hammered copper cylindrical vase, embossed with quatrefoils below a verdigris band of contrasting hammering, with Orb & Cross mark.

10in (25.5cm) high

£1,000-1,500   DRA

A pair of early Roycroft hammered copper candle sconces, of organic design, stamped with early Orb & Cross marks.

13in (33.5cm) high

£1,200-1,800   DRA

A pair of Roycroft hammered copper tall "strap" candlesticks, with Orb & Cross marks.

12in (30.5cm) high

£2,500-3,000   DRA

An early Roycroft hammered copper fernery/jardinière, on brass ball feet, incised with dogwood branches, stamped with early Orb & Cross mark.

1910-15   7.25in (18.5cm) high

£2,000-3,000   DRA

A Roycroft hammered copper cigarette box, with applied brass-washed pull and handles in a dogwood pattern, the base with unusual verdigris patina, with original cedar lining, with Orb & Cross mark.

10in (25.5cm) wide

£1,500-2,000   DRA

A Roycroft hammered copper desk set, designed by Walter Jennings, with Italian polychrome enamel, comprising bookends, letter-holder, pen tray and letter-opener, all with Orb & Cross marks except letter-opener.

£2,000-3,000   DRA

DECORATIVE ARTS

A WMF pewter-mounted wine jug, with tapering green glass body, the mounts cast with Art Nouveau maidens and flowering whiplash foliage, with stamped marks.

c1910 *17in (43cm) high*
£1,000-1,500 **L&T**

A pair of WMF plated candlesticks, stamped factory marks.

WMF (Württembergische Metallwarenfabrik) was founded in 1880 in Germany.

c1910 *11in (28cm) high*
£1,000-1,500 **L&T**

A pair of WMF plated pewter vases, the open-bottomed bodies with twin handles flanking a lady wearing a long dress, stamped.

14in (36cm) high
£2,000-2,500 **SWO**

A WMF silver-plated jardinière, model no.85, the original clear-glass liner with a cut pattern, featuring a partially moulded amorous couple and a floral garland at the front, with impressed factory marks.

c1900 *21in (53cm) long*
£4,000-5,000 **DOR**

A WMF silver-plated four-arm girandole, the clear glass cup decorated with a cut pattern, marked on the underside.

c1900-5 *18in (45.5cm) high*
£2,200-2,800 **DOR**

A WMF silver-plated wine cooler, model no.112, the shell-shaped bowl decorated with raised foliate motifs and a moulded mermaid and lizard, impressed factory marks to the underside.

c1900-5 *13in (33.5cm) high*
£1,500-2,000 **DOR**

A WMF silver-plated comport, model no.246, cast as an Art Nouveau winged maiden, the dish formed as lily pads and flowers with tendril base, stamped and cast marks.

c1900 *8in (20cm) high*
£800-1,200 **L&T**

A pair of WMF wine ewers, model no.138D, decorated in relief with floral motifs, with moulded mermaid handles, curved lancet-leaf finials, and with distributor's marks.

c1905 *15in (38cm) high*
£2,000-2,500 **DOR**

A WMF brass and copper tea service, comprising a spirit kettle-on-stand complete with burner, a teapot and a covered sugar bowl, with impressed marks to kettle, burner and sugar bowl.

c1910 *16in (40.5cm) high*
£250-350 **DA&H**

A Birmingham Guild of Handicraft silver pot and cover, circular bellied form, spot-hammered decoration, with a girdle of foliate decoration, on four bracket feet.

1904　　　*4.5in (11.5cm) diam 9oz*

£800-1,000　　　**WW**

A Boin-Taburet, Paris silver double sauce boat, the two sauce boats with intertwining handles and scalloped bowls, on fixed tray with conforming, decoration with two sterling silver liners.

12.25in (31cm) wide 69.7oz

£1,200-1,800　　　**LHA**

An Art Nouveau Christiania silver, enamel and carnelian-mounted ewer, by David Andersen, lid with small open wirework thumbpiece, the neck with openwork stylised leaftip, engraved at waist with organic roundels enamelled in mottled ochre and green.

c1876-88　　*10.25in (26cm) high 15oz*

£3,500-4,000　　　**SK**

An Arts and Crafts silver rose bowl, by F.S. Greenwood, London, with a chased foliate and floral girdle, with a pull-off wire-work grille and flower finial, on four bracket feet.

1912　　　*7.5in (19cm) diam 20oz*

£2,500-3,000　　　**WW**

A James Hardmann & Co silver-gilt chalice, Birmingham, in the manner of A.W.N. Pugin, with a border of fleur de lys, the knopped stem set with garnets, with stamped marks.

1867　　　*5in (12.5cm) high*

£1,200-1,800　　　**WW**

A W.H. Haseler & Co. Ltd. silver toast rack, by Archibald Knox, Birmingham, with entwined Celtic knot design, on squat bun feet.

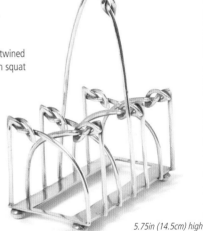

1906　　　*5.75in (14.5cm) high*

£7,000-8,000　　　**L&T**

A Reed & Barton "Diamond" pattern silver coffee service, by Gio Ponti, including coffee pot, cream pitcher, sugar dish and tray with black laminate centre, stamped "Reed & Barton Sterling", stamped "The Diamond".

Reed & Barton is a prominent silver maker, based in Taunton, Massachusetts since 1824.

Coffee pot 11.75in (30cm) high

£1,500-2,000　　　**DRA**

An Arts and Crafts twin-handled pedestal bowl, by Omar Ramsden, London, with applied cast nude figures entwined in plant growth, hammered effect, engraved "Omar Ramsden Me Fecit", maker's mark "Or".

1936　　　*7in (18cm) diam 14oz*

£2,500-3,000　　　**TEN**

A silvergilt commemorative cup, by Omar Ramsden, London, with a corded border, the bowl with a cast leaf calyx, an applied coat of arms and inscribed "IN COMMEMORATION OF ACCESSION OF KING GEORGE VI", "OMAR RAMSDEN ME FECIT".

1936　　　*7.5in (19cm) high 22oz*

£3,000-4,000　　　**WW**

A French Art Nouveau silver, copper, enamel and marble tazza, the plate with copper enamel roundel with three fish on a shaded blue and green ground accented with kelp, the rim embossed with stylised nautilus shells, on three slender curved uprights, on circular green marble foot.

8.25in (21cm) high

£3,000-4,000　　　**SK**

ESSENTIAL REFERENCE - JARVIE

The Jarvie Shop was established in Chicago in 1904 by Robert Riddle Jarvie (1865-1941).

● The company produced useful wares, such as bowls, vases, and trays, in simple, elegant shapes. They were sold through the Kalo Shop. Slender, elegant candlesticks were a speciality. These were named after Greek letters of the alphabet: Alpha, Beta, Lambda and Iota.

● Jarvie favoured copper, brass and bronze. Silver was used occasionally, notably on the "Paul Revere" tea sets.

● Some bronze pieces were treated with acids to achieve an antique-style green finish.

● Pieces are typically marked "Jarvie" in script. Some pieces are also inscribed with "The Jarvie Shop".

● The Jarvie Shop closed in 1917.

An Art Nouveau hammered copper tray, by Joseph Heinrichs, with silver bear heads and oak branches, stamped "Copper and Silver C160".

16.25in (41cm) long

£5,000-6,000   DRA

A large Newlyn copper wall sconce, by John D. Mackenzie and P. Hodder, repoussé-hammered with a speared serpent in an apple tree, based on the Earth design by J.D. Mackenzie, etched marks.

16.5in (41.5cm) high

£2,000-2,500   WW

A Jarvie hammered copper card tray, with embossed and textured rim, with medium patina, signed "The Jarvie Shop".

6in (15cm) diam

£800-1,200   DRA

An Onondaga Metal Shops hammered copper cigarette box, with stamped mark.

7.5in (19cm) wide

£1,500-2,000   DRA

An Onondaga Metal Shops hammered copper tray, with raised spade design, with "OMS" stamp "110".

15in (38cm) diam

£3,000-4,000   DRA

A John Pearson repoussé copper charger, hammered to the well with three flying birds, the rim with foliate and roundel motif stamped "JP" monogram.

15.5in (39cm) diam

£1,000-1,500   WW

A Glasgow School patinated-copper and enamel hall mirror, hammered in relief with stylised flower heads decorated with red enamel.

22in (56cm) high

£4,000-5,000   WW

ESSENTIAL REFERENCE - ERNESTINE MILLS

Ernestine Mills (1871-1959) was a noted enameller and metalworker, as well as a fervent political activist and suffragette.

- She studied at the Slade School and the Royal College of Art, both in London, under the celebrated enamellist Alexander Fisher (1864-1936), who helped to revive the art during the Arts and Crafts period.
- In 1901 Mills joined the British Society of Women Artists (est. 1865). She served as its Acting President 1943-4.
- She exhibited at various exhibitions (including the prestigious Walker Gallery in Liverpool 61 times), and was featured in the influential magazine "The International Studio".
- She is known to have produced enamelled badges promoting the Votes for Women movement.

An Arts and Crafts enamel-mounted silver-plate jewellery casket, by Ernestine Mills, with enamelled roundel of an angel, the lid chased and embossed with hammered lobing, with flower finial centred by a baroque pearl, with purple fabric lining, signed "Ernestine Mills" and "EM".

6in (15cm) wide

£3,000-4,000   SK

An Arts and Crafts Scottish enamelled metal box and cover, the front enamelled with domed panel of a Pre-Raphaelite maiden before trees, the cover and sides stamped in low relief with flocks of flying birds.

4.75in (12cm) wide

£2,500-3,500   WW

A J.A. Henckels chromium-plated "Aeroplane" travelling cocktail bar, with screw-top flask, cocktail shaker with strainer, four "tot" cups, and funnel, four stirring spoons, the "wings" are removable hip flasks, the tail contains a corkscrew, stamped "DRGM 89438" and "J.A. Henckels, Twin Works, Solinsen, Germany".

c1930   12.5in (32cm) long

£4,000-5,000   L&T

A Bernard Rice's Sons silver-plated Skyscraper candlestick, by Louis W. Rice, with copper handle, stamped "Skyscraper Des. Pat. Pending Apollo EPNS Made by Bernard Rice's Sons Inc. 5270".

c1928   9in (22cm) high

£4,000-5,000   DRA

A Scottish Arts and Crafts brass wall mirror, the frame repoussé-decorated with fruiting vines and embellished with riveted strapwork, set with Ruskin pottery cabochons.

c1900   33in (84cm) wide

£1,000-1,500   L&T

A rare E. & J. Bass Company Art Deco silver-plated nine-piece cocktail set, by Elsa Tennhardt, comprising six glasses, shaker, ice bucket and tray, marked "E.&J.B Pat.Apld For".

c1928   Tray 23.25in (59cm) wide

£20,000-25,000   DRA

A Gothic Revival brass cross, attributed to the Artificers' Guild, engraved with the lamb of God and four evangelists, with enamelled turquoise detailing.

20in (51cm) high

£3,000-4,000   WW

A Glasgow School embossed brass square planter, attributed to Margaret Gilmour.

8in (20cm) high

£300-400   DN

A gilded bronze figure of "Le Secret", by Pierre Félix-Masseau (French, 1869-1937), also known as Fix-Masseau, manufactured by Siot-Decauville, Paris, on a blue and grey marbled stone base, inscribed in the bronze, with foundry mark and impressed number "L 903".

The statue was designed in 1894. The 30in (76cm) high mahogany version with an ivory box is now in the Musée d'Orsay in Paris. A smaller version in bronze was cast by Siot-Decauville around 1900.

c1900   12in (30.5cm) high
£3,000-4,000   DOR

A bronze figure, of a mounted Cossack, by Vasili Grachev (Russian, 1831-1905), signed on the plinth "V. Grachev", foundry mark for F. Woerffel St. Petersburg.

14in (36cm) high
£12,000-14,000   DOR

A bronze figure of a female bather with panpipes, by Jean-Louis Gregoire (French, 1840-1890).

35.5in (90cm) high
£2,500-3,500   LHA

A French bronze figural sculpture of "Pêcheur", by Louis-Philippe Hébert (Canadian, 1850-1917), depicting a spear fisherman, with foundry mark of "R. Hohwiller, Paris", dated.

1916   26.75in (68cm) high
£10,000-15,000   LHA

A bronze group of "The Tsar's Falconer", by Eugène Alexandrovitsch Lanceray (Russian, 1848-1886), with dark brown patina, signed on the plinth "E. Lanceray", with foundry mark for Shtangel.

19in (48cm) high
£20,000-25,000   DOR

A bronze sculpture of an egret, by Jules Moigniez (French, 1835-1894), on naturalistic oval base, with raised foliage.

21.75in (54.5cm) high
£1,200-1,800   LHA

A bronze figure of seated Mercury, after Marius Pierre Montagne (French, 1828-1879), with medium brown patina, on pivoting circular base, inscribed "Montagne".

17.25in (44cm) high
£2,000-2,500   FRE

A late 19thC Russian bronze sculptural troika group, by E.Nahcepe (Austrian, 19thC), with possible foundry mark for "H.Wtahre".

20.75in (52.5cm) long
£12,000-14,000   LHA

A French bronze group of "Hebe on an Eagle", by Jules Pierre Roulleau (French, 1855-1895), on a square rouge marble plinth base.

26.5in (67cm) high
£6,000-7,000   LHA

A bronze figure group of "Ariadne on the Panther", on marble socle with overlaid coat of arms and the date "D. N 29. MAI 1839", one character missing.

1839   14in (36cm) high
£6,000-7,000   DOR

ESSENTIAL REFERENCE - FRANZ BERGMAN

Franz Xavier Bergman (1861-1936) was a Viennese sculptor, who created numerous colourful cold-painted bronze figures. His father, also Franz Bergman (1838–1894), founded a small bronze factory in Vienna in 1860. Franz Xavier inherited the company and opened a new foundry in 1900.

● Bergman created numerous figures, including Oriental and animal subjects, and erotic forms of naked young women. Other bronzes were based on designs by Franz Bergman, the elder.

● Bergman bronzes are usually marked with a "B" in a vase motif. Some are marked "Geschützt".

● His more erotic pieces were marked "Nam Greb" ("Bergman" in reverse).

A gilded and cold-painted bronze figure of a woman and her servant, by Franz Bergman, on a bowl-shaped marble base, hinged to lift the cloth concealing the woman's naked body, inscribed "Nam Greb", stamped amphora mark.

c1900
£7,000-8,000

12in (30.5cm) high
DOR

A cold-painted bronze figure of Cleopatra, by Franz Bergman, the semi-nude figure reclining on a chaise, holding an asp to her breast, signed "Nam Greb" with Amphora mark.

9.5in (24cm) long
£3,000-4,000   **FRE**

A large cold-painted bronze figural boudoir lamp formed as a mosque with a minaret, by Franz Bergman, with coloured glass window, with impressed amphora mark, electrified.

29in (73.5cm) high
£10,000-15,000   **SK**

A cold-painted bronze figural group of a Bedouin trader drinking coffee, by Franz Bergman.

3.5in (9cm) high
£750-850   **LHA**

A cold-painted bronze model of an elephant, by Franz Bergman, stamped "Geschützt 3412", with Bergman vase stamp.

9in (23cm) high
£8,000-10,000   **H&L**

A cold-painted bronze figure of a seated blackamoor playing a harp, by Franz Bergman, stamped with "B" within a vase twice, "3412" and "Geschützt".

9in (23cm) high
£2,000-2,500   **WW**

A cold-painted bronze figure of an Arab boy, by Franz Bergman, stamped "Geschützt" and numbered "3063".

8in (20cm) high
£1,000-1,500   **GORL**

A cold-painted bronze figure group of "Bedhouin in a Tent", by Franz Bergman, with many firm-marks.

c1900   *17in (43cm) high*
£7,500-8,500   **DOR**

A cold-painted bronze figure of a Native American warrior on horseback, by Franz Bergman, on a plain rectangular base, with amphora mark and stamped "GESCHÜTZT" and "3605".

12.5in (32cm) long
£3,000-4,000   **FRE**

DECORATIVE ARTS

A bronze figure "Seated Nude II", by Lucien Alliot (French, 1877-1956).
c1925   *15.5in (39cm) long*
£1,500-2,000   **LHA**

A French silvered- and cold-painted bronze figure of "The Fan Dancer", by Marcel Bouraine (French, 1886-1948) inscribed "Bouraine" and "Etling, Paris".
Bronze 17in (43cm) high
£3,000-4,000   **LHA**

A silvered- and gilt-bronze figure of a naked female dancer, by Demêtre H. Chiparus (Romanian, 1888-1950), on an onyx base, with incised signature.
19in (48cm) high
£6,000-7,000   **DN**

A cold-painted bronze figure of "Phoenician Dancer", by Demêtre H. Chiparus, signed "D.H. Chiparus".

c1926   *17in (43cm) high*
£5,500-6,500   **LHA**

A French bronze figure of "Crimean Dancer", by Claire Jeanne Robert Colinet (Belgian, 1880-1950), signed "C. J. Colinet", stamped "EL3".
c1925   *17in (43cm) high*
£5,000-6,000   **LHA**

A French bronze figure of "Theban Dancer", by Claire Jeanne Roberte Colinet (Belgian, 1880-1950), on a rectangular marble base, inscribed "Cl. J.R. Colinet".
22in (56cm) wide
£4,500-5,500   **LHA**

A patinated- and cold-painted bronze figure of "Egyptian Dancer", by Claire Jeanne Roberte Colinet, with cast signature "Cl. J R Colinet", on a variegated marble socle.
Figure 13in (33.5cm) high
£3,000-4,000   **SWO**

A silvered-bronze figure of a seated nude, by Maurice Guiraud-Rivière (French, 1881-1938), with Etling Paris foundry mark.
c1922   *14.5in (37cm) long*
£2,000-2,500   **LHA**

An American Bacchante patinated-bronze flower holder, by Maude Sherwood Jewett (American, 1873-1953), signed "Maude S. Jewett" and dated illegibly, impressed "Gorham Co. Founders OFAL".
10.5in (27cm) high
£4,000-5,000   **LHA**

A bronze figure, by Pierre La Faguays (French, 1870-1938), depicting an Art Deco girl with marionettes, the marble base inscribed "La Faguays".

bronze 15in (38cm) high

£3,500-4,500   LHA

A silvered bronze female dancer, by Josef Lorenzl (Austrian, 1892-1950), signed "Lorenzl", on an onyx base.

10in (25.5cm) high

£1,500-2,500   TEN

ESSENTIAL REFERENCE - LORENZL

Josef Lorenzl (1892-1950) was a popular and prolific Austrian Art Deco sculptor.

● His early 1920s pieces are more conventional in form and dress than the later sculptures he is better known for. Many are cold-painted.

● By the end of the 1920s his style had evolved. Figures (typically naked female dancers) were elongated, and often balanced precariously on tiptoe on top of an onyx plinth.

● Most figures are made from patinated bronze, with a silvered or gilt finish.

● They are usually signed with an impressed signature.

● He also designed ceramic figures for Goldscheider.

An Austrian cold-painted bronze figure of "Chinese Pheasant", by Lorenzl, depicting a standing female, her cape painted with exotic birds.

c1928   15in (38cm) high

£2,500-3,500   LHA

A cold-painted bronze figure of a dancer, by Josef Lorenzl, on an onyx socle, impressed "Lorenzl, Made in Austria".

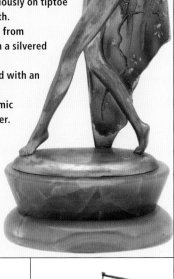

8.25in (21cm) high

£1,500-2,000   SWO

An Austrian bronze figural group of "Erotische Darstellung mit Frauenakt und Rokokodame " (Erotic depiction of a nude woman and a woman in a ball gown), by Heinrich Karl Scholz (Austrian, 1880-1937).

c1919   11.75in (30cm) high

£800-1,200   LHA

An Austrian bronze figure of a woman in a swimsuit, by Bruno Tuch.

c1925   13in (33.5cm) high

£1,000-1,500   LHA

An Art Deco silvered- and brown-patinated bronze figure of a female archer, by Bruno Zach (German, 1891-1935), signed "Zach", on a green onyx plinth.

15in (38cm) high

£2,500-3,000   TOV

A bronze, ivory and onyx figure of a draped woman, by Bessie Tough Callender (American, 1889-1951).

c1930 12.25in (31cm) high

£4,500-5,500 LHA

A patinated bronze and ivory figure of Pierrot, by Demêtre H. Chiparus (Romanian, 1888-1947), signed "D.H. Chiparus", damages.

c1928 12in (30.5cm) high

£1,500-2,500 L&T

A French bronze and ivory figure of a dancer, by Paul Philippe (French, 1870-1930).

c1925 13in (33.5cm) high

£7,000-8,000 LHA

A pair of bronze and ivory figures of "Hoop Girl" and "Sonny Boy", by Ferdinand Preiss (German, 1882-1943), on marble bases, etched "F Preiss".

8in (20cm) high

£6,500-7,500 WW

A marble, gilt-bronze and ivory figural group of "The Spring", by Ferdinand Preiss, depicting a standing Classical maiden before a fountain with grotesque mask.

6.5in (16cm) high

£4,500-5,500 LHA

A pair of gilt-bronze and ivory figures "Pierrot" and "Pierrette", by Peter Tereszczuk (Austrian, 1875-1963), on onyx bases, minor damages.

c1900 12in (30.5cm) high

£10,000-15,000 DOR

ESSENTIAL REFERENCE - FERDINAND PREISS

(Johann Philipp) Ferdinand Preiss (1882-1943) was born in Germany and studied sculpture in Paris. He is best known for the Art Deco chryselephantine (bronze and ivory) figures he produced from c1930.

- **He founded Preiss & Kassler with Walter Kassler in Berlin in 1906.**
- **Preiss' favourite subjects were sporting figures, children and dancers. He also made portraits of celebrities, such as pilot Amy Johnson.**
- **Over 90 models (including clocks) are recorded.**
- **Most are signed, either with a full signature or "PK" (Preiss & Kassler).**
- **Preiss & Kassler closed in 1943 after his death.**

A cold-painted bronze and ivory figure of "Fisher Boy", by Ferdinand Preiss, no.1229, with impressed Preiss Kassler logo, on a stepped onyx base signed "F Preiss".

12in (30.5cm) high

£4,500-5,500 TEN

A gilt bronze and ivory figure of a scantily clad maiden, by George Wagner (1915-1963), on a green marble plinth, with cast foundry marks "Akt Ges v H.Gladenbeck & Sohn, Berlin D 5013", plinth etched "G. Wagner".

c1910 11in (28cm) high

£4,000-5,000 L&T

A French silver and ivory figure of "Mysterious and Veiled 'Nature' Uncovering Herself Before Science", by Louis-Ernest Barrias (French, 1841-1905), made by Susse Frères foundry, part gilt, mounted with lapis lazuli accents, signed, bearing French .950 silver hallmarks, on porphyry base.

c1893-1908 16in (40.5cm) high

£30,000-40,000 SK

One of a pair of Arts and Crafts wool hangings, attributed to George Faulkner Armitage for Arthur H. Lee & Sons, woven with an allover design of flowering lilies and foliage on a deep blue ground.

c1900   97in (246cm) long
£2,500-3,500 pair   L&T

A printed cotton velvet tapestry, by Ruth Reeves for W. & J. Sloane, signed "Ruth Reeves" within print.

c1930   90in (229cm) long
£6,500-7,500   DRA

A silk embroidered "Faith" panel, by N. Victoria Wade, after a design by Sir Edward Coley Burne-Jones, depicting a Classical figure in a niche, in ebonised wood frame.

20in (51cm) high
£4,000-5,000   WW

A rare area rug, by Henry Varnum Poor, with stylised floral pattern in shades of purple, green and blue, woven "HVP" cypher.

71.5in (182cm) long
£2,500-3,500   DRA

A French ormolu inkstand, by Gustave Frédéric Michel (French, 1851-1924), modelled as two men wrestling on a shell, signed "G. MICHEL", with foundry seal "SIOT-PARIS".

16in (40.5cm) wide
£800-1,200   FRE

A silver and ivory desk seal carved as a girl, signed "E. Thomasson".

c1900   5.25in (13cm) high
£600-700   SWO

A pietra dura plaque with butterflies in mixed hardstone, by Richard Blow for Montici, in gilded frame, inlaid "M".

Plaque 9.25in (23.5cm) wide
£2,500-3,500   DRA

A Spartan Bluebird radio, by Walter Dorwin Teague, with polished chrome bands and ebonised ball feet, on blue glass base, with "Spartan" decal.

15in (38cm) high
£2,500-3,000   DRA

A pastel on paper design of a Pre-Raphaelite woman, by William De Morgan, in later frame, paper label to reverse image.

15in (38cm) high
£7,000-8,000   WW

MODERN DESIGN MARKET

The most explosive area in terms of demand, with the possible exception of the Chinese market, is without doubt furniture and accessories produced after World War II. The market has been driven by the influence of interior designers and modern homes magazines, and fed by the quantity of items available. While arguably an urban collecting area, the market is international and attracts a wide range of collectors.

The new breed of designer, who started working after World War II, was excited by the possibilities of new materials and the demands of an enthusiastic consumer class. Designers such as Charles and Ray Eames in the US said their mission was "getting the most of the best to the greatest number of people for the least amount of money".

Whether it is studio work from craftsmen such as George Nakashima, Paul Evans and Wharton Esherick, ceramics by Gertrude and Otto Natzler, Beatrice Wood and Peter Voulkos, or metalwork by Albert Paley, there is something in this area to suit all tastes and pockets. This section also covers furniture by interior designers including Tommi Parzinger, James Mont and Paul Laszlo, who were somewhat overlooked in the past.

While other established collecting areas may have struggled in the last few years, the interest in, and prices for, Post-War objects has, in many cases, quadrupled. Many pieces are found in large numbers and are consequently relatively affordable, making this area accessible to younger buyers. The choice of styles is also a major attraction. Many buyers favour the "soft modernism" of Vladimir Kagan and Arne Jacobsen, while others have started to buy and invest in 1960s plastic and Postmodernism by designers such as Joe Colombo and Ettore Sottsass.

Glass from the 20thC greats – the designers and factories of Scandinavia, Murano and Czechoslovakia (now the Czech Republic) – continue to sell really well. Buyers like the vibrant colours and modern forms. Big names are another plus factor. Look out for the Murano factories Barovier, Venini and Seguso, and designers such as Fulvio Bianconi and Dino Martens.

A newcomer to the growing 20thC glass stable is Post-War Czech glass. It's arguable that this vast, recently reappraised area is at the stage Murano glass was three decades ago. There's plenty of room for growth in both understanding and values. Currently, the low end of the market (£20-250) is the most populated, as collectors get to grips with "new" designs, designers, and factories. Meanwhile unique landmark studio works by greats such as František Vízner and Stanislav Libenský fetch the largest and most stable sums. It will be interesting to see how the vast middle market separates out over the next few years as collectors learn more and new discoveries are made.

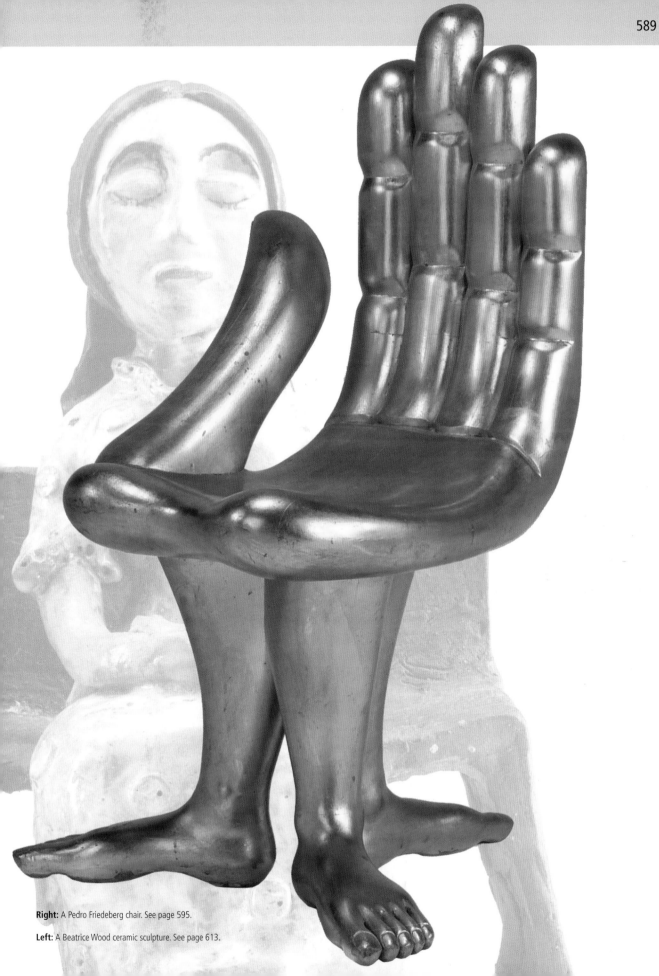

Right: A Pedro Friedeberg chair. See page 595.

Left: A Beatrice Wood ceramic sculpture. See page 613.

An Alvar Aalto "Tank" chair, upholstered in bouclé fabric on cantilevered laminated birch frame.

34in (87cm) high

£2,500-3,000　　　　　　　　**DRA**

A Jacques Adnet four-shelf open bookcase, with stitched black leather frames integrated with enamelled steel and brass hardware, and architectural laminate surfaces.

59in (150cm) high

£6,500-7,500　　　　　　　　**DRA**

A Jacques Adnet daybed, covered in stitched black leather with brass hardware and two bolster cushions.

75in (191cm) long

£6,500-7,500　　　　　　　　**DRA**

A pair of Jacques Adnet armchairs, with tufted and stitched black leather upholstery on faux bamboo brass legs.

35.5in (90cm) high

£6,000-7,000　　　　　　　　**DRA**

A R.&Y. Augousti shagreen console table.

84in (213cm) long

£2,200-2,800　　　　　　　　**DRA**

Judith Picks: Ron Arad sofa

I believe Ron Arad (b.1951) is one of the most influential designer-artists of our time. Constantly experimenting with technology and materials to feed the versatile nature of his work, he has produced an outstanding array of innovative objects over the past 25 years, from his "Well-tempered chair", made from salvaged bent sheet steel, to a one-off "tree" light on a concrete base.

Idiosyncratic and surprising, and also very beautiful, Arad's designs communicate the joy of invention, pleasure and humour.

This colourful "Big Easy" sofa, designed in 1988, makes a bold sculptural statement.

The prices for his pieces used to be a few hundred pounds but, as you can see, quality wins out, and they can now fetch several thousand.

A Ron Arad "Big Easy" sofa, upholstered in red wool.

72in (183cm) wide

£1,500-2,000　　　　　　　　**DRA**

An Edgar Bartolucci and Jack Walheim coffee table, with interchangeable and reversible panels to top within a birch frame, on iron legs.

One of seven originally made.

c1950   *48in (122cm) long*

£2,200-2,800   **DRA**

A pair of Milo Baughman and Thayer Coggin polished steel lounge chairs, with gold chenille upholstery.

30in (76cm) high

£2,500-3,500   **DRA**

A set of four Mario Bellini "Cab" armchairs, for Cassina, upholstered in stitched white leather, embossed Cassina mark.

32in (81cm) high

£1,200-1,800   **DRA**

A Richard Blow travertine-top coffee table, for Montici, with inlaid triangles in mixed hardstones, on walnut frame, inlaid "M".

28.5in (72cm) wide

£2,500-3,000   **DRA**

An Osvaldo Borsani elliptical dining table, with book-matched cherry top on bronze-clad splayed steel base.

77in (196cm) diam

£1,500-2,000   **DRA**

A Mark Brazier-Jones salvaged steel robot table, the square black granite top with canted edges above three "hinged" legs, with inset glass lights, with an adjustable hinged arm with further granite tier above.

c1990   *48in (122cm) high*

£1,200-1,800   **L&T**

A Marcel Breuer birch plywood desk chair.

33in (84cm) high

£2,000-3,000   **DRA**

A large Wendell Castle wall-hanging mirror, with sharp-angled frame, signed "Castle 96".

1996   *88in (224cm) high*

£5,500-6,500   **DRA**

A Wendell Castle table, with Macassar ebony top on mottled green, gold, and silver pedestal base, signed "Castle 97".

1997   *30in (76cm) high*

£2,500-3,000   **DRA**

ESSENTIAL REFERENCE - WENDELL CASTLE

Wendell Castle (1932-) studied sculpture at the University of Kansas. During the 1960s he became known for his highly sculptural furniture.

- **He has worked with moulded plastic and fibreglass, resulting in the "Castle" and "Molar" series (both 1969), as well as stacked and laminated woods and steel.**
- **In 1980 he founded The Wendell Castle Workshop to teach craftsmanship in wood.**
- **From the 1980s, many designs were inspired by Art Deco.**
- **Many of his pieces are unique commissions or limited editions of eight.**

A Norman Cherner "Pretzel" chair, for Plycraft, with bent walnut frame and grey vinyl seat pad.

A rare transitional piece between George Nelson's Pretzel chair and the later Plycraft bentwood chairs. Only a few examples are known.

c1955   *30.25in (77cm) high*

£1,500-2,000   **DRA**

A Michael Coffey "Pegasus" coffee table, in sculpted and laminated walnut with plexiglass support, carved "M. Coffey".

55in (140cm) long

£3,500-4,000   **DRA**

A Wendell Castle walnut coffee table, with tapering scalloped top on stack-laminated and cantilevered corkscrew base, signed "W. Castle 80".

1980   *53in (135cm) long*

£15,000-20,000   **DRA**

Judith Picks

I met Jon Brooks (the first pupil of one of my furniture design heroes, Wendell Castle) at a recent "Chairs" symposium at the Museum of Contemporary Art in Jacksonville, Florida.

He was inspirational and I would love to own one of his chairs, inspired by, and constructed from, the trunks and branches of trees surrounding his New Boston, New Hampshire, USA home.

As he himself says, "A chair is the only object of furniture you become physically involved with... It's also the most complicated piece to make precisely because it makes all these demands. You're limited to the shape of the human body and there are a lot of givens. I've held a fascination for making a chair which physically involves the viewer.".

A Jon Brooks carved black walnut stool with curvilinear ridges, carved "JB 1969".

1969   *24.5in (62cm) high*

£2,000-2,500   **DRA**

A Joe Colombo "Tube" chair, for Flexform, of arcipiuma plastic with coated foam upholstery, steel and rubber clips, comprising four plastic cylinders upholstered in soft vinyl-covered polyurethane foam.

Joe Colombo's "Tube" chair was one of the most innovative seating solutions of the 20thC. The different-sized seating tubes could be joined together in a number of configurations, which gave the design an inherent functional flexibility, while also offering a degree of playful user interaction. Importantly, the upholstered tubes could also be placed inside each other for easy transportation. This was absolutely in tune with the increasingly youthful, casual and nomadic lifestyles of the late 1960s.

1969   *44in (112cm) long*

£6,000-7,000   **DRA**

A Dominique rosewood sideboard with book-matched top, two parchment-covered doors with brass-mounted pulls and escutcheons, and fitted interior.

79in (201cm) wide

£7,500-8,500 **DRA**

A Dominique secrétaire, with four parchment patchwork doors within wood frame, branded "Dominique Paris".

47in (119cm) wide

£7,500-8,500 **DRA**

A Dunbar trapezoidal side table, in bleached mahogany with inset glass mosaic top, with rectangular brass Dunbar tag.

22.75in (58cm) wide

£4,000-5,000 **DRA**

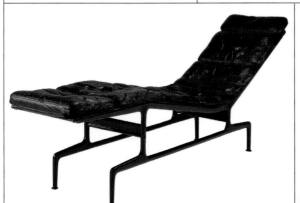

A Charles and Ray Eames "Billy Wilder" chaise lounge, for Herman Miller, in enamelled aluminium with black leather upholstery, with circular black and white Herman Miller tag.

77.5in (197cm) long

£1,200-1,800 **DRA**

A Charles Eames "ESU" eleven-drawer chest, for Herman Miller, in birch with multicoloured side and back panels.

47in (119cm) wide

£5,000-6,000 **DRA**

A Charles Eames first-generation "ESU" single-pedestal desk, for Herman Miller, with birch top and drawer fronts, zinc pulls, and multicoloured panels on angle-iron frame, with red, white and blue Herman Miller/Zeeland Michigan decal.

60in (152cm) long

£2,500-3,000 **DRA**

A Charles and Ray Eames "670"/"671" lounge chair and ottoman, for Herman Miller, with down-filled leather cushions on rosewood plywood frames, with Herman Miller circular tag.

Chair 33in (84cm) high

£2,000-2,500 **DRA**

A Wharton Esherick hammer-handle chair, with burgundy leather webbed seat.

30.25in (77cm) high

£8,000-12,000   **DRA**

ESSENTIAL REFERENCE - WHARTON ESHERICK

Wharton Esherick (1887-1970) was born in Philadelphia, PA, USA. He trained as a painter, but began creating furniture influenced by the Arts and Crafts movement in the late 1920s.

● By the 1930s he began to produce sculptural furniture, with very little surface decoration. At this time his work often featured sharp edges and crystalline forms, influenced by German Expressionism and Cubism. He is best known for the free-form curvilinear furniture he produced from the end of the decade.

● As well as furniture, he also designed interiors, including the Curtis Bok House, Radnor, PA, designed 1935–37, and his own Philadelphia studio, in Paoli, PA, which he worked on continually for 40 years. The studio is open to the public .

● In 1971, he was posthumously awarded the national Craftsmanship Medal by The American Institute of Architects.

A Wharton Esherick walnut buffet, with a sculpted top on curved solid base, with seven drawers flanked by two doors over blonde maple interior, signed "W.E. 1969".

1969   *117in (297cm) wide*

£200,000-250,000   **DRA**

Two of a set of four Paul Evans bronze patchwork and black leather dining chairs, on welded steel bases, signed "Paul Evans 70".

1970   *33in (85cm) high*

£4,000-5,000 set   **DRA**

A Paul Evans patinated and welded steel dining table, with plate-glass top, welded "PE 69".

1969   *96in (244cm) long*

£4,500-5,500   **DRA**

A Paul Evans sculpted bronze barrel chair, with original orange upholstery and swivel base.

33in (85cm) high

£6,000-7,000   **DRA**

A Paul Evans sculpted bronze dining table, with clip-corner rectangular plate-glass top on serpentine base, signed "PE 73".

1973   *82.75in (210cm) wide*

£6,000-7,000   **DRA**

A rare Paul Evans "Skyline" series sculpted steel and bronze dining table, with octagonal plate-glass top, signed "Paul Evans 70".

1970   *36in (91.5cm) wide*

£20,000-25,000   **DRA**

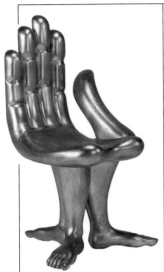

A Pedro Friedeberg "Hand Chair with Three Feet", with three-footed base and gilded finish, branded "Pedro Friedeberg".

Designed 1998   *35in (89cm) high*

£12,000-18,000   **DRA**

One of a pair of Garouste & Bonetti "Barbare" armless tall-back lounge chairs, of rounded metal barstock, with leather seats and two crystal circles atop each chair.

48in (122cm) high

£2,500-3,500 pair   **DRA**

A Goudji table, covered in thick, overlapping silver sheets held with silver nails, the arcaded sides with columnar angles surmounted by turreted capitals, each inlaid with Armour granite, front with an openwork panel moulded with a stag, set with rubies and framed with amphibolite, stamped "Sterling 925/"G"/Paris/Iranos".

Goudji Amashukeli was born in 1941 in Georgia, USSR. He moved to Moscow in 1964, where he became a member of the Union of Soviet Artists. In 1974 he settled in Paris. He became a French citizen in 1978, and a chevalier of the Ordre des Arts et des Lettres in 1986.

60in (152cm) wide

£9,000-11,000   **GORB**

A Pedro Friedeberg teak double dresser, for Urban Furniture Co., from the Swedish Guild Collection, with curved drawer fronts and sculpted exterior mounted legs.

78.5in (199cm) long

£2,000-2,500   **DRA**

A Klaus Grabe contoured slatted lounge chair in birch and plywood.

c1948   *63in (160cm) long*

£1,500-2,000   **DRA**

ESSENTIAL REFERENCE - PIERRE JEANNERET

Pierre Jeanneret (1896-1967) was a cousin of Le Corbusier (Charles-Édouard Jeanneret) and collaborated with him to produce numerous furniture and architectural designs.

- **He trained as an architect in Geneva.**
- **He went to work for Le Corbusier in Paris in 1922.**
- **With Charlotte Perriand, they designed a range of furniture including the "Basculant No. 301" chair (c1928) and the "B306" chaise longue (1928).**
- **He became a member of the UAM (Union des Artistes Modernes) in 1930. The furniture he designed with Le Corbusier and Perriand was shown at its first exhibition.**
- **Following World War II, he designed prefabricated housing with Jean Prouvé.**
- **From 1952 he worked with Le Corbusier on the urban plan and architecture for the city of Chandigarh in India.**

One of a pair of Pedro Friedeberg birch "Scissor" chairs, for Knoll, with webbed supports and red woven wool upholstery.

29.5in (75cm) high

£2,200-2,800 pair   **DRA**

One of a pair of Pierre Jeanneret teak armchairs, with woven cane seat and back, and fabric-upholstered seat pads (not shown).

26.5in (67cm) high

£3,500-4,000 pair   **DRA**

A rare Pierre Jeanneret single-pedestal desk, with burgundy leather inset to top, and open cubicles to back.

48in (122cm) wide

£5,500-6,500   **DRA**

A George Jouve quartered oak low table, the top with six tiles and three compartments, each with circular handles.

21.25in (54cm) wide

£4,000-5,000 DRA

A Finn Juhl "Judas" rosewood extension dining table, inlaid with silver buttons, with Illums Bohligus metal tag.

71in (180cm) wide

£2,200-2,800 DRA

A Finn Juhl double-pedestal "Diplomat" desk, for France & Son, in teak with brushed steel pulls, four locking drawers, and two pull-out shelves.

75in (191cm) wide

£3,000-4,000 DRA

A Vladimir Kagan contour rocker and ottoman, on sculpted walnut frames with beige fabric upholstery.

Chair 42in (107cm) long

£7,500-8,500 DRA

A Vladimir Kagan sculpted walnut dining table, for Dreyfuss, the boat-shaped top inset with glass tile panel surrounded by bronze trim, with pull-out extensions.

Closed 84.25in (214cm) long

£7,500-8,500 DRA

A set of four Vladimir Kagan sculpted walnut side chairs, for Kagan Dreyfuss, with black leather upholstery, branded "Kagan Dreyfuss New York".

36.5in (93cm) high

£6,000-7,000 DRA

A Vladimir Kagan serpentine sofa, upholstered in original Vladimir Kagan textured fabric on drum bases.

117in (297cm) long

£3,000-4,000 DRA

A Vladimir Kagan contour chair, in sculpted walnut with moss-green chenille upholstery.

39in (99cm) high

£5,000-6,000 DRA

ESSENTIAL REFERENCE - KNOLL

Hans Knoll (1914-1955), the son of German furniture maker Walter Knoll, founded his furniture company in New York City in 1937. In c1941 the company began producing modern furniture designed by Jens Risom.

- In 1943, Florence Schust (1917-), who had trained under Mies van der Rohe, was employed as an interior designer. Schust transformed the company, changing its style to a more international Modernism.
- She mixed woods and metals to great effect and added laminates as they came into fashion.
- In 1946 Florence and Hans married, and together founded Knoll Associates. The new company produced sculptural furniture by Eero Saarinen (who it commissioned to design the "Tulip" chair), Isamu Noguchi, Harry Bertoia and, from 1948, Mies van de Rohe.
- Florence Knoll oversaw all aspects of the company's image until her retirement as company President in 1960, and her later retirement as Director of Design in 1965.
- Today Knoll is one of the world's largest manufacturers of office furniture.

A Florence Knoll ten-drawer rosewood credenza, for Knoll, with finely grained marble top, with Knoll International label.

74.5in (189cm) long

£3,000-4,000   DRA

A Florence Knoll partners' desk, for Knoll, with rosewood top on chromed-steel pedestal with pencil drawers on both sides.

72in (183cm) long

£3,500-4,500   DRA

A Silas Kopf rosewood clock/cabinet, with marquetry inlays of springtime motifs depicting foliage and leaping frogs, with brass hands and German brass movement.

74.5in (189cm) high

£4,000-5,000   DRA

A cocktail table, in the style of Ibram Lassaw, with smoked plate-glass top over sculptural steel base in dark patinated finish.

60in (153cm) long

£3,500-4,500   DRA

A pair of Mogens Lassen sculpted solid teak stools, for K. Thomsen.

19.75in (50cm) high

£2,000-2,500   DRA

A Philip and Kelvin Laverne freeform bronze-clad coffee table, depicting Grecian figures on a raised and etched surface, with buttressed columnar legs, signed "Philip & Kelvin Laverne".

69in (175cm) long

£5,000-6,000   DRA

A Philip Laverne side table, with mottled and patinated metal finish, with Philip Laverne Collection paper label.

30.25in (76.5cm) diam

£3,000-4,000   DRA

A John Lewis purple-yellow cast-glass "Sphere" table, with textured top on three-wheeled base.
2003 *39in (99cm) diam*
£4,000-5,000 **DRA**

A John Lewis cast-glass "Glacier" coffee table, with textured top and white gold leaf accents to base.
2003 *59.5in (151cm) long*
£10,000-15,000 **DRA**

A Raymond Loewy "DF2000" eight-drawer valet chest, with red acrylic drawer fronts, in white laminate case, on castors, marked "BF2000 Made in France".
42in (107cm) high
£2,000-2,500 **DRA**

An Angelo Mangiarotti "T70" travertine dining table, with circular top over flared conical base.
47in (119cm) diam
£1,500-2,000 **DRA**

ESSENTIAL REFERENCE - JOHN LEWIS

John Lewis (1942-) was born in California, USA. He studied at the University of California, Berkeley, in the late 1960s, where he was taught by Professor Marvin Lipofsky.

● He initially worked with hot glass. From 1980, he began creating the cast-glass sculptures for which he is best known. For this he built a special furnace, which melted and poured glass.

● Lewis's work includes a wide range of cast-glass pieces, from decorative vessels to sculptural glass furniture and architectural installations. Pieces are typically solid and structural, often incorporating simple shapes.

● In 2000 his studio created the cast-glass used in the 168 empty chairs of the Oklahoma City Memorial Project.

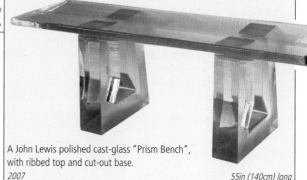

A John Lewis polished cast-glass "Prism Bench", with ribbed top and cut-out base.
2007 *55in (140cm) long*
£20,000-25,000 **DRA**

A Christian Liaigre coffee table/bench, for Holly Hunt, with maple top on contrasting oak legs, stamped "Christian Liaigre Holly Hunt".
59in (150cm) long
£2,000-2,500 **DRA**

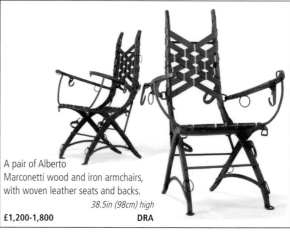

A pair of Alberto Marconetti wood and iron armchairs, with woven leather seats and backs.
38.5in (98cm) high
£1,200-1,800 **DRA**

MODERN DESIGN

An Alphonse Mattia whimsical architect's valet chair, of stained and painted wood, signed "Alphonse Mattia 1991 Westport MA KH".

1991   79in (201cm) high
£6,500-7,500   **DRA**

A Paul McCobb three-drawer maple dresser, with brass pulls.

36in (91.5cm) wide
£1,200-1,800   **DRA**

A Paul McCobb walnut dining table and six side chairs (not shown), for Calvin, with three extension leaves, chairs with Calvin paper labels.

Table closed 74.25in (189cm) long
£2,500-3,000 set   **DRA**

Judith Picks: Judy Kensley McKie

If I want to buy a piece of Modern classic furniture, I want to buy something firstly that I like, secondly that challenges my preconceptions, and thirdly that makes me smile. That is why I would choose the work of Judy Kensley McKie.

McKie is widely recognised as a premier figure in the American Studio Furniture movement. Her furniture occupies a singular position in the field and is particularly tactile. I challenge anyone who discovers a piece by her NOT to touch it! The work is infused with a lively awareness of Modernist and Contemporary art and

also of the approaches to design to be found in indigenous cultures throughout the world. Playfulness and power are summoned by her incorporation of sculptural, totemic animal forms.

A Judy Kensley McKie patinated bronze and glass "Serpent" side table, inscribed "15 of 16", each snake engraved "JKM 97" and "copyright".

1997   31in (79cm) high
£20,000-25,000   **DRA**

A Judy Kensley McKie patinated bronze "Jaguar" bench, inscribed "11 of 12, copyright, JKM 1992".

1992   57in (145cm) long
£45,000-55,000   **DRA**

A set of six Borge Mogensen oak dining chairs, for Fredericia Stolefabrik, with original leather seats.

28in (71cm) high
£2,000-3,000   **DRA**

MODERN DESIGN

A James Mont three-drawer dresser, in black enamel, with silver-leafed pulls, with branded mark.

46in (117cm) wide

£2,200-2,800   **DRA**

A pair of James Mont armless sleigh-shaped lounge chairs, with dark brown synthetic upholstery on cerused oak frames, one with James Mont paper label.

32.75in (83cm) high

£5,000-6,000   **DRA**

A set of eight George Nakashima walnut "Grass Seated" chairs.

27.5in (70cm) high

£7,500-8,500   **DRA**

A George Nakashima walnut "Conoid" dining table, with four rosewood keys on book-matched top, signed with client's name.

72in (183cm) long

£15,000-20,000   **DRA**

A George Nakashima figured walnut "Conoid" bench, with hickory spindles.

83in (211cm) long

£15,000-20,000   **DRA**

A set of three George Nakashima free-edge crotch walnut nesting tables, one with client's name.

Tallest 21.5in (55cm) wide

£6,500-7,500   **DRA**

A George Nakashima walnut seven-drawer tall chest, on planks, signed with client's name.

52.75in (134cm) high

£7,000-8,000   **DRA**

One of a pair of George Nakashima walnut "New" chairs, with hickory spindles and saddle seats.

36in (91cm) high

£2,500-3,000 pair   **DRA**

A George Nakashima walnut "Long Chair", with adjustable back and ivory-coloured cotton webbing.

60in (152cm) long

£10,000-15,000   **DRA**

Judith Picks: "Gluon"

Designed by Australian Marc Newson the "Gluon" chair displays a biomorphic shape which is typical of this designer's work.

Newson has been very influential in the establishment of a more playful strand of Post-Modernism in the 1990s. Personally, I think the "Gluon" chair looks fantastic – one of the most impressive "sculptural" chairs I've seen, and I tried it out when we photographed some of his designs for my "Chairs" book (Conran Octopus, 2009). Having eased myself down onto and back into it (it's quite a low chair, armless, and with a notably rounded profile to the seat and back) I instantly realised to stay on it would take a sense of balance far greater than one acquired from my sporadic evening classes in yoga – and then I made the huge mistake of slightly turning my head. Lying slightly concussed on an unforgiving metal floor (we shot it in a rather trendy converted warehouse) I realised that my small head movement had triggered a near-perfect, slapstick fall – sideways, down, and off the chair straight into a foetal position! How ironic! And how very Post-Modern!

A George Nelson rosewood "Thin Edge" double-chest, for Herman Miller, with eight drawers, porcelain pulls, on aluminium legs.

46.75in (119cm) wide
£2,200-2,800 DRA

A George Nelson "Coconut" chair, for Herman Miller, upholstered in royal blue vinyl.

41.5in (105cm) wide
£2,000-2,500 DRA

A Marc Newson "Gluon" chair and ottoman, upholstered in orange ultrasuede on swivel bases.

chair 35in (89cm) long
£3,000-4,000 DRA

An Isamu Noguchi coffee table, for Herman Miller, with shaped, pale yellow-green glass top over two-piece wooden base.

This is an early, first generation version of this table.

50in (127cm) long
£1,200-1,800 DRA

An Isamu Noguchi "Cyclone" dining table, for Knoll, with circular white laminate top on black enamelled base, with "Isamu Noguchi / Knoll Studio 1955" metal tag.

1955
43in (109cm) diam
£1,200-1,800 DRA

A John Nyquist sculpted black American walnut rocker, with dowelled and pinned joinery, and burgundy leather upholstery, carved "JN".

45in (114cm) high
£4,500-5,500 DRA

A Hovmand Olsen wall-hung rosewood server, with drop-front extension, and Hovmand Olsen foil label.

40.5in (103cm) wide
£1,500-2,000 DRA

A Pace executive double-pedestal desk, with burlwood and chromed-steel frame.

74in (188cm) wide

£1,500-2,000 DRA

An Albert Paley formed and fabricated steel pedestal dining table, with bevel-edged plate-glass top, stamped "Albert Paley 1996", with copyright.

1996 *53in (135cm) diam*

£18,000-22,000 DRA

A Verner Panton lounge chair, with orange wool upholstery, on ebonised ball feet.

42.5in (108cm) long

£1,500-2,000 DRA

ESSENTIAL REFERENCE - VERNER PANTON

Verner Panton (1926-1998) was a Danish architect and designer of Modern interiors, furniture, textiles, carpets and lighting. His style epitomises the 1960s.

- He worked for Arne Jacobsen between 1950 and 1952, before establishing his own studio in 1955.
- In 1955 he designed the cantilevered plywood "S"-chair in association with Thonet.
- His first solo project, designing the interior of the Kom-igen Inn on the Danish island of Fünen, was completed in 1958 and resulted in one of his most famous designs, the "Cone Chair". Along with the "Heart chair" (1959), the "Cone" was subsequently mass-produced by Plus-Linje.
- In 1960 he designed the world's first one-piece moulded plastic chair, the "Panton" chair. It was put into mass production in 1967 by Vitra in Switzerland and Herman Miller in the USA.

One of a set of four Verner Panton bentwood chairs, for Thonet, with red aniline-dyed finish, with Thonet paper labels.

33in (84cm) high

£7,000-8,000 set DRA

A Tommi Parzigner six-drawer maple chest, for Parzinger Originals, with brass pulls on curved legs, branded "Parzinger Originals".

70in (178cm) wide

£4,000-5,000 DRA

A Tommi Parzinger nine-drawer dresser, with etched-brass drop pulls and black lacquer finish.

95.25in (242cm) wide

£18,000-22,000 DRA

A Tommi Parzinger three-drawer chest, with etched-brass drop pulls and white lacquer finish.

47.75in (121cm) wide

£7,000-8,000 DRA

A pair of Tommi Parzinger two-drawer nightstands, with etched-brass drop pulls and black lacquer finish.

32in (81cm) wide

£10,000-15,000 DRA

A pair of Clifford Pascoe four-drawer birch dressers, for Pascoe Furniture, with recessed pulls.

c1938   *37.5in (95cm) wide*

£2,000-2,500   DRA

A Gio Ponti walnut writing desk, with two drawers.

A unique prototype produced for Ponti in the development of the "AP 1025" model, sold by the Altamira Company, New York.

c1953   *70in (178cm) wide*

£20,000-25,000   DRA

A set of ten Gio Ponti dark-stained oak dining chairs, with black leather upholstery.

36in (91.5cm) high

£2,000-2,500   DRA

A Phillip Lloyd Powell sculpted and chip-carved walnut seven-door credenza, with steel bolts and cleft slate top.

108in (274cm) long

£30,000-40,000   DRA

A mid- to late 1970s Phillip Lloyd Powell carved and painted front door.

This is the front door to Powell's own residence, on route 202, New Hope, PA, USA. The building has recently been demolished. The overall shape of the door, along with the many different layers of carving, show the influence his trips to India were to have on his designs, starting in the mid-1970s.

142in (361.5cm) high

£35,000-45,000   DRA

A Harvey Probber even-arm sofa, with royal blue ultrasuede upholstery on Lucite plank legs.

84.75in (215cm) long

£1,000-1,500   DRA

A Harvey Probber extension dining table, with corseted oak top on plank legs, and two leaves, stamped numbers to underside of table.

Closed 78.25in (199cm) long

£2,500-3,000   DRA

A Jean Prouvé oak full-size bed, with steel box spring.

76.5in (194cm) long

£3,000-4,000 **DRA**

A set of four Jean Prouvé "Standard" chairs, with enamelled-steel frames and bent plywood seats and backs.

32.25in (82cm) high

£15,000-25,000 **DRA**

A Jens Quistgaard aluminium, teak and suede open armchair, for Nissen Langaa, with swivel back, set within a tubular frame.

1966 *28.75in (73cm) high*

£1,500-2,000 **LHA**

A Carlos Riart rosewood rocker, for Knoll, upholstered in burgundy leather.

41.5in (105cm) high

£2,000-3,000 **DRA**

A Gerrit Rietveld parana pine and enamelled metal pew, made for the Hocksteen Church, Uithoorn, the Netherlands.

c1963 *86in (218cm) long*

£2,000-2,500 **DRA**

A T. H. Robsjohn-Gibbings dining room suite, for Widdicomb, comprising a drawleaf extension table and six upholstered side chairs, the table with rectangular top with two leaves.

Table 29in (74cm) high

£2,500-3,000 **LHA**

A rare T.H. Robsjohn-Gibbings side chair, for Widdicomb, with woven cotton webbings and sculpted birch frame on brass legs.

35in (89cm) high

£1,200-1,800 **DRA**

ESSENTIAL REFERENCE - T.H. ROBSJOHN-GIBBINGS

Terence Harold Robsjohn-Gibbings (1905–1976) was born in London, England. He became famous in America, which he moved to in 1930.

- After working as a salesman for an antiques dealer, he opened a showroom on Madison Avenue, New York in 1936. There he displayed pieces of furniture he had designed, based on drawings he had made at the British Museum.
- His designs featured Classical elements of Ancient Grecian and Art Deco design. He is best known for the Greek-style "Klismos" chair (1961).
- He disliked both Modernism and popular revival styles. He expressed this in satirical writings, such as "Goodbye, Mr. Chippendale" (1944).
- In 1948 he became the chief designer of the Widdicomb furniture company.
- In 1966 he moved permanently to Greece where he designed interiors for wealthy Athenians.

A T.H. Robsjohn-Gibbings chaise lounge, for Widdicomb, with original gold bouclé upholstery on walnut frame, with Widdicomb fabric label.

56in (142cm) long

£3,000-4,000   DRA

A T.H. Robsjohn-Gibbings armless sofa, for Widdicomb, in walnut with tufted fabric-upholstered cushions and webbed seat support, with Widdicomb fabric label.

90in (229cm) long

£3,000-4,000   DRA

A pair of T.H. Robsjohn-Gibbings two-tier "Klismos"-style walnut sofa tables, for Widdicomb, with Widdicomb decals and stencilled numbers.

32in (81cm) wide

£2,000-2,500   DRA

A T.H. Robsjohn-Gibbings "Mesa" freeform coffee table, for Widdicomb, with Widdicomb label, stamped "Sorrell" and numbers.

72in (183cm) long

£30,000-40,000   DRA

A Gilbert Rohde mahogany veneer "Paldao" desk, for Herman Miller, with leatherette-covered three-drawer pedestal and leg, with single pull-out shelf.

52in (132cm) wide

£1,500-2,000   DRA

A Gilbert Rohde "Paldao" four-door cabinet, for Herman Miller, with large etched-brass pulls, single shelf and interior shallow drawers, stencilled "4104".

66in (168cm) wide

£1,200-1,800   DRA

An Eliel Saarinen pedestal dining table, for Johnson Furniture, from the "Flexible Home Arrangements collection".

c1941   *52in (132cm) diam*

£4,500-5,500   DRA

A pair of Richard Schultz lounge chairs, by Knoll, in grey-enamelled metal with mesh and stitched leather seat covering.

54in (137cm) long

£1,500-2,000   DRA

MODERN DESIGN

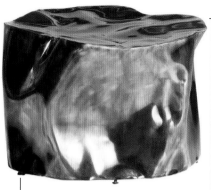

A Silas Seandel patinated bronze coffee table, with circular glass top (not shown), signed.

£2,500-3,500   DRA

A Karl Springer freeform coffee table, in solid brass with patinated finish, on adjustable feet.

56.5in (144cm) wide

£3,000-3,500   DRA

A Karl Springer brass, chrome and glass elliptical occasional table.

24in (61cm) high

£2,200-2,800   DRA

A pair of Philippe Starck lounge chairs, with black vinyl upholstery on fin-shaped aluminium front legs, stamped "Starck".

33.5in (85cm) high

£1,500-2,000   DRA

A Mies Van Der Rohe daybed, by Knoll, with tufted café-au-lait leather cushion and bolster on walnut and polished steel frame, with Knoll International factory tag.

78.5in (199cm) long

£2,000-2,500   DRA

Judith Picks: "Barcelona" chairs

Mies van der Rohe's stunningly Modern "MR90" or (as it's commonly known) "Barcelona" chair, is one of the brightest stars in the world of seating. Since it was designed in 1929, the "Barcelona" chair, or copies of it, can be seen everywhere, including in my "Chairs" book (Conran Octopus, 2009), and the foyer of our London offices where it shares floor space with Eileen Grey's "E-1057" tables.

Initially designed (by van der Rohe and his sadly less well-known partner, Lilly Reich) to furnish Germany's Pavilion at the 1929 International Exhibition, it has been mass-produced since 1953 by Knoll.

Classic colours for the removable seat and back cushions (now covered in bovine leather, rather than the original pigskin) are black, white and tan, although numerous other colours are available.

A pair of Mies van der Rohe "Barcelona" chairs, for Knoll International, with two rectangular cushions supported by leather straps attached to an X-form stainless steel frame.

Designed 1929   *30in (76cm) high*

£3,000-4,000   LHA

A pair of Mies van de Rohe "Barcelona" chairs, for Knoll, with chromed frames, the brown leather in very worn condition. .

Designed 1929   *38.5in (98cm) high*

£1,000-1,500   LHA

A Hans Wegner teak dining table set, for Fritz Hansen, model "FH-4103", comprising a circular dining table, and six matching chairs, maker's marks.

c1960   *Table 47.25in (120cm) diam*

£1,500-2,000   **L&T**

A Line Vautrin talosel "Saint-Hubert" mirror, incised "Line Vautrin" and "ROI".

c1960

£30,000-40,000   **SOT**

A Hans Wegner oak credenza, for R.Y. Mobler, with two sliding caned-front doors, over four sliding trays and four adjustable shelves, with contrasting aluminium and rosewood tipped feet, with branded mark.

78.75in (200cm) wide

£2,000-2,500   **DRA**

A Hans Wegner oak armchair, for Carl Hansen, with woven cord seat.

28.5in (72cm) high

£1,200-1,800   **DRA**

A Hans Wegner "Papa Bear" chair, for A.P. Stolen, with green fabric upholstery, with "A.P. Stolen" stamp mark, distressed.

38.5in (98cm) high

£3,000-4,000   **DRA**

A pair of Hans Wegner oak and teak "Peacock" chairs, for Johannes Hansen, with woven cord seat and fabric-upholstered seat cushions (not shown), with branded mark.

44in (112cm) high

£3,000-4,000   **DRA**

A Frank Lloyd Wright plywood chair, designed for the Meeting House of the First Unitarian Society in Madison, Wisconsin, USA.

27.5in (70cm) high

£1,200-1,800   **DRA**

ESSENTIAL REFERENCE - EDWARD WORMLEY

Edward Wormley (1907-1995) studied briefly at the Art Institute of Chicago, USA in 1926. In 1928 he worked for Marshall Fields & Company department store in their design studio.

● In 1931 he was hired to produce Modern-style pieces for Dunbar in Indiana. Wormley's furniture for Dunbar was simple and elegant. He took elements from Classical design and translated them into a Modern vernacular.

● He opened his own office in New York in 1945, staying on as a consultant to Dunbar.

● His most famous pieces are the 1946 "Long John" table and the 1948 "Listen-to-me" chaise longue. The "Janus" line (1957) of occasional tables featuring tiles by Tiffany and Otto Natzler was also very successful.

An Edward Wormley desk, for Dunbar, with combed oak top and brass frame legs and pulls, with brass "D" tag.

46in (117cm) wide

£2,000-2,500   DRA

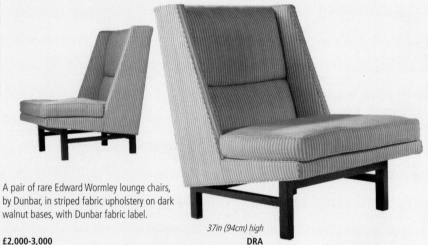

A pair of rare Edward Wormley lounge chairs, by Dunbar, in striped fabric upholstery on dark walnut bases, with Dunbar fabric label.

37in (94cm) high

£2,000-3,000   DRA

An Edward Wormley walnut pedestal side table, for Dunbar, inset with Tiffany Favrile tiles, on tripod base, with brass Dunbar tag.

13in (33.5cm) wide

£7,000-8,000   DRA

An Edward Wormley two-tier walnut table, for Dunbar, the top inset with three Natzler tiles in jade-coloured glazes, with rectangular brass Dunbar tag, and Dunbar factory tag.

29in (74cm) long

£3,500-4,000   DRA

A pair of Edward Wormley mahogany armchairs, by Dunbar, with dark green leather upholstery and pivoting backs, with green Dunbar metal tags.

28.25in (72cm) high

£2,000-2,500   DRA

An Edward Wormley mahogany chest, by Dunbar, with five drawers and recessed pulls flanked by two sliding doors concealing adjustable shelves, on tapering legs with brass-capped feet.

49in (124cm) wide

£2,000-3,000   DRA

One of a pair of Edward Wormley "Slipper" chairs, for Dunbar, with tufted fabric upholstery on dark-stained bases, with brass Dunbar tags.

31in (79cm) high

£2,500-3,000 pair   DRA

A Laura Andreson glazed stoneware vessel, with small prunts covered in a cinnabar and gunmetal glaze, incised "Laura Andreson 84".

1984 *8in (20cm) diam*

£1,500-2,000 **DRA**

An early Gordon Baldwin earthenware vase, painted with blue panels with painted black grid, on a speckled off-white ground, the interior a rich blue glaze, with incised marks and paper label.

c1963 *13in (33.5cm) diam*

£1,500-2,000 **WW**

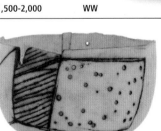

A Robert Arneson ceramic Trophy Bust of the artist, stamped "Arneson".

1979 *7.75in (19.5cm) high*

£7,000-8,000 **DRA**

A Gordon Baldwin earthenware coiled bowl, with pierced panels, with painted white and brown, painted "GB" signature, dated, minor restoration.

1986 *12in (30.5cm) diam*

£1,200-1,800 **WW**

A Bennett Bean glazed earthenware vessel, with gilded interior.

5.75in (14.5cm) diam

£1,200-1,800 **DRA**

An Alison Britton slab-built earthenware vase, painted in colours, incised "Alison Britton", dated.

1983 *12.5in (32cm) high*

£1,000-1,200 **WW**

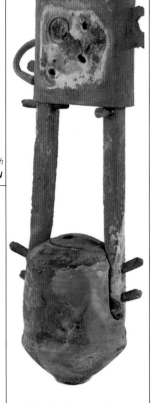

An early and large Claude Conover "Colima" stoneware vessel, signed, titled and numbered "91.2.40".

Educated at the Cleveland Institute of Art, Claude Conover (1907-93) was a commercial designer who also worked as a Studio Potter. From the 1960s onwards, he devoted himself to creating pots, which generally have low-level textured brown, beige, grey or black colouring and gentle, curving forms. Sizes can be large and monumental. Most bear incised or scratched patterns that suggest some mysterious primordial script.

17in (43cm) high

£12,000-18,000 **DRA**

A tall Kris Cox glazed earthenware sculpture.

49in (124.5cm) high

£400-500 **DRA**

A large Val Cushing bulbous stoneware vessel, with incised lines and random patches covered in gunmetal glaze, with incised mark.

22in (56cm) high

£1,500-2,000   **DRA**

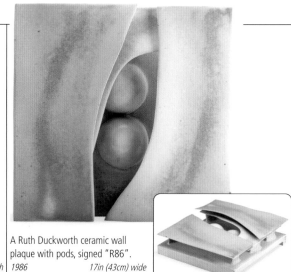

A Ruth Duckworth ceramic wall plaque with pods, signed "R86".

1986   *17in (43cm) wide*

£10,000-15,000   **DRA**

A large Ruth Duckworth stoneware vessel, with inlaid abstract designs in blue-greys, signed "R 80".

1980   *23.5in (60cm) diam*

£4,500-5,500   **DRA**

A Jack Earl "Covered Bridge" ceramic sculpture, inscribed "Jack Earl Lakeview Ohio".

1979   *9.75in (25cm) wide*

£3,500-4,500   **DRA**

A Jack Earl glazed ceramic sculptural vase, signed "Jack Earl 1976".

Made for the Kohler Foundation.

1976   *17in (43cm) high*

£2,000-2,500   **DRA**

A large Gustavsberg Berndt Friberg ceramic vessel, with hare's fur glaze, incised "Friberg" with studio hand mark.

15in (38cm) high

£3,000-4,000   **DRA**

A Jun Kaneko glazed earthenware "Dango" form, incised "Kaneko/98".

1998   *22.25in (56.5cm) high*

£8,000-10,000   **DRA**

A large Jun Kaneko glazed ceramic oval, with multicoloured spiral design, signed "Kaneko '79".

1979   *25in (63.5cm) diam*

£2,000-2,500   **DRA**

A Karen Karnes stoneware covered vessel, with split base in speckled blue, grey, and terracotta glaze, signed "Karen Karnes".

10.75in (27.5cm) diam

£1,500-2,500   **DRA**

A Jeff Koons "Balloon Dog" metalised porcelain sculpture, numbered "393/2300", with original box.

2002   *10.25in (26cm) diam*

£2,500-3,000   **DRA**

A Junko Kitamura bamboo-carved black stoneware bowl.

1992 *10.75in (27.5cm) diam*
£1,500-2,000 **DRA**

A Hui Ka Kwong earthenware bird vessel, signed.

1993 *20in (51cm) long*
£500-700 **DRA**

A Michael Lucero stoneware fish sculpture, with glazed panel of rocky landscape on the face and wind-blown tree on reverse.

17in (43cm) long
£600-800 **DRA**

A Glen Lukens ceramic bowl, covered in crackled glaze, inscribed "Glen Lukens".

8.25in (21.5cm) diam
£800-1,000 **DRA**

A Kate Malone stoneware "Millennium" jug, covered in a crystalline glaze, with etched signature.

11in (28cm) high
£2,000-2,500 **WW**

A large John Maltby slab vase, with flattened rim, painted in slip with flowers and geometric panels, the base with painted "Maltby" signature.

12.5in (32cm) high
£2,000-3,000 **WW**

A Harrison McIntosh glazed stoneware bottle, with paper label and "HM" stamp.

7in (18cm) high
£800-1,200 **DRA**

A Harrison McIntosh bottle-shaped stoneware vase, with chevron pattern in speckled ivory, olive, and light blue matte glaze, with Harrison McIntosh paper label, and impressed artist's cipher.

10in (25.5cm) high
£1,500-2,000 **DRA**

A Lanier Meaders face jug, in alkaline glaze, signed Lanier Meaders, dated.

1988 *10in (25.5cm) high*
£600-700 **DRA**

A rare Pillin tall cylindrical vase, signed "Pillin".

18.5in (47cm) high

£1,000-1,500   DRA

A Scheier glazed ceramic vessel, with couples, illegible signature.

13in (33.5cm) high

£1,500-2,000   DRA

A Scheier large glazed vase, with overlapping figures, inscribed "Scheier 83".

1983   12.25in (31cm) high

£4,000-5,000   DRA

A Don Reitz glazed stoneware single-handled footed sculptural vessel, signed and dated.

1973   18.5in (47cm) high

£2,000-2,500   DRA

An Axel Salto baluster-shaped private Studio vase, with corn-relief design, in speckled green and grey matte glaze, incised "Salto".

7in (18cm) high

£3,000-4,000   DRA

A large Richard Slee earthenware crinkled vase, the textured body glazed yellow with blue highlights, flaring cream rim, incised "Richard Slee" with paper collection label.

15in (38cm) high

£1,500-2,000   WW

A Royal Copenhagen ribbed porcelain bulbous vase, by Axel Salto, in flambé glaze, incised "Salto 20700" with Royal Copenhagen mark, and "520" and "521".

8in (20cm) high

£800-1,200   DRA

A small Royal Copenhagen stoneware budding vase, by Axel Salto, in a dripping blue semi-matt glaze, the clay showing through in spots, marked "Salto" with three-line Royal Copenhagen mark.

4.25in (11cm) diam

£1,200-1,800   DRA

A Toshiko Takaezu glazed stoneware "Moonpot", with rattle, incised "TT".

8.75in (22cm) high

£1,200-1,800   DRA

ESSENTIAL REFERENCE - PETER VOULKOS

American ceramicist Peter Voulkos (1924-2002) began his career producing dinnerware, but is best known for his Abstract Expressionist ceramic sculptures.

● He began producing sculptures in the mid-1950s, after establishing a department dedicated to Art Ceramics at the Otis College of Art and Design, Los Angeles, CA, USA.

● His ceramic pieces, typically created using coiling, are often decorated either by pounding, tearing and/or gouging, and are sometimes glazed or hand-painted.

● In the 1960s he set up a bronze foundry at the University of California, Berkeley, where he already ran a ceramics studio. He continued to make large bronze and ceramic sculptures at Berkeley until his retirement from teaching in 1985. He continued to work full time in his own workshop until his death.

A Peter Voulkos charger, the surface the result of wood ash fusing with clay in the firing process, signed and dated.

1997   *22in (56cm) diam*

£7,500-8,500   **DRA**

A Peter Voulkos stoneware bottle-form vase, in graded brown/black glazes, signed "Voulkos F".

5.5in (14cm) diam

£2,500-3,500   **DRA**

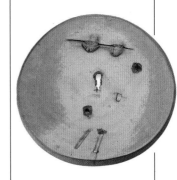

A Peter Voulkos charger, with pierced, gouged, and protruded surface, signed "Voulkos 73".

1973   *18.5in (47cm) diam*

£6,000-7,000   **DRA**

A tall Robert Washington stoneware vase, painted with a figure in rust in a pale blue ground, incised "R J W", dated.

1981   *19in (48cm) high*

£1,500-2,000   **WW**

A Marie Woo porcelain charger, with "torn" rim and gouged and applied surfaces, in peach and grey glazes, artist signed.

18.25in (46cm) diam

£1,500-2,000   **DRA**

A Beatrice Wood "Poor Man!" ceramic sculpture, signed and titled, repairs.

18.5in (47cm) wide

£2,000-2,500   **DRA**

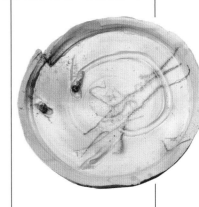

A Beatrice Wood chalice, in lustred volcanic glaze, signed "BEATO".

4.5in (11.5cm) high

£1,500-2,000   **DRA**

A May Yeung stoneware vase, of organic conch form with textured surface, the base with impressed seal mark.

12.5in (32cm) diam

£1,500-2,000   **WW**

A Sonja Blomdahl blown-glass vessel, inscribed "Sonja SP 2187".

13in (33.5cm) high

£800-1,200   DRA

A Ruth Brockman Venetian glass mask.

c1980   16.5in (42cm) high

£800-1,000   DRA

A Dale Chihuly "Seaforms" quadripartite, blown in an optic mould, with applied decoration, with vibro-engraved signature.

1984   18in (45.5cm) diam

£3,000-4,000   FIS

ESSENTIAL REFERENCE - DALE CHIHULY

Dale Chihuly (b.1941) trained in the USA, and at the Venini factory in Murano, Italy.

- In 1969 he began a glassworking programme at the Rhode Island School of Design, USA. For the next 11 years he trained pupils including Dan Dailey and "Toots" Zynsky.
- In 1971 he founded the Pilchuck Glass School near Stanwood, Washington.
- After losing the sight in one eye (1976), he stopped blowing his own glass in favour of directing a large team in the manner of the Murano glassblowers.
- He is known for his multi-part blown-glass organic shapes.
- In the early 1990s, he began producing massive "Chandeliers", including the 18ft (5.5m) example in the Victoria & Albert Museum in London.

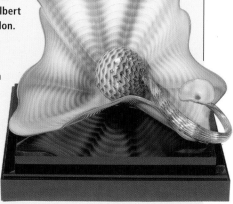

A Dale Chihuly green "Persian" hand-blown green glass sculpture, consisting of two pieces outlined in a thin red glass strip, signed "Chihuly", on base.

Designed 2001   including base 11in (28cm) high

£3,000-4,000   FRE

ESSENTIAL REFERENCE - DAN DAILEY

Dan Dailey (b.1947) trained at the Rhode Island School of Design, under Dale Chihuly.

- His glass sculpture often incorporates metalware. Pieces often show a variety of decorative techniques, such as acid-polishing, sandblasting or patination.
  - Dailey's work often shows a streamlined Art Deco influence.
  - In 1972, like Chihuly before him, he was invited to work at the Venini factory, in Murano, Italy. There he created a series of blown glass and brass sculptural lamps.
  - Since 1976 he has worked as an independent designer for Cristallerie Daum, France.
  - He has taught at many glass programmes, notably at the Massachusetts College of Art, where he founded the glass department in 1973.
  - In 2000, he was given the Libensky Award.

A large Dan Dailey "Picture Man" sculptural glass vessel, with title and "FV.40.90".

1990   23in (58cm) high

£12,000-14,000   DRA

A miniature Dan Dailey and Lino Tagliapietra glass vase, with stylised landscape in polychrome, marked "Dailey Tagliapietra", with their initials inside a grid.

Vases of this type were miniature replicas of collaborative pieces that Dailey and Tagliapietra executed in Murano, Italy, and also during a joint fellowship at the Creative Glass Center in Millville, New Jersey, USA, between 1989 and 1994.

c1990   3.25in (8.5cm) high

£1,000-1,500   DRA

An Erwin Eisch "My Ring Finger" black glass vase, with deep engraving with gold painting, engraved "J.S. E. Eisch 81".

1981

£800-1,200   FIS

A Jon Kuhn blown-glass sculptural vase, inscribed "Jon Kuhn Nov 1979".
1979   *7in (18cm) high*
£800-1,000   DRA

CLOSER LOOK - "GENGI MONOGATARI"

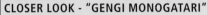

"Genji Monogatari" ("The Tale of Genji"), written c1000 is a classic work of Japanese literature, sometimes referred to as the first modern novel. Attributed to the noblewoman Murosaki Shikubi, it is a romantic and sad story of the decadent aristocracy at the court in Kyoto.

The purple colour of the box is a reference to Genji's wife, Murosaki, whose name translates as "purple" or "violet". Murosaki Shikubi was not the author's real name. She was nicknamed "Murosaki" at court after the character.

Creating this shade of purple glass is difficult and requires extraordinary craftsmanship

The box is an unusual seven sided shape.

The edge of the cover and box are lined with silver bands.

A rare Kyohei Fujita "Genji Monogatari" silver-mounted glass box, with purple, pink, blue and white glass over clear glass core, with applied gold leaf, base engraved "K. Fujita", in original box.
                                    6.5in (16cm) diam
£5,000-6,000   FIS

A Dominick Labino glass sculpture, from the "Emergence" series, inscribed "Labino 12-1982".
1982   *9in (23cm) high*
£5,500-6,500   DRA

A Maria Lugossy "Stages" tripartite sculpture, comprising three blocks of grey laminated plate-glass, set with bronze face, engraved signature "LUGOSSY".
1993   *12.5in (32cm) high*
£5,000-6,000   FIS

1988
£3,000-4,000

A miniature Richard Marquis blown-glass teapot, with polychrome murrines, inscribed "Thanx Scott Marquis, copyright 1988".
                    4in (10cm) high
                              DRA

A large William Morris glass vase, from the "Stonehenge Series", signed and dated.
1984   *16.5in (42cm) high*
£7,000-8,000   DRA

A Stephen Rolfe Powell "Tangerine Buns Smith" vase, with horizontal ribbons of melted coloured murrine honeycomb.
1994
£4,000-5,000   FIS

An Ann Robinson "Yellow Ice Bowl", engraved "N.a. Robinson '94 I/I".

1994   *15.75in (40cm) wide*
£2,500-3,000   **FIS**

A Livio Seguso "Bolle" crystal glass sculpture, internally-decorated with a cluster of submerged bubbles and single amber streak, artist-signed.

c1978   *9.75in (25cm) wide*
£1,200-1,800   **DRA**

A 1980s Memphis "SOL" glass tazza, by Ettore Sottsass, the blue bowl lined in white on a clear hollow stem and red and white domed foot, engraved mark "E. Sottsass per Memphis".

12in (30.5cm) diam
£500-600   **L&T**

A large Lino Tagliapietra "Fazzoletto" glass vase, etched "Lino Tagliapietra/Effetre International/Murano Italy/1986, 17/100".

1986   *14in (36cm) diam*
£2,000-2,500   **DRA**

A "Fazzoletto" glass vase, by Lino Tagliapietra, with vertical stripes and ochre lip wrap, etched "Lino Tagliapietra/ Effetre International/Murano Italy/1987, 27/100".

1987   *13.5in (34.5cm) high*
£1,200-1,800   **DRA**

A Howard Ben Tré "Stone for casting no. 4" green blow-formed glass object, partially etched, with bronze powder.

1992   *16.5in (42cm)*
£4,000-5,000   **FIS**

A Karla Trinkley pâte-de-verre vase, with grey, blue and green colouring, with vibro-engraved signature "Karla Trinkley".

c1985   *11in (28cm) high*
£4,500-5,500   **FIS**

A large Kosta Boda vase, by Bertil Vallien, with sand-blasted designs, engraved "Kosta Unik 6685 B. Vallien".

1985   *11.5in (29cm) diam*
£700-800   **FIS**

A large Veart four-sided lobed vessel, by Toni Zuccheri, with rippled panels.

14.75in (37.5cm) wide
£700-800   **DRA**

A Mary Ann "Toots" Zynsky "Night Out" glass shell, composed of fused coloured-glass threads, signed "Z" in melted thread.

c1993   *9.5in (24cm) diam*
£5,500-6,500   **FIS**

ESSENTIAL REFERENCE - LIBENSKÝ AND BRYCHTOVÁ

Husband and wife team, Stanislav Libenský (1921-2002) and Jaroslava Brychtová (b.1924) are the most influential figures in the field of optical-glass sculpture.

- Their work is characterised by bold, blocky shapes.
- They first worked together in 1954 in Železný Brod, Czechoslovakia (now Czech Republic), where Libenský was principal at the Glasfachschule (Special School for Glassmaking) and Bryctová head of the Department of Architectural Glass at the glass factory. Their first work together was the famous "Head Bowl" in c1957.
- During the 1970s they worked predominantly in colourless glass, introducing colour in the mid-1980s.
- While teaching at the Prague Academy (1963-1986) Libenský taught students including Jirí Harcuba, František Janák, Marian Karel, and Yan Zoritchak.
- Brychtová continues to produce castings today.

A Stanislav Libenský and Jaroslava Brychtová "Cross Head" red optical-glass sculpture, polished and acid-frosted, with vibro-engraved signature "S. LIBENSKY J. BRYCHTOVA 1988.89".

1988/89　　　　　*32in (81cm) high*
£35,000-40,000　　　　　**FIS**

A Stanislav Libenský and Jaroslava Brychtová "Space III" optical-glass sculpture, partly polished and acid-frosted, with vibro-engraved signature "S. LIBENSKY J. BRYCHTOVA 91-92".

1991/1992　　　　　*13.75in (35.5cm) wide*
£20,000-25,000　　　　　**FIS**

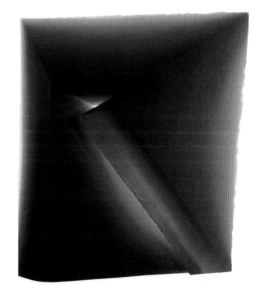

A Stanislav Libenský and Jaroslava Brychtová "Diagonale" red optical-glass sculpture, polished and acid-frosted, with vibro-engraved signature "S. LIBENSKY J. BRYCHTOVA 1989".

1989　　　　　*30in (76cm) high*
£40,000-50,000　　　　　**FIS**

A Jaromir Rybak colourless and blue pâte-de-verre glass sculpture, with gold and silver highlights, signed "Jaromir Rybak".

1990　　*19.5in (49.5cm) high*
£3,000-4,000　　　　　**FIS**

A Frantisek Vízner thick green optical-glass vase, polished and acid-frosted, with diamond-point engraved signature "VIZNER".

6.75in (17cm) high
£4,500-5,500　　　　　**FIS**

One of a set of nine Dana Zámecníková "Little Italy" flat glasses, sandblasted, etched, enamelled, painted, engraved, laminated.

c1988-1990　　　　　*18in (46cm) high*
£4,000-5,000 set　　　　　**FIS**

ESSENTIAL REFERENCE - RON ARAD

Israeli-born British architect and designer, Ron Arad (b.1951) trained at the Jerusalem Academy of Art before continuing his studies in London from 1974.

- **In 1981 he founded the company "One Off" with Caroline Thorman.**
- **In 1989 he founded the larger company, "Ron Arad Associates".**
- **Many of his early designs were art furniture, created from existing objects. These included the famous "Rover" chair (1981), made from a used car seat mounted on a steel frame.**
- **His later designs, such as the "Tom Vac" stacking chair (1997) are more sculptural.**
- **He is currently head of Product Design at the Royal College of Art, London.**

A Ron Arad tree floor lamp, with two flexible tubular steel arms, on cement base.

78in (198cm) high

£2,500-3,000   DRA

One of a pair of Martinelli Luce "Pipistrello" table lamps, by Gae Aulenti, each with moulded plastic shade, and four sockets, on chromed and enamelled metal base, with embossed mark.

28in (71cm) high

£1,500-2,000 pair   DRA

A Camer Crystal eight-socket hanging fixture, with crystal prisms on anodised metal frame.

28in (71cm) diam

£1,500-2,000   DRA

A pair of Orgues "Charles & Fils" floor lamps, in polished and brushed stainless steel, on black marble bases, with stamped signature.

12in (30.5cm) high

£6,000-7,000   DRA

A Dan Dailey metal, blown-glass and vitrolite figural table lamp, stamped signature.

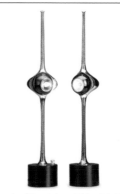

31.5in (80cm) high

£12,000-14,000   DRA

A Willy Daro pyrite table lamp, with polished brass mount and dark brown silk shade.

21.75in (54.5cm) high

£2,200-2,800   DRA

A Fontana Arte brass, glass, and enamelled metal desk lamp, with adjustable shade.

25in (63.5cm) high

£3,000-4,000   DRA

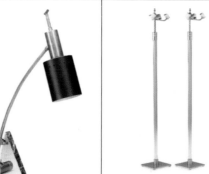

A pair of Hansen floor lamps, with crystal shafts and brushed nickel-plate on solid brass, embossed "Hansen New York".

9in (23cm) wide

£1,500-2,000   DRA

A pair of Arredoluce "Cobra" table lights, by Angelo Lelli, with magnetic adjustable metal shades.

4.75in (12cm) diam

£2,200-2,800   DRA

A pair of Angelo Mangiarotti white and clear glass table lamps, each with single socket.

19.5in (50cm) high

£2,000-2,500   DRA

An Angelo Mangiarotti chandelier, with interlocking clear and coloured loop-shaped glass elements suspended from a polished steel frame.

fixture only 46in (117cm) long

£1,200-1,800   DRA

A James Mont table lamp, in limed oak and brass with two stylised birds, topped by a flared burlap-covered shade.

23.25in (59cm) high

£2,200-2,800   DRA

A Fondica sculptural gilded-bronze table lamp base, by Mathias, signed "Mathias Fondica C.E. L.MATH07".

17.5in (44cm) high

£750-850   DRA

A Mazegga lighting fixture, with green glass drops, suspended on chains hanging from a circular steel frame with four sockets.

24in (61cm) diam

£1,500-2,000   DRA

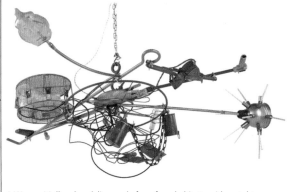

A Warren Muller chandelier, made from found objects, with metal tag, marked "Warren Muller #3".

62in (157cm) diam

£1,500-2,000   DRA

An Idee aluminium "Super Guppy" floor lamp, by Marc Newson, on castors, with Idee label.

73in (185.5cm) high

£2,500-3,500   DRA

A Verner Panton floor lamp, with ceramic base, chrome hardware and original printed fabric shade.

72in (183cm) high

£900-1,100   DRA

A pair of table lamps, attributed to Verner Panton, with enamelled metal shafts and shades on marble bases.

8in (20cm) diam

£250-300   DRA

A pair of Hansen brass floor lamps, by T.H. Robsjohn-Gibbings, each with three sockets and original linen shades.

56in (142cm) high

£4,000-5,000 **DRA**

An Arredoluce "Triennale" floor lamp, by Gino Sarfatti, with three adjustable arms in brass and enamelled metal on white marble base, marked "#1864 Made in Italy" in black crayon.

62in (157cm) high

£1,500-2,000 **DRA**

A Jonathan Singleton "Little Buildings" polished stainless steel floor lamp, with small cut-outs, with metal tag, "Jonathan Singleton SIG Furniture".

74.75in (190cm) high

£1,200-1,800 **DRA**

A Memphis "Tahiti" enamelled metal and printed laminates table lamp, by Ettore Sottsass.

c1980 *26in (66cm) high*

£1,200-1,800 **L&T**

An Arredoluce enamelled metal and brass single-arm floor lamp, by Ettore Sottsass.

64in (163cm) high

£3,000-4,000 **DRA**

A Taito solid brass desk lamp, by Paavo Tynell, with two sockets, stamped "TY1005 TAITO TT Made in Finland".

17.25in (43.5cm) high

DRA

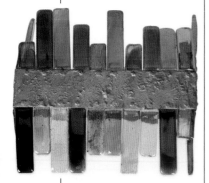

A Venini wall sconce, with golden and amber-toned glass elements, in patinated steel frame.

17in (43cm) wide

£750-850 **DRA**

A Vistosi glass disc chandelier, with coloured cased-glass discs on steel frame.

25in (64cm) diam

£2,500-3,500 **DRA**

An Edward Zucca "Tolstoy or TV Guide" sculptural lamp, in mahogany, brass, copper, aluminium, plexiglass and masonite, signed, titled and dated.

2006 *27in (69cm) high*

£1,800-2,200 **DRA**

An Alexander Archipenko polished terracotta sculpture, "Round Torso", inscribed and dated 37.

46in (117cm) high

£70,000-80,000　　　LHA

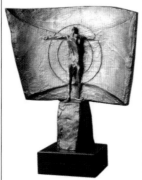

A Michael Ayrton bronze sculpture, "Icarus II".

12.5in (32cm) high

£6,000-7,000　　　SWO

A Michael Ayrton bronze sculpture, "Re-Entry", edition 3/6.

1968　　22in (56cm) high

£7,000-8,000　　　LHA

A Harry Bertoia bronze and copper "Bush" sculpture.

11in (28cm) diam

£12,000-18,000　　　DRA

A Harry Bertoia beryllium copper "sonambient" sculpture, with 16 rods arranged in an alternating pattern on square base.

12in (30.5cm) wide

£10,000-15,000　　　DRA

A Deborah Butterfield mixed media sculpture, "Horse".

46in (117cm) long

£12,000-18,000　　　LHA

A Lynn Chadwick bronze sculpture, "Two", no.1/6, inscribed.

1970　　29in (74cm) high

£35,000-45,000　　　LHA

An Arthur Court cast aluminium sculpture of a Kudu antelope skull, stamped "Arthur Court Designs Copyrighted 1982".

1982　　39.5in (100cm) high

£1,200-1,800　　　DRA

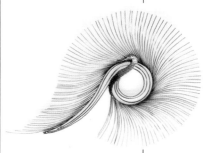

A Curtis Jere brass and copper peacock wall sculpture, signed copyright "C Jere 1989".

1989　　58.25in (148cm) long

£500-700　　　DRA

A Jose de Rivera brass sculpture, "Construction 174".

1976   *9.5in (24cm) diam*
£5,000-6,000   **LHA**

A Claire Falkenstein welded-copper and Venetian glass sculpture.

20in (51cm) diam
£4,000-5,000   **DRA**

A David Hare cast-bronze sculpture, "Couple", incised with the artist's signature, date and numbered "4/7".

1950   *13.75in (35cm) high*
£4,500-5,500   **SWA**

A John Henry aluminium sculpture, "Tiny Red", inscribed.

10in (25.5cm) high
£1,000-1,500   **LHA**

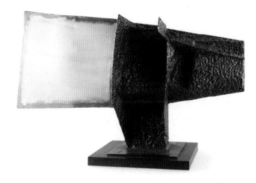

A John Hoskin abstract steel sculpture, "Subject Unknown", on slate base.

28in (71cm) high
£3,500-4,500   **GORL**

A Richard Howard Hunt bronze figural sculpture, no.1/15, dated.

1984   *19in (48cm) high*
£3,000-4,000   **LHA**

A Klaus Ihlenfeld phophorus bronze sculpture, "Sunflower", stamped "K".

1970   *6in (15cm) diam*
£1,200-1,800   **DRA**

A Roy Lichtenstein "Modern Sculpture with Apertures", of screenprinted enamel on interlocking Plexiglas forms with mirrored silver Mylar, signed and numbered in ink, printed by Maurel Studios, New York, published by the artist.

1967   *16.5in (42cm) high*
£3,000-4,000   **SWA**

A Densaburou Oku fused and patinated found objects and glass fish sculpture.

27.5in (70cm) high
£1,500-2,000   **DRA**

A Tom Otterness cast bronze sculpture, "Mother and Daughter", incised with the artist's initials, date and numbered 1/3.

1984   *18in (45.5cm) high*
£2,500-3,000   **SWA**

A Man Ray cast metal sculpture, "Cadeau", signed and titled in white ink, initialled and numbered "XLI/CCC" on printed paper justification card, cast by the Mirano Foundry, Venice.

1974   *6.5in (16cm) high*
£2,000-2,500   **SWA**

A Silas Seandel wall sculpture, composed of horizontal and vertical rectangular forms in a variety of finishes, signed "Silas Seandel 73".

1973   *59.5in (151cm) wide*
£2,000-2,500   **DRA**

A Daisuke Shintani patinated bronze and glass sculpture, signed "D. Shintani".

20in (51cm) high
£1,500-2,000   **DRA**

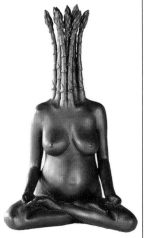

A Jack Thompson large figural ceramic sculpture, "Asparagus Buddess", with painted gunmetal finish.

2001   *42in (107cm) high*
£2,000-2,500   **DRA**

A Steve Tobin patinated bronze "Syntax" sculpture, inscribed "Tobin".

15in (38cm) high
£2,000-2,500   **DRA**

A Steve Tobin bronze sculpture with vintage car, inscribed "Tobin".

18.5in (47cm) high
£1,500-2,000   **DRA**

A Fritz Wotruba bronze sculpture, "Standing Figure", no. 2/6.

1964   *16.5in (42cm) high*
£15,000-20,000   **LHA**

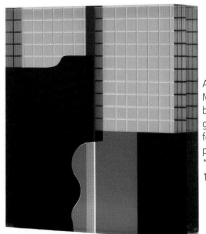

A Vasa (Velizar Mihich) large acrylic block sculpture, with grid- and puzzle-form-patterns in polychrome, signed "#2939 Vasa @ 1989".

1989   *18in (45.5cm) wide*
£1,500-2,500   **DRA**

An Edward Zucca sculpture, "Jailbird Set Free", in painted-brass, wood and resin, signed, titled and dated.

2005   *14in (36cm) high*
£1,500-2,000   **DRA**

A Yaacov Agam "Festival" square wool carpet, signed in field and tag on verso.

1982   *82in (208cm) wide*

£1,200-1,800   DRA

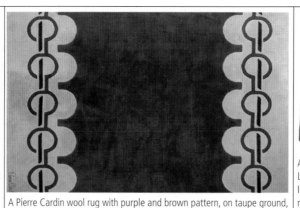

A Pierre Cardin wool rug with purple and brown pattern, on taupe ground, signed.

130in (330cm) long

£3,500-4,500   DRA

A Robert Indiana "Philadelphia Love" wool rug, signed "R. Indiana", signed in ink marker and numbered "130/300", with fabric certificate verso.

1995   *72in (183cm) wide*

£1,500-2,000   FRE

A Bon-Art "Circus" maguey fibre tapestry, by Alexander Calder, woven "Calder 75", no. "78 of 100" with copyright and fabric label.

1975   *84.5in (215cm) long*

£5,500-6,500   DRA

A Bon-Art "Moon" maguey fibre tapestry, by Alexander Calder, with Bon-Art label and woven "CA 74", numbered "72/100", with copyright.

Maguey comes from the "leaves" of a large cactus that grows in Mesoamerica – the same catcus is used in the production of tequila.

1974   *85in (216cm) long*

£6,000-7,000   DRA

A David Shaw Nicholls Maui hand-knotted runner, in silk and wool, marked with Nicholls fabric label.

232.5in (590cm) long

£4,000-5,000   DRA

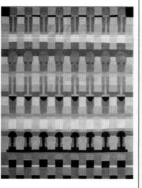

A David Shaw Nicholls Carlisle hand-knotted carpet, in silk and wool, with Nicholls fabric label.

117.25in (298cm) long

£3,500-4,500   DRA

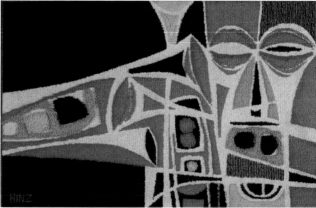

A tapestry with stylised depiction of a jazz musician, by Bill Hinz, in orange, yellow, black and white, with woven signature.

61in (155cm) wide

£1,800-2,200   DRA

U.K. PERIOD	US. PERIOD	FRENCH PERIOD	GERMAN PERIOD
Elizabethan *Elizabeth I (1558-1603)*		**Renaissance**	**Renaissance** *(to c1650)*
Jacobean *James I (1603-1625)*			
Carolean *Charles I (1625-1649)*	**Early Colonial**	**Louis XIII** *(1610-1643)*	
Cromwellian *Commonwealth (1649-1660)*			**Renaissance/** **Baroque** *(c1650-1700)*
Restoration *Charles II (1660-1685)* *James II (1685-1688)*		**Louis XIV** *(1643-1715)*	
William and Mary *(1689-1694)*	**William and Mary** *(1689-1694)*		
William III *(1694-1702)*	**Dutch Colonial**		
Queen Anne *(1702-1714)*	**Queen Anne**		**Baroque** *(c1700-1730)*
Early Georgian *George I (1714-1727)* *George II (1727-1760)*		**Régence** *(1715-1723)*	
	Chipendale *From 1750*	**Louis XV** *(1723-1774)*	**Rococo** *(c1730-1760)*
		Louis XVI *(1774-1792)*	**Neoclassicism** *(c1760-1800)*
Late Georgian *George III (1760-1811)*	**EARLY FEDERAL** *(1790-1810)* *American Directoire* *(1798-1804)* *American Empire* *(1804-1815)*	**Directoire** *(1792-1799)*	**Empire** *(c1800-1815)*
		Empire *(1799-1815)*	
Regency *George III (1812-1820)*		**Restauration** *(1815-1830)*	**Biedermeier** *(c1815-1848)*
George IV *(1820-1830)*	**Later Federal** *(1810-1830)*	*Louis XVIII (1814-1824)* *Charles X (1824-1830)*	
William IV *(1830-1837)*		**Louis Phillipe** *(1830-1848)*	**Revivale** *(c1830-1880)*
Victorian *Victoria (1837-1901)*	**Victorian**	**2nd Empire** *(1848-1870)*	
Edwardian *Edward VII (1901-1910)*		**3rd Republic** *(1871-1940)*	**Jugendstil** *(c1880-1920)*

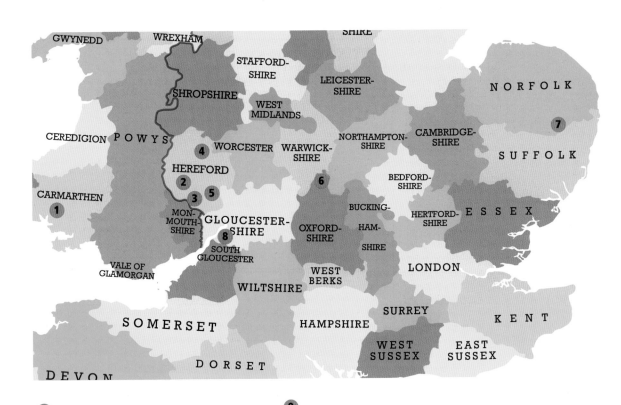

ADVERTISERS

Every antique illustrated in Miller's Antiques has a letter code which identifies the dealer or auction house that sold it. The list below is a key to these codes. In the list, auction houses are shown by the letter A and dealers by the letter D. Some items may have come from a private collection, in which case the code in the list is accompanied by the letters PC. Inclusion in this book in no way constitutes or implies a contract or a binding offer on the part of any of our contributors to supply or sell the goods illustrated, or similar items, at the prices stated.

A&G Ⓐ
ANDERSON & GARLAND
Anderson House, Crispin Court,
Newbiggin Lane, Westerhope,
Newcastle upon Tyne,
Tyne and Wear, NE5 1BF
Tel: 0191 430 3000
www.andersonandgarland.com

AH & HT Ⓐ
HARTLEY'S
Victoria Hall, Little Lane,
Ilkley, West Yorkshire, LS29 8EA
Tel: 01943 816363
www.andrewhartleyfinearts.co.uk

ANDG Ⓓ
ANCIENT & GOTHIC
PO Box 5390, Bournemouth,
Dorset, BH7 6XR
Tel: 01202 431721

BE & HL Ⓐ
BEARNES, HAMPTON &
LITTLEWOOD
St Edmund's Court,
Okehampton Street,
Exeter, Devon, EX4 1DU
Tel: 01392 413100
www.bearnes.co.uk

BEJ Ⓓ
BÉBÉS ET JOUETS
c/o Lochend Post Office,
165 Restalrig Road,
Edinburgh, EH7 6HW
Tel: 0131 3325650
bebesetjouets@tiscali.co.uk

BELL Ⓐ
BELLMANS
New Pound Wisborough Green,
Billingshurst, West Sussex,
RH14 0AZ
Tel: 01403 700858
www.bellmans.co.uk

BER Ⓐ
BERTOIA AUCTIONS
2141 Demarco Drive,
Vineland, NJ 08360, USA
Tel: 001 856 692 1881
www.bertoiaauctions.com

BLNY Ⓐ
BLOOMSBURY AUCTIONS
6 West 48th Street,
New York, NY 10036 1902, USA
Tel: 001 212 719 1000
ny.bloomsburyauctions.com

BLO Ⓐ
BLOOMSBURY AUCTIONS
Bloomsbury House,
24 Maddox Street,
London, W1 S1PP
Tel: 020 7495 9494
www.bloomsburyauctions.com

BZ Ⓟ
BASIA ZARZYCKA
52 Sloane Square,
London, SW1W 8AX
Tel: 0207730 1660
www.basia-zarzycka.com

CANS Ⓓ
CANDY SAYS
39 Elm Road, Leigh-on-Sea,
Essex, SS9 1SW
Tel: 01277 212134
www.candysays.co.uk

CAPE Ⓐ
CAPES DUNN & CO.
The Auction Galleries, 38 Charles
Street, Manchester, M17DB
Tel: 0161 2731911
www.capesdunn.com

CHEF Ⓐ
CHEFFINS
Clifton House, 1 & 2 Clifton Road,
Cambridge, Cambridgeshire,
CB1 7EA
Tel: 01223 213343
www.cheffins.co.uk

CHT Ⓐ
CHARTERHOUSE
The Long Street Salerooms,
Sherborne, Dorset, DT9 3BS
Tel: 01935 812277
www.charterhouse-auctions.co.uk

CRIS Ⓓ
CRISTOBAL
26 Church Street, Marylebone,
London, NW8 8EP
Tel: 020 7724 7230
www.cristobal.co.uk

CSB Ⓐ
CHENU SCRIVE BERARD
Hôtel des Ventes Lyon Presqu'île,
Groupe Ivoire, 6, rue Marcel
Rivière, 69002 Lyon, France
Tel: 003 472777801
www.chenu-scrive.com

DA&H Ⓐ
DEE, ATKINSON & HARRISON
The Exchange Saleroom, Driffield,
East Yorkshire, YO25 6LD
Tel : 01377 253151
www.dahauctions.com

DCB Ⓐ
DELORME ET COLLIN DU
BOCAGE
11, rue de Miromesnil 75008
Paris, France
Tel: 003 158183905
www.parisencheres.com

DCP Ⓓ
THE DUNLOP COLLECTION
PO Box 6269, Statesville,
NC 28687, USA
Tel: 001 871 2626
dunloppaperweights@mac.com

DN Ⓐ
DREWEATTS
Donnington Priory Salerooms,
Donnington, Newbury,
Berkshire, RG14 2JE
Tel: 01635 553553
www.dnfa.com/donnington

DOR Ⓐ
DOROTHEUM
Palais Dorotheum,
Dorotheergasse 17,
1010 Vienna, Austria
Tel: 0043 1515600
www.dorotheum.com

DR Ⓓ
DEREK ROBERTS ANTIQUES
25 Shipbourne Road,
Tonbridge, Kent, TN10 3DN
Tel: 01732 358986
www.qualityantiqueclocks.com

DS Ⓐ
DUNBAR SLOANE
12 Akepiro Street, Mt Eden,
Auckland, New Zealand
Tel: 0064 4721367
www.dunbarsloane.co.nz

DRA Ⓐ
DAVID RAGO AUCTIONS
333 North Main Street,
Lambertville, NJ 08530, USA
Tel: 001 609 397 9374
www.ragoarts.com

DUK Ⓐ
HY DUKE & SON
The Dorchester Fine Art
Salerooms, Weymouth Avenue,
Dorchester, Dorset, DT1 1QS
Tel: 01305 265080
www.dukes-auctions.com

EAL Ⓓ
EXETER ANTIQUE LIGHTING
43, The Quay, Exeter, Devon,
EX2 4AN
Tel: 01392 433604
www.antiquelightingcompany.
com

ECGW Ⓐ
EWBANK CLARKE GAMMON
WELLERS
The Burnt Common Auction
Rooms, London Road, Send,
Woking, Surrey, GU23 7LN
Tel: 01483 223101
www.ewbankauctions.co.uk

FIS Ⓐ
AUKTIONHAUS DR FISCHER
Trappensee-Schößchen, D-74074
Heilbronn, Germany
Tel: 0049 7131155570
www.auctions-fischer.de

FLD Ⓐ
FIELDINGS AUCTIONEERS
Mill Race Lane, Stourbridge,
West Midlands, DY8 1JN
Tel: 01384 444140
www.fieldingsauctioneers.co.uk

FRE Ⓐ
FREEMAN'S
1808 Chestnut Street,
Philadelphia, PA 19103, USA
Tel: 001 215 563 9275
www.freemansauction.com

G&M Ⓐ
GORNY & MOSCH
Maximiliansplatz 20,
80333 Munich, Germany
Tel: 0049 89/24 22 643-0
www.gmcoinart.de

GBA Ⓐ
GRAHAM BUDD AUCTIONS
PO Box 47519,
London, N14 6XD
Tel: 020 83662525
www.grahambuddauctions.co.uk

GEOA Ⓓ
GEORGIAN ANTIQUES
10 Pattison Street, Leith Links,
Edinburgh, Midlothian, EH6 7HF
Tel: 0131 5537286
www.georgianantiques.net

GHOU Ⓐ
GARDINER HOULGATE
Bath Auction Rooms,
9 Leafield Way,
Corsham, Wiltshire, SN13 9SW
Tel: 01225 812912
www.gardinerhoulgate.co.uk

GORB Ⓐ
GORRINGES
Terminus Road, Bexhill-on-Sea,
East Sussex, TN39 3LR
Tel: 01424 212994
www.gorringes.co.uk

GORL Ⓐ
GORRINGES
15 North Street,
Lewes, East Sussex, BN7 2PD
Tel: 01273 472503
www.gorringes.co.uk

GUK Ⓓ
GLITZ UK
www.glitzuk.co.uk

HANDC Ⓐ
HISTORICAL & COLLECTABLE
Kennetholme, Midgham
Reading, Berkshire, RG7 5UX
Tel: 01189 712420
www.historicalandcollectable.com

IMC Ⓐ
I. M. CHAIT
9330 Civic Center Drive
Beverly Hills, CA 90210, USA
Tel: 001 310 2850182
www.chait.com

JA Ⓐ
LEONARD JOEL
333 Malvern Road,
South Yarra, 3141, Victoria,
Melbourne, Australia
Tel : 0061 3 98264333
www.leonardjoel.com.au

JDJ Ⓐ
JAMES D JULIA INC
PO Box 830, Fairfield,
ME 04937, USA
Tel: 001 207 453 7125
www.juliaauctions.com

JPOT Ⓐ
JONATHAN POTTER LTD
125 New Bond Street, London,
W1S 1DY
Tel: 020 7491 3520
www.jpmaps.co.uk

L&T Ⓐ
LYON AND TURNBULL
33 Broughton Place,
Edinburgh, Midlothian, EH1 3RR
Tel: 0131 5578844
www.lyonandturnbull.com

LAW Ⓐ
LAWRENCES AUCTIONEERS
Norfolk House, High Street,
Bletchingley, Surrey, RH1 4PA
Tel: 01883 743323
www.lawrencesbletchingley.co.uk

LC Ⓐ
LAWRENCE'S FINE ART AUCTIONEERS
The Linen Yard, South Street,
Crewkerne, Somerset, TA18 8AB
Tel: 01460 73041
www.lawrences.co.uk

LDY ⒫Ⓒ
LADY DOUBLE YOU
info@ladydoubleyou.com
www.ladydoubleyou.com

LHA Ⓐ
LESLIE HINDMAN AUCTIONEERS
1338 West Lake Street, Chicago,
IL 60607, USA
Tel: 001 312 280 1212
www.lesliehindman.com

LOC Ⓐ
LOCKE & ENGLAND
18 Guy Street, Leamington Spa,
Warwickshire, CV32 4RT
Tel: 01926 889100
www.leauction.co.uk

LOW Ⓐ
LOWESTOFT PORCELAIN
Surrey Street, Lowestoft,
Suffolk, NR32 1LJ
Tel: 01296 892736
www.lowestoftchina.co.uk

LSK Ⓐ
LACY SCOTT & KNIGHT
10 Risbygate Street, Bury St.
Edmunds, Suffolk, IP33 3AA
Tel: 01284 748600
www.lsk.co.uk

LT Ⓐ
LOUIS TAYLOR AUCTIONEERS
10 Town Road, Hanley,
Staffordshire ST1 2QG
Tel: 01782 214111
www.louistaylorfineart.co.uk

MACK Ⓓ
MACKLOWE GALLERY
667 Madison Avenue, New York,
NY 10021, USA
Tel: 001 212 644 6400
www.macklowegallery.com

MAR Ⓐ
MARSHALLS
Marshall House, Church Hill,
Knutsford, Cheshire, WA16 6DH
Tel: 01565 653284
www.frankmarshall.co.uk

MDM Ⓓ
M&D MOIR
www.manddmoir.co.uk

MILA Ⓓ
MILLER'S ANTIQUES
Netherbrook House, 86
Christchurch Road, Ringwood,
Hampshire, BH24 1DR
Tel: 01425 472062
www.millers-antiques.co.uk

MOR Ⓓ
MORPHETS
6 Albert Street, Harrogate,
North Yorkshire, HG1 1JL
Tel: 01423 530030
www.morphets.co.uk

MTB Ⓓ
MAGIC TOY BOX
210 Havant Road, Drayton,
Portsmouth, Hampshire, PO6 2EH
Tel: 02392 221307
www.magictoybox.co.uk

PC ⒫Ⓒ
PRIVATE COLLECTION

PIA Ⓐ
PIASA
5, rue Doruot, 75009 Paris, France
Tel: 0033 153341010
www.piasa.auction.fr

POOK Ⓐ
POOK & POOK
463 East Lancaster Avenue,
Downington,
PA 19335, USA
Tel: 001 610 269 4040
www.pookandpook.com

QU Ⓐ
QUITTENBAUM
Theresienstrasse 60, D-80333
Munich, Germany
Tel. 0049 89 273702125
www.quittenbaum.dem

RELL Ⓓ
RELLIK
8 Golborne Road, London,
W10 5NW
Tel: 0208 9620089
www.relliklondon.co.uk

RMAA Ⓓ
ROBERT MILLS ARCHITECTURAL ANTIQUES
Narroways Road, Eastville,
Bristol, BS2 9XB
Tel: 0117 95565429

ROS Ⓐ
ROSEBERY'S
74-76 Knight's Hill,
West Norwood,
London, SE27 0JD
Tel: 020 8761 2522
www.roseberys.co.uk

RTC Ⓐ
RITCHIES
No longer trading

SAS Ⓐ
SPECIAL AUCTION SERVICES
81 New Greenham Park,
Newbury, Berkshire, RG19 6HW
Tel: 08456 044 669
www.specialauctionservices.com

SBG Ⓓ
SWEETBRIAR GALLERY LTD
No longer trading.

SCG Ⓓ
GALLERY 1930
18 Church Street, Marylebone,
London, NW8 8EP
Tel: 020 7723 1555
www.susiecooperceramics.com

SHAP Ⓐ
SHAPES
Bankhead Medway, Sighthill,
Edinburgh, Midlothian, EH11 4BY
Tel: 0131 4533222
www.shapesauctioneers.co.uk

SK Ⓐ
SKINNER INC.
The Heritage on the Garden,
63 Park Plaza,
Boston, MA 02116, USA
Tel: 001 617 350 5400
www.skinnerinc.com

SOT Ⓐ
SOTHEBY'S (US)
1334 York Avenue,
New York, NY 10021, USA
Tel: 001 212 606 7000
www.sothebys.com

SOTH Ⓐ
SOTHEBY'S (LONDON)
34-35 New Bond Street,
London, W1A 2AA
Tel: 020 7293 5000
www.sothebys.com

SWA Ⓐ
SWANN GALLERIES
104 East 25th Street, New York,
New York 10010, USA
Tel: 001 212 254 4710
www.swanngalleries.com

SWO Ⓐ
SWORDERS
14 Cambridge Road, Stansted
Mountfitchet, Essex, CM24 8GE
Tel: 01279 817778
www.sworder.co.uk

TBW Ⓓ
TEDDY BEARS OF WITNEY
99 High Street, Witney,
Oxfordshire, OX28 6HY
Tel: 01993 706616
www.teddybears.co.uk

TDM Ⓐ
THOMAS DEL MAR LTD
25 Blythe Road,
London, W14 0PD
Tel: 0207 602 4805
www.thomasdelmar.com

TEN Ⓐ
TENNANTS
The Auction Centre, Leyburn,
North Yorkshire, DL8 5SG
Tel: 01969 623780
www.tennants.co.uk

TOV Ⓐ
TOOVEY'S
Spring Gardens, Washington,
West Sussex, RH20 3BS
Tel: 01903 891955
www.tooveys.com

VEC Ⓐ
VECTIS AUCTIONS
Fleck Way, Thornaby, Stockton on
Tees, County Durham, TS17 9JZ
Tel: 01642 750616
www.vectis.co.uk

W&W Ⓐ
WALLIS AND WALLIS
West Street Auction Galleries,
Lewes, East Sussex, BN7 2NJ
Tel: 01273 480208
www.wallisandwallis.co.uk

WAD Ⓐ
WADDINGTON'S
111 Bathurst St., Toronto,
Ontario M5V 2R1, Canada
Tel: 001 416 504 9100
www.waddingtons.ca

WEB Ⓐ
WEBBS
18 Manukau Road, PO Box 99
251, Newmarket, Auckland 1000,
New Zealand
Tel: 0064 9 5246804
www.webbs.co.nz

WES Ⓐ
WESCHLER'S
909 E Street NW, Washington,
DC 20004 USA
Tel: 001 202 628 1281
www.weschlers.com

WHP Ⓐ
W. & H. PEACOCK
26 Newnham Street,
Bedford, Bedforshire, MK40 3JR
Tel: 01234 266 366
www.peacockauction.co.uk

WKA Ⓐ
WIENER KUNST AUKTIONEN - PALAIS KINSKY
Freyung 4,
1010 Vienna, Austria
Tel: 0043 15324200
www.palais-kinsky.com

WW Ⓐ
WOOLLEY & WALLIS
51-61 Castle Street,
Salisbury, Wiltshire, SP13SU
Tel: 01722 424500
www.woolleyandwallis.co.uk

NOTE

For valuations, it is advisable to contact the dealer or auction house in advance to confirm that they will perform this service and whether any charge is involved. Telephone valuations are not possible, so it will be necessary to send details, including a photograph, of the object, along with a stamped addressed envelope for response. While most dealers will be happy to help you, do remember that they are busy people. Please mention Miller's Antiques when making an enquiry.

This is a list of auctioneers that conduct regular sales. Auction houses that would like to be included in the next edition should contact us at info@millers.uk.com.

LONDON

Angling Auctions
PO Box 2095, W12 8RU
Tel: 020 8749 4175
angling-auctions.co.uk

Auction Atrium
101B Kensington Church Street,
W8 7LN
Tel: 020 7792 9020
www.auctionatrium.com

Baldwins
11 Adelphi Terrace, WC2N 6BJ
Tel: 020 7930 6879
www.baldwin.co.uk

Bloomsbury
24 Maddox Street, W1 S1PP
Tel: 020 7495 9494
www.bloomsbury-book-auct.com

Bonhams
101 New Bond Street, W1S 1SR
Tel: 020 7447 7447
www.bonhams.com

Graham Budd Auctions Ltd.
P.O. Box 47519, N14 6XD
Tel: 020 8366 2525
www.grahambuddauctions.co.uk

Chiswick Auctions
1 Colville Road, Acton, W3 8BL
Tel: 020 8992 4442
www.chiswickauctions.co.uk

Christie's
8 King Street, St. James's, SW1Y 6QT
Tel: 020 7839 9060
85 Old Brompton Road, SW7 3LD
Tel: 020 7930 6074
www.christies.com

Criterion Auctioneers
53 Essex Road, N1 2SF
Tel: 020 7359 5707
www.criterionauctions.co.uk

Dix-Noonan-Webb
16 Bolton Street, W1J 8BQ
Tel: 020 7016 1700
www.dnw.co.uk

Lots Road Galleries
71-73 Lots Road, SW10 0RN
Tel: 020 7376 6800
www.lotsroad.com

Rosebery's
74-76 Knights Hill, SE27 0JD
Tel: 020 8761 2522
www.roseberys.co.uk

Sotheby's
34-35 New Bond Street, W1A 2AA
Tel: 020 7293 5000
www.sothebys.com

Spink & Son Ltd.
69 Southampton Row, WC1B 4ET
Tel: 020 7563 4000
www.spink.com

Kerry Taylor Auctions
Unit C25 Parkhall Rd Trading Estate,
40 Martell Rd, Dulwich SE21 8EN
Tel: 020 8676 4600
www.kerrytaylorauctions.com

AVON

Aldridges of Bath
Newark House, 26-45 Cheltenham
Street, Bath BA2 3EX
Tel: 01225 462830
www.aldridgesofbath.com

Gardiner Houlgate
9 Leafield Way, Corsham SN13 9SW
Tel: 01225 812912
www.gardinerhoulgate.co.uk

BEDFORDSHIRE

W. & H. Peacock
26 Newnham Street, Bedford MK40 3JR
Tel: 01234 266366
www.peacockauction.co.uk

BERKSHIRE

Cameo Auctions
Kennet Holme Farm, Bath Road,
Midgham, Reading, RG7 5UX
Tel: 01189 713772
www.cameo-auctioneers.co.uk

Dreweatts
Donnington Priory, Donnington,
Nr Newbury RG14 2JE
Tel: 01635 553553
www.dnfa.com

Special Auction Services
81 New Greenham Park, Newbury,
Berkshire, RG19 6HW
Tel: 08456 044 669
www.specialauctionservices.com

BUCKINGHAMSHIRE

Amersham Auction Rooms
Station Road, Amersham, HP7 0AH
Tel: 01494 729292
www.amershamauctionrooms.co.uk

Bourne End Auction Rooms
Station Approach, Bourne End SL8 5QH
Tel: 01628 531500
www.bourneendauctionrooms.com

Dickins Auctioneers
Claydon House Park, Calvert Rd,
Middle Claydon MK18 2EZ
Tel: 01296 714 434
www.dickins-auctioneers.com

CAMBRIDGESHIRE

Cheffins
Clifton House, 1 & 2 Clifton Road,
Cambridge CB1 7EA
Tel: 01223 213 343
www.cheffins.co.uk

Hyperion Auctions Ltd
Station Road, St. Ives PE27 5BH
Tel: 01480 464140
www.hyperionauctions.co.uk

Rowley Fine Art Auctioneers
8 Downham Road, Ely CB6 1AH
Tel: 01353 653020
www.rowleyfineart.com

CHANNEL ISLANDS

Martel Maides
Martel Maides Auctions,
Cornet Street, St. Peter Port,
Guernsey GY1 1LF
Tel: 01481 722700
www.martelmaides.co.uk

CHESHIRE

Frank R. Marshall & Co.
Marshall House, Church Hill, Knutsford
WA16 6DH
Tel: 01565 653284
www.frankmarshall.co.uk

Halls Fine Art Auctions
Booth Mansion, 30 Watergate Street,
Chester CH1 2LA
Tel: 01244 312300
www.hallsestateagents.co.uk

Maxwells of Wilmslow
133A Woodford Road, Woodford,
SK7 1QD
Tel: 01614 395182
www.maxwells-auctioneers.co.uk

Peter Wilson Auctioneers
Victoria Gallery, Market Street,
Nantwich CW5 5DG
Tel: 01270 623878
www.peterwilson.co.uk

CORNWALL

W. H. Lane & Son
Jubilee House, Queen Street, Penzance
TR18 4DF
Tel: 01736 361447
www.whlaneauctioneersandvaluers.
co.uk

David Lay FRICS
The Penzance Auction House
Alverton, Penzance TR18 4RE
Tel: 01736 361414
www.davidlay.co.uk

CUMBRIA

Penrith Farmers' & Kidd's
Skirsgill Salesrooms, Penrith CA11 0DN
Tel: 01768 890781
www.pfkauctions.co.uk

Thomson, Roddick & Medcalf
Coleridge House, Shaddongate,
Carlisle CA2 5TU
Tel: 01228 528939
www.thomsonroddick.com

DERBYSHIRE

Bamfords Ltd
The Old Picture Palace, 133 Dale Road,
Matlock, DE4 3LU
www.bamfords-auctions.co.uk

DEVON

Bearnes Hampton & Littlewood
St Edmund's Court, Okehampton Street,
Exeter EX4 1DU
Tel: 01392 413100
www.bhandl.co.uk

S. J. Hales Auctioneers
Tracey House, Newton Road, Bovey
Tracey, Newton Abbot TQ13 9AZ
Tel: 01626 836 684
www.sjhales.com

The Plymouth Auction Rooms,
Faraday Mill Trade Park,
Cattedown, Plymouth,
PL4 0SF
Tel: 01752 254 740
www.plymouthauctions.co.uk

DORSET

Charterhouse
The Long Street Salerooms,
Sherborne DT9 3BS
Tel: 01935 812277
www.charterhouse-auctions.co.uk

Cottees Auctions Ltd.
The Market, East Street, Wareham
BH20 4NR
Tel: 01929 552826
www.auctionsatcottees.co.uk

Dalkeith Auctions
Dalkeith Hall, Dalkeith Steps, 81 Old
Christchurch Rd, Bournemouth,
BH1 1EW
Tel: 01202 292905
www.dalkeith-auctions.co.uk

Hy. Duke & Son
The Dorchester Fine Art Saleroom,
Weymouth Avenue, Dorchester DT1 1QS
Tel: 01305 265080
www.dukes-auctions.com

Onslows
The Coach House, Manor Road,
Stourpaine DT11 8TQ
Tel: 01258 488 838
www.onslows.co.uk

Riddetts of Bournemouth
177 Holdenhurst Road, Bournemouth
BH8 8DG
Tel: 01202 555686

DURHAM

Vectis Auctions Limited
Fleck Way, Thornaby, Stockton on Tees
TS17 9JZ
Tel: 01642 750 616
www.vectis.co.uk

ESSEX

Sworders
14 Cambridge Road,
Stansted Mountfitchet CM24 8GE
Tel: 01279 817778
www.sworder.co.uk

GLOUCESTERSHIRE

Clevedon Salerooms
The Auction Centre, Kenn Road, Kenn,
Clevedon, Bristol BS21 6TT
Tel: 01934 830111
www.clevedon-salerooms.com

The Cotswold Auction Co. Ltd.
The Coach House, Swan Yard,
9-13 West Market Place,
Cirencester, GL7 2NH
Tel: 01285 642420
www.cotswoldauction.co.uk

Dreweatts
St. John's Place, Apsley Road, Clifton
Bristol BS8 2ST
Tel: 0117 973 7201
www.dnfa.com/bristol

Mallams Fine Art Auctioneers
26 Grosvenor Street, Cheltenham
GL52 2SG
Tel: 01242 235712
www.mallams.co.uk

Moore, Allen & Innocent
33 Castle St, Cirencester, GL7 1QD
Tel: 01285 646050
www.mooreallen.com/cat

Tayler & Fletcher
London House, High Street, Bourton-
on-the-Water, Cheltenham GL54 2AP
Tel: 01451 821666
www.taylerfletcher.com

Dominic Winter Book Auctions
Mallard House, Broadway Lane,
South Cerney GL7 5UQ
Tel: 01285 860006
www.dominicwinter.co.uk

Wotton Auction Rooms Ltd
Tabernacle Road,
Wotton-under-Edge GL12 7EB
Tel: 01453 844733
www.wottonauctionrooms.co.uk

HAMPSHIRE
Andrew Smith & Son
Manor Farm, Itchen Stoke SO24 0QT
Tel: 01962 735988
www.andrewsmithandson.com

George Kidner Auctioneers
The Lymington Saleroom,Emsworth
Road, Lymington SO41 9BL
Tel: 01590 670070
www.georgekidner.co.uk

Jacobs & Hunt Auctioneers
Lavant Street, Petersfield GU32 3EF
Tel: 01730 233933
www.jacobsandhunt.com

D.M. Nesbit & Co.
Southsea Salerooms, 7 Clarendon Road,
Southsea PO5 2ED
Tel: 02392 295568
www.nesbits.co.uk

HEREFORDSHIRE
Brightwells
The Fine Art Saleroom,
Easters Court, Leominster HR6 0DE
Tel: 01568 611122
www.brightwells.com

Morris Bricknell
Stroud House, 30 Gloucester Road,
Ross-on-Wye HR9 5LE
Tel: 01989 768320
www.morrisbricknell.com

Nigel Ward & Co.
The Border Property Centre, Pontrilas
HR2 0EH
Tel: 01981 240140
www.nigel-ward.co.ukm

R. G. & R. B. Williams
Ross Auction Rooms, Ross-on-Wye,
HR9 7QQ
Tel: 01989 762225

HERTFORDSHIRE
Sworders
42 St Andrew St, Hertford SG14 1JA
Tel: 01992 583508
www.sworder.co.uk

Tring Market Auctions
Brook Street, Tring HP23 5EF
Tel: 01442 826446
www.tringmarketauctions.co.uk

ISLE OF WIGHT
Shanklin Auction Rooms
79 Regent Street, Shanklin PO37 7AP
Tel: 01983 863441
www.shanklinauctionrooms.co.uk

KENT
Bentley's Fine Art Auctioneers
The Old Granary, Waterloo Road,
Cranbrook TN17 3JQ
Tel: 01580 715857
www.bentleysfineartauctioneers.co.uk

Canterbury Auction Galleries
40 Station Rd, Canterbury CT2 8AN
Tel: 01227 763337
www.thecanterburyauctiongalleries.com

Dreweatts
(consignment only)
10 Mount Ephraim, Tunbridge Wells,
TN4 8AS
Tel: 01892 544500
www.dnfa.com/tunbridgewells

Gorringes
(consignment only)
85 Mount Pleasant Road, Tunbridge
Wells TN1 1PX
Tel: 01892 619670
www.gorringes.co.uk

Ibbett Mosely
125 High Street,Sevenoaks TN13 1UT
Tel: 01732 456731
www.ibbettmosely.co.uk

Lambert & Foster Auction
77 Commercial Road,
Paddock Wood, TN12 6DR
Tel: 01892 832325
www.lambertandfoster.co.uk

Mervyn Carey
Twysden Cottage, Benenden,
Cranbrook TN17 4LD
Tel: 01580 240283

LANCASHIRE
Smythes Fine Art
174 Victoria Road West, Cleveleys
FY5 3NE
Tel: 01253 852184
www.smythes.net

LEICESTERSHIRE
Gilding's Auctioneers & Valuers
64 Roman Way, Market Harborough
LE16 7PQ
Tel: 01858 410414
www.gildings.co.uk

Tennants Auctioneers
Millhouse, South Street, Oakham,
Rutland LE15 6BG
Tel: 01572 724666
www.tennants.co.uk

LINCOLNSHIRE
Eleys Auctioneers
Old Wharf Road, Grantham NG31 7AA
Tel: 01476 575202
www.eleys-auctions.co.uk

Marilyn Swain
Northend Farm, Long Street, Foston,
Grantham NG32 2LD
Tel: 01400 283377
www.marilynswainauctions.co.uk

MANCHESTER
Capes, Dunn & Co.
The Auction Galleries, 38 Charles
Street, Manchester, M17DB
Tel: 0161 2731911
www.capesdunn.com

MERSEYSIDE
Cato Crane & Co.
6 Stanhope St, Liverpool L8 5RF
Tel: 01517 095559
www.cato-crane.co.uk

NORFOLK
Garry M. Emms & Co. Ltd.
Beevor Road, Great Yarmouth
NR30 3QQ
Tel: 01493 332668
www.greatyarmouthauctions.com

T.W. Gaze
Roydon Road, Diss IP22 4LN
Tel: 01379 650306
www.twgaze.com

Holt's Auctioneers
Church Farm Barns, Walferton
PE31 6HA
Tel: 01485 542822
www.holtandcompany.co.uk

Keys Auctioneers & Valuers
Aylsham Salerooms, Palmers Lane,
Aylsham, NR11 6JA
Tel: 01263 733195
www.keysauctions.co.uk

NOTTINGHAMSHIRE
Mellors & Kirk
Gregory Street, Nottingham,
NG7 2NL
Tel: 0115 979 0000
www.mellorsandkirk.com

Dreweatts
(consignment only)
192 Mansfield Road,
Nottingham NG1 3HU
Tel: 0115 962 4141
www.dnfa.com/nottingham

John Pye & Sons
James Shipstone House,
Radford Rd, Nottingham NG7 7EA
Tel: 0870 910 9000
www.johnpye.co.uk

T Vennett-Smith Auctioneers
11 Nottingham Rd, Gotham NG11 0HE
Tel: 0115 9830541
www.vennett-smith.com

OXFORDSHIRE
Holloway's
49 Parsons Street, Banbury OX16 5NB
Tel: 01295 817777
www.hollowaysauctioneers.co.uk

Jones & Jacob Ltd.
Watcombe Manor Saleroom
Ingham Lane, Watlington OX49 5EJ
Tel 01491 612810
www.jonesandjacob.com

Mallams Fine Art Auctioneers
Bocardo House, 24a St. Michael's St,
Oxford OX1 2EB
Tel: 01865 241358
www.mallams.co.uk

SHROPSHIRE
Brettells Antiques & Fine Art
58 High Street, Newport TF10 7AQ
Tel: 01952 815925
www.brettells.com

Halls Fine Art
Welsh Bridge, Shrewsbury SY3 8LA
Tel: 01743 284777
www.hallsestateagents.co.uk/fine-art

Walker Barnett & Hill
Cosford Auction Rooms, Long Lane,
Cosford TF11 8PJ
Tel: 01902 375555

SOMERSET
Greenslade Taylor Hunt
The Priory Saleroom, Winchester St,
Taunton TA1 1QE
Tel: 01823 332525
www.gth.net

Lawrence's Fine Art Auctioneers
The Linen Yard, South Street,
Crewkerne TA18 8AB
Tel: 01460 73041
www.lawrences.co.uk

Dreweatts
St Johns Place, Apsley Rd, Clifton BS8 2ST
Tel: 01179 737201
www.dnfa.com/bristol

STAFFORDSHIRE
Louis Taylor Auctioneers
10 Town Road, Hanley ST1 2QG
Tel: 01782 214111
www.louistaylorfineart.co.uk

Potteries Specialist Auctions
271 Waterloo Road, Cobridge ST6 3HR
Tel: 01782 286622
www.potteriesauctions.com

Richard Winterton Auctioneers
Main Midland Saleroom, Hawkins Lane,
Burton-on-Trent DE14 1PT
Tel: 01283 511224
www.richardwinterton.co.uk

Wintertons
Uttoxeter Auction Centre, Short St,
Uttoxeter ST14 7LH
Tel: 01889 564385
www.wintertons.co.uk

SUFFOLK
Lacy Scott and Knight Fine Art
10 Risbygate Street, Bury St. Edmunds
IP33 3AA
Tel: 01284 748600
www.lsk.co.uk

Neal Sons & Fletcher
26 Church Street, Woodbridge
IP12 1DP
Tel: 01394 382263
www.nsf.co.uk

Sworders
The Saleroom, Burkitts Lane, Sudbury
CO10 1HB
Tel: 01787 880305
www.sworder.co.uk

SURREY
Clarke Gammon Wellers
4 Quarry St, Guildford, GU1 3TY
Tel: 01483 880900
www.clarkegammon.co.uk

Crows Auction Gallery
Reigate Road, Dorking RH4 1SG
Tel: 01306 740382
www.crowsauctions.co.uk

Ewbank Clarke Gammon Wellers
Burnt Common Auction Rooms, London
Rd, Send, Woking GU23 7LN
Tel: 01483 223101
www.ewbankauctions.co.uk

Dreweatts
Baverstock House, 93 High Street,
Godalming GU7 1AL
Tel: 01483 423 567
www.dnfa.com/godalming

John Nicholson
Longfield, Midhurst Road, Haslemere
GU27 3HA
Tel: 01428 653727
www.johnnicholsons.com

Lawrences Auctioneers Ltd.
Norfolk House, 80 High Street,
Bletchingley RH1 4PA
Tel: 01883 743323
www.lawrencesbletchingley.co.uk

Weller's
70 Guildford Street, Chertsey, KT16 9BB
Tel: 01932 568678
www.wellers-auctions.co.uk

P.F. Windibank Auctioneers
Dorking Halls, Reigate Road, Dorking
RH4 1SG
Tel: 01306 884556/876280
www.windibank.co.uk

EAST SUSSEX
Burstow & Hewett
Lower Lake, Battle, TN33 0AT
Tel: 01424 772374
www.burstowandhewett.co.uk

Dreweatts
46-50 South Street,Eastbourne BN21 4XB
Tel: 01323 410419
www.dnfa.com/eastbourne

Eastbourne Auction Rooms
Auction House, Finmere Road,
Eastbourne BN22 8QL
Tel: 01323 431444
www.eastbourneauction.com

Gorringes Auction Galleries
Terminus Road, Bexhill-on-Sea
TN39 3LR
Tel: 01424 212994
15 North Street, Lewes BN7 2PD
Tel: 01273 472503
www.gorringes.co.uk

Raymond P. Inman
The Auction Galleries, 98A Coleridge
Street, Hove BN3 5 AA
Tel: 01273 774777
www.invaluable.com/raymondinman

Rye Auction Galleries
Rock Channel, Rye TN31 7HL
Tel: 01797 222124
www.ryeauctiongalleries.co.uk

Wallis & Wallis
West Street Auction Galleries,
Lewes BN7 2NJ
Tel: 01273 480208
www.wallisandwallis.co.uk

WEST SUSSEX
Henry Adams Fine Art
Baffins Hall, Baffins Lane,
Chichester PO19 1UA
Tel: 01243 532223
www.henryadamsfineart.co.uk

Bellmans
New Pound, Wisborough Green,
Billingshurst RH14 0AZ
Tel: 01403 700858
www.bellmans.co.uk

Toovey's
Spring Gdns, Washington RH20 3BS
Tel: 01903 891955
www.tooveys.com

TYNE AND WEAR
Anderson & Garland
Anderson House, Crispin Court,
Newbiggin Lane, Westerhope,
Newcastle upon Tyne NE5 1BF
Tel: 0191 430 3000
www.andersonandgarland.com

WARWICKSHIRE
Bigwood Auctioneers Ltd
The Old School, Tiddington CV37 7AW
Tel: 01789 269415
www.bigwoodauctioneers.co.uk

Locke & England
18 Guy Street, Leamington Spa
CV32 4RT
Tel: 01926 889100
www.leauction.co.uk

WEST MIDLANDS
Biddle & Webb
Ladywood, Middleway, Birmingham
B16 0PP
Tel: 0121 455 8042
www.biddleandwebb.co.uk

Fellows & Sons
Augusta House, 19 Augusta Street,
Hockley, Birmingham B18 6JA
Tel: 0121 212 2131
www.fellows.co.uk

Fieldings
Mill Race Lane, Stourbridge, DY8 1JN
Tel: 01384 444140
www.fieldingsauctioneers.co.uk

WILTSHIRE
Henry Aldridge & Son
Unit 1 Bath Road Business Centre
Bath Road, Devizes SN10 1XA
Tel: 01380 729199
www.henry-aldridge.co.uk

Gardiner Houlgate
Bath Auction Rooms, 9 Leafield Way,
Corsham, SN13 9SW
Tel: 01225 812912
www.gardinerhoulgate.co.uk

Woolley & Wallis
51-61 Castle Street, Salisbury SP1 3SU
Tel: 01722 424500
www.woolleyandwallis.co.uk

WORCESTERSHIRE
Andrew Grant Auctioneers
5 New Road, Bromsgrove, B60 2HX
Tel: 01527 579977
www.andrew-grant.co.uk

Philip Serrell Auctioneers
Barnards Green Road, Malvern
WR14 3LW
Tel: 01684 892314
www.serrell.com

EAST YORKSHIRE
Dee Atkinson & Harrison
The Exchange Saleroom, Driffield
YO25 6LD
Tel: 01377 253151
www.dee-atkinson-harrison.co.uk

NORTH YORKSHIRE
Boulton & Cooper
St Michael's House, Market Place,
Malton YO17 7LL
Tel: 01653 696151
www.boultoncooper.co.uk

David Duggleby Fine Art
The Vine Street Salerooms, Scarborough
YO11 1XN
Tel: 01723 507111
www.davidduggleby.com

Lithgow Sons & Partner
The Auction Houses, Station Road,
Stokesley, Middlesbrough TS9 7AB
Tel: 01642 710158
www.lithgowsauctions.com

Morphets of Harrogate
6 Albert Street, Harrogate HG1 1JL
Tel: 01423 530030
www.morphets.co.uk

Tennants
The Auction Centre, Leyburn DL8 5SG
Tel: 01969 623780
www.tennants.co.uk

SOUTH YORKSHIRE
BBR Auctions
Elsecar Heritage Centre, Barnsley S74 8HJ
Tel: 01226 745156
www.onlinebbr.com

ELR Auctions Ltd.
The Sheffield Saleroom, The Nichols
Building, Shalesmoor, Sheffield S3 8UJ
Tel: 0114 281 6161
www.elrauctions.com

WEST YORKSHIRE
Hartley's
Victoria Hall Salerooms,
Little Lane, Ilkley LS29 8EA
Tel: 01943 816363
www.hartleyauctions.co.uk

John Walsh & Co. Auctioneers
55 Jenkin Road, Horbury, Wakefield,
WF4 6DP
Tel: 01924 271710
www.john-walsh.co.uk

SCOTLAND
Bonhams
22 Queen St, Edinburgh EH2 2JL
Tel: 0131 225 2266
www.bonhams.com

Loves Auction Rooms
Arran House, Arran Road, Perth PH1 3DZ
Tel: 01738 633337

Lyon & Turnbull Ltd.
33 Broughton Place,
Edinburgh EH1 3RR
Tel: 0131 557 8844
www.lyonandturnbull.com

D.J. Manning Auctioneers
Bridgeness Road, Bo'ness,
West Lothian EH51 9SF
Tel: 01506 827693
www.djmanning.co.uk

McTear's
Meiklewood Gate, 31 Meiklewood
Road, Glasgow G51 4EU
Tel: 0141 810 2886
www.mctears.co.uk

Shapes
Bankhead Medway, Sighthill, Edinburgh,
EH11 4BY
Tel: 0131 4533222
www.shapesauctioneers.co.uk

Sotheby's
7 Howe Street, Edinburgh EH3 6TE
Tel: 0131 558 7799
www.sothebys.com

Thomson, Roddick & Medcalf
Carnethie St, Rosewell, Edinburgh
EH24 9AL
Tel: 0131 440 2448
Irongray Road, Dumfries DG2 OJE
Tel: 01387 721635
www.thomsonroddick.com

WALES
Anthemion Auctions
15 Norwich Road, Cardiff CF23 9AB
Tel: 029 2047 2444
www.anthemionauctions.com

Bonhams
9-10 Park Place, Cardiff, CF10 3DP
Tel: 02920 727980
13 Spilman Street, Carmarthen
SA31 1JY
Tel: 01267 238231
www.bonhams.com

Morgan Evans & Co. Ltd
28-30 Church Street, Llangefni, Isle of
Anglesey LL77 7DU
Tel: 01248 723303/421582
www.morganevans.com

Peter Francis
Towyside Salerooms, Old Station Road,
Carmarthen, SA31 1JN
Tel: 01267 233456
www.peterfrancis.co.uk

Rogers Jones Co.
The Auction Rooms, 33 Abergele Road,
Colwyn Bay LL29 7RU
Tel: 01492 532176
www.rogersjones.co.uk

Welsh Country Auctions
2 Carmarthen Road, Cross Hands,
Llanelli, Carmarthenshire SA14 6SP
Tel: 01269 844428
www.welshcountryauctions.co.uk

Wingetts Auction Gallery
29 Holt Street, Wrexham,
Clwyd LL13 8DH
Tel: 01978 353553
www.wingetts.co.uk

IRELAND
Limerick Auction Rooms
Hamptons House, Garryglass Industrial
Estate, Ballysimon Road, Limerick
Tel: 00353 61422143
www.lar.ie

AUSTRALIA
Bonhams & Goodman
76 Paddington Street, Paddington,
Sydney, NSW 2021
Tel: 0061 2 8412 2222
www.bonhams.com/au

Deutscher-Menzies
12 Todman Avenue, Kensington, Sydney
NSW 2033
Tel: 0061 2 8344 5404
www.deutschermenzies.com

Leonard Joel
333 Malvern Road, South Yarra,
3141, Victoria, Melbourne,
Tel : 0061 3 98264333
www.leonardjoel.com.au

Lawsons
1A The Crescent, Annadale 2038
Tel: 0061 2 9566 2377
www.lawsons.com.au

Shapiro
162 Queen Street, Woollahra, Sydney
NSW 2025
Tel: 0061 2 9326 1588
www.shapiroauctioneers.com.au

NEW ZEALAND
Dunbar Sloane
12 Akepiro Street, Mt Eden, Auckland,
Tel: 0064 4721367
www.dunbarsloane.co.nz

Webb's
18 Manukau Road, PO Box 99 251,
Newmarket, Auckland 1000
Tel: 0064 9 524 6804
www.webbs.co.nz

Specialists who would like to be listed in the next edition, or have a new address or telephone number, should contact us at info@millers.uk.com. Readers should contact dealers before visiting to avoid a wasted journey.

ANTIQUITIES
Ancient Art
85 The Vale, London N14 6AT
Tel: 020 8882 1509
www.ancientart.co.uk

Finch & Co.
Suite No 744, 2 Old Brompton Rd,
London SW7 3DQ
Tel: 020 7413 9937
www.finch-and-co.co.uk

John A. Pearson
Horton Lodge, Horton Rd, Horton, Near
Slough, Berkshire SL3 9NU
Tel: 01753 682136

Rupert Wace Ancient Art Ltd.
14 Old Bond St, London W1S 4PP
Tel: 020 7495 1623
www.rupertwace.co.uk

Ancient & Gothic
PO Box 5390, Bournemouth, Dorset,
BH7 6XR
Tel: 01202 431721

ARCHITECTURAL
Joanna Booth
P.O. Box 50886, London SW3 5YH
Tel: 020 7352 8998
www.joannabooth.co.uk

LASSCO
30 Wandsworth Rd, London SW8 2LG
Tel: 0207 394 2100
www.lassco.co.uk

Sweerts de Landas
Dunsborough Park, Ripley, Surrey
GU23 6AL
Tel: 01483 225366
www.sweerts.com

Robert Mills Ltd.
Narroways Rd, Eastville, Bristol BS2 9XB
Tel: 0117 955 6542
www.rmills.co.uk

ARMS & MILITARIA
Q&C Militaria
22 Suffolk Road, Cheltenham,
Gloucestershire GL50 2AQ
Tel: 01242 519815
www.qcmilitaria.com

Garth Vincent
The Old Manner House, Allington,
Nr Grantham, Lincolnshire NG32 2DH
Tel: 01400 281358
www.guns.uk.com

West Street Antiques
63 West Street, Dorking, Surrey
RH4 1BS
Tel: 01306 883487
www.antiquearmsandarmour.com

BAROGRAPHS
Richard Twort
Tel: 01934 612439
walls@mirage-interiors.com

CARPETS & RUGS
Gallery Yacou
127 Fulham Rd, London SW3 6RT
Tel: 020 7584 2929
www.galleryyacou.com

Gideon Hatch
21 Lambourn Rd, London SW4 0LS
Tel: 0207 720 7543
www.gideonhatch.co.uk

John Eskenazi Ltd.
P.O. Box 55621, London W9 2XA
Tel: 020 7409 3001
www.john-eskenazi.com

Karel Weijand
Lion & Lamb Courtyard, Farnham,
Surrey GU9 7LL
Tel: 01252 726215
www.karelweijand.com

Lindfield Galleries
62 High Street, Lindfield, West Sussex
RH16 2HL
Tel: 01444 483817
david@orientalandantiquerugs.com

Wadsworth's
Marehill, Pulborough, West Sussex RH20
2DY
Tel: 01798 873 555
www.wadsworthsrugs.com

BOOKS
Barter Books
Alnwick Station, Alnwick,
Northumberland NE66 2NP
Tel: 01665 604888
www.barterbooks.co.uk

George Bayntun
Manvers Street, Bath BA1 1JW
Tel: 01225 466000
www.georgebayntun.com

David Aldous-Cook
PO Box 413, Sutton, Surrey SM3 8SZ
Tel: 020 8642 4842
www.ukbookworld.com/members/
aldouscook

BOXES
Alan & Kathy Stacey
www.antiqueboxes.uk.com

Mostly Boxes
93 High Street, Eton,
Windsor, Berkshire SL4 6AF
Tel: 01753 858 470

CERAMICS
Albert Amor Ltd.
7 Bury Street, London SW1Y 6AU
Tel: 020 7930 2444
www.albertamor.co.uk

Andrew Dando
34 Market Street, Bradford-on-Avon,
Wiltshire BA15 1LL
Tel: 01225 865444
www.andrewdando.co.uk

Brian & Angela Downes
PO Box 431, Chippenham,
Wiltshire SN14 6SZ
Tel/Fax: 01454 238134

Clive & Lynne Jackson
Cheltenham, Gloucestershire
Open by appointment only
Tel: 01242 254 3751

Davies Antiques
c/o Cadogan Tate, Unit 6, 6-12 Ponton
Road, London SW8 5BA
Tel: 020 8947 1902
www.antique-meissen.com

E & H Manners
66A Kensington Church Street, London
W8 4BY
Tel: 020 7229 5516
www.europeanporcelain.com

Garry Atkins
P.O. Box 50415, London W8 7XY
Tel: 020 7727 8737
www.englishpottery.com

John Howard at Heritage
6 Market Place, Woodstock, Oxfordshire
OX20 1TA
Tel: 01993 812580
www.antiquepottery.co.uk

**Mary Wise and Grosvenor
Antiques**
58 Kensington Church Street, London
W8 4DB
Tel: 020 7937 8649
www.wiseantiques.com

Roderick Jellicoe
P.O. Box No. 50732 London NW6 6XW
Tel: 020 7624 6471
www.englishporcelain.com

Rogers de Rin
76 Royal Hospital Road, Paradise Walk,
Chelsea,London SW3 4HN
Tel: 020 7352 9007
www.rogersderin.co.uk

Roy W. Bunn Antiques
Tel: 01282 813703
www.roywbunnantiques.co.uk

Steppes Hill Farm Antiques
Steppes Hill Farm, Stockbury,
Sittingbourne, Kent ME9 7RB
Tel: 01795 842205
www.steppeshillfarm.com

Stockspring Antiques
114 Kensington Church Street, London
W8 4BH
Tel: 020 7727 7995
www.antique-porcelain.co.uk

T.C.S. Brooke
The Grange, 57 Norwich Road,
Wroxham, Norfolk NR12 8RX
Tel: 01603 782644

Valerie Main
PO Box 92, Carlisle, Cumbria CA5 7GD
Tel: 01228 711342
www.valeriemain.co.uk

W.W. Warner Antiques
The Green, High Street,
Brasted, Kent, Westerham, TN16 1JL
Tel: 01959 563698

Yvonne Adams Antiques
The Coffee House, 3 & 4 Church St,
Stow on the Wold, Gloucestershire
GL54 1BB
Tel: 01451 832 015
www.antiquemeissen.co.uk

Barling Porcelain
Tel: 01621 890058

Greystoke Antiques
4 Swan Yard, Sherborne, Dorset
DT9 3AX
Tel: 01935 812833

Winson Antiques
Unit 11, Langston Priory Workshops,
Kingham, Oxfordshire OX7 6UP
Tel: 01608 658856 / 07764 476776
www.clivepayne.co.uk

CLOCKS, WATCHES & BAROMETERS
P.A. Oxley
The Old Rectory, Cherhill, Calne,
Wiltshire, SN11 8UX
Tel: 01249 816227
www.british-antiqueclocks.com

Coppelia Antiques
Holford Lodge, Plumley Moor Rd,
Plumley, Cheshire WA16 9RS
Tel: 01565 722197
www.coppeliaantiques.co.uk

The Grandfather Clock Shop
Sheep Street, Stow-on-the-Wold,
Gloucestershire GL54 1JS
Tel: 01451 830455
www.stylesofstow.co.uk

Woodward Antique Clocks
21 Suffolk Parade, Cheltenham,
Gloucestershire GL50 2AE
Tel: 01242 245667

Northern Clocks
Boothsbank Farm, Worsley,
Manchester M28 1LL
Tel: 0161 790 8414
www.northernclocks.co.uk

The Clock-Work-Shop
6A Parchment Street
Winchester, Hampshire SO23 8AT
Tel: 01962 842331
www.clock-work-shop.co.uk

The Clock Clinic Ltd.
85 Lower Richmond Road,
Putney, LondonSW15 1EU
Tel: 020 8788 1407
www.clockclinic.co.uk

Roderick Antique Clocks
23 Vicarage Gate, London W8 4AA
Tel: 020 79378517
www.roderickantiqueclocks.com

Allan Smith Clocks
Amity Cottage, 162 Beechcroft Rd,
Upper Stratton, Swindon SN2 7QE
Tel: 01793 822977
www.allansmithantiqueclocks.co.uk

Brian Loomes
Calf Haugh Farm, Pateley Bridge,
Yorkshire HG3 5HW
Tel: 01423 711163
www.brianloomes.com

Alan Walker
Halfway Manor, Halfway, Nr. Newbury,
Berkshire RG20 8NR
Tel: 01488 657670
www.alanwalker-barometers.com

Baskerville Antiques
Saddlers House, Saddlers Row,
Petworth, West Sussex GU28 0AN
Tel: 01798 342067
brianbaskerville@aol.com

Derek and Tina Rayment
Orchard House, Barton Rd, Barton,
Nr. Farndon, Cheshire SY14 7HT
Tel: 01829 270429
www.antique-barometers.com

Derek Roberts
25 Shipbourne Road,
Tonbridge, Kent TN10 3DN
Tel: 01732 358986
www.quallityantiqueclocks.com

Pendulum of Mayfair
51 Maddox St, London W1S 2PJ
Tel: 020 7629 6606
www.pendulumofmayfair.co.uk

Raffety & Walwyn Ltd.
79 Kensington Church Street,
London W8 4BG
Tel: 020 7938 1100
www.raffetyantiqueclocks.com

Somlo Antiques
35-36 Burlington Arcade, London
N1J 0QB
Tel: 020 7499 6526
www.somlo.com

The Watch Gallery
129 Fulham Rd, London SW3 6RT
Tel: 020 7581 3239
www.thewatchgallery.co.uk

Anthony Woodburn Ltd.
PO Box 2669, Lewes,
East Sussex BN7 3JE
Tel: 01273 486666
www.anthonywoodburn.com

Horological Workshops
204 Worplesdon Road, Guildford,
Surrey GU2 6UY
Tel: 01483 576496
www.horologicalworkshops.com

**COSTUME JEWELLERY &
ACCESSORIES**
Cristobal
26 Church St, London NW8 8EP
Tel: 020 7724 7230
www.cristobal.co.uk

Linda Bee
Grays Antique Dealers, 58 Davies St &
1-7 Davies Mews, London W1K 5AB
Tel: 020 7493 9344
www.graysantiques.com

Richard Gibbon
neljeweluk@aol.com

Glitz UK
www.glitzuk.co.uk

William Wain at Antiquarius
Stand J6, Antiquarius, 135 Kings Road,
Chelsea, London SW3 4PW
Tel: 020 7351 4905
williamwain@btopenworld.com

DECORATIVE ARTS
Adrian Sassoon
14 Rutland Gate, London SW7 1BB
Tel: 020 7581 9888
www.adriansassoon.com

Aesthetics
Stand V2, Antiquarius, 131-141 Kings
Road, London SW3 4PW
Tel: 020 7352 0395

Arenski Fine Arts Ltd.
The Coach House, Ledbury Mews
North, London W11 2AF
Tel: 020 8202 3075
www.arenski.com

Art Deco Etc.
73 Upper Gloucester Road, Brighton,
Sussex BN1 3LQ
Tel: 01273 202 937
decojohn@hotmail.com

Art Nouveau Originals c.1900
The Bindery Gallery, 69 High St,
Broadway, Worcestershire WR12 7DP
Tel: 01386 854645

Beth
Stand G043/46, Alfies Antiques Market,
13-25 Church St, London NW8 8DT
Mob: 07776 136 003

Circa 1900
6 Camden Passage, London N1 8ED
Mob: 0771 370 9211
www.circa1900.org

Clarion Antiques & Fine Art
Ground Floor, 2 St Georges Sq,
Lancashire, FY8 2NY
Tel: 01253 721903

Crafts Noveau
112 Alexandra Park Road,
Muswell Hill, London, N10 2AE
Tel: 0208 444 3300
www.craftsnoveau.co.uk

Fay Lucas Art Metal
Christie's Fine Art Security,
42 Ponton Rd, London SW8 5RA
Tel: 020 7371 4404
www.faylucas.com

**Gallery 1930/Susie Cooper
Ceramics**
18 Church St, London NW8 8EP
Tel: 020 7723 1555
www.susiecooperceramics.com

Garret & Hurst Sculpture
PO Box 658, East Grinstead,
West Sussex, RH19 3GH
Tel: 01342 311729
www.garretandhurst.co.uk

Halcyon Days Ltd.
14 Brook St, London W1S 1BD
Tel: 020 7629 8811
www.halcyondays.co.uk

Hall-Bakker at Heritage
6 Market Place, Woodstock, Oxfordshire
OX20 1TA
Tel: 01993 811 332
www.hallbakker.co.uk

Mitofsky Antiques
8 Rathfarnham Road,
Terenure, Dublin 6, Eire
Tel: +353 1 4920033
www.mitofskyantiques.com

Mike Weedon
7 Camden Passage, Islington,
London N1 8EA
Tel: 020 7226 5319
www.mikeweedonantiques.com

Mike & Debby Moir
www.manddmoir.co.uk

Richard Gardner Antiques
Swan House, Market Square,
Petworth, West Sussex GU28 0AH
Tel: 01798 343 411
www.richardgardenerantiques.co.uk

Robert Bowman Ltd.
34 Duke Street, St James's,
London SW1Y 6DF
Tel: 020 7930 8003
www.robertbowman.com

Rumours
4 The Mall Antiques Arcade,
359 Upper St, London N1 0PD
Tel: 020 7704 6549

Spencer Swaffer Antiques
30 High Street, Arundel, West Sussex
BN18 9AB
Tel: 01903 882132
www.spencerswaffer.co.uk

Style Gallery
10 Camden Passage, London N1 8ED
Tel: 020 7359 7867
www.styleantiques.co.uk

Tadema Gallery
10 Charlton Place, Camden Passage,
London N1 8AJ
Tel: 020 7359 1055
www.tademagallery.com

The Country Seat
Huntercombe Manor Barn, Nr. Henley
on Thames, Oxfordshire RG9 5RY
Tel: 01491 641349
www.thecountryseat.com

The Design Gallery
5 The Green, Westerham,
Kent TN16 1AS
Tel: 01959 561234
www.designgallery.co.uk

The Red House
Duncombe Place, York, North Yorkshire
YO1 7ED
Tel: 01904 637 000
www.redhouseyork.co.uk

Titus Omega
Tel: 020 7688 1295
www.titusomega.com

Van Den Bosch
123 Grays, 58 Davies St,
London W1K 5LP
Tel: 020 7629 1900
www.vandenbosch.co.uk

DOLLS AND TOYS
Bébés et Jouets
Tel: 0131 332 5650
bebesetjouets@tiscali.uk

Collectors Old Toy Shop & Antiques
89 Northgate, Halifax,
West Yorkshire HX1 1XF
Tel: 01422 360434
www.collectorsoldtoyshop.com

Sue Pearson
147 High St, Lewes, East Sussex
BN7 1XT
Tel: 01273 442677
www.suepearson.co.uk

Victoriana Dolls
101 Portobello Road,
London W11 2BQ
Tel: 01737 249 525
heather.bond@homecall.co.uk

Teddy Bears of Whitney
99 High St, Witney, OX28 6HY
Tel: 01993 706616
www.teddybears.co.uk

FISHING
The Old Tackle Box
PO Box 55, High Street,
Cranbrook, TN17 3ZU
Tel: 01580 713979
www.oldtacklebox.com

FURNITURE
Alistair Sampson Antiques
120 Mount St, London W1K 3NN
Tel: 020 7409 1799
www.alistairsampson.com

Anthemion
Cartmel, Grange-over-Sands, Cumbria
LA11 6QB
Tel: 015395 36295
www.anthemionantiques.co.uk

The Antiques Warehouse
25 Lightwood Road, Buxton,
Derbyshire SK17 7BJ
Tel: 01298 72967

Antony Preston Antiques Ltd.
The Square, Stow-on-the-Wold,
Cheltenam, Gloucestershire, GL54 1AB
Tel: 01451 831586
www.antonypreston.com

Avon Antiques
25-27 Market Street, Bradford-on-
Avon, Wiltshire BA15 1LL
Tel: 01225 862052
www.avon-antiques.co.uk

Baggott Church Street Ltd.
Church Street, Stow-on-the-Wold,
Gloucestershire GL54 1BB
Tel: 01451 831392
www.baggottantiques.com

Blanchard Ltd.
86/88 Pimlico Road, London SW1W 8PL
Tel: 020 7823 6310
piers@jwblanchard.com

Charles Lumb & Sons Ltd.
1 Montpellier Gardens, Harrogate,
North Yorkshire HG1 2TF
Tel: 01423 504118
www.harrogateantiques.com

Cheverons Antiques Ltd
Unit 8, New Place, Blackboys Road,
Framfield, East Sussex TN22 5EQ
Tel: 01825 890 223
www.chevertons.com

Christopher Buck Antiques
56-60 Sandgate High St, Sandgate,
Folkestone, Kent CT20 3AP
Tel: 01303 221229
chrisbuck@throwley.freeserve.co.uk

Country Antiques (Wales) Ltd.
Castle Mill, Kidwelly Carmarthenshire,
SA17 5AJ
Tel: 01554 890534
www.welshantiques.com

Cross Hayes Antiques
Unit 6, Westbrook Farm, Draycot,
Chippenham, Wiltshire SN15 5LH
Tel: 01249 720033
www.crosshayes.co.uk

David Love
10 Royal Parade, Harrogate,
North Yorkshire HG1 2SZ
Tel: 01423 565797
david.love@btconnect.com

Denzil Grant
Green Farm Gallery, Thurston, Bury St
Edmunds, Suffolk IP31 35N
Tel: 01359 230888
www.denzilgrant.com

Destiny Antiques, Art & Design
Perth Airport,
Scone, Perthshire, PH2 6PL
Tel: 01738 553273
www.destinyantiques.co.uk

Elaine Phillips Antiques Ltd.
1 & 2 Royal Parade, Harrogate,
North Yorkshire HG1 2SZ
Tel: 01423 569 745
www.elainephillipsantiques.co.uk

Freeman & Lloyd
44 Sandgate High St, Sandgate,
Folkestone, Kent CT20 3AP
Tel: 01303 248986
www.freemanandlloyd.com

Georgian Antiques
10 Pattison St, Leith Links, Edinburgh
EH6 7HF, Scotland
Tel: 0131 553 7286
www.georgianantiques.net

John Bly
By appointment London SW1Y 6AL
Tel: 01442 823030
Showroom: Woburn Abbey Antiques,
Woburn, Bedfordshire MK17 9WA
www.johnbly.com

John Hobbs Ltd.
107A Pimlico Road, London SW1W 8PH
Tel: 020 7730 8369
www.johnhobbs.co.uk

Lennox Cato Antiques
1 The Square, Church Street,
Edenbridge, Kent TN8 5BD
Tel: 01732 865 988
www.lennoxcato.com

Lorraine Spooner Antiques
211 Watling Street West,
Towcester, Northamptonshire
NN12 6BX
Tel: 01327 358777
www.lsantiques.com

Lucy Johnson
PO Box 84, Carterton, Burford,
Oxfordshire OX18 4AT
Tel: 07071 881232
www.lucy-johnson.com

Mac Humble Antiques
7-9 Woolley Street, Bradford-on-Avon,
Wiltshire BA15 1AD
Tel: 01225 866329

Oswald Simpson
Hall St, Long Malford, Suffolk
CO10 9JL
Tel: 01787 377523

Owen Humble Antiques
By appointment only
Newcastle Upon Tyne, NE2 4RP
Tel: 01912 812100

Patrick Sandberg Antiques
150-152 Kensington Church Street,
London W8 4BN
Tel: 020 7229 0373
www.antiquefurniture.net

Paul Hopwell Antiques
30 High Street, West Haddon,
Northamptonshire NN6 7AP
Tel: 01788 510636
www.antiqueoak.co.uk

Peter Bunting
Harthill Hall, Alport, Bakewell,
Derbyshire DE45 1LH
Tel: 01629 636203
www.countryoak.co.uk

Peter Foyle Hunwick
The Old Malthouse,
15 Bridge Street, Hungerford, Berkshire
RG17 0EG
Tel/Fax: 01488 682209

Phillips of Hitchin (Antiques)
The Manor House, Hitchin,
Hertfordshire SG5 1JW
Tel: 01462 432067

Pugh's Antiques
Portley House, North Road,
Leominster, Herefordshire H36 0AA
Tel: 01568 616546
www.pughsantiques.com

R G Cave & Sons Ltd.
Walcote House, 17 Broad Street,
Ludlow, Shropshire SY8 1NG
Tel: 01584 873568

R N Myers & Son Ltd.
Endsleigh House, High Street, Gargrave,
Skipton, North Yorkshire BD23 3LX
Tel: 01756 749587
rnmyersson@aol.com

Reindeer Antiques Ltd.
81 Kensington Church Street, London
W8 4BG
Tel: 020 7937 3754
43 Watling Street, Potterspury,
Northamptonshire NN12 7QD
Tel: 01908 542407
www.reindeerantiques.co.uk

Robert Young Antiques
68 Battersea Bridge Road,
London SW11 3AG
Tel: 020 7228 7847
www.robertyoungantiques.com

Roderick Butler
Marwood House, Honiton,
Devon EX14 1PY
Tel: 01404 42169

S.W. Antiques
Abbey Showrooms,
Newlands Road, Pershore,
Worcestershire, WR10 1BP
Tel: 01386 555580
www.sw-antiques.co.uk

Thomas Coulborn & Sons
Vesey Manor, 64 Birmingham Road,
Sutton Coldfield B72 1QP
Tel: 0121 354 3974
www.coulborn.com

Tobias Jellinek Antiques
20 Park Road, East Twickenham,
Middlesex TW1 2PX
Tel: 020 8892 6892
toby@jellinek.com

W A Pinn & Sons
124 Swan Street, Sible Hedingham,
Essex CO9 3HP
Tel: 01787 461127

W R Harvey & Co Ltd.
86 Corn Street, Witney,
Oxfordshire OX8 7BU
Tel: 01993 706501
www.wrharvey.co.uk

Wakelin & Linfield
PO Box 48, Billingshurst,
West Sussex RH14 0YZ
Tel: 01403 700004
www.wakelin-linfield.com

Witney Antiques
96-100 Corn Street, Witney,
Oxfordshire OX28 6BU
Tel: 01993 703902
www.witneyantiques.com

GENERAL
Alfies Antique Market
13-25 Church Street, Marylebone,
London NW8 8DT
Tel: 020 7723 6066
www.alfiesantiques.com

Antiquarius
131-141 Kings Road London SW3 4PW
Tel: 020 7823 3900
www.antiquarius.co.uk

Grays Antiques Markets
1-7 Davies Mews & 58 Davies St,
London W1K 5AB
Tel: 020 7629 7034
www.graysantiques.com

Heritage
6 Market Place, Woodstock,
Oxfordshire OX20 1TA
Tel: 01993 811332
www.atheritage.co.uk

Otford Antiques & Collectors Centre
26-28 High Street, Otford, Kent
TN14 5PQ
Tel: 01959 522025
www.otfordantiques.co.uk

Pantiles Spa Antiques
4-6 Union House, The Pantiles,
Tunbridge Wells, Kent TN4 8HE
Tel: 01892 541377
www.pantiles-spa-antiques.co.uk

The Ginnel Antiques Centre
Off Parliament Street,
Harrogate, North Yorkshire HG1 2RB
Tel: 01423 508 857 www.theginnel.co.uk

The Swan at Tetsworth
5 High St, Tetswoth, Oxfordshire
OX9 7AB
Tel: 01844 281777

Woburn Abbey Antiques Centre
Woburn Abbey, Woburn,
Bedfordshire, MK17 9WA
www.woburn.co.uk/antiques

GLASS
Andrew Lineham Fine Glass
PO Box 465, Chichester, West Sussex
PO18 8WZ.
Tel: 01243 576 241
www.antiquecolouredglass.com

Frank Dux Antiques
33 Belvedere, Lansdown Road
Bath, Avon BA1 5HR
Tel: 01225 312367
www.antique-glass.co.uk

Christine Bridge Antiques
78 Castelnau, London SW13 9EX Tel:
0208 741 5501
www.bridge-antiques.com

Delomosne & Son Ltd.
Court Close, North Wraxall,
Chippenham, Wiltshire SN14 7AD
Tel: 01225 891505
www.delomosne.co.uk

Jeanette Hayhurst Fine Glass
www.antiqueglasslondon.com

JEWELLERY
N. Bloom & Son (1912) Ltd.
www.nbloom.com

J H Bonnar
72 Thistle Street, Edinburgh, EH2 1EN
Tel: 0131 226 2811

MODERN
Fragile Design
14-15 The Custard Factory, Digbeth,
Birmingham, West Midlands B9 4AA
Tel: 0121 224 7378
www.fragiledesign.com

Francesca Martire
1st Floor, Alfies Antique Market, 13-25
Church Street, London NW8 8DT
Tel: 020 7724 4802 www.francesca-martire.com

Rennies Seaside Modern
47 The Old High St
Folkestone, Kent CT20 2RN
Tel: 01303 242427
www.rennart.co.uk

Twentieth Century Marks
Whitegates, Rectory Rd, Little Burstead,
Nr Billericay, Essex CM12 9TR
Tel: 01474 872460
www.20thcenturymarks.co.uk

MUSIC
Stephen T. P. Kember Ltd,
3 The Corn Exchange, The Pantiles,
Tunbridge Wells, Kent, TN2 5TE
Tel: 01959 574067/07850 358067
www.antique-musicboxes.co.uk

Turner Violins
1-5 Lily Grove, Beeston,
Nottinghmshire, NG9 1QL
Tel: 0115 943 0333
www.turnerviolins.co.uk

ORIENTAL AND ASIAN
Guest & Gray
1-7 Davies Mews, London W1K 5AB
Tel: 020 7408 1252
www.chinese-porcelain-art.com

Roger Bradbury
Church Street, Coltishall, Norwich,
Norfolk NR12 7DJ
Tel: 01603 737 444

R & G McPherson Antiques
40 Kensington Church Street,
London W8 4BX
Tel: 020 7937 0812
www.orientalceramics.com

SCIENTIFIC INSTRUMENTS
Charles Tomlinson
Chester
Tel: 01244 318395
charlestomlinson@tiscali.co.uk

SILVER
B. Silverman
4 Campden Street, Off Kensington
Church Street, London W8 7EP
Tel: 020 7985 0555
www.silverman-london.com

Didier Antiques
58-60 Kensington Church Street,
London W8 4DB
Tel: 020 7938 2537
www.didierantiques.com

Fay Lucas Artmetal
Christies Fine Art Securities
42 Ponton Road, London SW9 5RA
Tel: 020 7371 4404
www.faylucas.com

Goodwins Antiques Ltd
15 & 16 Queensferry Street,
Edinburgh EH2 4QW
Tel: 0131 225 4717
www.goodwinsantiques.com

Mary Cooke Antiques
12 The Old Power Station,121 Mortlake
High Street, London SW14 8SN
Tel: 020 8876 5777
www.marycooke.co.uk

Nicholas Shaw Antiques
Virginia Cottage, Lombard Street,
Petworth, West Sussex GU28 0AG
Tel: 01798 345 146
www.nicholas-shaw.com

Paul Bennett
48a George Street, London W1U 7DY
Tel: 020 7935 1555
www.paulbennettonline.com

Payne & Son (Goldsmiths) Ltd
131 High Street
Oxford, Oxfordshire OX1 4DH
Tel: 01865 243 787
www.goldandsilverjewellery.co.uk

Peter Cameron Antique Silver
PO Box LB739, London W1A 9LB
petercameron@idnet.co.uk

Peter Szuhay
302-303 Grays Antiques Market,
58 Davies Street, London W1Y 2LB
Tel: 020 7408 0154
pgszuhay@aol.com
www.peterszuhay.co.uk

Sanda Lipton
28a Devonshire Street, London
W1G 6PS
Tel: 020 7431 0688
www.antique-silver.com

S & J Stodel
Vault 24, London Silver Vaults,
Chancery Lane, London WC2A 1QS
Tel: 020 7405 7009
www.chinesesilver.com

Shapiro & Company
380 Grays Antiques Markets,
58 Davies Street, London W1K 5LP
Tel: 020 7491 2710

Smith & Robinson
101 Portobello Road, London W11 2QB
Tel: 020 7371 0552
www.smithandrobinson.com

Steppes Hill Farm Antiques
Steppes Hill Farm, Stockbury,
Sittingbourne, Kent ME9 7RB
Tel: 01795 842205
www.steppeshillfarm.com

Van Den Bosch
123 Grays, 58 Davies St, London
W1K 3LP
Tel: 020 7629 1900
www.vandenbosch.co.uk

William Walter Antiques Ltd
London Silver Vaults, Chancery House,
Chancery Lane, London, WC2A 1QS
Tel:020 7242 3248
www.williamwalter.co.uk

Daniel Bexfield Antiques
26 Burlington Arcade, W1J 0PU
Tel: 020 7491 1720
www.bexfield.co.uk

TEXTILES
Antique Textiles and Lighting
34 Belvedere, Lansdowne Road, Bath,
Avon BA1 5HR
Tel: 01225 310 795/443884
www.antiquesofbath.com

Esther Fitzgerald Rare Textiles
28 Church Row, London NW3 6UP
Tel: 020 7431 3076
www.estherfitzgerald.co.uk

Junnaa & Thomi Wroblewski
78 Marylebone High Street,
Box 39, London W1U 5AP
Tel: 020 7499 7793
junnaa@wroblewski.eu.com
thomi@wroblewski.eu.com

Rellick
8 Golborne Road,
London W10 5NW
Tel: 020 8962 0089

Vintage to Vogue
28 Milsom Street, Bath,
Avon BA1 1DG
Tel: 01225 337 323

Erna Hiscock & John Shepherd
Barn Owls, Finn Farm Road, Kings
North, Ashford, Kent TN23 3EX
Tel: 01233 661407
www.ernahiscockantiques.com

TRIBAL ART
Jean-Baptiste Bacquart
62 Gloucester Place, London W1U 8HW
Tel: 020 7224 0282 www.
AfricanAndOceanicArt.com

Michael Graham Stewart
173 New Bond Street
London W1S 4RF
Tel: 020 7495 4001

Owen Hargreaves & Jasmine Dahl
9 Corsham Street
London N1 6DP
Tel: 020 7253 2669
www.owenhargreaves.com

SPORTING
Manfred Schotten Antiques
109 High Street, Burford, Oxfordshire
OX18 4RG
Tel: 01993 822302
www.schotten.com

WINE ANTIQUES
Christopher Sykes
The Old Parsonage
Woburn, Milton Keynes,
Buckinghamshire MK17 9QL
Tel: 01525 290259

INDEX TO ADVERTISERS

Alan Walker Barometers	299	Robert Mills Ltd	399
Ancient & Gothic	483	Special Auction Services	450
Bagnam Barn	199	Special Auction Services	452
Dominic Winter Book Auctions	437	Stephen T.P. Kember Ltd.	307
Dorking Desk Shop	249	Styles of Stow	285
Dreweatt Neate	361	Teddy Bears of Witney	449
Exeter Antique Lighting	570	Turner Violins	485
Georgian Antiques	199	Wallis & Wallis	471
Historical and Collectable	71	Woburn Abbey	163
J. Hartley Antiques Ltd	199	Woolley & Wallis	499
Lyon & Turnbull	569		
The Old Brigade	481		
Q & C Militaria	481		

Page numbers in **bold** refer
pages with special features.

Aalto, Alvar 590
Abbott, Thomas 350
"Act of Parliament" clocks 291
Adam, Stephen & Son 562
Adam style
 sideboards 240
 tables 192, 193
Adams, George 298
Adams, George II **303**
Adams, Hannah 298
Adie, A. 299
Adnet, Jacques 590
Aesthetic movement
 ceramics 505
 furniture 533–4
 glass 562
 silver 575
African tribal art 459–61
Agam, Yaacov 624
agate 143
Alaïa 429
albarellos 64–5
Alcock, Samuel 89
Alden and Harlow 542
Aldridge, Edward 332
Alekseev, Nikolaj V. 388
Alleine, Jonathan 313
Allen, F. 495
Allen, Joseph 435
Allen & Hanburys 458
Alliot, Lucien 584
altar tables 153, 154
Althof Bergmann 447
American
 armchairs 173, 174, 177
 arms and armour 473, 474,
  476, 477, **478**
 automaton 445
 beds 262
 bookcases 229
 boxes 271–3
 bureaux **247**, 247
 cabinets 237
 carvings 275
 chairs 160, 162, **168**, 168
 chests 219
 chests-of-drawers 220–2
 chests-on-chests 226, 227
 chests-on-stands 225
 clocks 286, 289
 cupboards 215–17
 desks 242, 243
 dolls 440
 engines 305
 étagères 254
 jewellery 365
 lighting 354
 metalware 340, 584
 mirrors 250
 money banks 446
 nautical antiques 309
 needlework 417, 419–21
 objets de vertu 376, 383
 quilts 413–14
 rugs and carpets 412
 sideboards **239**, 239
 silver 315, 320–3, 329, 331,
  332, 334
 sofas 183
 stoneware **84**, 84–5
 tables 186, 189, 191,
  204–8, 211
 teddies 449
 telescopes 304
 tribal art 464–7
 watches 294
 weather vanes 400
American Encaustic Tiling
 Co. 527
Amphora 488
Andersen, David 579
Anderson, Robert 476
andirons 396
Andreson, Laura 609
aneroid barometers 302
Angell, Joseph Jr 322
Angell, Joseph Snr 322
Anglo-Dutch tables 206
Anglo-Indian
 boxes 266, 270, 272, 273
 chairs 176
 chests-on-stands 225
 jardinières 258
 tables 189, 190
Anglo-Saxon antiquities **483**
animals
 Bernard Moore 508

Black Forest carvings 260
Bow 12
chalkware **86**
Chinese ceramics 93, 95,
 107, 111
creamware 68
Doulton 496
Dutch Delft 61
faience 63
garden antiques 398
ivory 131, 382
jade 137, 141
Japanese metalware 127
lapis lazuli 143
Louis Wain **519**, 519
Meissen 31, 32
Middle Eastern ceramics 123
netsuke 135
pearlware 70
Prattware 75
redware 86
Russian antiques 393
Samson 37
silver 335, 337, 338
Staffordshire 53, **74**, 74–7
weather vanes 400
Wemyss 523–5
see also birds
Anne Marie of Paris 427
annuals, sporting 455
antiquities 482–3
Antwerp 268
appliqué 413–14, 421
Arad, Ron **590**, **618**
Archipenko, Alexander 621
architect's tables 201
architectural antiques 394–401
 fire accessories 396
 fire grates 395
 fire surrounds 394
 garden antiques 398
 garden furniture 397
 trade signs 401
 weather vanes 400
Arequipa 489
argand lamps 355
Argy-Rousseau, Gabriel 559
Arita 121
armchairs
 Art Deco 545
 Art Nouveau 543, 544
 Arts and Crafts
  536, 538, 542
 bergères **178**, 178
 Gothic Revival 535
 library 173, 176, 178,
  179, 182
 modern 590, 595, 596, 598,
  604, 606–8
 open armchairs **172**, 172–7
 upholstered armchairs
  179–81
 Windsor 160–1
Armfelt, Karl Gustav Hjalmar 391
armillary spheres 306
Armingaud 286
Armitage, George Faulkner
 533, 587
armoires 546
armorial Chinese ceramics 113
arms, armour and militaria
 470–81
 armour 481
 badges 480
 edged weapons 476–7
 guns 470–5
 medals 479
 powder horns 478
 uniform 481
Arneson, Robert 609
Arnett, Hugh 311
Arnstadt 63
Arrowsmith, Aaron **435**, 435
Art Deco
 ceramics 500
 clocks 565
 furniture 545–6
 jewellery 364
 lighting 572, 573
 metalware 581
 posters 628
 sculpture 584
 smoker's compendiums 379
Art Nouveau
 ceramics 488
 fire surrounds 394
 furniture 543–4
 jewellery 362
 lighting 572

metalware 580
 posters 625–7
 silver 579
Artificers Guild 581
Arts and Crafts
 clocks 564
 furniture 536–42
 jewellery 363, 365
 metalware 581
 silver 579
 stained glass 562
 textiles 587
Ashbee, Charles Robert 559
ashtrays 458
Asprey, Charles & Son 270
Aston and Son 370
Atkin, Henry 331
Atkins, Sam 293
Atkins Bros 335
Aubusson 416
Augousti, R. & Y. 590
Auguste, Robert-Joseph 392
Aulenti, Gae 618
Austrian
 cabinets 236
 carvings 274–5
 clocks 286, 292
 containers 260
 cupboards 214, 215
 dolls 439
 glass 343, 344, 561
 objets de vertu 382, 387
 sculpture 585
 silver 313, 321, 337
 stools 171
 tables **189**, 195, 206
Austro-Hungarian
 objets de vertu 381
 tables 191
automata **378**, 444–5
Avery, John 305
Ayrton, Michael 621

B
Baccarat 347, 348
Bach, Oscar 572
badges, military 480
Baggs, Arthur 502, 527
Baker, Oliver 574
Baldwin 400
Baldwin, Gordon 609
Baldwyn, Charles 49
Ball, Black & Co. 321, 331
Ball, Edward Oakes 18
balls, golf 457
balustrades 399
bamboo 144
bangles 358
bar cabinets 546
Barbadian stools 170
Barbedienne, F. 350, 381
Barber, James 336, 380
Barber, Jonas Jnr 281
Barberi, Gioacchino 387
barber's bowls 63
Barlow, Florence 495
Barlow, Hannah 495
barographs **304**, 304
barometers **298**, 298–302
Baroque **212**
 armchairs 172
 cabinets 234
 commodes 223
 cupboards 214–16
 mirrors 250
 tables 194
Barovier, Giuseppe 557
Barr, Flight & Barr 47
Barratt, John 430
Barrias, Louis-Ernest 586
Barrie, J.M. 432
Bartolozzi, Francesco 21
Bartolucci, Edgar 591
basalt, black **81**, 81
baseball 458
basins, Chinese ceramics 111
baskets
 ceramic 16, 60, 523
 silver 332
 tribal art 465, 467
Bass, E. & J. Company 581
Bateman, Ann 319
Bateman, Hester 336
Bateman, Jonathan 319
Bateman, Peter 319
bats, cricket 456
Battersea enamel 381
Bauer, Johann Bernhard 306
Baughman, Milo 591
Bawden, Edward 397

Baxter, Thomas 48, 284
Bayes, Gilbert 496
Bayler, Richard 318
beadwork 421, 464, 466
beakers
 Chelsea 14
 glass 344, 345
 Meissen 29
Bean, Bennett 609
Beauvarlet 278
Beck, R. & J. 303
bed steps 263
bedroom suites 262
beds 262, 604
bedside cabinets 241, 541
Beeson 451
Behrens, Balthazar Friedrich **312**
Beilby, William and Mary 342
Belgian
 boxes 270
 lanterns 353
 silver 314
 tapestries 416
Bell, John 34, 430
Bell, S. & Sons 86
bell pulls and pushes 381, 390
bellamine jugs 83
Bellini, Mario 591
bells, nautical antiques 310
Ben Tré, Howard 616
benches
 Black Forest 169
 Chinese 154
 garden 397
 modern 599, 600
Benham & Froud 394
Bennett, John 527
Bennett, Thomas 300
Bennett & Lacy 472
Benson, W.A.S. 540, **573**
Bentley, Percival Arthur 292
Berganti, Piero 64
Bergdoll, Adam 54
bergères **178**, 178
Bergman, Franz **583**
Berlin porcelain **10**, 10–11
Bermudan chests 218
Berthoud, Ferdinand 305
Bertoia, Harry 621
Bianconi, Fulvio 556
bible boxes 272
Bibles 430
Bickerstaff, William 283
bidets 263
Biedermeier **179**
 armchairs 179
 chairs 167
 clocks 286, 292
 glass 343
 silver 337
 tables 195, 206
Billington, Dora M. 508
Bilston enamel 373
Bilton, Eli I 326
Bing 447, 449
Birch, William Russell 386
birds
 chalkware 86
 Derby 20
 ivory 134
 jade 140
 Lowestoft 28
 Martin Brothers **504**, 504
 Meissen 31
 pearlware 70
 Samson 37
 Staffordshire 74, 76, 77
 Zsolnay 526
Birthray, Stephen 300
biscuit barrels 491
bisque dolls 441–3
black basalt **81**, 81
Black Forest **260**
 benches 169
 clocks 287
 garden furniture 397
 hall stands 260
blanc de chine 95
blankets, tribal art 464
Bliss, John & Co. 302
Blom, Johan Henrik 392
Blomdahl, Sonja 614
Bloor Derby 21, 22
Blow, Richard 587, 591
blue and white Chinese ceramics
 99–106
blue john 398
boats see ships
Boch Frères 527
Bode, Johann Elert 306

bodkin cases 382
Bohemian
 arms and armour 474
 glass 344–6
Bointaburet 579
Bolek, Hans 321
Bolin, C.E. 388
Bolton, Thomas 322
bonheurs du jour 248
book tables 209
bookcases 229–33, **231**
 Aesthetic movement 533
 Art Deco 546
 Art Nouveau 543
 Arts and Crafts 537, 539,
  541
 Gothic Revival 535
 modern 590
bookends 537, 561
books and prints **430**, 430–8,
 433, 456
Boosey & Hawkes 485
boots 428, 429
Borbon, P. & Co. 300
Borsani, Osvaldo 591
Boston & Sandwich Glass
 Co. 348
Böttger 37
bottles, snuff see snuff bottles
bough pots 69, 73
Boulanger, Jean Nicolas 320
Boulle, André-Charles 242
boullework **242**
 clocks 278, 279
 jardinières 258
Boulton, Matthew 339
Bouraine 584
Boutet, Nicholas Noel 470, 472
Bow 12
Bowles, H. 435
bowls
 Cantagalli 508
 Chelsea **15**
 Chinese ceramics 96–102,
  104, 107, 108, 110, 112–15
 Clarice Cliff 490
 cloisonné 124, 125, 389
 glass 146, 346, 347, 548,
  550, 553, 556,
  559–61, 616
 ironstone 79
 jade 139
 Japanese ceramics 118, 119
 Japanese metalware 128
 Korean ceramics 122
 lapis lazuli 143
 maiolica 65
 Mochaware 88
 modern ceramics 609, 611
 New Hall 36
 Persian ceramics 123
 redware 87
 Rockingham 52
 Royal Worcester 44
 Russian antiques 391, 392
 Samson 37
 Sèvres 39
 silver 333, 575, 576
 studio pottery 532
 transfer printed 72
 treen 376
 Wedgwood 520
 Worcester 44
boxes 264–73
 Chinese ceramics 94
 Chinese lacquer 145
 cloisonné 124, 389
 decanter boxes 270
 dressing boxes 270
 enamel 381
 glass 553, 615
 ivory 134, 383
 jewellery 381
 knife boxes **271**, 271
 pill 390
 silver 372, 576
 snuff boxes **372**, 372–5
 table cabinets 267–8, **268**
 tea caddies 264–5
 tobacco 372, 374
 treen 378
 wood 144
 work boxes 266
 writing boxes **269**, 269
Boyton, Charles 343
bracelets 358, 360, 366, 367
bracket clocks **278**, 278–9
brackets 263
Bradley & Hubbard 286
Brander & Potts 472

Brandt, Edgar 545
brass 340
    andirons 396
    candlesticks 349
    clocks 288
    fire accessories 394
    fire grates 395
    lighting 353–5
Braun, Martin 295
Brazier-Jones, Mark 591
breakfast tables 190
breakfront bookcases 231
Breguet 295
Breitling 295
Breuer, Marcel 591
Bridgens, Richard 395
Bristol
    delftware 59
    glass 343
    porcelain 52
Britton, Alison 609
Broad, John 495
Brockman, Ruth 614
Brocot, Achille 287
Brogden, John 359
Broggi, Fratelli 339
bronze
    andirons 396
    candelabra 350, 351
    chandeliers 352
    Chinese 126
    garden antiques 398
    Japanese 127–8
    lighting 354
    sculpture 582–6, 621–3
brooches 356–68
Brooks 300, 542
Brooks, Jon 592
Broun, Andrew 280
Brown, George 447
Browne, Henry and Son 310
brush pots
    bamboo 144
    Chinese ceramics 101, 103,
        106–8, 111
    ivory 132, 134
    jade 137, 137, 138
brush washers
    Chinese ceramics 97, 98,
        117
    jade 139
Brychtová, Jaroslava 617, 617
buckles 362
Buddhist Emblems 145
Buff & Buff 304
buffets 594
Bugatti, Carlo 543
bulb jars 47
Buquoy, Count 344
bureau bookcases 231
bureaux 196, 245–7
bureaux plat 202, 203
Burmantofts 527
Burnap, Daniel 305
Burne-Jones, Edward 508
Burrell 453
Burrows, George 325
Burwash, W. 334
Buschman, John 293
Bushey Heath Pottery 527
busts
    Goldscheider 497
    ivory 382, 384
    Lenci 500
    modern ceramics 609
    parian 19
    pearlware 69
    Wedgwood 81, 82, 501
butler's trays 259
Butterfield, Deborah 621

C
cabinet cups 47
cabinets 196
    Aesthetic movement
        533, 534
    Art Deco 546
    Art Nouveau 544
    Arts and Crafts 536, 538,
        539, 541
    bar 546
    bedside 241, 541
    bureau 230
    cabinets on stands 233–4
    Chinese 155, 155
    corner 534
    display 235, 535, 544
    Dresden 25
    Gothic Revival 535
    modern 605
    side 236, 236–7, 533
    table 267–8, 268, 382

Cable, Margaret 510
caddies see tea caddies
caddy spoons 325
Cahusac, Thomas 485
Caille 308
Calder, Alexander 624
Caldwell 354
Callaghan 298
Callender, Bessie Tough 586
Callowhill, James 49
Cambrian Pottery 70
cameos 356, 359
Camer Crystal 618
campaign furniture
    butler's trays 259
    toilet boxes 270
Canadian samplers 419
canapés 184
candelabra 573
    brass 350
    bronze 350–1
    ormolu 350, 351
    silver 314
    silver plate 339
candlesticks 349–51
    Berlin 10
    Bow 12
    Chinese cloisonné 125
    Derby 20, 21
    Minton 34
    pewter 574
    Roycroft 570, 577
    Russian antiques 392
    Tiffany 567
    silver 311–13
    silver plate 581
    WMF 578
Cantagalli 508
canterburies 249, 249
Capodimonte 55
card cases 370–1, 389
card tables 205, 205–6, 206
Cardew, Michael 532
Cardin, Pierre 424, 624
Carnegie, Hattie 368
carpets and rugs 402–12,
        587, 624
carriage clocks 288, 288
Carrington & Co. 323, 338, 380
cars, toy 447
cartel clocks 291
Carter, John 313
Cartier 295, 379, 426, 565
Carver, S. 435
carvings 274–5, 394, 397
Cary, John 435
Caselli, Giovanni 55
cassones 218, 219
cast iron see iron
Castel Durante 64
Castelli 64
casters, silver 334
Castle, Wendell 592, 592
Catteau, Charles 527
Cattle, Robert 336, 380
Caucasian rugs and carpets
        408–9
caudle cups 316
Caughley 13, 13
celadon 96
cellarets 256–7
Cellarius, Andreas 435
cellos 485
Cenedese 557
censers
    Chinese ceramics 95, 96
    Chinese cloisonné 124, 125
    Chinese metalware 126
    ivory 134
    jade 139–41
    Japanese ceramics 120
    silver 337
centre bowls 40
centre tables 191, 191–2,
        534, 540
centrepieces
    Amphora 488
    Dresden 25
    Meissen 33
    Royal Dux 516
    silver plate 339
ceramics
    Chinese 93–117
    decorative arts 488–532
    Japanese 118–21
    Korean 122, 122
    modern 609–13
    Oriental 92–125
Chadwick, James 315
Chadwick, Lynn 621
Chaffers Liverpool 26
chairs 160–82

Art Deco 545
Art Nouveau 543
Arts and Crafts 536,
        537, 542
    Chinese 152, 152
    corner 168
    country 160–1
    desk 196, 591
    dining 162–6, 537, 545,
        594, 599, 603
    Gothic Revival 535
    hall 169
    library 536
    lounge 591, 593, 595, 600,
        602, 605, 606
    modern 591, 592, 594, 595,
        599–608
    nursing 180
    Oriental 152
    rocking 538, 601, 604
    side 167–8, 596, 604
chaise longues 183, 593, 605
chalices 317, 340, 388
chalkware 86
chamber pots 71
Chamberlain's Worcester 48, 48
chambersticks 32, 575
chandeliers 352, 573, 619, 620
Chanel 366, 424, 426
Channel Islands silver 333
Chantilly 54
chargers
    Chinese ceramics 96, 99, 114
    Clarice Cliff 491
    delftware 59
    maiolica 65
    Minton 505
    modern ceramics 613
    redware 87
    slipware 66
    studio pottery 532
    Vietnamese 123
    William de Morgan 493
Charles I, King 438
Chase, Martha 441
Chawner, Henry 324
cheese bells 502
cheese dishes 512
Chelsea 14–17, 15
Chelsea Keramic Art Works 489
Cherner, Norman 592
chess sets 450
Chesterfield sofas 184
chests 218–19
chests-of-drawers 220–2
    Aesthetic movement 533
    Arts and Crafts 536
    feet 221
    modern 593, 598, 599, 601,
        602, 608
chests-on-chests 226–7
chests-on-stands 225
cheval mirrors 253
chicken feeders, stoneware 85
chiffoniers 238
Chihuly, Dale 614, 614
children's
    chairs 161
    desks 242
Chiltern 449
chimneypieces 394
Chinese
    bamboo 144
    cloisonné 124, 124–5, 125
    coral 142, 147, 148
    dolls 443
    embroidery and textiles 151
    fans 422
    furniture 152–7, 153
    glass 145, 146, 146
    ivory 130–4, 371, 371
    jade 137, 137–41, 140,
        147, 148, 156, 157
    lacquer 145, 145
    lapis lazuli 143
    metalware 126
    objets de vertu 374
    paintings 149–50
    rhino horn 136, 136
    rugs and carpets 411
    snuff bottles 147–8, 148
Chinese ceramics 93–117
    ancient 93, 93–4, 94
    armorial 113
    blanc de chine 95
    blue and white 99–106
    celadon 96
    doucai 113, 113
    export porcelain 100
    famille jaune 112
    famille noir 112
    famille rose 109–11, 111

famille verte 107, 107–8
    monochrome 98
    polychrome 115–17
    rose medallion 112
    sang de boeuf 97
    wucai 114
chinoiserie
    andirons 396
    armchairs 175
    bookcases 231
    cabinets 234, 235
    desks 243
    screens 261
    secrétaires 228
    teapoys 255
Chiparus, Demêtre H. 486-7,
        584, 586
Chippendale, Thomas 166, 226,
        430, 530
Chippendale style 226
    armchairs 174
    brackets 263
    bureaux 247
    chairs 162, 166, 168
    chests-of-drawers 220–2
    chests-on-chests 226, 227
    lanterns 353
    wine coolers 256
Chivers, Frederick H. 18
chocolate pots 30
Chodowiecki, Daniel Nikolaus
        385
christening bowls 333
christening cups 574
Christiania 579
Christie, Agatha 432
chronometers 302
Chulot, Louis-Gabriel 38
churns, stoneware 84
cigar cases 273
cigarette boxes 577, 580
cigarette cases 379, 390
cisterns, Chinese ceramics 103
Claire, Peter 283
claret jugs 322, 343, 574
clarinets 485
Claudin, F. 472
Clay, Henry 264
Clemens, Andrew 310
Clewell 489
Clichy 348
Cliff, Clarice 490, 490–2, 492
clocks 276–92
    bracket 278, 278–9
    carriage 288, 288
    ceramic 497
    decorative arts 564–5
    garnitures 290
    glass 553
    lantern 288
    longcase 280–5, 537, 564
    mantel 286–7, 504,
        529, 564
    modern 597
    wall 291–2
clockwork toys 443, 447
cloisonné
    Chinese 124, 124–5, 125
    Japanese 127
    Russian 388–9
Closon, Peter 288
clothes see costume
coal scuttles 263
Coalbrookdale 397
Coalport 18
coasters 336, 387
Cobb, John 224
Cobb, Cambridge 282
coffee cups and cans
    Coalport 18
    Longton Hall 27
    Meissen 31
    Worcester 45
coffee grinders 378
coffee pots
    Caughley 13
    creamware 67
    Lowestoft 28
    Quimper 512
    silver 320
    toleware 340
    Worcester 46
coffee services
    Berlin 10
    Derby 23
    Fabergé 391
    Meissen 29
    Paris 36
    silver 321, 574, 576, 579
    Wedgwood 521
coffee tables 591, 592, 597,

598, 601, 605, 606
coffers 218–19
Coffey, Michael 592
Coggin, Thayer 591
Cohen & Charles 338
Coker, Ebenezer 330
Cole, Henry 234
Coleman, John 289
Coles, Abraham 282
Coles, Lawrence 326
Colin, Jean-Baptiste 484
Colinet, Claire Jeanne
        Roberte 584
collectors' cabinets 236, 268
Collot, A. 40
Colombo, Joe 592
Colt 473
Comberbach, E.S. 301
commemorative glass 343
commodes 223–4, 224
Compass Artist 262, 272
compasses, nautical
    antiques 310
comports 52, 578
concertinas 485
Coney, John 315
Conover, Claude 609
console tables 193–4, 545, 590
Continental
    andirons 396
    armchairs 173, 180–2
    bedside cupboards 241
    carvings 274
    chairs 197
    clocks 287, 290
    desks 243
    faience 63
    glass 342
    jewellery 365
    lighting 354
    music boxes 308
    objets de vertu 375,
        381, 383
    pewter 340
    porcelain 54
    silver 335
    silver plate 339
    tables 191, 192, 194
    tapestries 415, 416
conversational settees 184
Cooke, Thomas 301
Cooke, Thomas II 316, 334
Copeland 19, 19, 458
Coper, Hans 531, 531
copper 340
    decorative arts 577, 580
    weather vanes 400
Coppolo and Toppo 368
coquilla nut snuff boxes 375
coral 142, 147, 148, 358
Corden, William 22
corner chairs 168
corner cupboards 216, 216, 534
Coro 366
Correani, Ugo 368
Corum 295
costrels 66
costume 423, 423–5, 424
    Chinese 151
    sporting 454–5, 456, 458
costume jewellery 365–8
couches 544
country chairs 160–1
Court, Arthur 621
Courtauld, Augustine 324
cow creamers 68, 70
Cowden & Wilcox 85
Cowham, Thomas 284
Cox, Kris 609
Cozzi 55
Crace and Sons 175
Craddock, Joseph 337
cradles 262, 466
creamware 67, 67–8, 68, 82
credenzas 238, 597, 603, 607
cricket 456
cricket cages 134
Crimp, Francis 332
crocks, stoneware 85
Crouch, Henry 304
Crucefix, John 280
cruets
    cloisonné 389
    creamware 68
    silver 334
    treen 378
cufflinks 359, 364
Cuno & Otto 441
cupboards 214–17
    Chinese 155
    corner 216, 216, 534
    linen presses 217, 217

Oriental 155
cups and saucers
Bow 12
Bristol 52
Capodimonte 55
Chinese ceramics 103, 111, 113, 117
glass 146
ivory 383
Meissen 29
rhino horn 136
Royal Copenhagen 55
Sèvres 38
silver 315–17
slipware 66
treen 376
Vienna **42**, 42
Worcester 46
Cushing, Val 610
cushions 421
custard cups 28
cutlery boxes 271
Czech silver 325

D
Da Venezia, Domenego 64
Dailey, Dan **614**, 614, 618
Dakon, Stephan 498
Dangel, F. Josef 41
Danish porcelain 55
Dante Alighieri **430**
Daro, Willy 618
Darwin, Charles 430, 438
Dasson, Henry 197, 287, 351
Daum 547–8, **548**, 571, 573
Davenport 89
davenports 248
Davie, Thomas 327
Davies, Frederick 563
Davies, John **306**
Davis, Harry 49–51
Dawson & Co 71
Day, Josephine 489
daybeds 171, 590, 606
De Leth, A. & H. 435
de Morgan, William **493**, 493–4, **494**, 587
decanter boxes 270
decanters 343
DeCharmes, Simon 278
decorative arts 486–587
ceramics 488–532
clocks 564–5
furniture 533–46
glass 547–63
lighting 566–73
metalware 574–81
sculpture 581–6
textiles 586, 587
découpage screens 261
Dedham 528
delftware **58**, 58–60, **59**
Della Robbia 528
Dent 288, 293
Derby 20–3, **21**
desk boxes 269
desk chairs 196, 591
desk lamps 618, 620
desk sets 575, 577
Deskey, Donald 573
desks 242–4, **244**, **247**, 247
Art Nouveau 543, 544
Arts and Crafts 539, 542
Chinese 154
modern 593, 595–7, 602, 603, 605, 608
Shaker 210
dessert services
Coalport 18
Derby 23
Dresden 24
ironstone 79
Minton 34
New Hall 36
transfer printed 73
Worcester 48
Devez 559
diamonds 356–61, 363, 364
Dickens, Charles 430
Dieppe ivory **384**
Diers, Ed 514
dining chairs 162–6, 537, 545, 594, 599, 603
dining tables 186, 188–9, 538, 545, 591, 594, 596, 598–603, 605, 607
dinner services
Derby 22, 23
ironstone 79
transfer printed 73

Wedgwood 82, 521
Worcester 48
Dior, Christian 366, 424, 425
dioramas, marine 309
dishes
Caughley 13
Chelsea 15, 16
Chinese ceramics 94, 97, 99, 103, 104, 107, 111, 114, 117
Chinese lacquer 145
delftware 60
Dutch Delft 61
faience 63
Iznik 123
Japanese ceramics 118, 119, 121
Japanese metalware 128
Liverpool 26
Longton Hall 27
maiolica 64, 65
majolica 501
Minton 34
Nantgarw 35
New Hall 36
redware 87
Royal Worcester 50
Safavid 123
silver **333**
studio pottery 610
William de Morgan 493
Worcester 44–6
display cabinets 235, 535, 544
display stands 155
diving helmets 310
Doccia **55**, 55
Dodin, Charles-Nicolas 38
dog baskets 263
dog's bowls 72
Dollond 298
Dollond, Peter **303**
dolls **439**, 439–43, 466–7
dolls' house pottery 62
dolls' houses 443
Dominick & Haff 333
Dominique 593
Donaldson of Edinburgh 306
Donyatt 88
doors, modern 603
doorstops 378, 528
doucai **113**, 113
Doulton 456, 457, 495–6, **496**
dower chests 219
Doyle, Sir Arthur Conan 430
draughtsman's tables 201
Drbal, Constantin 171, 260
Dresden 24–5
Dresser, Dr.Christopher 394, 505, 529, 533, 560
dressers 212–13, **213**
modern 595, 600, 603
dressing boxes 270
dressing table mirrors **253**, 253
dressing tables 208
Art Deco 546
Arts and Crafts 537, 540
Dreyfuss 596
drinking glasses 343
drop-leaf tables **187**, 187, 188
drug jars
Alcock 89
delftware **58**, 58, 60
faience 63
maiolica 64
Du Maurier, Daphne 432
Dubuis, Roger 295
Duckworth, Ruth 610
duet stands 260
Dulac, Edmund 438
dumb waiters 254
Dunbar 593, 608
Dunleavy, Anthony 514
Durand 559
Dutch
barometers 298–300
bureaux 246
cabinets 234, 235
clocks 281, 282
cupboards 216
metalware 340
pot cupboards 241
screens 261
silver 334
tables 204

E
écuelles 15, 38
Eagle, Nathaniel 293
Eames, Charles 593
Eames, Ray 593

Earl, Jack 610
earrings 365, 366, 368
easel stands 260
Eastlake, Charles Locke 535
Ebel 295
Edwards, Edward 369
Edwards & Roberts 200, 203, 224, 244, 533
Effetre International 616
Eger boxes 272
Egermann, Friedrich 344
eggcup stands 72
eggs, transfer printed 72
Egyptian antiquities **482**, 482
Egyptian Revival candelabra 350
Einco 447
Eisch, Erwin 614
Eley, Fearn & Chawner 327
Eliot, T.S. 432
Elizabeth, The Queen Mother **424**
Elizabeth II, Queen 424
Elkington, Frederick 317
Elkington & Co. 339, 380
Ellerton, Thomas 319
Ellicot, John 279
Elliot, John & Sons 250
Elliott, John 279
Ellis, Harvey 538
Ellwood, George Montague 540
Elsner, Joseph 292
embroidery 151, 417–20
Emery, Josiah **282**
Empire style
armchairs 180
bergères 178
cabinets 235
candelabra 351
clocks 286, 290
lighting 355
mirrors 253
tables 194, 202
enamel 381
Chinese cloisonné **124**, 124–5, **125**
cloisonné 388–9
Japanese 381
jewellery 358, 362–3, 367
snuff bottles 147
snuff boxes 372, 373
table cabinets 268
engines 305
Engleheart, George 385
Ennutsiak 462
Enterprise Mfg. Co. 446
entrée dishes 328
epergnes, silver 337
ephemera 521
Erat, J. 485
Erhald & Sons 571
Esherick, Wharton **594**, 594
Estwick, Thomas 281
étagères 254
Etondeur 527
étuis 381
Evans, Paul 594
ewers
Amphora 488
Chinese ceramics 94, 101, 103, 117
Derby 23
Doulton 495
ironstone 79
metalware 575
Minton 34
Royal Worcester 49
Safavid 123
Samson 37
Wedgwood 81, 82, 501
Wemyss 523, 525
extending tables 188–9, **189**
Eyre, George 81

F
Fabergé 390–1
Faenza 64
Fahrmer 368
faience 62–3, **63**
Falkenstein, Claire 622
famille jaune 112
famille noir 112
famille rose 109–11, **111**
famille verte **107**, 107–8
Fang art **461**
fans 422
Farnell 449
Farrer, Joseph 283
Faure, Camille 529
fauteuils 177
Federal

chests-of-drawers 222
cupboards 216
knife boxes 271
mirrors 250
sideboards 239
feet
chests-of-drawers **221**
tables **209**
Felkl, Jan & Son 306
felt pictures 421
Fender 484
Field, Robert **386**
figures
antiquities 482
bamboo 144
Bow 12
carvings 274–5
Chelsea 16
Chinese ceramics 93, 95, 108, 111, 117
Chinese cloisonné 125
Chinese metalware 126
coral 142
Cozzi 55
Derby 20–1
Doccia 55
Doulton **496**, 496
Dresden 24, 25
German porcelain 54
glass 553
Goldscheider 498
ivory 130–1, 275, 382, 384
jade 135
Japanese ceramics 121
Japanese metalware 127
Lenci 500
Meissen 29, 30–3
parian 19, **34**, 34
pearlware 69
Prattware 75
Royal Dux **516**, 516
Royal Worcester 49, 50
Russian porcelain 393
silver 338
Staffordshire 53, **74**, 74–7, **76**
trade signs 401
treen 378
tribal art 459–62, 464, 468, 469
Vienna 41, 41
Wedgwood 80, 81
wood 144
Finaughty, William 430
finger bowls, Chelsea **15**
fire accessories 396
fire grates 395
fire screens 261
fire surrounds 394
first editions 432–4
Fisher, Alexander 535
fishing 458
flagons, faience 62
flasks
Chinese ceramics 112
Minton 505
redware 86
slipware 66
flatware, silver 330–1
Fleming, Ian 432
Fleming, William 372
Flemish
arms and armour 481
cabinets 233
carvings 274
cupboards 214
embroidery 418
table cabinets 267
tapestries 415, 416
Fletcher, T.S. 323
Flight, Barr & Barr 47
floor lamps 618–20
floral stands, Meissen 33
flower troughs 49
flutes 485
folk art dolls 439
Folkingham, Thomas 320
Folwell, Samuel 385
Fontana Arte 618
football **454**, 454–5
footbaths 523
Fordney, Melchior 474
Forestville Manufacturing Company 289
Forsyth, Gordon 529
four-poster beds 262
Fourdrinier, R. 298
Fowler 453
Fox, A.H. 475
Fox, Isaac 279

Frank, Jean-Michel 541
Frankenthal 54
Frankl, Paul 546
Franz, Johann Georg 306
Freeman, John 51
French
architectural antiques 399
armchairs 175–7, 181
arms and armour 470, 472
Art Deco furniture 545, 546
automaton 445
barometers 301
bedroom suites 262
bookcases 232
boxes 266, 270, 273
bureaux 196
cabinets 234–6
candelabra 350, 351
canterburies 249
chairs 196
chandeliers 352
clocks 278, 279, 282–4, 286–8, 290
commodes 223, 224
costume 423
desks 243, 244
engines 305
étagères 254
faience 62
garden furniture 397
glass 343
jardinières 258
jewellery 356, 362–5
lighting 354, 573
metalware 340
mirrors 251
objets de vertu 372–5, 377, 381–4, 386, 387
pedestals 260
porcelain 54
rugs and carpets 411
sculpture 582, 584–6
silver 312, 320, 321, 329, 334, 392, 579
sofas 184
tables 185, 192, 194–9, 201, 202
tapestries **415**, 415
toys 447
trade signs 401
watches 293
writing slopes 269
Friberg, Berndt 610
Friedeberg, Pedro 595
Fu Baoshi 149
fuddling cups 59, 66
Fuga, Anzolo 557
Fujita, Kyohei **615**
Fukugawa 121
Fuller, Loie **571**
Fulper 528
furniture 158–263
Chinese 152–7, **153**
decorative arts 533–46
garden furniture 397
modern 590–608
Oriental 152–7
Furstenburg 54

G
Gainsborough armchairs 174
Gallé, Emile 528, 543, **549**, 549–50, 571
game pie dishes 501
games tables 203, 205–6, **206**
Gamon, John 316
Gane, P.E. 543
garden antiques 398
garden furniture 397
garden seats, ceramic 106, 501, 525
Gardner, Francis 393
Garnier, Jean-Paul 288
garnitures
clocks 290
Derby 22
Dutch Delft 61
ironstone 79
Vienna 43
Garouste & Bonetti 595
Garrard, James 329
Garrard, R. & S. 334
Garrard, Robert 314, 331
Garrard, S. 317
Garrard, Sebastian 335
Garrard & Co. 313, 458
Gaskin, Arthur and Georgie 365
gateleg tables 186
Gatti, Giovanni Battista 209
Gaultier, François 441

Gérard, Noël **223**
Gerike, Gebrüder 328
German
   arms and armour 470, 476,
      478, 481
   boxes 272
   cabinets 236
   carvings 274
   clocks 287, 289
   coffers 218
   commodes 223
   cupboards 214, 215
   dolls **439**, 439–40
   engines 305
   faience 61, 63
   garden furniture 397
   glass 345
   hall stands 260
   music boxes 308
   musical instruments 484
   nautical antiques 310
   objets de vertu 373, 374,
      379, 382–4
   porcelain 54
   silver **312**, 312–17, 324,
      325, 328, 330
   stoneware 83
   tables 203
   toys 447, 450
   watches 296
   writing boxes 269
Ghigo, Camillo 500
Gibbons, John 333
Gibson 291, 484
Gibson, John 19
Gibson, William 331
Gill & Knubley 470
Gillows **200**
   armchairs 174, 182
   bedside cupboards 241
   bookcases 233, 533
   cabinets 237, 534
   chairs 164, 169
   chests-of-drawers 222
   secrétaires 228
   stools 171
   tables 188, 190, 200, 203,
      210, 211
   wine coolers 257
Gilmour, Margaret 581
Gimson, Ernest **536**, 536
Giner, Johann the Elder 275
girandoles 251, 346
'Girl on a Swing' factory **17**, 17
Giuliano, Carlo 363
Glasby, William 562
Glasgow School 580, 581
glass 341–8
   antiquities 483
   Bohemian 344–6
   Chinese 145, **146**, 146
   decorative arts 547–63
   drinking glasses 343
   jewellery 366, 368
   modern 614–17
   paperweights 348
   scent bottles 563
   snuff bottles 147, **148**, 148
   stained glass 562
   wine glasses 341–2
glass holders 391
Glen, James 316, 318
Glenny, Alexander 327
globes 306, 377
Glynne, Richard 278
'Goat and Bee' jugs **14**
Gobelins Tapestry Factory **415**
goblets
   glass 343, 345, 346
   silver 392
   treen **376**, 376
Godson, William 436
Godwin, Edward William 533
gold
   cigarette cases 379
   Fabergé 390, 391
   Japanese 128
   jewellery 356–65
   medals **454**, 454, 456
   snuff boxes **372**, 372, 373
   watches 293–7
Goldscheider **497**, 497–8
golf 457
Goossens, Robert 366
Gordon, David 281
Gordon, Hugh 323
Gorham Mfg. Co 322, 362
Gosselin 278
Gothic Revival
   architectural antiques 399

candlesticks 351
davenports 248
furniture 535
metalware 581
sideboards 240
silver 317
Goudji 595
Gould, William 312
Gouvion, Colonel Jean Baptiste
   436
Grabe, Klaus 595
Grachev, Mikhail 392
Grachev, Vasil 582
Graham, Charles 528
Graham, George 293
Grahame, Kenneth 431
Grainger's Worcester 47
Grand Feu 528
Grand Tour **380**
Gray, Benjamin 281
Greek
   antiquities 482, 483
   jewellery 356
Green, Richard 318
Greene, Graham 432
Greenwood, F.S. 579
Gregoire, Jean-Louis 582
Gregory, Albert 23
Greiner, Ludwig 440
Grendey, Giles **162**, 167
Gresley, Cuthbert 23
Grey & Co. 338
Griffin, Joseph 470
Gripoix, Maison 368
Grodnertal 439
Grove, Richard 291
Grundy, William 312, 323
Grunsteidel, Christian 305
Guarnerio, P. 301
Gubisch, F. 568
Gucci 426
Guggiari, D. 301
Guild of Handicraft 559, 579
Guiraud-Rivière, Maurice 584
guitars 484
guns 470–5
Gunthermann 447
Gurney, Joseph 291
Gurney, Richard 316, 334
Gustavsberg 610
Gyokuzan 119

H
Haab, Konrad 41
Hagler, Stanley 366
Haile, Sam 531
Haines & Co. 436
Hale, F.G. 363
hall chairs 169
hall seats 542
hall stands 260, 543
Halston 425
Hamada, Shoji 531
Hanau 63
Hancock, Robert 44
hand warmers, ceramic 62, 106
handbags 426–7
Handel 568–9
Hansen 618, 620
Har 366
Harden 542
Hardman, James & Co. 579
Hardman, John and Co. 317
Hare, David 622
Harper, J.M. 446
harps 485
Harris, Charles Stuart 332
Harris, Samuel 281
Haseler, W.H. 579
Haskell, Miriam 367
Hatfield, Chas. 330
Haüer, Bonaventura Gottlieb 30
Havilland, Terry de 429
Hawkes & Co. 477
Hawkins, W.A. 51
Hazlehurst, Thomas 385
Heal's **213**
Heath, S. 182
Hébert, Louis-Philippe 582
Heinrichs, Joseph 580
helmets
   antiquities 483
   military 481
Henckels, J.A. 581
Henderson, Henry 309
Hennell, James Barclay 317, 335
Hennell, Robert 328, 336
Hennell, Robert II 331
Henry 475
Henry, J.S. 540

Henry, John 622
Hentschel, William 514
Hepplewhite style
   knife boxes 271
   sofas 183
   window seats 171
Herculaneum 68
Hericourt, Antoine 224
Hermann 449
Hermès 426
Hertel and Schwab 441
Heubach, Gebruder 441
Highley, John 284
Hilliard & Thomason 325, 338
Hinz, Bill 63
Hitchcock, Samuel 326
Höchst 54
Hodder, P. 580
Hodler, Joseph 502
Hoenig, Lazlo 545, 546
Hoffmann, Josef 554
Hofstötter, Franz 554
Holdcroft, Joseph 502
Holland & Sons 200
Holloway, John 82
Holmden, John George 300
Holubetz, Robert 554
Homann, J.B. 436
Homer, Michael 319
Hondius, Jodocus 436
horn
   jewellery 362
   powder horns **478**, 478
   rhino horn **136**, 136
   scrimshaw **309**, 309
Hornby 451
Hornby, William 335
Horner, R.J. 283
horse racing 458
Hoskin, John 622
Hotham, Henry 288
Houle, Daniel & Charles 331
How, Frances Thalia 363
Howard, Thomas 279
Hozan, Matsumoto 119
Huang Bin-Hung 149
Huang Hsiang Chien 149
Huber, J.S. 293
Huckfield, Flora 510
Hughes, W.C. **450**
Humbert and Sohn 313
Humphreys, Richard 322
Hunt, John Samuel 321, **322**
Hunt, Richard Howard 622
Hunt & Roskell 322, 328, 363
hunt tables 187
Hunter, Dard **570**, 570
Hurley, E.T. 513–14

I
ice pails 18, 25
icons 393
Idee 619
Ihlenfeld, Klaus 622
Iksiktaaryuk, Luke 462
Imari 118, 118
incense burners 95
Indian
   arms and armour 472, 474,
      476, 478
   beds 262
   boxes 266
   carvings 275
   chests-of-drawers 222
   ivory 382
   rugs and carpets 411–12
   table cabinets 267, 268
   tea caddies 265
Indiana, Robert 624
Indo-Portuguese
   coffers 219
   table cabinets 267, 268
   writing boxes 269
Ingermann, Christian Erich 314
inkstands 380, 381, 587
inkstones, jade 139
inkwells
   Lowestoft 28
   treen 377, 378
Inuit sculpture **462**, 462
Inukpuk, Johnny 462
invalid chairs 182
Ipeelee, Osuitok 462
Irish
   arms and armour 470
   barometers 300
   chairs 164, 166
   clocks 281
   objets de vertu 372
   silver 313, 319, 322, 330,
      332, 336

tables 187, 195, 205,
   207, 209
window seats 171
wine coolers 257
iron
   architectural antiques 399
   clocks 286
   fire grates 395
   fire surrounds 394
   garden furniture 397
   Japanese 128
   money banks 446
ironstone 79
Irvine, Sadie 509
Issod, Thomas 326
Italian
   architectural antiques 399
   armchairs 172–4, 176, 182
   arms and armour 476
   boxes 272
   bureaux 246
   cabinets 230
   candlesticks 349
   carvings 275
   chests 218, 219
   chests-of-drawers 220
   commodes 223, 224
   cupboards 214, **216**
   faience 63
   garden antiques 398
   maiolica 64–5
   mirrors 250–2
   objets de vertu 387
   porcelain 55
   prie-dieus 263
   silver 313, 314
   silver plate 339
   sofas 183
   table cabinets 267, 268
   tables 192–4, 197, 208,
      209, 211
ivory
   boxes 266, 270
   card cases **371**, 371
   Chinese 130–4, **371**, 371
   fans 422
   figures 130–1, 275, 382, 384
   Japanese **131**, 131
   netsuke **135**, 135
   objets de vertu
      382, 382–4, **384**
   snuff boxes 374
   table cabinets 267, 268
   tea caddies 265
   tobacco boxes 374
Iznik 123

J
Jacopi, A. 500
jade **137**, 137–41, **140**, 147–8,
   156, 157
Jaeger LeCoultre 295
James, P.D. 433
Jamieson, William 336
Japanese
   arms and armour 472, 476, 477
   ceramics 118–21
   furniture 155, 157
   ivory **131**, 131–2
   metalware 127–8
   netsuke **135**, 135
   objets de vertu 371
   wood 144
japanned
   armchairs 175
   bureaux 245
   clocks 281, 291
   secrétaires 228
   tables 195
   tea caddies 265
jardinière stands 154
jardinières 258
   Chinese ceramics 105, 106
   Chinese metalware 126
   Dresden 24
   Japanese ceramics 121
   marble 399
   Moorcroft 506
   silver-plate 578
   Weller 522
   Zsolnay 526
jars
   Bernard Moore 508
   Chinese ceramics 94, 100,
      103, 105–7, 113, 114
   Chinese metalware 126
   drug jars 58, 60, 63, 64, 89
   Dutch Delft 61
   glass 146, 347, 560
   jade 139, 140

Japanese ceramics 120
Korean ceramics 122
Martin Brothers 504
Moorcroft 507
Roseville 515
Royal Worcester 51
slipware 66
stoneware 85
studio pottery 531
Wemyss 523
Jarvie **580**
Jarvis, Leonard 78
Jasperware **80**, 80
Jeanneret, Pierre **595**, 595
Jeanselme 177
Jeckyll, Thomas 171
Jeffries, C. 485
Jenkins, Thomas 315
Jennings, Walter 577
Jensen, Georg **576**, 576
Jere, Curtis 621
Jervis 528
Jewell, S. & H. 231
Jewell, W.E. Co. 400
jewellery 356–68
   Art Deco 364
   Art Nouveau 362
   Arts and Crafts 363, 365
   costume jewellery 365–8
   early 356
   Edwardian 363
   Georgian 357
   language of stones 359
   Victorian 358–60
jewellery boxes 272, 273, 381
Jewett, Maude Sherwood 584
Jiajing ceramics 99
Jiaqing ceramics 105
Jin Cheng 149
Johnson, John 484
Johnson, W. & A.K. 306
Jones, George **501**, 501
Jones, Owen **530**
Jones, Thomas W. Company 400
Jones and Schofield 314
Joseff of Hollywood 367
Jouve, George 596
Jover 472
Joyner 470
jugs
   Caughley 13
   Chelsea 15
   claret 343, 574
   Clarice Cliff 491, 492
   creamware 67, 68
   faience 63
   George Ohr 511
   glass 548
   'Goat and Bee' **14**
   ironstone 79
   Iznik 123
   Longton Hall 27
   Lowestoft 28
   lustre 71
   Martin Brothers 503
   Meissen 30
   Mochaware 88
   modern ceramics 611
   pearlware 69
   puzzle jugs 59, 69, 88
   redware 86
   silver **322**, 322, 575
   sporting antiques 456, 458
   Staffordshire 74
   stoneware 83–5
   studio pottery 531
   Toby jugs **78**, 78
   transfer printed 72
   Worcester 44, 45
Juhl, Finn 596
Jumeau Bebe 441
Juster, Joe 493

K
Kagan, Vladimir 596
kaleidoscopes 450
Kämmer & Reinhardt 441–2
Kändler, J.J. 30–3
Kaneko, Jun 610
Kangxi ceramics 101–3
Kao Feng-Han 149
Karnes, Karen 610
Kashan rugs 403–4, **404**
Kempe, Charles Edward 562
Kendall, John & Co. 237
Kennedy, Thomas 474
Kennon, Roberta B. 509
Kent, William 193, 197
Kenton 446
Ker, Thomas 338

Kerouac, Jack 433
Kerr and Binns 47
Kestner 442
kettle stands 260
kettles, copper 340
Khlebnikov, Ivan 388, 389
Killiktee, Shorty 462
King, Jessie M. 363, 365, 574
King, Leonard 527
Kinkozan family 119, 120
Kipling, Rudyard 431
Kitamura, Junko 611
kitchen tables 211
Klinkosch, J.C. 314
Kloch, Pieter 281
Klotz, Joseph 484
Knibb, John **280**
Knibb, Joseph **280**, 280
knife boxes **271**, 271
Knight, Dame Laura 492
Knight & Sons 168
Knoll **597**, 601, 604–6
Knoll, Florence **597**
Knox, Archibald 564, 574, 579
Kollin, Erik 391
Konrad, Anton 476
Koons, Jeff 610
Kopf, Silas 597
Korean ceramics **122**, 122
Kosmos Brenner 573
Kosta Boda 616
kovshes 388, 390–1
Kowalskij, Andrej 393
Kozan, Miyagawa (Makuzu) 120
KPM 440
Kramer, Georg 286
Kray, Wilhelm 11
Kringle, Kris 440
Kruse, Käthe 442
Ku-Yin 149
Kuhn, Jon 615
Kurliukov, Orest 389
Kutani 121
Kwong, Hui Ka 611

L
La Faguays, Pierre 585
labels, wine 336
Labino, Dominick 615
Laborde, Guillermo 455
Lacloche Frères 364
lacquer
    cabinets 230, 234, 235
    Chinese **145**, 145
    tables 195
    teapoys 255
Lacroix, Christian 425
ladder back chairs 161, 162
Lagerfeld, Karl 368
Lakeside Crafters 542
Lakin, T. & Sons 72
Lalique, René
    glass 551–3
    jewellery 362
    lighting 571
    perfume bottles 563
Lallemant, Robert 529
Lamb of Manchester **533**, 533
Lambeth delftware 59
Lamerie, Paul de 311, **333**
lamps see lighting
Lancaster, William 279
Lanceray, Eugène Alexandrovitsch 582
Lane, Kenneth Jay 368
Lange, A. & Sohne 296
Langman, John 331
language of stones 359
lantern clocks 288
lanterns 353
    Chinese ceramics 117
    nautical antiques 310
lapis lazuli 143
Lapparra, Henri 321
Larche, François-Raoul 571
Lassaw, Ibram 597
Lassen, Mogens 597
Laver, William 328
Laverne, Philip and Kelvin 597
Law, Andrew II 315
Lawrence, John 325
le Bass, James 458
Le Maire 470
Le Mere, Thomas 438
Leach, Bernard 532
Leach, John 333
Leach Pottery 531–2
leather screens 261
LeBlanc, Marie De Hoa 509
lecterns 340, 542

Leeds creamware **67**, 67
Lehmann 447
Leiber, Judith 427
Leleu, George 572
Leleu, Jules 546
Lelli, Angelo 618
Lenci **500**, 500
Leonard, Agathon 571
Lepori, Joseph & Co. 300
Leroy, Desire 23
letter holders 133
letters 438
Lewis, C.S. 433
Lewis, Harvey 332
Lewis, John **598**, 598
Leyniers, U. 416
Liaigre, Christian 598
Lias Brothers 327
libation cups 136
Libenský, Stanislav **617**, 617
Liberty & Co.
    clocks **564**, 564
    furniture 540
    jewellery 363, 365
    metalware 574
    silver 574
library armchairs 173, 176, 178, 179, 182
library bookcases 232
library chairs 536
library davenports 248
library steps 263
library tables 200, 536
Lichtenstein, Roy 368, 622
Lidston, G. 299
lighting 349–55
    candlesticks 349–51
    chandeliers 352
    decorative arts 566–73
    desk lamps 618, 620
    floor lamps 618–20
    Japanese ceramics 121
    lanterns 353
    modern 618–20
    oil lamps 355, 572
    table lamps 355, 618–20
    wall lighting 354
Limbert 536
Limoges 529
Lin Fengmian **149**
Lindley, John 288
linen presses **217**, 217
Linke, François **196**
Linthorpe Pottery 529
Linwood, Matthew 369
Liszt, Anton 292
Lithyalin glass 344
Liverpool
    creamware 67
    delftware 60
    porcelain **26**, 26
Lock, Nathaniel 311
lockets 357
Loetz **554**, 554–5, 571
Loewy, Raymond 598
Loft, Matthew 303
longcase clocks 280–5, 537, 564
Longines 296
Longton Hall 27
Longwy **529**, 529
Lorenzl, Josef 498, **585**, 585
Loudon 249
lounge chairs 591, 593, 595, 600, 602, 605, 606
love spoons 377
loving cups
    delftware 59
    pearlware 69
    Wemyss 525
low tables 596
lowboys **208**
Lowenthal & Co. 439
Lowestoft 28
lucite jewellery 366
Ludwig, Bernhard 189
Ludwigsburg 54
Lugossy, Maria 615
Lukens, Glen 611
Lumpkins, Robert 291
Lunan, C. 292
lusters, glass 345
lustre pottery 71

M
McCandless, Cora 529
McCobb, Paul 599
McGregor, D. & Co. 284, 301
McIntire, Samuel Field 222
McIntosh, Harrison 611
Macintyre, James & Co. 506

Mack, Lajos 526
MacKenzie, Colin **318**
Mackenzie, Joseph D. 580
McKie, Judy Kensley **599**, 599
Mackley, James C. 86
McLaughlin 522
MacMillan, Hugh 309
Macrae, John 325
Maer, Mitchell 366
Maffezzoli, Giovanni 224
magazine stands 539
magic lanterns **450**
Mahood, Marguerite 529
maiolica 64–5
Maison Millet 351
majolica **501**, 501–2
Makeig-Jones, Daisy 520
Malone, Kate 611
Maltby, John 611
Mangiarotti, Angelo 598, 619
mangle boards 275
Manton, Joseph 472, 474
maps **435**, 435–7, **436**, **437**
marble
    architectural antiques 399
    clocks 287, 290
    fire surrounds 394
    garden furniture 397
    inkstands 380
    lighting 355
Marblehead 502
Marcolini Meissen 31
Marconetti, Alberto 598
Märklin 451
marks
    Chinese porcelain 92
    Derby 21
    Meissen 31
    Sèvres 38
    Worcester 47
Marks, Henry Stacy 505
marquetry **235**
    bonheurs du jour 248
    boxes 272
    cabinets 234–7
    clocks 280–2
    credenzas 238
    cupboards 214, 216
    desks 243
    jardinières 258
    mirrors 250
    music boxes 307
    pot cupboards 241
    table cabinets 267, 268
    tables 192, 198, 204, 206, 208
    tea caddies 264
    teapoys 255
Marquis, Richard 615
Marseille, Armand 442
Marshall, Mark V. 495
Martens, John 557
Marti, Samuel 290
Martin, C.F. & Co. 484
Martin Brothers 503–4, **504**
Martinelli Luce 618
Martinuzzi, Napoleone 556
masks
    glass 614
    tribal art 459–61, 464, 465
Mason's Ironstone 79
Masseau, Pierre Felix 582
Massier, Delphine 502
match-holders 391
Mathias 249
Mattia, Alphonse 599
Mattson, Julia 510
Mayerhofer & Klinkosch 343
Mazezga 619
Meaders, Lanier 611
Measham 89
meat dishes, transfer printed 72, 73
medals
    military 479
    sporting **454**, 454, 456
Medinger, Jacob 86
Meert, D.J. 353
Megrini, C. 301
Meissen **29**, 29–33, **31**, 374
Meizan, Yabu 120
Memphis 616, 620
Meriton, Samuel 338
Mermod Frères 307
Merry, Thomas I 311
metalware
    decorative arts 574–81
    Oriental 126–9

see also brass; bronze; copper; gold; iron; silver; silver plate
metamorphic armchairs 182
Mewis & Co. 474
Mexborough Pottery 89
Mexican tribal art 468
Michel, E. 559
Michel, Gustave Frédéric 587
Michigan Chair Co. 542
micro-mosaic 387
microscopes 303
Mies van der Rohe, Ludwig **606**, 606
Miki, Andy 462
militaria 470–81
Miller, F.M. 19
Miller, Herman 565, 593, 601, 605
Miller, Howard 565
Miller, Patrick 431
Mills, Dorothy 323
Mills, Ernestine 581
Mills, Nathaniel 369, 370
Milne, Jean 363
Ming porcelain 92
Minic 453
Minoan antiquities 482
Minton **34**, 34, 394, 501, 505
Mira 308
mirrors **250**, 250–3, **253**
    Aesthetic movement 534
    Arts and Crafts 539
    decorative arts 574, 580, 581
    Dresden 25
    Fabergé 391
    ivory 383
    modern 592, 607
Mitchell, Henry 34
Miyake, Issey 425
models 453
modern design 590–624
    ceramics 609–13
    furniture 590–608
    glass 614–17
    lighting 618–20
    sculpture 621–3
    textiles 624
Mogensen, Borge 599
Mohn, Gottlob 344
Moigniez, Jules 582
Moll, Herman 437
Monart **559**
money banks and boxes
    iron 446
    pearlware 69
    pottery 88, 89
monkey band, Meissen **31**
Mont, James 600, 619
Montagne, Marius Pierre 582
monteiths 333
Montelupo 64
Monti, Raffaelle 19
Moorcroft **506**, 506–7
Moore, Bernard 508
Moore, James 336
Moore, Santiago James 284
Mordan, Sampson & Co. 270, 338, 370, 379
Morgan & Stanley 182
Morgan Colt 573
Morin, Jean-Louis 38
Morris, William 615
Morris & Co. 508, **540**, 540
mortars and pestles 376, 378, **382**
Mortlake Factory 415
Mortlock, John 501
Morton, Richard & Co. 318
Moschino 427
Moser, Kolo 571
mother-of-pearl
    card cases 371
    fans 422
    snuff boxes 373
    tea caddies 265
Mottheau, Maison 354
Mountlow, Henry 280
Moyr Smith, John 562
muffineers 378
muffs 443
mugs
    creamware 67
    delftware 60
    Doulton 495
    George Ohr 511
    Liverpool 26
    Longton Hall 27
    Lowestoft 28
    lustre 71

Newcomb College 509
    Plymouth 52
    stoneware 83–5
    Wemyss 523–5
    Worcester 45
Müller, Adolf 445
Muller, Frank 296
Muller, Warren 619
Muller Frères 560, 573
Mumbouer, Conrad 87
Murray, Keith 521
Murrle Bennet & Co 363
music boxes 307–8
music seats 182
musical clocks **281**
musical instruments 484–5
muskets 474
Mussill, Wenceslas 505
Mycock, William S. 529

N
Nahcepe, E. 582
Nairne, Edward 303
Nakashima, George 600
Nantgarw **35**, 35
Napoleon Bonaparte 438
Nardi 314
Natzler 532
nautical antiques 309–10
Neale & Co 78
nécessaires 387
Necker, Jacques 431
necklaces 358, 360–8, 467
needle cases 387
needlework 417–20
Negretti & Zambra 302, 304
Nekola, Joe 523, 524
Nekola, Karel 523, 525
Nelson, Admiral 357
Nelson, George **565**, 565, 592, 601
Neo-classical **193**
    candlesticks 349
    clocks 287
    jardinières 258
    lighting 350, 354
    mirrors 252
    silver 314, 336
    tables 193
Nepomuk, Alois 313
Nereshimer 317
Nesterow, Semen Bogdanovich 392
netsuke **135**, 135
Nevalainen, Anders 391
New Hall **36**, 36
Newcomb College 509
Newlyn 580
Newson, Marc **601**, 619
Newton & Co. 303
Nichols & Plinke 392
Nicolason, Mat.s 289
Nicole Frères 307
Noah's Arks 450
Noble, Matthew 384
Nock, Samuel 472
Noguchi, Isamu 601
Noke, Charles 495, 496
Norell, Norman 424
North Dakota School of Mines **510**, 510
North East Potteries 70
Northern Song dynasty 94
Nossiter, Dorrie 365
Nourse, E. 513
Nove 62
novelties, silver 335
Nowlan, William 332
nursing chairs 180
nutmeg graters 338
Nyburg, Soloman & Co. 317
Nyquist, John 601

O
Oakley, George 210
objets de vertu 369–93
    card cases 370–1
    enamel 381
    inkstands 380
    ivory **382**, 382–4, **384**
    miniatures 385–6
    Russian antiques 388–93
    snuff boxes **372**, 372–5
    treen 375–8, **376**, **378**
    vesta cases 379
occasional tables 198–9, 606
Oceania, tribal art 469
Oertel 561
Ohr, George 511
Öhrström, Edvin 560

oil lamps 355, 572
Oku, Densaburou 622
Oldfield, Thomas 431
Oliphant, Ebenezer 320
Olsen, Hovmand 601
Omega 296
O'Neale, Jefferyes Hammett 46
Onondaga Metal Shops 580
Orgues 618
Oriental
  ceramics 92–125
  coral 142
  embroidery and textiles 151
  furniture 152–7
  glass 145
  ivory 130–4
  jade 137–41
  lacquer 145
  lapis lazuli 143
  metalware 126–9
  netsuke 135
  paintings 149–50
  rhino horn 136
  snuff bottles 147–8
  wood and bamboo 144
Orkney chairs 182
ormolu
  cabinets 236
  candlesticks 350, 351
  chandeliers 352
  Chinese 126
  clocks 279, 282, 283, 286, 287
  inkstands 380, 587
  lighting 354
  tables 202
Orrefors 560
orreries **306**
Orwell, George **433**, 433
Otterness, Tom 622
Ottoman
  silver 325
  watches 294
ottomans 593, 596, 601
Ovchinnikov, M. 388
Ovchinnikov, Pavel 389
overmantel mirrors 251
overmantels 394
Owens Pottery 529

P
Pace 602
Pace, John **289**
paintings
  Chinese 149–50
  miniatures 385–6, **386**
  Oriental 149–50
Paley, Albert 602
Pangnark 462
Panton, Verner **602**, 602, 619
pantry tables 211
paperweights 348, 553
papier-mâché
  automata 445
  coasters 387
  dolls 439–40
  snuff boxes **373**, 373
  tea caddies 264
  trays 259
parian
  Copeland **19**, 19
  Minton **34**, 34
  Wedgwood 82
Paris porcelain 36
Parker, John 313
Parker & Wakelin 312, 330
parquetry
  music boxes 307
  tables 190
  tea caddies 264
partners' desks 242, 243
Parzinger, Tommi 602
Pascoe, Clifford 603
Passenger, Charles 493
Passenger, Fred 527
patchwork **413**
Patek Philippe 294, 296
pattern books **530**
Pearce, J.R. 373
Peard, John I 326
pearls 359–61, 363, 367
pearlware 69–70, 73, 74, 78, 82
Pearson, John 580
Peaston, William 323
Peche, Dagobert 561
pedestal tables 186
pedestals 260
Pemberton, Samuel 325, 338
Pembroke tables **204**, 204
pendants 356, 357, 359–63, 365
  jade 140, 141

Penn, F.J. & Company 310
Pennington, John 26
Pennsylvania Dutch **273**
penwork boxes 273
pepper pots
  Mochaware 88
  pearlware 69
  silver 335
Perchin, Michael 390
Perelda, Pollio 557
perfume bottles see scent bottles
Perry & Co. 304
Persian
  arms and armour 476
  ceramics 123
  cushions 421
  rugs and carpets 402–7,
    404, 407
Peters, Henry **176**
Petite, Jacob 290
Pettifer, David 370
Pewabic 512
pewter 340, 564, 578
Philippe, Alfred 367
Philippe, Edward 367
Phillips, Edward 431
Phorzeim 362
photograph frames 391
photographs 438
piano stools 170
pianos 485
Pianon, Alexandro 557
picture frames 575
pier glasses 250
pier tables 193–4
Pierre, Georges 362
pietra dura 587
Pilkington's 529
pill boxes 390
pill slabs 60
Pilleau, Pezé 320
Pillin 612
Pillsbury, Hester 522
Pini, Joseph 301
Pinney, Francis 301
pipe boxes 272
pipe tampers 377
pipes, stoneware 83
pistols 470–2
pitchers
  Newcomb College 509
  redware 86
  stoneware 85
Pitts, Thomas 337
Pitts, William 314
Plail Brothers 542
planetariums 306
Plant, James 22
plaques
  Berlin 11
  Chinese ceramics 111
  Clarice Cliff 490–2
  Dresden 25
  ivory 133
  modern ceramics 610
  pietra dura 587
  Rookwood 514
  Royal Worcester 51
  Sèvres 39
  Wedgwood 82, 520
plates
  Berlin 10
  Bow 12
  Chelsea 14–16
  Chinese ceramics 103,
    107, 113
  Clarice Cliff 492
  Coalport 18
  delftware 60
  Derby 21, 22
  Dresden 25
  Dutch Delft 61
  faience 62
  jade 140
  Japanese ceramics 119
  Japanese metalware 128
  Lowestoft 28
  maiolica 65
  Meissen 30, 31
  Minton 34
  Nantgarw 35
  Pewabic 512
  pewter 340
  Quimper 512
  redware 87
  Sèvres 39
  Swansea 35
  transfer printed 73
  Vienna 42, 43

Worcester 46, 48
Plath, C. 310
Plath, Sylvia 433
platinum jewellery 364
platters
  spatterware **89**
  transfer printed 72, **73**, 73
Plymouth porcelain 52
pocket watches 293–4
Pocock, Edward 311, 320
Poli, Flavio 557
Pollard, William 53
Pollion, O. Dioniusius 41
polychrome Chinese
  ceramics 115–17
Pond Farm 532
Ponti, Gio 579, 603
Poor, Henry Varnum 532, 587
porcelain 10–55
  Berlin **10**, 10–11
  Bow 12
  Caughley **13**, 13
  Chamberlain's Worcester
    48, 48
  Chelsea 14–17, **15**
  Chinese 92
  Coalport 18
  Copeland **19**, 19
  Derby 20–3, **21**
  dolls 440
  Dresden 24–5
  'Goat and Bee' jugs **14**
  Liverpool **26**, 26
  Longton Hall 27
  Lowestoft 28
  Meissen **29**, 29–33, **31**
  Minton **34**, 34
  Nantgarw **35**, 35
  New Hall **36**, 36
  Paris 36
  Royal Worcester 49–51
  Russian antiques 393
  Samson **37**, 37
  Sèvres **38**, 38–40, **40**
  snuff boxes 374
  Vienna 41, 41–3, **42**
  Worcester **44**, 44–7, **47**
Porter, Thea 425
porter's chairs 169
Portuguese ceramics 502
posters 625–30
  Art Deco 628
  Art Nouveau 625–7
  sporting 455, 457
  travel 629
pot cupboards 241
potpourri vases
  ironstone 79
  Meissen 30, 32
  Royal Worcester 49–51
  Sèvres 38, 40
pottery 56–89
  antiquities 482
  creamware 67, 67–8, **68**
  delftware **58**, 58–60, **59**
  Dutch Delft 61
  European stoneware 83
  faience 62–3, **63**
  ironstone 79
  lustre 71
  maiolica 64–5
  Mochaware **88**, 88
  pearlware 69–70
  Prattware **75**, 75
  redware 86–7
  slipware 66
  sporting 456
  Staffordshire figures **74**,
    74–7, **76**
  studio pottery 531–2
  Toby jugs **78**, 78
  transfer printed 72–3, **73**
  tribal art 467
  Wedgwood **80**, 80–2, **81**
pounce pots 376
Pound, Ezra 434
powder horns **478**, 478
Powell, Anthony 434
Powell, Philip Lloyd 603
Pradier, Jean-Jacques 349
Prattware **75**, 75
Pre-Columbian tribal art 468
Preedy, Joseph 314
Preiss, Ferdinand **586**, 586
Price, Horace 51
prie-dieus 163
Priess, Leonard John 63
Priest, William 318
prisoner of war work **309**
Probber, Harvey 603

programmes, sporting 455, 458
Protat, Hugues 82
Prouve, Jean 604
provenance **144**, **294**
Puente del Arzobispo 65
Pugin, A.W.N. 535, 579
Pugin, Edward Welby 535
punch bowls
  Chinese ceramics 110,
    113, 115
  glass 347
  silver 333
punch pots, creamware 67
punch sets 392, 553
puzzle jugs 59, 69, 88
Pyne, Nathaniel 280

Q
Qianlong ceramics **104**, 104
Qing porcelain 92
quaiches 376
Quantock, John 312
quartetto tables 154, 198
Queensware 82
Quezal 560, 572
Quick, John 326
quill work boxes 266
Quimper **512**, 512
Quistgaard, Jens 604

R
Radiguet 453
radios 587
Ramsden, Omar 579
Rappoport, Julius 391
Rathbone, Harold Steward 528
Ravilious, Eric 521
Rawlings, John Henry 332
Ray, Man 623
Reballio, A. 299, 300
redware 86–7
Reed, Olga G. 513
Reed & Barton 321, 579
Reeves, Ruth 587
Regina Music Box Company **308**
regulators 284
Reid, Alexander 326
Reid, John 169
Reily, John 338
Reinicke, Peter 30, 31
Reisener, Jean-Henri 197
Reitz, Don 612
reliquaries 272, 356
Remington 473
Remmey, Richard 84
Renaissance carvings 274
Renaissance Revival
  cabinets 237
  cassones 219
  coal scuttles 263
  desks 243
  mirrors 252
Renou, Timothy 325
Restauration
  clocks 286
  lighting 354
revolvers **473**, 473
Rhead, Frederic 527
Rhenish stoneware 83
rhino horn **136**, 136
Rhodes, David 67
Riach, John and Patrick 327
Riart, Carlos 604
Ricardo, Halsey 493
Rice, Bernard 581
Rice, Louis W. 581
Richardson, H.G. 560
Richardson, Joseph and
  Nathaniel 320
Ricketts, William 50
Ridgway 579
Rie, Lucy 532
Riesener, Jean-Henri 224, 283
Riessner, Stellmacher &
  Kessel 488
Rietveld, Gerrit 604
rifles 474–5, **475**
rings 356–61, 363, 364
Rivera, José de 622
Robb, Samuel A. 401
Robb, William 325
Robertson, Hugh 489, 528
Robineau, Adelaide 530
Robinson, Ann 63
Robjohn-Gibbings, T.H. 604–5,
  605, 620
rock crystal 147
rocking chairs 161, 538, 539,

  542, 601, 604
Rockingham 52
Rococo
  armchairs 182
  mirrors 252
  silver 314
Roentgen, David 234
Rogers & Spencer 473
Rohde, Gilbert 565, 605
Rohmer 442
Rolex 297
Rolfe Powell, Stephen 615
Roman antiquities **482**, 483
Romilly 293
roof tiles, Chinese 117
Rookwood **513**, 513–14
Roosevelt, Theodore **475**
Roquelon 279
rose bowls 579
rose medallion, Chinese
  ceramics 112
Roseville 514–15
Rouen, faience 62
Roulleau, Jules Pierre 582
Roullet & Decamps 445
Roux, Alexander 254
Rowley, Isaac 369
Rowling, J.K. 434
Royal Copenhagen 55, 612
Royal Crown Derby 21, 23
Royal Doulton 495, 496
Royal Dux **516**, 516, 572
Royal Flemish 560
Royal Pavilion, Brighton **175**
Royal Worcester 47, 49–51, **502**
Roycroft 542, 570, 577
Rückert, Feodor 389, 390
Rudal Carte & Co. 485
rugby 458
rugs and carpets 402–12,
  587, 624
rummers 343
Rundell, Bridge & Rundell
  336, 337
Rundell, Philip 316, 328, 331,
  336, 337
Rushton, Josiah **502**
Ruskin Pottery **517**, 517
Russell, Gordon **541**
Russell, Thomas & Son 294
Russian 388–93
  armchairs **175**
  cloisonné 388–9
  Fabergé 390–1
  sculpture 582
  silver 392
  stools 170
Rybak, Jaromir 617
Ryozan 119, 120

S
Saarinen, Eliel 605
Safavid ceramics 123
Saila, Pauta 462
St Cloud 374
Saint Laurent, Yves 368, 425
St. Louis 348
saltglazed stoneware 83
Salto, Axel 612
salts
  Bow 12
  glass 347
  maiolica 65
  treen 376
salvers, silver 330–1
samplers 419–20, **420**
Samson **37**, 37
sand pictures 310
Sandilands Drinkwater 336
Sandland, Edwin 524
Sandwich Glass Co 347
sang de boeuf 97
Sansovino, Jacopo d'Antonio 214
Sanster, George 325
Sarfatti, Gino 620
Satsuma **119**, 119–20, **120**
sauceboats
  Liverpool 26
  Longton Hall 27
  silver 323, 579
  Worcester 45
saucepans 340
saucers
  Chelsea 14
  see also cups and saucers
Savone 63
Sax, Sarah 513
saxophones 485
Sazikov 392
Scandinavian carvings 275

Scarpa, Carlo 556
Scavini, Helen König 500
scent bottles
  Chelsea 17
  Derby 22
  Fabergé 390
  glass 563
  Ruskin Pottery 517
  treen 377
  triple **17**
Schaffhausen International Watch
  Co. 297
Scheier 612
Schiaparelli 367
Schiffer, Franz 337
Schimmel, Wilhelm 275
Schleissner, J.D. and Sons 314
Schlesinger, Franz 321
Schneider 560
Schneider, Charles 572
Schoenhut 450
Scholz, Heinrich Karl 585
Schonheit, Johann Carl 31
Schultz, Richard 605
Schulz, Franz 42
Schwanthaler, Johann Josef 274
Schwinger, Hermann 345
scientific instruments
  barographs 304
  barometers 298–302
  engines 305
  microscopes 303
  telescopes 304
Sclater, Philip Lutley 431
Scofield, John 331
sconces 354, 577, 580
Scott, James 330
Scottish
  arms and armour 474,
    476, 476–8
  Arts and Crafts 541
  barometers 299–301
  chairs 164
  clocks 280, 283, 284, 292
  jewellery 356
  metalware 581
  objets de vertu 369, 375
  pearlware 70
  samplers 419
  silver 315, 316, 318–20, 323,
    325–7, 338
screens **261**, 261
  Arts and Crafts 541, 542
  firescreens 396
  Oriental **156**, 156–7
scrimshaw 309, 309, **478**
sculpture 581–5
  decorative arts 582–6
  glass 557, 614–17
  Inuit 462
  modern ceramics
    609–11, 613
  modern 621–3
seals
  ivory 133, 587
  objets de vertu 387, 390, 391
Seandel, Silas 606, 623
Sebright, Richard 50, 51
Secessionist lighting 571
secrétaire bookcases 229
secrétaires **228**, 228, 593
Seddon, John Pollard 169, 535
Seguso, Livio 616
Seguso Vetri D'Arte 557
Selmer 485
Sergeni and Aine 270
serving tables 211
settees 183–4
settles 539, 541, 542
Seville, W. 386
Sèvres **38**, 38–40, **40**, 286
sewing boxes 266
sewing cases, enamel 381
Shaker **210**
  desks 210
  tables 189, 211
Shapland & Petter 543
Sharp, James 523
Sharp, Robert 319
Shaw, Richard Norman 535
Shaw, Robert 291
Shaw, William II 318
Shaw Nicholls, David 624
Shawsheen 530
Shenfelder, Daniel 85
Shepherd, J.B. 442
Sheraton style
  desks 244
  sideboards 240
  sofas 184

tables 195, 197
shibayama 128
Shigeyoshi 531
Shin-Lou-Shan-Jen 150
Shintani, Daisuke 623
ships
  nautical antiques 309–10
  silver models 337
  toy 447
Shirayamadani, K. 513
Shirrell, Charles 385
shoes 428–9, 465
shotguns **475**
Sibley, R. 334
Sibley, Richard I 319
side cabinets **236**, 236–7, 533
side chairs 167–8, 596, 604
side tables 195–7, **197**, 535,
  536, 593, 597
sideboards **239**, 239–40, **240**
  Art Deco 546
  Arts and Crafts 537, 539–41
  modern 593
signs, trade 401
silhouettes 386
silk embroideries 417–18
silkwork, work boxes 266
silver 311–38
  baskets 332
  bowls 333, 575, 576
  boxes 372
  caddy spoons 325
  candelabra 314
  candlesticks 311–13, **312**
  card cases 370–1
  Chinese 126
  cigarette cases 379
  clocks 564
  coffee pots 320
  cruets 334
  cups 315–17
  decorative arts 574–6, 579
  Fabergé 391
  flatware 330–1
  inkstands 380
  Japanese 128
  jewellery 356–7, 362–3,
    365, 367
  jugs **322**, 322, 575
  novelties 335
  Russian antiques 392
  sauce boats 323
  spoons 326–7
  tea and coffee sets 321
  tea caddies **324**, 324–5
  teapots **318**, 318–19
  tongs 327
  tureens **328**, 328–9, **329**
  vesta cases 379
  vinaigrettes 369–70
  watches 293
  wine antiques 336
silver-plate 339, 578
silver tables **207**, 207
Simmance, Eliza 495
Simon & Halbig 443
Simpson, A.F. 509–10
Singleton, Jonathan 620
Siot-Decauville **571**, 582
Sitzendorf 54
Skeggs, William 278
skeleton clocks 289
Slee, Richard 612
slippers 428
slipware 66
Smith, Benjamin II 317
Smith, Charles and Son 306
Smith, Helen 515
Smith, S. & Son 294
Smith, Stephen 337
smoker's compendiums 379
snuff bottles 147–8, **148**
snuff boxes **372**, 372–5
snuff rasps 382
Sobey, W.R. 336
sofa tables 203
sofas 183–4
  Aesthetic movement 533
  modern 590, 596, 603, 605
Sosuke, Namikawa 127
Sottsass, Ettore 616, 620
Soumin, Avenir I. 393
soup bowls 72
soup plates 45
Southey, William 334
Spackman, William 322
Spanish
  bookcases 230
  cabinets 234

candlesticks 349
maiolica 65
silver 337
tables 185, 191, 193
spatterware **89**
Spelzini, J. 299
spice cabinets 267
spill vases 48, 76, 77
Spode 73
spoon trays 60
spoon warmers 504
Spooner, Clowes & Co. 321
spoons
  caddy 325
  Caughley 13
  love 377
  silver 326–7
sporting antiques 454–8
Springer, Karl 606
Staffordshire
  creamware 67–8
  enamels 381
  figures **74**, 74–7, **76**
  pearlware 70
  porcelain 53
  Prattware 75
  slipware 66
  Toby jugs 78
  transfer printed pottery 72
Stahl, Isaac S. 87
stained glass 562
Stamp, James 319
Stampa, L. 300
stands 260
Starck, Philippe 606
Starr and Hurry 269
statues, garden antiques 398
steam engines 452–3
Steiff **448**, 448
Steiner 443
Steinway & Sons 485
Stellmacher, Eduard 488
Stenglin, Philipp 316
steps 263
Steuben 560
Stevens, J. & E. 446
Stevens & Williams 563
Stevenson, Robert Louis 431
Stewart, R. 283
Stewart, Thomas 327
Stickley, Gustav 538–9
Stickley, L. & J.G. 538
Stiegel 347
Stinton, Harry 49–51
Stinton, James 50
Stinton, John Jr 50, 51
stirrup cups 317
Stobwasser **373**
Stoker, Bram 431
stone, garden antiques 398
stoneware **83**, 83–5, **84**
stools **170**, 170–1
  Arts and Crafts 540, 542
  Chinese 152
  modern 592, 597
Storr, Paul **329**, 334
Stourbridge glass 563
Strange, Robert 385
straw splitters 378
studio pottery 531–2
sucriers 53
sugar bowls
  silver 333, 576
  treen 377
sugar sifters 490–2
Suisse Frères 349
suitcases 427
suites
  bedroom 262
  dining room 604
supper sets 72
Susse Frères 571
Swansea 53, 70
Swedish armchairs 175
Swift, John 319
Swiss
  engines 305
  music boxes 307, 308
  singing bird boxes 387
  watches 294
swords 476–7, **483**
Syng, Richard 311
Szyk, Arthur 434

T
table cabinets 267–8, **268**, 382
table clocks 278, 289
table lamps 618–20
table screens 133, 143, 156–7

tables 185–211
  Aesthetic movement 534
  altar 153, 154
  Art Deco 545
  Art Nouveau 543
  Arts and Crafts 536–8,
    540, 541
  breakfast 190
  card **205**, 205–6, **206**
  centre **191**, 191–2, 534, 540
  Chinese 153–4
  coffee 591, 592, 597, 598,
    601, 605, 606
  console 545, 590
  dining 186, 188–9, 538, 545,
    591, 594, 596, 598–603,
    605, 607
  dressing 208
  drop-leaf **187**, 187, 188
  extending 188–9, **189**
  feet **209**
  games 203, 205–6, **206**
  gateleg 186
  Gothic Revival 535
  library 200, 536
  low 596
  modern 590–603, 605–8
  nesting 600
  occasional 198–9, 606
  Oriental 153–4
  pedestal 186
  Pembroke **204**, 204
  pier and console 193–4
  quartetto 154, 198
  refectory 185
  side 195–7, **197**, 535, 536,
    543, 593, 597
  sofa 203
  tea 207
  tripod 209
  work 210
  writing 201–2, 545
Tagliapietra, Lino 614, 616
Takaezu, Toshiko 612
Takebe, Shoko 119
Talavera 65
Talbert, Bruce 533, **534**
tankards
  cloisonné 388
  faience 63
  ivory 383
  lustre 71
  Russian antiques 392
  silver 315, 316, 575
  stoneware **83**
  Wedgwood 521
  Worcester 44
tapestries 415–16, 587, 624
tartanware
  card cases 371
  tea caddies 265
tavern clocks 291
Tavernier 291
Taylor, Alfred 372
Taylor, Joseph 325
Taylor, Samuel 324
Taylor & Hinsdale 331
tazzas 389, 558, 579, 616
tea **264**, 264
tea caddies 264–5, **265**
  Japanese ceramics 120
  Japanese metalware 128
  Russian cloisonné 389, 390
  silver **324**, 324–5
tea cups see cups and saucers
tea services
  brass and copper 578
  Clarice Cliff 491
  cloisonné 389
  Derby 23
  Fabergé 391
  glass 344
  Liberty & Co. 574
  Meissen 29
  silver 321, 576
tea strainers 390
tea tables 207
tea urns 319, 340
teabowls
  Chinese ceramics 115
  Liverpool 26
  Meissen 30
  Worcester 45
Teague, Walter Dorwin 587
teapots
  Chinese ceramics 104, 111
  Clarice Cliff 492
  creamware 67, 68
  Doccia 55
  glass 615

Liverpool 26
Meissen 29
silver **318**, 318–19
Wedgwood 82
Worcester 44, 46
teapoys **255**, 255
Teco 517
teddies **448**, 448–9
Tegelsten, Carl 392
telescopes 304
Tereszczuk, Peter 586
tester bedsteads 262
tete-a-tetes **53**
Teufel, Johann 42
textiles 402–29
  Chinese 151
  costume 423–5
  decorative arts 586, 587
  embroidery 417–20
  fans 422
  handbags 426–7
  modern 624
  Oriental 151
  quilts 413–14, **414**
  rugs and carpets
    402–12
  samplers 419–20, **420**
  shoes 428–9
  tapestries 415–16
Theed, William 19
Thieme, Carl 24, 25
Thomas, John 34
Thomasson, E. 587
Thompson, Jack 623
Thompson, Robert "Mouseman"
  537
Thormodsgard, Marie B. 510
Thornhill, Walter 335
Thornton, John **437**
Thwaites, Jonathan 283
Tiffany & Co.
  clocks 290
  glass **558**, 558, 563
  lighting **566**, 566–7
  silver 328, 575
  tiles 608
Tiffany Studios 564, 566–7, 575
tiles
  American Encaustic
    Tiling Co. 527
  Marblehead 502
  Minton 505
  Morris & Co. 508
  studio pottery 532
  Walrath 519
  William de Morgan **494**, 494
tinplate toys 447
Tinworth, George 496
Tittensor, Harry 496
toast racks 579
tobacco boxes 74, 372, 374
tobacco jars 375
Tobin, Steve 623
Toby jugs **78**, 78
toilet boxes 270
toleware 340
Tolkien, J.R.R. 434
Tompion, Thomas **280**
tongs, silver 327
torchères 258–9, 260
tortoiseshell
  boxes 273
  cabinets **233**
  card cases 371
  clocks 291
  snuff boxes 373
  table cabinets 267, 268
  tea caddies 264, **265**, 265
Toso, Aureliano 557
Toso, Fratelli 557
totem poles 464, 465
Townsend, Edward 50
toys and dolls 439–53
trade signs 401
trains 451–2
transfer printed pottery 72–3, **73**
Tranter, W. 473
travel posters 629
trays 259
  Chinese lacquer 145
  copper 580
  faience 62
  Japanese cloisonné 127
  silver 330–1
treen 375–7, **376**, **378**
tribal art 459–69, **460**, **461**
Trifari 367
Trinkley, Karla 616
trios 45, 46
tripod tables 209

triptychs 383, 535
trophies 458
Trotter, William 203
trunks 427
Tso Tzu Yang 150
tubas 485
Tuch, Bruno 585
Tucker & Sherrard 473
tulip mania **219**, 219
tumbler cups 316
tureens
    Chinese ceramics 111
    enamel 381
    faience 62
    ironstone 79
    Longton Hall 27
    Nantgarw 35
    silver **328**, 328–9, **329**
    Worcester 48
Turkish
    arms and armour 477
    ceramics 123
    rugs and carpets 410–11
Turner Simpson 322
Twell, William 316
Tycos, Short & Mason 304
tygs 456
Tynell, Paavo 620

U
Underhill, T. 299
uniforms, military 481
Universal Geneve 297
University City 530
Urban Furniture Co. 595
urns
    architectural antiques
        398,
    Berlin 10
    Chelsea Keramic Art
        Works 489
    Derby 21
    enamel 381
    faience 62
    ivory 132
    Japanese metalware 128
    maiolica 65
    redware 86
    Royal Worcester **502**
    Sèvres 39, **40**, 40
    toleware 340
    Vienna 43
    Worcester 47

V
Vacheron & Constantin 297
Vallien, Bertil 616
Van Briggle **518**, 518
Van de Voords, George 380
Van Loo 386
Vance Faïence Company 530
varguenos 234
Vasa 623
vases
    Amphora 488

Arequipa 489
Berlin 10
Bernard Moore 508
Bow 12
Chelsea Keramic Art
    Works 489
Chinese ceramics 96–102,
    104–9, 112–14, 116
Chinese ceramics 124, 125
Chinese lacquer 145
Chinese metalware 126
Clarice Cliff **490**, 490–2
Clewell 489
Coalport 18
copper 577
creamware 67
delftware 59, 60
Derby 22, 23
Doulton 495
Dresden 24, 25
Dutch Delft 61
George Ohr 511
glass 146, 344, 346, 347,
    547–61, **548**, 614–17
ironstone 79
ivory 132
jade 137, 140, 141
Japanese ceramics 118,
    120, 121
Japanese cloisonné 127
Japanese metalware 128
Korean ceramics 122
lapis lazuli 143
Lenci 500
Liverpool 26
Longton Hall 27
maiolica 65
Marblehead 502
Martin Brothers 503
Meissen 30, 32
Minton 505
modern ceramics 609–13
Moorcroft **506**, 506–7
nephrite 393
Newcomb College 509–10
North Dakota School
    of Mines 510
Paris 36
Pewabic 512
pewter 578
Prattware 75
Ridgway 52
Rookwood 513–14
Roseville 514–15
Royal Worcester 49–51
Ruskin Pottery 517
Samson 37
Sèvres 39, 40
silver **337**
Sitzendorf 54
studio pottery 531–2
Teco 517
Van Briggle 518
Vienna 42–3
Walrath 519

Wedgwood 80–2, 520–1
Weller 522
Wemyss 524, 525
William de Morgan 493
Worcester 44, 45, 47, 48
Zsolnay 526
Vautrin, Line 607
Veart 616
V.E.M. 557
Venetian maiolica 64
Venini, Paolo **556**, 556, 620
Le Verre Français 561
Versace, Gianni 425, 429
vesta cases 379
Vichy **444**, 444
Vickery, James 270
Victorian style **165**
Videau, Ayme 316
Vieillard, J. & Co. 290
Viennese
    clocks 286
    enamel 381
    porcelain **41**, 41–3, **42**
    table cabinets 268
Vietnamese ceramics 123
vinaigrettes 369–70
Vincennes **38**
violins 484
Vistosi 557, 620
Vizagapatam 265, **266**, 266, 268
Vizner, Frantisek 617
Volk, E. 25
Volkmar 530
Volkstedt 530
Volmer 573
Vonham, Frederick 313
Voulkos, Peter **613**, 613
Voysey, C.F.A. 543
Vuitton, Louis 427
Vulliamy 282

W
Wade, N. Victoria 587
Wadsworth, John 505
Wagner, George 586
Wain, Louis **519**, 519
'wake' tables 187
Wakelin, Edward 313
Wäkevä, Alexander 391
Wäkeva, Stefan 391
Walheim, Jack 591
Walker, Izannah 440
wall clocks 291–2
wall lighting 354
wall masks
    Clarice Cliff 492
    Goldscheider 497
    Lenci 500
wall mirrors 250–2
wall pockets 86
Wallis, J. 437
Walrath 519
Walter, Amalric 561
Walton, George **541**, 541, 564
Walton, Isaac 74

Wang Chen 150
Wang Ti-Ying 150
Wang Yun 150
Wanli ceramics 100
Warburton, John 68
Warega art **460**
Warhol, Andy 424
warming pans 340
Warnberger, Erhard 330
Warren, James 313
wash stands 260
Washington, George 438
Washington, Robert 613
Wast, P. & Zoon 298
watches 293–7
water coolers 84
water droppers 122
waterpots 94
Waterhouse & Co. 332
Waugh, Evelyn 434
weapons 470–7
weather vanes 400
Weaver-Bridgeman, Montague
    A. 81
Webb, Philip 540
Webb, Thomas & Sons 561, **563**
Weber, Jonas 273
Wedgwood
    creamware 67
    Fairyland Lustre **520**, 520
    Keith Murray 521
    majolica 501
    porcelain **53**, 53
    pottery **80**, 80–2, **81**
    transfer printed pottery 73
Weeden Mfg. Co. 446
Wegner, Hans 607
Wehrle, P. 291
Weisweiler, Adam 234
Weller 522
Wellington chests 227, 228
Welsh treen 377
Wemyss 523–5, **525**
Wenford Bridge 532
West, Matthew 330
Westerwald 83
Westley Richards 474
Westwood, Vivienne 429
Weygandt, Cornelius 376
Wheatley, William 278
Whipham & Wright 320
White, Fuller 323
Whytock & Reid 244
wicker chairs 538
Wickes, George **328**
Widdicomb 604–5
Wiener Werkstätte 561
Wiggan, Thomas 282
Wigstrom, Henrik 390
Wilde, Oscar 431
Wildenhain, Marguerite 532
Willems, Joseph 16
Wilmore, Joseph 336, 370
Winchester 475

window seats 171
Windsor chairs 160–1
wine antiques, silver 336
wine bottles, Korean
    ceramics 122
wine coolers 256–7, **257**
    pottery 89
    Samson 37
    silver 336, 339
    silver plate 578
wine glasses 341–2
WMF 578
Wodehouse, P.G. 434
Woo, Marie 613
wood **227**
    carvings 274–5
    Oriental 144
    treen 375–8, **376**, **378**
Wood, Beatrice 613
Wood, Enoch 70, 77
Wood, Ralph 74
Woods & Brettle 72
Woodward, Artemas 227
Woolf, Virginia 434
woolwork 418
Wooton desks 243
Worcester **44**, 44–7, **47**
work boxes 266
work tables 210
Works Progress Administration
    (WPA) 630
Wormley, Edward **608**, 608
Wotruba, Fritz 623
Wright, Charles 320
Wright, Frank Lloyd 607
Wright, William Thomas 563
wrist rests 133, 134
wristwatches 295–7
writing boxes and slopes **269**, 269
writing tables 201–2, 545
wrought iron see iron
Wu Ku-Hsiang 150
wucai 114
Wyburg, Leonard 540
Wyke, John 305
Wyon, E.W. 82

Y
Yasuyuki, Namikawa 127
Yeung, Mae 613
Yorkshire pottery 67–70, 75
Young, J.M. 542
Young, Peter 340
Yuan ceramics 99

Z
Zach, Bruno 585
Zámecníková, Dana 617
Ziegler & Co. **407**, 407
Zsolnay **526**, 526
Zucca, Edward 620, 623
Zwierzina, Otto 43
Zynsky, Mary Ann "Toots" 616